ON THE ETERNAL IN MAN

ON THE ETERNAL
IN MAN

MAX SCHELER

Translated by
Bernard Noble

ARCHON BOOKS
1972

Library of Congress Cataloging in Publication Data

Scheler, Max Ferdinand, 1874–1928.
   On the eternal in man.

   Translation of Vom Ewigen im Menschen.
   "Bibliography of Scheler's published works": p.
   1. Philosophy   and   religion.   2. Religion–Philosophy.
I. Title.
[BL51.S423 1972]   100   72-6599
ISBN 0-208-01280-X

Printed in the United States of America

CONTENTS

Foreword by August Brunner   7

Translator's note   10

Preface to first German edition   11

Preface to second German edition   15

REPENTANCE AND REBIRTH   33

THE NATURE OF PHILOSOPHY AND THE MORAL PRECONDITIONS OF
PHILOSOPHICAL KNOWLEDGE   67

  1. The autonomy of philosophy   70

  2. The philosophical attitude (the idea of the philosopher)   72

  3. Analysis of the moral upsurge   89
    A. The moral upsurge as a personal act of 'the whole man'
    B. Starting-point and elements of the moral upsurge

  4. Philosophy's object and cognitive attitude   98

PROBLEMS OF RELIGION   105
  The renewal of religion

  1. Religion and Philosophy   128
  Existing views typified
    The types of partial and total identity
    Dualistic views
  The system of conformity

  2. The Essential Phenomenology of Religion   161
  Branches of study
  The Divine
    Basic character of the divine
    The attributes of God in natural religion
    Growth and decline of the natural knowledge of God
    Attributes of the divine mind
  The religious act
    The immanent aspects of the religious act
    Religious acts are a law unto themselves
    The religious act in its internal and external, individual and social aspects
    No man can avoid the religious act
  Some recent basic theories of natural religion

3. Why no New Religion?   332
  The idea of a personal God conflicts with the expectation of a new
  religion
  The prospects of a 'new religion', seen in the light of the socio-
  historical distribution of cognitive aptitudes

CHRISTIAN LOVE AND THE TWENTIETH CENTURY: An Address   357
  1. Humanitarianism and the Christian commandment of love   367
  2. The Christian idea of community   373
  3. The present relevance of the Christian idea of community   378

THE RECONSTRUCTION OF EUROPEAN CULTURE: An Address   403
  1. The political framework and moral conditions of cultural   405
     reconstruction in Europe
  2. The formative powers available for the spiritual renewal of
     Europe   422

Editorial Notice, by Frau Maria Scheler   449

Bibliography of Scheler's published works   457

Annotations, by Frau Scheler   462

A Note on the Author, by I. M. Bochenski   471

Index of Names   479

FOREWORD

Max Scheler (1874–1928) is one of the philosophers who decisively influenced German philosophy in the period after the first World War, a time of upheaval and of new beginnings. Without him and Husserl the problems of German philosophy today and its attempts to solve them would be quite inconceivable. Husserl introduced into philosophy the new method of phenomenology. Reality was to be realized and described—'to be brought to self-givenness in immediate intuitive evidence' —in those very structures and contents which both everyday and scientific cognition leave unregarded. Those things 'given' by reality, things which cannot be reduced to other things and cannot be explained from them, were to be looked at and represented, since a definition, in the strict sense of the word, was impossible. These are the '*Washeiten*' or phenomenological essences (*Wesenheiten*), which must not be confused with the 'essences' of ancient philosophy. Further, the necessary connections between the essences had to be explored. These connections are always and everywhere valid where these essences have been realized. Such laws are valid before every induction and only they make one possible (cf. p. 279). Thus the *a-priori* received a new significance and an immensely enlarged field of application. The result was a 'radical empiricism' compared to which ordinary empiricism proved to be a restriction of the view. From it the way to a metaphysics stood open once more. Thus phenomenology is not a school but an attitude of mind.

Husserl came to philosophy from mathematics. For this reason he tried above all to establish the validity, first of mathematical knowledge and then of all logical structures, independently of every psychological mode of thought, of heredity, custom, etc. This explains why Husserl finally came to rest in a transcendental idealism.

Scheler was not really a pupil of Husserl. He started out from Eucken and his doctrine of the spiritual life as a final reality. But his intuitive inclinations were very soon bound to feel attracted by the new method and to recognize in it a tool suitable for his own interests. The thing that was new in his philosophy was in fact that he used phenomenology for the investigation of spiritual realities. 'Repentance and Rebirth' in this volume is a good example of this.

Opposed to this enterprise was the dominant neo-Kantianism. This regarded knowledge as the formation by the Categories of something given by the senses. According to neo-Kantianism, a direct view of things that are spiritually given and which man meets with is not only impossible but nonsense—contradicting the essential nature of knowledge.

Scheler came to grips with Kantianism in his *Der Formalismus in der Ethik und die materiale Wertethik*. In this work he showed that ethics are built upon really objective values that can be recognized as such; that a purely formal principle like Kant's is not enough and that, above all, it fails to recognize the actual essential nature of morality and therefore of man. Before that there had appeared the book *Zur Phänomenologie und Theorie der Sympathiegefühle und von Liebe und Hass*.

The subject of the present work, *Vom Ewigen im Menschen*, is the divine and its reality, 'the originality and non-derivation of religious experience' (p. 173). Attempts had been made for a long time to explain religion from extra-religious spheres. Kant himself had as good as completely let it dissolve in morality. Throughout the whole of the nineteenth century similar attempts were carried on; of these psychologism and materialism are still widespread today. Over against this Scheler shows the characteristic quality of that which is religious. It is a particular essence, which cannot be reduced to anything else. It is a sphere that belongs essentially to man; without it he would not be man. If genuine fulfilment is denied it, substitutes come into being. This religious sphere is the most essential, the decisive one. It determines man's basic attitude towards reality and thus in a sense the colour, extent and position of all the other human domains in life. It forms the basis for all sorts of views about life and thought.

One cannot possibly go into detail in a short introduction. The reader must first seek to understand Scheler's arguments and then carry them out after him. In the nature of the case there cannot be a proof in the ordinary sense. In the place of proof we here have insight. We shall then find that the work is of an unusual richness. Perceptions of all kinds crowd in upon one, relationships that are not obvious at first shine out; the old the accustomed, gleams in a new light. And these perceptions do not leave the reader cold: he feels how they can enter into his spiritual being, enrich it and fulfil it. It is a knowledge that is alive, near to actual reality and decisive for that which is human. There will be few philosophical writers whose insights spring forth just in this way, and in whom one feels such freshness and directness.

Scheler has not infrequently been rebuked for discovering all too precipitately insights into being when it was a question of historically determined connections—as too, in his interpretation of historical characters and systems, his judgment was often not free from preconceived ideas, from sympathetic and antipathetic feelings. Further, the fact that the phenomenological method was new made it inevitable that too much was expected of it. Husserl believed that he had found in the phenomenological method an exact method—like that of natural science —by which all differences of opinion between philosophers could be abolished. This expectation was not fulfilled and, considering the nature of philosophy, could not be fulfilled.

Scheler was emphatically an intuitive philosopher. It is therefore not surprising that his systematic thinking is rather weak. He never succeeded in solving really satisfactorily the basic question of the relation between value and being. In his separation of the two, and thus in his system of conformity, some people have seen an after-effect of the Kantian doctrine of theoretical and practical reason. In Scheler's later works the break between them—between being as the almighty but blind rage and value as the knowing but powerless spirit—has become complete and makes of man a split being. Personal experiences may be reflected here. The development of Scheler's work as a whole was very dependent on his personal experiences. It is this that gives Scheler's work its liveliness but endangers its validity.

The system of conformity is no doubt right in so far as that which is religious must have been experienced, that it cannot be explained or constructed from elements that are strange to it. And in the book there are enough passages about the relation of being and value in which this point appears (pp. 138, 151f., 163, 173). A *summum bonum* that does not exist would be an unreal God and an *ens a se* that is not *summum bonum* would not be God. Scheler saw that too. But he did not draw the conclusion which is really implicit in his doctrine, that the metaphysical is a part of the impulse of religious knowledge and can be lifted out from it. These parts of this book have not had any great effect. What remains are the many insights and, above all, the fundamental recognition that the spiritual is a reality directly accessible to our knowledge. This is a great enlargement of the philosophical view and the re-awakening of a metaphysics near to reality.

AUGUST BRUNNER

Munich

TRANSLATOR'S NOTE

Notes are the author's except those beginning or ending '*Translator*'.
Asterisks refer to Frau Scheler's Annotations.

'Realize' is used in the sense of 'make real', and 'sensual' means simply
'of the senses'; readers are referred to my note on page 215 for discussion
of the special use of 'insight' and 'perception', and to those on pages 182
and 190 for remarks on the translation of *Geist* ('mind' or 'spirit'). Otherwise terminology is that of common rather than technical usage, though
'intention' usually has its epistemological sense.

The author's inconsistency of self-reference (as both 'I' and 'we')
has been retained.

I wish to make known my deep indebtedness and gratitude to Dr
Austin Farrer, then Chaplain and Fellow of Trinity College, Oxford,
now Warden of Keble College, for his help of many occasions.

B. N.

PREFACE TO FIRST GERMAN EDITION

(Leipzig 1921)

The work whose first[1] volume is now to be published—considerably delayed by the inauspicious conditions of the times—contains essays and studies which in essence are devoted to problems of ethics and the philosophy of religion. Partly they are intended to serve as the precursors of systematic works on a larger scale, which the author has in hand, and partly to develop and apply what he has already established in such works, particularly *Der Formalismus in der Ethik und die materiale Wertethik* (Halle 1916). The essays on repentance and rebirth, the Christian ideas of love and community, the nature of philosophy and on the cultural reconstruction of Europe have already been published in the periodicals *Summa* and *Hochland,* and appear here in only slightly altered forms.* What is new is the second, greater part of the book, on 'Religious Renewal',*[2] which is an attempt to draft the lines on which religion may be understood and provided with a philosophical and phenomenological basis.

The overall title of *Vom Ewigen im Menschen* should suffice to indicate that the author is consciously anxious to lift up his thoughts above the storm and turmoil of the age and into a purer atmosphere, fastening them on that in man which makes him man, that whereby he has part in the eternal. To few is granted grace to abide in happy wonder in the eternal and to conceive the rest of life as only a tortuous path to this highest goal. Here the author will settle for a lesser thing; it is to show how, from those spiritual sources in man where divine and merely human streams commingle, the thirst of the hour can be satisfied, and the hope of a *vita nuova* restored to those who in these times have suffered most affliction and distress. The quest of that *how* is the bond which unites in spirit the

[1] *Vom Ewigen im Menschen* was envisaged as the title of a three-volume work. The other two volumes did not appear (*Translator*).

[2] By this title Scheler referred to the whole of this work. He calls 'Problems of Religion' the second part because it was printed last in order in the first two editions, the essays forming a first half. However, the introductory pages of 'Problems of Religion', a section which *also* bears the title of 'Religious Renewal', are in fact the only part of that work which was not new, since, as Frau Scheler informs us in her *Notice,* they were published in *Hochland* during 1918 (*Translator*).

writings published here. And that is why an essay on such a topic as Europe's cultural reconstruction has a place with the rest.

A man has a poor conception of the eternal if, merely grasping its contrast to the flow of time, he is unable to hear the soft voice of eternity in the most momentary demand which is made on the individual in the here and now. For, rightly conceived, the eternal is not sealed away from time in a simple juxtaposition: it timelessly embraces the content of time and its fulness, pervading each of its moments.

And so the eternal can be no *asylum* into which a man may flee, thinking himself unable to endure any more of history and life. No good 'eternalist' can devote himself to the contemplation of eternity if flight from history is his only motive. Yet considerable numbers of young people today are determined by motives of escapism. Some flee to the mysticism of higher things, things superior to history; some take refuge where history is a flow apart, in the idyll of the naturalist, botanist, astronomer; others, and these are the least edifying, fly to the subhistorical world of the pleasure of the moment, this being the antipole of eternity. Though the author finds these tendencies understandable, he is unable to give them his blessing. To acknowledge history, to see it in its hard reality— but to revive it with the water of eternal springs—that is worthier than flight and more fitting to the age.

This first volume, devoted to philosophical and religious trends of thought, begins with an endeavour to analyse more deeply than has been the case the great phenomenon of conscience—*repentance*. This is because the mind of man has no moral religious act more commensurate to the age, none which should prove more fruitful to it than the act of repentance. It alone holds out a promise of rebirth.

The treatment of *religion* has only a loose tie with present exigencies. It offers to the public for the first time a few fruits of the work on the philosophy of religion which has occupied the author for many years*—the underlying bases for the systematic construction of a 'natural theology'. The author believes these fundamentals, despite all foreseen objections, to be more assured than traditional bases and also of a nature to encounter a deeper understanding and sounder appreciation from the man of today than the traditional systems of religious theory which lean either to Aquinas or to Kant and Schleiermacher. In the same way as what Kant called the 'scandal of philosophy', it is a scandal of theology and philosophy *alike* that the questions of natural theology, *i.e.* the very thing designed to *unite* minds irrespective of sectarian differences, should divide minds even more deeply than points of confessional dogma. It is a further scandal that whatever knowledge of God men owe solely to the spontaneous reason in every man, that which should therefore enable us to see the true bounds of tradition and revelation, is for the most part cultivated in purely *traditional* systems of doctrine.

The author is profoundly convinced, for reasons he cannot embark on here, that natural theology is unable to perform its task of *unification* either on a basis of Thomism or on a basis derived from the philosophical era ushered in by Kant.

This task it can only perform once it has delivered the kernel of Augustinism from the husklike accretions of history, and employed phenomenological philosophy to provide it with a fresh and more deeply rooted foundation. (Phenomenological philosophy is one which undertakes to look on the essential fundamentals of all existence with rinsed eyes, and redeems the bills of exchange which an over-complex civilization has drawn on them in terms of symbol upon symbol.) When this has been done, natural theology will more and more clearly reveal and demonstrate that *immediate* contact of the soul with God which Augustine, from the experience of his great heart, was striving with the apparatus of neo-Platonism to capture and fix in words. Only a theology of the *essential experience of divinity* can open our eyes to the lost truths of Augustine.

The present volume is not intended to form an elaborate systematic philosophy of religion. That must be reserved for some future work. In particular, the *system* proper of the kinds of evidence for God's existence is less developed here on paper than in our mind; we have set down no more than selected parts of it.

Work on the second and third volumes is steadily proceeding, and it is hoped that both will appear before long. The principal section of the second will be devoted to a definitive completion of the author's *ethics*. Herein will be considered the importance of the *personal exemplar* of all kinds for the moral and religious being of man as well as for historical variations in forms of ethos. The special function of the third volume will be to treat the *interrelation of love and knowledge* (a historical typology of theories about this interrelation was elaborated in an earlier work) in a purely objective and *systematic* way, and to propose an irreducible basis for a 'sociology of cognition' which the author is also reserving for a later systematic treatment.*

As the author sees it, philosophy should be systematic—but should result in a 'system' which does not rest on deduction from a few simple fundamental propositions, but *acquires* an ever-renewed sustenance and content from the searching *analysis of the various domains* of existence—a system which is never closed but *grows in life* and *by* the continual rethinking of life.

A system is either a gift of grace to the fulness and unity of the person who philosophizes, or it is an *artificial* fabrication of the arbitrary intellect. Once for all, the author will desist from a 'system' of the latter variety. And yet the reader should in fairness not ignore what these essays contribute in certain directions to uncovering the systematic complex of the author's thought.

Cologne,   MAX SCHELER
17th October, 1920

PREFACE TO SECOND GERMAN EDITION
(Leipzig 1923)

A year after its first appearance it has become necessary to reprint this book. There are no changes in this second edition. The more convenient format obtained by division into two volumes (a step most generously taken by the publisher at the author's request, despite a considerable increase in expense) will certainly not be unwelcome to readers.

The reception accorded to the work in reports, reviews and criticisms by the public and critics at home and abroad was on the whole most reassuring for the author. He may perhaps take this opportunity of remarking how eagerly receptive are the minds of people today (especially young people) toward the questions treated in this book, particularly the problem of the philosophical basis of religion; and he would like also to remark how easily debate and discussion flow nowadays between one confession and another, not to say between the confessions in general and independent religious thinkers, at least in respect of the *general* problems, outside the scope and competence of confessional dogma, which concern the primal nature and truths of religion. He may surely take it as a sign of this new *loosening of traditional rigidity* of thought and tenet that his book has encountered much the same keen interest and comprehensive criticism not only in Catholic, Protestant and Jewish theological and philosophical circles, but even in the theologically unclassified circles represented by sects and groups of various persuasions. The situation which the preface of the first edition sharply castigated as the 'scandal of theology and philosophy alike'—that thinkers were even more deeply divided by the problems of pre-dogmatic 'natural' theology than by dogma itself—does seem, in this country at any rate, to be on the decline.

But what struck the author as even more important and encouraging than this most valuable, but still negative, breaking down of mistakenly interposed barriers was the appearance of a number of works reaching essentially the author's conclusions about the origin of all religious knowledge. Some had written independently of the author's theories; others even took them in some way as their starting-point. About the time of this book's publication positions at least very similar had been taken up by Rudolf Otto in his work on *Das Heilige* and by K. T. Österreich in his

Religionspsychologie and his article '*Über die religiöse Erfahrung*', and now the
following writers must be noted as contributors to the same line of
thought: H. Scholz, who in a fine, pregnant work, *Religionsphilosophie* (two
editions), likewise bases religion on irreducible elementary phenomena
in the mystic experience of divinity, I. K. Girgensohn, with his book,
Der seelische Aufbau des religiösen Erlebens, O. Gründler in his phenomenological philosophy of religion and Josef Heiler, author of *Das Absolute*;
on this point even E. Troeltsch appears to have approached a kindred
position as a result of his re-appraisal of certain elements in the teachings
of Malebranche.[1] These names are introduced merely to show how something for which the author hardly dared hope when he penned the first
preface has today grown into a well-founded and most important prospect,
that of a genuinely *unified*, essentially supra-confessional philosophy concerning the nature of religion and the true seat and origin of religious
knowledge in 'religious acts' of an 'original religious experience irreducible in terms of the secular empirical'. There are also attendant signs that
both Thomism and Kantianism, whose supremacy over whole insulated
groups had until lately blocked the path to union, are being radically
called into question. When these facts are taken in conjunction with
the ever-growing interest of learned Catholic circles in the Platonic-
Augustinian tradition of thought,[2] and with the close affinity between
their positions and the arguing of philosophy from phenomenological
premises, they provide the most hopeful signs the author has observed in
the past year and would bring to his readers' attention.

With reference to the extremely comprehensive criticism to which the
book has been subjected, it is noteworthy that the treatment of 'Repentance and Rebirth' and 'The Nature of Philosophy' has received more
universal and undivided agreement and appreciation than that of the
'Problems of Religion'. Independently of the author, Nicolai Hartmann,
in his penetrating *Metaphysik der Erkenntnis*, has attempted to satisfy the
requirement that philosophy should base the concept of 'knowing' on an
ontic relationship, on the relationship of 'participation' of an entity A in
the thusness of a second entity B: a connection of such a kind that its
taking effect determines no corresponding change in B. Since the appearance of the first edition of the present work the author himself has carried
out the plan, adumbrated in 'The Nature of Philosophy', of setting out

---

[1] Cf. Troeltsch, '*Die Logik des historischen Entwicklungsbegriffes*' (*Kantstudien*,
Vol. XXVII, Nos. 3/4) and *Der Historismus und seine Probleme*, I, pp. 166 *et seq.*,
& II, p. 615.

[2] Cf. *inter alia* the article of the Tübingen dogmatist K. Adam, '*Glaube und
Glaubenswissenschaft*'.

from this dominant principle to formulate a new kind of realistic epistemology, one which diverges considerably from the existing forms of
scholastic, 'critical' and intuitive realism; it is his intention to publish this
research during the coming year under the title of *Phänomenologische
Reduktion und voluntativer Realismus—eine Einleitung in die Theorie der Erkenntnis*.[1] The essay on 'Repentance and Rebirth' is the section of the book
which (at least in its psychological analysis) has been received with the
most unanimous applause of the critics—even of those who felt obliged to
reject the author's philosophy of religion.

The last part of the book, 'Problems of Religion', has encountered a
very different reception. The unusually numerous public utterances on the
subject of the author's inquiry, not to mention the no less numerous
epistolary utterances, showed an *extremely* wide variation in the extent to
which his intentions and the meaning of his arguments had been *understood*. To take an example: the author was and remains clearly conscious
of having strictly distinguished on all occasions between what rests in his
theses on essential *insight* and what is matter of positive faith. In spite of
that, certain people of a strictly ecclesiastical outlook have accused him of
wishing to deduce propositions of positive dogma philosophically. Now,
apart from a specific rational element, philosophically necessary, in the
idea of the Fall (in the absence of which he still believes any kind of theism
to be a totally nonsensical system), such an intention was wholly remote
from the author's mind. At some points the understanding of his statements has been adversely affected by the fact that the reader has taken
purely hypothetical statements of philosophical insight to be categorical
existential propositions of, moreover, a positive religious nature; in other
words, certain readers who have *themselves* confused matters of faith with
philosophical insights have attributed the same confusion to the author.
Thus when for example the author says that (on theistic premises) it lies
in the nature of the 'original holy one'[2] to be not 'one of many' but 'the
one and *only*' person through whom God reveals himself, the inattentive
reader replaces this hypothetical statement with concurrence in the two
articles of faith: there is a personal God, and Christ is that one and only
person. This is just as if the author had not in fact *demonstrated* the logical
unprovability of theistic personalism, and the hypothetical statement did
not leave it open for anyone to put a quite different 'one and only'
person—Mohammed, say—instead of Christ. That this unique person *is*

[1] In this connection, cf. the author's essay, '*Die deutsche Philosophie der Gegenwart*'
in *Deutsches Leben der Gegenwart*, ed. P. Wittkop, Bücherfreunde-Verlag, Berlin
1922.*
[2] Literal sense. See pp. 341 *et seq.*, in 'Problems of Religion', Section 3
(*Translator*).

Christ is a *pure* judgment from faith, and it has never entered the author's mind to wish to 'prove' it philosophically. Again, on p. 699 (of the first edition)[1] the author seeks to show that the hypothetical assumptions of a loving God, of the primacy of love over knowledge, of a divine self-revelation through a historical human person *necessitate*, when taken in conjunction, an infallible authority in matters of salvation of the Church *qua* Church, as guardian and dispenser of the blessings of salvation presented by the 'one and only' man of God. In consequence some readers appear to have assumed that the author wished to 'prove' the infallibility of the Roman papacy, although the conditions of the above proposition could be no less satisfied by the institution of the Dalai Lama, or by the absolute doctrinal authority of a *concilium*, or by a holy synod which expounds 'the holy tradition', as in the Orthodox Church. It must have been due to *this* type of misunderstanding if extra- and anti-ecclesiastical circles have made the converse reproach against the author, that he has pressed philosophical method into the service of the apologetics of a positive Church and its dogma—turning phenomenology, as one critic put it, into a 'common whore'. Here the following needs to be said: The descriptive method, *not* aiming at essential philosophical insights, of reducing given religious and metaphysical systems (*e.g.* Buddhism, August-inism, the philosophies of Plato, Aristotle, Schopenhauer) to their *original empirical contents, i.e.* of *reconstructing* and re-intuiting the basis of what appears in them as matured, developed, rationalized, ossified,—thereby revitalizing its *original meaning* and restoring its perceptual validity for today—*this*, as the method used in the descriptive study of Weltan-schauungen, is in fact a 'common whore'. It is in the very fact that it *is* a 'common whore' that its outstanding, positive value lies. But it goes without saying that this reconstructive phenomenology cannot be *productive*: proceeding as it does from *given* 'ideas', it can only rediscover, therefore produce nothing new, for one cannot *re*discover what no one has ever observed. It is likewise unable to determine the positive cognitive value of the system under investigation: it cannot, that is to say, determine the degree of adequacy or inadequacy of the underlying perceptual intuitions to the full objective content of the object; nor the degree to which, if at all, the existence of the objects of the given knowledge is dependent on, or a function of, the existence and mode of being of the subject; nor the truth or falsity, or formal correctness (logical consequence), of the correspond-ing judgments, inferences and organized propositions. Hence reconstruc-tive phenomenology must and *should* be *unlimitedly* 'relativistic'. But it is no less clear that *essential* phenomenology—including of course the

---

[1] See p. 343 (*Translator*).

essential phenomenology of religion—is able to go much further. Although, like reconstructive phenomenology, it on *no* occasion enables one to assert the *reality* of a given object (for the simple reason that one begins with a conscious renunciation of one's competence to deal with the existential coefficient of the objects under review), one yet knows *a priori* that the 'essential correlations' which it discovers, since they are true of the *essence* of this or that object, are also true of all possible contingent objects of the same 'nature' or essence, whence it follows that it can make true judgments about those objects. But reality itself can only be established, 'in accordance with' these essential co-relations, by some kind of *contingent* experience (taking into account its subsequent thinking over, development, supplementation), and for supersensual objects this implies either *metaphysics* or God's *positive self-communication, i.e.* 'revelation', whose assumption thereupon is enacted solely in receptive acts of faith. It may be contended, however, that in the course of argument the author has not always kept apart these four cognitive forms or procedures—descriptive phenomenology, essential phenomenology, metaphysical discourse and whatever he may have affirmed subjectively here and there as articles of faith (though in the last instance he has always expressly made this affirmation known as applying to an act of *faith*). Against any such contention the author would invoke the fact that it is quite impossible, in the course of investigating any given object to set down, step by step, the underlying epistemology of the investigation. But, in fact, the author believes that he has even distinguished more clearly than has been done before what he considers metaphysically (not phenomenologically) demonstrable in the idea of God, what (secondly) can rest solely on the basis of the essential elementary phenomena, accessible to all men, of *all* religion ('natural revelation')—and what finally can rest, in his theory, *only* on judgment from faith and positive revelation. Only one who knows nothing but 'causal' and other 'inferences' from empirical data to supersensual things or, conversely, positive revelation and its dogmatic formulation—only one therefore who does not acknowledge any *primordial* religious phenomena or, alternatively, any special, specifically religious experience in specifically '*religious acts*'—can from *his* standpoint, which our book precisely refutes and replaces, find 'confusion' where he is in fact in presence of a new and deeper *clarification* of the different sources of knowledge of God.

That the *neo-Thomist* trend of metaphysics and theology would inevitably reject the author's representations, of that much the author was certain before ever the matter was put to the test. Indeed he has rather marvelled at the mostly mild and qualified objections that have come

from that quarter. On the other hand K. Eschweiler's[1] illuminating
account of the differences between genuine mediaeval Thomism and the
far more thoroughgoing rationalization of Thomism in the age of Enlightenment (which is to say the form of Thomism by far the most prevalent still, especially in German universities, and the form which the author
himself confesses to have equated too closely in his book with the original
Thomism)—this account has taught the author that he had been inclined
more to overrate than underrate in a number of instances the distance
which separates him from the old Thomistic system. The many accusa-
tions of 'ontologism' or 'fideism' which have represented the party-cries of
the strict Thomists leave him unintimidated, not only because the same
objections could be raised (and would *have* to be raised if one were logical
and refrained from Thomistic 'interpretations' of all pre-Thomist philosophy) against the whole of patristic theology and the whole pre-Thomist
manner of justifying natural religion, but also because these party-
slogans—which should be evaluated under the heading more of Church
politics than of philosophy—are in fact quite *in*applicable to his
theories. Neither have the Thomist critics of our work had any more
success than these parrot-cries in convincing us that the traditional
doctrine of proofs of God, in particular that of the 'cosmological causal
proof', really has the stringency imputed to it, while our own conception
and teachings have no more than a 'psychological significance' for the
subjective paths by which men may come to believe in God's existence.
Far from observing that our propositions have been confuted, we have
not anywhere seen our thorough treatment of this question put to the
test. So far as the argument is concerned that our theory has no more than
'psychological' significance, we thoroughly examined this expected
reproach in the very text of the book, and rejected it for reasons which are
exhaustively stated. Far from agreeing with *this* objection from that
quarter, we would say that, as Kant glimpsed and Hegel plainly saw, it
is the traditional 'proofs of God' which have no more significance than to
describe, in the form of artificial rational formulae, the *ways* by which a
man, having *already* accepted the existence of an infinite and spiritual
ens a se, which he knows from sources quite *independent* of these 'proofs',
can retrospectively clarify his notions of the manifold *relationships* which
God *may* possess to the *world* and its given essential constitution.

If the school-philosophy of German neo-Thomism has objected that our
position makes much too little account of spontaneous reason as a source
of knowledge and deductive thought as a theological method, the ranks
of Protestant theology have again and again raised the opposite objection,

[1] See *Hochland*, 19th Year, Nos. 3 & 4, 1921-22: '*Religion und Metaphysik*'.

that we acknowledge any 'natural theology' at all and that we have allotted metaphysics much too important a place in the book, in relation to knowledge of God.[1] For some I prove too little, for others too much; some find my theories too 'irrationalistic', others too 'rationalistic' in questions of theology. There are those who think in terms more of cultural politics than of philosophy, those who, when anything appears which is new by comparison with time-honoured school- or party-views, see it only in its 'position relative' to those views. Such men will readily declare, in the favourite phrase, that I have 'fallen between two stools'. Before proceeding, however, I will allow myself to assume that I am sitting on a perfectly serviceable stool, while my critics are unknowingly squatting to right and left of me on the floor—where they find themselves thanks to taking sides in the polemical shuttlecock of *false antitheses* produced one by another in endless dialectic.

The circles which stand opposed to all confessionalism and are seeking a new form of religious awareness have also not refrained from criticism. A. Horneffer[2] for example finds that I argue in terms which are far too definite and decisive, that I speak with far too much assurance on things which are open to question, that in this way I am putting opinions in the reader's mind rather than seeking to convince him. He takes particular offence at the fact that I not only consider a 'new religion' to be a contradiction in principle of the theistic idea of God, but also think it unlikely on historico-philosophical and sociological grounds that any such novelty could arise. To critics in this camp I can reply that I too have known the deepest skepticism in relation to all human expressions and concepts concerning the being commonly called 'God', and that I have for that very reason put negative theology and the conceptually unformulable experience of divinity much more in the foreground than is customary; for that reason, too, I laid the most definite emphasis on the 'supraconceptuality' of the idea of God and the merely *symbolically analogical* character of all positive definitions of God. But I must confess myself unable to go all the way with those who at the name of 'God' are content with *only* pointing to their hearts and feel no need of clear, definite ideas about the objective entity which moves their hearts in this ineffable way—or who feel no need, even, of any definite account of the kinds of attitude, any setting into relief of the mental *acts*, by adoption or performance of which we may bring this objective entity, which by nature can *only* be intuited or sensed by us, within range of our apprehension. But

[1] Thus for example R. H. Grützmacher in *Kritiker und Neuschöpfer der Religion im 20. Jahrhundert*, 1921.

[2] See *Deutsche Pfeiler*, 2nd Year, 1922, No. 3.

I am amply compensated for this judgment on my 'dogmatism' when I hear Catholics call me 'properly' a skeptic. For from that I may infer that I have not failed, not *quite* so lamentably as these critics on both sides believe, to strike a just balance between that shy awe which the very mystery of God and the world seems to demand of our souls, and a strictly practical attitude.

With regard, however, to my theses concerning any 'new religion', the first of them does not *have* to carry weight with the adherents of any monistic or pantheistic doctrine, since it is expressly related to the supposition of a personalistic theism or panentheism. With regard to the second contention—the unlikelihood of a new religion—I would have been more interested if A. Horneffer, who so seriously entertains the possibility of new religions, had seriously invalidated my grounds for the opposite view (reasons I had set no higher than 'grounds of probability') rather than subjected them to a dogmatic contradiction which gives the impression that I categorically excluded what in fact I only described as improbable. For the rest, I would refer all readers who are imperfectly satisfied with this section to my *Wesen und Formen der Sympathie*[1] (second edition, Bonn 1923), wherein I bring forward numerous illustrations of the general fact that in all 'psycho-mental' evolution (animal to man, savagery to civilization, child to adult) there is no unqualified gain in cognitive powers, since one can also discern recession, diminution or total *loss* of aptitudes for knowing whole realms of objects.

Finally I would like to take this opportunity of forestalling a number of further misunderstandings which I think possible in the light of the effect my book has already produced. From one quarter, from a contributor to German academic philosophy whom I hold in the highest esteem,[2] I have received a letter objecting that in my book, as in all my writings, I lean much too heavily on the epistemological principle of self-evidence. Other men, the writer says, who live in other circumstances or have other types of character also know other kinds of self-evidence. He therefore considers that I am far too inclined to credit universal validity to kinds of self-evidence that have only the character of 'subjective certainty'. To this my answer is as follows: For me the principle of self-evidence, rightly understood, is constituted by the fact that an intentional object, whether entity or value, is clear to the mind in its essential *thusness* (hence is '*itself*' present in the mind as the correlate of an intentional act), when there is an utter *congruence* among the contents of all noetic acts which are

---

[1] English translation, *The Nature of Sympathy*, London 1954 (*Translator*).

[2] I refer to Ernst Troeltsch, whose recent death was a grievous loss to German philosophy.

possible with reference to *that* object. I said its 'thusness', *i.e.* its state, qualities and essence, because its *existence* always remains *extramental* and is not in any way apprehensible by intellectual acts: it can only be apprehended as a resistance to acts of a volitional nature. Nevertheless, 'in' this very *congruence* as such the very object *itself* is given, as I said; what is given, then, is in no way a mere 'image', 'copy' or 'symbol' of it. To me, at any rate, this principle is the *ultimate* criterion of knowledge, the most *decisive* we have. It has not the slightest resemblance to any mere 'certainty' or even any so-called 'feelings of self-evidence'. All proving and in general all indirect thought, all ideal construction (as in mathematics), all technical extrapolation from our sensory experience, all psycho-technical or noetic methods of arriving at the particular psychic and mental *states* wherein it is supposed that a particular *range* of phenomena may be encountered—all these are in the final analysis only *means* of producing the 'self-evidence' I have described above or of guiding the subject to the 'threshold' of it.

Now, in *my* teaching this does not preclude the possibility that self-evidence may at the same time be the most individually personal evidence for the existence and constitution of the given object. But in this connection 'individually personal' means anything but 'subjective'. In *my* teaching, moreover, self-evidence is not *necessarily* restricted to the sphere of knowledge which is of potentially *universal* validity. Just as there is a good which is *intrinsically* of potentially universal validity, and is, therefore, also of objective universal validity, as well as a good intrinsically of potential and objective *individual* validity,[1] so there can certainly be also an 'intrinsically universally valid truth' *and* an 'intrinsically individually valid truth'. *Both* can and must rest on manifest *insight*. It is the attempts, much favoured by Kantian schools, to reduce the concept of *objective* knowledge to mere 'universal validity of knowledge' or knowledge by a 'transcendental subject' which represent distinctly *subjectivistic* doctrines. For what reason is there to rule out the possibility that certain objective entities or values are cognitively accessible only to *one* particular individual person, or to *one* particular *individual civilization or culture* or to *one* particular phase of historical development?

Suppose there is a subject A who finds a certain object or state of things *x* 'self-evident', and a subject B for whom this is not the case; if A and B have exhausted all *possible* called-for ways whereby the self-evidence of *x* might have been invincibly demonstrated to B, if *all* attempts to achieve this by methodical argument, or by exposition of technically receptive states of mind, have failed, then only one conclusion is to be drawn from

[1] Cf. my *Der Formalismus in der Ethik und die materiale Wertethik.**

the impasse: that the 'conflict'—the 'phenomenological conflict', as I call it,* *i.e.* the deepest conflict there is—is *socially* just unresolvable, that one, therefore, can only leave the other person 'be' and allow him to go his separate way. What certainly does not follow is the wholly unfounded rationalistic prejudice that for any 'given' objective entity there *must* be a 'universally valid' knowledge, hence knowledge of whose validity any person can *in principle* be persuaded. Still less does it follow that *only* knowledge with this property *can* be knowledge adequate to the content of the objective entity. On the contrary, we trust that we have demonstrated elsewhere that universally valid knowledge can be objectively valid and of more than formal significance *only* in regard to objects which belong *not* to the metaphysical (*i.e.* '*absolute*') order of being but only to a plane of being whereon the existence of objects is *relative* to what is *general* in human nature. Such objects are for example those of the positive sciences. Given that, as we maintain, the personal—indeed the individually personal—form of existence extends into the very depth of the world-basis, the validity of absolute *metaphysical* truth, when it is given and received as 'adequately' as is humanly possible, can *only* be entirely cogent in the direct individual subject of its knowledge.

And so if the objection is made to us that what is self-evident to us is not so to 'other men', it is of course quite *possible* that we are the prey to an *illusion* of self-evidence, for we do not contest the possibility of such illusions. If such is the case, and if this illusion is an expression and consequence of circumstances like heredity, natural proclivities, historical environment, then the fact is deplorable, no less. But it is no less deplorable if similar factors have blinded others to *intrinsically* manifest truths which at the same time we must suppose to be universally apprehensible. If, however, there is no explaining away the 'phenomenological conflict' by such 'subjective' influences, which can in principle be eliminated— if the conflict is in fact unresolvable, it does not in the least follow that the principle of self-evidence ought to be subordinated to an allegedly 'higher' principle, the principle of 'provability'. On the contrary, the position is rather that, as says the Latin tag,[1] there is no arguing with one who denies the existence of common ground, of principles directly accepted as manifest by both disputants; hence nothing may here be indirectly proved. If, as every philosophy must assume which envisages knowledge as an ontic relationship, the sphere of what a man may cognitively apprehend depends on and is determined by the state and quality of his own mental personality, it *must* be the case that, even in relation to truths of absolute being, no two individual minds find *exactly* the same set of

[1] *Contra principia negantem non est disputandum.*

cognitive data 'self-evident'. Henceforth, therefore, let a sharp distinction be made between the 'universally' and the 'objectively' valid, as well as between the 'personal' and the 'subjective'.

Here in fact our opinion is the following: Beyond what knowledge of God is, potentially, *universally* self-evident (and this we delineate in our book), only the fulness of *all* the ages, all their separate religious outlooks and their cultures, only the fulness of *all* nations and peoples, but—most of all—only the fulness of all *individual personal minds*, that 'rest' in the divine, where they find their ideal, characteristic essence, can, in *solidary co-operation and intercompletion*, make as it were a full circuit round the *inexhaustible fulness* of the deity, and see all humanly accessible aspects of the divine—see it even then only to the degree of adequacy with which it is given to the specific nature of man to apprehend the divine.

A second point which—as I gather from the letter of an English scholar, but also from conversations and printed criticisms—has raised many difficulties even for the *good* reader is my view on the knowability of the *personality* of God. A contradiction is seen in my saying that metaphysics, to which I attribute the ability to know spontaneously the spirituality[1] of a supramundane *ens a se*, is, nevertheless, incapable of knowing that this spirit[1] has a personal form of existence; it is thought inconsistent that I should claim ability to 'prove' the *unprovability* of God-as-a-person from the nature of all possible knowledge of persons. On the grounds of two principles which I have previously expounded in my ethics*—1. personal value is highest value, 2. concrete spirit postulates a person as subject— and on the grounds of the (by my theory) metaphysically knowable propositions that (*a*) God is the *summum bonum*, (*b*) God is infinite spirit, it is thought that I should be able to infer, purely syllogistically, that the *summun bonum* or infinite spirit must be a person. From those idea-relations, taken with the attributes of the deity which I hold to be metaphysically knowable (*ens a se*, infinite spirit, etc.), it is said to follow indirectly, but automatically. and necessarily, that God—if he exists at all—must be a person, and it is said that this refutes my proposition of the 'provability of the unprovability of God as a person' or my proposition that it is always God who, as a person, first discloses his own *existence* as a person in his own voluntary self-revelation.

Now, I must first of all point out that there is an important difference between knowing God to be a person and knowing that a person, who first announces himself to me through his own divulgence or communication, is *God*. Indirect knowledge of God as a person refers to the first, but it

---

[1] More correctly, I feel, in the last analysis: 'mental-ity' and 'mind' (the German of course has *Geistigkeit* and *Geist*). Cf. my note on p. 182 (*Translator*).

is to the second that my thesis of the unprovability, the very provability of the unprovability, of God as a person refers. Furthermore, when I said that metaphysics could not know the personality of God, I was speaking only of metaphysics, not *also* of ethics; and I had in mind, moreover (though this I did not say plainly enough) only the metaphysics of the subhuman world, in which the idea of *personalitas* is not yet realized. That with the help of ethical principles *and* a metaphysics—or rather meta-psychology—of the human spiritual soul we may indirectly know that the infinite spiritual *ens a se* must be 'personal' in its essence and quality—that is something which I had no wish to deny; on the contrary I raised this very point on p. 633 (of the first edition).[1] Nevertheless, this last-mentioned knowledge does not yet seem to me to imply knowledge of the 'existence of the personal God'—*not in the sense in which I deny* indirect knowledge of such existence.

For there is a great difference between my knowing an apprehended person 'as' God and my only attributing the personal form and mode of being to the unity and manifoldness of an already known spiritual deity. One instance in which this becomes very clear is in comparing Jewish theism and the Christian doctrine of the Trinity. The latter rests on the rational knowledge that God must have a personal form of existence *and* on the revealed doctrine that in his existence he comprises not one but three persons. In contrast, unitarian monotheism does not distinguish between God's existential form as personality and God's concrete existence as a person. The existential form of *personalitas* is only an attribute of *deity*, not of the real *God*, and this existential form is exactly the same in both the unitarian and the trinitarian ideas of God. But the existence of a personal God is not yet implied with the personal *form* of divine being, and it is the mistake of the ontological proof of God to assume this im-plication. Thus the existence of God as a person is left purely to the *experience* of a divine communication, however much any preceding in-ference that the divine spirit must be personal may *incline* the soul to heed such a communication or prepare it for such an experience.

But what kind of 'experience' is in question here? What kind of ex-perience is a minimal condition for knowledge of the personality of God? I do not believe—and this point has also been misunderstood—that only the experience which the theologies of the Church call 'positive revelation' affords the possibility of such knowledge. No, I believe that, given pre-disposing conditions and a certain inner preparation, the experience of divinity which is possible to any man in the ground of his personality is sufficient, and the mystical contact with the deity which the personal

[1] See p. 308 of this edition (*Translator*).

nucleus of his soul can make. Undoubtedly, as accords with the principle of the unprovability of God as a person, this experience depends unconditionally on a 'revelation' and 'communication' of God to men. But it is *natural, universal* 'revelation', *already* given in the very constitution and form of existence of the human mind—but of course given *only* there, and not in the extra-human, though animate natural world—: it is that revelation which we place in the centre, as a *third* principle of supersensory knowledge, between spontaneous, indirect rational knowledge and positive revelation to founders of religion.

Only in this third epistemological principle, which without postulating positive revelation is *purely* religious, not metaphysical simply, does all specific mysticism (*supraconfessional* as such) receive its due place, which in essence—if not in any given form—is independent of metaphysics and positive religion: its eternal place among the essential forms of human experience.

On this point our opinion differs by a wide margin from that of (*inter alios*) H. Scholz[1] (see pp. 149 *et seq.* of his *Religionsphilosophie*, first edition). We agree with Scholz that this grasp of reality, knowledge of God as a person, is an intense, rare and commonly short experience to which a man can only prepare himself by definite psychic techniques, and that its access is more or less difficult according to the character of the man. Nevertheless, we believe it represents a form of experience which in principle is accessible to all men, hence one potentially of universal validity: it is not—as Scholz thinks—something one might liken to musical talent, sense of absolute pitch and other unteachable things which one man may have and another not. If we differ from Scholz here it is not as a result of inductions as to how many and what kinds of men find or have found the way to this experience; the difference derives from our divergent views of human nature and its constitutional structure.

My conviction, as carefully formulated in the book, is that this experience by man at the very core of his being of personal contact with God *always* and *necessarily* accompanies the fulfilment of two conditions, one positive, one negative. The negative is what I have called disillusion with idols, *i.e.* removal from the centre of the *absolute* sphere (always given to human consciousness as the uppermost sphere of its intentional objects and values) of all finite things and finite goods, with a consequent release from conscious or subconscious self-identification with any finite object

---

[1] On the relation to our views of H. Scholz's philosophy of religion, cf. his *Religionsphilosophie*, first edition, p. 468, n.1, and K. Adam's excellent critique of Scholz in *Glaube und Glaubenswissenschaft im Katholizismus*, Rottenburg 1923.

of 'faith' and love (cf. pp. 550 *et seq.* of this book, first edition[1]). The positive condition is that the spiritual person itself, hence also its acts, as distinct from the principle of physical life (and its functions), which in all natural, non-mystical experience it only serves, or serves to some extent— that the spiritual person should be *independently* active and active of its own spontaneous accord, and at the same time see this principle, with its mechanical teleological functions, 'below' it in a figurative sense as its purely objective area of *command.* Thus this positive condition is more than a question of the autonomously regular functioning of particular *kinds* oı noetic act, with as little disturbance and influence as possible from the physical principle. For *wherever* man judges rightly and truly, has a clear and unadulterated vision of truth, wherever he grasps and wills the objective good, this positive condition applies. It is most eminently fulfilled in the genius, who in a given sphere of spiritual activity, released from determination by his biological impulses, their specific sensual—and attendant intellectual—phenomena (e.g. sensory perceptions, reproductive processes and even discursive thought), devotes himself to the matter in hand and its value-demands in an attitude of spiritual love which transcends the bounds of all mere 'life'; in the intensest moments he is devoted to his task with the devotion I would term ecstatic—that is, in such a way that the nucleus of the Self and the devotion are wholly given up to interfulfilment and self-intensification, and cease to be registered in paraconsciousness. (Here we speak only of the 'inspiration of genius'—not of mystical experience.) Not, we believe, when the person merely 'judges' itself free, but when, in predisposing acts of the utmost *concentration* on the part of the spiritual person as such, it directly possesses the sense and experience of being free, autonomous and essentially, existentially independent of the principle of physical life—then, in our opinion, there takes place that direct empirical contact with the deity as a person which we would call a '*mystical*' contact.

The kernel of our meaning is therefore this: if these *two* conditions are fulfilled, the negative and the positive, and if in the progress of concentration it attains to its own substance, *i.e.* detaches itself and knows itself detached from all control by the physical principle, the person *necessarily* attains at one and the same moment, in an *indivisible and indestructible unitary experience*, to its substance in *God*, while in it the reality of God as a person becomes simultaneously discernible. But since the structural nexus comprised by the personal soul, the physical principle and everything here mentioned forms the essential constituents of human nature, this experience, given rightness of ethical conditions and a technique for preparing the appropriate states of mind, *cannot* in *principle* be inaccessible

[1] See pp. 267 *et seq.* of this translated edition (*Translator*).

to any man—even if (as I am naturally willing to grant Scholz) it is in fact inaccessible in a given case in one degree or another. I will also gladly concede that heredity may *empirically* exclude actualization of this possible experience, quite apart from an individual's blameworthy neglect of the conducive moral acts or lack of proficiency in the technique of concentration, etc. Of course heredity may exclude a thousand possibilities which definitely lie in the ideal, essential potentiality of human nature—even, as in congenital idiots, the simplest mental arithmetic. What I must contest with Scholz is not that predispositions can in fact preclude the experience but that specific, positive predispositions (such as is musical talent, for example) are unequivocally the *preconditions* of mystical experience, so that one might say a man simply *was not* 'religious' as another *is* simply unmusical. I must confess that if Scholz could persuade me of the truth of his proposition I would immediately abandon a view that I have hitherto shared with him, namely belief in the empirical nature of conviction, at least in relation to the existence of God as a person.

For in the first place his suggestion of positive religious 'talent' would stand in direct contradiction of my conception of the positive condition for this experience, which postulates a supra-biological spiritual person and a regularity of noetic acts which is independent of the body (however much their taking place may be conditioned bio-psychologically here and now, hence indirectly physiologically). It goes without saying that the existence and essence of this person cannot depend on a 'predisposition': it is what of course constitutes the *essence* of man (as distinct from the animal) and therefore the very precondition for the various proclivities of the principle of physical life. But Scholz's proposition also contradicts the content of every arguable *idea* of God, inasmuch as a God who grants to one group of men special 'talents' for knowing him which he refuses to other groups could be anything but a *God*.

It may be that this view of Scholz's, which differs so greatly from mine, derives from the fact that—like the disciples of Kant—he simply overestimates, by a quite considerable amount, the unity and universal validity of what he calls 'natural experience'. Primitive men have an entirely different *structure* of even 'natural experience' from that possessed by civilized men; moreover, race and culture determine such a wide range of 'relatively natural' structures, which condition all perception and insight via different hereditary sets of instincts and differing traditions, that *absolutely* natural experience is at bottom no more than a terminal concept, though admittedly a necessary one.[1] Furthermore, Scholz's

---

[1] Cf. my article '*Weltanschauungslehre, Soziologie und Weltanscahuungssetzung*' in *Moralia* (Vol. 1 of *Schriften zur Soziologie und Weltanschauungslehre*), Leipzig 1923.

theory rests on no less considerable an *underestimate* of the possible *unity* and universality of mystical contact with God as a person, because he takes insufficient notice of the *psychic techniques* which necessarily belong to mystical experience; in his comparative ignorance here he is a true son of the Protestant culture which rejects such psychic disciplines root and branch. There is, as you know, a prejudice shared by rationalists, ecclesiolaters and adherents (like Scholz) of a wayward individualistic, aristocratic religiosity to the effect that no mystical 'experimental theology' could ever acquire any kind of consistent universal validity in the sphere of religious experience or for the theory of such experience. But it seems to me that the reason for this prejudice does not lie in the first place in the existence (which I admit) of predispositions and their greater or lesser allotment to individuals, but in the lack of knowledge and appreciation of psychic techniques as a means not to ethical, practical ends but to an increase in *religious knowledge:* it is a lack which has diminished the attention paid to such disciplines and has therefore militated against their uniform exercise—it is a more or less constitutional deficiency over the whole of modern Europe. It follows that our theses depend for their full elaboration and verification on something which is absent from this book but which we hope to pursue systematically elsewhere,[1] namely a fundamental treatment, in accordance with our present psychology, of the *technique* appertaining to the mystical experience of divinity and the corresponding living network of procedures and states of mind.

One possible misunderstanding remains to be forestalled. The reader would completely misunderstand my book, in particular 'Problems of Religion', if he were to seek my *metaphysics* in it, or if he were to believe that he learned something essential in it about my metaphysical beliefs and theories, as I have been expounding them for years in, for example, my academic lectures on metaphysics—and as I hope to publish them shortly in quite another connection, without a word on religion. Of course, here and there certain very formal propositions belonging to metaphysics have been drawn into the argument, but only in so far as required by the formal object *ens a se,* which belongs simultaneously and identically to both metaphysics and religion. Our view of the total *independence and freedom from preconceptions* of metaphysics in regard to religion would alone suffice to preclude our attaching a metaphysics *en appendice* to a book on the philosophy of religion. Metaphysics must be based on the whole diverse

[1] On techniques of patience and suffering see certain passages in my essay '*Vom Sinne des Leides*' (in *Moralia*); on the technique of concentration see my *Wesen und Formen der Sympathie.* Cf. also C. Hock's much-discussed *Die Übung der Vergegenwärtigung Gottes,* Würzburg 1919, and criticisms of it by A. Mager and J. Lindworsky.

reality of experience in life, learning and history, and at the same time on the *whole* ideal, essential ontology of the world and its modes of being—either that, or it has no right at all to exist. As to how metaphysics and religion should come to terms, if that be so, that is a second question, another problem. *A priori* neither of them has an obligation to 'agree' of its own accord with the other: any consciously tendentious relationship of dependence or subservience is wholly wrong. It is of course desirable—though no more is desirable—that each should *voluntarily* extend a hand to the other, in the sense of what I have termed the 'system of conformity' of faith and knowledge. Again, it is true that in ascribing predicates to the *ens a se* neither may contradict the other, but this is a requirement which lies in the *nature* of the *ens* and of the human mind. On the other hand one may not legitimately demand that metaphysics should predicate the *same* constitutive attributes to the *ens a se* which the religious consciousness ascribes to it. Religious experience can discover attributes which will always be hidden to metaphysics, but metaphysics can also discover attributes which religion could never discover by its own procedures. For metaphysics the object *ens a se*, in its concrete hypostasis, can only be likened to an *infinitely remote* point towards which converge all the *substantial* utterances of the metaphysician, *i.e.* those which go beyond formal ontology and have essentially no more than *probable* validity. In contrast to this restriction, religious experience enables the personal self to transpose itself *directly* into the godhead, and seeks from that position, and from what it has learned and experienced in it, to understand the meaning of this *world*.

Cologne,   MAX SCHELER
Christmas 1922

REPENTANCE AND REBIRTH

REPENTANCE AND REBIRTH

BEHIND the stirrings of the conscience, its warnings, its counsel, its condemnations, the spiritual eye of Faith is ever aware of the outline of an invisible, everlasting Judge. These stirrings seem to form a wordless natural discourse from God to the soul, prompting the course of its salvation and the world's. It is here an open question whether it is at all possible to separate the peculiar unity and the sense of the so-called *stirrings* of conscience from this view of them as a secret 'voice' and symbolic language of God, and yet preserve intact the unity of what we call conscience itself. I doubt it, and believe rather that if it were not for the participation of a divine Judge those very stirrings would disintegrate into a host of phenomena—feelings, images, opinions—and that there would no longer remain any basis for conceiving them as a unity. Furthermore, it seems to me that no positive act of interpretation is demanded before we attribute the function of adumbrating such a judge to the psychic material of these stirrings: on the contrary they exercise of their own accord this God-intimating function, and one would have to close or avert one's eyes to avoid experiencing it as an integral part of them. Just as phenomena of pitch and colour, unlike pain and well-being, do not present themselves as mere sensations of our bodies (which are simply 'what they are') but from the outset as objective phenomena that cannot be 'sensed' apart from their function of bringing us, with their own content, information about a real world, just so there dwells from the outset within these stirrings of conscience the implication of some invisible Order, and of some spiritual, personal Subject presiding thereover. We are no more led by a 'causal inference' from these stirrings to God's existence than we are led to the existence of a red ball by a 'causal inference' from its extended red appearance. But in both cases something *is presented* in the act of experience: something transcending the medium of presentation, yet nevertheless apprehended in it.

Among the stirrings of conscience Repentance is the one whose characteristic is to judge, and to concern itself with our past lives.

Its nature, its meaning, its connection with the whole course and purpose of our life have been so frequently, profoundly and fundamentally misunderstood by the *désordre du cœur* of the present age that it is essential to clear the ground for the proper determination of its positive nature. We must therefore subject the modern theories of its origin, sense and worth, which for the most part are altogether facile and superficial, to a critical examination:

Modern philosophy almost invariably sees in Repentance merely a negative and, so to speak, highly uneconomical, even superfluous act—a disharmony of the mind which may be ascribed to lack of thought, or to sickness, or to illusions of the most diverse kind.

When the medical layman observes rashes, purulence or boils on a body, or those unattractive deformations of skin and tissue associated with healing wounds, he can for the most part see nothing more therein than a symptom of one sickness or another. It takes the pathologist to show him in detail how these phenomena are at the same time highly developed and ingenious methods whereby the organism rids itself of certain poisons in order to heal itself, and how indeed pernicious conditions which the organism would otherwise suffer are often checked in advance by their intervention. Even mere shivering is more than a symptom of chill: it is also a means of warming us. Our nature comprises distinct stages of being, which may not, as superficial monisms will have it, be reduced to a single one: mind, soul; flesh, body. Nevertheless, certain comparable regularities are to be found in the first three stages, which exhibit a profound common analogy. Thus Repentance too has, together with, and even in consequence of, its negative, demolishing function, another which is positive, liberating and constructive. It is only to the casual observer that Repentance appears as a mere symptom of some disharmony of the mind or even as a useless deadweight which is more of a hindrance than a help along the way. People say: 'Surely having regrets leads us to dwell morbidly on a past which is done with and unalterable, and whose content—as determinists maintain—happened exactly as it had to happen, given all the causes of our regretted behaviour?' And 'No regrets!—just try harder next time!' is the jovial slogan of the plain man, with his indulgent smile and well-meaning impatience.

Thus judged, Repentance is not only a 'useless deadweight': it originates moreover, in a form of peculiar self-deception. This supposedly consists first in our setting our faces against past reality and absurdly attempting both to eject that reality from the world and to reverse the current of the river of time in which our life flows by; but it is said also to consist in our subconsciously equating the Self that regrets the deed with the Self that performed it, whereas (through subsequent mental events, and even through the deed itself and its sequel) the Self has become, by any test of identity, something constitutionally different. Because we like to think that we could now refrain from the deed, we imagine—so it is said—the possibility that we could have refrained from it when we performed it. Others go even further, maintaining that in the act of repentance we confound our memory-image of the deed with the deed itself. It is then, they would have us know, to this *image* that the pain, suffering and grief comprised in Repentance adhere; they do not adhere to the deed itself, which lies behind us so still and silent, speaking to our understanding only through its effects, of which the image is just another one. But inasmuch as we now transpose this present memory back to the time and place of the deed, the deed itself is clothed for us in that character which is no more than an emotional reaction to the effect of the present image.

Such is the 'psychological' way in which for example Nietzsche has sought to explain away Repentance as a kind of inner deception. The repentant lawbreaker, in his opinion, cannot endure the 'image of his deed', and 'calumniates' the deed itself through this 'image'. According to Nietzsche, Repentance, like 'bad conscience' in general, arose when passions of hate, revenge, cruelty and spite of all kinds, which once were allowed free play against fellow-men, came to be dammed in by State, Law and Civilization, and thereupon turned for their satisfaction against the life-matter of those who felt them. 'In times of peace, man the warrior must needs attack himself.'

Rather less 'wild' than this hypothesis is the suggestion that Repentance is a kind of revenge upon oneself, a reflexive tit-for-tat, the mere carrying out of a kind of self-punishment, which in its most primitive form is not necessarily directed exclusively against what is considered 'wicked', but is also exemplified in such expressions as 'I could tear my hair for doing that!' or 'I could kick myself!', on occasions when it is plain in the event that one has acted against one's own interests or otherwise made some 'slip'. If the revenge-animus of a wronged man B against wrongdoer A may find satisfaction through the action of some—as it were—depersonalized force of retribution (whether it be a sympathetic third party or, at a later stage, government and authority in a similar rôle), it can be imagined that the retributive impulse set going by any 'wrong' might avail itself of the urge to self-punishment which has just been described, and that in this way retribution comes to be exacted even in cases where one is oneself the author of a reprehensible deed or injustice. It is noticeable that this theory envisages the will to make reparation and do penance as a stage prior to true Repentance, and as rather its cause than its consequence. By this reading, Repentance is an intensified will to reparation.

Finally, I shall mention three more 'modern views' of Repentance which are much in favour: the Fear-theory, the 'Hangover'-theory, and that view of Repentance as a psychological malady which is different only in degree —not in essence—from pathological self-accusation, from masochism, from 'self-indulgent wallowing in one's own sins', etcetera—in short, from any kind of mental self-torture.

The Fear-theory is probably the prevalent conception in the theology, philosophy and psychology of recent times. According to this, Repentance is 'nothing but' (as you know, most 'modern' theories take this 'nothing-but' form) '—nothing but a kind of wish that one hadn't done something', which wish is founded in a fear, that has become as it were pointless, of possible punishment. Therefore, no Repentance but for a pre-existent system of punishment! The only thing by which the anguish of contrition differs from ordinary fear of punishment is the absence of any particular-ized image of the pain of punishment, of the agent of punishment, of the type and method of punishment, or of the time and place of its carrying out. Repentance is thus a hereditary echo of earlier experiences of punishment, where, however, the middle terms are missing in the chain of association between the mental image of the relevant deed and the pain of punishment felt long ago; perhaps it is itself, as Darwinists like further to maintain, a beaten path of association between the two things, which has become an inheritance of the individual. By this interpretation Repent-ance is a kind of cowardice grown systematic, which refuses to accept the consequences of one's actions and is at the same time a weakness of the memory which serves the interests of the race.

It is not then, in this view, a pointer to a divine Judge. It is, rather, an interiorization of yesterday's policeman.

The second point of view, the 'Hangover'-theory, is somewhat more rarely encountered in philosophy, but all the more often in everyday life. Repentance is said to be basically a state of depression which normally supervenes once the tensions accompanying an action have been relaxed, whenever the after-effects have proved harmful and unpleasant. Thus Repentance is by nature a kind of 'moral hangover', which admittedly finds a subsequent 'higher significance' in the act of judgment. In par-ticular, excesses in the satisfaction of sensual instincts (in eating, drinking, sexual intercourse, fine living, etc.) and their depressive after-effects form, in this view, the basis of a melancholy state of mind in which we after-wards repudiate these excesses: *Omne animal post coïtum triste*, and 'Young whores make old penitents'. The doubtless correct observation that, even outside this sphere of what is harmful to health, other mishaps may dispose one to repentance, appears to lend support to this point of view.

For every one of the above-mentioned attitudes, Repentance represents, naturally, behaviour as pointless as it is senseless. 'Pointless' is indeed the favourite epithet with which it is dismissed by the mass of people today. Really clever people add that Repentance is not only pointless but also 'harmful', since its effect can only be to hamper our living and acting, and since it resembles nakedly retributive punishment in having something distasteful about it which its capacity for increasing the sum of pleasure in life-as-a-whole can by no means justify. For even if Repentance is occasionally productive of good resolve and improvement, it is not, so they say, essential to the purpose, and can very well be dispensed with. And at the end of life, of what use is a deathbed repentance, a customary and particularly forceful instance, if it results in nothing but, just now and again, this trend of improvement? It is much truer to say that, far from improving matters, it hampers life while life is still running its course, in that it chains us to an unalterable past.

All these explanations and indictments of Repentance, from Spinoza via Kant to Nietzsche, rest upon grave errors. Repentance is neither a spiritual deadweight nor a self-deception, it is neither a mere symptom of mental disharmony nor an absurd attempt on the part of the human soul to cast out what is past and immutable.

On the contrary, Repentance, even from the purely ethical aspect, is a form of self-healing of the soul, is in fact its only way of regaining its lost powers. And in religion it is something yet more: it is the natural function with which God endowed the soul, in order that the soul might return to him whenever it strayed from him.

One of the principal causes of the misconception of Repentance (and one which underlies all the supposed 'explanations') is a false notion of the internal structure of our spiritual life. One can in no way fully understand Repentance unless one places it within a deeper overall conception of the nature of our temporal life-stream in relation to our permanent personal Self.* That becomes at once apparent if one examines the sense of the argument that Repentance is the meaningless attempt to turn a past act into something which has never happened. If our existence as a person were a kind of river which flowed past in the same objective Time wherein natural events take place, resembling that stream even if differing in content, this way of talking might be justified. No 'afterwards' part of the river could then turn back over a part 'gone before' or effect any kind of alteration in it. But standing in opposition to the continuous flux of inanimate nature with its movements and changes—whose 'Time' is a uniform one-dimensional and one-directional continuum, lacking the tripartition into past, present and future—there are present to us in the experience of every one of our indivisible, temporal moments of life the structure and idea of the *entirety* of our life and personal Selfhood. Every single one of these life-moments, corresponding with just one indivisible point of objective Time, contains within itself its three extensions: the experienced past, the present being experienced and the future, whose ingredients are constituted by awareness, immediate memory and immediate expectation. It is by virtue of this wonderful fact that—perhaps not the material reality—but the *sense* and *worth* of the whole of our life still come, at every moment of our life, within the scope of our *freedom* of action. We are not the disposers merely of our future; there is also no part of our past life which—while its component natural reality is of course less freely alterable than the future—might not still be genuinely altered in its *meaning* and *worth*, through entering our life's total significance as a constituent of the self-revision which is always possible.

Let us imagine our experiences up to a given point in time as the parts of a line P(ast)-F(uture), which represents a section of objective Time.

$$\overset{\displaystyle R}{\overbrace{}}$$

$$\text{P} \qquad a \quad b \quad c \quad d \quad e \quad f \quad g \qquad \text{F}$$

It would not then be the case, as in inanimate nature, that b was determined unequivocally at a given moment by a, then c by b, d by c, and so on. Rather is it the case that g, the latest event, is in principle determined through the whole row R (a to f), and that moreover every one of the events a, b, c, d and e are capable of becoming once more 'effective' upon g and upon all the events to come. The event lying in the past has this capability without first entering (whether as itself or as a so-called 'image' of itself) as a component into the position f immediately preceding g. Since, however, the total efficacy of an event is, in the texture of life, bound up with its *full* significance and *final* value, every event of our past remains *indeterminate* in significance and *incomplete* in value until it has yielded *all* its potential effects. Only when seen in the whole context of life, only when we are dead (which, however, implies 'never', if we assume an after-life), does such an event take on the completed significance and 'unalterability' which render it a fact such as past events in nature are from their inception. Before our life comes to an end the whole of the past, at least with respect to its significance, never ceases to present us with the problem of *what we are going to make of it*. For no sooner does a section of objective time enter into that extension-category of our experience which we know as our past, than it is deprived of that fatality and completion which past events in nature possess. As *past* this time-content becomes 'ours'—is subordinated to the power of the *personal Self*. Therefore, the extent and nature of the effects that every part of our past may exercise upon the sense of our life lie still within our power at *every* moment of our life. This proposition is valid for every 'fact' in 'historical reality', whether in the history of the individual, the race or the world. *'Historical reality' is incomplete and, so to speak, redeemable.* I grant that everything about the death of Cæsar which appertains to the events of nature is as complete and invariable as the eclipse of the sun which Thales prophesied. But whatever belonged on that occasion to 'historical reality', whatever is woven of it as meaning and effect into the fabric of man's history, is an incomplete thing, and will not be complete until the end of world-history.

Now, our nature possesses wonderful powers of releasing itself from the further effects of one or other member in the chain of past experiences. Even the clear, objective remembering of the event in question, though this mental function is commonly misconstrued as a factor without which the past may not take effect upon our life, is such a power. For the act of remembering depends for its effectiveness upon a source of strength identical with the life-nerve of that force which, in accordance with the above principle of psychic efficacy, goes on mysteriously living and acting within us; that force, then, receives a vital hurt from the objectification, the precise locating of time and place, to which the remembering mind directs its cool perception. If a falling stone were able, in a given phase of its fall, to remember the preceding phase—which alone is determining it to fall through the succeeding phase according to a prevailing law—the law of gravitation would immediately be nullified. For remembering is the beginning of *freedom* from the covert power of the remembered thing and occurrence. It is precisely by being remembered that experiences usually make their exit from the inner temple of our life; it is the way in which they become detached from the centre of the Self whose attitude to the world they formerly helped to form, and in which they lose their direct impact. Memory, then, is so far from being a factor in the 'stream of psychic causality' that it really interrupts this stream and brings parts of it to a halt, is so far from transmitting the effect of our past upon our present life that on the contrary it liberates us from the determining power of that effect.

History comprehended frees us from the power of the history we live. Likewise the *knowledge* of history (as distinct from that saga of human and intellectual adventures which 'tradition' hallows) is first and foremost a *liberator* from historical determination.

The phenomenon of Repentance also has its place in this general scheme of ideas. Repenting is equivalent to re-appraising part of one's past life and shaping for it a mint-new worth and significance. People tell us that Repentance is a senseless attempt to drive out something 'unalterable'. But nothing in this life is 'unalterable' in the sense of this argument. Even this 'senseless' attempt alters the 'unalterable' and places the regretted conduct or attitude in a new relation within the totality of one's life, setting it to work in a new direction. People tell us Repentance is absurd, since we enjoyed no freedom and everything had to happen as it did. It is true that no one would be free who could not repent. But only repent—and see how as a result of the act you acquire what in the beginning you unwisely deemed a prerequisite of that act as you saw it—*freedom*! You are now *free* from the floodtide of bygone guilt and wickedness that was sweeping you relentlessly away, *free* from that rigid chain of effect, such as subsisted before repentance, which produces ever new guilt from old so that the pressure grows like an avalanche.

It is not repented but only unrepented guilt that holds the power to bind and determine the future. Repentance kills the life-nerve of guilt's action and continuance. It drives motive and deed—the deed with its root—*out* of the living centre of the Self, and thereby enables life to begin, with a spontaneous, virginal beginning, a new course springing forth from the centre of the personality which, by virtue of the act of repentance, is no longer in bonds.

Thus Repentance effects moral rejuvenation. Young forces, as yet guiltless, are dormant in every soul. But they are hampered, indeed smothered, by the tangled growths of oppressive guilt which in the course of time have gathered and thickened within the soul. Tear away the undergrowth, and those forces will rise up of their own accord.

You may choose always to resemble Prometheus and never Epimetheus. But the more 'progressively' you speed forward, borne down the stream of life, the more you are *dependent* on this pressure of past guilt, and the more you are *bound* by it. You are merely fleeing your guilt while you think to take the crown of life by storm, for your *storming* is your secret flight. The more you close your eyes to what should be a subject of repentance, the more tightly you bind on your feet the chains that encumber your progress.

But even the ordinary upholder of free-will errs when he speaks of Repentance. He mistakenly insists that it is conditional upon that new freedom which is in fact first *realized* in the act of repentance. Well may the plain man say, 'No regrets!—just resolve to do better in future'. But what the plain man fails to tell us is where we may find strength to make those resolutions, still less the strength to carry them out, if Repentance has not first liberated the personal Self and empowered it to combat the determining force of the past. Resolutions not intimately linked with a consciousness of strength and ability to carry them out are precisely those good intentions with which the 'road to Hell' is so invitingly paved. There indeed we have a profound proverb which is vindicated by the principle that every good resolve which does not carry within it the strength for its execution does not merely reveal its uselessness by maintaining the existing torment of mind, but adds to the Self a new and positive defeat, which it even serves to entrench and consolidate. The path to the utmost self-contempt passes nearly always through unfulfilled resolutions which were not preceded by any *genuine* repentance. After any non-fulfilled resolution the Self is no longer on the same level, but finds itself far more deeply degraded than before. This therefore is the paradoxical position: Even supposing it were true that the sole value of Repentance lay in its possible amendment of future intention and conduct, the immanent *sense* of the act of repentance would still have to relate exclusively to the past misdemeanour, without any surreptitious regards to future reformation. But the supposition is erroneous.

As for the objection that the act of repentance does not affect deed an conduct during the deed but only the memory-*image*, which itself has not arisen uninfluenced by the deed and its sequel, it is in like case: an entirely false conception of memory underlies such talk. Memory does not consist in there being in our present consciousness a pre-existent 'image', which is referred to something in the past only by conscious adjudgment. On the contrary, the original act of remembering comprises a kind of re-possession *of the very situation* appearing in the phenomenal past, a living and dwelling within *that*, not the possession of a present image which must await inspection before being referred to the past or 'assumed' to be there. Whatever memory-images are present during the act of remembering are, moreover, conditioned by the trend and purpose of the *intention* of that act. The images follow this intention and change in accordance with it; the intention does not follow in haphazard or mechanical fashion a train of images linked by mental association.

What we call the *Person* or personal Self, that central concretion of our responsible acts ranging over the course of time, can of its nature— *de jure*—contemplate every part of our past life, can lay hold of its sense and worth. The only factors which are dependent on prevailing physiological conditions, on the reproductive causes which they govern and on the associated principles of this reproduction, are those which determine what *selection* is made from that life-realm which is in principle accessible

to the act of remembering. Therefore Repentance is in the act a true
incursion into the past sphere of our life, and a genuinely effective en-
croachment upon it. Repentance genuinely extinguishes the element of
moral detraction, the quality of 'wickedness', of the conduct in question,
it genuinely relieves the pressure of the guilt which spreads in all directions
from that wickedness, and at the same time deprives evil of that power
of reproduction by which it must always bring forth more evil. In accordance with the general rule whereby the value-qualities of our life are
presented to the memory before any other of its significant qualities,*
readiness to repent provides a light which shines into our past to such
good effect that we begin to summon up images of many things which we
did not previously recall. Repentance breaks down that barrier of pride
which restricts resurgence to such past events as furnish pride with
satisfaction and justification; it relieves one from the repressive force
of 'natural' pride; it thus becomes a vehicle of truth against oneself.

At this point the special connection of readiness to repent with the
system of virtues in the soul becomes clearly apparent. Just as in its
absence truth against oneself is impossible, so readiness to repent is itself
impossible in the absence of *humility*, which works against the natural
pride ensnaring the soul in the focal here-and-now of the active Self.
It is only possible when humility, resulting from steady self-reform, inspired by that clear idea of absolute good which we know to measure our
inadequacy, dispels the repressive, hardening and obdurative tendencies
of pride and sets the active Self, which pride had isolated from the dynamic
of the life-stream, once more in a fluid relation with this stream and the
world. Man is rendered obdurate far more by pride and presumption
than by the fear of punishment born of his concupiscence, and the more
deeply guilt is embedded in him, the more it has become, as it were, *part*
of him, the greater is his obduracy. It is not confession, but the initial
surrender of himself, which is so difficult for the hardened impenitent.
He who repents his deed also confesses his deed and overcomes himself—
overcomes even the shame which would close his lips at the last moment.[1]

It follows that Repentance must therefore be generally misunderstood
in its nature, sense and achievement where it is confused (in conformity
with that theory of memory which reduces the function of remembering
to the reproduction of 'memory-images') with conditions which may well
pre-dispose and facilitate it, but by no means constitute Repentance itself.

---

[1] Church doctrine correctly assumes that the 'perfect' repentance which washes
away all guilt automatically produces the readiness to make both inner acknowledgment and oral confession, and that where such readiness is lacking the
repentance may not be deemed perfect.

It is quite correct that the failure or unhappy consequences of 'wicked' conduct more easily dispose human weakness to repentance than positive success, that thus for example injury to health, etc., resulting from guilty excesses, or punishment and disgrace imposed by society, frequently *induce* the act of repentance in cases where it might not otherwise have been induced. Nevertheless, the suffering attendant on Repentance *per se* is divided by a deep gulf from all these various revulsions conducive to rueful introspection. Quite a host of fallacious psychological theories of repentance fall into this basic error—among others—of confusing the act of repentance with its *predisposing circumstances*.

The peculiar nature of the rôle which memory plays in the act of repentance is not, however, exhausted by the foregoing. There are two basically different types of memory, which may be differentiated as static and dynamic, or *phenomenal* and *functional* memory. In remembering of the first type we do not relive isolated incidents or situations of our past but reinhabit the central *attitude* to the world which we then adopted, together with its *tendencies* of thought and will, love and hate; we conform to our total attitude of that time, in other words to the identity and disposition of the Self which then prevailed. This is a distinction which certain pathological phenomena bring into sharp focus. In a German lunatic asylum, some years ago, I came across an old man of seventy who was experiencing his entire environment on the plane of development reached in his nineteenth year. That doesn't mean that the man was still lost amid the actual *objects* making up his world when he was a boy of eighteen, that he saw his home of those days, with its attendant people, streets, towns, etc. No, he saw, heard and experienced nothing but what was going on around him in the room, but he lived it all *as* the boy of eighteen he once was, with all that boy's individual and general impulses and ambitions, hopes and fears. The special kind of re-living in memory which is here demonstrated in its extreme form and as a self-sufficient system enables us to know not only what we in fact did and how in fact we reacted to our environment, but also what we would have done, what indeed we *could have wanted* to do, how we *would have* reacted, when confronted by this or that circumstance. In this kind of remembering the path does not lead from the content of our life to the Self which lived it, but from the experiencing Self into which we displace ourselves to the specific content of the life.

But the kind of remembering which contributes to the deeper and more important type of Repentance comes under the heading of functional memory. In this case, although the past deed appears in memory and is related to the unworthiness of our conduct in performing it, the deed is not the actual object of repentance. Instead, the constituent Self in our total Person out of whose roots the deed, the act of will, arose is re-experienced and, in the course of repentance, cast down and thrust out of the totality of the personal Self. Where then certain writers distinguish between a *repentance of being* and a *repentance of conduct*, or even between 'repentance' and 'rueful introspection', they can only be referring to whether it is the objective disvalue of the past constituent Self or that of the momentary active Self performing the deed which preponderates in the repentant memory. Schopenhauer in particular used to stress that the deepest state of repentance is not expressed in the formula 'Alas! what have I done?' but in the more radical 'Alas! what kind of a person I am!' or even 'What sort of person *must* I be, to have been *capable* of such an action!' It is, moreover, his intention to illustrate that although empirical determinism first lends repentance its proper weight, the far deeper and more overwhelming character of that second form of repentance is a proof that our 'intelligible character' (which Schopenhauer inaccurately equates with 'innate character') is nevertheless regarded as a consequence of the exercise of free will.

But this is a theory which rends asunder the whole meaning of Repentance. It is implicitly not possible to repent one's very person in its quintessential Being. We may, I grant, be *sorry* that we are what we are, or even be shocked, but—quite apart from the fact that our sorrow itself would be coloured by our essential nature—we cannot repent our Being. Once we cease to regard exclusively the details of our past conduct, the only thing left for us to repent is that we *then* were such a person as *could* do that deed! It is not the deed, and certainly not our essential Self, that in this act of repentance lie both 'behind' and 'below' us, but that concretion of the Self from which memory showed us the deed arising—'*necessarily*' arising, if such a concretion may be at all supposed.

The unique impact and significance of the deeper act of repentance —which impels no mere adjustment of outlook or good resolve but a veritable *transformation* of outlook—can be understood only if we take account of the following. The manner in which we reflexively experience ourselves has definite *levels* of concentration and self-appraisal, and the change from one level to another is not unreservedly determined by the overall psychic causality which determines psychic processes within any one level. Relatively to the causal pattern which governs the empirical contents on each level, a radical alteration of the very level, or range of levels, whereon the personality currently dwells is a *free act* of our total personal Self. And in the last resort it is to this total Self that all the successive concretions of Self belong as empirical constituents out of which, as this or that circumstance is revealed by memory, we see *the deed* arising. It is when such a freely effected alteration of the focal *level* of our whole inner life is seen to be its attendant phenomenon that the deeper act of repentance becomes fully comprehensible. However necessary the deed appears to us on the level of our existence at that time, however 'understandable' it is, down to its smallest details, in the strict historical sense—once we are confident of having 'placed' that level—there was no *like* necessity for us to *have been* on that level. We could have altered that level. Not only could we have *willed* and *acted* otherwise, we 'could' equally have *been* other than we were. Therefore this *ability to have been other than we were* is no mere illusory and misconceived back-dating of the quite separate fact that we *now* could act otherwise or think that we could. On the contrary, the act of repentance shows us this ability, this central will-power, as an ingredient pervading the whole earlier situation.

However, present acknowledgment of evil in the old Self, and present awareness of the better beings we could have been or better things we could have done, have their way of bursting through once we know from present experience our capacity for improvement of conduct. One might conclude that it is not the act of repentance which effects the alteration of level, that this act is only a sign and consequence of our present superiority to the old Self and its deed. From this point of view we could now repent only *because* we are now freer and better. Indeed, when measured against the newly-felt capacity for improvement there evidently falls across the earlier deed and situation the shadow of a guilty constraint, in which we see them now lying far below us. But this is not a matter which may be reduced to such a simple, rational either/or.

For it is the peculiar nature of Repentance that in the very act which is so painfully destructive we gain our first complete insight into the badness of our Self and conduct, and that in the same act which seems rationally comprehensible only from the 'freer' vantage point of the new plane of existence, this very vantage point is attained. So the act of repentance precedes in a certain sense both its point of departure and its point of arrival, its *terminus a quo* and its *terminus ad quem*.

It is Repentance, then, which first brings home to us the knowledge of a past capacity for better conduct. But this knowledge is in no way *productive*; it is mere awareness, a penetration of the instinctual fog which blinded us. It produces nothing: it only informs.

Thus the continuous dynamic of Repentance enables us to glimpse the attainment of an altogether higher, ideal existence—the raising through firm self-revision of the whole plane of our moral existence—and lays open to our gaze, far below us, the whole condition of the old Self. This is the deepest mystery of that vital, deeper act of repentance, and it has given rise to many difficulties in systematic theology. We find, in particular, an analogous problem underlying the interaction between divine remission of guilt and the new quality of man initiated by sanctifying grace. It appears that only the free grace entering with 'perfect' repentance can truly erase and eradicate the guilt of sin—not merely so order matters, as Luther would have it, that God closes his eyes to guilt and 'counts it not', while man lingers on in sin and guilt. And yet again the admission of grace would seem *conditional* upon the removal of guilt. For grace, like the higher existence conditional upon it, can only make inroads into the human being in so far as guilt is removed. Many theologians (Scheeben for example) make use at this juncture of a felicitous simile: guilt, they say, retreats before the advance of grace into the soul 'as darkness before light'.[1] In this way Repentance no longer appears to presuppose the very upraising of the moral being which it is assumed to initiate. It is therefore one and the same act which effects both the Self's upstriving to its potential height of ideal existence and the perceptible descent of the old Self, its destruction and expulsion.

Just as, when climbing a mountain, we see both the summit's approach, and the valley sinking beneath our feet, each picture entering our experience under the control of the one act, so in Repentance the Person mounts, and in mounting sees below it the former constituent Selves.

The more Repentance ceases to be mere repentance of conduct and becomes repentance of Being, the more it grasps the *root* of guilt perceived, to pluck it out of the Person and restore the latter's freedom, and the more also it makes the transition from shame over a particular deed to that completeness of 'hearty contrition' out of which an indwelling force of regeneration builds up a 'new heart' and a 'new man'. To that extent, then, Repentance even assumes the character of a true *repentance of conversion* and leads finally from good resolutions through a deeper alteration of outlook to *transformation* of outlook—that is, to a positive 'rebirth'—wherein, without detriment to its formal and individual identity, the spiritual core of the Person, which is the ultimate root of our moral acts, appears to burn away all remnant of the objects of its former regard and to build itself anew.

Something remains to be said about two of the skeptical theses mentioned earlier: the Fear-theory and the Revenge-theory.

The Fear-theory was already to the fore in the early history of

[1] Matthias Scheeben: *Die Mysterien des Christentums* (Freiburg 1912), p. 531,

Protestantism. Luther and Calvin find the essence of contrition itself in the *terrores conscientiae*, in that fear of Hell whose onset succeeds man's perception of his inadequacy to observe God's law. For Luther this terror is the only motive driving man, aware of his burden of sin and of his necessary insufficiency before the law, to secure justification through faith in Jesu's redeeming blood and in the atonement and divine mercy which that blood obtained. In that Jesus 'shields' the heart of man, sinful now and sinful to remain until death, from the eye of God with the fulness of his merits, 'the sin is not counted' against the sinner; in other words, the punishment of the sin is remitted. 'Good resolve', as well as a certain diminution of sinfulness, are expected to ensue when man is fully conscious of the wholly undeserved mercy of God and its attendant state of grace. And so resolve is here completely divorced from Repentance. In this view the divine 'forgiveness' of sin has the sense of neither a true extinction of guilt as a pre-existent condition, nor a healing displacement of guilt by a new sanctifying quality within the soul. Its whole meaning resides in the remission of punishment and in the assumption by the sinner that God now 'turns a blind eye' upon his sin—a somewhat unintelligible assumption, and one which runs altogether counter to the omniscience of God.

But more recent secular philosophy also takes the Fear-theory as a point of departure:

'Repentance[1] is no virtue, and does not spring from reason; but whosoever repents a deed is doubly oppressed and incapable.' 'For whosoever repents a deed suffers doubly, in that he permits himself to be overcome first by a reprehensible desire and thereafter by disgust concerning it.' Spinoza is also one of those who find in fear the origin of Repentance, that 'disgust, accompanied by the idea of the deed, which we believe we have performed out of a free decision of the mind', to quote his untenable definition. According to his further explanation, Repentance is a consequence of blame and of penalties imposed by society, with an attendant fear, based on observed effect, that attaches itself to the idea of any deed we come to regard as 'wrong'. 'Thus does man according to his education repent or glory in a deed.' Spinoza therefore sees in Repentance no more than a relative virtue, a virtue for the common herd. 'The people should be feared in so far as they do not fear.' But Repentance is no virtue for the 'free man'; *he* is guided by reason itself.

What radically contradicts the Fear-theory is above all the fact that it is on the contrary fear which normally prevents us from reaching that mental level of unflinching self-'possession' in which true Repentance

[1] Spinoza: *Ethics* IV, Proposition 45.

becomes possible. Fear directs our attention and interest outward—to face oncoming danger. An active type of criminal, while he knows himself the object of a hue and cry, will defiantly stand by his crime, devoting all his energies to 'not letting himself be caught'. One of more passive disposition will allow fear to cow him and reluctantly submit to his fate. In either case, even were nothing else to hinder repentance, fear would prevent it. A man must know himself out of immediate danger before he can come to that self-possession which is a prerequisite of true Repentance. Then for the first time he can find that *being alone* with oneself and one's deed, without which there is no Repentance. Apart from that, we are able to make a very clear conscious distinction between retrospective repentance of a deed and the simultaneous fear which looks future-wards; at the same time we confirm that the two occur in—so to speak—entirely different *strata* of our existence. We see how the fear breaks forth from the centre of our consciousness of life, and would be completely removed if its vehicle, the body and its sensations, were abstracted: Repentance, on the other hand, is felt to flow forth from the psychic centre of personality, and after abstraction of our tenement of clay would not only remain possible but be enabled to reach *perfection*, through our release from the strait-jacket of fleshly instincts, which distract us from perception of our wickedness. This independent but *simultaneous* existence of fear and Repentance in relation to the same valuation of the deed shows at once that Repentance cannot be a psychic 'evolved form' of fear, since if that were so the fear would have had to be consumed and transmuted in forming the new pattern of Repentance; therefore it could not still pervasively *co*-exist in us with Repentance.*

These naturally remain valid propositions when we consider fear of divine punishment. Mere fear of the pain of punishment—'servile fear'— has nothing in common with Repentance. Nor is it even *attritio*, which theology rightly distinguishes from *contritio*—that is, from 'perfect' Repentance founded on the act of loving God as the highest good and intrinsically the most worthy of love. No, *attritio* neither *is* fear of the mere pain of punishment, nor is it even based on such fear. Certainly it may be '*triggered*' by fear of the punishment itself as an utterance of divine justice, but never by fear of pain *qua* pain. But even then Repentance proper stands apart from this 'triggering' process as something altogether new and distinct from fear of punishment. Moreover, the so-called fear of (eternal or temporal) punishment is powerless to precipitate genuine Repentance unless its primary object is not the mere *pain* but the punishment itself as an act and expression of eternal justice, unless therefore its roots lie also in *reverence* and respect for the divinity administering this justice and meting out punishment. If then *attritio* represents a stage inferior to *contritio*, it must also be true that whenever *contritio* is possible for a person, mere *attritio* presents a positive hindrance to the admission of *contritio*, according to the rule whereby in general fear hampers rather than assists the development of Repentance.

From the viewpoint of a philosophy of fear it is no less difficult to grasp how it comes about that fear is transmuted into Repentance only when the thing or conduct detracting from the Person has some *moral* and *religious* significance. How is it that for example an ugly face, organic defect or deficiency of talent—things that are always coming to light, things one is unhappily obliged to encounter again and again—how is it that all these factors of detraction are never the object of Repentance but at the most objects of self-torture, of grief, of self-loathing, of revenge upon oneself? How is it that we never repent an unsuccessful venture, or a work of art that falls short of an ideal, in the same way as a theft or forgery? 'Never'; that is, save in so far as we are forced to ascribe poor achievement to *moral* insufficiency in the exercise of requisite skills: we never repent our deficiency of talent. Do we then feel that the sheer disgust which may arise from such defects, from unintelligence or inadequacy of disposition, is intrinsically any the less important?—and is there any the less cause for fear and disgust in 'the idea of oneself as the cause of our disgust'? Of course not. Notwithstanding, in such cases everything is lacking that could be called Repentance.

Now, if it is a necessary part of Repentance that the repented deficiency should be of that quality which is specified as 'evil', and that it should be discovered in the sensing of evil which goes to the making of Repentance, why should not this deficiency, that is the inner *character* of evil, in itself suffice to determine its emotional negation in the act of repentance? What does there remain for a fear of consequences to contribute, as a superfluous vehicle of the quality 'evil'? Or what need is there that the after-effects of this fear should intervene, to assist the realization of Repentance? Fear does from time to time occasion Repentance, but still more often— such is the general finding—it *adulterates* Repentance. In every possible form fear, even devoid of any specific object, is a presentiment, a premonition, *before* the actual hurt, of danger or of harm to life: Repentance *necessarily* is retrospective.

The Revenge-theory cuts rather deeper. There is undoubtedly an impulse to revenge directed against oneself. When a child hits itself for doing something 'wrong', when we 'could tear our hair' for acting in this or that way, when countless forms of self-punishment known to history do not necessarily represent religious penance or mortification of the flesh but bear all the marks of natural expiation or revenge upon the Self, then it appears one may correctly assume that a man possesses a primordial revenge-impulse even against himself. For it is hardly feasible to reduce such an impulse to a mere psychic infection with foreseen social blame or, as Adam Smith does in his fallacious doctrine of sympathy,[1] to an involuntary sympathy with the revenge-impulse of another—that is to say, a collaboration, against our will or without its participation, in the fulfilment of revenge against ourself. The revenge-impulse thus precedes primordially the specific choice between Self and not-Self for its object. In its original nature it can as well turn against our-self as against other persons.

There are today writers whose whole output seems—if one may speak thus—to feed upon a savage inner thirst for revenge against themselves and everything with which they are associated. In their satires they only *appear* to let fly against their invented characters: it is themselves alone whom they have in mind. It is therefore scarcely necessary to regard, with Nietzsche, such self-revenge as primarily a consequence and extreme retroversion of revenge-feelings against others, and similar impulses that are frustrated of outlet. *Both* the unbridled revenge-impulse and its rational, civilized form, the impulse to mete out proportional retribution, represent an immediate reaction to certain kinds of faulty conduct which from their nature 'demand to be expiated'.[2] It is noteworthy that the impulse to retribution ensues *before* the perpetrator is known or envisaged: the search for an object is a later step, and therefore does not exclude admitting *oneself* to be the uncovered perpetrator.

Yet no matter how one 'spiritualizes' these two impulses, the reality of Repentance remains unexplained! Well may the Revenge-theory appear to elucidate many features of Repentance which are quite unamenable to (*inter alia*) the Fear-theory: features such as the essential necessity of reference to the past, the peculiarly overwhelming keenness of remorse, the urge to expiate and repair the wrong, etc., etc. Nevertheless, the hypothesis still fails entirely to illuminate the dark core of the act as a whole. The attributes particularly lacking in revenge and self-retribution which would lend them an affinity, albeit at one remove, with Repentance are 1. spirituality[3] and inwardness, together with the medium of calm, repose, gravity and 'self-possession' in which Repentance is embedded; 2. the ascent to a higher plane of life which is realized in Repentance and is accompanied by the envisaging of the ideal worth, indeed the very

---

[1] See my book, *Zur Phänomenologie der Sympathiegefühle.**
[2] Cf. my analysis of expiation in *Formalismus in der Ethik und die materiale Wertethik.*
[3] Cf. my remarks on p. 50 concerning the possible abstraction of the body.

salvation, of our Person—that is, by an image once hidden from us to which we are now drawn in love, in 'love of our eternal good'; 3. the strengthening through Repentance and the liberation of our moral Self for good resolve and amendment of outlook; 4. restriction of reference to evil and moral guilt; this is characteristic only of Repentance, whereas revenge may attack any kind of suspected personal defect and any cause of faulty conduct. Revenge against the Self is undertaken in a mood of excitation, *devoid* of any foundation in a positive guiding-image of the Self's being and development; in these circumstances the attitude remains quite fruitless.

One thing, I grant, is beyond dispute: that in regard to any condition of self-torture or self-loathing, no matter how determined—be it even pathologically—which has resulted in a certain situation or course of conduct, we do have a strong tendency to *mistake* it (if at all possible) for genuine Repentance or to put it to our credit *as* Repentance. But such self-deceptions, which so often lead to the deception of others, *pre*suppose both the phenomenon of genuine Repentance and its positive valuation. In their cruelty to themselves, in their morbid love of pain, which 'wallows in suffering for sin', in their thirst for revenge against themselves, in their moral debilities, in their secret fear of the past or their obsessive brooding on it, in that jaundiced eye which they from time to time cast on themselves and all the world, in these men do indeed tend to *fancy* the image, well-pleasing to God, of a contrite heart, and to mask these their secret vices or mental illnesses under the semblance of a virtue. But this fate, which Repentance shares with every virtue, not to say every merit, that it can be *simulated* to the delusion of oneself and others, should give no cause for anybody who considers himself a psychologist to lose sight of Repentance itself behind its array of semblances.

Repentance is not, as is generally the first assumption, an inert 'feeling of disgust' attached to certain 'ideas' concerning conduct of which a man acknowledges himself to be the author. Let us put on one side this platitude of orthodox associational psychology. Repentance is on the contrary a purposeful *movement* of the mind in relation to guilt, aimed at whatever guilt has accumulated in the human being. The goal of this 'movement' is an emotional negation and neutralization of guilt's continuing effectiveness, an inner striving to drive guilt out of the vital core of the Person, to make that Person whole. What creates the *anguish* of Repentance is the reaction *against* this movement of the pressure of guilt, which is immediately increased in the act of repentance. As the unyielding quality of guilt increases, so does the anguish, and the deeper guilt is embedded in the core, the more it is unyielding. The first thing, then, is not the anguish, but the *movement* against guilt and the threat to its continuance; the anguish is secondary and consequent. The anguish of Repentance is by nature keen, burning, overwhelming; it has no dulness. But apart from this quality of pain there arises from the whole process a simultaneous peace and contentment which may rise to the height of bliss. Peace and enjoyment have nothing in common with discontent and disgust; yet see, this more deeply felt appeasement rises even as the anguish gains in force. Can it then be the inward perception that in this pain guilt's expiation lies —is it to this that the contentment testifies? Or to the removal of guilt's pressure as Repentance takes its course? One could assume the first if Repentance were envisaged as a kind of mental, reflexive retribution. But this assumption has been shown to be false. When one bows to a demand for expiation, one does *penance*, one does not repent. Such obedience is even possible without any basis of repentance. For though willingness to do penance is a necessary consequence of Repentance—as necessary as readiness to confess—it is not conversely true that Repentance must result from willingness to do penance. Still less is such willingness identical with Repentance. Least of all is Repentance a self-gratifying pain, though this may appear to be so when the place of genuine Repentance is usurped by an illusion of repentance founded on love of pain. Among others, the Pietists have often confused the two things: hence the highly sensual, almost masochistic colouring of their writings on Repentance.

And so progressive contentment is in fact a consequence of the gradual lifting of the pressure of guilt. It comes automatically to fruition as guilt is objectified and displaced from the centre of the Person.

If Repentance is a neutralization of guilt, then there must be guilt somewhere when the reaction of Repentance sets in.

But what is this 'guilt' then? It is that quality of 'evil' which in the course of time has accreted to the Person, the very seat of action, through its evil acts. And so guilt is a *quality*, not a 'feeling'. What is known as a 'sense of guilt' differs from other feelings only in its inner reference to this quality. So whether one feels guilty or not, the guilt sticks fast. It is most important to distinguish between on the one hand the existence of guilt and its measure, and on the other the varying subtlety or obtuseness of the sense of guilt, that is, the liminal values of the sensing of guilt. For one of the most mysterious ways in which guilt works is that it *provides its own concealment* and blunts all sensitivity to its existence. And conversely it is characteristic of the growth of humility and holiness in a person that, as the life of every saint bears witness, sensitivity to guilt *becomes more acute* functionally as guilt is objectively removed, and that therefore smaller and smaller failings are felt to be grave. And so the act of repentance is directed throughout not against the sense of guilt—which it is quite likely to extend and expand—but against the *objective quality* of guilt itself. But it is 'through' sensitivity to guilt that it is directed against guilt, just as the act of focusing one's own or someone else's attention is directed to an object through listening to or through seeing that object. In every case, then, the act of repentance must be *induced* by some feeling of guilt, usually unaccompanied at first by any pinpointing of the 'how?' and 'towards whom?' But only in and through the act of repentance does the sense of guilt normally find its expansion, location, direction and depth— often even its specific object in, say, this deed or that one. Admittedly, if guilt has grown so great that it entirely or almost stifles all feeling of its existence, it has indeed come to that partial or total hardening through which Repentance can no longer break, or break only with difficulty. Since guilt is a quality of the Person, the centre of action of the human being, and has through the Person's acts and deeds accreted to it as a pervasive 'complement', it remains latent, as long as it persists, in *every* act performed by the Person. It is not necessarily the real, causal consequences in nature of evil deeds which produce further evil: in a purely causal sense they are just as likely to issue in good or indifferent effects. There is no moral causality in that sense. But guilt, the dark work of these deeds in the very soul, enters into everything a man wills and does, and it determines, without his knowing, that he shall proceed in its direction. And so to this extent every repentance of conduct is not repentance directly concerning a deed, but repentance concerning the *guiltiness* which the deed has imposed on the Person. Nevertheless, repentance of conduct still differs from repentance of Being in its primary concern with the moral deficiency of the deed.

But what may Repentance accomplish in its attack upon guilt? Two things—of which it alone, and nothing else, is capable. It cannot drive out of the world the external natural reality of the deed and its causal consequences, nor the evil character which the deed acquires *ipso facto*. All that stays in the world. But it can totally kill and extinguish the *reactive* effect of the deed within the human soul, and with it the root of an eternity of renewed guilt and evil. Repentance, at least in its perfect form, genuinely annihilates the psychic quality called 'guilt'. And so it bursts the chain of evil's reproductive power which is transmitted through the growth in evil of men and times. This then is the way in which it enables men to embark on new and guiltless courses. Repentance is the mighty power of self-regeneration of the moral world, whose decay it is constantly working to avert.

There lies the great paradox of Repentance, that it sorrowfully *looks* back to the past while *working* mightily and joyfully for the future, for renewal, for release from moral death. Its mental concern and its living action are in diametric opposition. The progressive, the meliorist, the perfectionist, they all say *No regrets!—but do better in future.* Why, to them, even, Good is no more than the Better of tomorrow! But here is another paradox:—The more such people look to the future, the more projects for 'improvement' they continue, in their fear of inaction, to turn over in their minds, the more terribly all their inner activity is hounded by past guilt, hounded not merely in the execution but before that, in the selection of material for schemes and resolutions. *Thus* the eternal fugitive from his present and past sinks deeper and deeper into the dead arms of that very past. For the less one sees the guilt of history objectively, to repent it, the more mightily it is at work. And so the rubric is rightly not 'Forget Repentance and vow past action to future amendment' but '*Repent*, and *therefore* do better!'

Not utopianism but Repentance is the most *revolutionary* force in the moral world.

When we thus consider good resolve, amendment and transformation of outlook, the 'change of heart', we see they are not arbitrary measures subsequent upon, but divorced from, Repentance, nor are they a kind of by-product, dispensable and inessential. They all spring from Repentance as of their own accord. This is simply the fruit of the *natural* activity of a soul which has yielded itself to be cleansed from guilt and reinstated in its original and rightful eminence. The less the intention of 'good resolve' is contained in the initial act of repentance, the more powerful it is in the end, raised up out of Repentance as if by its own strength and almost without the assistance of conscious will. Moreover, the less the penitent allows his spiritual attention to digress towards the goodness of his newly repentant Self, turning Repentance into a fresh occasion for vanity and private glorification in his own or even in God's eyes, and the more painfully he is as *lost* in the depth of his guilt, the more majestically his god-created soul, all unbeknown, is rising to its height out of the dust of earthliness that used to stifle and pervade it. Meanwhile, the more deeply Repentance penetrates into the roots of being of a Person's source of action, the more it appears the equivalent, on a higher, spiritual plane, of that most elementary phenomenon of biology, described by A. Goette, in which the death and rebirth of an animal coincide as if one sole process, and the self-destroying animal builds itself anew.

For there is no Repentance which does not from its inception enclose the blueprint of a new heart. Repentance kills only to create. It annihilates only to rebuild. It is already building secretly where it still seems to destroy. So it is that Repentance forms the driving power of that miraculous process which the Gospels call the 'rebirth' of a new man out of the 'old Adam', the acquiring of a 'new heart'.

It is very superficial to imagine that the only occasions of Repentance should be certain quite special and obvious misdeeds and moral failures, forming a concrete debit, which must then be balanced by an equal credit of likewise quantitative repentance. The dark earth-realm of guilt we are discussing has such deeds and failures only as its visible peaks. Within the soul, guilt itself is the hidden reservoir which feeds each individual moral failure. Into this subterranean realm of the soul, into the hidden realm of its guilt, Repentance must descend, must as it follows down the slope awaken a new *consciousness* of this dark and hidden existence. If any therefore should say, 'I am not conscious of any guilt in myself, therefore I have nothing to repent'—he must surely be either a god or an animal. If however the speaker is a man, he as yet knows nothing of the nature of guilt.

A man should also be sure of this: Repentance is not only a process in the individual soul; like guilt it is basically also a social, historical, collective phenomenon. The great principle of the solidarity[1] of all the children of Adam in responsibility, guilt and merit implies that the subsistence of collective responsibility, together with each individual's awareness that he does in fact share responsibility for *all* events of the moral cosmos, has no primary connection with those perceptible, demonstrable *effects* which individuals exercise on one another whether directly or through whatever middle-terms, in the causal context of society and history, and which are accessible to their understanding. On the contrary, these effects, and our awareness of them, serve only to *locate* those points of the moral cosmos for which we can *know* with certainty our collective responsibility. But they do not *create* this responsibility, nor the feeling for it which—in so far as we are morally awakened—is our constant companion. There is, however, a pure form of collective responsibility: it comprises an unceasing awareness that even the *total* moral world of all past and future, of all stars and heavens, could be radically different if 'I' were only 'different'; it comprises a deep intuition that the mysterious laws of the interresonance of love and hate, the laws of their

[1] See my formal deduction of the principle of solidarity in *Formalismus in der Ethik, etc.*, Part 2.

propagation through infinity, gather all stirrings of all finite hearts either into an occasionally varied concord or into a disharmony that is incessantly varied, all being heard and judged by the ear of God as an indivisible whole. This *fundamental* sense of collective responsibility is just as essential to the subsistence of a moral subject as the sense of responsibility for itself. Collective responsibility is not first assumed by special acts of obligation or by pledging oneself to others; indeed such engagements are implicitly conditional on its pre-existence.

And so Repentance is as fundamentally concerned with our share in all guilt as with our individual culpability; it is as fundamentally concerned with the tragic guilt to which we blamelessly fall a prey as with the guilt which we freely incur; with the collective and hereditary guilt of communities, families, peoples and all humanity as with individual guilt.* Considering that the principle of solidarity lies at the roots of Christian doctrine, it is very superficial to say that one should rest content with 'not judging' the guilt of others but rather be mindful of one's own individual guilt. Now this is the true meaning of the doctrine: that one should not only be mindful of one's own guilt but feel oneself genuinely implicated in this guilt of others and furthermore in the collective guilt of one's age; one should therefore regard such guilt as also one's 'own', and share in the repenting of it. That is the true sense of *mea culpa, mea culpa, mea maxima culpa!*

Similarly we see even in history how Repentance can grow into a mighty torrent; how it rushes for a generation through whole peoples and civilizations; how it opens obdurate hearts to compassion; how it historically illumines the past of nations which was hidden by racial pride; how it broadens the once ever-narrowing future into a broad, bright plain of possibilities—and so prepares the way for the regeneration of a *collective* moral existence. Such processes of communal Repentance—for an accumulation of communal guilt—recur, with a rhythm all their own, throughout the history of nearly all great communities. They have the most diverse forms and modes of expression, according to the social system of the people concerned, and according to its positive religion and morality. It was not least through the invincible tears of its Repentance that early Christianity renewed the outgoing world of antiquity, hardened by pleasure-seeking, by lust for power and glory, and poured into that world a feeling of rejuvenation. How great a part of all the thoughts and feelings of patristic literature is shot through with this Repentance! Yet another mighty wave of Repentance ran through the peoples of Europe after the increasingly savage, life-destroying brutality of the eleventh century had taken hold. On this occasion Repentance put an end to the final, desperate utopian hope, for the end of the world and the Second Coming were thought to be imminent, and thus it prepared the ground for that spiritual and religious rebirth whose greatest leader was to be Saint Bernard of Clairvaux. *Dona lacrimarum*— such was the name given to the gift, bestowed by grace, of a new will to penance and repentance, which brought Europe to its senses for the great enterprise of the Crusades and ensured the revival of a Church formerly paralysed by a withering and coarsening of spirituality and by the un-bridled, arbitrary tyranny of worldly powers. 'There awoke out of the raging passions and outbreaks of brutal force a mighty feeling of penance.'[1] Construction, paralysis and cultural fragmentation, then once again resolution through Repentance and re-acceptance of the old ingredients into a new, creative will to life and spirit of total rebirth: it is not only the little individual soul which breathes in this rhythm, but the great soul of mankind in history. Even in the field of history, the more deeply searching eye will fail to discern in any direction the spectacle of continuous 'pro-gress'—that mirage which for so long mocked our nineteenth century and hid from our eyes the more beautiful, more sublime law which compre-hends all progress, the law of *death and transmutation*.

Borne on such an outburst of feeling, commensurate in power and extent with the collective guilt of Europe, which in the last war was in-curred more expressly and publicly than before,—borne on a wave of Repentance, that conversion will also come to pass which is intrinsically the sole condition for the formation of a new political system of European union. No new juristic wisdom, no diplomatic good will (no matter *how* good), not even any 'revolution' nor any 'new men' can take the place of this *change of heart* among the peoples. For this great object, too, the conversion of the soul is the inevitable form of the new dispensation. Here, too, the necessary form of consciousness, out of which alone can be born new positive attitudes and finally new plans of political reconstruction, is that recent feeling of profound *revulsion* from the man-made historical system as it existed before the war; it is the gradual revelation, under the spur of Repentance, that the roots of that event sprang from the cata-combs in the soul of the type of man foremost in every nation.

All those numerous philosophies which modern man has cultivated and excogitated in evasion of the guilt growing within him—they will all have to be smashed in the process. For the latest type of man, who would seem finally to have crossed the bounds of Christianity, to have left its framework of vital acquisitions, has now reached the following basic position: Having allowed the guilt of the age to grow to the point where he *dared* not feel or

[1] Neander: *Der heilige Bernhard und sein Zeitalter*, 1848.

think—much less expiate—it, he finds the guilt he guiltily obscures confronting him as, apparently, a purely objective force of 'related circumstances' (*e.g.* economic circumstances), before which one must uncomplainingly bow. To him, then, I would say: *Tear off the mask from your 'related circumstances', and you will see guilt.* His own unrepented guilt, or that of his forefathers, takes on for modern man the outward form of a spectre in which his soul no longer recognizes itself. Guilt stands before his bewildered mind in the guise of a new thing, an external power, a 'fate'. The spectre demands whole complex, scientific theories for its 'explanation'. All historico-deterministic theories (*e.g.* the economic view of history) in fact subconsciously derive their sustenance from this feeling of helpless constraint, which is no more than the natural consequence of a spiritual condition and attitude that, systematically and on principle, excludes the only answer to the recurring necessity for liberation, the unfailing air-duct which may rescue the Self from suffocation under the weight of history—the way of Repentance. Self-deception over guilt which, though scarcely felt any more, is all the more effective; self-deception through boundless activity, elevating the simple process of work to an absolute value, or self-deception through the headlong plunge into the primitive pleasure-world of sensuality; eternally provisional life, postponing automatically all assessment of life to the future, to the death-bed, to the 'next time', and then seeking a logical and moral justification in the doctrine of the will to 'progress'—that is the *kind* of 'system' prevailing today.

We said at the beginning that in the stirrings of our conscience we become aware of an invisible order, concerning our soul and its relation with its lord and Creator, which presents itself spontaneously, without interpretation on our part. Likewise Repentance assumes its full meaning and becomes, as it were, fully articulate only when we come to envisage it (over and above its neutralization of guilt, which still belongs to the order of nature) within the universal framework of metaphysics and religion. It assumes its full meaning when it no longer strikes at the merely 'bad', but at the 'bad' which is sin in the eyes of God. As it thus looks up to God the soul learns to understand the renewal and peace of Repentance as the mysterious process known as 'forgiveness of sin' and as an infusion of new strength from the Centre of things. Grace is the name of this strength. It may depend on very many conditions what form the representations and attendant dogmatic concepts of this great process take, and how the system of a Church presents Repentance, confession, penance, justification, reconciliation and sanctification as positive institutions of salvation. The root of all such representations and institutions is, however, always one and the same. They are all founded in the fact that Repentance, though it is directed as a personal act against our own guilt-laden heart, of its nature yet *transcends* our heart, and looks beyond the confines of its impotence to assist its re-immersion in a suspected Centre of things, the eternal source of all strength. Such, in the full measure of the experience, is the immanent 'sense' of Repentance.

Even if there were nothing else in the world from which we might create the idea of God, Repentance alone could draw our attention to God's existence. Repentance begins with an indictment! But before *whom* do we indict ourselves? Is it not then in the nature of an indictment that there should be a person who receives it and before whom the charge is laid? . . . Repentance is, furthermore, an inward *confession* of our guilt. But to *whom* do we then confess, when lips are sealed and we are alone with our soul? And to *whom* do we owe the debt of guilt which oppresses us? . . . Repentance ends with a clear consciousness of the removal, the annihilation of guilt. But *who* has taken the guilt from us? Who or what is capable of such a thing? . . . Repentance pronounces its verdict according to a *law* felt to be holy, which we could not have prescribed to ourselves but which nevertheless dwells within our hearts. Yet almost in the same breath Repentance releases us from the consequences of this law for us and our conduct! But where is the *giver* of this law, and who but the lawgiver could restrain the law's consequences? . . . Repentance endows us with a new strength of resolution and, in certain cases, a new heart risen from the ashes of the old. But where is the *source* of strength, and where the *idea* for the construction of this new heart, and where the effective power for its making?

And so every manifestation of this great moral process sets in motion a purposeful reaching out to an invisible world, and if we leave this movement to itself, if we refrain from diverting it with premature interpretations, it will of its own accord bring before our minds the mysterious outline of an eternal and infinite Judge, an eternal and infinite mercy, an infinite might, an eternal source of life.

The foregoing is still not specifically a Christian thought, and is far from resting on any positive revelation. It is Christian only in the sense that the soul itself is, as Tertullian says, *anima naturaliter christiana*. And yet it is only in the Christian Church that even these natural functions of Repentance have retained their full meaning and illumination. For it is only through Christian teaching that we are able to understand why Repentance should possess the central function of Rebirth in the life of man.

It is a fearful thing that we can win life only on the dark *via dolorosa* of Repentance. But it is glorious that we have *any* way to life. And do we not *necessarily* lose it through the accumulation of guilt?

What kind of a world must it be, and how created, in which such a thing should be both necessary and possible? In what strange relation to its Creator must such a world stand? And how is it that this thing is necessary *always* and *for everybody*? I answer with a thought from Cardinal Newman's *Apologia pro vita sua*:

'. . . either there is no Creator, or this living society of men is in a true sense discarded from His presence. . . .—*if* there be a God, *since* there is a God, the human race is implicated in some terrible aboriginal calamity. It is out of joint with the purposes of its Creator. This is a fact, a fact as true as the fact of its existence; and thus the doctrine of what is theologically called original sin becomes to me almost as certain as that the world exists, and as the existence of God.'[1]

This thought of Newman's, as simple as it is great, we would ourselves formulate as follows: I possess a perfectly clear and self-evident mental vision of the nature[2] of a possible God as that of an infinite Being and a *summum bonum*. I ascertain that I have neither received this idea from any factual form in the internal or external real world, nor in any way deduced or borrowed it therefrom. The contrary is rather the case: that I apprehend the world, just as I apprehend myself, in the light of this idea—*in lumine Dei*, to use Augustine's phrase. It is, moreover, an essential feature of the fully developed idea of a spiritual Person that only a reality corresponding to it—if such there be—can attest it to man: attest it in self-revelation.[3] Therefore: if there is a reality corresponding to this idea, I can never be in a position to confirm this reality through spontaneous and conscious acts. It is evident to me that I could never distinguish the non-existence of a reality which in its nature exactly corresponds to my clear idea of a personal God from the mere *enduring silence*, the withholding of such a reality. But I believe that, after traces of it had become visible at various points, with more or less clarity, in the universal revelation inspiring history, the reality of this Being was manifested in the Old Covenant and, in the completest form, in Christ.

Such are some of the bases of my knowledge of God. If I know accordingly of God's reality, without having concluded or borrowed this reality from the existence of the world, I next have good grounds for assuming

[1] Part VII, 'General Answer to Mr. Kingsley', para. 7 (*Translator*).

[2] It is not a question here of the revealed nature of God *per se* (independently of God's relation to the world), but only of the essential content of the natural idea of God.

[3] Scheler's thought is less elliptically expressed on pp. 333 *et seq.* of this work, in 'Problems of Religion' (*Translator*).

that this world is not absolutely self-sufficient, and does not originate before God, but has proceeded from his creating hands.[1] Yet now that I have reached that conclusion, I cast my eye over this world, such as it *is*, and on man, such as he appears in the total trend of his activity throughout the history accessible to me. Now can world and man have proceeded, such as they *are*, from the hands of the Creator? Everything in me answers *No!* But at once there spontaneously arises the idea of some kind of Fall, of taint and inherited sin, as the sole explanation of the difference between a world created by the absolute perfection of God and the world as it is known to me in reality.*

It is in this context that Repentance, like so much else, acquires its full meaning—at least it is in this way that it becomes the enduring *necessity* which we earlier saw it to be.

Guilt stands at the beginning of the history of this world! How then could eternal regeneration take any other form than Repentance?

I have hitherto made no comment on the Christian doctrine of Contrition, and the forms which this doctrine has assumed in Christian Churches and sects, for it was my intention to show how far one may be taken by purely philosophical considerations. But if I now compare what I have established with these doctrines, I find that the deepest understanding of the meaning and significance of Repentance is to be encountered in Christianity and, within Christianity, in the Catholic Church. Setting aside all tenets of justification, two things particularly seem to me to characterize the Christian concept of Repentance: first, the blatantly paradoxical notion that not only does the rhythm of culpability and repentance *necessarily* belong to the life of fallen man, but perfect Repentance even raises man above the state of innocence into a higher existence which, but for prior sin and subsequent repentance, would have been unattainable. This thought is expressed macrocosmically, as it were, in the doctrine that Christ's act of redemption did not merely erase the sin of Adam, but brought man henceforth into a communion with God that was deeper and holier than Adam enjoyed—although the person redeemed by the effects of faith does not regain the full integrity of Adam, and undisciplined longings, 'concupiscence', persist. We have a further instance of the same rhythm—falling, then rising above the primal status—in the proposition of the evangelist that there is more joy in Heaven over one repentant sinner than over a thousand of the righteous.

The first of these two thoughts, especially, illumines the full sublimity of man's fall in Adam, and his raising to divine communion through Christ's

[1] Creation in Time is here left undecided.

assumption of humanity. Almost from the beginning it was felt by Christian theologians that scant justice was done to the sublime nature of the Incarnation by a concept which placed its essence and purpose exclusively in God's compassionate mercy for fallen man, in simply a healing and restoration to which God was—so to speak—obliged by the Fall and original sin. God could have found other ways to save and forgive than that he—the Infinite—should himself become flesh and man. On the other hand, the Incarnation—according to the universal teaching of theology—could have ensued without the Fall, without original sin. And so the Incarnation remains a free act of God. Yet there is an absurd disproportion between a mere restoration of man to his natural height before the Fall, and the eternally sublime action of the Lord of things who takes on the form of man. The only reason why the Church may sing its *felix culpa* with respect to the Fall is that the raising of man and the world through God's entry into humanity lifts man to a plane incomparably more lofty than that on which he dwelt in the origin of things. 'Since the fulness of the human race', says Saint Leo, in accord with many others, 'fell in our first parents, the merciful God wished so to succour the creature made in his image, through his only-begotten Son Jesus Christ, that the restoration of the same should not lie outside nature, and that the second state should exceed the dignity of that creature's origin. Happy creature, if it had not fallen away from that which God had made; *happier still*, if it abide in that which he has restored! It was something great to have received form from Christ; but it is a greater thing to have one's substance in Christ.'[1] Therefore, it must be thought that in the depth of his eternal wisdom God designed the Incarnation for the exigency of the Fall, which was foreseen from eternity; but at the same time it has also to be assumed that man was, in the Fall, permitted freely to incur the guilt of sin only because the Incarnation was already decided in God's eternal wisdom. In this way we are led to a full understanding of the idea that God, through the Incarnation, is performing a greater work than a mere coming to the rescue of man in his wilful guilt, that he is primarily, and out of that infinite love which continues the immanent witness of the Son, glorifying himself and also taking up man—likewise the world in this its noblest part—into his glorification.—But we are straying beyond our theme.

There is a second momentous factor, inseparable from the foregoing: the new relation between Repentance and *love*. In both senses of the phrase, 'perfect' Repentance seems borne on the love *of* God. Firstly, in

[1] Leo the Great: Second Sermon *De Resurrectione* (Sermon 72, section 2).

that God's love, constantly knocking at the door of the soul, sets up before man, as it were, the portrait of an ideal Being and enables man to appreciate for the first time, in comparison with this vision, how base and restricted is his real condition. Secondly, in that man, after the spontaneous consummation of Repentance, and in growing awareness of forgiveness and sanctification, comes finally to the knowledge that he has received strength for that consummation as a token of God's love and mercy. This he knows inasmuch as his loving approach toward God, rendered first possible in the process of Repentance, gradually restores his full capacity for loving God, and, through removal of his guilty limitations and the barriers guilt has interposed, effects his reconciliation and reunion with the Centre of things.

Love stirred within us. At first we thought it our love—love of God— our love of him. We came to know it for his love—the love of God. His love of us.

c

THE NATURE OF PHILOSOPHY
AND THE MORAL PRECONDITIONS
OF PHILOSOPHICAL KNOWLEDGE

THE NATURE OF PHILOSOPHY
AND THE MORAL PRECONDITIONS
OF PHILOSOPHICAL KNOWLEDGE

THE question *What is philosophy?* is beset with difficulties, not out of any human inadequacy but in the very nature of the case. These difficulties are not to be compared with those which normally arise in attempts to define the proper sphere and limits of the various positive sciences, though they too are far from negligible. For, however difficult it may be, for example, to make a sharp distinction between physics and chemistry (especially with the advent of physical chemistry) or to state what psychology is, it is at least in these cases practicable and advisable, when in doubt, to resort to philosophically clarified basic conceptions, such as *matter, bodies, energy,* or *consciousness, life, psyche,* in other words to conceptions whose nature it is undoubtedly the very business of philosophy to elucidate. Nothing of the kind is on the other hand open to philosophy, unless it is prepared—at the cost of falling into a circular argument—to resort to the teachings of a particular department of self-sought philosophy, that is to some particular philosophical *doctrine* or so-called philosophical 'system', for philosophy must first, as it were, *constitute itself* by asking what its own nature may be. The ability to decide not only whether such teachings are true and can withstand criticism but whether they are even philosophical presupposes that very knowledge of what philosophy is and what its object. When, moreover, one reviews the history of philosophy, one can do no more, without conscious or semi-conscious recourse to some accepted idea of philosophy, than demonstrate the existence of that one thing which has been *called* 'philosophy' by various authors at various times, and of whatever common features are to be found in the products of these various minds. Such a review fails to relieve philosophy of the task which I have called 'self-constitution'. What can reasonably be expected of such a methodical, historical inquiry into bygone philosophy is only a certain verification and *exemplification* of a self-knowledge won by philosophy in the process of 'self-constitution', the verification and exemplification necessarily resting for their disclosure on the fact that basically different enterprises, each *called* philosophy, reveal for the first time, in the light of the acquired self-knowledge, a *unified* significance and a positive, meaningful interrelation of historical development.

The peculiarity of the task which I have called 'philosophy's self-knowledge through philosophy' is further evident in that it is in every case the intention of philosophical inquiry to establish *knowledge independent of hypotheses*, or let us say—to avoid anticipating any philosophical judgment here—knowledge as independent of hypotheses as is objectively *possible*. The conclusion of all the foregoing is that philosophy may not presume the truth of the acquisitions either of history (including the history of philosophy), or of 'science' in general or of any individual science, or of revelation, or of the 'common-sense' attitude and its observations. This remains so however much all these kinds of knowledge and materials of knowledge come—from one aspect, which evolves in the course of philosophy's self-constitution—within the scope of those objects which philosophy has to comprehend (*e.g.* the essential *nature* of historical knowledge, of the history of ideas, of revealed knowledge, of the 'common-sense' attitude). Any alleged philosophy, therefore, whose exponents deliberately make such presumptions at once fails to satisfy the first essential criterion of philosophy, that it should represent knowledge independent of hypotheses—unless indeed it should have been established as a *result* of non-hypothetical inquiry *that* the task of philosophy obliges it to make specific presumptions of this kind.

At this point it would be as well to mention the special names given to certain inquiries that are contrary to the true spirit of philosophy. The names depend on the branch of knowledge whose truth, from a certain stage onward, they presume: if it is history, then 'traditionalism'; if science, 'scientism'; if revelation, 'fideism'; if 'common-sense' observation, then 'healthy empiricism'. I shall on the other hand call any philosophy whose constitution avoids these faults and is genuinely free of presumptions *autonomous* philosophy, *i.e.* philosophy which seeks and finds its essence and principle exclusively *through itself*, in itself and its constitution.

1. THE AUTONOMY OF PHILOSOPHY

There is a certain prejudice in epistemology which in recent times has become so general as scarcely to be felt as a prejudice any more. It consists in the opinion that it is easier to define a 'sphere of relevance' or a 'problem' than to describe or descry the type of *person* who possesses genuine competence in that sphere and for that problem—competence not merely to treat and solve, but in the first place even to define and delimit them. If one were to say that art is what the true artist produces, religion what the true saint feels, represents and preaches, *and* that philosophy is likewise the true philosopher's relationship to things and *his* manner of regarding them, I am afraid that many people would laugh one to scorn. Yet I am convinced that, heuristically at least (thus apart from the objective precedence of one definition over another), this method of determining a sphere of relevance by reference to the type of person is both more certain and less equivocal in its results than any other procedure.

How much easier it is for us to make up our minds whether a man is a true artist or true saint than to decide what art is and what religion! However, even if to that extent our decision is easier and more sure, we must still, in judging whether a Plato, Aristotle, Descartes or other man is a 'true philosopher', be *guided* by something which is certainly no *empirical* abstraction—for it is precisely this something whose range of application and *sphere* (from which we could have elicited typological characteristics) we wish to locate and determine. And again this guiding something is not a concept we have derived from within the field of philosophy itself, for there groping and anomaly are all the greater, and this domain, too, has first to be discovered in reference to the type of man who rightly wields authority within it. No, this 'something' can be no other than the *idea*, as yet hidden from our judging, conceptual consciousness, of a certain universally human, pre-eminently intellectual basic *attitude* to things, an attitude of which we have, constituted as an objective *personality*, a mental image enabling us, without determining the attitude's positive *content*, to say whether an object conforms to or deviates from it.

I grant there are conspicuous limits to the utility of this procedure whereby the nature of a sphere or 'problem' is elicited in the first place not from themselves but via an earlier decision of what constitutes such a basic personal *attitude*—is found, that is, not *from* but *in* the works, for example, of the philosophers. It is, for instance, quite unthinkable that we should want to find out by this method the realm of physics, zoology, etc., etc. The procedure is possible, meaningful and heuristically necessary only for those absolutely autonomous regions of being and value which may be defined neither through empirically determinable object-groups nor through any positive human need which arose *before* the attitude and its resultant activity, and demanded to be 'met'. In these cases entities and values form closed, self-contained, self-consistent realms.

Thus the possibility I have indicated, of setting out to discover the domain of philosophy from that 'idea' which leads us to call certain men philosophers, is bound to present one more retrospective confirmation of philosophy's autonomy. But here let us guard against a misunderstanding which will leap into minds imbued with modern bad habits of thought. It consists in jumping to the conclusion that, if the above procedure is possible and necessary, philosophy absolutely *could not* have a particular sphere all its own, could not have any peculiar *object*-world, and that it is therefore merely a special *way* of knowing about all possibles—*i.e.* the same objects with which, for example the sciences also deal—only from a differently chosen subjective viewpoint; similarly many thinkers today are of the opinion (which I consider erroneous) that the unity of psychology is comprised not in a factual world of its own but merely in the unity of a 'viewpoint of observation' of all possible facts. Of course, it may be so— I grant the possibility—but it in no wise *must* be so! In any case, the point of outset chosen for the examination of the nature of philosophy does not in any way prejudice the issue. For it may well be that the ideal, typical unity of mental attitude which guides us when we decide *what* a philosopher is, though it indeed form the essentially *necessary* subjective *approach*, is *no more than* the approach and way to a special world of facts and objects—*i.e.* an object-world so disposed as to appear *only* in this one attitude of the cognizant mind, and which, though for heuristic purposes we seek to capture its essence and singularity by circumscribing that attitude, exists as independently of the attitude as the star, invisible to the naked eye, of the telescope that reveals it. But just one thing is certain *a priori*: whatever forms the peculiar 'object' of philosophy, it cannot consist of groups and kinds of objects empirically delimitable and definable *per species et genus proximum*, but only of a whole world of objects, any insight into which is essentially connected with the attitude and types of cognition immanent within it.

What is the nature of this 'world'? What types of cognition correspond to it? If we wish to answer these questions we must elucidate that philosophical frame of mind which hovers darkly before us when we are trying to decide whether *A. B.* is a philosopher.

2. THE PHILOSOPHICAL ATTITUDE
(THE IDEA OF THE PHILOSOPHER)

The great philosophers of antiquity were free from the pedantry I have deprecated—of defining philosophy either as an answer to some pre-existent need felt by a social organization or as a province of knowledge easily demonstrable to *all*, and presumed to lie within the data accessible to the common-sense view of the world. However much they, as opposed to the moderns, discovered the object of philosophy in a particular realm of *being* and not, like modern philosophy, which is essentially inclined towards epistemology, in *knowledge* of being, they yet knew that the possibility of contact between the mind and this realm of being is bound up with a function of the whole personality, a function not available to man in the common-sense outlook. This function—which we are to examine in greater detail—was for the Ancients one primarily of a *moral*, but not for that reason exclusively volitional nature. It did not appear to them as an act in which a specifically envisaged goal was to be attained, or an 'aim' realized, but as one through whose agency the mind should be rid of a *hindrance* natural to all common-sense attitudes and preventing the mind, as the *ens* of philosophy, from making possible contact with the realm of true entity; it was for them an act through which a constitutional bond of human nature should be burst asunder and a veil that conceals Being lifted from the eye of the mind.

When Plato wishes to guide his pupil to the nature of philosophy, he never tires of casting fresh light on this operation in continually new aspects. He calls it in one phrase, as plastic as it is profound, the 'movement of the soul's wings' and elsewhere, the soaring of the personality's heart and soul upwards to Reality, not as if this 'reality' were a special object comparable with empirical objects, but to the essential reality in all individual possibles together. And he describes the *dynamis* at the centre of the Person, the mainspring, the Something which produces the soaring to the Real world, as the highest and purest form of what he calls *eros*— that is, as what he was later to call (here indeed anticipating the outcome of his philosophy) the indwelling tendency of all imperfect being towards perfect being or, more exactly, of μὴ ὄν towards ὄντως ὄν. The very name 'Philosophy', *love of essential Reality*, still bears the clear and ineffaceable stamp of Plato's basic meaning, inasmuch as the *x* borne up by *eros* to the full height of Being is no nondescript entity but the *special case* of a human soul.

If this assimilation of the highest form of love to the tendency of not-being towards being is too charged with special elements of Platonic doctrine for us to take it as a basis, this is still more the case with Plato's description of the activity typifying the philosopher as no more than *conflict*, wresting, opposition to the body and all life in the senses and the flesh. This interpretation finally leads to seeing the goal of the activity (*i.e.* the state at which the soul must arrive before the object of philosophy is unveiled to the mind's eye) not in an eternal *life* of the mind within 'Reality' but in *dying to all eternity*. For these further definitions postulate the rationalistic Platonic theory and the opinion of Plato (which we consider false) that 1. all perceptual (*i.e.* non-conceptual) knowledge is sensorily conditioned within the specific sensory organization of the subject (subjectivity of all qualities), and 2. the obstacle which must be overcome in order to 'participate in Reality' is not only such a dependence on our physical nature but that nature itself in its basic integrity. In other words, when Plato calls the life of the philosopher an 'eternal dying' he postulates the asceticism consequent upon the rationale of his epistemology. Indeed he regards this ascesis as the attitude and way of life which *disposes the philosopher to knowledge*; without it philosophical knowledge is impossible.

Here, concerned as we are, not with the particulars of Platonic doctrine, but with the essential nature of philosophy, let us dwell awhile on the two basic definitions wherewith Plato opened the door to philosophy for all times and all men:

1. An *integral movement* of the inmost personal Self, such as is *not* within the capacity of the common-sense outlook or of any cognitive desire which is founded therein.

This is necessary even to bring the object of philosophy before the mind's eye. Further, this movement is founded in—

2. An Act, which in essence is a *love* with a special character.

And so, even before we proceed to a separate analysis of this act, we may define the nature of the mental attitude which underlies all philosophical thinking as: *a love-determined movement of the inmost personal Self of a finite being toward participation in the essential reality of all possibles.* A man who takes up this attitude to the world belongs, in so far as he does take it up, to the essential type 'philosopher'.

But have we now sufficiently defined the general mental attitude of philosophy? I think not. For we have left out a factor of great importance which it is unthinkable to withhold from the ideas of philosophy and the philosopher—the fact that philosophy is *knowing* and the philosopher one who knows. It is a secondary question whether the philosopher is enhanced by this underlying fact, whether it promotes him and his activity to the highest rank of existence possible to man or allots him merely a rank, somehow subordinate, on an intermediate level. At all events, philosophy is *knowing*. If therefore it should be possible for the inmost personal Self of a finite human being to achieve a participation in essential reality which was something other than knowledge or which somehow excelled the knowledge possessed by the subject, it would follow not that the philosopher is not one who knows, but that philosophy is quite simply not the most *direct and ultimate* participation in Reality which is granted to man.

In this methodological sense, then, *every* possible philosophy, no matter what the *content* of its findings, is 'intellectualistic'. It is quite certain that whether it is in the nature of *philosophy* (meaning spontaneous knowledge *proceeding* from the human subject) to be able to achieve the inmost, ultimate 'participation' depends wholly on the substantial content and ordering of the essentials of things; in the last resort it depends on the content of an essence which we may be permitted to call the primal essence of all essences. For it is in accordance with the *content* of that primal essence that participation in it naturally has its underlying form. The devotee of Orpheus, to whom the 'thing given' in the state of ecstasy was a chaotic, inarticulate, creative cosmic drive, had naturally to deny that the Apollonian art of philosophy could achieve this participation. For him the *methodos* of ultimate participation in the primal essence was not knowledge but supreme dionysiac rapture. If the content of the primal essence is a cosmic drive and thrust, then the right way to achieve the most direct and intimate participation can only be to share in the thrusting; if, as Fichte teaches, it is an eternal obligation, it can only be to share that obligation; if it is a universal love, in the Johannine Christian sense, then only to share in the activity of love; if it is a cosmic vitality (in the sense, say, of Bergson's *élan vital*), then the right method can only be a living, parallel with or drawing upon that vitality, in empathy and sympathy toward all things as transitory forms of the cosmic life. If the primal essence is, in the ancient Indian sense, an all-dreaming Brahma, then our dreaming the Brahma's dreams will be the deepest, the final participation; if it is, in Buddha's sense, a non-essence or nothingness, then it will be the removal of our very being in absolute death—the 'entry into Nirvana'. But *if* one of these cases, or an analogous case, were valid, it would never follow under any circumstances that philosophy was anything *other* than knowing; that is, than that particular form of participation in Reality which is called *knowledge*. The philosopher—supposing he arrived at one of these termini—could not *qua* philosopher cease to be a philosopher till he came to the very end of his journey and saw the really Real lying even then, so to speak, on the other bank; even then he could not set *philosophy* any other task than to know. And not until *after* the occurrence of such a non-cognitive participation in Reality could the philosopher, reflecting on the course which led to this achievement, describe this course in an account of the inner 'technique of participation'. Anyone, then, who would like to escape this *formal* 'intellectualism' of philosophy does not know what he is asking. One can only say to him that he has mistaken his vocation, but that he has no right to make out philosophy and the philosopher to be other than they are.

No less senseless than to deny philosophy's *formal* intellectualism would be the other extreme of seeking to infer from it something about the material content of the Reality in which the philosopher seeks fundamentally to participate. For though it is certain that the philosopher is bound to seek participation through knowledge (so far as possible), it is just as certain that the primal essence is not *a priori* in duty bound to grant ultimate participation to the knower *qua* knower. For the form which participation takes is governed exclusively by the essential *content* of the primal essence—not by the 'cognitive' aspect of that content *qua* essence. And so it is quite senseless, even if fashionable, to conclude from the methodic intellectualism of philosophy that its object is the knowable, or the possible 'knowledge' of the world. It would likewise be quite fallacious to think there was some logical theoretical basis for the proposition that philosophy is concerned from the beginning not with the Reality of things but with knowledge of things as an end in itself, and that every other possible aspect of things is merely 'the rest' and 'does not concern' the philosopher. It is not a logical but a *moral* cause, the philosopher's vice of *intellectual pride*, which underlies the fallacy of excluding *a priori* the possibility that the strictly intellectual method of philosophical thought could lead (after moral defeat of the natural hindrances to knowledge) to such a content of Reality as would of *its* nature demand of the philosopher, as his final act, a *self-limitation*, both voluntary and consonant with philosophical autonomy, of philosophy as philosophy; this means excluding, therefore, the possibility that the content of the primal essence could ultimately *necessitate* an appropriate form of participation which would be other than the cognitive approach of philosophy. Now it may very well be that the philosopher *must* freely and autonomously subordinate himself, in strictest *consequence* of his philosophical thinking, to another and higher form of participation in Reality; that in fact he should offer himself as a philosopher, together with the rational tools of philosophy, in free *sacrifice* to the non-philosophical kind of participation demanded by the content of the primal essence. Far from surrendering or abandoning his autonomous methodological principles of cognition or capitulating, as it were, to something extra-philosophical, he would, provided his philosophy *had* led him to this conclusion, be simply bowing to the logical outcome of those very principles if he were to subordinate both self and principles to the positive *content* of the Reality he has come to know, or freely sacrifice them to the *form* of participation which alone is commensurate to that content. In fact, if the accusation of philosophical heteronomy and prejudice, or lack of 'freedom from preconceptions', can fairly be levelled anywhere, it is against those who, quite *regardless* of the positive content of Reality and the primal essence of all things, have decided from the outset, with a mere 'fiat' of personal velleity, not under any circumstances to perform that act of sacrifice. For *they* have quite arbitrarily supposed Reality to be of such a composition that full participation in it can be reached via its 'human' object-aspect (as distinct, for example, from its *act*ual identity from its own point of view). But we have to make the *sharpest possible distinction* between the *being* of objects (and non-objects) and the *object*-ive identity of that being; *a priori*, the final limits of that identity are also the limits to which the object may be known. The entity *may* in fact extend far *beyond* the objectifiable identity. Only *if* the being of Reality—of the primal essence—is of a wholly *objectifiable* composition will *knowledge* truly be the adequate form of possible participation, and in this case philosophy will not have to limit itself in the sense above. But to state *a priori* that this is so would be a pure prejudice, a downright *alogical* hypothesis, and we must radically deny the predicate of genuine autonomy and independence of hypotheses to any philosophy which makes that supposition.

Here let me give an example which will also serve us as more than an example. The great progenitors of European philosophy, Plato and Aristotle, started out quite rightly from the idea that the goal of philosophy was human participation in absolute Reality. Since in the *outcome* their philosophy defined the primal essence as an objectifiable entity and therefore a possible correlate of knowledge, they had also to regard knowledge (or a particular kind of knowledge) as the definitive, ultimate participation in Reality which man might attain. Attain, be it noted, through spontaneous acts of the mind. Accordingly they could not but see the highest and most perfect form of human being in the *philosophos*, the 'wise one'. For the same reason they felt no call, at the issue of their philosophical thinking, to perform an act in essential limitation of philosophy itself. The very idea of God had to present itself to them in the idea of an infinitely wise being, or of an 'infinite knowing of knowing', as Aristotle puts it.

Now there had to be a complete change, though stemming directly from the great Ancients' philosophical principle—being indeed its very *consequence*—when at the beginning of the Christian era the primal Reality was, rightly or wrongly, thought and felt to consist in an endless activity of creative and merciful *love*. For, given that philosophy 1. has the final end of participation in the absolute being of Reality, and 2. is essentially cognition, philosophy could in this event *no longer*, as peculiarly knowledge, attain its self-prescribed purpose. For human participation in an entity which is not objective but *active* in essence cannot be other than a collaboration in this activity, and therefore evidently not knowledge of objects. Furthermore such participation must first have been *completed*, by the entry of the inmost human personality, inasmuch as it is the seat of love (not knowledge) as well as action, into the Real primal entity, if philosophy wishes to attain *its own* particular kind of participation, or even to *initiate* it with regard to the primal Reality. It followed, therefore, in strict logic—postulating love as the content and activity as the mode of primal Reality—that philosophy, *by virtue of its own principle*, freely and autonomously limited itself and, when occasion arose, as freely and autonomously sacrificed itself and its source of knowledge, reason, to an *essentially different form of participation* in Reality. In other words, philosophy had freely and autonomously to acknowledge itself the 'handmaid of faith'[1]—not faith as a subjective function but faith as an objective *substance*, since faith in the words of Christ, as the person whom one presumed to have achieved the ultimate union with the underlying Reality of this new content, must be regarded as more immediate a participation, and one more consonant with that Reality's mode and content, than that through knowledge. If the philosopher at all accepted this Christian definition of the ultimate Reality, philosophy could be regarded only as the forerunner of and *way to* an altogether different kind of participation, just as, from the methodological viewpoint, would have to be the case if Fichte's doctrine of infinite obligation or Bergson's of *élan vital* were true. Accordingly, the status of the 'philosopher' or 'wise one' had to take second place after that of the 'saint'—and the philosopher had consciously to adjust himself to the inferior position. Similarly, under Kant's hypothesis of the 'primacy' of practical reason[2] the philosopher must consider himself the inferior and voluntary servant (*ancilla*) of the morally exemplary man of practical wisdom, while under Fichte's hypothesis he must yield to the practical, ethical reformer. Under Bergson's hypothesis he must subserve the empathetic and sympathetic observer of the universal march of life. The philosopher must even be prepared to regard these types of man as his most authoritative source of material for philosophical reflection—material which is 'given' to his 'knowledge' just as the data of empirical observation are given to the mind in the common-sense outlook. It should go without saying that (within the scope of our example) philosophy retains that ancient dignity which it possessed for Plato and Aristotle, of being not 'a science' but the

---

[1] Not necessarily the 'handmaid of theology'! For the theologian is related to the saint as the dabbler in theories or expert on philosophy to the philosopher himself.

[2] Kant makes a logically necessary distinction between the 'cosmic' and 'academic' concepts of philosophy.

autonomous *queen* of sciences—retains it throughout its new Christian historical environment. But, presuming the truth of the new definition of the nature of Reality, there accrued to philosophy a new and manifestly far more lofty dignity, surpassing that of *regina scientiarum*—that of *ancilla*, *i.e.* the willing[1] servant and (when apposite) *threshold* of faith: *praeambula fidei*. This step of *voluntary* and objectively *necessary* philosophical self-limitation of philosophy was only the ultimate realization of its *true* autonomy; it was exactly opposite to the introduction of a heteronomous principle limiting philosophy *from without*, and it was also the opposite of that other limitation which would restrict philosophy according to knowable objects (not in an agnostic sense, or with reference to the phenomenal aspect, but rather in the Kantian sense relating to the thing-in-itself). For indeed throughout the whole era of European-Christian philosophy philosophy has been held to be absolutely *unlimited* in its range of objects, in that it claimed to be metaphysics, having as such the right to know every being in its ultimate root and basis.

However, it is now clear that the internal self-development of 'modern philosophy' up to the present has finally led it (not, I admit, unerringly, but in spasmodic stages) to a position almost exactly the opposite of that expressed in the double claim of the older idea—that philosophy was at one and the same time the free handmaid of faith (its highest dignity) and, as second highest dignity, queen of the sciences. Over wide areas faith's erstwhile 'free handmaid' has become its *usurper*, but at the same time it has become *ancilla scientiarum* in various senses, being allotted the tasks either of 'uniting' the conflicting results of the individual sciences into a homogeneous '*Weltanschauung*' (I refer to positivism) or, as a kind of science-police, of laying down their premises and methods with greater exactitude than they can themselves achieve (this is critical or '*scientific*' philosophy).

It can easily be shown—on the evidence—that the *new* basic relationship of philosophy to faith and the sciences represents the most deep-seated, far-reaching and consequential *perversion of the true relationship* that the European mentality has ever attained, and that even this perversion is no more than one instance of a far more all-embracing phenomenon—the internal *overthrow of all order of values*, that disorder of mind and heart which forms the soul of the bourgeois-capitalist age. What we are witnessing is in fact the *slave-rebellion in the world of intellect*, and together with closely associated similar uprisings of lower against higher in other fields it offers the symptomatic evidence of that general overthrow of

[1] In accordance with the beatitude, 'Blest are the (*voluntarily*) poor in spirit'— μακάριοι οἱ πτωχοὶ τῷ πνεύματι.

values. Thus in ethics egocentric individualism has rebelled against the principle of solidarity, utilitarian criteria have asserted their supremacy over values of culture and intellect, but even these have in turn revolted against spiritual values;* in institutions, State first rose against Church, then Nation against State, finally economic institutions against Nation *and* State; in society, class has risen against position; in history, technicalism and economics are supplanting classical theories; in the arts, '*engagement*' is preferred to form, commercialism has invaded art, the producer dominates the poetic stage; instances multiply. . . .

But it ought not to surprise us at all that philosophy should have become (via the Renaissance) a 'worldly wisdom' not merely hostile to faith but even usurping its place—and *simultaneously* a slave and whore progressively cheapened in traffic from science to science (in the service now of geometry, now of mechanics, now psychology, and so on). The two processes are in essence one. Each illustrates in the closest way the following principle: it beseems reason, as of *eternal* right, to exercise *autonomy*, and power and authority over all instinctual life and wherever its laws 'apply' among the myriads of sensory phenomena; but at the same time it befits reason to hold itself in a free and humble, yet self-imposed subjection to the order of divine revelation; thus reason is of such a nature that it *must of necessity* fall into heteronomous slavery to that extent to which it repudiates as slavery the very intrinsic *condition* of its right to full autonomy—that is, its vital connection with God as the source-light of life, a connection founded in humility and in capacity for *sacrifice*. Only *as* the 'free handmaid' of faith can philosophy preserve the dignity of *queen* of sciences, and if it makes bold to assert a domination over faith it cannot *avoid* becoming the handmaid, the slave and whore of the 'sciences'.

If I use 'philosophy' and 'the sciences' as terms of distinction and deny that philosophy, while queen of the sciences, strictly belongs *among* them, I should like to justify this unorthodox usage without further delay. It would be particularly apposite to defend it against that of Edmund Husserl, who, while his idea of philosophy is in a material sense closest to that here expounded, expressly terms philosophy 'a science'.

In effect, there is no material disagreement between us but only a terminological difference of opinion which does not touch the heart of the matter. Husserl distinguishes—just as I do in principle at a later stage* —self-evident knowledge of essences from positive knowledge (*Realerkenntnis*). Positive knowledge remains by nature in the sphere of probability; however, philosophy in its basic discipline is self-evident knowledge of essences. Husserl further distinguishes philosophy from the deductive sciences of (in his terminology) 'ideal objects'—logic, theory of numbers and pure mathematics. In so doing he does appear to express a higher esteem for any phenomenology of subjective behaviour or the psychic than for the phenomenologies of the various impersonal fields, such as that of natural objects; in itself I consider this preference unwarranted. But since Husserl not only demands (with my entire agreement) that philosophy should be 'strict' but also bestows on it the title of 'science' he is at once obliged to employ the name 'science' with two distinct meanings —one for philosophy as self-evident knowledge of essences and the other for the positive formal sciences of ideal objects as well as for all inductive empirical sciences. Since, however, we already possess the tried and honourable name of *philosophy* for the first usage there seems to be no reason why we should needlessly employ one name for two things. It is also quite groundless to fear that if philosophy were not subsumed under 'science' it would have to fall under the heading of some analogous super-concept, such as 'art', for not all things have to be subsumed—certain things, as autonomous realms of objects and activities, have in fact the right to decline subsumption. Philosophy is pre-eminently one of these: it really is nothing else than simply philosophy: it even possesses its own idea of 'strictness', its disciplines, and therefore is in no way obliged to be ruled by some ideal notion of scientific discipline, which in measuring and counting is called exactitude.

But there is also a historical background to the matter. I believe that to designate philosophy Husserl employs that Greek concept of science which coincides in range of meaning with the Platonic ἐπιστήμη, to which Plato opposes the sphere of δόξα (*i.e. all* kinds of probable knowledge). In this case, it must be admitted, philosophy would not be 'a' strict science but *the only true science*, and everything else would basically be not science at all in the strictest sense. It must now be clear that the practical linguistic usage has over the centuries been not merely altered but *reversed*, and for the deepest cultural and historical reasons. It is precisely what, with the exception of the formal sciences, Plato called the sphere of δόξα that has become the concept underlying what, for some centuries past, has been called 'science' and 'the sciences' in nearly every nation. I at least have not met anybody, either personally or in books, who on mention of the word 'science' did not immediately think of so-called positive science but thought instead of Plato's ἐπιστήμη, or of philosophy, as a 'strict science' in Husserl's sense—but *not* however including all deductive mathematics. Is it now practical and historically justified to wish to revert from the modern to the ancient Greek usage? I cannot believe that it is. Unless one wished to give eternal sanction to a frightful equivocation, one would have to deny the name of science to all inductive empirical sciences, which is certainly not what Husserl wishes.

But it is not only in the usage of the words philosophy and science that Husserl's usage and mine diverge: they do so even more sharply in respect of the words *Weltanschauung* and *Weltanschauungsphilosophie*.[1] The plastic expression 'Weltanschauung', which was given to our language by that outstanding historian of the mind, Wilhelm von Humboldt, denotes primarily those forms of 'apprehending' and envisaging the world which prevail at a given time over a given area (forms not necessarily conscious or acknowledged) as well as the distribution of distinctive sectors of value-perception according to the aptitudes of various social units (peoples, nations, civilizations). These Weltanschauungen may be found and explored in the syntaxes of languages, but also in religion, ethics and so forth. What I call the 'natural metaphysics' of peoples should also come within the scope of Weltanschauung. Now what I understand by '*Weltanschauungsphilosophie*' is philosophy of the Weltanschauungen which remain constant as 'natural' to the species man and of those variants which are particular and transitory; this is a very important discipline, as Dilthey in particular recognized in his recent well-considered proposal that it should be used to lay the *philosophical* foundation of humane studies. Husserl on the other hand gives the name *Weltanschauungsphilosophie* to exactly what I call, with far more historical justification, '*scientific philosophy*', that is the attempt either (in the spirit of positivism) to shape the available 'results' of science into a 'definitive' metaphysics or Weltanschauung, or to reduce philosophy to scientific *doctrine*, *i.e.* theory of scientific methods and principles. Husserl himself, in most well-chosen words, castigates such attempts to fabricate a metaphysics out of the concepts underlying a particular science (*e.g.* 'energy', 'will', 'sensation') or science in general, and he cites the attempts of *inter alios* Ostwald, Verworn, Haeckel and Mach as examples showing how *arbitrarily* the —in principle—never-ending progress of scientific perception, observation and examination is thereby halted at one point or other. I agree whole-heartedly with this analysis. 'Scientific philosophy' is in fact a monstrous freak, since positive science has to lay down *its own* premises, *itself* draw out all their possible consequences, and even reconcile its own

[1] It may be left to Scheler's text to clarify the meaning of *Weltanschauung* in this book. But it should be remarked that to understand Scheler's concept fully it is necessary to understand what he means by *Anschauung* in general and to digest his theory of the 'functionalization of essential insights', expounded pp. 201 *et seq.* below. My note on *Anschauung*, p. 215, may possibly serve as a point of departure (*Translator*).

contradictions, but philosophy rightly stands aloof when science seeks to draw her in. Not until the whole of the sciences may be considered together, *with* all their premises (*e.g.* mathematics *with* its underlying axioms and discovered principles) do they form an object of phenomenology, in the sense that they become reduced to phenomenological homogeneity, are set, as it were, in inverted commas and may be examined in their substratum of essential insights. It does not seem right to me that Husserl should christen the abortive brain-children of would-be philosopher specialists—(*all* sciences are specializations)—should christen 'scientific philosophy', then, with the good name of *Weltanschauungsphilosophie*. Weltanschauungen are not thought up by savants: they evolve and grow. And as Husserl rightly maintains, philosophy itself can never be Weltanschauung but at most involve a theory of Weltanschauungen. If it should be thought, however, that the study of Weltanschauungen, though an important task, is not one for philosophy but one for history, anthropology, sociology and other organized humane studies, I would say this was undoubtedly true for the study of positive, individual Weltanschauungen such as the Indian, the Christian and so on. But there is another philosophy, concerned in the first place with the 'natural' Weltanschauung and thereafter with the range of 'possible' variants, which forms the historical basis for treating the humane problems relevant to a theory of *positive* Weltanschauungen.* And with the aid of a pure, truly comprehensive philosophical phenomenology such a theory would be in a position to assess the cognitive value of any given Weltanschauung. It could also show that in contrast to the ephemeral, journalistic products of 'scientific philosophy' the structures of the prevailing Weltanschauungen both occasion and control the structure, character and level of science effective in a society at a given time—in fact that they determine whether 'science' in the west-European sense exists or does not exist; furthermore it could be shown that every variation in the structure of science has been *preceded* by an analogous variation of principle in the overall Weltanschauung. Here perhaps we do at last encounter a *material* cleavage of opinion between Husserl and myself, in that Husserl is inclined to concede to the positive sciences a far greater actual independence of Weltanschauungen, which evolve very slowly and painfully—on quite another time-scale than the advances of positive science. For it seems to me that the *structures* of science, by which I mean prevailing systems of basic concepts and principles, change abruptly in history when the Weltanschauung changes, and I conceive the possibilities of progress in a given scientific system, though they are in principle unbounded, to lie *within* the limiting structure of the overriding—say, the European—Weltanschauung.

Confronted by my contention that it is a *moral* attitude which in the nature of things is a necessary prerequisite for the special kind of knowledge called philosophical, many readers may have recalled certain teachings that have found a strong following, particularly from Kant and Fichte to the present day. I have in mind the doctrine which Kant was the first to entitle the 'primacy of practical over theoretical reason'. But in fact W. Windelband—to give an example—has in his well-known book on Plato connected the Socratic reform and its Platonic development with Kant's doctrine in a way not merely untenable but involving a radical misconception of what Plato and Socrates (with whom we are in basic agreement) really meant. It is not simply that any doctrine of the 'primacy' of practical over theoretical reason is unknown to the great progenitors of European philosophy: it is as clear as day that on the contrary they accord to the theoretic life (θεωρεῖν) an unconditional precedence over the practical life (πράττειν). However, it is precisely this priority of esteem which is denied by every form which the doctrine of practical reason's primacy has taken since Kant. Now this is the true relationship of the two points of view: Antiquity teaches that a definite moral attitude (the soaring of the whole man to Reality) is the *sine qua non* of philosophical *cognition, i.e.* the condition of penetrating the *real* object-world of philosophy or of attaining its threshold, and that this *moral* attitude has as its task and aim, among other things, to overcome all merely *practical* attitudes to life. On the other hand Kant is of the opinion that theoretical philosophy does not postulate *any* specific moral condition in the philosopher, but that even in the hypothetical case of philosophical perfection a sense of *obligation and duty* is required before we may participate in that 'metaphysical' order which, he says, theoretical reason will seek to penetrate only in vain and at the risk of eventual self-delusion. Fichte, yet again (together with the present school headed by H. Rickert, who derive from him their teaching on this point), turned theoretical into a formation of practical reason by equating the being of things with the mere demand (the ideal obligation) that they should be acknowledged by the act of judgment; he thus permits the *being* of things to be founded on the obligatory acknowledgment of their truth-*value*, if he does not exactly fuse it with that acknowledgment. What then is for Plato a purely *subjective*, though no less necessary prerequisite for the attainment of philosophy's goal (the theoretic knowledge of being) is for these thinkers a primacy of the moral in the very *objective* order of things—whereas the Ancients thought almost exactly the contrary, seeing even in good itself only a supreme *degree* of being (ὄντως ὄν). And so we have in this doctrine of the primacy of practical reason the chief cause of the shattering and summary repudiation of the idea that a certain *moral way of life* is the *sine qua non* for the pure knowledge of definite objective entities—and that metaphysical illusions are bound up with the 'natural' and predominantly 'practical' way of looking at things.

The thesis we here present is not *exactly* congruent with either of these circles of ideas, though it has a strong preponderance in favour of the ancient rather than the modern view. It is clear, first, that in all instances of the perception and cognition of *values* (which unlike the Ancients I can no more regard as a mere function of the cognition of objects than the positive value itself as a higher degree of being) it is the antecedent intention and conduct which principally motivate any value-*illusions*, when the subject remains blind to true values. For that very reason authority and education must from the beginning train the human being to will and act in such a way that these motives of illusion are removed from his value-insight, if he is at all to *attain* a true value-insight and thereafter will and act in accordance with *its* dictates. A man has first to learn in a more or less blind way to will and act rightly and well, objectively speaking, before he is in a position to see good *intuitively* as good and *intuitively* to will and actualize what is good. For though (with modifications I have put forward elsewhere)[1] Socrates' proposition that whoever clearly recognizes good also wills and does it remains correct, inasmuch as good conduct comprises not only the willed thing's objective goodness but also the clear perception of its objectively based *value*-primacy as 'best', it is none the less valid that the acquisition of subjective aptitude for such insights is in turn related to the *sweeping away of motives of illusion*—and these originate above all in ways of life wherein willing and doing what is objectively bad have become ingrained. There are always certain practical ways of life which, having taken the wrong course at some time in the past, draw *down* our sense of values and relative worth and thereby lead us into blindness to values or illusions of value-perception. If this is admitted we still may not assume without further evidence that *theoretical* knowledge of things—as distinct from all grasp of values via emotional acts (intimations, preferences, loving)—is contingent on some relevant 'practical moral condition'. But further evidence is indeed available from the essential connection between value-cognition and cognition of entities. And there it seems to me that the system of our mind, in both its higher acts and the more lowly functions which supply them with material, is such that in the *objective* sphere value-qualities and value-units are received as data *before* anything belonging to the value-*free* sector of the object, so that no information at all of an utterly value-free nature can become the *original*

[1] Cf. Part 1 of my *Der Formalismus in der Ethik und die materiale Wertethik.**

content of a perception, memory or expectation—subsequently an object of thought and judgment—unless we have been given beforehand, in some way, the *value*-quality of the entity or its value-relation to some other thing (equality, difference, etc.); here 'beforehand' does not necessarily imply duration of perception or chronological sequence but refers only to the priorities of data-reception. Thus any value-free or value-neuter entity is in the first place such for us by virtue of a more or less artificial *abstraction*, whereby we set aside the value-quality which is given not merely together with but *before* the object. In the scholar this kind of abstraction can become so habitual, so much his 'second nature', that he is in fact inclined to regard the value-free entity of both psychic and natural phenomena not only as more fundamental *in esse* than their value-qualities but even as preceding them in order of perception. Consequently he casts about, on this false assumption, for some kind of 'yardstick' or 'norms' which might restore value-distinctions to his value-free entity.

For these reasons alone it is difficult for the natural man to think 'psychologically'—*i.e.* in a value-free manner.* As comparative organology of the senses will corroborate, the range of sensual modalities and qualities at the disposal of a species is dependent from the outset on whichever sector out of all *possible* qualities is able to acquire the signalizing function for the things and typical processes which are of *vital* importance for the particular animal organism. Originally qualities are only 'given' as signals for 'friend or foe'.[1] A child knows that sugar is nice sooner than that it is sweet (on which account he may have phases of calling all similarly nice things sugar) and he knows that medicine is nasty (*i.e.* 'bitter' in the value-sense) before he knows that it is bitter (in the qualitative sense of the sensual quality). I have demonstrated thoroughly elsewhere that the same holds true in any given context for remembering, expectation and all concrete instances of perception, and I hope I may be excused from repeating myself here.[2]

It is true even of whole peoples and civilizations that the structures of their *value*-consciousness dictate the ultimate *formative* principle within their collective Weltanschauung. And it holds true for all progress of knowledge in history that the objects touched upon by this cognitive process must first be loved or hated before they may be intellectually known, analysed and judged. Everywhere the 'amateur' precedes the 'savant', and there is no realm of objects, whether numbers, stars, plants,

[1] What this principle means for certain groups of facts in sensory physiology and psychology, as well as for the evolutionary history of the animal world, is shown in the third volume of the present work.*

[2] In this connection, and with reference to what follows, see *Der Formalismus in der Ethik*, etc.

historical reality, matters of divinity, etc., whose exploration did not pass through a phase of *bias* before entering the impartial phase of value-*free* analysis—a first phase which mostly coincided with a kind of meta-physicalization, a mistaken transposition of the object-realm into the world of 'absolute meaning'. To the Pythagoreans numbers, even, were 'divinities' before their interrelations were examined. For its discoverer, Descartes, analytical geometry had an entirely metaphysical meaning, coinciding with the absolutely valid in physics: matter he now envisaged as a congelation of space. To Leibniz differential calculus presented itself as a special case of his metaphysically conceived *lex continui*; originally, at any rate, he regarded it not as reason's artefact but as an expression of the essential becoming of things. Again, in the nineteenth century, it was thanks to the new, climactic interest taken in economic processes by a class which was suffering economic hardship that the embryo of economics was able to take form within the shell of the metaphysical concept of economic history. The strictly scientific investigation of nature was preceded, during the Renaissance, by a redirection of European man's interest; this took the shape of fantastic speculation about nature, flowering into a mighty outburst of quasi-pantheistic enthusiasm. The visible heavens, too, before they were genuinely explored by exact astronomy, were for Giordano Bruno the object of a new enthusiasm; he hailed Copernicanism not for its negative implication—that there no longer existed any such 'heaven' as that of the Middle Ages, no pre-Copernican world of supposedly infinite globes, with its own forms of matter and motion, its own sphere-spirits etc.—but for its positive implication: that Copernicus had discovered a new star in heaven—the Earth—and that we were 'already in Heaven', so that conversely the mediaeval conception of the merely 'earthly' was invalidated. In the same way alchemy preceded strict chemistry; likewise botanical and zoological gardens, as objects of a new *enjoyment* and valuation of nature, preceded the initiation of a more exact, scientific botany and zoology. Similarly a romantic 'love' for the Middle Ages preceded their strict historical exploration; Hellenic philology and archaeology, conducted for reasons of pure science and historical scholarship, were preceded by the amateur's congenial delight in the various aspects of Greek culture (think of Winckelmann and the plastic arts; the upholding of Greek poesy as the eternal model in the 'classical' era of modern philology). Moreover, it is wellnigh a *communis opinio* of great theologians that in the investigation of divine things all proofs of their existence are and must needs be preceded by an emotional contact with God in the love of God, a feeling of his presence as a *summum bonum*—when, as it is put by the great

Oratorians Malebranche and Thomassin, in concert with the neo-Platonists and the Greek Fathers, the 'sense of the divine' is aroused—since herein lies the ultimate source of the materials of demonstration.*

If this priority of value over entity as objects of perception may thus draw illustrations—I have offered but a few—from so many fields, and be demonstrated in accordance with the most diverse methods by which we can test cognition of values and entities, nevertheless it in no way follows that there is any *intrinsic* priority of value over being. Here, too, the thing which 'in itself is the later' *can* be 'the earlier for us', as Aristotle maintained to be the general rule for the interrelation of cognition and being. Indeed, it is reasonable to say that however much they may be *perceptible* in separation from their vehicles and however much they are subordinated to some essential order, based on their content, existing among themselves, there *'belongs'* to all qualities a subsistent entity in which they inhere. And for this reason Aristotle's principle not only *can* but *must* hold good in this case.

Now when the data-precedence of value over being is taken in conjunction with the earlier principle, whereby the (self-evident) perception of values in turn postulates a 'moral condition' (and the less relative the values, the more forcefully this applies), it follows that access to the *absolute entity* is itself *indirectly* dependent on this 'moral condition'.

The peculiarity of the relationship which we thus affirm between on the one hand value and being and on the other hand theory and morality is as follows: Value-insight has an *objective* priority over good volition and conduct, for only what is unmistakenly willed as good is, if it be also objectively good, *perfectly* good. But at the same time true value-insight is subjectively dependent on, hence posterior to, objectively good volition and conduct. Furthermore, true value-insight has a subjective priority over perception of entities, though value itself is no more than an attribute of the absolute entity. So we may go on to say that the specific 'emotional' acts through which we come to apprehend values and which are consequently the source of all value-*judgments* as well as of all norms and decisions of obligation, constitute the unifying factor which is *common* to our practical conduct and all our theoretical knowing and thinking. But since, within the group of these emotional acts, *love and hate* are the most fundamental, embracing and underlying all other kinds (interest, 'feeling of . . .', preference, etc.), they also constitute the common *roots* of our practical and theoretical behaviour; they are the *basic acts* in which alone our theoretic and our practical life discovers and conserves its ultimate *unity*.

Now it is evident that the doctrine here established differs sharply from all doctrines of a primacy of will or of intellect in our minds, since it asserts a *primacy of love and hate* not only over all forms of volition but over all forms of 'representation' and judgment. For, as has elsewhere been shown, it is not in any way feasible to subsume the acts of taking interest, attending or loving and hating under the heads of conation and volition, neither is it tenable to reduce them to mere adjustments of representational content.[1]

3. ANALYSIS OF THE MORAL UPSURGE

Within the integral whole of that upward movement, the *dynamis*, through which the inmost personal Self strives after participation in Reality by knowledge, there are various factors discernible. Supposing these had been distinguished and characterized, three things would remain to be investigated: firstly the stable cognitive *position* which is peculiarly attained by this upsurge of the whole person, secondly the cognitive *principle* in accordance with which things are discovered by the philosophical attitude, thirdly—the last and most important considera-tion—the nature and structure of the *object-world* which, in that stable position of the subject, replaces the perceptual world of the common-sense outlook or natural Weltanschauung.

Only when this task has been performed can we develop philosophical *disciplines* and ascertain the relationship of philosophy to all kinds of non-philosophical knowledge—1. to the natural Weltanschauung, 2. to science, 3. to art, religion and myth.

A. THE MORAL UPSURGE AS A PERSONAL ACT OF 'THE WHOLE MAN'

It is not the characteristic of any particular philosophy, but is in the nature of philosophy as a whole that in it the *whole* man comes into action, with the concentrated sum of his highest mental power. This corresponds on the subjective side to the basic fact that philosophy is *one*, in contrast with the sciences, which—essentially—are many. Even at this stage we find in oneness and multiplicity a difference of principle between philo-sophy and science.[2] By virtue of the special nature of their objects (numbers,

---

[1] For a more precise treatment of the essential relations between love and hate on the one hand and acts of cognition and volition on the other, see in volume 3 of this work the section entitled '*Erkenntnis und Liebe*'. Cf. also the historical typology of this problem, under the heading of '*Liebe und Erkenntnis*', in my *Krieg und Aufbau*, as well as my book on sympathy.*

[2] 'Science' does not exist: there are only sciences.

geometric forms, animals, plants, animate or inanimate things) the sciences demand the exercise of quite distinct *partial* functions of the human mind; one, for example, will require more skill in reasoning or observation, another greater ability to draw conclusions or make intuitive discoveries; furthermore the principal branches of science demand their own special forms of one-sided insight for the acquisition of material, forms corresponding to their objects' particular *forms of existence*. Thus, natural science requires an extraverted, psychology an introverted professional attitude. Moreover, sciences whose spheres of interest are inextricable from certain kinds of value (art, law, government, etc.), require a special *one-sidedly* developed exercise of the emotional functions (*e.g.* the sense of quality in art, of right and fairness in jurisprudence) through which values of this kind announce themselves to consciousness.

In philosophy it is otherwise. From the outset the *concrete whole* of the human mind engages in philosophical thinking, and that in a sense which I would describe as 'bracing and embracing' (*überspannend*) whatever particular group of functions is active at a given time. Even in the minutest subsidiary problem of philosophy the *whole man* philosophizes.

There is one task which the philosopher can perform which cannot be performed by any of those who live and work in the sciences, or in art and religion. This task he can perform and only *could* perform inasmuch as he directly *reintegrates*, in his innermost self, the intrinsically disintegral forms of insight and mental orientation which are accepted in the sciences, arts or religion as separate and distinct, related as they are to the specific conditions and possibilities of whatever regions of value and being are relevant to a given branch of knowledge. The task is that of demonstrating and clearly delineating the essential differences in these *forms* of insight and their attendant modes of existence and perception; furthermore—and this is the important point—the philosopher can as it were focus an as yet undifferentiated and completely *simple glance* of attention upon the *forms* of insight, thought and feeling by which scientists, artists and divines live: he can subject them to that glance (*without*, objectively, sharing them) as objects still *substantially* distinct; he is able to *objectify* them and confront them with a *pure and formless* insight, or pure and formless way of thought.

The old Platonic requirement that in philosophy the whole man, not only his isolated intellect or isolated sensibility, etc., should seek participation in Reality is therefore not, as many very childishly assume, merely a *psychological* feature of Plato's character; it is a requirement lying in the true *oneness* of philosophy and its *objective* problematic structure and governed by the intrinsic possibilities of knowing the *object* of philosophy. It is

a requirement whose basis is neither psychological, nor purely epistemological, but *ontic*. For the essentially different regions of being cannot
themselves be in general apprehended *as* essentially different in kind until
the forms of insight and act, etc., peculiar to them have been reintegrated
within the *centre* of a person and concentrated upon a *single* point of
union and origin. It is only when that psycho-physical object known as
'man' is substituted for the concrete '*act-centre*' *of the mind*, as if *this* 'man'
too might be allowed to obtrude his peculiarities into philosophy and so
turn it into a travesty of its founder's intentions, that the proposition of
the 'whole man' is radically misunderstood. It is another misreading to
follow the sense of Fichte's proposition—which is quite different from
Plato's—that 'one's philosophy is governed by the kind of man one is',
and to regard moral character as responsible for the *content*, the *result*
of one's philosophy, instead of only for the moral upsurge (that is, for its
magnitude, purity and force) which first opens to us the cognitive
possibilities of the self-contained realm of being that is philosophy's
concern.

Lastly, our proposition would still be misunderstood unless one were to
appreciate that while the whole man's every conclusive act of philosophical
thinking must be a *cognitive* act—in ethics, for example, as well as in
knowledge of entities—, nevertheless the particular *datum* underlying such
cognition may very well—indeed sometimes *must*—be ascribed to non-
cognitive functions of the concrete mind. It seems to me, for example, that
Wilhelm Dilthey did not always make a precise enough distinction in his
writings between the mind's data-supplying functions and acts, in philosophical thinking, and those others which make cognitive conclusions. In
this way he opened the door to certain ill-conceived rationalistic criticisms
of his doctrine. Undoubtedly there is today some kind of move towards a
'philosophy of experience', enshrining the basic error that philosophy
could be something other than knowledge, strictly objective *knowledge*,
determined *through* the object and through nothing else—that it could be,
say, 'experience' too, or pass judgments on this or that fortuitous experience, such as the purely emotional convictions which impose themselves from time to time.[1] However, there are also, more notably,
philosophers who regard even the *essential* emotional forms of value-
perception and the *superabundance*, diversely rich for each philosopher, of
knowable *materials* (whose *subjective perceptibility*, not subsistent entity,

[1] Even my article '*Versuche einer Philosophie des Lebens*' (in the collection entitled
Umsturz der Werte) has been subjected to this psychological misinterpretation.
That this could happen is no more than symptomatic of the depth of ignorance at
which these critics or self-appointed disciples exist.

depends on the moral upsurge) as merely a 'fortuitous fact of psychic experience', and therefore hold the immeasurably naïve opinion that to be philosophers they need only be able to pass proper judgments and draw proper conclusions about anything they please.

In seeking to lift itself up to participation in Reality, the goal of the whole man's concrete 'act-centre' is *direct union* between its being and that of Reality; it is in other words man's goal to 'become' the central correlative subject of all possible essential reality, within the *order* immanent in the world of the absolute. This implies that the act-centre must realize its essential nature and eternalize its ontic self in this participation, and implies equally that the essential qualities of Reality must be carried over into the entire ontological form and range of the *personality*. However— as will become evident*—in so far as the idea of an (infinite) concrete personal act-centre as a correlate of *all* possible real essences is identical with the idea of God (or at least with *a* basic definition of the idea), the attempted moral upsurge of the whole mental man is always simultaneously man's attempt to *transcend* himself as a finite natural being, to make himself divine or like to God (cf. Platonic doctrine). Indeed, an essential feature of the upsurge we are examining is the constant endeavour actually to detach one's own mental act-centre from the psycho-physical nexus of human biology[1] (an attempt carried forward in ever-renewed impulses by the operation of the centre, not simply through a theoretical abstraction or 'disregard' of this cohesion), and to transpose it into the universal act-centre corresponding to the idea of God, so that from the vantage-point and, so to speak, 'in' the strength of that centre one may look upon the being of all things. Whether it is ontically possible, and how far it is possible, for this attempt to succeed is quite another question, which is irrelevant to the origin of the philosophical *attitude* and the intention essentially one with it; it relates to the content of philosophy.

[1] The procedures (later* to be established) whereby one 'reduces' the existential modes of objects in order to look through them and discover for oneself the objects' pure perseity or essence—procedures recently called 'phenomenological reduction' by E. Husserl, who describes them as simply 'abstraction', *i.e.* 'setting-aside' or 'bracketing-off', of the existential modes (not of the actual existence, as he assumes)—presuppose this endeavour to detach, at least in a *functional* sense, the act-centre from the psycho-physical nexus, and they thus presuppose some process of being, some evolution and transmutation on the part of the human subject. For this reason the mental cognitive technique of this personal transposition must precede these purely logical abstractive procedures.

B. STARTING-POINT AND ELEMENTS OF THE MORAL UPSURGE

In studying the upsurge which leads to the philosophical attitude and opens the way to philosophy itself and its object we must distinguish two things—its point of outset and its goal. Now the point of outset *common* to all kinds of higher mental activity related to the group of values which I called in my *Ethik* 'spiritual values' (whether scientific, philosophical, aesthetic, artistic, religious or ethical) is man's natural Weltanschauung[1] with its attendant categories of value and being. But the *identically* common requirement of the different acts and approaches which lead away from the 'natural' point of outset in the direction of some *supra*vital region is the *objective attitude*. This is the attitude essentially related to supravital values as such. If then we are to study how to overcome the 'moral impediment' —an operation which is part of the upsurge and depends on it for success —we must first arrive at a general understanding of the natural Weltanschauung and the human attitude which inhabits it and is conditioned by the same circumstantial factors. And it is no less our task to seek out the crucial personal factor which underlies, first, a generally objective attitude, then more particularly, the philosophical attitude. In this connection we shall find it especially important to bear in mind the three distinct procedural attitudes toward the cognition of objects: 1. the natural Weltanschauung, 2. the philosophical Weltanschauung, 3. the general scientific conception—and grasp their *correct* interrelation.*

A primary feature of the natural Weltanschauung is that the subject takes the environing world of the moment, or all possible human-environmental worlds, to be *the* world-being.* And this applies in all directions, in space, in time, externally, internally, and in respect of the divine as well as of ideal objects. For in all these directions there is indeed an 'environment', which partakes of an essential *structure* which makes it the environment, although its specific content varies according to the individual subject or collectivity (peoples, races, the species man) and the different levels of organized life. In the case of the natural environment this structure consists of the system of natural existential forms (things, events, the natural reactions to time and space) together with the corresponding *forms* of perception, thought and expression (plain common-sense and ordinary ways of speech). This demands the detailed study of a 'phenomenology of the natural Weltanschauung', which should be quite distinct both from 'science's' study of *categories* and from the study of

[1] Likewise the 'natural forms of behaviour', the 'natural value-attitude', etc., etc.

ontological and cognitive forms which is the proper concern of philosophy *qua* philosophy, once it has attained full access to its special object
and stands in the position of knowing it.

But however the structure of general environment appears to man it is
in any case peculiar both to the environment's objective being and to its
structure that their existence is *relative* to the *special bio-organism* of man as a
particular species of universal life; this existential relativity, this inex-
tricability from the organism, applies just as much to the structure and
the content (the component essences) of the separate ingredients of this
environment as to their actual existence and forms of existence. Here we
find ourselves in the world of *doxa*—in accordance with the Platonic
distinction between δόξα and ἐπιστήμη. Moreover, this holds good
whether we refer to the special environment of an individual, race, tribe
or people or to the general environment of natural man as representing
the species *homo*. But scientific, 'universally valid' cognition undertakes a
reduction in respect of the being and content of general environment: it
undertakes to know and to 'think' entities in a consistent ontic relativity
to life in general, in such a way that they can be considered, as much
'in the round' as possible and following a principle of strict detachment
from all essential or existential relativity to individuals or particular
collectivities, *purely* in their relativity to the generic human organism and
its identical counterpart as a component of every human being. Nevertheless, the underlying fact that, out of the vastness of the subsistent
cosmos, only those things enter the sphere of human environment which
fulfil, thwart or in some other way respond to man's instinctual and
corresponding sensory structure is true as much for the general environment (even when stripped of all particular reference) as for the more
specific environments of an individual, a race and so on.

Thus 'scientific' cognition retains the shell, the structural *forms*, of the
natural Weltanschauung, even if it discards many of the contents. But
philosophical cognition is *not* directed to such an extension of cognitive
participation in the being of environing worlds, nor does it seek to extract
an environment of 'universal' (human) validity. No; philosophical
cognition is aimed into an entirely *different* sphere of being, which lies
outside and beyond any mere environment. This explains the necessity
of the moral upsurge: only by its means can man hoist himself to the
plane of being of the *cosmos itself*. In other words, a special combination of
moral acts is needed in order as far as possible to perform for the inquiring
mind the service of removing those *bonds* which restrict it to the natural—
environmental—Weltanschauung. Within the scope of that outlook,
whether in its common-sense form or in its scientific refinement, the mind's

only possible objects must be ontically relative to life, relative to 'the vital' in general, hence *also*—of necessity—relative to some specific corporeal, instinctual, sensory system. The moral acts are needed so that the mind may be enabled to *eschew* on principle the merely life-*relative*, the being which is being 'for' life and therein 'for' man as a living creature; they are needed that the mind may begin to participate in being *per se et in se*.[1]

Within this combination of basic moral acts conducive to philosophical cognition we discern one of positive and two of negative character; they must work together in unitary interaction if a man is to reach the threshold of knowing the object of philosophy:

1. *the whole spiritual person must love absolute value and being;*
2. *the natural self and ego must be humbled;*
3. *self-mastery must be achieved*: in this way it is possible to objectify the instinctual impulses of life, which are 'given' and experienced as 'of the flesh' and which must needs exert a constant influence on natural sensory perception.

In systematic interaction these—and only these—moral acts lead the spiritual person, as the potential subject of participation in absolute being, out of the environmental sphere, that of ontic *relativity*, and into the cosmic—toward *absolute* being. They neutralize man's natural egocentricity, life-engrossment and anthropomorphism, all characteristic of the natural Weltanschauung, and remove the corresponding material characteristics of the environment as such. This they do in various ways:

Love of absolute value and being counteracts, at its source in man, the ontic relativity of the environmental.

Self-humbling overcomes natural pride and is the moral precondition for the simultaneous 1. discard of the modes of contingent existence of pure substantive *entia* (a condition of 'seeing' pure essences) and 2. deliverance from the actual entanglement of the cognitive act in the economy of a psycho-physical organism. Be it noted that the above modes and the entanglement are *essentially* interdependent, standing and falling together.

Self-mastery, as a means of restraining and objectifying the instinctual impulses, overcomes natural concupiscence and is the moral condition of *adequate* perception of objects in the *cosmic* sphere. For according to the

---

[1] Since in principle these acts can be performed in all possible grades of human being, the attainment of the object of philosophy (the absolute being—essence and existence—of all objects) is possible in all degrees of adequacy and completion. For that reason, if for no other, we are debarred from saying that any person can know everything, or nothing, or just as much or just as little as another, about absolute things and values. Whatever a person *can* know depends rather on the degree of upsurge.

extent of the subject's instinctual 'blindness' this perception may have any degree of adequacy, from none to perfection.

Thus to these three moral acts, as conditions of full knowledge, there correspond three independently variable *criteria* of all knowledge:

1. its object's kind and degree of ontological *relativity*;
2. whether it is *self-evident knowledge of essences* or *inductive existential knowledge*;
3. the extent of its *adequacy* to the fulness of the object.

Love, which may be thought of as the heart and soul of the entire complex of acts, leads us in the direction of the absolute. It thus takes us *beyond* objects existing only *relatively* to *our* being.

Humility leads us away from the contingent existence of something-or-other (and all the forms and interconnections of being which belong to *that* sphere) toward the *essence*, the pure substantive content of the cosmos.

Self-mastery leads from inadequate knowledge—in the extreme case of an object's merely 'standing for *x*', from no knowledge at all—toward full *adequacy* of cognitive insight.

The connection which obtains between these moral attitudes and the possibility of advance in knowledge along *any* of these basic paths (toward absolute being or self-evident insight or full cognitive adequacy) is no fortuitous or empirical psychological fact but an *essential* bond wherein the moral and the theoretic worlds are eternally tied—as if riveted— together. For the factors within us from which we are delivered by humility are those corresponding to this fact: that in the natural Weltanschauung and its involvement with the environmental (even in 'science'), we *primarily* perceive the object's contingent existence, not its essence. Humility thus removes the systematic moral impediment which those factors, occluding the mental eye, set up as a barrier to the pure knowledge of essences.

Only one of these three basic moral acts will be found a moral condition not only of philosophical but also of scientific cognition, in this case as distinct from the natural Weltanschauung. This is self-mastery—the domination of the instinctual impulses by the rational will, a condition of adequate knowledge. This situation accords precisely with the fact that science, as opposed to philosophy, moves—whether by inductive or deductive method—in the sphere of contingency, even when it seeks and finds the universal laws of nature; it does indeed postulate knowledge of essences, but this it does not itself provide. Likewise, the object of its knowledge is not absolute Reality but only the sum of entities when they are still ontically relative and as such open to the possibility of *control and modification* by means of a rational will which is itself guided, but also *bound*, by possible anthropocentric aims and values. For, however much it succeeds in extinguishing the individual, collective and racial relativity of things, even if it succeeds in excluding the generic reference to man's positive natural organism—and therewith the phase of natural Weltanschauung—science and its object-world remain bound of *necessity* to two fundamental facts of man: 1. his 'wilful' nature, 2. his *universal* bio-economic characteristics. The reason for this lies in the fundamental constitutional reference of all possible being to *possible control* by a *finite rational will* governed by the possible ends of universal life in general. But these two are the very facts which, as centres of reference and selection-mechanism, correspond in all non-philosophical attitudes so exactly to the primary perception of contingent and relative being that but for them the very primacy of such data would be rescinded. These, too, are the facts which tend to banish and preclude love of absolute being and humility toward the pure *quid-est* of the cosmos and its contents (no matter how this *quid-est* and its structure are distributed, in accordance with the laws of time, space, number, causality, etc., over the sphere of contingent existence).

So, once again, it is not by chance but in the nature of things that even the scientist's basic *moral* attitude to the world and his task in it is, and should be, totally different from that of the philosopher. In positive research the scientist's will to know is primarily inspired by a will to *master* and, thence arising, a will to *order* the whole of nature: it is for that very reason that 'laws', in *obedience* to which nature lets herself be governed, represent the highest goal of his endeavour. What interests him is not *what* the world is, but how it may be considered as *constructed*, so that, within the scope of this highest goal, it may be regarded as practically *modifiable*.

For this reason his basic ethos is not love and not humility, but it *is* self-domination—self-mastery for the sake of potential world-mastery. This is not to say that the scientist, too, may not be moved by love of *knowledge* of things: just as science presupposes philosophy, knowledge of the contingent presupposes knowledge of essences. But not—like the philosopher—by love of the very *being* of objects. And even his love of knowledge is only love of a certain kind of knowledge—the kind which, *in addition* to satisfying all criteria of adequacy and logical correctness (two yardsticks valid for all knowledge), assists the realization of a potential mastery of the world, but mastery, be it noted, *for its own sake*—not, then, for any specific use or purpose.

Conversely, this is not to say that the philosopher is not guided also by self-mastery; but it guides him only as a rule of heuristic discipline, so that, having with its aid come to the maximum adequacy of cognition, he may strike away the 'contingency' adherent to the being of the object—an operation which he is enabled to perform by reason of the utter humiliation of his wilful self—and look upon its *quid-est*, its eternal *essence*, to the exclusion of all else. Once over the threshold of knowledge, the philosopher must again bar the door to the will, which is *in essence* the correlative subject of all contingent existence, and wholly 'devote' himself to the absolute reality of his object.

4. PHILOSOPHY'S OBJECT AND COGNITIVE ATTITUDE

The question of which is the first self-evident insight has rightly been placed at the head of all 'classical' philosophy, and rightly, too, the great phases of philosophy have been primarily classified according to the insight allotted this place as the most obvious 'starting-point' of all philosophy. The most important dividing-line in the history of European thought is furthermore correctly seen in the fact that since Descartes the problem of *knowing* has displaced from the front rank the problem of the being of things in themselves.* Ancient and mediaeval philosophy are predominantly ontological; the modern, with few exceptions, epistemological. But whether philosophy takes shape in one or in the other of these radically divergent directions depends essentially on what is declared to be that primal self-evident insight, the one most unhypothetical, incontrovertible—and what the order of origin, postulation and consequence in which other insights follow. For this reason every inquiry into the nature of philosophy must also begin with this problem of the *order of fundamental self-evident insights*.

But the *first* and most direct self-evident insight is that already postulated in establishing the sense of the expression 'doubt about something' (about the being of something, the truth of a proposition, etc.) : put in the form of a judgment it states that *there is something* (in general) or, to put it more acutely, that *there is not nothing*—the word 'nothing' here denoting not simply the not-being-anything or non-existence of a thing, but that *absolute nothing* whose negation of being does *not* 'as yet' discriminate in the negated being between thusness (*So-sein*), or essence, and existence (*Da-sein*). The situation that *there is not nothing* is at one and the same time the object of the first and most direct self-evident insight and the object of the most intense, the ultimate philosophical *wonder*, though I grant that this emotional response cannot come to fruition until it has been preceded, among the emotional acts conducive to the philosophical attitude, by the adoption of that humility which abolishes the taken-for-granted, self-evident character of being as a fundamental fact and even undermines it as an *obvious* fact. *This* insight, then, is evident to me with invincible clarity, no matter where I turn my attention, whatever I look upon and however it be more closely determined according to secondary categories of being—whether it be quality or existence, noumenal or phenomenal, a real or objective non-real entity, an object or subject, an ideal or a resistant object, valuate or value-neuter 'existential' being; whether it be substantial, attributive, accidental or relational; possible, necessary or actual; timeless, purely durational, past, present or future; true (as *e.g.* a proposition), valid or pre-logical; purely mental and fictive (like the wholly imaginary 'mountain of gold' or a merely imagined feeling) or extra-mental or both mental and extra-mental. Choose where you will, with *every* example within one or more interlinked and overlapping 'kinds' of being, as with every one of these categories themselves, the clarity of this primary insight is such that it outshines *everything* which can in any conceivable way be brought into comparison with it. But whoever has not, so to speak, looked into the *abyss of absolute nothing* will indeed completely overlook the eminent positivity inherent in the insight that there is something and not rather nothing; he will begin with one or other of the perhaps no less self-evident insights which are, nevertheless, posterior and subordinate in self-evidence to this insight, as for example the insight implicit in *cogito ergo sum*, or such intuitions as that there is truth, that there is judgment, that there are feelings, or that we have a 'picture' of the world.

The insight under discussion would not be self-evident, still less the most fundamental, if it had to be 'founded'. On the other hand the *assertion that* it and no other is the primary insight, the one least assailable, requires foundation. For it is precisely this that the majority of philosophers deny —philosophers, for example, who insist that this insight is excelled in self-evidence by the insight that *knowledge*—or, as others prefer, truth, validity or even value—exists. We have therefore to find special, universally recognized methods of confirming the primacy of this insight over all others. After that, every attempt to supplant it with some other insight would have to be refuted *in extenso* with the help of these methods.[1]

But before these methods are developed and set to work on examples a *second* insight may be adduced which is grounded in the first and also in a

---

[1] I intend to carry out this task exhaustively in my next book, *Die Welt und ihre Erkenntnis: Versuch einer Lösung des Erkenntnisproblems** (The World and knowledge of it: an approach to a solution of the problem of knowledge).

classification of being which overlies all other internal distinctions and therefore cannot fail to cut across them. The distinction I here refer to concerns the difference between one non-nonentity and another with respect to whether it 'is' only by virtue of a one-way or mutual dependence on another entity or 'is' in exclusion of any possible dependence on another entity—'is', that is, in an *absolute* way. An entity which—if it is—simply *is*, which has its being in itself and *only* in itself, thus not holding it in fee from anything else, we shall therefore call the *absolute entity*, however it may otherwise be qualified by subsequent ontological distinctions. The absolute entity may be variously conceived or abstracted in *relation* to other ontological distinctions without their being present in it. For instance it may be denoted the 'entity for itself' (*ens pro se*) in relation to the entire sphere of possible object-hood; as distinct from all entities conditional on the *conceivability* of a judgment of acknowledgment or propositional 'verification' of their existence, it may be denoted the *ens a se*; as distinct from all entities which 'are' only 'through' or by reason of another entity (be it only logically or also causally) it may be denoted the *ens per se*. In relation to all such absolute being as is only the absolute being of a merely 'intended'—in the sense of mental or fictive—existence, it may be called that absolute entity which is not merely relative to the content of intention but is also the absolutely absolute entity in respect of all mental intention. All the foregoing and like designations are but relatively meaningful connotations of the absolute entity: they are justified, but may not be imported into its innermost self-being.

And so the insight that there is an absolute entity, or an entity through which every non-absolute entity has and holds its attributive being, forms the *second self-evident insight.* For if (as we clearly recognize with each example of an entity, no matter what) there is something (in general) rather than nothing, then in our 'examples' to be reviewed at will that part of them which is relative not-being (both not-being-anything and non-existence) can indeed be attributed to the possible contingencies and relativities which their being possesses from other entities (including even the knowing subject), but this is never possible in respect of their positive being itself. It is no inference merely, but a direct intuition, which tells us that this being demands a source in an entity pure and simple which is *devoid* of any more restrictive determination. To anyone who denies this proposition one can only show that the mere *attempt* of denial and all his arguments presuppose that even in his own intention the absolute entity is in fact *given* to him and is in fact acknowledged by him. In every one of his mental intentions he in fact looks it 'in the eye'—so much is as clear as day once one makes the intellectual effort to *remove* it. Looking through the web of any relative entity—thus of any relative non-entity—he looks *through*, but in the *direction* of the absolute entity. But in order to look in its direction he must also see the goal in so far as it is nothing more than the absolute entity—not to define it more closely.

Of course, the light of this truth does not shine in the first place by courtesy of chop-logic. Just as insight into the first proposition depends on one's having not merely brought to occasional judgment the undoubted objective possibility that there is *nothing*, but also consciously entertained it, 'lived' in it in such a way that the subsistence of every entity has seemed a miraculous repealing of that possibility, an eternally astonishing *roofing of the abyss* of absolute nothing—just so the illumination of this second insight depends on one's awareness of not only the being but also the relative *non-being* in all relative, contingent entities (within oneself in the first place), so that one does not—without properly noticing the fact—privately identify one or other relative entity with the absolute entity. It is therefore *not* a question of whether men bring their thoughts and intentions to bear on absolute being in every conscious moment of their lives, but only a question of whether it stands for them in sufficient relief and sharp enough distinction from relative being, or whether it secretly merges in their consciousness with this or that part of relative being because, unaware of the latter's relative non-entity, they consciously or unconsciously equate that with, and substitute it for, absolute being. Whoever raises a relative to an *absolute* being must needs become what is known as a relativist, since he no longer perceives the absolute in separation from the relative. Indeed *always*—without exception—the relativist is the absolutist of the relative.

Even at this stage of inquiry we see that our earlier assertion, that a certain moral attitude of the whole person is a *sine qua non* in philosophy, is valid here for the clarity of vision in self-evident insights. For only a man who, in the value-aspect of the world and of himself, is conscious that beside the relative 'pride' adherent to the being and positive value of every thing there is a measure of peculiarly fitting 'humility', lying in its relative non-entity, hence negative value, will be able to satisfy those moral conditions without whose fulfilment the light of neither insight shall shine upon him. And this man will be one whose love is clearly directed to what has absolute and positive value (the *summum bonum*) as to a special good divorced in his mind from all relative goods. For both the 'taken-for-granted' quality of being, the very thing which obstructs clear perception of the immeasurable positivity of the fact *there is something* rather than nothing, and the denial of the relative non-entity in things—their relative 'nothingness'—, which denial proceeds from different subjects in different ways and with reference to different zones of being, are dependent functions of 'natural pride', that natural and instinctive self-overvaluation (which has admittedly its biological purposes) and that consequent self-confidence of existence which permit one so remarkably, in—so to speak—the teeth of one's awareness, to deny death itself and the infinity of time when we were not and shall not be. And only when we have learned to marvel *that we ourselves do not not-exist* shall we also be able to receive the full illumination of the two insights and their primacy in self-evidence over all others.

The *third* insight to follow in the 'order of self-evidence'—'follows', that is, in such a way that we have essentially completed our perception of the preceding member of the order, so that it now makes sense to *wish* to perceive the next, or, to put it differently, in such a way that it is still possible for us to 'doubt' the next insight while we can no longer doubt the antecedent—the third insight corresponds, expressed in the form of a judgment, to the proposition that every possible entity must *necessarily* possess a qualitative *quid-est*, an essence, and also an *existentia*. These they possess without regard to what they otherwise may be or to the sphere of being they inhabit by reason of possible subdivision into ontological forms and categories. Here, too, you may choose an entity at random—let it be agent or object, an *ens in abstracto* or even some particular *form* of being such as reality and objective non-reality or subsistent and inherent being— any entity will serve to illustrate the divisibility into *essence* and *existence* which holds good for all possibles, and to assist us to perceive that any entity must *of necessity* possess both essence and existence. Even realness, for example, has its own particular essence.

It follows that to every essence of a thing some kind of existence must belong, and to every existence a particular essence—though *knowledge of essences* is entirely different from existential knowledge, different as much in its self-evidence as in its range of values and human attainability. For our knowledge of the existence of things, and of the interrelations of existences, is far more *limited* than our knowledge of the essences in the world and of their interrelations. But perhaps we may be permitted to express here and now the underlying principle that whatever is contained in the essence of an object, or is true of that object *qua* essence, is *a priori* and of necessity also contained in, or true of, all possible existents having the same essence, whether or not these existents or part of them are knowable by us; whereas by no means everything which is contained in or true of objects known and considered as existents is also contained in or true of the essence of these objects.[1]

---

[1] Since the formal and substantive *a-priori* content of the essence is not only valid 'for' the particular existent in which it happens to be found and which lies within the bounds of *our* existential experience, but is also predicable of any existent

Once we have fully perceived the pure essential content of an object (or an act), or a particular arrangement or interrelation of such essences, our knowledge has peculiarities which fundamentally distinguish it from all knowledge of the realm of relative and contingent existence. It is *definitive*, thus incapable of increase or diminution—that is to say, it is strictly *self-evident*, whereas knowledge of contingency, however attained, whether by direct perception or the drawing of inferences, never arrives at more than presumptive truth, certainty conditional on the findings of later experience or on adjustment to a more conclusive context; to express it in the form of an objective judgment, then, it arrives not at truth but at probability. To pursue, perception of essences is *insight* and (as judged) is 'true' *a priori* of all possible existents having the same essence, those it is quite impossible for us to know, as much as those we merely happen not to know. It follows that all true a-priority is, as such, essential a-priority. Again, as pure insight essential knowledge may be as successfully (indeed often more easily) applied to the wholly notional entity of *ficta* having a given essence as to genuine existents which have that essence. If, for example, I deludedly think something to be live which is not live, the liveness of the object delusively envisaged being thus a fiction, then the essence of liveness must be as much part of the *fictum* as of the idea we have of a thing both envisaged as live and in fact live. But one must add with sole reference to the absolute entity (whose perceptual status, still undivided into essence and existence, *precedes*—not follows—this dichotomy and the true principles connected with it) that, since by concept and definition it depends on no other entity and *cannot* exist as contingent, its existence must be so determined as to be only a necessary consequence of its very essence, whatever that may be. While, therefore, the division of all relative entities into essence and existence is an *ontic* distinction which lies not in our understanding but in the being of *things themselves*, in respect of the absolute entity, whatever that may be, it is no true dichotomy but one epistemologically relative to a cognitive subject. Within the absolute entity essence and existence are fused in one—but in such a way, to be sure, that envisaged *hypothetically* as a dichotomy, its existence follows from its essence, but not conversely its essence from its existence.

having the same essence which lies *outside and beyond* the sphere of our possible existential experience, we do possess in this *a-priori*, at all events, a knowledge which, though it does not necessarily *exhaust* the essences of the transcendental sphere, is nevertheless *also* valid for existents in that sphere. On this basis it is possible to arrive at a positive solution of the problem whether metaphysics is possible, but here is not the place for such a demonstration, which is therefore held in reserve for a systematic treatment of the epistemological question.*

At this stage, though we have not assembled all the materials needed to define the object of philosophy, we are already in possession of some. We may say: *In essence philosophy is strictly self-evident insight, which cannot be either augmented or nullified by induction and which has a-priori validity for contingent existents: insight into all such essences and essential interrelations of beings as are accessible to us from available instances, in the order and hierarchy as they stand in relation to the absolute entity and its essence.*

The direction of cognition toward the *absolute* sphere or toward the relationship to the absolute of all objectifiable being, and the concentration of cognition on the *essential* as distinct from contingent existential sphere of objectifiable being: these characteristics, and these alone, constitute the primary nature of philosophical knowing. Herein it stands in strictest contradistinction to the sciences, which are just as necessarily concerned with the multifarious forms of ontically *relative* being—relative both in essence and existence—and which, even if they set out from 'axiomatic' bases founded in essential insight, derive all their knowledge either from the intramental entities of pure *ficta* (as in the whole of mathematics) or from contingent existence and the structure thereof.

For the rest, we must acknowledge that in this incomplete definition of philosophy's object, as in all our earlier remarks, a certain concept has come to the fore which has so far gone untested, though, when we call to mind the dominant trend of post-Cartesian philosophy, this is a fact which appears to cast a shadow of doubt over all our statements. This is the concept of *knowledge*—with all its attendant concepts. Indeed, it is now our task to say what kind of being is the *being of knowledge,* and it is all the more our bounden duty for having set out, when determining the order of self-evident insights or the stages whereby we might uncover them by skepsis, without a tested postulate—such as Descartes, Locke or Kant employed—of 'knowledge' or 'thought' or 'consciousness' or some kind of 'subject' or 'judgment' and so on, notions with whose aid one might uncover the basic ontic concepts. In fact we shall not be able to uphold *conclusively* the order of self-evidence we have established unless we refute the orders accepted by the above thinkers not only by arguing from our own but by showing *positively* what knowledge itself really is and means in a world of pure being, a world of 'things' which 'are'.

We hope to air this problem, already stretching far beyond the definition of the nature of philosophy and its moral preconditions, in the first pages of a new study of 'the world and knowledge of it'; this is the next work we intend to lay before the public.

PROBLEMS OF RELIGION

PROBLEMS OF RELIGION

THE RENEWAL OF RELIGION

WHENEVER man is seized in his deepest being and overwhelmed —whether by rapture or grief—the hour does not pass before he has beheld, with the inner eye of the mind, the eternal and absolute, nor before that sight has wrung from him a loud, or muffled, or secret, or even inarticulate—cry of longing. For in the person whole and undivided, in the core of the human person—not, like the springs of social activity, in partial and peripheral functions, talents, needs of the person; not close by the surface of the psychic stream—in our deepest depth, then, there lies that wonderful mainspring which, mostly unnoticed and disregarded in wonted circumstances, is ever latent and active to lead us upward, over and beyond ourselves and all things finite, to the divine. When therefore such an event as awakens the core of the human soul and unpinions this mainspring for greater activity impinges not only on the individual soul, in the dumb secrecy of its suffering and struggle, but on the community of men; when it impinges on the world-wide community, divided in peoples, which has nothing over it but its God; when its impact is greater than that of any event in the whole of history; when the event is in addition so unimaginably saturated with tears, suffering, lifeblood as the late war—*then* one may expect the call to a renewal of religion to resound through the world with such power and strength as has not been for centuries.

Today this call takes on a singularly historic character in that what is stricken to the heart is nothing less than the *whole of humanity*, nothing less than this mysterious planetary species in its undivided state—that is, like one man, a man cast into the boundlessness of time and space, cast into a mute uncomprehending nature: he bends every member in a solidarity of effort to win the fight for existence, but it is also a fight for the meaning of his life and for his worth and dignity. Whatever exists in material reality apart from this species—flora and fauna, the sun and stars—man knows that everything is *beneath* him, beneath him in status and value, even in strength. But what does this creature, that knows everything beneath itself and learns to master it, know to be above it save the pitiless stars—save God? Where could this creature find something stronger and worthier than itself? Countless sufferings in its struggles with nature and internecine conflicts has this species undergone, and countless themselves have been the struggles and conflicts throughout the course of its dark history, a history illumined with but one thread of light at its medial point. But wherever these vicissitudes appeared, whatever aspect they assumed, always, until the outbreak of the Great War, the subject that fought and suffered, the people and the nations, had at least one thing *above* it, above it in worth and strength: there was, then, something above man to which he imputed as it were a moral office of judge over himself, but something in which he could at the same time place a deep trust and hope and in whose bosom he could at least believe himself to lie in some way sheltered. This one thing was—*humanity*. The part had a right of appeal to the whole, the part had a right to hope through the whole. Every suffering and every despair could say: 'The whole is not suffering, the whole does not despair.' Today that appeal is no more. For the first time, no more, since as far as thought can reach. Gone is the right to say: 'For mankind as a *whole*, the future remains, and the wealth of humanity, and undiminished strength.' Gone, because this war, rightly called the World War, was the first experience to be undergone by humanity as *its collective* experience. It was not a thing taking place in only one section of humanity and reaching all other sections only as foreign rumour and report; nor was it an affair wherein one section fights and suffers, while the others look on merely to applaud or commiserate. And yet every contention known to us in history has hitherto been of that kind. The issue of world-war and world-peace is an issue common to all mankind, affecting directly every member of the race—to a greater or lesser degree—in life, in body, in soul.

Up to the time of the outbreak there existed in Europe a certain widespread fashion of thought. In philosophy it was called *positivism*, and it was also busily active in poetry and art. This way of thinking shifted all the love and veneration which man formerly brought in offering to his God, his invisible lord and creator, on to the 'great being' —as A. Comte called humanity. 'God was my first, reason my second, man my final thought' were the words of Ludwig Feuerbach even in the Germany of the 1860's. And so what Comte, Feuerbach, Zola called the great being of humanity was inflated to something distant and holy, to be approached in fear and trembling. A similar quasi-religious pathos over humanity is to be found in Friedrich Schiller, especially in the productions of his youth. It was to humanity that the cry of the injured and insulted went out, of all those, were they individuals or whole peoples, who felt themselves unjustly humbled and oppressed. Where is, where ever was, this humanity, which still seemed enthroned *above* us all as the *'grand être'* ? The war, unlike all previous wars in history, was no longer within humanity, no longer in one of its sections. Humanity itself was in the war. Where now was that which used not to suffer, but reposed in remote sublimity while peoples suffered? Humanity itself was suffering violence committed by humanity. Where was the seat of the wicked, where the source of disturbance and peril, where the demonic element of turmoil and faction which attacked a people and made them to suffer, that humanity might arm to punish the transgressors? Let the politicians peer through their spectacles and seek it as best they may: it is nowhere. For it is in the whole of humanity itself and it *is* humanity itself, suffering the violence upon violence which it inflicts upon itself. Where is the whole which, when a part strayed into evil ways, could yet lead the part back, teach it and educate it? Nowhere! For mankind has learned how to master everything *beneath* it—plants and animals, sunlight and all kinds of energy—but *one* thing alone it has not learned to master: *itself.* Where is the *grand être* to whom the people look up in reverence? It has been convulsed with pain and bloodletting, and is truly no more the 'great being'. It is only a small being, a quite small, suffering, being. For the first time humanity feels *alone* in the wide universe. It has seen that the god it made of itself was an idol —the basest of idols since time began—baser than graven images of wood, marble and gold.

This, then, is the new thing in the present call to religious renewal: *humanity* is rejecting its *idol-self*, and the *'grand être'* which so long hid God from sight, as a cloud veils the sun, has been blown away. In some unprecedented way humanity has become aware of its weakness, its lowliness, its crooked timber, as Kant put it. For this reason it is hard to understand why, precisely when the *grand être* has become so small and— like a caterpillar inquisitively swaying its head beyond the edge of the leaf—is powerlessly scanning its surroundings for some force that might help it to escape the clutches of the frightful mechanism in which it has trapped itself,—why at this moment Alfred Loisy[1] is able to write a book which, on the basis of a wealth of religious scholarship, seeks to breathe new life into Comte's religion of humanity. Moral 'obligation'? —that is supposed to be no more than the sense of what we owe to the work of past humanity. What *we*—owe to past humanity? Come now, whatever we owe to past humanity, 'they' are indebted to *us* for the entire sum of human suffering endured by youth in the Great War: for that they are indebted to us, since to *them* we are indebted for the war. Without further investigating the extraordinary apparition of this somewhat

[1] A. Loisy, *La Religion*: Paris, Émile Nourry, 1917.

belated book, we may affirm that *positivistic faith in humanity*, as a chosen makeshift for genuine religion, has collapsed in ruin.

It had necessarily to collapse at a time when mankind, divided into states and peoples, is at least showing the *first will* to embody itself in a league which represents *more* than a bare sum of compacts between states, in an independent, real and collective moral corporation, armed with power and enthroned above peoples and states, a body which, like a state over its citizens, seeks to settle all disputes between states and peoples according to universally recognized norms and laws of right, and to enforce the idea of justice embodied in these laws even, if need be, between separate *sections* of humanity. For it is precisely this legislative moral *embodiment*, for the first time realizing the abstract natural concept of humanity in a 'league of nations', which finally and emphatically precludes any deification of the object of that concept. Only while 'humanity', as an ultimate unit of right and morality, still remained merely a distant *Utopia*, a shining figment of dreams and mystery, or at its highest a splendid vision of poet and seer, could it appear to certain intellectual groups as a substitute for the idea of God. The humanity *realizing* itself in humanity's world-war—the humanity now making the first attempt in its history to master itself and control its destiny in freedom according to supra-national law—can no longer be open to this delusion. Even as the age-old vision begins to be realized, in a realization hampered, like *every* realization, by obstacles, imperfections and disturbances, even the *apparent* gratification of religious cravings which the substance of the vision offers is eschewed. Likewise exactly, the *grand être* is left to fall into desuetude in accordance with that law of the soul whereby the realization of socialism has already begun to expose the redundance of the sham religious gratification offered by the quasi-messianic 'ideal state'. This is the law whereby, in general terms, every realization of the simplest dream of youth, let it be ever so perfect, destroys the power of the fantasy to shine and enchant. For it is only through the transforming psychic power of *longing*, which bathes everything in an ineffable medium of light and splendour, that essentially finite contents of our thoughts and aspirations can assume even an apparent power to satisfy the *religious* craving of our mind, to satisfy the demands of our reason for the final realization of our ideal of the world. Disenchantment ensues even when the substance of the ideal, as envisaged in the longing mind, is fully realized. For one element is bound to be absent from the *realization*—the shining splendour which *longing* itself cast over the ideal.

Nowadays humanity, as realized in one concrete, real and effective subject, will *finally* cease to mistake itself for God. The humanity which in the sphere of earthly justice has no longer any earthly thing above it, the humanity which has pledged itself to the task of eliminating, as far as possible, the blind hazards of chance and fatality from the relations between its parts, will doubly need some insight into an *eternal* order of good and right, by whose light it is taking the first great step towards the genuine mastery of itself.

In Germany, positivism and its religious pathos over humanity was never a considerable force. The more active, on the other hand, among our intellectuals, were the manifold forms of *pantheism*, bequeathed by classicism to our poetry and philosophy. For long it persisted in dilute form—though basically *counter* to the actual feeling of the times. But it is probably no exaggeration to say that of all philosophical attitudes and ways of life, idealistic pantheism is the one which has been struck the hardest blow by the deep revelation of the *nature of things* which the experiences of the Great War have brought in their wake. It has been stricken to the roots.

Pierre Bayle was perhaps the first to ask the ironic question (in his Dictionary's article, 'Spinoza') whether God is at war with himself in time of war. But how more profoundly shattered is pantheism now than was indicated in that question! The seeds of its destruction were already sown in the development of pantheistic thought and feeling over the course of the nineteenth century and during the two decades of the twentieth.

Pantheism's system of thought and feeling rests more or less on the equation *God = World*. Its first error is the unproven hypothesis that the multiplicity of things, forces, relations surrounding us men form *one* world (not an unrestricted number of worlds, as was taught by every logically consequent materialism from Democritus on), and that it forms moreover, a *world* (not a *chaos*), hence one 'sensibly' ordered whole. For this assumption is already founded on the unity and cosmic supremacy of a *single* creator-god.* It is not only in a historical sense that one may demonstrate the truth of Christoph von Sigwart's dictum,[1] which is that if man ceased to countenance the notion of regions of being without causal contact (the idea latent in all true polytheism) and instead envisaged a single, internally consistent cosmic whole, with its parts all in systematic relation, this change of attitude was a fruit of philosophical monotheism. It is also logically and objectively true that the assumption of cosmic unity and singularity *follows* from—before anything else—the assumption of a single creator-god. (For that reason, by the way, it is not quite so easy as is commonly believed to demonstrate the existence of God from

[1] Cf. Sigwart, *Vermischte Schriften*: '*Über den Zweck*'.

the necessity of a first cause for the 'world'.) The world is world (not chaos), and the world is one world, only if and *because* it is God's world—if and because *one and the same* infinite will and spirit is latent and active in every entity. Just as the unity of human nature does not in the last resort lie in man's demonstrable natural characteristics but in his likeness to God, and just as humanity as a whole is only *one* humanity if all its component persons are, by virtue of their connection with God, also truly and morally bound one to another, so the world is *one* world only by virtue of *God's* oneness. Pantheism, which begins by postulating the world-character of subsistent being and the unity of the world, both independently of God, is only guilty—in a more blatant way—of the error committed by those who conclude the existence of God from a presupposed oneness and unity of a world-reality. From this we understand that wherever pantheism has made an appearance in history it has been always an end, never a beginning, never the dawning red of a sunrise of belief but always a sunset glow. It invariably rests on the fact that, in their outlook on the world, men cling to some of the consequences of a positive religious attitude, though its root and basis be forgotten. For the most part therefore, it is the way of thought typical of mature, synthetic, silver-age civilizations, and as such it may be endowed with a marvellous nobility, a greatness truly felicitous and harmonious. The god of pantheism is always a reflection of theistic belief, and is frequently of greater warmth and beauty than the theistic God. Few have so profoundly recognized this as Schopenhauer, who regarded all the pantheism of his age (represented by Fichte, Schelling and Hegel) as a residue of theistic attitudes—and for that very reason poured the more scorn on it. In ages of cataclysmic change and rebirth pantheism not only retreats in the face of reason (which has always put it to rout) but renounces the attempt to gratify religious cravings. It is even by reason of its endeavours to reconcile and harmonize, which leave no place for the moral either-or (the form of experience imposed by such ages), that pantheism is obliged to abdicate in crucial periods of history.

Pantheism can derive its equation of god and world either from an existing idea of world or from an existing idea of god. Before Hegel, a new and deeper understanding of Spinoza had been adumbrated by Jacobi, in his dispute with Lessing over that philosopher, and achieved an early fruition in Novalis's enlightening reference to 'Spinoza, drunk with God'. This *aperçu* was summarized by Hegel in the dictum that, far from being the 'atheism' which Frederick the Great and his century had declared it, Spinoza's doctrine represented a form of *acosmism*.* In his god-intoxication the Jewish apostate overlooked the right and might proper to the world itself, the world's substantial existence. He identified the world with an existing God, not God with the world. It was the same tendency of pantheistic thought and feeling which flared into the suicidal visions of Giordano Bruno and underlies the more dynamic and historic-ally-aware rational pantheism of the German speculative school. Hegel, and those of the Hegelian 'right wing' who closely follow the 'Master', did not, for example, think to deny the divinity of Christ—in the manner of Renan, Strauss, Feuerbach and later 'liberal theology'. On the contrary, they upheld the viewpoint and emotional content of the doctrine of the Incarnation, as well as of Consubstantiality, but (in effect) they reduced Christ to a mere *teacher* who happened to be the first of men to *recognize* in himself a special relation to God which was universally endemic in the human soul. Thus for Christ's personal act of redemption they substituted a simple recognition, and allowed the doctrines of his dual nature and divine superiority to be supplanted by a negation of the autonomy of human nature, together with the (presumptive) elevation of all men to the same sonship of God which he is supposed to have been merely the first to recognize. Hence for these thinkers the Christian religion became simply the 'perfected awareness of God in man'.

However false pantheism is in *every* form, one must nevertheless, make a distinction among pantheisms between a *noble* and a *base* form. These forms correspond respectively to the essentially acosmic and the essentially atheistic forms. In the first place this distinction concerns the dynamic tendency that carries the mind to the equation God = World. Once the distinction is made one may proceed to the following generalization about the evolution of pantheism up to the outbreak of the Great War: *Pantheism was tending more and more away from its noble to its base form, from acosmism to atheism.* This is glaringly true of 'monism' (the systems of Haeckel and Ostwald, etc.) and its satellite theories: there is no need to discuss them here. But the proposition is equally true (if less obvious) of systems of thought and belief conceived, after the hey-day of materialism, on an altogether higher plane. It is true of idealistic systems such as those of Fechner, Paulsen, W. Wundt and so on—down to the last exiguous shred of 'general consciousness'[1] (said by some to exist, by others to be 'existing in effect' as a universal postulate) gratefully received by the pantheistic idealists into our teeming academic theories. These doctrines too, which —historically—trace their ancestry to Kant's theory of reason, in par-ticular to his doctrine of transcendental synthetic apperception (also the

[1] *Bewusstsein überhaupt*—otherwise absolute, abstract (non-concrete) conscious-ness. Scheler's unfavourable opinion of this notion is elaborated on pp. 312 *et seq.* (*Translator*).

starting-point of Hegel's system and Fichte's early pantheism)—these, too, possess the sure sign of pantheism: man's spiritual and mental individuality is either (as in Averroes) said to lie merely in the restriction which the body imposes on the epistemological subject identical in all men, or is equated with the purely fortuitous phenomenal *content* of the empirical consciousness.

It should occasion no astonishment that pantheism has developed in this direction. Pantheism was able—with certain allowances—to express as it were the religious formulation of the German temperament so long as the nation's intellectual life was lost in dreams of an ideal world of the spirit, representing the true homeland of man (for 'man' read 'German') —so long as the nation thought and felt itself to be first and foremost a *Kulturnation*; so long, finally, as there still existed an 'art and science' of which one might still say with some claim to *sense* that whoever possessed them possessed religion, and that only those excluded from the cultural aristocracy need take to heart Goethe's famous *mot*, 'If any possess not these two, let *him* possess religion!' For just as that art was an art of ideas with little tendency to specialization, that 'science' was a synthetic, autodidactic pursuit of cultivated men in a strictly local *culture*, a science strongly coloured by theology—most of the German speculative philosophers were former Protestant theologians. To say anything similar about the art of our time and its science, geared as it is to *work* and *research*, and specialized in the extreme, would be not only incorrect—as also is Goethe's dictum, by the way—but absurd and ridiculous. If then these German pantheistic traditions are to return in backwash to our present world, they must automatically take the shape of some highly-coloured and enticingly dangled *lie*, some illusionistic evasion of reality.

From this implicit association of German idealist and acosmic pantheism with a stage in German civilization that is played out in all respects, we may be led to consider that the many and various attempts to restore these systems to a place in our academic philosophy do not promise any true furtherance or underpinning of either *philosophy* or *religion*. That much may be said regardless of whether the attempt is made under the banner of Fichte, Hegel or Schelling. In principle such traditionalism stands in the way of a new and vital contact of thought and attitude with the facts and objects of philosophy—the subsistent constants of the universe, its order and its structure. It likewise hinders any solid application of the substantial facts concerning the nature of things which have been uncovered in the history of humanity between then and now, and the full exploitation of religion's world-wide immensity of new experience. This kind of artificial philosophical refurbishing can only draw up barriers between philosophical research and any international co-operation among philosophers. For deeply implanted in this philosophy, seen in its historical origins, is its connection with the German nation. Moreover, national connections as such lie in the nature of pantheism, inasmuch as it is a *cultural* religion—whether or not it *means* to be national. Likewise, that the sociological form called 'school of philosophers' should be the natural breeding-ground of pantheisms belongs to their nature as closed *systematic philosophies*. However, in the sense in which the German speculatives strove for it, the system would be an obsolete philosophical ideal if we were able to reject the epistemological assumption that reason (embracing all subjective *a-priori* forms and functions) is itself a closed system, if we could maintain that on the contrary there is a reciprocal *functionalizing* effect between the mind and the data it receives, so that the mind genuinely *grows* in and from its history—a growth basically different from an accumulation of random empirical facts on a *given* level of subjective apparatus, functioning as a constant *a-priori*. This, however, is what we maintain—and we shall give our reasons elsewhere.* The 'system' as a form is itself a consequence of the transcendental subjectivism of all these systems, however they may differ in content. For that matter, the form of the system (which fundamentally precludes any co-operation on a common ground of philosophy, co-operation between one generation and another as much as between co-eval groups of thinkers) is the consequence of an implicit affirmation which all these philosophies have as a common underlying factor. If the human mind as such—not then an assemblage of its discoveries and products—grows not simply 'through' but in *direct* instrumental relation with the *history* of its various real embodiments, *i.e.* the flowering of one new essential outlook after another, and if *this* kind of growth is independent of the biological constancy or inconstancy of the natural species man, then in general terms one cannot expect any proper ideal philosophy in the form of a *system*. One may indeed go so far as to say that a systematic philosophy is false from the outset *because* it has the form of a system—without regard to the content—or that it is a 'will to lie', as Nietzsche once happily phrased it.

But pantheistic thought shows yet another very characteristic tendency. In order to uphold the equation world=god against theism and atheism, in the face of the immense flood of new reality pouring in from the course of history itself as well as from the new discoveries of history and natural science, an ever lengthening succession of *irrational*, non-divine and, in the event, even *counter*-divine factors had to be accepted within the frame of the pantheistic idea of the world. Even Hegel—the romantic poet of logic —had long ago to accept movement and counteraction, evolution and development (even if he will not admit it) into the idea of God, if world-history was to represent the process explaining the idea of God as that historical pantheist conceived it.[1] After the failure of the 1848 revolution and the disillusion of the subsequent period of restoration, which Schopenhauer's at first quite unnoticed work helped to spread among the intellectuals, pantheism—still preserving the basic error of *monism*—underwent a brief transition into pandemonism. For Schopenhauer's 'will' is no god—not even a pantheistic god—but a dark demon. But it remained a pandemonism attached to *Christian values* or at least premises of value similar to those of the Christian ethic. By this I mean that what Schopenhauer maintained to be the basis of the world—the blind, unresting 'urge' to life and being which he calls 'will'—was envisaged by this solitary thinker, who stood with one foot in the old, humanistic Germany and the other already in the new and realistic, as something bad, wild and fearful which must therefore be overcome in visionary ascesis through *repudiation* of the will to life. Nietzsche and, in a somewhat diluted, Gallic form, Henri Bergson were the first to accept as a basis of the world the *same* thing which Schopenhauer had already seen and felt as *his* world-basis —that thrusting, covetous, demonic power, throwing out new forms of existence in ever greater profusion—and to refuse to bewail it pessimistically, suffer it resignedly or flee it ascetically, but to welcome it, acclaim it in jubilation and demand of man that he should throw himself unhesitatingly into the dynamo, dive into the raging torrent. To this end the system of *values* must naturally be altered from top to bottom, and there was nothing for it but to reject out of hand all the morals of Christianity and humanism alike. It is not the metaphysical conception as such, but the new system of values, which distinguishes Nietzsche from Schopenhauer. Nietzsche once applied the term 'my *ipsissimum*' to 'dionysian pessimism'—which as an aesthetic view of history may also be found, inert and innocuous, in Jakob Burckhardt and Nietzsche's friend Erwin Rohde. Thus what Schopenhauer lamented in the manner of a Christian is now the object of Dionysian rejoicing. The *esprit nouveau* of young France before the war[2] had its philosophical counterpart in Bergson's '*élan vital*' and '*évolution créatrice*'—which at bottom is a self-contradiction, since creation and evolution are different in kind. To say the least, his philosophy closely resembles dionysian pessimism, not only as an irrational pantheism

---

[1] For the rest, error and wickedness had to belie their true nature and agree to be construed as the ever renewed and *necessary* spur to the realization of the good and true, if mere *world-history* itself was to embody the tribunal of the world.

[2] Cf. E. R. Curtius, *Die literarischen Wegbereiter des neuen Frankreichs*, Kiepenheuer, Potsdam 1919.

but as sharing the positive emphasis on novel values. Finally, E. von Hartmann, who—without any metaphysical innovations—most deeply and comprehensively formulated pantheistic thought from the logical viewpoint and in a manner typical of the thoroughness and profundity with which he treats the whole history of ideas, had felt compelled, in order to uphold the pantheist-monistic equation against theism and atheism, to introduce before Nietzsche and Bergson a completely *blind dynamic* factor into his idea of god, which is divested of characteristics deduced from awareness of love and goodness. But the work of this all too learned syncretic thinker was never really alive and effective, and may be passed over here, where we are not concerned to evaluate its considerable merits in other, purely philosophical, fields.

If one looks at philosophical trends not only for their absolute truth but for their value as indices of the historical evolution of human life, one can learn a great deal from this tendency of pantheistic thought. At first one sees how open to suggestions is the god of pantheism—more than beseems a god. He meekly complies with the veering currents of history—just like the 'intellectuals' who are the channel of this 'cultural religion'; in turn he puts on a front of rigid geometry, then of visionary euphoria, another of passion-spurred suffering, after that one of devotion to passion and suffering actually combined with dionysian jubilation. All the sublime dignity of supremacy over time and space, which has been the mark even of polytheistic gods, is wanting in this Proteus. Next we see how in this process of pantheistic thought the psychic attitude of pantheism prepares as it were to destroy itself. The pantheism of the nineteenth century is not only a Proteus: it is also its own dissolution. Pantheism, pandemonism, pansatanism—and self-destruction in the flames of the Great War: that is its course.

The literary historian Walzel was right some time ago when he maintained with reference to our modern literature that within it—within this sometimes noble, sometimes ignoble cry of a downtrodden, scandalized youth—the universal *feeling* of pantheism had lost any kind of meaning. To that extent we Germans of the present—in spite of all the literary attempts at restoration such as every war brings in its train, efforts to enhance the continuity of national culture—have become separated more than ever before from our classical writers, both philosophers and poets. Quite apart from its errors, pantheism in every form has no more future, even as a form of religious consciousness, than positivist faith in humanity. It is in fact the most exhausted seam among all European forms of religious consciousness. In its dogmas and philosophy, as much as in its

sociological nature, it is the religion of a self-conscious cultural aristocracy taking its stand against the 'people'. The present wave of democratic
feeling, if nothing else, would bring it to the grave—but thither it has
already dragged itself.

If these two worlds of thought, the positivist and the pantheistic, are
unable to give *any* answer to the call for religious renewal, what is the
significance of that call? It can signify a great deal, but it can also come
and go like the call for help of a man who remains *unanswered* in the
extremest danger of drowning. For however strong may be a pressure, a
need, a deeply felt want, an emptiness in the heart that might be filled,
the pressure itself, the need itself, have *not* the power nor the means to
achieve their own satisfaction. Yet the attempt has been made to turn
the need, the lack, the necessity into the creator of cultural and technical
civilization.* The great physiologist A. Pflüger even tried to prove that
in the life of the bodily organism every need became ultimately the cause
of its own satisfaction. Lamarck built the whole of his theory of evolution
on a similar proposition. There is likewise the German proverb 'Need
teaches to pray', and it is true that we Germans are traditionally all too
fond of believing in, and appealing to, the creative force of 'holy' need.
But in *no* field of human values is this proposition true in the sense in
which it is meant. *Least of all* is it true in the field of religion.

With regard to higher culture, the free creations of the mind, philosophy
and art, never and nowhere spring from necessity and dire need, but
always from disengaged leisure. The ancients knew it well. Even technical
skills and inventions, for which need and necessity mean considerably
more, spring from them only in the sense that they control the choice of
direction exercised by the mind's *inventive activity*—which, however, must
always be present. But even in this case the very 'needs' which are satisfied by the invented tool or machine are of *historical* origin; they have
arisen through adaptation of instinctual life to types of good which as
types were already present before they were, types which were thus
already formed before the corresponding need, types which—finally—
did *not* themselves proceed from needs, but from the free and positive
creative force of the mind. Nearly everything which today is a need of the
masses was once a luxury of the few.

The higher we climb from the utilitarian in the realm of values, the
more *erroneous* the proposition becomes. For that reason it is at its most
erroneous where types of the *highest*, the *religious*, the *truly holy good* are
concerned. 'Need teaches to pray'—certainly. But the fundamental act of
the mind whereby we first open our inner eye to the eternal and are first

enabled to pray to it, the act of *worship*, and thereafter the acts of reverence and devotion—these are *not* taught by need. And yet there is never
any prayer without worship beforehand—neither thanksgiving, supplication, nor any kind of prayer. But at least pure need, necessity, emptiness,
do tell us something about *what* we worship, what we pray to, what we
pray, and how we should pray. There are Negroes in Africa dwelling in
tribes by lakes with abundant fish, yet many die of starvation every year,
since the dire need of hunger has not been able to provoke the invention
of the angler's hook. How much easier it is to imagine that so great a
need for religious renewal should remain without positive consequence.
It is possible for the world's cry of need to hold great meaning only when
it generates motion and activity in man's positive springs of religion,
only when it brings our reason to act in renewed concentration on the idea
of God and opens our mental eye to the positive benefits of revelation and
grace which are already *present* in the world, though great multitudes are
blind to them. Need, the empty heart, the heartfelt want, can and should
have this effect: to that extent they are beacons, drawing souls on to
explore new ground. But *more* they cannot do. For this world and human
nature are everywhere so ordered that the lower, natural and instinctual
forces can unleash higher forms of activity, but cannot create them;
they bid them seek, but not *necessarily* bring them to find. The mental
force which creates and finds is invariably a higher force, working according to its own inner law and owing nothing of its goal, substance and
principle to that which merely set it in motion.

So the 'intellect', which operates in the exact sciences and which
mentally converts, as thoroughly as possible, the phenomena of the
internal and external worlds to dependent functions of a dynamic mechanism, is in all things directed, by the basic values of a living creature,
towards the greatest possible control and mastery of things by the will
and action of that creature; but therein lies also its restriction and
limitation. The 'intellect' is chained to the service of the needs of human
life: its object is not the universal cosmos, but the *general environmental*
world of man. For only in so far as the world is comparable to a perfect
mechanism is the general environmental world susceptible of control by
mechanical acts of a living creature, through implements, machines—
in short, technology. *Is* therefore the world nothing more than a very
complicated game of billiards? Of course not. For one thing, *reason* itself,
which shapes our *philosophical* image of the world and frees itself from
the service of vital need—reason, which seeks to present an image of the
world not so that things may be *mastered* but that they may be *adequately
known*, and which regards the world not only from here below but also

from above—reason can show us that all possible mechanisms, including even the whole mechanism of the world, are enslaved to activities realizing *forms*, *goals* and *values*, through which some system of ideas is striving to fulfilment.[1] But only powers higher than reason—*revelation* and *grace*—bring us light on the inner nature of God and bring us strength from him: a light and a strength which no reason may see, and which we do not deserve. Reason may yet indicate their essential necessity and their validity *once* an almighty, omniscient and supremely good thing has been shown to lie at the basis of things. Nevertheless, the substance of revelation lies outside the span and reach of reason. We must receive it in the free act of faith.

Thus the needs of human life release the activity of the practical intellect, giving its questionings a goal and a direction. Thus the work of the intellect releases the activity of reason, at the same time posing it the question of what *ends* are served by the presence of this mechanism; what system, what eternal ideas and values, are finding a realization therein. And thus reason itself, attaining its *own* true limit—not simply the provisional limits of its former works—unbinds our eyes to the possibility of revelation, and bids our heart seek it. Everywhere on the plane which corresponds to the nature of man the lower must freely subordinate itself to the higher—*freely*, because it acts from strictly positive perception of its own limitations—and only in *serving freely* the higher may it preserve *its own* entire liberty within *its own* sphere. On the other hand, whenever it seeks to step beyond that sphere, to rule the higher instead of serving it freely, it becomes the bondslave of that which is even lower.

The foregoing indicates what the call to religious renewal may *never* mean: a call from mere need to renew—or renovate—religion. To seek religion, not in the sense merely of piety or inner adherence to an existing positive religion, but in the sense of new faith-inspired thinking about the objective realm of religion, is an attitude which is completely misunderstood by men in the present state of the world. False belief in the inventive, creative or even revelatory power of need has led very many people today to the opinion that the Great War must of itself bring to birth a *new religion* or perhaps a new phase in the development of religion, as it were a miraculous pin-bright new Word in answer to the Question of suffering humanity, which I described at the beginning. Unhappily such wishful thinking is apt to receive sustenance from certain reflections about Christianity.

[1] Since it is not unusual, in English usage, to regard reason as a function of a faculty called intellect, it should be pointed out that Scheler limits intellect (*Verstand*) to a practical or technical, specialized function of a very general faculty called reason (*Vernunft*) (*Translator*).

Christianity, some say, is bankrupt; No—simply the Churches, say others; Just this Church and that one, say others yet again. All these theses were prevalent long ago—long before the war. Among the older voices only *one* is almost wholly unheard today—the one which says, Religion itself is bankrupt: it is only an atavism in historical evolution. That this voice is missing shows that we should expect at all events an age of extreme *vitality* in matters of religion, an age characterized by quite new kinds of mighty spiritual conflicts. But for precisely that reason, in the coming age every existing positive religion and Church must cease to be a mere ice-box for old truths—as it was recently put by a Swiss theologian. No doctrinal position—unless it wishes to surrender entirely—will be able to content itself with a mere wish to maintain its *status quo*; every such position will have to exert itself in addition to demonstrate positively to the world its overriding worth—and to be the warrant of its own truth. There we have certainly a new situation, to which none may remain blind. Consider the person who wishes merely to *preserve*, or at the most defend, his religious position: if he dare not see in it the positive means of salvation for suffering humanity, and will not extend to humanity this means in a gift of joy and love, then he will find even his more modest goal of self-preservation *no longer* attainable. As men reckon, his cause will vanish from the face of the earth. For this is how things stand: neither mass-indifference, however widespread, nor even heresy and unbelief, nor sham piety nor superstition were ever a real, an ultimate danger to the existence of a positive religion and Church. Rather the opposite—the outworn, the decadent, custom and inertia were never so mightily propped and preserved in Church-religion as by—*inter alia*—indifference and unbelief. Especially among the educated. Only one true possible danger threatens the existence of a positive religion—the greater enthusiasm and the deeper faith of those who practise *another religion*. It was skeptic indifference and unbelief which enabled the Churches to live such an easy life before the war and to be so content with 'maintaining' their position. But the time will come when unbelief's sterile negation and the apparent tolerance of religion by lazy indifference will have come to an end. Then religion will once again be recognized and attacked from all sides for what it is—the highest concern of man. Then will be an end of the easy life. And with it there will cease the perfunctory frontier-patrol of one's values and ideas, or the airtight, quasi-paralysed self-mummification in the coffin of exclusive organizations and places apart. Only one alternative will then be valid—either one must gird up one's loins and with open, succouring arms *give*, present or lavish something on humanity, heal its heart's open wound, or one must be prepared to find that the world, though thirsting feverishly for religion, believes one has nothing to give; to find, even, that one no longer feels oneself wholly in the right or in possession of the true and the good—of, in short, the divine verities. But in the latter case one must also be prepared to find that this catalytic conviction also penetrates one's own ranks, and that the mere policy of 'holding fast'—that gesture of pride and avarice—brings on the destruction of the very things which one wished to preserve. Any positive religion which today fails in the above sense to carry out its spiritual mission, to bear new and living witness to its cause in every way, is most certainly doomed to defeat and decline in the spiritual struggles which we have before us. Not in the sense of outward power and might, but in the sense of the proofs of heart and soul, every positive religion must win victory *or* suffer defeat. He who has nothing to give in *this* crisis of the world will lose what he possesses.

Two further things may serve to characterize the new position:

I said that in those circles where religious renewal is understood in the sense of a demand for new religion, people are also apt to speak of the 'bankruptcy of Christianity'. If one blurs the distinction between the subjective act of faith and Christianity's objective merits as a faith, and if one refrains from probing the underlying causes of the recent conflagration, the judgment is not so incomprehensible. In spite of the ambiguity and obscurity of their proposition, these people are right in *one* respect. If Christianity, as subjective faith, and the human governance of the Churches in which it has its being were in such good condition and so splendidly placed as many of the faithful would so often have us believe, one might fairly declare that the civilization of modern Europe has remained *Christian* over the past few centuries, at least in the ramified roots of its way of life. But who in that case could dare *deny* the objective sense of the opinion that Christianity is bankrupt? For this much is as clear as the day: if the teaching of Christianity really *prevailed and ruled* in the times, in the peoples, their morals and social order, from which this war arose, or if it was but the *leading* spirit of the age, then by any light of reason *Christianity also, as a positive religion, stands condemned.* True Christianity can be true and divine only in so far as it did not prevail in that time, but was *hidden* and *suppressed*. To recognize in some way its truth and divinity thus entails an accompanying negative proof that the hidden causes of the cataclysm are to be found where Christianity as a subjective faith was suppressed or precluded—in other words, not in Christian Europe but in extra-Christian, *anti-Christian* Europe. This further implies a confession that the Churches were inwardly far weaker than they used to think, whether by their own fault, or the fault of others, or both together. It is impossible that one should wish to prove *both* that before the

war Europe represented a truly *Christian civilization* and that Christianity is
not bankrupt—that the Churches, or the aggregate of the true Church,
retained even an averagely good position of inward normality and external power and authority, such as befitted their dignity, and that
Christianity still is *not* bankrupt. No: if the Churches were indeed so well
placed, then Christianity *is* well and truly bankrupt, and with it the
Church which derives ultimately from the merits and authority of Christ.

The cry that Christianity is bankrupt does therefore include a comparatively justified riposte to the many false zealots who are unable to paint in
colours too optimistic the position of the Church and the level of Christian
awareness in Europe—though their gestures are for the most part confined
to pharisaic nationalism on behalf of the countries and peoples to whom
they themselves belong. For the sake of the power they have been
accustomed to share they have thought out a complete system for muffling
their Christian conscience. Not for the sake of Christ's eternal claims, but
to preserve their power and live comfortably as before, they declare that
Europe—or perhaps their country—lies still within the 'fold' of Christian
civilization. If these zealots are right in their utterances, then for sure
Christianity *is* bankrupt. If nationalistic passions, if capitalism of
bourgeois and worker alike, if the system of radical mistrust and the
consequent arms-race (which ruled and rules not only actual policies but
the very theory of politics), if the godless insolence of imperialism ('dividing
the globe' in utter disregard of European solidarity and the right of non-
European, non-American peoples to exist), if all these, these forces destined
to lead Europe into world-war, are compatible with the spirit of Christ, or
if they are mere 'distortions' of mighty and rightful endeavours, and not
perversions and damnable *mockeries* of Christianity with their roots in the
core of European life—then Christianity is bankrupt. Either one admits
Europe's deep and widespread *falling-away* from Christ, and confesses that
his representatives have been woefully weak and made inexcusable
compact with the spirit of anti-Christ—or one confesses Christianity
bankrupt! One must *choose* one of these two things. And the decision is
utterly divorced from the question of who was *guilty* among the parties to
the late war. It is no verdict for or against Germany, for or against France,
for or against England and so on. What do I care *who* is 'guilty' among the
members of a family, when I can see from afar that as a *whole* it is sapped
and rotten at the core, a family dwelling in a stricken house, where palpable hate and desolate confusion leer out from walls and pictures,
cupboards and chairs? All and none are guilty: so everyone must conclude,
to the extent of his penetration into the hearts of the family and the
relations within it. On the surface guilt always lies on one side—in depth

always on either side, just as the world itself is in theory always one-dimensional on the surface, in its causal mechanism, but at bottom remains a multi-dimensional reciprocation.

There is a degree of total human catastrophe where it becomes pure childishness to apportion individual guilt. Strindberg—so great in spirit, so desolate and hateful of soul, but for just that reason the purest poetic exponent of his time, an epitome of modern Europe's basic instincts and conversely for *that* reason, in the tragedy of a poet called to express an age accursed, a man of *necessity* so hateful and desolate—Strindberg wrote a play he called *The Funeral Pyre*, in which just such a family as I have described goes up in flames with its house. One of the children—the one to suffer most from the ruin it knows to be closing on and strangling its life—sets fire to the house, so that the house and family may be removed from God's world in a single act of entire, inseparable destruction, and the child's own suffering and horror be thereby extinguished. In the Aeschylean fate of this house, which possessed all the profound adaptability of a symbol, the wartime spectators of this play's numerous performances saw a prefigurement of Europe's fate. And this, too, is the judgment of the Japanese who speaks of Europe's *hara-kiri*.

It is certainly quite foolish and mistaken to confuse different *levels of attitude* to events. The politician must think differently from the man who thinks religiously and looks for a change of heart. The politician may dispute over the 'guilt' of the Great War, in the sense of the responsibility of factions. He even *must* so dispute, and I would not deny his right to do so. It is at one's greatest peril that one confuses the problem of Europe's comprehensive moral and religious condition with things of quite another order of value and magnitude, questions concerning the political adjustment of its parts. One should not talk like a divine when the politician ought to come to the fore. Many of us have fallen into such confusion, seeing all too one-sidedly a merely German guilt, where in fact there subsisted a collective guilt of Europe. But if such an attitude is tasteless and tiresome, if it testifies to some deficiency in the internal structure of the personality, a combined lack of purity and clarity, even, in its moral and religious thought and feeling, it remains true that the organic *in*ability to lift oneself above the whole *sphere* of the merely political, and see the condition of Europe—or indeed the condition of humanity—in the sunlight of Christ the Word, is lamentable and Philistine.

There is nothing so clear as this: only the gradual raising of the whole of the European heart, mind and judgment to that sunlit plateau, only the clear vision of Europe's—and indeed the world's—inseparably inter-woven *common guilt* for the late war, can even *begin* any edifice of religious renewal. The cry goes out to all men: Arise! set your feet to the holy mountain of your consciences, with Christ's help. From its sunbathed peak you may look down into the maelstrom of Europe's common guilt, as into a valley of fearfulness, of sin and tears! Look down upon it as Moses saw the Jews dancing round the golden calf, when, drunk with God, he strode quietly down the hillside; look down from your summit of conscience, still bathed in the splendour of your humble prayers, and see how Europe dances round its stupid, ludicrous idols! Only one who does not dance in the depth of his soul, but who yet knows that his body is swayed by the rhythm, can discern the dance. Whoever dances the dance with heart and soul cannot discern it. Whoever pharisaically sees only 'the others' dance— he cannot discern it. Neither does he discern it who fails to see his shadow, his own grotesque, misshapen figure, fails to see *himself* in the dance of death, all conscious of his share in the common guilt.

The first thing which can bring us back to a real perception of the *collective guilt* for the late war as an *instance* unique in history is the religious moral principle of general *solidarity*, which modern Europe has torn to shreds, the principle that in the realm of finite minds and *all* their groupings all moral actions and values are reciprocal and interdependent. It is this which can teach us once again to see and feel that at every juncture this world is rising to God or falling from God as a *single*, indivisible whole, a morally compact mass, and that all therein answer for all, and all for the whole, before the highest judge. Furthermore, only this perception of collective guilt can awaken in us, out of the will to reconciliation, which still today holds back in shame and trembling, the great pathos of mutual pardon with collective repentance and atonement for this guilt.*

But, let us admit it, prudence here bids us not expect too much from this collective moral impulse which is sweeping through the youth of the nations. Let us, though, make no mistake: it is the first of the starting-points necessary to any renewal of religion. But it is not the renewal itself. It is the only *common* starting-point of all those who feel the general necessity for a religious renewal—however may vary the *content* of the religion they have in mind. But one may only hope for a genuine religious renewal when longing for *positive* convictions, and a new *form* of moral and religious *will*, raise their heads above the cross-currents of feeling which are sapping heart and soul, and today possess all our poetic youth to the point of emotional anarchy. Over wide circles in the belligerent nations this new pathos has become powerful, perhaps over-powerful. All hearts have been seized, especially young hearts, with an unprecedented urge to take their fate in their hands and join forces across all frontiers; it is an urge to warm away in contacts the icy cold of the times—just as, in Tolstoy's *Master and Man*, the bodies of the serf and his master, in danger of freezing to death, seek the warmth of each other in the snowy plain. No less violent is the urge to forgive each other everything, to fly into each other's arms in mutual pardon and remorse, crying Brother! Brother! There can be no doubt that the heartfelt movement described in these words has been the strongest stimulus behind the many new ventures in art and literature to which the War has given rise. A mystical democratic feeling—quite different from political and social democracy, but the underground source of these universal trends—is flooding through the younger generation in all countries and cannot be withstood. It ordains that art shall once again be concerned with the great *typical* figures, sufferings, destinies of mankind, the *essential* situations in this riddle called human life. 'Man' is art's object. 'Men' and the individual have become uninteresting. A something which, though Aeschylean in its conception and typology of life, has a specific content of present realities, pervades this wild, expressionist art. A cosmic feeling, a mystic, evanescent hypersensitivity, now tinged with Christian, now with demonic elements, an attitude bent more on realizing the full range and power of infinitely shaded emotions than on the achievement of purity, form and depth in feeling and idea; and with it a manner of thought and feeling which seems it would gladly leave (or oblige) all structures, forms and orderings that are the established products of culture and history to sink and drown, or bathe and be cleansed in the flaming tide of man's primordial longings (all kinds of love, and tenderness, and pity, and conjubilation), the tide which, fearfully dammed back in the heart by war, is now breaking forth in thousandfold strength:— this is by far the most significant new *ferment* in man's outlook on the world to have been born of the Great War.

At all events, it is scarcely possible to exaggerate the importance of this new spiritual current for the religious situation. The ice in men's souls has begun to melt and, like curiously shaped islets of ice in a half-thawed lake, the fragments of castaway ideologies, for the most part half-understood, often quite misconceived, are eddying in froth and scum. It is quite undeniable that such a liquidation and dissolution, such a reduction-process in the over-solidified organization of the European soul, is necessary, if religious renewal is to be at all possible. But, for all that, one should always bear in mind that the present orgy of emotional self-indulgence has not yet left the stage of a '*glorious shake-up*', in which the highest lies next to the lowest, the dark urge next to the shining intuition, the demonic next to the divine, and the nihilistic impulse to throw oneself into the abyss of one's own heart lies next to an edified heart's approach to God. Least of all should one forget that this whole movement is nothing *more* than *raw material* for the *true architect* of moral and religious renewal. For how much in all this flux is only exhaustion and release from tension! How much, again, is the rapidly subsiding breakthrough of emotional forces too long repressed! How much of it all is simply idle and amorphous negation, concealed by impressive names! Where in all this is the hold of sickness and death broken, where the wonderful *release* of the soul that must herald all change of heart and any conversion? For any who fully grasp the implications, that is a riddle of dark mystery—and no one has hitherto been able to give an answer.

So far as I can see, the new psychic force I have described is, as hitherto shaped and expressed, only the psychic preparation of collective repentance—its psychic medium and, so to speak, the bed of its healing stream. As yet it is not the repentance itself.

In the situation I have described, *philosophy*, too, has a new and special task, in so far as religion is its concern. This task is not the highest among those which must be devoted to the renewal of religious awareness. For this highest task will always fall to the lot of the *homo religiosus* himself, the man who has God in his heart and God in his actions, who in his own *spiritual figure* is a transformer of souls and is able in new ways to infuse the word of God into hearts that have softened and yield. But since the being and presence of such men come as the most wonderful of mercies that can fall to mankind's lot, there is something intrinsically repugnant to sense not only in wishing to produce such men but even in seeking and expecting them. Only readiness to hear them, if they should appear, and ability to see them, when and wherever they offer themselves, are things one can prepare and *cultivate*. However, this religious receptivity is in the highest degree dependent on the ideas one adopts concerning the *nature of religion*, the forms *underlying* the highest ultimate verities, the place of religion in the structure of human reason, the principles of the origin of all true religion, and the way the sources of religious knowledge and life are ordered and combined.

This circle of questions is to be our object in the following pages. But a strictly systematic treatment of the questions touched upon here must be held over to a work which for some years past has been growing in my desk, though the unpropitious times have so far hindered me from finishing it.* Here I must be content to develop the main ideas,—which in the work I have just mentioned are to offer religion a more rigorous, comprehensive foundation and justification,—for what is intended to be more than a narrowly philosophical circle of readers, and in a form which may not lay claim to the degree of precision which hovers before me as an ideal, since it ignores much desirable historical and psychological material. These reservations apply above all to the methods of proving and demonstrating the principal truths of religion. This subject is not systematically treated here; neither is the criticism of traditional proofs of God.

1. RELIGION AND PHILOSOPHY

On the question of whether and to what extent the objects of religious belief—the existence and nature of God, the immortality of the soul, etc. —together with belief itself and the existential context of these objects, are also objects of philosophical cognition, the views of philosophers and theologians were and are divided. Examination will show that in contrast to the doctrines which prevailed with seeming uniformity over European minds from the thirteenth to the end of the eighteenth century, the nineteenth century brought forth an unconscionable number of 'viewpoints' on this question, which have not found acceptance outside rather narrow academic circles and have contended one against the other to the present day, with no sign that any one will prevail. This phenomenon is not simply the product of the doubt and confusion into which the development of modern civilization threw the whole question of *religion*: it is just as much a product of growing uncertainty over *philosophy's* nature and task. When not only *one* of the things whose essential relationship we wish to know has become indefinite and uncertain, but *both* together, the attainment of this knowledge is ten times more difficult. The optimistic assumption that this intellectual position at least bears witness to a deep, strong, rich and diversified intellectual life—a wrestling of minds with these matters—may not be altogether incorrect with respect to strictly limited periods within the narrow confines of general philosophical movements in certain countries. It may at least claim an appearance of validity in the case of German culture from the death of Lessing and the appearance of Kant's critique up to the exit of so-called 'classical speculation'. Applied to the present it would be quite meaningless. For these 'viewpoints' have for a long time now resided, isolated from each other, next to each other, sealed in and buttressed—not to say cocooned and petrified—in the 'organization' of narrow academic circles which are quite unheeded by the *formative* elements of European civilization; they scarcely pay much attention to each other, and scarcely ever arrive even at any vital and fruitful statement of differences. The multiplicity of 'viewpoints' has led in the outcome not to any vital 'wrestling of minds' but to the most arid academicism, whose maxim is *Quieta non movere*. Since the 'viewpoints' rest for the most part on traditionalist attempts to refurbish elderly philosophical systems—with trivial deviations at the most, and so-called 'concessions' to 'opponents'—a serious will to reach a common understanding was never much to be expected from their 'representatives'. For such an understanding would be possible only if one sought to look upon the very facts of the case with a new, unclouded eye, without previous reference to mere tradition and with the intention of bringing newly won results into contact with living or dead traditions at a subsequent stage. Only one subordinate and, of its kind, very problematical branch of the studies concerned with religion has proceeded on these lines, and that is the 'psychology of religion', of which we shall have something to say later: at all events, it is quite powerless in all matters connected with the foundation and justification of religion. In the *philosophy* of religion, on the other hand, it is the 'system' which holds sway as in former times, nurtured by tradition in the narrowest of academic circles, the systems for example of Thomism and neo-Thomism, or of the Kantian, positivist, Hegelian and neo-Hegelian philosophical and theological schools. Even the modern pragmatical philosophy of religion is simply a more conscious formulation of age-old English academic traditions.

The above-mentioned traditionalist 'viewpoints'—if only because they are originally the offspring of great minds—can adduce at least one thing in their favour: that their 'representatives' treat questions with a certain methodic rigour and *sub specie aeternitatis*. However, there also exists a self-consciously up-to-date kind of popular philosophy which, if only because of its lack of method and lack of serious consideration for the eternal significance of its subject-matter, has lost *any* kind of contact and continuity, whether historically or objectively, with the historic landmarks in its chosen fields. Whether this modern kind of popular philosophy and edifying literature is cultivated by scientists like Ostwald, who heedless of the limits of their 'subject' turn its technical categories into universal concepts, or pedagogues like Frau W. Förster, or 'writers' like Nietzsche, or preachers and reformers like Johannes Müller and others, this 'philosophy' of frontier-violation or, shall we say, of 'good ideas' and aphorisms uncritically culled from raw observation cannot seriously claim to have solved all problems in such a way that the solutions can be universally disseminated and digested. No, this it cannot do, however valuable it may be for the rest, and however genuinely it may claim to be the only real sustenance of an age so deeply depressed, spiritually, as ours.

I should like to introduce my endeavour to arrive from the natures of philosophy and religion at a corresponding *determination of their relationship*

E

with a short account of the typical solutions which the problem has received hitherto. At the conclusion of this study of these types, I wish to develop the idea of a *philosophical analysis of the forms* (eidology) *of the object and act of religion.* This may claim to be the basic philosophical discipline offering a common foundation for the construction not only of all further philosophical disciplines concerned with religion (epistemology and axiology of the religious act, metaphysics of religion, historical philosophy of religion) but also of any *science* of religion (by which I mean the psychology of religion, the history of religion and finally the many branches of theology).*

EXISTING VIEWS TYPIFIED

The types of partial and total identity

Doctrines of the relationship between religion and philosophy fall into two categories: those which assert a total or partial *identity* of essence between religion and that part of philosophy called since Aristotle the 'prime philosophy' or later metaphysics, and those which assert an essential *difference* between religion and philosophy.

Only in the latter case has the expression 'philosophy of religion' a sense. For only in that case is religion itself and not religion's object—God —the object of philosophy. However, the expression 'philosophy of religion' is of recent date. It is completely absent from the entire literature of philosophy before Kant and Schleiermacher, neither did theology know any discipline of that name. Furthermore, the name itself conceals a definite theory of the relation between religion and philosophy, the idea that if philosophy has any concern with God, its concern is not direct, but must always pass *through* the mediation of religion. So long as there was understood to be a special branch of metaphysics which had the nature and existence of God for its direct object of cognition, no one spoke of a 'philosophy of religion'. This branch was called natural theology or rational theology. Natural theology passed as a branch *common* to both theology as a whole and philosophical metaphysics. In this way positive or revealed theology, with its essentially new sources of knowledge (God's self-communication in individuals and traditions, the corpus of dogma), was built up directly on the basis of natural theology without the intermediary of any so-called philosophy of religion.

1. The *system of partial identity* between religion and (metaphysical) philosophy is the type of their defined relationship which in Europe has prevailed for the greatest length of time and enjoyed the widest dissemination, especially in the teaching of the Church. Since Aquinas this system has dominated at least the main stream of academic traditions in

philosophy and theology up to the present day. The heirs of this tradition defend the system with energy against all doctrines which are willing to concede to religion (even natural religion) a different source of knowledge from the source open to philosophy (this is fideism), as well as the systems of total identity (gnosis and traditionalism) which in some form—that is, in favour of one or other side—remove the distinction between a natural and a positive revealed religion: a distinction holding dogmatic validity for the Catholic Church by reason of the well-known words of Saint Paul. Man can gain sure knowledge of God's existence with the help of philosophical reason, but can penetrate God's intrinsic nature (or his nature divested of his external relation to the world) only if he faithfully accept the content, as revealed in positive theology, of the revelation in Christ. Since Leo XIII's revival of Thomism the 'sure knowledge' is conceived as a knowledge which is indirect or may be gained exclusively by inferences from the existence and constitution of the created world. The doctrine which goes back to Augustinian tradition and was held esoterically by the Oratorians of Port-Royal—that there is a natural *imm*ediate knowledge of God or the divine—is, usually without any closer differentiation among the various forms this doctrine can take and has taken, given short shrift, for the most part being dismissed as 'ontologism', like the 'ontological' proof of God with which it has a close affinity.

2. We can divide the *systems of total identity* into the gnostic and the traditionalist, according to whether the whole of theology is to be merged in philosophy or philosophy (at least as metaphysics) wholly in (positive) theology.

The essence of *gnostic* systems of identity is that religion, both positive and natural, is regarded merely as a *lower stage of knowledge* on the path to metaphysical knowledge. In this view religion is therefore at bottom itself a metaphysic, but a second-class metaphysic, metaphysic 'in pictures and symbols', metaphysic by 'the people', for 'the people'. And so gnosis represents religion as an attempt to treat the same questions and satisfy the same basic needs of the human spirit that metaphysics explores, solves and satisfies, but an attempt without methodical thinking and un-connected with science, exercising the human mind in types of operation identical in essence with those of philosophy, and enjoying no sources of material for perception and experience essentially different from those sources which stand at the disposal of philosophy. But religion is defective in procedure, relying on symbol and image and making far greater concessions to the needs of the human heart in the latter's historical con-formations, where metaphysics on the contrary proceeds with systematic perfection by the use of rational concepts, hand in hand with science. In the last resort this distinction in the gnostic conception may be explained sociologically, inasmuch as metaphysics is the religion of *thinkers*, while religion is the metaphysics of the *masses*. A characteristic opposition of exotericism and esotericism is therefore essential to this point of view. The symbolic and allegorical interpretation of writings which religion accounts 'holy' becomes a means of overcoming this dichotomy, so that the already-won results of gnostic metaphysical speculation are sought behind the holy words as their 'proper sense'. In this theory there is *no* specifically religious group of objects and values, such as would be accessible only to a peculiar class of acts—religious acts like belief, worship, veneration, avowal of insufficiency or redemption, etc. No more is there any special good end for man—salvation—attainable only through religion and not through metaphysics. Neither, according to the gnostics, is there any special positive self-communication of God concerning himself to special persons: there is no such source of religion, *i.e.* no revelation—at least no such revelation as could be different from the natural philosophical sources of knowledge in reason and experience (of self, world and fellow-men) at the height of intellectual activity, in moments, for example, of philosophical or artistic 'inspiration'.

Historically we find that this conception achieved its most widespread dissemination in Buddhism, neo-Platonism and the gnostic sects; we find it again in the extravagant mysticism of mediaeval Germany, in Spinoza, and above all as an explicit or more often tacit assumption in the German philosophers of 'classical' speculation, in Fichte, Hegel, Schelling—and quite explicitly in Schopenhauer and E. von Hartmann. Hegel expresses this conception when he defines philosophy as 'absolute knowledge in the form of concept' and religion as 'absolute knowledge in the form of representation'. Schopenhauer never tires of asserting that religion is 'metaphysics for the people' and all churches, dogmas, cults memorials of man's 'metaphysical craving'. But Eduard von Hartmann and his pupil A. Drews have for their part developed an entirely new dogmatic system, which corresponds to the findings of their metaphysics and is supposedly destined to replace positive Christian dogma. When Drews seeks to buttress Hartmann's assertion—that Paul, not Jesus, was the founder of the Christian Church—with a denial of Jesus' existence and an attempt to prove the corollary, that the ideal content of Christian dogmas is a mere communal product from the many and various elements in the history of religion, it is the gnostic hypothesis that religion is an inferior form of answer to metaphysical cravings which has methodically led him to that position.

Certain quite definite conceptions of religion and everything to do with religion belong *essentially* to the gnostic viewpoint:

(*a*) Religion does not find its most perfect archetype and basic norm in the being and essence of a holy *person*, whose declarations about God are true because it is *this* person who utters them, but in a *system of ideas* free from all personal connections, which should be assessed in the light of purely objective, extrapersonal norms. Hence the 'saint' neither effects a new relation of man to God nor mediates any divine action and efficacy such as might give rise to a new relation. He is only a special kind of *teacher*, or man who as a *metaphysician* has reached greater depths of knowledge and spoken what he has known.

(*b*) Correspondingly, the sociological form in which knowledge of God is acquired is not the Church but a kind of *school*, and the religious form of teaching is not the representation of the holy benefits of faith, to be dutifully received in faith, but *instruction* in a metaphysical theory.

(*c*) The act of belief is an imperfect act of knowing, and invariably grasps only through some *image* or *symbol*, which metaphysics has to construe, what the metaphysician expounds in the adequate form of concepts.

(*d*) Revelation as a communicated knowledge is replaced by a knowledge spontaneously acquired by man.

(*e*) Since finally, as we shall more closely show, a *person* may not be spontaneously known, either as existing or as of a certain nature, without its free consent, the gnostic viewpoint must deny, if only because of the *method* peculiar to it, that the divine has a personal form of being. It regards the divine as a substance, a thing, an order, a logical subject—but on no account a concrete person. How rich this is in consequences, we have yet to see.

Let it be shortly remarked in passing—none of the views it is possible to hold on the relation of religion and philosophy is so erroneous and inadequate as this one. Moreover, none so directly and irremediably conflicts with everything we know today about the nature and history of religion, and the psychology of the religious life. Today, when religious positions are otherwise more widely divergent than ever, nothing perhaps is accepted with greater agreement and assurance, among those who treat of religion with understanding, than this: religion's origin in the human mind is *fundamentally and essentially different* from that of philosophy and metaphysics; the founders of religions—the great *homines religiosi*—have always belonged to a type of human intellect entirely different from philosophers and metaphysicians; furthermore, the great historical changes in the structures of religion have never and nowhere been *consequent upon* a new metaphysics, but have ensued in an entirely different way. And so even if there is such a thing as a metaphysic—a rational knowledge of the ultimate bases of the world's being and essence—the impulse which leads to it, as well as its methods of procedure, its goal and object must be basically and essentially different from religion's stimulus, method, goal and object. I personally, as a philosopher, believe *unreservedly* that a metaphysic is possible. None the less, any doctrine which sees in metaphysics, even if we suppose it perfect and universally valid, any kind of substitute for religion, or a higher goal towards which religion may develop, remains at bottom fallacious.

Religion's God and the world-basis of metaphysics may be *identical in reality*, but as *intentional* objects they are *different in essence*. The God of religious consciousness 'is' and lives exclusively in the religious act, not in metaphysical thinking about realities extraneous to religion. The goal of religion is not rational knowledge of the basis of the world but the *salvation of man* through vital communion with God—apotheosis. The religious subject is not the 'solitary thinker', for from the beginning it comprises the *reciprocal collectivity* of the group—humanity in the last analysis—as much as the individual thirsting for salvation. *The God of religion is the god of the saints and the god of the people, not the cerebral god of the 'intellectuals'.* The fount of all religious truth is not scientific utterance but *faith* in the words of the *homo religiosus*, the 'holy man'—that is, a type of man who may be known by the following signs: 1. As a *whole and undivided* person he possesses a *charismatic quality* peculiar to no other outstanding type of humanity, such as the genius or hero. By virtue of this quality he encounters belief, simply because it is *he*—the bearer of this quality—who is talking, acting, expressing himself. 2. He lives in his own peculiar, real and vital relationship to the divine as the eternal source of salvation, and bases his utterances and precepts, deeds and authority on this relation. By virtue of his charismatic quality his disciples believe in his words as subjectively and objectively true. Unlike the sayings of the genius, of the hero, etc., his utterances are never tested for truth and justness against objective norms *external* to himself—norms of morality, logic and ethics—and recognized only because his words, deeds and work are found to be in general agreement with those norms. On the contrary, *he* as a *person* is the norm of his utterances, with the sole authority of his relation to the divine.*

However, the *second* definition of the relationship between philosophy and religion is no less erroneous. Certain Fathers of the Church leaned towards it, and not long ago we find it much more outspokenly in the so-called *traditionalists*, such as Joseph de Maistre and Lamennais. By this definition philosophy—at least in so far as it is metaphysical—should merge in *religion* as revealed doctrine. The traditionalist uses concepts and ideas derived in fact from metaphysics in order to rationalize, systematize and formulate a body of belief which has a genuinely religious origin. Thus it was that the great Fathers and teachers of the Christian Church employed the two great philosophical systems of the Greeks, Platonism and, in the second rank, Aristotelianism, in order to penetrate and illumine with reason the truth within Christian faith. There was no room here for an *independent* philosophy. But certain tendencies in Protestant theology also come near to this type of solution. Luther himself tried to topple philosophy from a position of privilege and establish positive theology's self-sufficiency and independence of it. And in his recent theology, which has been so well received, the only philosophical basis which Albert Ritschl would allow was an essentially negative epistemology limiting human cognition: taking authority sometimes from Kant and sometimes from an agnostic positivism, he roundly *repudiates* both metaphysics and natural theology, so that metaphysics must be swallowed by *religion*.

Once again, this definition of the relationship is quite certainly wrong from the beginning. As the first definition failed to give due acknowledgment to the primary, *ab origine* nature of religion, so this second form, asserting the total identity of religion and philosophy (*qua metaphysics*), fails to do justice to philosophy's *independent origin* in the human mind, its *special object and goal*.

One must admit that the traditionalist can with a certain appearance of justification call in support the historical fact that the metaphysical systems which come to mind all exhibit certain *structural analogies* with the positive religious outlooks under whose inescapable influence their creators' minds were formed and in whose historical reign they arose. Thus, in spite of the fact that Greek philosophy is far more clearly separate from Greek religion than, say, Indian philosophy from brahmanism, and despite the widely differing methods and results of the individual systems, certain deep-rooted and significant features of Greek religion are rediscovered in Greek philosophy. The multiplicity of relative juxtapositions and the floating, hovering character of Plato's 'ideas' (which Augustine was the first consciously to imagine as 'God's thoughts') has a certain formal and structural affinity with Greek polytheism. Malebranche was of the opinion, historically perhaps not incorrect, that Aristotle's entelechies, those independent bundles of energy, were only the rationalized naturegods of Greek 'heathendom'. In this he was followed by Auguste Comte's theory of the 'age of metaphysics'. Erwin Rohde has shown thoroughly in his *Psyche* how deeply conceptions of soul originating in Asiatic religion were implanted in nearly every Greek philosopher's doctrine of the soul—

if indeed they were not chiefly instrumental in *shaping* those doctrines. Plato's and Aristotle's organological view of the world, which seeks to incorporate not only all inanimate processes but the soul and the cosmos into conceptual categories doubtless derived from the living animal organism, presents a similar analogy with the Greeks' religion, which has the same kind of organological horizon. It is not therefore accidental that the idea of creation should be absent from both Greek philosophy and Greek religion. A spatially static (hence non-temporal) idea of all exist-ence is to be found in both, likewise the model of physical sight for all noesis (ἰδεῖν τῶν ἰδέων) with a resultant predominance of the intellect-ual and contemplative aspects in the Greek attitude to the universe. How many similar instances might be enumerated!—far beyond the demon-strable influence of, for example, Greek and Asiatic religions on Platonism and Pythagorism.

Moreover, if one is more and more inclined, in Christian philosophy up to the late Scholastics, to assume that by purely rational means, without recourse to revelation, one may employ Aristotelian apparatus to prove propositions from whose acceptance Aristotle himself was far removed (*e.g.* the Creation, the personal nature of God, individual immortality— propositions even demonstrably contradictory of that apparatus), it is not hard to understand why many thinkers should maintain that philo-sophy is procuring an unfair advantage from religion, in other words that the pre-existing wholly rational way of thinking, alleged to be producing proofs, is from the outset secretly and unconsciously nourished by religious tradition. And in a completely analogous way one can find in Kant's teaching, despite its opposition to Lutheranism and Calvin-ism on many essential points, very many structural similarities to those established forms of Protestantism.

The above merely samples a well-nigh countless host of instances. One might be tempted to draw from such facts the conclusion that the self-sufficiency of philosophy, when more than logic or scientific theory, is a merely ostensible independence—that really it is metaphysics living secretly on religious capital, acquired by false pretences from the savings of faith and converted into a currency of rational forms to which it would be wrong to ascribe an issuing authority of rational thought. If anyone should wish to make that inference, he will not find evidence unforth-coming. Both anti-religious positivism and pro-religious traditionalism— each based, it may be noted, on the same sensualist epistemology—have adduced the relevant material to the point of satiety. To Auguste Comte, for example, the whole 'metaphysical age' of human thought and activity is at bottom no more than a period of *watered, mock-rational religion*, a

period which, assessed as a whole, is vastly inferior in worth and significance both to the age of personalistic religion and to the positive age
which Comte found in the making.*

The traditionalist theory of the relation between religion and philosophy arose in its first exponents (Joseph de Maistre, Bonald, Lamennais)
as a reaction consciously biassed against the philosophy of the Enlightenment, against its revolutionary 'natural' theology, which rejected all
positive religion, and its revolutionary notions of natural right. It has
therefore all the marks of a one-sided *philosophy of reaction.* At the same time
it is romanticism based in western and Catholic tradition. It tends to
reduce thought and reason to language, and logical to grammatical
categories. Language itself it traces back to the original divine revelation.
Just as sensualism proposes sensory feeling and perception as the ultimate
source of all knowledge, ascribing tradition and memory to sensual
sources, as being the faded residue of bygone sensations, so the traditionalists tried to establish memory, including the *collective* memory of
mankind, as the ultimate and original source of knowledge. The
concrete mind of the individual is, they allege, wrought by received
tradition into such a deep and lasting conformation that it can never
be wholly 'pure'—never purged of conformity. Therefore it cannot
be accounted a new source of knowledge but only an occasional,
supplementary contributor to the traditional categories of thought.
Even so, sensualism was wrong to assume that memory and tradition
themselves originate in earlier sensational contact between the mind
and the actual world; no, they hail from the original revelation of the
Word of God.

It was an important effect of traditionalism that it strongly reasserted
the essential *communal* aspect of religion and philosophy against the
religious individualism of Protestant confessions. Lamennais carried this
idea to the utterly mistaken extreme of insisting that the so-called proof of
God from the *consensus gentium* was the principal and most fundamental
proof of God, since he believed that the consensus offered the highest
criterion of truth. However, he failed to observe that he was thereby
betraying the idea of a truly universal community of religion by restricting
it to groups sharing the communal tradition, and that he was also falling
foul of the creationist doctrine of the human soul, and the doctrine of the
absolute value of the individual soul.

More recently traditionalism has been revived with all kinds of modifications by such men as Brunetière and Maurice Barrès in France, James
Balfour in England. Philosophically, and sometimes epistemologically, it
is not far removed from Henri Bergson, inasmuch as he reduces reason to

an *original mindfulness* whose contents may not be identified with sensual perception.

Traditionalism is a system raising the *independence* of religion to a kind of *despotism* which corresponds to neither the nature of religion nor the nature of philosophy.

The first consideration which it fails to acknowledge is that as a need, as a problem, as an object and as a method of knowing—*metaphysics struck root in the human mind independently of religion.*

The so-called metaphysical urge is distinct from the motivation of religion. The fount of all interest in metaphysics is *astonishment that anything at all should exist.** It is a quite definite *emotion* which generates that peculiar liminal question of all man's speculation which we call the metaphysical question. It is in a certain sense the root of that question. This astonishment condenses to inquiry concerning the nature of *that which is*—independently of the interpreting human organism—and the nature of whatever it may be which upholds, determines and effects all other entities within that self-constituting entity. The cathexis of metaphysics is curiosity about the nature of the world subsisting in ipseity and the nature of its conditioning basis.

Religion is, in contrast, founded in the love of God and longing for a final *salvation* of man himself and all things. Religion is thus pre-eminently a *way of salvation*. The *first* intentional object of the religious act is not the absolutely real and its essence, but the *summum bonum.*

This difference in the permanent and essential subjective sources of metaphysics and religion does not exclude a connection lying in the nature of the intentional *objects* on both sides—a connection of the respective intentions in the human mind and a possible connection of the two intentional objects in one and the same reality. For *a priori* this much is clear: the essential peculiarity of the absolutely real—the reality underlying all things real—must of necessity be that which decides the salvation or non-salvation of all things, including men. It is, so to speak, the last court of appeal for this salvation. And this is also clear *a priori*: the absolutely holy and divine, whose nature is to satisfy the longing of things, can only do this if it is in addition the absolute reality on which all else depends. But this intrinsic positive connection between the intentional objects of metaphysics and religion in no way invalidates the basic difference between their *essential intentions*, and the consequent difference between the laws and procedures by which they develop. The question of salvation remains secondary for the metaphysician, and knowledge of absolute reality remains secondary to the man of religion. Salvation and love for the salvation of all things remain self-sufficient and fundamental categories of religion; the entity in its selfhood remains the self-sufficient, fundamental category of metaphysics. The idea of that-which-founds-salvation as the absolutely holy and therefore divine, which idea stands before all religious questing as its ultimate goal and indeed endows it with its unity *qua* religious, can never be analytically deduced from the idea of the absolutely real. Neither, conversely, may the latter idea ever be deduced from the former. Only one thing stands firm: that metaphysics and religion—should they ever achieve their goals—must needs lead to one *identical* reality, a reality which lends real and ultimate meaning to the two essentially different intentional objects.

For that matter there is an *identical component* even in the intentional objects of religion and metaphysics, and on it there also rests in the last resort their necessary connection in the human mind. This component is the object of the concept *ens a se*, when *ens* is so conceived as to be still *indifferent* as against the concept of the absolutely real and also as against that of the absolutely holy good. But it would be as wrong to say that religion takes the idea of the *ens a se* from metaphysics as to propose the converse. The *ens a se* is thus always the ultimate *logical* subject of all metaphysical and religious predications. But the manner of its intentional conception and the essential aspect it presents to cognition, together with the manner in which it is brought into relation and connection with any *ens ab alio*, remain *different* in metaphysics and religion. The course of religion always begins with the conceptual datum of a thing which is *absolutely holy* and strong to save, whence it is shown (as a side-issue) that this *ens a se* is *also* the absolute basis of the reality of things. The course of metaphysics always begins with a definition of the nature of the *absolutely real*, whence it is shown (as a side-issue) that personal union with this *ens a se* will *also* lead man to his salvation (or that conformity with it will lead things to their final good).

And so the question of how far the metaphysical quest for the world-basis may also establish what is contained in the idea of God found in religious experience evidently *pre*-supposes knowledge of what essentially constitutes religious experience: its constitution always requires separate examination. Faith in God, or religion, even *natural* religious faith, does not live by the grace of metaphysics, any more than knowledge of the world-basis by the grace of religious faith. Both *entia intentionalia*, therefore, *may* in fact follow widely divergent paths, in spite of their a-priori, necessary, real identity. For this *real* identity, or perception of it, does not rest on a pre-established identity of *content* between the two *entia*, but on an *a-priori* proposition. The foundation of this proposition is the *unity of the human mind* and the necessary compossibility of all its findings. It is precisely on this account that (subjective) reason and religious acts (as conceptual forms of all revelation, both natural and supernatural) may very well lead to different elements of *content* within the *ens a se*, and yet not bring into doubt the real identity of the metaphysical world-basis with the God of religion.

The above theory enables us to avoid a host of dangers which threaten the right founding of religion:

1. The danger of excessive rationalism, such as might wish to deduce matters of revelation (God's love and mercy, for example, his long-suffering and his goodness in the moral sense, not in the sense of onto-logical perfection) directly from the *ens a se*—without, that is, any *new* sources for religious attitudes and evaluations—and would finally dispense with revelation for the sake of appearing *consistent*.

2. The other danger—supposing this fault were avoided and this or that restriction placed on rational deduction, for example by authority of the Church—the danger of calling an *arbitrary* halt to logical development, without any objective justification. This is how many neo-scholastics proceed; as faithful members of the Church they do indeed curb their rational constructive method where matters of revelation most obviously begin, but by reason of their very method they are unable to provide any *firm basis* for anything, simply because they applied the ban *at that moment* and not earlier or later.

3. The danger of overlooking the *necessary* differences in content between the metaphysical and religious God with his attributes. For example, the God with whom religion is concerned knows wrath, vengeance and love, and knows them in turn according to situations. The metaphysical God is an absolutely unalterable *ens* and is *totally devoid* of such possible predicates. Religious 'God' turns his face to me or to whole peoples (more intensively during prayer); sometimes he is friendly to me, sometimes he chides me for my sin. The metaphysical God cannot act in this way or be these things. The God of religion smites sinners with new sin, distributes his grace and disfavour after free and inscrutable self-debate; the metaphysical God is a fixed entity in which everything is eternal (supratemporal) and necessary. The religious God is the 'living God'—which leaves nothing essential unsaid.

The perception *a priori* of the *real identity* of the metaphysical and religious Gods demands a *true and proper* resolution of the seeming contradiction. By which I mean something quite different from 'overlooking' the contradiction. Moreover, a resolution is something quite different from the perpetuation of a game of false pretences, wherein one either impregnates the metaphysical idea with material and features taken from the God envisaged by prayer and faith, thinking to have discovered them analytically, or conversely brings to the God of religious intention metaphysical attributes which he does not possess. This contradiction *can* be resolved. In principle it can be resolved if one ascribes the apparently changing and changeable elements which are *essential* to the (intentional) God of prayer, including his 'anthropopathetic' attributes (wrath, etc.), to the result of changes from one viewpoint to another on the part of the finite creature in his relations with God; or, with regard to the seemingly anthropopathetic, one may ascribe it to analogies that in fact hit upon *something essential in God* which the rational idea of God *cannot* provide, but which may only be regarded as analogies, not as adequate descriptions of God.

4. Further, through acknowledging this 'seeming contradiction' we *avoid* thinking that either the metaphysical God's 'necessary appearance' of emptiness and fixity or the religious God's necessary appearance of anthropopathy are full and exhaustive concepts. For not only the religious but also the metaphysical God is necessarily an *incomplete* object of intention. God is not sempiternal (ever-being) but eternal (supratemporal). And it is the eternality of God which not merely permits but demands that to a finite creature, whose life proceeds in Time, the eternal supratemporal being shall *appear* in any vital communion between them not as sempiternal, filling all Time, but as changing; though God *is* not changing, and eternity *also* contains the being and essential identity of the eternal one in every part of Time. However, such sempiternity does not *exhaust* eternity. The eternal also bears within it the *contents* of all possible change—though the form of change is lacking. If metaphysics represents the eternal's temporal form of being, *i.e.* sempiternity, religion represents the *fulness* of the eternal, as a sublimity above change and duration. Only by putting religion and metaphysics together can we obtain an—inadequate—picture, an—inadequate—expression of the eternal.

5. We cannot now avoid seeing that the most adequate possession of God, the maximal participation of our being in his, cannot be achieved unless we first attain to a *simultaneous vision*, free from all contradictions and incompatibilities, of the religious God and the metaphysical 'world-basis' together. It follows that we cannot achieve this goal by wholly or partly making either the religious God or the metaphysical 'God' the yardstick against which we measure the *other* intentional object.

To choose the metaphysical God for this purpose is the basic error of that way of thinking which maintains that natural *theology* (not natural religion) is the *objective* pre-requisite for the empirical theology of revelation. For even natural religion is *religion*—not simply an imperfect and unmethodical jumping to conclusions. It lives in religious acts. The natural revelation of God in his works, as the apostle has in mind, rests on a *symbolic relationship to God* in nature and soul, in nature's 'mirror of divinity', in a pointing of *things themselves* and their (objective) *meaning* to God as the world's root-meaning. These are things which only the religious act grasps and can grasp, in (reverent) contemplation of nature and the soul, but reason cannot grasp them as it argues from *causality* in psychology and natural science.

To set up the religious God as the criterion of the metaphysical is on the other hand the basic error of fideism and traditionalism, the former particularly as found among Protestants. It is a tendency which denies the authenticity of metaphysics and natural theology, and, being necessarily obliged to particularize the idea of God, undermines the universality of religion. The truth of the matter may be expressed in the following summary form:

The *true* God is less empty and fixed than the God of metaphysics.

The *true* God is less narrow and 'human' (life-like) than the God of simple faith.

6. The oneness and indivisibility of God requires that we should strictly avoid obtruding into his very essence the differentiation of *ways* to the *ens a se* which, as 'different', are constitutive of a finite and divisible mentality. If, however, the God of either metaphysics or religion, or alternatively either one of the *entia intentionalia* of reason or faith, is made into the yardstick of the other, such a wrongful obtrusion becomes necessary and inevitable.

Dualistic views

The three definitions of the relation between metaphysics and religion which we have so far studied presuppose the existence and possibility of metaphysics. Wholly fresh endeavours to find a definition were necessitated when the possibility and justness of any metaphysics were *disputed*—as they have been by widespread philosophical tendencies. For all those who had wholly or partially identified religion with metaphysics, religion was thereupon *destroyed* in its roots. Since, however, religion was much more deeply implanted than metaphysics in the being and life of the nations, it was this very abandonment of metaphysics by the various forms of *metaphysical agnosticism* which provided the stimulus to separate religion wholly and utterly from metaphysics and attempt to furnish it with a basis of another kind. This basis had inevitably to be atheoretic, in the sense that one no longer sought a foundation for religion in general *ontological* knowledge but in some regularity of principle in atheoretical acts, whether with reference (as in Kant) to the order of ethical and practical life or (as in

Schleiermacher) to acts of a specifically religious kind. It was from this position that the systems of an exclusive moral theology and of 'fideism' arose.*

On the other hand, the metaphysically agnostic trends of philosophy arrive at a rejection of theoretical metaphysics on entirely different grounds. Here let a difference be noted in passing which has often been overlooked and is yet of great importance for the relating of agnostic philosophies to religion. Positivist, sensualist agnosticism not only is inimical to all possible *answers* to and *solutions* of metaphysical questions and problems, but denies all meaning and validity to the *questions* themselves. Therein lies the difference of principle between it and the schools of Kantian agnosticism, which leave intact the meaning and validity of metaphysical questions and problems, and only deny the possibility of theoretically solving them through operations of the human *intellect*. Thus for Kant the 'rational ideas' of soul, world and God, as ideas of the totality of preconditions for everything respectively psychic, physical and in being, can no more be traced back to sensations than can the categorical forms of intellect and the forms of pure intuition. They are 'ideas' which the reason spontaneously, necessarily produces as its eternal, problematic correlates, but ideas whose objects are with like necessity unknowable, so that they cannot yield to theory any meaning of genuinely constitutive importance; they are confined to the merely regulative importance of enabling a maximal uniformity of connotation to be established in the quest for laws of interrelation. For practical reason these ideas are useful as demarcating, so to speak, the perimeter of realms of possible objects, realms which are definitively circumscribed but void of theoretical knowledge, it being the subsequent concern of natural moral theology to occupy them with rationally imperative 'postulates'.

In contrast positivism proceeds in accordance with a maxim enunciated by E. Mach and exactly corresponding to its sensualist epistemology: either a question must be answerable or its meaninglessness must be demonstrable. If no possible combination of sense-data can be aptly assigned to the purpose of answering a given question, then either the question itself is meaningless, or the included concepts are being non-sensically combined, or an illicit construction is being placed on them. Thus sensualist positivism asserts far more than the theoretic unanswerability of metaphysical questions: it asserts their *nonsensicality*. This is of far-reaching importance for the historical view of metaphysics and religion. From this assertion positivism develops the basic opinion that the religious-cum-metaphysical problem of existence is not of man's spiritual *essence* (hence not of historical permanence), but represents no more than a 'historical category' at a definite level of historical and social evolution, one which should—and will—be completely discarded at some future stage. In his growing adaptation to the universe man will cease to ask metaphysical and religious questions, since he will have grasped their meaninglessness. On the other side we still have the agnosticism of Kant and his followers, for whom metaphysical and religious questions retain a permanent sense and validity, though they regard them as—with equal permanence—theoretically unanswerable.

It is now clear why only theoretic agnosticism of the second type can accept an essential relationship between philosophy and religion. In the face of religion and metaphysics positivist agnosticism can acknowledge only one theoretical task: to describe them as psychic phenomena of human life and provide these phenomena with a psychological, historical and sociological explanation. At the most generous, it may include an appreciation of their biological and sociological *utility* for certain epochs.

Many and various were the forms of basis for religion that derived from the other type of metaphysical agnosticism, and here we cannot follow them into their individual variations.[1] Within this type, at all events, there remains full scope for a *religious epistemology and axiology*. These would have to lay bare the permanent roots of religion in the human mind and determine the underlying common factor in the variety of acts through which religious objects are presented and realized. Anything lying outside the competence of this transcendental philosophy and psychology of religion would *ipso facto* fall to the portion of historical philosophy, as the exposition of the stages and route whereby this transcendental underlay of the rational mind worked towards historical realization.

This latter definition of the relation between philosophy and religion presents a schema which is followed by a considerable number of attempts to argue a basis for religion, some of which we owe to modern philosophers, others to Protestant theologians. Let us mention here the endeavours of Ritschl and his pupils Kaftan and Herrmann, who are the most resolute in shutting the door against metaphysics (the first on more positivist, the last-named on neo-Kantian grounds). Then there is Ernst Troeltsch, who, in spite of all kinds of concessions to a metaphysic influenced by Hegel and Eucken, sees the fundamental recipe for a theory of religion in a renewal by transcendental philosophy of the rational roots of religion, taking the very possibility of religion as starting-point. Next we have Wobbermin,

---

[1] Neither positivist nor Kantian agnosticism is tenable. No; metaphysics has a clearly laid-down eternal task, and it is possible to demonstrate epistemologically with certainty that metaphysics is possible with the employment of the mind's purely theoretic equipment.

who in a 'transcendental psychology' of religion seeks to form a typology of the religious object from the empirical material of religious life. Finally there is Rudolf Otto, who, in spite of preparing his definitions of the holy with phenomenological preliminaries of quite another kind, reverts at the conclusion of his profound and beautiful *Das Heilige*[1] to a conception of the holy, leaning on Kant and Fries, as a subjective rational category 'coined' for certain sense-data (and so not pre-existent as an attribute of the object).

We consider that, like the preceding, these dualistic definitions of the relation between philosophy and religion *conflict with the natures* of religion and philosophy.

A whole succession of principles, which religion declares true from the logic of religious acts *themselves*, can *in addition* be demonstrated philosophically with the help of metaphysics. In these I include, by way of example, the existence of an entity whose existence proceeds solely from its very essence; the existence of this *ens a se* as prime cause of every contingent existent (as a fragment of the whole of essential possibility, by eidological deduction); the nature of this *ens a se* as a rational and intelligent spirit, and as the *summum bonum* and final goal of all activities in the world; its infinitude. What I certainly do not include is its *actual personality*. To the philosophically knowable there also belong the specific intelligent spirituality and rationality of the human soul, its essential belonging to a body and—notwithstanding—its real separability from the latter's existence; the *idea* of the essence of higher and purer minds than are represented by the mentality of human souls; the personal continuance of the human soul after death (but not its general immortality); lastly in our examples, the idea that the mind, especially the will, enjoys a freedom which *specifically* transcends every form of regularity in man's submental processes and the rest of nature.

Nevertheless, I would most categorically deny, taking of course my stand against the system of partial identity, that religion in any way *founds* its own fundamental articles (including those of natural religion) on these metaphysical propositions in the sense that these articles would lack evidence, or be unfounded and false, if no appeal were made to metaphysics.

In so far as some of the theories here called 'dualistic' assert only the independence of religion (from metaphysics as well as philosophy), our

---

[1] Rudolf Otto, *Das Heilige*, Breslau 1917. (Translation by J. W. Harvey, *The Idea of the Holy*, London 1923, and as Pelican Book 1959—*Translator*.)

inclination is to applaud them. We would only demur at the manner in which they establish this independence. Of that, more later.

The thesis that religion (including natural religion) is independent and founded in itself does not exclude a definition of its relation to metaphysics which I call the *system of conformity* between religion and metaphysics, and which I would oppose to the above-named dualistic systems as well as to the systems of total or partial identity.

THE SYSTEM OF CONFORMITY

The first advantage of the system of conformity is that it permits one to uphold both the *unity of religion* and the *unity of metaphysics* without, like the dualistic systems, tearing faith apart from knowledge or doing violence to that great saying, *Gratia perficit naturam, non negat.**

1. Let us be clear that whatever form it may take religion is religion and not metaphysics. Even the elementary distinction between natural and revealed religion is a distinction *within* religion. Moreover, it is not a distinction to be met in any form in religion's realm of objects or corpus of truth. There is not one natural God and another of revelation, but just one God. Even in a living religious *act* there are no partial functions corresponding to this distinction. The only difference which this distinction may indicate is in the *source of knowledge* from which definite attributes of God (and of other religious objects) are subsequently elicited, and certified to the rational (theological) consciousness. Unless this relationship between natural and revealed religion is rigorously respected, the *unity of religious truth* and still more of religious *life* stands in great danger. The danger is that natural religion will declare its independence, as it did, from Herbert of Cherbury onwards, in the eighteenth century's religion of nature and reason. It then happens that 'natural religion' no longer appears as a mere stage of foundation-laying for a true and undivided religion, but sets itself up as the norm and yardstick of positive religion. And the danger grows the more serious when (as in the system of partial identity) 'natural religion' is equated with a totally different kind of knowledge—namely, metaphysical knowledge. Then even the concept of 'belief in the existence of God' becomes evidently senseless, since we can no longer hold any belief concerning God's existence, but only have knowledge of it. If we also look at the matter historically it should not be very difficult to show that the eighteenth century's gross error and desertion to deism and the religion of reason had its fount and sustenance in that very system we have called that of partial identity. In all the rich abundance of its many forms, religion ever flows from one source: objectively from the '*revelation*' of God, which itself proceeds by

degrees and has many stages; subjectively from *faith*. By 'revelation' I here intend to designate not what positive theologians call '*the* revelation', nor any actual revealing, much less 'positive' revelation, but solely the specific manner in which any kind of data relating to an object of divine and holy nature is *received* into the mind via observation or experience. I refer, in other words, to the specific manner in which it is actually or potentially *imparted* as perceptual data, whether directly or indirectly. The nature of this type of cognition is such that it stands in contrast to *all spontaneous cognitive acts*, and here it is not a question of distinguishing objectively between two modes of causality by which knowledge may enter the mind, but of recognizing a peculiar mode of evidence-forming which is latent in the observable cognitive process and basically different from all other modes. All *religious* knowledge of God is also knowledge *through* God, in the sense of the manner of its reception. Only this great, ancient and fundamental proposition can give religion that ultimate *unity* which it needs. Even the necessary distinction between natural and positive revealed religion cannot dislodge it. It must—and does—allow itself to be adapted to that distinction by means of an expanded doctrine of the structure and stages of revelation (in the most formal sense of the word, as in the philosophy of religion).

That, in complete disregard of the above, metaphysics should arrive by the free deployment of its own resources at insights held in common with religion in the higher stages of its own autonomous development—this is a sure sign of that deeper *unity* of human nature, mind and being, which, beyond all 'unity' of an intentional, merely 'deliberate' kind (this invariably, if truth were known, is too narrow and papers over unwelcome cracks), is certain to break through of its own accord and is never more in evidence than when everything within us that is truly 'of the spirit' is guaranteed free scope to develop according to its own principles.

2. But only the system of conformity assures the independence of *metaphysics* and its full potential scope for making acquisitions. If metaphysics, or its central part, *theory of the world-basis*, is also to do duty as the natural theology which positive theology requires as its basis, then however sincerely one strives to separate free rational inquiry from *de fide* propositions there can at bottom be only one outcome: history will produce a particular metaphysic with its own definite method of inquiry and at length a whole school accepting that method as valid; thence will flow a succession of results, and these will assume the character of presumptive *religious truth*. But it is logically perverse to inflict not only on certain specific results, but even on a particular rational *method* of producing them, an official sanction that reduces their dialectic respectability to

positive revelation. Revelation may with just reason determine *ex se* the limits of its validity in relation to man's spontaneous rational activity, which is in principle what Paul was doing when he spoke of the natural knowledge of the divine craftsman through his works. But the authority of positive religion *cannot* be said to extend to the passing of any *competent* judgment of dogmatic force concerning the positive *method* by which such knowledge is to be acquired. Any who, nevertheless, insist on proceeding with such a judgment are responsible for turning some particular *school of metaphysics,* and indirectly some complete philosophy, into a body of dogma and religious learning. This is extremely harmful for religion itself, since it is thereby set on a presumptive foundation which is in *essence* less durable than faith, and it is no less harmful for metaphysics. For the sector of metaphysics that is to serve religion as a basis is so to speak *broken away* from the body of philosophy and is so paralysed and stultified that it can be neither tested nor further developed by living thought. It is then very understandable if those who do not venerate the positive faith for which this sector is to be the 'foundation' react by assuming that this ostensibly *free and spontaneous rational metaphysic* was designed from the beginning to serve as basis for that positive faith. The consequence is that on principle they regard this metaphysic with so deep a mistrust that they overlook its truth, or eternal elements of truth, and no longer wish even to examine the questions which it answers. A paradoxical situation of this kind has been a reality for a long time now. For is there anything more paradoxical than that the branch of theology which, independently of positive and thus confessional content, was to establish the highest and most fundamental religious truths, so providing a *common forum* for all subsequent religious and ecclesiastical debate, performs and supplies the exact *opposite* of what it *should*—and is in fact the part of theology which divides opinion the most sharply? But when things which are rationally perceptible become *de facto* obligatory items of traditional faith, and when opinions are most divided by the very thing which was intended to establish an irreducible minimum of agreement among the adherents of different positive religions, then the meaning of all natural theology is *twisted into its exact opposite.*

The system of conformity precludes this situation, precludes it in such a way that, subject to a fresh testing, neither the results of metaphysics nor any proposition of positive theology need necessarily be altered, since only their supposed 'foundation' relationship is relegated by the conformity.

3. The system of conformity is no less successful in revealing the proper *stature and importance* of metaphysics. Metaphysics achieves its full value

as a branch of learning only when it is grounded, as to its object, in the full depth, range and variety of existence and the world, and when, as to its origin, it springs from the root of a comprehensive spiritual life and arises from its era as a collective historical phenomenon. Knowledge of the 'world-basis' is only its final and highest, and truly not its first nor its only object. Properly it represents for metaphysics the intellectual grasp of the point where all those countless threads intersect which lead us from glimpsed essences and essential correlations (these being latent in the empirically known, contingent and objectively real entities of positive science) across the frontiers of the empirically known and in the *direction* of the *absolutely real*. The essential meaning of metaphysics indicated in this description is quite independent of a system's truth or falsity. In this sense the metaphysical systems of, for example, Aristotle, Leibniz, Hegel, Schelling, Fechner, Schopenhauer, Hartmann or Bergson are 'genuine' metaphysical systems—regardless of whatever measure of falsity they contain. Their separate ideas of the world-basis are only the concluding, synthetic formulations of the end-points x, y, z, to which the threads of all the world's things and circumstances lead these thinkers if they pursue them beyond the sphere of the objectively real but (in comparison with suprasensual, absolute reality) existentially *relative*, and as far as their common root in absolute existence. None of these metaphysicians confines himself to making formal and abstract affirmations about the world-basis, paying no attention to the world itself and the rich store of its contents, taking no account of his own personal state of knowledge and that of the times in which he lives. Each of their metaphysical systems is pregnant with 'world' and empirical matters and seeks to show how this world is deeply rooted in the 'world-basis'. But while their highest and ultimate truths partly overlap the fundamental propositions of the developed religious consciousness, they in some way *anchor* these truths —without formulating their religious 'basis'—in the *plenitude of experience of world and self*: this cannot be done by religion alone and unaided. For religion proceeds directly from that basic definition of the absolutely real (of the *ens a se*) which is inaccessible to unaided metaphysics—the personality of God, which attests its existence in revelation. But metaphysics on the other hand is able to demonstrate that the *ens a se* must have, as an objective condition, certain definitive attributes if it is to be both real and personal. It must, that is, possess above all *rationality* and *intelligent spirituality*. However, the personality of God is withheld from every kind of *spontaneous* rational cognition in finite beings—not on account of any alleged limitations of the cognitive faculty, but because it belongs to the nature of a *purely* spiritual person in its objective aspect that its existence (*if* it exists) can only be known as a result of self-communication, *i.e.* revelation.

Nevertheless, metaphysics *cannot* thus freely and independently 'anchor' religion's fundamental propositions if it is previously conceived *as* the means of underpinning religious faith and if its character as a foundation is to be given the seal of a *religious* truth.

In that case metaphysics is denied any expansion from the rich field of essential knowledge presented by the realm of existent objects (including the exact and positive sciences)—and the denial is scarcely mitigated by the fact that metaphysics has its origin in the living totality of the mind. It now becomes a *summa* of petrified formal propositions—propositions which, truth to tell, are much too congested with circumstantial matter to be as easily deducible by pure analysis from the *ens a se* as is supposed, in the absence of fresh empirical data. It becomes an academic tradition drained of spirit, unworthy—as it stands—of the attention of those outside the tradition. In contrast the system of conformity envisages religion and metaphysics as hands extended *freely* in mutual assistance; neither hand has secretly compelled the other to support its authority while claiming to have received that support as a willing gift.

It is not here our business to demonstrate *in extenso* the possibility of a metaphysic in accordance with the above—still less to develop it in detail.

4. But there is one more decisive reason for rejecting metaphysics as the prop of natural theology and religion. Only two propositions of metaphysics—the most *formal* known to ontology—are utterly self-evident: first, the proposition that there is an *ens a se*—or existent whose existence is a consequence of its essence—which differs from the whole of all contingent things, events, realities, *i.e.* from the whole of the 'world', and secondly, the proposition that this *ens a se* is the prime cause and basis of the fact that out of all intrinsically possible worlds this one contingent world is real. (Here the idea of creation is not yet present, since 'creation' presupposes the personality of God, to which religion alone has access.) All further definitions of the world-basis have two peculiarities which are in radical contrast with the nature of religious self-evidence. The judgments which they express are permanently *hypotheses*, which are never strictly verifiable and never more than presumptively evident (*i.e. probable*), in accordance with the logical rule that 'the conclusion accepts the weaker premise'—since, in addition to their basis in manifest, but non-existential, knowledge of essences and essential relations, they must constantly and necessarily seek support *also* from the material inductions of the positive sciences. For all judgments of positive science are by *nature*

probably, and not manifestly, true. Every one of these judgments may be robbed of its validity by the progress of observation. For, as Husserl has strikingly demonstrated, every real thing or phenomenon, however small and trivial it may be in relation to other phenomena, is essentially *inexhaustible* in purely inductive material, and determinable only within an *infinite* process of determination. It is only manifest knowledge of essences which is conclusive (*i.e.* not interminable like inductive knowledge) and may call a halt at any point of the endless, feverish process of inductive inquiry and redefinition. Nevertheless, essential knowledge, as ignorant of existents, can never yield *unaided* a metaphysical knowledge which of its nature is knowledge of existent realities.

Now it is out of the question that a religious judgment (that is, a judgment from faith) should possess the characteristics proper to any metaphysical judgment defining attributes of the world-basis beyond the above propositions of the *ens a se* and prime cause. True faith is either visionary faith or blind faith—the rest is heresy, superstition or hypocrisy.

There is no such thing as probable faith; no such thing as hypothetical faith. The 'rocksteady certitude' built on the evidence of faith is utterly different from all forms of presumptive knowledge. That evidence and that certitude are made possible only by the freedom of the act of faith, in contrast to acts of the practical intellect which are bound by circumstantial objects. Faith is the free *option of the person*, the innermost person, for the religious truth and benefit held out to faith; the *judgment* of faith is simply judgment concerning the substance of that which is received in the act of faith. For hypotheses and probabilities—or acts of assumption and presumption—there can be no place within faith or faith's object.

It clearly follows that no metaphysical proposition which offers an attributive definition of the world-basis can be a sufficient ground for accepting a religious truth, *i.e.* one which is the natural object of belief. For how can a thing hypothetically true 'found' anything absolutely true, or a presumption found a self-evident knowledge (such as, subjectively, the knowledge of faith), or a probability found a truth? Here it can be a question only of 'corroboration' (in some other way) and never of 'foundation'.

From this divergence, in the matter of evidence, between natural and religious knowledge there follows a most important proposition concerning the basic relation to *history* of the acquisitions respectively of faith and of natural knowledge (including more-than-formal metaphysics). The acquisitions of faith, and the 'dogmas' in which they are formulated, are by nature and meaning *eternal* truths and acquisitions: those of metaphysics are necessarily parts of the historical process—the history of metaphysical inquiry. What is therefore the implication of basing faith on non-formal metaphysical propositions? Such a proceeding implies either drawing 'eternal' religious truths down into the flux proper to metaphysical knowledge as spontaneous and probable, or the elevation of this or that rational metaphysical proposition into dogma, which is tantamount to misunderstanding the merely probable character of metaphysical knowledge and promoting its propositions to the level of the absolutely evident. This way lies paralysis and death for free, rational inquiry. The first course is the path of gnosis, the second has often been the path taken by an overweening sense of ecclesiastical authority. Both are courses of evil, equally harmful to both religion and philosophy.

The practical *independence* of metaphysics from religion, which the foregoing establishes, should not, however, be confused with the question of how far all possible metaphysics (including therefore all metaphysics historically encountered) is independent from religion in its (possible) *origin* and *initial formation* within the mind of man. For in the matter of this independence it is a question of the philosopher's *intention*, or the extent to which his inquiry and will to inquire are in intention *free of religious preconceptions*. If they are truly free it becomes a question of the origin of metaphysical cognition *including* the accompanying intention. This last question will receive different answers according to the way in which this further question is decided: is religious or metaphysical awareness, both constitutive to the human mind, the earlier to be actualized? I do not think there can be any doubt that the *religious* is the earlier, the more *original*—not only in the empirical, psycho-genetic sense but also in the sense of the actual order in which the two types of knowledge originated in the mind of man.

The human being always 'has' some kind of credence and assumption concerning his own and the world's *weal* or way of salvation before ever he adopts the metaphysical frame of mind. He 'necessarily' has this assumption, whether he will or no, and whether or not he is reflexively aware of it. For in order of origin—which no matter-of-fact historical test can prove or refute—the religious act is *antecedent* to the act of philosophical cognition. The historical fact, demonstrable in detail, that every metaphysic there has ever been has kept within the scope of fundamental religious categories which religion has marked out for metaphysics, is only a *verification* (not a proof) of the order in which the activities of religious and metaphysical cognition and conduct originated.

The numerous metaphysical systems of the Indians, the Greeks and the Christian era represent families of metaphysical systems which each preserve *one* overall character in spite of the great disparity of their parts.

And what endows them with these overall unities of character is in the last resort the essential disparity of the religions in whose spheres of influence they originated.

However firmly we are obliged to reject the 'dualistic' systems in principle, the intellectual toil which went to their making has not been entirely in vain. They were wrong when they denied the possibility of a metaphysic or the respective organic unity of metaphysics and religion; they were wrong when they applied false yardsticks to the historical findings of metaphysics (Kant, for example, the criterion of mathematical evidence; 'inductive' metaphysicians, the *kind* of progress and degree of certainty epitomized by positive science)—and thereafter felt obliged to abandon metaphysics as historically 'untenable'. They were wrong because it is not on account of some supposedly just claim to full objective truth that mathematics enjoys its own peculiar kind of evidence, but by virtue of its far more significant renunciation of real asseverations and on account of its greater economy and adequacy to purely logical 'correctness'. Moreover, positive science is so much more rapid and continuous in its progress than metaphysics not on account of its full objective truth, but on account of its comparative abstention from such truth—that is, positively speaking, because it limits itself to as much objective truth as is necessitated by its goal (governed by the conditions of human life) of practical world-mastery and control. A further reason is that it breaks down the work of cognition into 'departments' (the essential multiplicity of the sciences) according to purely subjective points of view, and by this dismemberment (which is not demanded by the objects themselves, but only by the social and economic principle of the division of labour) 'scientific' truth loses as much in *concrete* objective truth as it gains in capacity for progress. For there is no mechanical, physical, chemical, biological, psychic, intellectual, historical 'world', but only *one* concrete world-reality, which as such is in its entirety a single and unique, effluxive continuum, with never twice the same 'occurrence'. It is possible to confirm the hypothesis of regularity only in the objects of the predefined *departmental* sciences, since these objects are detached from the world-reality by the process of abstraction. But it is the entire *concrete* world-reality which metaphysics, in accordance with autonomous and self-prescribed essential principles, seeks to approach by means of a complete synopsis and philosophical collation of positive scientific results.

Yet, however false may be the epistemology underlying the dualistic systems, with their mistrust of metaphysics, and however false their manner of estimating the worth of metaphysics, these systems possess one indisputable merit: *they recognize the independence of religious constructs, their autonomy of principle* and the independence of the self-evidence of faith from the self-evidence of theoretical knowledge. In this respect, and in this respect only, they are superior to the systems of identity. Even so, this superiority applies only on one side—the *subjective* side—of religion, with reference to the irreducibility and essential independence of the *religious act*. In other words, all these systems—even including the profound and reformative work of Otto, which at least may here be considered more in the right direction—share in some form the *universal* constant of error which is endemic in 'modern' philosophy, namely, epistemological subjectivism, or the basic proposition that an ontic realm of objects may be determined—if not actually created or 'generated'—solely by the nature of the acts and intellectual operations through which alone it is accessible to man. It is not their assertion of religion's independence and autonomy (as is often thought), but this subjective *conception* of its independence, which both justifies and enjoins us to condemn them with the name of '*fideism*'—that is, the doctrine that mankind taken as a whole possesses a faith to which there belongs no objective religious good or blessing of salvation.

The true counter to this basic error is not the doctrine that the natural part of these blessings of faith must be grounded in metaphysics and rational conclusions, as so many think. The answer is rather a thorough examination, on the basis of religion's independence, into the general peculiarities of the *objects* and *values* of faith—an examination which, since everywhere the entity precedes cognition, the value the estimate, and peculiarities of circumstance determine 'acts', would leave the nature of religious *acts* to a secondary stage of inquiry.

But such a religious phenomenology and theory of objects we possess only in some few, mostly unsystematic beginnings, and we are no better provided with any universal religious philosophy concerning the types of revelation. This latter would have to stand apart from all theological questions of true or false, genuine or spurious revelation, since it would be concerned only with the various ways in which objects of a religious kind present themselves to, and are received by, the empirical consciousness.

Moreover, the philosophical doctrine of religious acts—which must follow, not precede, the ontology of the divine essence—must be most sharply separated from the '*psychology of religion*'. For it is not 'religious psychology' but religious *noetics*. But since an essential *ontology* of religious objects was unknown to existing doctrines of the 'independence of religion', which evolved on a basis of subjective and individualistic Protestantism, these doctrines have invariably declined more or less into mere religious psychology. At all events they presumed they would be able to describe the nature (and types) of the religious act with abstractional methods and resources which, deprived of bearings upon the objects of religion, were consciously or—which is worse—unconsciously biassed toward the sphere of psychology. Of this the best proof is offered by their basically erroneous questions, for it is in the questions, before ever they propose an answer, that these theories are on the wrong track. They ask for example whether the religious act is primarily a 'feeling' (*e.g.* Schleiermacher's feeling of utter dependence) or, as according to Ritschl, a type of comportment proper to the volitional sphere or, as the Schoolmen and the religious rationalists maintain, a way of thought. They go on to ask whether 'religious experience' is mediated or not mediated through the 'subconscious' of our psychic life. Yet all these are distinctions which overlook the nature of the religious act completely and from the outset, because its ideal unity is the *unity of operation* of the mind *trained upon the object*, and is therefore in no way similar to psychological concepts. The psychological processes which, as observable by introspection, are active within the praying subject, and the manner of the activity—these are matters as indifferent for the nature of the act of prayer as are a mathematician's indigestion or his fantasies, while he thinks a problem over, for the noetics of mathematics. The act of prayer can be defined only from the *meaning* of prayer, and the manner in which the psychic materials deployed in the act are psychologically composed—out of what particular combination of sensations, emotions, imaginings, intentional acts, apostrophes, ejaculations and other expressive behaviour—holds not the slightest interest for the noetics of religion.

If the doctrine of the independence of religion has hitherto been closely connected, historically, with the so-called religion and theology of sentiment or with moralistic voluntarism,* it has needless to say followed a path of error, but the error arose from historical accident and is not of the essence of the doctrine. Even the thinking comprised in the religious act (and, in our view, even forming the leading element) is embraced from the outset by the act's specific, noetic unity of operation: it has an object exclusive to *religious* thought—available to no other kind. One may go much further: it is even incorrect to associate the religious act more with the 'internal' than with the external world. For, as regarded not in its subjective *meaning* but according to the manner of its actualization in a human being, the religious act certainly does not present itself as purely psychic, but as psycho-physical.* It presents itself, for example, as just as much an outward act of worship as an internal process in the human soul—and this with utter continuity and no possibility of dis-memberment into external and internal, physical and psychic halves. To every prayer there belongs an expressive action or posture—it may be individual and occasional or general, with an established outward form of prayerful attitude. Even in this sense the concept of the religious act has nothing in common with any psychological concept.

Nevertheless, the psychology of religion, which is so favoured and overrated today, needs to be methodologically redirected within its proper boundaries.[1]

The modern psychology of religion, in its essentials, originated histori-cally in the spirit of positivism. (Among the moderns David Hume was its progenitor.) This is of course no accident. For inasmuch as religion's claim to truth was meeting a *rebuff* of one kind or another, it was to be expected that the religion of the positivists should decline to nothing more than a collection of psychic phenomena, which required to be described, causally explained, and at best conceived teleologically (from the biological aspect) as a particular stage in man's adaptation to his environment. But apart from the historical origin of modern religious psychology it is a misrepresentation to argue according to the following favourite method of outlining its sense and purpose:

'Whatever one thinks of religion's truth, affirming or denying, whatever the religion to whose milieu one belongs, *in any case* religion is a collection of psychic phenomena and experiences, and as such is indubitably an object for psychology. The appropriate branch of psychology is called the psychology of religion, and this psychology of religion is a science which can be practised just as well by Christians as by Muslims, by atheists as by believers, etc., etc. It is thus entirely *free of preconceptions* and *inter-confessional.*'

This argument is purely specious and of no account. No one who makes use of it can have clearly grasped the question of what the conditions are under which *anything whatsoever* becomes the object of psychological elucidation, and what the objective premises (or preconceptions) from which every branch of explanatory psychology must operate.

To the nature of psychology, or rather to the type of perception and perceptual state in which a datum of the type 'psychic' can enter a cognitive consciousness, two things belong: always the psychic is *primarily* the object of a perception of *otherness*, not a perception of a thing proper to the subject; secondly, it is invariably the case that the psychic is primarily

[1] The question of the pragmatic theory and psychology of religion is taken up on a later page. See p. 291.

something which is held to be error, delusion or in some way *abnormal*. Now, while it is true that reflexive perception of things proper to the subject, together with all kinds of 'self-observation', need not necessarily have been genetically formed under the influence of an already exercised perception of extraneous things, such perception is nevertheless in essence (as a *type* of act and mental disposition) simply extra-perception to which—by chance—the object assigned is not that which is adequate to perception of that kind (*i.e.* some instance of the 'alien' and 'other'), but the modifications of the reflexive self. Or we may thus express it: to adopt a 'psychological' attitude to oneself is to behave towards oneself *as if one were a stranger or 'someone else'*.

Again: it is impossible to adopt a psychological attitude toward the 'other' until one has by some method relinquished the natural relationships subsisting between spiritual subjects (*shared experience* of the same objects, values, etc., the relationship of *understanding*). Not until the personal quality of the other has vanished or appears to have done so (madness is the clearest instance), or until we exercise an artificial abstraction upon his being, upon the significant content of his intentions, thus upon the intentions themselves, does the other yield a potential object of psychology. By strict analogy, I must also abstract my own free person and its mental intentions—must feign to remove them—if I wish to adopt an attitude of self-perception toward myself.

Finally: if a person judges that twice two are four, it is absurd to demand a psychological explanation of the fact. The only meaningful question to ask in these circumstances is why he so judges now, in this connection and not in that one. But if a person judges that twice two make five, then the content of his judgment, not only the occasion of his judging, is a possible object of psychological elucidation.

Psychology, then, is primarily always psychology of the *other, divested of spirit and personality*, and psychology of that which is held to be false or nonsensical at its intentional face-value.

But this noetic origin of explanatory psychology (in the modern sense of the word) is also of some importance for the so-called psychology of religion. Religion simply is not, as that argument would have it, 'in any case' a psychic phenomenon. It is *that* only on occasions when—and to the extent that—it rests on delusion and error, or is perhaps already seen as delusion. So anyone investigating religion as an object of psychology has already emptied it of meaning and intention—even if only in a feigned and tentative manner, for the purposes of research. But if anyone deprive religion of all possible truth, he should not claim that he can still practise the psychology of religion. He should rather say: 'There is nothing left of what men called religion. There is only a collection of psychic phenomena, which as "religion" used mistakenly to be considered the essential embodiment of certain acts directed to a common object, and these morbid phenomena of the *psyche* I will investigate.' This is a sensible way of talking, whereas the other is senseless.

If the modern explanatory psychology of religion is obviously preoccupied with the abnormal, *pathological* phenomena of religious life, it is clear that this is no accidental penchant but derives from its very nature and origin.

Methodologically it is no less erroneous to believe that a psychology of religion *free* of religious or confessional premises is possible—other than one merely descriptive.

For explanatory psychology, in *all* its branches, presupposes the reality of the objective field whose action and reaction on the *psyche* it is investigating. Thus all explanatory sensual psychology postulates the concept of attraction, *i.e.* a real causal relation between the organism and physical bodies or kinds of energy. On the other hand all descriptive sensual psychology postulates a bare minimum of definite objective phenomena, such as colours or sounds. If we apply this principle to our present field of inquiry we ascertain that specific real, religious objects must be postulated before the attempt can be made to investigate their effect on the human *psyche*.

But on what basis are they to be postulated? It is the answer to *this* question which decisively precludes an interconfessional psychology of religion. For this is the answer: Since it is of the *essence* of a religious object that it can attest its possible reality only through and in an act of *faith*, all those who do not possess the appropriate belief in a religious reality fail to satisfy the *precondition* for empirically knowing and observing the action of the religious object on the *psyche*.

To give an example, it is clear that nobody who does not possess *belief* in the Real Presence of Christ in the Sacrament can seek even to *describe* the psychic experiences induced by a Catholic's pious assistance at the holy Mass. He is as little able to do so as a person totally blind is able to describe the sensation and mood produced by colours vivid to unimpaired perception. Therefore, a psychological investigation of this religious object is only possible among those who believe the relevant dogma—not, then, among a group of people some of whom believe it and some of whom do not. The psychology of religion is confronted by this wholly peculiar situation, that the reality of the object whose reaction on the psyche it seeks to examine can only be received in the state of faith. Even the much-bruited 'empathy', by which one may enter the religious act of another, is no kind of substitute for the real performance of the act. For it is only the *reality* of the religious object and material, a reality experienced in real and genuine faith but necessarily wanting in the object of merely empathetic faith, which can faithfully reproduce the psychic condition that is required for inspection.

Thus it is that merely descriptive religious psychology, as distinct from the explanatory—which can only be practised from premises of unbelief— is upheld in its well-defined and limited rights. But even this type of religious psychology is only meaningful and possible within a single religious community and not among different communities or their individual members—at least, not as applied to the psychic action of objects affected by the disparity of religious viewpoints. There are there- fore as many psychologies of religion as there are *separate confessions*. For the psychic condition which is here to be 'psychologically' explored, the psychic experiences induced by the conceptual possession of religious objects, *arise* in the first place under the influence of different metaphysical and dogmatic systems.

There is to be sure another quite separate line of inquiry, in addition to the spurious, atheistic, explanatory religious psychology and the kind of psychology which is conditional on the unity of the religious community. It is best described as the *concrete* phenomenology of religious objects and acts. There is naturally a fundamental difference between this and all types of eidological or *essential* phenomenology of religion, such as envisage the 'essence' of the act or object. This is because it seeks to understand as fully as possible the meaning of one or a number of religious constructs, and attempts an intelligent reconstruction of the acts through which their meanings were or are transmitted. Thus I can describe the polytheistic world corresponding to a particular phase of Greek religion and can give a *direct* account of its material content, *i.e.* not merely a description of the Greeks' own representations of that world. I can investigate its hierarchic system, demonstrate its relation to the world and the life of man. In the same manner I can treat of the acts of worship—their forms and types–in which the Greek of that era turned to his gods, in homage, in supplication, etc. But of psychology here there is no question, since all I am doing is lifting the concrete material of intentions and acts, in its intentional relation to its objects' positive meaning, out of the context of the 'spiritual world' existing among the Greeks of those days—and in this the reality of the objects stands disregarded. There is here no question of psychologically describing the internal repercussion of the gods (felt as their spontaneous action) upon the psychic life of the Greeks, and it goes without saying that there is also no question of any objectively real action of the gods, since (according to our own religious notions) they did not really exist.

This concrete phenomenology of religions is a basic discipline for the positive, systematic study of religion and at the same time a *sine qua non* for all religious history concerned with the *evolution* of religions; this latter study may be as strictly distinguished from the systematic science of religions, which *itself* descriptively and comparatively investigates the structure and ramification of mankind's religious object-world, as the jurist has long been wont to distinguish (for example) an inquiry into the doctrine and system of Roman law—at a particular moment in Roman history—from legal *history*, whose business it is to trace legal concepts in their evolution from the collective influences of earlier civilization.[1]

Now, *fundamentally* different from all the above religious disciplines is the *essential philosophy of religion.*

It is not metaphysics, neither is it natural theology, nor epistemology, nor explanatory and descriptive psychology, nor the concrete phenomenology of religion, but it is the ultimate *philosophical foundation* of *all and every* other philosophical and scientific study of religion. It must be perfected before we may clearly know the declared *independence of religion*, as much in its *ontological* and *objective* aspect as in that of *active* religion. But in process of demonstrating this independence it also performs a second valuable function: by concentrating on the essence of religion it disengages from the religious objects found as items of faith in religions, as positively studied, the essences, the essential correlative principles and structures, which are realized in all the religious realities we have before us in positive religions. Thus it uncovers what we would call the logic of religious acts, *i.e.* the active principles of *religious* reason. These are not in themselves 'norms' but essentially principles of construction and logical development by which religious acts themselves combine or evolve one from another. But they *become* norms for the empirical subject 'man'. However, since all religious knowledge has its final source in some kind of revelation (in that sense of the word which is defined on an earlier page), the whole of religious logic has simply the one significance: it shows the manner and principles whereby religious reason leads man to readiness to receive the light of revelation —light from all the basically different gradations of revelation. Thus, even if we follow these 'norms' they lead us only to the threshold of obtaining revelation, whose substance must then be grasped in the act of faith, grasped as evident in evident faith; they do not lead to any spontaneous cognition of God or (as many seem to think) to any *ex*cogitation or construction of religious objects.

[1] Similarly Utitz is right to distinguish the systematic study of art from the history of art.*

2. THE ESSENTIAL[1] PHENOMENOLOGY OF RELIGION

BRANCHES OF STUDY

The essential phenomenology of religion has three ends: 1. the essential nature of the divine; 2. the study of the forms of revelation in which the divine intimates and manifests itself to man; 3. the study of the religious act through which man prepares himself to receive the content of revelation, and through which he takes it to himself in faith.

In so far as the divine presents and manifests itself in things, events and orders which belong to the natural reality accessible in principle to all, to the reality of the mind, to the social reality of history, we shall refer to *natural revelation*, whose subjective correlate is *natural religion*. In so far as the divine on the other hand presents or announces itself through the medium of the word and through persons (*homines religiosi* in the most eminent sense), let us speak of *positive* revelation. In so far as the divine— the 'godly'—is a being taking the form of *personality*, it can *only* reveal itself in the second, positive form of revelation; and only while it does *not* contain the idea of a person as ontological form—*e.g.* while it is defined only as *ens a se*, infinite being, eternal reason, spirit, etc.—can it also present itself to man in the form of natural revelation.

Furthermore, there is one essential study of the stages of natural revelation and another of the stages of positive revelation. For if the divine reveals itself in some way at all levels of being, it reveals different characteristics of its essence on different levels, and reveals itself with different degrees of adequacy. The way of its revelation also varies as between different *general* forms of contingent existence—inanimate nature, living nature, the soul of man, society, history. And its various outward forms of revelation are grasped by various kinds of religious act. The fact remains that in so far as the divine is a person and manifests itself to us in persons, its only possible medium of revelation is the *word*. But the positive forms of revelation also have their essential stages, according to whether the divine reveals merely a limited something of itself—a particle of knowledge, thought, will, as offered to the intelligence—or its whole personal essence and being: thus there is functional revelation and self-revelation.

Again, there correspond to the different forms in which the divine communicates itself in and through persons the different *essential types of 'homines religiosi'*, the recognition of which offers another very important

---

[1] In his preface to the second German edition, Max Scheler stresses the crucial distinction between essential phenomenology and descriptive or reconstructive phenomenology. See p. 18 l. 18 of this edition (*Translator*).

F

field of research to the essential phenomenology of religion. They begin with the lowest forms and rise to the highest imaginable. The wizard, the magician, the seer, the sage, the prophet, the lawgiver and judge, the king and hero, the priest, the saviour, the redeemer, the mediator, the messiah, and finally the idea of the highest conceivable form, the *essential idea of the person* to whom God has imparted his own personal essence and being: these are examples whose nature and gradation must be thoroughly examined. We must therefore first establish the essential difference between the *homo religiosus* or 'holy man' and other value-types of person, such as the genius, the hero, etc., and so a thoroughgoing investigation of these types must form the basis of our inquiry.[1] Furthermore, the difference between the so-called founder of religion (the original holy man) and the merely derivative *homines religiosi* must also be clearly established. (Among the 'derivative' I include the apostle, the patriarch, the dogmatist, the 'reformer', the 'witness', and the saint within the established fold.)

In view of the essentially *social* nature of all religion, another discipline which must be accepted into the essential phenomenology of religion is the study of the *essential forms of sociological structure* taken by communities to whom revelation is proclaimed as collective revelation (as opposed to grace and individual illumination) by the medium of a 'representative'. Directly relevant to this field of study is what is predicated of the nature of God as lord, protector, head, lawgiver, judge and king of communities (including the nation, the family, the professions and kindred vocational groups, the Church, etc.), as are collective acts of worship and liturgy, communal prayer, forms of homage and devotion.

Finally, the essential phenomenology of religion must submit to scrutiny the *historical* order of succession of the natural and positive revealed forms of the divine. This study must form the basis of any historical philosophy of religion, just as the preceding one must underlie the theory of religious communities (Church, sect, school, monastic order and the rest).

It is not, however, our present intention to construct the entire phenomenology of religion. We will confine ourselves in general to examining the *religious act* in more elaborate detail. For it is from that act and its internal logic that we may most plainly see how there may come into being a religious self-evidence which, residing in faith, resides in itself, and how religion proceeds to unfold and throw out new and higher structures in conformity with its own autonomous laws.

But if we are to observe the proper order for treating these problems

[1] See Volume 2.*

(as we have previously determined it*), we must first say a few words about the *essential definitions of the nature* of the divine.

Basic character of the divine

Just as in all fields of knowledge the being and the object are given to man earlier than knowledge of the being, and earlier still than the *manner* of acquiring such knowledge, so the objects of the essence called 'divine'—God or the gods—also belong directly to the *primal datum* of the human consciousness. In and through all other things which are given to him as existent and possessing such and such qualities, man has learned by dint of natural religious acts to see, sense or imagine that an entity is being disclosed ('revealed') to him which possesses at least two essential attributes: *it 'is' in absolute being, and it is holy.* However many additional attributes this holy and absolute being may receive from religions both primitive and developed, it invariably possesses *these.* Always it is given to man as an 'absolute entity', *i.e.* as one which is unconditionally superior to all others (including the *ego* so thinking) in capacity for sheer 'being', and one on which man is therefore utterly dependent in his whole existence. Yet the 'absolute entity' is not inferred, constructed or excogitated from an initial sense of awareness of utter dependence: such a feeling could always be ascribed to weakness in the subject—his inadequate reserves of will-power or the underdevelopment (by himself or society) of his latent capabilities. No; what happens is that the positive attribute of *supremacy* in a being X (implying the dynamic predicates of might, power and the like) becomes perspicuous to intuition 'in' some one contingent entity. Furthermore, it is not himself alone whom the individual subject sees to be dependent on this absolute being—this entity founded in and 'resting on' itself—but also, even without inductive scrutiny of their being and qualities, all other entities there are; indeed it is as a *part* of contingent being in general that he feels himself dependent.

This unconditional self-inclusion in the sphere of relative being—to the last jot of selfhood—is the foremost characteristic in the religious conception of this first attribute of divinity. On this point there is no reservation on the ground of distinctions between soul and body, spirit and flesh, I and thou, etc. No; utter dependence affects the human being as an undivided whole, as a simple fragment of this 'world'—'world' being the heading under which man subsumes the totality of relative being. In the *religious* conception of this primary content of the divine essence there is no question either of an 'inference' or of any theoretical, philosophical perception such as underlies the 'proof from contingency'. If for no other reason, this is so because only the relative entity, whichever it may be, that exercises the *primary* indicative function of pointing the way to the absolute being could be the starting-point of such an inference, and this entity does not acquire any special religious significance until there is a reflexive retrospection to the fact that it *has* shown the way to the absolute, *i.e.* the divine. But here too, as everywhere, 'to stand revealed' means to have been the reverse of extrapolated, inferred, abstracted. It means that when the absolute being of an object qualified as 'divine' becomes, of and *out of* itself, 'trans-parent' and 'trans-lucent' (in the active senses) within an empirical object from the relative sphere, it is only the operation of the shining and looking through which lifts the latter object into prominence and singles it out from among all other objects of relative existence. Just as, when a man or woman looks out of a window, that window becomes from the very fact conspicuous beyond the others in its row, so the finite object becomes 'special' and 'holy' from the fact that it is symbolizing the absolute being.

If the metaphysical idea of the *ens a se* coincides in this way with the primary *religious* definition of the divine, it none the less remains true that the religious and metaphysical paths to knowledge are altogether different. The correlative religious act *accepts* a thing in *process* of revelation and self-presentation within another thing: the act of metaphysical cognition *goes to meet it* spontaneously in logical operations. The relation inherent in a thing's 'process of revelation' (the objective *standing* for something, one object's pointing on to another or, in the case of higher forms of revelation, a self-annunciation, self-communication, self-expression)—belongs to the class of symbolic and intuitive relations. In this there is no more question of abstracted relational *concepts* than of inferential or interpretative, meaning-seizing operations of the intellect. Again, the symbolic relation of self-presentation certainly does not originate in an item contained by the human mind—as happens when the meaning of a word presents itself on its utterance—but in the very *object* of the relative entity 'in' which the possessor of absolute being presents or 'discloses himself'. Hence we are dealing with an *objective* relation, not one objectively logical (such as identity or similarity), not one objectively causal, but a symbolic and, in the event, *intuitive* relation. The mind discovers it only in the religious act. Hence another vast distinction: the metaphysical thought-process leading to the *ens a se* can be applied quite indiscriminately to *any* contingent, relative existent, whereas in the religious conception of this basic definition of the divine, the divine invariably reveals itself in specific, *isolated* or strictly limited *concrete things* and *happenings*, including *also* such psychic experiences as may arise. All further substantive definition of the 'gods' or 'God' beyond the general essential category of the divine is always determined subsequently in various ways from the essential material of these things and happenings.

Even the world's *'dependence'* on the absolute being thus disclosed is given only in the religious act. It is not a logically objective or objectively causal dependence, corresponding to the relations of reason and consequence or cause and effect. It rests rather on the intuitively evident activity of the 'effecting process', which enters into all observable causal connections as an irreducible phenomenal factor. This activity is distinguished by the fact that God equated with the *ens a se* appears as the *utterly* active, strong and almighty, and everything else as the utterly passive and enacted—appears enacted in that the active presents itself, in turn, *dynamically* and *symbolically*. In the purely objective causal connection of two events or things (in the case of direct interaction) the cause does not in any way present itself *in* the effect; one cannot tell from the effect alone what thing is its cause; inductive practical knowledge must precede the connection of C and E, if one wishes to conclude C from E, and C is to be more than 'some cause unknown'. It is otherwise in the religious act, which conceives the finite and contingent entity as the *'creature'* of the mighty or (in monotheism) almighty deity. Here the creatureliness of the creature bears the original stamp of a *phenomenal characteristic*: thus it points to a symbolic connection with the creator and 'mirrors' him in its own defective and inadequate way. It is true that in this way the relations of reason and consequence, cause and effect, enter into the content of the religious act. But here these relations are *sensed*, not excogitated, and are always also *symbolic*. For that reason there can *here* be no question of metaphysical inferences.

In varying ways—some illustrating the purity and sublimity of religion, some the different attributes of God—'God expresses himself' in the events of nature. All nature is indeed the field of his expression, just as a human face is available to express joy or grief in smiles or tears. Or God proclaims and manifests himself in nature as mighty and active. Everywhere there lies in or beside the intuitive causal connection one other symbolic relation which is not present in simple objective causality. That a certain acid will turn litmus-paper blue or red is not something we can deduce from the acid alone, however exactly we know its constituents. Still less, conversely, can we deduce from a blueness the actual cause of blueness. We may not come to any conclusion in the matter until we have made many inductions on the hypothesis of regularity. The substance of the effect is not contained in the substance of the cause. If, as here, where we are dealing not with a multiplicity of gods and worlds but with the concrete causal relationship between *one world* and *one God*, there is (from the fact of uniqueness) a complete absence of regularity, we cannot make any statement about the nature of the world-cause from the *mere* objective causality subsisting between God and the world. However, we have quite a different situation when we come, for example, to the relationship of a work of art to the mind of the artist and the individual nature of that mind. Certainly the artist is *likewise* the cause of his work. But beyond that fact, the work also contains *phenomenally* something of the artist's individual spirit and essence: it mirrors him, his spirit lives in it—is present to us in his work. Here the substance of the effect is itself a pointer to the nature of its author, even though we have no previous knowledge of him. Thus the work is 'a Rembrandt', 'a Grünewald' and so on. Yet take but one step down from art to craft, and the same is no longer true. The craftsman has merely clothed a traditional form with material (*e.g.* the form of a table with wood). Nevertheless, we conclude as to the cause of the table in the way in which we conclude as to the cause of a natural event. For before we know the craftsman we see from the table *itself* that it is the 'work of man' or that reason and industry had their parts in its production. A presence of God in the creature, *analogous to the presence of the artist in the work of art*, is visible and sensible in the religious act.

To these two basic definitions of the divine, the *ens a se* and the mightiest or almighty active principle, there exactly correpond two empirically known *reactions* to the *divine apprehended in self-revelation* in the religious act —the sense of the partial *nothingness* and impotence of all *relative* being, and the sense of the *creatureliness* of all relative being and of one's own being as part or member thereof.

These two experiences cannot take shape *unless* both basic definitions of the divine have already been apprehended in the religious act, or can only enter the mind to the extent that these definitions are apprehended and present within it. In no sense, therefore, are they the first experiences from which one either can or should infer God. For it is only when *God* is confronted as the *ens a se* that there ensues an extremely characteristic 'conversion' of whatever existential phenomenon is the immediate object of experience—a transformation whereby that which *before* the religious act was perceived as positively existing now appears relatively non-existent, a relative nonentity. Anybody who experiences a *transition* from a state outside to one inside the active religious sphere may observe the nature of this *conversion of perspective* in his own person. It is not in the presence of the purely conceptual idea of the *ens a se*, but in the presence of the *ens a se* naturally revealing itself via the religious act in an object of some kind, that *all* other existing entities acquire with varying intensity their character of *nothingness*. 'I nothing—Thou all' is always the most primitive expression of the religious consciousness in the *first* stage of its evolution. The second experience, of *createdness* and *creatureliness*, can enter only when we reflect on the positive entity which every thing still *is* and we as men still are—regardless of that partial non-entity and nothingness which we first apprehended in the presence of God. In that reflection both things are made plain, both the nothingness experienced in submission to God and the positive selfhood grasped in the self-assertion of the positive entity we 'still' bear within us. 'I am not utterly nothing, but a creature of God' is the sense of the second experience.

Here, too, we are concerned with a *sense of enactment*, not a conclusion from effect to cause. As such it precedes the experience of creatureliness proper, which postulates the analogy with personal human volitional activity, in other words the idea of the divine as personal and intelligent. For to *create* is something other than to be the mere cause, and implies the intelligent personality of the cause in question. So it is in the first place on theistic religious grounds that the sense of enactment becomes that of creatureliness. Nevertheless, metaphysics can for *its* part demonstrate three things: 1. it is intrinsic in the contingent existence of an object in *any* given sphere of being that the existence must have an effective cause; 2. the phenomenon of reality is originally given only in the empirically known *resistance* of an object to the exercise of volition;* 3. the only model on which we apprehend the mode of *possible* realization of a purely qualitative essence is that of the manner in which we apprehend the original realization of a merely imagined thing when, in and through volition, we enact a project of the will—irrespective of the intermediary processes of a psychophysical organism and mechanism.

Unlike the above-described prime causality, all kinds of *lateral* causality between contingent existents affect not the realness or realization of such existents but only their *arrangement in time and space*; they are therefore subordinate to the idea of the initial causation of *any* given existent by an *ens a se*.

But, however much the religious act in which we apprehend our own and the world's createdness conforms to these metaphysical perceptions and accords with them in results, the logical operations which give rise to the perceptions are wholly *absent* from the natural religious act which teaches us our created status as a work of God. One may therefore have the sense of that status *without* thought or conclusion, and one may think and conclude yet not have it. Suppose, moreover, one were to formulate the following conclusion: the cause of human reason, and the cause of the existence of forms of being which correspond to its thought-forms, must likewise be rational—indeed, by virtue of the formally absolute and infinite character bestowed on all divine attributes by the nature of the *ens a se*, it must be 'absolutely and infinitely rational'. Such a conclusion would be utterly different from the *experience* of infinite reason as it pours its light into finite reason and shines forth out of created things. This sense of the godly attribute shining into the light of finite reason is expressed in the thought of Saint Augustine that in so far as we truly understand all things, *i.e.* as they are in themselves, we understand them '*in lumine Dei*'— though perhaps we may not see God thereby.

In the idea of the divine there is a direct, necessary and real connection for the religious consciousness between the *ens a se*, the all-pervading active force and the *value*-modality known as *holiness*, with all its attendant wealth of value-qualities.

Metaphysics may try by various means of deduction and proof to represent this connection as logically necessary. Thus, for example the attempt has been made, taking the idea of the *ens a se* as an ideal limit, to arrange every kind of entity in a sequence of such a nature that the things within it would be ordered according to the degree in which they owed their being to themselves or derived it *ab alio*. In this sense the concept of the *degree* of being is meaningful and justified. Thus there can be no doubt that as an autonomous rational being man is an *ens* which is self-dependent to a higher degree than the living creature devoid of reason; but this latter in turn, as an *auto*motive phenomenon, is at a higher degree than the inanimate body which *as* inanimate must clearly be determined in its movements by bodies *other* than itself. Believing that these degrees of ontological perfection might also be regarded as the measure of *an entity's perfection of value*, the metaphysician now proceeded with an appearance of strict *analytical* logic from the ontological to the value-definitions of the divine. And so without more ado the *ens a se* was to be the *ens perfectissimum* because its being is the most complete; hence, it becomes the *summum bonum*, hence again, the absolutely holy. It is possible to go yet farther. Since freedom and intelligence (=ability to be cause rather than effect) represent the highest degree of ontological perfection, as pre-eminently enjoyed by the human spirit among all *entia ab alio*, it seems inherent in the concept of *ens a se*=*ens perfectissimum* that if it is real at all it should also be absolutely spiritual, intelligent, free and rational.

Whatever justice may lie in these deductions' claim to logic, this much is certain: the *religious* consciousness does not arrive by this route at the idea of a holy God. For the *religious* consciousness it is a composite axiom about the nature of things that what is absolutely valuable must also exist—that is, what has value only *through* and *in* itself (not that the absolute entity is necessarily also valuable in itself). In this connection, by the way, it is immaterial what the people (or other repository of religious awareness) actually *consider* to be of absolute value. For that reason love of God, in a special sense, and fear of God for that matter, *precedes*, in the evolution of a given individual religious consciousness, even the religious act in which the existence of the 'godly' thing is posited; here 'love of God' is understood *not* as love of a deity whose existence is already assumed, but as the qualitative *character* of the act of loving when addressed to 'something' within the *value-modality* of holiness. And again it is for the religious consciousness a composite axiom about the nature of things that whatever has 'absolute' value derived exclusively from itself belongs to the value-*category* of the holy, which category cannot be resolved into any other group of values, whether logical cognitive values, or axiological, moral, aesthetic values, etc.

Within the multiplicity of positive religions the value-category 'holy' may appear very elastic in its separate *qualities* and their *combination*. As a *category* it is an absolutely stable quantum which has not 'evolved' from anything else. All that the history of human value-preferences can show is that many kinds and qualities of value, which in earlier stages of development had 'right of entry' into the category of holiness, possessed religious 'sanction', have gradually lost that right and become extra-religious, profane values.

As a further proposition it is also axiomatic that the holy (*i.e.* whatever is of holy worth at a given time) is to be preferred before all other values, and has therefore the intrinsic right to demand the free *sacrifice* of every good belonging to another value-category.[1] This is the *basic liaison-principle* linking religion and morality. 'Sacrifice to holiness' is not only the very morality of religion, but also the religion of morality.

A most estimable writer on the philosophy of religion, Rudolf Otto, has recently expounded the qualities of holiness with remarkable depth and subtlety. In his book *Das Heilige*[2] he distinguishes a number of elements in that part of the holy which may be considered an 'irrational' supplement to those attributes of the divine which he groups together as 'rational'. To these elements Otto gives special Latin names in order to distinguish them clearly from similar but *extra*-religious values. Thus he adduces the *mysterium tremendum*, the element of *maiestas*, the elements of the

---

[1] See my classification of value-categories in *Der Formalismus in der Ethik und die materiale Wertethik*, Section IIB.

[2] Rudolf Otto, *Das Heilige: über das Irrationale in der Idee des Göttlichen und sein Verhältnis zum Rationalen*, Breslau 1917.

energeticum, mysteriosum, fascinosum (this last being that of attraction and
enticement, which counteracts the deterrent *tremendum*), the element
affording protection or atonement, etc. Little as I can accept the religious
epistemology which Otto develops in the later sections of his book, I the
more gladly salute in its purely *descriptive* section the first serious endeavour
to analyse the chief qualities of the value-modality 'holy'—the objective
characteristic of all and every religion—by the dialectical method of
phenomenology. In the true spirit of the phenomenological method
Otto rightly says of his own procedure: 'This (the category of holiness) is
perfectly *sui generis* and irreducible to any other; and therefore, like every
absolutely primary and elementary datum, while it admits of being discussed, it cannot be strictly defined. There is only one way to help
another to an understanding of it. He must be guided and led on by
consideration and discussion of the matter through the ways of his own
mind, until he reach the point at which "the numinous" in him perforce
begins to stir, to start into life and into consciousness. We can co-operate
in this process by bringing before his notice all that can be found in other
regions of the mind, already known and familiar, to resemble, or again to
afford some special contrast to, the particular experience we wish to
elucidate. Then we must add: "This *X* of ours is not precisely *this* experience, but akin to this one and the opposite of that other. Cannot you now
realize for yourself what it is?" In other words our *X* cannot, strictly
speaking, be taught, it can only be evoked, awakened in the mind; as
everything that comes "of the spirit" must be awakened' (*op. cit.*, p. 7)
[E.T. 1923 ed., p. 7, 1959 ed., p. 21].

This on the whole negative method of successively peeling away the
correlates and contraries that are felt to offer progressive indications to
the 'phenomenon *demonstrandum*', with the consequent laying bare of the
phenomenon and its presence to the inspecting mind, is the way which
leads to the *phenomenological scrutiny of the essence*. The indefinability of the *X*
under investigation (*per genus et differentia specifica*) is a sure sign that in
this *X* we have a genuine elementary essence which underlies ultimate
concepts but is itself 'inconceivable'. For 'to conceive' means to reduce the
object of a concept in terms of other concepts. It is not surprising that the
rationalistic philosopher decries this method as generally fruitless.
Unaware of its character as a mind-awakening and guiding procedure
(into which indirect thinking in judgments and inferences enters only as a
means of leading the mind to the threshold of discovery), he sees only
those judgments and inferences and overlooks the sense and nerve of the
whole procedure. He then agrees with the finding of Wilhelm Wundt[1]

---

[1] Cf. Wundt's criticism of Edmund Husserl's *Logische Untersuchungen.**

that phenomenology is a wholly profitless affair, since it consists in negative judgments and always ends in a tautology (such as that the holy is simply—the holy). Where this priceless verdict is unutterably mistaken is in this: Wundt takes the negative judgments—which in this method are no more than dialectic invitations to redirect the mind's attention closer to the all-important object—to imply theoretical rational definitions of some *thing*, and even the so-called tautology he regards as a theoretical rational definition instead of merely the concluding invitation to look here and now upon the *supraconceptual datum* which can *only* be beheld, to gaze directly upon its *pure* self-given state, now that the husks of approximation have been stripped away. Nobody in his senses could believe, however, that *as a theoretical rational definition* the 'tautology' would be anything but absurd.

Many who make use of this method (in our present field or any other) are surprisingly unaware that as a method it is basically none other than that of 'negative theology'. For the method of 'negative theology' itself arose purely from the deep conviction that the *divine* and holy form as such a prime elementary quality which can only be demonstrated by a slow process of elimination and analogy, a quality which must satisfy all concepts of the divine—positive and negative—but itself remains inconceivable. There is no doubt that as an approach and method phenomenology was first employed, in the time of Plotinus, in exactly this theological context. 'Negative theology' has also been a frequent victim of the misunderstanding that it employed negations to define the divine theoretically and not on the contrary to prevent its being prematurely defined in rational terms *before* its essence had been grasped. But to understand the meaning of negative theology one need only be clear about *one* constantly recurring fact concerning all religious discourse. This is the enormous disproportion subsisting, in rational linguistic expression describing religious experience of divinity, between what is truly and positively vouchsafed to mental vision and its often, indeed mostly, negative definitions. Otto himself gives an example which is very much to the point—indeed conclusive: ' "Eye hath not seen, nor ear heard, neither have entered into the heart of man, the things which God hath prepared for them that love him." Who does not feel the exalted sound of these words and the "Dionysiac" element of transport and fervour in them? It is instructive that in such phrases as these, in which consciousness would fain put its highest consummation into words, "all images fall away" and the mind turns from them to grasp expressions that are purely negative. And *it is still more instructive that in reading and hearing such words their merely negative character simply is not noticed;* that we can let whole chains of such negations enrapture, even intoxicate us, and that . . . deeply impressive hymns—have been composed, in which there is really nothing positive at all! All this teaches us the independence of the positive content of this experience from the implications of its overt conceptual expression, and how it can be firmly grasped, thoroughly understood, and profoundly appreciated, purely in, with, and from the feeling itself' (*op. cit.*, p. 36) [E.T. 1923 ed., p. 34, 1959 ed., p. 48].

Now if negative theology is rationalistically misunderstood, the reader or hearer is left with only the negative propositions in place of the positive datum which these propositions single out for us from the chaos of the finite, non-divine or merely analogically similar and seek to place before the mind's eye. And this is also true: if negative theology, which by nature is mystical technique rather than theory, is accepted, even by its champion, as *rational* theory, it must necessarily lead to religious nihilism—even to atheism. For an object whose every definition is negative is—even apart from formal categorical exactitude—nothing. So the result of such misunderstanding is that the most positive, most high repository of being and value is supplanted by its exact opposite—nothing.

But if negative theology, or rather its method, is understood properly in accordance with the business in hand, the proposition that it is the *basis of all positive theology* (and not *vice versa*) is as certainly true as that the eidetic phenomenology of any object-group is the ultimate basis of the positive science concerned with that group. All *positive* conceptual definitions of God are therefore by nature (*i.e.* as conceptual) no more than quasi-definitions or *analogical* definitions. Measuring the varying *nearness* of these analogical definitions to the intentional object is a task demanding more than simply an investigation of their obvious rational interconnection—though that they *should* so interlock is a requirement whose observance undoubtedly helps the progress of religious cognition. But the *final decision* as to the possibility or extent of *cognitive* value in any such analogy (or, for that matter, in any positive conceptual definition) lies with the religious consciousness, to be settled according to its own autonomous principles and in the light of that quality of divinity *self-'given'* to it (by negative theology, demonstrably *self*-given if at all)— together with a normative notion of the divine's internal consistency.

The attributes of God in natural religion

The three attributes *ens a se* (infinitude),* omnipotence and holiness are the most formal attributes of a being and object of 'divine' essence. It is as such that they have developed in the intentional objects of every religion, of the lowest as of the highest and absolute. They are the *only* attributes which unquestionably constitute and demarcate the objective domain of a mode of religious consciousness—in distinction from all other possible objects of consciousness.

In principle these attributes can become manifest, to the appropriate religious acts, in any entity whatsoever—no matter to what order of creation it belong, whether to nature, history or the soul of man. They are not limited to any one material realm of being. Neither do they 'derive' from any realm in the sense of having been in some way abstracted from objects of *pre*-religious experience or obtained from them by idealizing or analogizing processes. The extra-religious empirical object has always but two functions so far as they are concerned: for the subject it provides the springboard from which the religious act may leap up to them; for the immediate reality of the divine it is the object in and through which it becomes manifest.

Religious acts, with their objective domain of being and value, thus form a basically closed system—more or less in the same way as do acts of external perception taken in conjunction with the external world. If we examine them for their essential content, our inquiry is not concerned in any way with the question of which acts of a religious kind are 'right' or 'wrong' and which objects of a religious kind are 'real' or 'imaginary'. Just as any astronomical theory, *e.g.* that of Thales concerning the sun, is not necessarily 'right', though as 'astronomical' it remains different in kind from, say, a psychological theory, so a religious object—say Apollo, Artemis, the most primitive fetish—does not have to correspond to true religion and its God. Notwithstanding its possible falsity it still *'belongs to a sphere' of reality and value* which from the beginning of things has subsisted as surely and irrefutably as the constellations in *their* sphere—however falteringly the images and concepts of either sphere have developed in human history.

This is therefore the *first sure truth* of all religious phenomenology: on whatever level of his *religious development* he may be, the human being is *invariably* looking into a realm of being and value which is in basis and origin utterly different from the whole remaining empirical world; it is not inferred from that other world, neither won from it by idealization, and access to it is possible solely in the religious act.

This is the proposition of the *originality and non-derivation of religious experience*.

All genetic problems of natural religion, all questions regarding the truth or falsity of positive religion, and so all problems of justification, assume this proposition; while it is still in doubt they may not be fruitfully discussed.

However manifold and abundant the progress and development of religion, the *whole* development—so far as it is not distracted by extra-religious cultural forces—takes place solely *within* the sphere of the religious realm of being and of the religious act by which access is had to that realm.

For that reason it is senseless to wish to trace a development of man *towards* religion.

Just as senseless is any question concerning the genesis of the religious object from the human soul or the genesis of religious objectification as such. It is only meaningful to ask in this respect how the *material* of one objective representation arose *determined* by another. Religion—so far as it does develop—develops not heterogenetically but autogenetically; or rather religions, apart from special acts of God, are transformed one from another.

Thus the much-favoured question of religion's historical *origin* is as senseless as the question of the historical origin of speech and reason. Just as the possession of word and reason is what first makes us man[1] (and different in kind from the animal) but also first circumscribes the whole domain of *possible* historical experience and knowledge, so man's connection with the divine through the religious act and divine manifestation is an inherent element in *essential human nature.* In this respect Otto has something very apposite and imaginative to say with reference to all attempts (such as that of Paul Natorp) to find a 'religion within the bounds of pure reason' or 'humanity': 'And for that matter, this proceeding of constructing a "humanity" prior to and apart from the most central and potent of human capacities is like nothing so much as the attempt to frame a standard idea of the human body after previously cutting off the head'.[2]

No less senseless is any question which asks how ever man came from pre-religious knowledge to the *divine.* For all ideas and representations of profane and finite reality (which only within the zone of *theistic* civilization appears as that *single, ordered whole* we call 'world') have always and everywhere been formed under the determining influence of *existing* religious ideas. This has been the case even when the existence of divinity has been deliberately discounted, or its reality denied, in the course of investigating the finite world. Correspondingly, all rational knowledge concerned with the world as a whole—'worldly wisdom'—everywhere moves, and has always moved, within the *scope* of possibilities prescribed to it by the prevailing formal categories of natural religion (not positive religion revealed through persons). Here 'prescribed' is not used in the

---

[1] Cf. '*Zur Idee des Menschen*' in my collection of essays, *Vom Umsturz der Werte.*
[2] *Op. cit.*, p. 40 [E.T. 1923 ed., p. 37, 1959 ed., p. 51].

sense of conscious prescription but in the sense of *principles* offered to the human mind as a *foundation* for the exercise of its cognitive abilities within the order of its modes of cognition. Whatever he bends his will to in the matter, man can only know and 'think' the world in a manner consonant with the possibility of its being a dependency or effect of that reality which he primarily considers 'divine'—'divine' of course only within the variation-limits of the three formal constituents of divinity we have listed. Thus for example only the unity of God guarantees the unity of the world.*

The position is different—different in principle—when we advance beyond those three formal attributes of divinity and the *possible* objects comprised in its essence and seek new attributes of the reality given or suspected as divine. For the essential structure of facts and values belonging to the finite world, a structure revealed to man through his experience here-below and *in terms of which* he conceives all contingent entities, now enters as *co-determinant* of all further attributes.

It is not until we come to these supraformal attributes (*e.g.* spirit, mind, reason, will, love, mercy, omniscience, goodness, creatorship) that we find in the religious act (as opposed here to metaphysics) the way of thinking of the real embodiment of the 'divine' essence as if he were so constituted that this world is the possible and natural *revelation of his nature*—his *work*, his creation. In other words, once we possess the religious assurance that God *is*, that the world *is*, being in its qualitative substance God's manifestation and in its reality his work, we continue our task of defining God by passing repeatedly from the essential, supraformal *material* of the world to predication of God's attributes. Though in the process we do not make philosophical inferences, the procedure adopted by the religious act may be expressed in the *form* of conclusions. That is to say, though there are 'inferences' of a kind, they are not causal but *analogical* inferences; moreover, the sole ingredients of the operation are intuited essences and general principles of relation which apply *a priori* to any possible world. Thus *empirical abstractions* and principles of inter-relation between *contingent facts* can never form part of these *quasi-*inferences. What is ascertained is not the *fact* of God's causal relation to the world, nor the *fact* of his self-revelation in it, but only what God 'must' be if such things are possible as the content of natural revelation and that part of his universal activity which he discloses in the world. If it is necessary to attribute, in absolute form and infinite degree, the essences of this world to God, this is not because God is the cause of the world and the effect cannot be more perfect than the cause (or because the cause must contain the perfections of the effect). For in itself this causal hypothesis is by no means certain; in fact we constantly encounter instances when in strict regularity the more perfect is created from the less—that is even the kind of causation which all modern 'evolutionary' theories consider to govern the world. No: if such an attribution is necessary it is because God is *revealed* in the world and its structure, because it symbolically mirrors him, because its essential unities hold 'traces', indications of his nature, pointers to his essence. And if, notwithstanding, the causal hypothesis holds good, it is only because God is also the cause of *reality* for some of these essences. But it may not in this connection be applied to God as a mere 'instance of applicability' of some universally valid causal principle. It is thus not the causal but the *symbolic* connection between God and the world which leads to the attribution, the predicative transference.

It is this *transference* which initiates and underlies a *natural theology*, *ascribing positive attributes to God*—this in distinction from the method of negative theology, which (rightly understood) remains the basis of the other. The price, however, paid for positively defining the holy, infinite, omnipotent *ens a se* is that the definitions shall be of utterly *inadequate*, *inexplicit and merely analogical validity*.

First, their *inadequacy*. It is from the outset clear to us in natural religion and theology that, beyond his formal essential definitions, the nature of God must be infinitely richer than this method can help us men to know. For even if the essential qualities and relations found or discoverable in this actual world have limitless validity beyond the mere fact of *this* world—validity for all *possible* worlds—they are still infinitely far from representing the sum total of *all* possible essences. For the only essences to which we have access are those which are realized in *this* world in some form—albeit as possible fictions. But God, as *ens a se*, is the sum and epitome not only of essences realized in this world but of *all possible essences*. For that reason we can acquire a *natural* knowledge of his attributes only in so far as he reveals himself in *this* world. Only a positive self-revelation in holy persons could—and can—lead us further and instruct us in the manner of his essential being, independently of his natural *manifestation* in this world. The inadequacy of our acquaintance with God—his infinite overflowing of the borders of inner vision, which the believer must feel even if he adequately knew all the essences of the world—these remain directly present to us in the act of veneration. We yet know that we do not know that part of him which is not mirrored in *our* world's essential character.*

Again, the positive definitions offer no more than *inexplicit* 'attributes' of God. That is to say that when we use expressions such as 'the mind of

God', 'the reason, will of God' and the like, we know that they do not in any way correspond to parts of God, whether real or abstract, but merely enhance certain classifiable similarities which subsist between on the one hand a perfectly single, homogeneous and indivisible being and, on the other, the differently *ordered* being and nature of a divisible and finite creature.[1] Or we may express it thus: since God of his nature *transcends* the categorical divison of the entity into substantial and attributive being (a division applicable therefore only to finite being as such), each substantive attribute represents *in toto* the *whole* of his being, and each attributive quality represents the *whole* spectrum of his single, homogeneous, indivisible essence.

Positive specifications of God are *analogical* in that they *parallel* the absolute and infinite nature of divine being by themselves being absolute and infinite. But in spite of God's essential similarity 'as' mind to the finite mind, or 'as' rational will to finite rational will, etc., there is not only an existential difference between God, as *infinite* will, reason, etc., and finite will or reason, but also an *essential difference*, which does not of course preclude essential similarity (of any degree), for only things different in quality can be similar.

Like the inadequacy of natural knowledge, the *inexplicit* character and the *analogical* nature of divine attributes are qualities of which we first become conscious in the performance of religious acts. Of *inexplicitness* the believer grows aware when, immersed in prayer and devotion, he finds that the nearer his approach to God the *more* urgently he must envisage God as ἄρρητον, *i.e.* that which arouses reluctance to apply to it the categories of human thought and speech. For even if there are *genuine* categories of the 'supersensual' (*i.e.* the above-mentioned purely formal categories), as a *whole* the categories of our thinking and of life in this world—the categories of both internal and external worlds—are obviously insufficient to describe the *being* and essence of God. If for example we try to relate the categories of substance, power and activity, we are obliged to say that God's power coincides with his substance, but that his power also coincides with his activity, that—in a word—all coalesce in *one*. And so it is with all other categories of finite being.[2]

That our knowledge of the positive attributes of God is *analogical* by

[1] Thus here the similarity does not rest on a part-for-part *identitas partium*; the quasi-identity which we imply in propositions such as 'God is mind, reason, will, etc.', rests only on God's assimilability to the essential *substratum* of such concepts as mind and reason.

[2] Self-evidently, the same applies to the categories of cause-effect, end-means. For example, the prime cause is not only a different cause from all other known causes, but its very causal *quality* is different from all other kinds of causality.

nature is made clear in the great *freedom of imagery* found in religious language, though in serious religious experience the images are never accepted as anything more than images. To that extent the linguistic usages of religion are for the most part more judicious and sensitive, but also more adequate, than those of metaphysics and theology. The method they follow is this: the pious spirit, in truly *religious* awareness that God's positive qualities transcend all 'concepts', employs a great number of images, often unashamedly concrete images, with reference to God, so that by a process one can call reciprocal interference he may express what is real and present to the religious act in a *supraconceptual* way. The justification of this religious linguistic method[1] lies in the very intuition that in principle all positive definitions of God are of a uniformly *analogical* character. It is no less clear that the supersensory vision of God which is given to the mind in religious acts, and only in their living performance, is not only 'single' in relation to the multiplicity of images; it is also 'simple' where the images may be more or less elaborately figurative and possess a greater or lesser degree of resemblance to the 'real' intentional object they symbolically express.[2] For in the 'intersection of images' the conjunction is catalytic for their truly meaningful elements, which are enabled to flow together in *one* indivisible impression, while in the clash of inessentials the dross of '*mere*' figure and likeness is cast out and purged from the intentional meaning; but this is only possible if the mind *notices* and as it were *estimates* the way in which, and the extent to which, the individual images find *fulfilment* in the object of the religious act.

It is the profound error of all gnosticism (that is, any attempt to merge natural—if not all—religion in conceptual metaphysics or regard the latter as a 'higher' form of theology) that it fails to appreciate that all *positive* definitions of God are necessarily of no more than an *analogical* character. It assumes the positive predicates of God in a categorical sense and turns them into (at least) abstract or 'metaphysical' parts of God instead of seeing that they are only approximations to analogies existing between an aspect of the single and indivisible divine essence and a similar thing in the finite world. Seen from the viewpoint of this error, which is founded in the *religious* defect of approaching God without due awe, as if he might be directly and adequately 'conceived' in explicit and

[1] A full exposition of the inner methodology of religious language would require a special and searchingly detailed examination of instances, such as is impossible in the present context. Let the reader, for example, consider the range of expressions designating the Mother of God in the Litany of Loretto.

[2] How else could the greater or lesser congruence of images, and the aptness of similes and analogies be consciously noted, if the simple datum offered to the religious act did not provide a *yardstick*?

non-figurative terms, the language of religion, with its frequent use of emphatically concrete images, appears to gnosticism as 'anthropomorphism' or mere 'metaphysics for the people'. That is the verdict of Spinoza, Hegel, Fichte and Hartmann *inter alia*. But in fact precisely the *reverse* is true. It is at the door of Doctor Metaphysicus that we may lay the charge of *anthropomorphism*, in that he understands neither God's transcendence in *principle* of finite intellectual categories nor the essential difference between all divine positive attributes and human attributes bearing the same name (the German pantheists, for example, identify divine with human reason); thus apart from recognizing a quantitative difference (finite against infinite) he supposes an *essential identity*. The religious man, on the other hand, even the most uncultivated, knows very well that all the thousand and one names and images he bestows on God are 'only' names and images, and that all their purpose is to clarify, or perhaps awaken in others, the *one and undivided* substance of the intentional object, which is inadequately present to him in the religious act itself. Nobody who calls God 'Our Father' in the Lord's Prayer looks upon the 'Father' as more than an expression of the *analogical* father-child relationship of God and man, and even this analogy is not held to extend beyond the *essence* of fatherliness and childhood, certainly not into all that actual fathers and children have empirically in common. So far from its being true that religion is 'the people's metaphysics', this gnostic kind of metaphysics is rather the *professional snob-'religion'* of the intellectual caste. For, whatever is genuinely religious in the gnostic concepts of God elaborated by these pantheistic metaphysicians has evolved only by learned filtration of traditional religious language—from which it is distinguished not by its direct conceptual expression, as against indirect and figurative meaning, but by the *flatness and bloodlessness* of its imagery.

The positive natural attributes of God are taken, as I have said, from the essential materials of the world. Before I ask what these attributes are, as distinct from those we called formal and as distinct from those which can only be ascribed to God's positive self-revelation in holy persons, let me ask how the sphere of *natural religion* derives them from the world.

Although in this sphere man's idea of God shows itself dependent on his *idea* of the nature of the world, in this differing from the formal definitions,[1]

[1] Of the formal definitions it is also true to say that we know the world's existence and essence, from the outset, 'in the light' of a (formal) divinity—whose subjective conception is itself, of course, variable by historical and social factors. But of the supraformal, substantive definitions of God's natural attributes the contrary is true: we first know them only in the light of our insight into the nature of the

on which, as we have seen, the idea of the *world* is on the contrary dependent, it is by no means from the reasoned philosophical form of the world-
idea that natural religion derives the positive attributes which it predicates
of God. It is only natural *theology*, not natural religion, which depends on
philosophy and its special methods of cognition. No, the natural religion
which is a constituent of any concrete religion depends on the *prevailing
historical variant of the natural Weltanschauung*—the Weltanschauung of the
race in the relevant ages and societies of history.[1]

What determines a community's living, positive idea of God is the overall structure and system of the cosmic object which, underwritten by the
prevailing order of values (the 'ethos'*), stands in the mind of the
community. But the form of Weltanschauung differs according to race,
civilization, nation, calling,[2] though of course always within the general
limits of the forms of Weltanschauung natural to the species man. It may
be widely divergent from the *doctrinal* formulae of a traditional religious
system, indeed it may—all unbeknown to the members of the community
—be standing in rudest opposition. To give an example, men may be
firmly convinced with their conscious judgment that they profess the
Christian idea of God, with all the traditional attributes of spirituality,
love, goodness, mercy, righteousness. But at the same time, as to the actual
form of their Weltanschauung, they may be ruled by a totally different
idea of God. For the structure of the natural religious consciousness can
only include God's love (for example) *if* love corresponds to the prevalent
form of Weltanschauung: that is, only if men live with a sense that *love* is
what leads, governs, prevails in their midst—not if completely different
things (power, economic expansion, etc.), are so 'felt'. Therefore not the
slightest inference as to a community's true natural beliefs may be drawn
from the fact that its intellectuals (philosophers, theologians) *teach* in
schools the Christian concept of God and reject in theory, say, Nietzsche's
doctrine of power. The community's natural Weltanschauung and
religion, and those very intellectuals too, may in fact be controlled by
quite a different concept of God—perhaps one corresponding in ideas and
values with Nietzsche's 'will to power'. Germany before 1914 was for
example obviously militaristic in its dominant forms of Weltanschauung

world; here we no longer know the world in the light of God but know God in the
mirror of the world. Quite apart from the qualitative variability of the conception of
formal divinity, the variability of the conception of God's positive attributes is
not only quantitatively greater but of an entirely different order of magnitude.

[1] The reader is referred to the definition of 'Weltanschauung' in 'The Nature of
Philosophy' (pp. 82 *et seq.*).

[2] Cf. a typology of various group-Weltanschauungen in my *Der Genius des
Krieges*, especially the chapter entitled '*Die geistige Einheit Europas*'.

and world-values; its 'religion' was the will to power through economic and military expansion. It happens that Nietzsche's metaphysical formulae fitted its actual Weltanschauung extremely well. In the circumstances it could hardly, seen as a whole, have been moved by a natural religion corresponding to the proposition that 'God is love' or 'God is mind'. But that certainly did not prevent the proposition that 'God is mind' from being taught in all schools, nor the majority of philosophers and theologians from teaching and seeking to prove it in *Hochschulen*; nor did it mean that Nietzsche's metaphysics found a conscious following outside very small groups.

Neither is there any limit to the extent by which natural theology may diverge from the prevailing natural religion. For that reason it is no use pointing to the widespread dissemination of 'true doctrine' in order to prove that the German Weltanschauung has been more attuned to Christianity than to the formulae of Nietzsche. It is much rather the rule, even, that the prevailing forms of Weltanschauung, if they are openly expressed at all, are expressed only by a tiny minority, while the overwhelming majority, though in fact sharing the same Weltanschauung, still cling (in the sphere of considered judgment) to convictions which have been handed down and do *not* assort with the Weltanschauung that overrules them. The living, belief-implying act may widely diverge from the belief-expressing *judgment*. For the most part group-Weltanschauungen are not generally known for what they are until they *change*. While they yet reign, they are as a faith taken for granted, unsensed and unremarked— like the pressure of the air.

Hence it is a matter of great difficulty to know, first, a community's natural historical forms of Weltanschauung and ethos, and subsequently its natural religion. For it is a matter of looking *behind* expressed judgments and formulae—behind the whole sphere of conscious reflection—to discover that hidden, hovering, intuitive element which, on the farther side of speech and judgment, *moves* and *governs* the mind of the group. The identity of religious language or formulae of belief in different periods, within different nations or among people of differing occupations (*e.g.* smallholders or industrial workers) still leaves natural belief the widest scope with regard to that *content* of the idea of God which hovers and *presides* over the implementation of beliefs. And it is the hovering *X*, steering and ruling the movements of thought and volition, which belongs to the very constitution of natural religion as well as its *pro tempore* form—certainly not learned theories or traditional formulae got by rote.

Natural *theology*, on the other hand, as belonging to the sphere of

conscious reflection, must employ throughout the discipline of *philosophical*
cognition, and must apply *this* to the essential reality of the world, if it
wishes to know the positive attributes of God.

Once, independently of all inferences from the nature and constitution
of the world, there is an unassailable religious certainty of an absolutely
holy and infinite *ens a se,* and once the religious act grasps the utter dependence of every finite *ens ab alio* on this formal God (since in so far as it
is real it is instituted, borne and sustained by the *ens a se*), then all such
religious knowledge of God as may further arise from observation of the
world can only relate to the constitutional *qualities* of the *ens a se.*

But the most fundamental and the principal positive (analogical)
attribute of God is *mentality.*[1]

Our task, then, is to characterize the *religious* origin and meaning of the
religious intuition, amounting as it does to a qualitative—not existential—
inference from this world that *what* is revealed of God and proclaimed in
this world as its basis is more thàn a blind *omnipotence*, more than a driving
force, more than a passive cosmic *soul*, more than a cosmic *life*—is more,
needless to say, than any physical or corporeal being—: is *mind.*

The word *mind* designates something which man finds or can find,
empirically, only in the world and only in that part of the world *which he
is.* But how does man come to bestow on God, as basis of the whole world
(which is not simply mind, but contains apart from mind quite other
groups of facts and *types of cause*), a positive attribute discoverable only in
so *minute* a part of the world as the human race—one race living in the
cosmic isolation of this little planet? Since it is certainly not possible to
develop the mentality of God analytically from the concepts *ens a se* or
holiness, the only meaningful basis for the assumption (meaningful
objectively as well as in its justification) must lie in the presumable fact
that, quite independently of the premise that God exists, man feels and
considers not only himself but the whole world to be *inspirited*, pervaded by
mind. It is possible to ascribe *mentality* to God by analogy only if the
complex of meaningful acts and correlates found in man and called 'mind'

---

[1] *Geistigkeit.* The incongruity of German and English terminologies forces a
decision between 'mind' and 'spirit' as a translation of *Geist.* If 'mind', 'mental'
and 'mentality' have been preferred to 'spirit' and its derivatives, this is principally because they are more concrete and imply intelligence and volition. This
will be found to accord with Scheler's concept, as it may be inferred from his
arguments. Furthermore, if, as Scheler insists, we are to treat God's positive
attributions as analogical, the analogy we make in this instance is surely with the
mind of which we have concrete empirical knowledge, rather than with the
Protean abstraction known as 'spirit'. There are further reasons for the choice
which it would be inappropriate to detail here. The special sense of 'mentality'
here will be self-evident to the reader (*Translator*).

is *more* than, and another kind of thing from, a *mere* 'piece' or 'part' of the world.

Now the noetic principles whereby the religious act comes to understand God as mind—rules which it 'follows' without having to consider them—are at bottom *perfectly simple* in character.

The first condition is that the human agent of the religious act should have a vital sense that his core—the seat of his selfhood—abides in the 'act-centre' of his *mental* acts—not, then, primarily in his body or in his perceptible psychical states. Mental acts are not inwardly perceptible, observable; they have *being* only *as* performable acts and exist only in their execution.[1] But the *manner* and *essential aspect* in which man becomes perceptible to himself may vary within a wide range of possibilities. In this respect I have elsewhere described two basic phenomena.[2] In the first of these the human being has a vital sense that the nucleus of his mental acts is his *core*, the master of his instincts, *governor* and *guide* of his sensory functions; moreover, he feels it as the *constant* round which his instinctual impulses and sensations flow eddying by. In the second, a phenomenon in polar opposition, he locates the seat of his selfhood in the *body*, and regards everything within him which pertains to mental acts as fleeting insubstantiality, as secondary phenomena attendant on the body-constant. Of these polarized types of *self-appraisal*, the second precludes, in so far as it is actualized, the completion of the religious act whereby the believer knows that 'God is mind'. Thus, the first type is a permanent and fundamental *condition* for the execution of that cognitive religious act. As the apostle says, it is only in so far as a man *lives* in the spirit (or *mind*), and not in the belly, that he can know in a religious act that *God is mind*. Herein lies yet another basic difference between metaphysical and religious knowledge. For the truth that the world-basis is by nature mental or spiritual is one that metaphysics can also know *without* this personal moral condition of 'living in the spirit', of *having one's substance* in the mind. But the mere possession of this knowledge in the judicative sector of consciousness means absolutely nothing in a *religious* sense. A man may form this judgment and yet be feeling that his centre, his *ego*, resides not in his mental 'act-centre' but in his belly. In that case he has no kind of *religious* knowledge that God is mind. The converse is not unthinkable: a man may be naturalist or materialist in theory, through the effects of tradition and intellectual environment, yet may fulfil the *precondition* of knowing God as mind in a

[1] . . . or in empirical stirrings of activity, which attest consciousness of the specific 'ability' to perform this kind of act, *i.e.* act-potentiality.

[2] Cf. the discussion of body and person in *Formalismus in der Ethik, etc.*, Section VIA, subsection 3f.

religious way. Of course his metaphysics and his religious consciousness are then contradictory and incompatible. Yet in a religious sense he stands nearer the truth than the 'spiritualistic' metaphysician who lives in the belly.

Once one is firmly persuaded that God is mind, one cannot remain unaware of an instantly perceptible *interrelation of the world and mental acts*, which may be described as follows in the language of philosophical apperception. The *being* and *thus*ness of the world (or of any given object in external or internal worlds) are self-evidently *in*dependent of the here-and-now existence of any individual or act envisaging that being as an object. Whether or not the entity enters into any one of the following ontic relations with a human mind—cognition/intentionality, liking/value, volition/resistance—is a consideration which, one way or the other, can neither posit nor delete its being. This truth is evident to us in every act of cognition and, generally speaking, in every mental act. It is inseparable from the sense of the words 'being' and 'object'.[1] It is not necessary to compare a number of acts or their identifiable content, neither need we examine relationships or classify the object-entities. Such procedure may be important for determining the being's formal or typical properties and assigning it to predetermined classes of essence or quality—but that is another matter.

But in spite of every entity's essential independence and transcendence of the here-and-now act, and indifference in this respect to the existence of the individual performing the act, it is *no less* evident that every possible extra-mental entity stands *in (inter-) dependence on a possible mental entity*. To all knowledge (and indeed all intentional acts) a being must correspond, and to every being a possible knowledge. Similarly, to all liking and preference there must correspond a value-bearing entity, and to every such entity a liking or preference. That is the essential relation which subsists between the act *qua* merely performable being and the object *qua* existent being (these representing their intrinsic and essential capacities). It is a relation which I have developed elsewhere as one of philosophy's most fundamental axioms.[2]

But what is true of the nature of the mental act and of the nature of the existent object, as such, must also be true for every particular *contingent entity*, which corresponds to either one 'nature' or the other.

The idea of an *absolutely* unknowable being is therefore, by the principle

---

[1] Here the object's 'independence' of the mind—and thus of all here-and-now empirical consciousness of a thing—is a *consequence* of the being of the object, and not an *inherent property of the entity*.

[2] See *Formalismus in der Ethik*, Section VIA, subsection 3.

of contradiction and in the light of this generalization, self-contradictory. But it is not self-contradictory in a purely analytical sense,[1] *i.e. only* by the principle of contradiction. By *that* principle, on the other hand, it is equally senseless to envisage some pre-existent *cognitive intention* corresponding to no kind of existent.

This fundamental axiom, though it is found in the human mind, and can indeed be found in every act of the human mind, is nevertheless quite independent of the purely contingent existence of the *human* mind or of man himself. It does not have any kind of special application to the particular attributes of mind as *human* mind, but refers to the *eternal essence of mind* in general. It refers solely to an essential constitutional relationship between mind and world in relation to which it is merely a gratuitous fact that it is found *in* man and his contingent empirical world. Its validity thus enjoys a like independence of this contingent world's existence: it is true for *any possible world.*

We have now come to the point where we may consider *together* and as one the *two* fundamental axioms which yield the (in itself) unitary basic religious intuition that 'God is mind'—*i.e.* that the holy *ens a se* is mind. Thus we may simultaneously envisage the world's radical existential independence of the concrete human mind, or its evident transcendence (in each of its objects) of every datum of itself that may become immanent in human consciousness, *and*—notwithstanding—its essential *dependence* on *mind in general, i.e.* on something which man has in common with the *essence of mind.* For it directly follows that the same entity which is given to the human mind as independent of it and transcending it in every object, being *thus* superior to the *human* consciousness, must nevertheless, for the sake *solely* of its being,[2] have a mental power as its correlate—a mental power standing in a relationship to the world in ipseity similar to that of the mental subject man to the immediate environment over which *he* has powers of disposition. A similar—not the same relationship. For the first of the two axioms, that of every entity's independence of the human mind and transcendence, as an object, of any human consciousness, already indicates a disparity in the two relationships and thereby precludes anthropomorphism. The being which 'is' independently of the being of human mind, postulates, on the grounds of being's essential dependence on mind in general, a simultaneous and unconditional ontological dependence on some mind unknown, *X,* which cannot possibly be the

[1] This is the erroneous belief of the idealism of subjective consciousness, which posits *esse = percipi,* whereupon the *idea* of a non-perceptible being would of course also be analytically self-contradictory.

[2] Not therefore for the sake of its mere properties: its regular ordering or teleological structure.

human mind; the being of the object, evidently transcending human consciousness, requires to be fully *immanent* in a mind which, by an intrinsic impossibility, *cannot*, again, be the human mind.

We are now in a position to see in the relation of the human mind to the world an essential interdependence of world and mind in general, with reference to which it is nevertheless obvious that the existent mind which, in accordance with this general principle, corresponds to the existent world is by no means the human mind—and indeed *cannot* be a mind of the nature of the human. For it is as evident that this world exists independently of the existence and essence of the human mind, as that mind and world stand in general mutual dependence. That which is existentially independent (as the existing world, of the existing human mind) is at the same time essentially dependent, given the general nature of *world* and *mind*.

We may also express the position in the *form* of a syllogism, whose steps are as follows:

1. The being of this world is independent of the existence of *my* mental act and the existence of *any* act of the same nature; each one of the world's objects is, if immanent at all, only *partly* and inadequately immanent in such mental acts.

2. Nevertheless, to the being of any possible world there corresponds a possible mind, and to every object there belongs *full possible immanence* in that mind.

3. Thus there corresponds to the world a mind which, *if* I posit the world, I must necessarily posit with it and which (by the first premise) cannot be the human mind—either in existence or essence.

However this syllogism is not traced through afresh in the religious act of knowing God as mind. One may only say that the religious act proceeds in *conformity* with the sense of the above propositions, that in apprehending the human mind as the 'type' of mind, and the relation of human mind to the world as altogether an essential relation of mind and world, it immediately transfers the *idea* of this type to the holy *ens a se* of whose existence it is already certain.[1]

---

[1] Admittedly there are theoretical philosophies which—if true—would destroy this implicit logic of the religious act. Among them is epistemological 'idealism' (Berkeley, Fichte), which thinks fit to degrade all being to the possible content of consciousness and thereby misrepresents the meaning of the concept 'being', the nature of the transcendence of the object and the nature of transcendental consciousness. For the para-logical *motive* for the turning of attention to the mind of God lies only in the clearly seen and experienced *conflict* and *tension* between the world's real transcendence of the human consciousness and the essential connection, found notwithstanding in the human mind, of mind and world in their generality. But absolute ontologism is no less destructive of the implicit logic of the

The task of describing and illuminating the nature of this religious transaction in accurate detail, of making it—so to speak—visible to the reader, is attended with difficulties so great that at this point I feel more than ever the utter inadequacy of human language. It is like some unheard-of, mysterious diama in the soul's deepest depths, through which the *religious* knowledge that the *holy ens a se* must be a *spirit of the kind called mind* is gradually pieced together. Man must have a clear and lively sense—in his every awareness and feeling of the world, in all his acting on the world, or any one of its objects—of how utterly *indifferent* a thing he is, how indifferent his *ego* and consciousness, for the world's existence, and how *impotent* his mind against the world's fulness of being, or even one element of that fulness. The guiding genius which will lead him to the sense of his indifference is the virtue of *humility* of mind, for which he has been prepared by his formal knowledge of the holy *ens a se* and of his own nothingness. He must feel plainly in his heart, and not merely know, how sublimely *indifferent* it is to the sun whether or not it is perceived, thought of or valued by him and his like—by any 'I' at all. To the sense of impotence he is led by another guiding genius, the virtue of *awe*, which I have elsewhere described as the emotional consciousness of the *real* insufficiency of our knowledge of any object, which is equivalent to a genuine (even perfect, invincible) *knowledge* of our partial incapacity for knowledge.[1] Awe simply gives plain expression, in the 'feeling of . . .' form, to something which accompanies every intentional act of for example perception, every act of thought and representation, namely, direct objective evidence not only that any intentional content is inadequate to the object-in-entirety, but that even an *infinite sum* of such contents would still be inadequate, since with every cognitive advance the object offers a proportional *increase* in the number of 'unknown' aspects and features which, while yet unknown, are presented as knowable and, in general essence, pre-intended.

But with awareness of the 'utterly indifferent' significance of one's own and all human 'thinking' for the subsistence and modification of things there must be intimately connected a direct insight into the *essential reference* of all possible objects and existence in general to something of the

religious act. (It is, for example, a basic premise of all kinds of materialism and naturalism.) In this view, as opposed to epistemological idealism, it is the essential relationship of act and object, mind and world, which is misunderstood—that relationship which, despite the world-reality's evident independence of the existence and contingent nature of the human mind, and despite also the object's transcendence of the human mind, yet demands *a* mind on whose essence and existence the world is dependent, and in which the object can be fully immanent.

[1] See '*Zur Rehabilitierung der Tugend*' in collected essays *Vom Umsturz der Werte*.

On the Eternal in Man

nature, broadly speaking, of mind. However *fortuitously* concrete acts *A* or *B* encounter object *a* or object *b*, the bond between the nature of the intentional act and the nature of the existent object (in a resistance- or value-capacity) remains an *essential, eternal and indestructible bond*.[1] There is a *dignity and sublimity* of the mind *as* mind, in virtue of which, even if the concrete human mind is but part and parcel of the world, mind itself cannot of its nature be *nothing but* a part of the world: it must at the same time be 'that' wherein the being of all things is conjoined and inter-related, 'that' which renders possible one entity's *ideal* participation in the being of another, 'that' wherein all things can be concentrated in unity *without* alteration of their qualitative modes of existence. To be alive to, to feel this eternal dignity and sublimity of mind, to feel it *in* and *with* the unutterable frailty, fallibility and instability of the *existing* human mind which is the only example directly vouchsafed to us of anything of the nature of mind—that is the *second* act of that mysterious drama in which the religious knowledge of *God as mind* takes shape. The third and last is the act of attaching the attribute 'mind' to the holy *ens a se* of which we already feel assured, and to this is joined the experience of the shining of infinite reason—its manifestation—into all rightful activity of finite reason; or the suffusion of the *world's objects and their meaning* by the ideas and values which stand, in their hierarchy, as correlates of the action of infinite reason.[2]

---

[1] It is only for the nature of the mental act and the nature of an existence itself, in their pure and naked state, that this essential bond is directly and absolutely self-evident. At this stage *forms* of objects (their objective forms) and *forms* and functions of mental acts are not envisaged.

[2] Perhaps no man's thought revolved so searchingly and profoundly round this inner drama as that of Blaise Pascal in his day. Descartes had brought the mind's dignity and sublimity to his attention in the inadequate form of *cogito ergo sum*; Pascal seized upon the simultaneous frailty of the human mind.

In the following words E. von Hartmann makes a deep and striking appraisal of the right relation of the human mind to nature and God—while at the same time properly castigating the false theories of naturalism and transcendental idealism:

'From the standpoint of *naturalism*, where nature is an ultimate, setting an impassable frontier to induction, natural laws and forces necessarily appear as *non-derived* and therefore eternal, immutable. Here, then, the *respect* felt for them by the conscious mind can *never be too great*: the individual consciousness, briefly emerging and soon to fade, must bow in humility before the omnipotence of eternal nature, whose mere fleeting product it is. The mind stands *impotent* in the sense of its littleness and nothingness before nature's immeasurable greatness in time, space and dynamic force. For the earth is but a speck of dust in the edifice of the world, and yet the smallest fragment of the earth can, in the shape of a stone, smash the life of a man and extinguish his consciousness. The mood appropriate to naturalism is *terror* of nature's immensity and *dread* of her might, of the inexorable regularity of her pulverizing wheels (*Preussisches Jahrbuch*, Vol. 101, No. 2, pp. 228-36).

'From the standpoint of *transcendental idealism*, on the other hand, nature is a *pure illusion*, and a self-delusion of the conscious mind. Its immensity, power and apparent infinitude are merely bestowed upon it by the mind, and as a dreamer ceases to be frightened by the spectres of a nightmare when it "dawns" upon him that he dreams, so all the transcendental idealist's respect for nature vanishes as soon as it occurs to him that nature is but *his creation*—an *illusion* which he is impelled to conjure up for himself. Thereupon, respect for the grandeur of nature, the might of her forces, the inviolability of her laws, is converted into respect for the might and grandeur of his own mind and the inviolability of its psychological laws. With sovereign arbitrariness the mind could play tricks with its nature (*mit seiner Natur*), did not the psychological laws of its *modus operandi* set bounds to its arbitrary power. But always it remains the *possessor* and its nature (*seine Natur*) the *property* of its consciousness. The mood appropriate to transcendental idealism is *contempt* for nature and overweening *pride* in the conscious mind (Fichte, Stirner, Nietzsche).

'*Transcendental realism* cuts away what is incorrect in these two viewpoints and makes a synthesis of that which is right. It cannot share naturalism's veneration of nature, which it regards as a mere product of mind, the prime cause. Mind posited it at the beginning of finite time and will take it back at the end of finite time; it is not eternal, but once was not, and "one day" will again not be. Only the mind that can posit and remove it is eternal. The laws of nature are immutable only for the finite duration of the world-process with which they begin and end. Before *the mind which posited nature* and continues to posit it, before that mind's grandeur and might, the conscious mind *bows in veneration*. Before its created *work*—never! For man knows that he himself is mind of that mind, that it stands much closer to him than nature, that in him that creator-mind has come to its own, that in him nature has most nearly attained the purpose for which it was created. The spatial immensity of nature can *no longer impress* him who knows that what matters is not that, but the inner recesses of the mind, which have nothing in common with spatial extension. The immeasurable duration of the natural process shrivels to nothing beside the eternity of mind, of which the human mind partakes in essence if not in its consciousness. The raw violence of natural forces may crush the body of man, because it is a part of nature; but against his mind they dash themselves in vain, even when they destroy with the body the condition of his individual consciousness. The mind is infinitely more *powerful* than the gathered forces of nature; all her mechanical forces are but splinters from the power of the mind that created her.

'But if nature ceases to impress the transcendental realist, he does *not*, however, regard her with contempt. For he knows that, both in the shape of his own body and in the shape of the external world which extends and reprieves his life, nature is the indispensable condition and essentially co-operative factor for the arising and subsistence of his individual consciousness. The transcendental idealist also sees nature as the condition of his noetic life, but only as an unreal and illusory condition, projected like a mirror's virtual image, just as a dreamer rightly regards the stoutness of a dream-bridge as the condition of his not dreaming of breaking through and falling in the water; if awareness rises in him that he is only dreaming, he no longer fears breaking through, however unsafe the bridge in his dream. Only for the simple objective realist and the transcendental realist is nature the *real* condition of the conscious mind; only they can value nature in accordance with the truth of her being, or can cultivate her with understanding, for what she is.

'As in the estimation of nature, so in that of *conscious* mind, transcendental realism holds the *balance* between naturalism and transcendental idealism. While the first of these extremes sees in the conscious mind an unaccountable illusion in

The formal attributes of *absoluteness* and *infinitude*—two properties which, as we have shown, are inherent in the relationship to contingent things of the absolutely holy *ens a se*—are moreover immediately transferred, in this act of ascription, to *God as mind*.

The first implies that divine mind, as an attribute of the holy *ens a se*, must also be understood as *absolute mind*, that is as *a mind founded solely in itself*. But this is tantamount to asserting the *absolute freedom* of the mentality of God, or the *self-determination of the divine mind*—a predicate *accreting* to the concept *ens a se* only now that God is known as *mind*. And only now can the manner of his acting and en-acting or effecting be understood as analogous to volitional acts, or his supreme causality be seen as the mind-like causality of *creative power and freedom*.

Once again, a quite special experience of being underlies the *idea of creation*. Before this idea can enter the mind, the pure fortuitousness of the contingent world-reality must first be grasped in relation to worlds essentially no less possible, worlds as subjected and obedient to the general

nature, with no proper right to existence and as nothing in the face of nature, and while the second on the other hand puffs it up into the almighty maker of heaven and earth, transcendental realism sees in it neither the one thing nor the other, but the *product of a collaboration between unconscious mind and nature*. In the presence of absolute unconscious mind, which produces it partly directly through synthetic categorical functions and partly indirectly by collaboration with nature, the restricted conscious mind feels its utter dependence, impotence and nothingness, and behaves with deference and humility. On the other hand it rightly feels itself incomparably *superior* to nature, being the end for which nature is the means, and standing closer to the absolute mind, with whom it knows its unity and whose ends it serves with will and consciousness. Lifted above time and space by its intellectual being, it enjoys eternal life in unity with eternal mind and can *look down indulgently* on the temporal extension of the natural process, which at any given instant is equally remote and excluded from eternity. Here there is no more foolish shuddering and dread before nature, neither those delusions of grandeur which induce the conscious mind to claim an impossible supremacy, but consciousness and nature *together* are *subordinated*, as phenomenal spheres of the world, to the metaphysical sphere, while that phenomenal sphere which is subjective and ideal is allowed a *teleological* superiority over the objective and real.' (Hartmann, *System der Philosophie im Grundriss*, Vol. 2, pp. 12-15.)

Hartmann's words are coloured here and there by his acceptance of an absolute unconscious mind, but allowance can be made for this without harming the general truth of the passage.

(*Translator's note:* Hartmann's concept of *unbewusster Geist*, paradoxical enough in German, seems a contradiction in terms when we render it as 'unconscious mind'. In this connection the following may be said: 1. It is necessary to Hartmann's critical argument that one should not use one word for his *Geist* and another for that of idealism; the idealist—and Schelerian—*Geist* is patently more 'mind' than 'spirit'. 2. Scheler was of course much exercised by such noetic paradoxes. Readers curious to know the exact content of his concept of *Geist* at this period are urged to consider his various references to Hartmann and Kant in conjunction with his critique of Windelband, below, pp. 309 *et seq.*)

cohesion of essences as is the real world. But the reality of any object is given in the empirical *resistance* which it offers as an intentional object to the (mental) interest or aversion of the experiencing subject.[1] If we had no kind of volitional relationship to the world, we could never have any consciousness of reality. When we encounter a resistance, its point of origin is felt to be a *nucleus of activity*, the nature of which varies according to the kind of resistant. Thus we experience perhaps a nucleus of latent *physical* forces (inanimate objects), of *biophysical* forces (animate objects), of *instinctual* forces (our own bodies) or of *alien volition* (fellowmen).

The principle of the sufficient cause, which postulates a cause (of being rather than not-being) for all contingent existents (real or ideal), leads to the proposition that all real existence is effected in an *activity*. Now, within the whole range of our world-experience we know only one case, one empirical datum, in which a contingent existence is not merely altered, modified or transformed but actually created by the action of another. That is the form, shape, idea which the originally 'creative' human act of will imposes on a given material. And it is only in this one set of circumstances that we may see an ideal thing (the content of the volitional project) 'become' real. This crucial perception is quite independent of the question how this happens, *i.e.* all questions of psycho-physical volitional causality. *That* this artefact or that painting is a work of mental volition, posited and carried out by it, is evident, however obscure the paths by which this action of 'my' will comes to impinge upon the limbs of my body. For in the process of imagining and creating I see directly that the material more and more closely resembles the content of the project, see the material 'growing into' the idea of the project and at the same time know that this is happening 'through me'. But from that we may clearly see that in so far as there is any question of its *general realness* (as distinct from its mere realness here-and-now, in this or that situation, with these or those properties), the reality of *any contingent real existent* must have been effected by the agency of some kind of *volition*. In other words, a volition must have created any real contingent existent.

This argument is not followed through in the religious act, neither in this case are the stages of the perception given in the manner developed here. It is more correct to say that whenever and however it leads to the idea of creation, the religious act operates on these general lines.

In that it designates the mentality of an infinite being (a consequence of the *ens a se*), the divine mind also assumes the attribute of *infinitude*. And it is only as infinite mind (*i.e.* not as the unqualified *ens a se*) that

---

[1] A detailed proof of this principle is offered in my forthcoming outline of an epistemology, *Die Welt als Erkenntnis* (*The world as knowledge*).*

God acquires essential predicates which in various ways relate the qualitative infinitude of his being (*qua* being) to the formal modes of ordering which belong to the nature of finite things as possible correlates of infinite mind. The most important are *number, time, space* and *magnitude*.

In relation to all possible multiplicity of *numbers* or *quantities*, God is the being which of its nature has no quantitative restriction and is therefore *incalculable*. In other words, he is the being to whose very *essence* it belongs to be the *unique* instance of its species. Thus, God is God as the *absolutely unique*. And so to God's absolute unity and formal simplicity we must add his absolute *uniqueness*. As such it precludes any numerical definition—and of course even the numerical definition represented by the figure 'one'. 'The' unique being just is not 'one'—it is by nature that which is innumerable.

In relation to *time* the infinite mind bears the name of the *eternal*. This is not simply the sempiternal, that which has absolute duration or fills all time, for that is an attribute which may at least meaningfully be predicated of matter and energy. No, what it expresses is that God, as '*supratemporal*', may (just as he please) be also intratemporal, is *able* to fill every instant and period of time in a manner and order chosen by himself and *not* prescribed to him by the order of time (that is, the natural laws appropriate to time). Precisely *by virtue of* his eternity God is also able to enter *any* irrevocable moment of history in his oneness and undivided state, without thereby detracting one jot from his eternity.

In relation to space the infinite mind has the property of *ubiquity*. This means that because of his absolute superiority over space God can in one and the same act be everywhere and act everywhere, without having in his being to partake of the divisibility and natural laws of space, and without submitting his located presence to geometric and kinetic laws.[1] Thus ubiquity is as distinct from *omnipresence* (in the sense of being at every point in space) as God's eternity is from *sempiternity*. It signifies that God,

---

[1] Here I leave on one side the task of characterizing the religious acts corresponding to the religious comprehension of these attributes of God. However, the task is not impossible. All love for a one and (in fact) only individual is analogous to the special character of the love of God, which enables us in a religious sense to grasp God's absolute *uniqueness* with special clarity. All acts of the human mind in which it takes a group of empirical and cognitive data, which have reached it in temporal succession, and comprehends them as a unity—as *one* undivided effective unit or *one* intuition—is an analogy for the eternity of mind. 'History' (in the sense not of historical knowledge but of the historicity of life) is a drive toward natural eternalization. (Cf. my theoretical conception of memory in *Der Formalismus in der Ethik und die materiale Wertethik.**) Whenever in the development of civilization thought overcomes that bondage to the here-and-now which is the lot of beasts, the achievement offers a progressive analogical image of the ubiquity of God.

as *supraspatial*, can be and act whole and undivided (being simple) at *whatever point in space he choose.*

In relation to all that partakes of the form of being, and of the corresponding ideal form, known as *magnitude*, God's infinity of being bears the name of *immeasurability*. This does not mean that God has magnitude, which, however, is *infinite* and therefore not measurable, but rather that as an *absolutely* simple being God has no part at all in the category of *divisible* magnitude and is immeasurable only because whatever is measurable *postulates magnitude*. God can therefore *be and act whole and undivided* in whatever thing he choose that possesses magnitude, whatever be that magnitude.

And so God, who as the *ens a se* is already infinite, unitary and simple, is in his attributive definition as *mind* also *unique, eternal, ubiquitous* and *immeasurable*.

Finally, God has omnipresence: the *immanentia Dei in mundo* belongs to the essence of God. God is in every existent, so far as it *is*. Omnipresence is not exhausted by the fact that God effects (creates and sustains) every thing, has power over all and knows all. On the contrary, it underlies his omnipotence and omniscience as a *precondition*. Both knowledge of a thing and power over a thing are but specified modes of participation in one being by another. God *is* in everything according to his very essence and existence, and only for that reason is he *able* to know everything and have power over everything. But it is not correct to say also that everything is in him, as is said in panentheism and acosmic pantheism; there is no *immanentia mundi in Deo*. For the world is according to reality distinct from God, and only because God is infinite mind can God notwithstanding be in everything.

Just as God's infinity of being (following upon his original definition as an *ens a se*) acquires these differentiations when conceived in conjunction with the analogical definition 'mind', so God's relationship to the real world is differentiated when we analogically apprehend him as mind.

When God is seen as mind his all-causality, which was *empirically* grasped in the most formal religious act, becomes '*creation*', and by the same token his manifestation in finite things a *revelation*—that is, the consequence of a *self-revealing*.

But there are mental creatures which as such—no matter what their separate places in the scale of rank—are the foremost *creations of God* as well as the first *recipients* of his self-revelation as infinite mind. And as such they are known to themselves as images and reflections of divinity.

For that reason the human mind, in the religious act of belief in God, is

G

felt to have a *twofold* reference to the divine mind: to be the work of God which he both *effected* and continuously *sustains*, and to be in its qualitative aspect the foremost natural *revelation of God* as infinite *mind*. And so we are not here confronted by a merely inferred causal connection of objective reality between infinite and finite reason. It is nearer the truth to say that against the background of its existing awareness that all finite things are created the human mind has an *empirical sense* of being God's *principal* creation and of being at the same time permanently rooted in him, 'grounded' on him and moved by him in the execution of its acts.[1] Thus the mere causal inference would have no significance at all for the religious connection between the human mind and the divine, however important it may be for metaphysics. Similarly the religious conception of the human mind as of God's principal natural revelation means more than that the human mind is '*like*' the divine in the sense of being its clouded miniature. More is concerned in the religious act than this judgment of relation. We are dealing with an experience of the relation, with an experience of the human mind as the reflected splendour and living mirror of the divine. Not only do we know all things '*per*' *lumine Dei* but also and at the same time '*in*' *lumine Dei*. The religious man apprehends empirically—not merely by judgment—that the human mind is only a reflected glory, the faithful image and first sign in creation of the creator of all finite things.[2] Or we may say: in devout recollection and self-immersion in the fount of his spiritual being, the believer comes finally into the palpable *vicinity* of a position where he may directly see his mind as 'cherished', 'nourished', 'founded' and 'sustained' by the mind of God—and yet have not the remotest glimpse of the correlate 'divine mind' *itself*. Thus the human mind's faithful likeness to God is *engraved* in the mind itself, in its very *being*, without its having to establish that likeness through a natural perception of the original. And even this *being* itself (as in acts of the mind contrasted with psychical states and phenomena) is an initial knowledge of self, if only potentially. For the 'act-centre' of the human mind—the spirit (*die Geistseele*)—is of course, in contrast with *actus purus*, a permanent *centre of potential activity*.

This highly individual basic phenomenon, in which the human mind 'knows' of the divine mind in a religious way and with this knowledge enters for the first time into full possession of itself (and thus must also

[1] Thus the 'person' is itself God's natural revelation and the highest natural revelation.

[2] In no sense, however, is the mind's knowledge that it springs from God's, is rooted in and moved by it, merely a special case of the universal *concursus Dei*, so-called, which, operating in '*causae secundae*', may be postulated of any effect which one has on another.

possess God, if it is to possess itself completely and with perfect mastery), can all too easily be flawed in the telling, and it is no wonder that for centuries the greatest thinkers have wrestled with language in quest of its cogent expression.

Pantheism offers an entirely crude theory of the relation, one which makes play with physical analogies. It not only envisages the light of the divine mind as mysteriously penetrating the mind of man, but makes the human an actual *part*, a *beam*, a *function* of the divine mind. Averroes, Spinoza, Fichte, Hegel and Hartmann are at one in this, however differently they formulate the idea. They fail to observe that by wishing to intensify the relation of similarity to the point of identity, they destroy that very similarity. For if the human mind is to be no more than *similar* to the mind of God, it must resemble it in *independence* of being and *freedom and spontaneity* of action. But these mental characteristics immediately vanish if it is not man *himself* who thinks, but only 'God thinking in him'. Or if, as Hegel and Hartmann say, it is God becoming first conscious of himself in man. Furthermore, the pantheists fail to notice that with the apparently most intimate participation in the mind of God, which they think to vouchsafe to the human mind by their doctrine of identity, they are in fact forcing open a fearful chasm between it and God. For if error, guilt and sin are not a consequence of the human mind's *voluntary deviation* from the divine mind's eternal laws which shine within it, they could in this case arise because it is not the *whole* mind of God which is at work in any man but only a part, a function. But this would be to nullify the formal simplicity of God. Alternatively they could arise because the divine mind has compacted with a finite body; in that case error, sin and guilt are *necessary* and *essential* human attributes which *cannot* be actively overcome or redeemed through God. There would then exist in the *nature of things* a chasm between the necessarily erring, guilty and sinful man and the spirit of truth and goodness. This in turn would render impossible any inward approach to God through self-sanctification. In that case sin and evil must be irremediably inherent in the fact of instinctual life in the body. So we see that every supposed *advance* to identity is in fact a recession. All the burning ardour of love for God is here extinguished at the outset in that its place is taken by the mere presumptive knowledge that one *is* already a part or function of God. God did not in Christ condescend to man in the act of redemption, in essential self-communication, but Christ was merely the first to *recognize* godmanhood in himself. The miracle of mystical union with God, that everrenewed resolution of the tension of nearness and distance between man and God, becomes a flatly naturalistic 'fusion' in the material sense, in that distance is completely removed from the relationship. There is a power possessed by persons, as spiritual beings of free and autonomous reality, a power serving to counteract all naturalistic images, of each accepting into the self and there emotionally affirming the essential individuality of another—*without* losing independent reality but rather on the contrary *gaining* the true self for the first time. It is in this power that the mystery of all love between human beings resides. But in pantheism love is stripped of its moral activity and of its sense as the unification of *two*. For it becomes mere *knowledge* that in reality there is no true *multiplicity* of independent, individual spirits—becomes mere removal of the illusion of dualities. There is purportedly just one infinite egoist who, when creatures think not that they enjoy but that they *love*, and that they love not God but *one another*, is in reality taking pleasure in himself through creatures. The many-membered realm of love, with its separate and autonomous foci, here congeals to the amorphous image of an undifferentiated mass.[1] Just as certainly this partial identification abolishes that veneration of the mind of God which is a *sine qua non* for any religious relationship with him.

But if we are content to accept any kind of causal connection *inferred* from the natural principle of causality, the relation of the divine to the human mind is as misrepresented as in pantheism. This we have already shown.

Hitherto, in finding a basis for the proposition that 'God is mind', we have not been concerned with the order and quality of the *world*— at least the world apart from the human mind. Neither have we considered the various *interests* of the human mind, its different forms and qualities of action, such as thinking, knowing, loving, wishing, etc.

Knowledge of the world, without knowledge of the intellectual nature of the human soul as the first work in creation, the most immediate and best approximation to its creator, will never suffice to render God *knowable to us as mind*, though to this end knowledge of man's own 'mentality' is conversely sufficient *without* any premise of the extra-mental world. *One* soul would therefore suffice to teach us that God is mind: the world would *not* suffice. Even though we possessed the concept 'mind', an ordering power or an apotheosis of 'order' would be enough to make the existence of the world understandable. But that notion is very far from that of the personal

---

[1] Cf. my phenomenological analysis of love and sympathy in *Zur Phänomenologie und Theorie der Sympathiegefühle** and the reference to the proposition that 'the love-for-others of the parts is the self-love of the whole'. This is the proposition which underlies all pantheistic theories of love.

God who is mind and not merely reason—who is, that is to say, a concrete unity of all essential mental-spiritual tendencies (thus love and a sense of value, as well as reason, etc.). The only thing which can take us *further* in natural knowledge of the divine mind is insight into the way in which the human mind's formal and functional laws are *ideally* related to forms of objective being, sense, value, purpose and instrumentality. This insight must be a product of the whole of noetic studies: epistemology and ontology, theory of values and axiology, theory of will and ontic teleology, etc. But *direct study of the factual world and its ordering cannot take us forward.* Though there be *objectively* a direct connection between the mentality of God and the world, what we may *know* is only a connection *mediated* through *essential* knowledge of the human mind and of *its* connection with the objective, essential constitution of the world. Because the world has an essential reference to the formal bases of the human mind, while the mind is the 'most original' mirror of the world's creator and is indeed a mirror conscious of its function, the world (whatever its properties) must *also* be the work of a mental cause. Taken by itself, the extra-mental world would lead us to the assumption of a force active at the origin and in the continuance of the world, a constantly active force, guiding things in conformity with the laws of reason—but not an agent working on rational principles;[1] it would not exclude the possibility that beside and outside this dominant (but not necessarily infinite and omnipotent) force there might be another underlying principle, one just as fundamental as the first—a blind energy or a substance co-original with God. In other words dualism, as in the religions of the Manichees and the ancient Persians, would not be precluded; on the contrary it would be probable.[2] The idea of creation, in which the all-causality of the *ens a se* combines with mentality in the unity of an *idea*, supposes that the at least comparatively creative power which the human mind possesses in the project-forming will (the *one* place where there is not only remodelling but free shaping, not only self-propagation and growth but genuine 'creation') is previously felt and known, so that it may be transferred to God in a *formally absolute and infinite* form.

In principle, therefore, Augustine's doctrine remains correct: the religious knowledge of God as mind is not dependent on a previous knowledge of the extra-mental world's existence or on a knowledge of its character—thus we do not know God as mind *in lumine mundi*, but on the contrary know the world *in lumine Dei*.

[1] Cf. Chr. von Ehrenfels, *Kosmogenie*, Jena 1916.

[2] A certain revival of Manicheeism is to be seen in the later doctrines of Schelling and in those of his disciple on this point, Hartmann.

It follows methodically that we must know and think of the world and its fortunes in such a manner that in all circumstances the proposition that its divine author is mind (which is manifest, true and valid quite independently of the world's existence or character) *remains true.* Our very confidence that essential, intrinsically evident relations between things, whether formal or material, may be grasped by our reason—the confidence on whose basis we wield our knowledge of the world and even postulate a world transcending human consciousness—*pre*-supposes that we know and feel our finite reason to be rooted in an infinite reason out of which it rises as object to the other's subject.

Not until we have reached this position does our general conviction of the mentality of God become so independent of all possible disturbances to our idea of the world that no upheaval can make us waver in this belief or compel us to final skepticism over the possibility that the mind can know the world. In these circumstances any upheaval, the most profound even, can only stimulate us to create for ourselves a more adequate image of the world.

And so, if the character of the extra-mental world has anything to teach us of the mentality of God, it cannot be that mentality itself but can only refer to his *manner* of being mind. And even that is only possible if the ontic structure of the universe is constantly observed in conjunction with the limiting structure of the human mind.

But before I turn to the determination of the divine mind's attributes, I should like to say certain things about the evolution of our knowledge of God's mentality.

Growth and decline of the natural knowledge of God

Our mind possesses no *innate* ideas, whether intrinsic or merely latent. Not even the *idea of God* is innate. And even the idea of the *ens a se* postulates acquaintance with some or other contingent entity and is elicited from that example only as the obvious precondition of any contingent being. That the intellectual soul of man is an image and mirror of God-the-mind in no way implies the innate *idea* of an infinite mind. Neither is knowledge of that likeness inborn in the mind. The mind first acquires that knowledge in the way described, through reflection on its nature and in the religious act I have discussed wherein God is grasped as the underlying mind. It is not through an idea, but through its very life and *being*, that it is rooted in God. And only because all being of mind *qua* mind is always likewise potential knowledge of itself—not because it possesses an innate idea of God—can the possibility of a direct knowledge of itself as similar be assumed with its *de facto* similarity. All that is assumed with the being of the spiritual soul is the potentiality of *religious* acts, as a special class of acts whereby it may *acquire* religious knowledge.

It is only because there is *no* innate idea of God that in principle there may be *unlimited growth of the natural knowledge of God* through constant acts of cognitive acquisition spread over the history of the human mind. Through the special conditions of this acquisition (in particular through the individuality of 'acquirers' according to their race, nation, historical and social milieu) the natural cognition of God produces, however, widely differing results, and thus there arises a multiplicity of natural religions.

No more than innate ideas, the human mind contains intrinsically no synthetic functional forms and laws (what Kant calls 'categories') which could bestow on the inchoate 'material' of a sense-datum (Kant's 'sensations' and instinctive impulses) the objective formal characteristics of an entity. Our mere thought and cognition are incapable of 'creating', 'producing', 'forming' anything—unless it be figments and cyphers. Both the inchoate, amorphous material of sensation and the nowhere-to-be-found functions of regular synthesis—the categorical functions—are pure inventions of Kant, each conditional on the other. The formal unities which Kant adduces as examples of his 'categories', as well as many another which he does not adduce, are *dispositions of the object* and pertain as such to the 'given' thing itself: here I include substance and causality, relations, shapes, etc. The perceptual content of our intuitive grasp of an object is incomparably *richer* than the partial content corresponding to a pure sensation (by 'pure' I mean as conditioned only by external stimulus) —and within the sensation to the various modalities of sensation. And even this 'partial content' is never a real part of the datum but only a fictional product of comparison, derived from the comparison of separate unitary acts of intentional perception whose functional components vary, even if the stimuli are constant.

Thus forms are given perceptually, not bestowed by the subject, and sensational elements are given with forms only in so far as they serve to implement or supplement the unitary perceptual intention. From these two principles we may infer the following: our mind has a form of contact with things which in itself is *unmediated* by the sensory organism of our body and is basic and *unitary*, in contrast to the multiplicity of sensory functions.[1] The senses merely *analyse* this mental contact in different ways. They are not creators but only analysts of our mind's total unitary perception, and as analysts they are 'concerned' to assess the value of the datum as a biological stimulus, according to whether it may induce beneficial or harmful

---

[1] My long note on page 215 is relevant here. See also the passage on 'the given', pp. 256 *et seq.* (*Translator*).

reactions in the organism which belongs to the mental person as the subject of the overall perception.* On the other hand there is no foundation at all for the hypothesis of Kantian epistemology that anything in the empirical datum which reaches *beyond* the 'previously given' sensational content (objecthood, being, realness, unitary forms of substance and causality, relations, shapes, values, the intuited complexity underlying space, time, magnitude, quantity, number, etc., etc.) must first have been produced or introduced by the *activity* of the human mind. This is of the very πρῶτον ψεῦδος of Kant's philosophy. The human mind has no such world-constructing gift as that which Kant attributes to it. To envisage it on that model is to confuse it with the mind of God. Moreover, if we attribute creative power at the level of thought and cognition, it becomes impossible to see the true importance of that conduct and volition which alone can create.[1]

But false as are these two forms of the old '*a priori*' teachings—the doctrine of innate ideas and that of synthetic categorical functions—the great distinction of *a priori* and *a posteriori* must still be jealously guarded, though in quite *another* form—as a distinction inhering in the object itself.*

Within any perceptual datum everything is *a priori* which belongs to the sphere of *pure 'identity' and essence, i.e.* the assemblage of all those *qualitative* dispositions of the object (left after discarding its existential modes) which as qualitative are indefinable and therefore taken as irreducible in any attempt at definition. These, then, are essences and can only be 'seen'. Any other element of the perceptual datum is *a posteriori*.

Now the principle governing the relation between essential and contingent facts, that everything true of an object's essence is *unconditionally* true of all possibles sharing that essence, holds good without our first having to be assured of its validity through an induction.[2] The categorical forms of being are then only the essential facts subdividing the being-real of objects into *basic modes* of realness (or of becoming real). Thus, though they do form part of the *a-priori* they form *only* a part—the *formal* part, and in fact the formal part which has to do not with objects in general but with the modes of realness of objects. Over against them stand the absolutely formal truths of the pure theory of objects—those truths, that

---

[1] If we look more closely at our Kantians, Fichteans, etc.—at any of those who would have it that cognition 'forms', 'shapes', 'produces'—we soon notice that these are people who for the most part lack all practical contact with the world. No wonder! What need have they to will, act, form or shape, since they believe they can—or must—perform by dint of mere cognition things which are exclusively the province of will and action? Their epistemological voluntarism leads to atrophy of the will proper.

[2] The *a-priori* datum is not altogether independent of the experience and perception of objects, but only of the quantity of experience.

is, which apply to every thing in so far as it possesses the essence of object-hood—and also the supraformal, *substantial a-priori truths* which describe the specific identity and content of real objects.

Knowledge of the a-priori sector of a datum is neither inborn nor as to content a pure product of the mind, but is intrinsically just as much a *'receptio'* as any knowledge of a given thing. Knowledge of the a-priori is therefore *in no way a-priori knowledge.* However, while a-posteriori (though not for that reason acquired by induction), it is knowledge which is *a priori* true of all objects provided they share the essence in question—even if they are unknown and perhaps unknowable at any stage of 'my' empirical knowledge. Consequently any self-evident insight into *a-priori* reality (be it perception of separate essences, essential correlations or essential structures) can be neither 'proved', destroyed nor refuted by (inductive) experience of contingent facts.

Thence derives the first important characteristic of knowledge of any essence, that once historically gained it cannot be called into question or modified by any subsequent experience. In this it differs from all knowledge of contingent facts and thus of all relations of principle between contingent facts. It is only possible that essential knowledge should be enriched and develop (by the steady addition of new essential data to old) or that more and more connections should be made between one item of such knowledge and another. Besides this, it is possible that an item of essential knowledge gained in the course of history should be lost and require to be discovered anew.

To this first is connected a second characteristic, which of all the properties of essential knowledge is nevertheless one of the least remarked: *essential knowledge is functionally transmuted into a law governing the very 'employment' of the intellect with regard to contingent facts; under its guidance the intellect conceives, analyses, regards and judges the contingent factual world as 'determined' in 'accordance' with the principles concerning the cohesion of essences.* What before was a thing *becomes* a form of thinking about things; what was an object of love becomes a form of love, in which a limitless number of objects can now be loved; what was an object of will becomes a form of volition, and so on. Whenever we, for example, conclude *according* to a principle without concluding 'from' it, or obey an aesthetic rule (like the creative artist) without in the remotest sense possessing that rule itself as a principle formulated in the mind, essential insights are 'functioning'— coming into play—though they are in no way explicitly 'visible' to the mind. It is only when we sense incorrectness, deviation from a law not consciously present to us as a law, that we have a glimmer of awareness that an insight has been leading and guiding us. This is what happens for

example in all stirrings of conscience, which rather protest against the
wrong than point away from it to the good: but behind them there nevertheless stands a *positive* insight into the good and into a positive ideal of
our individual and universal human life.* In that essential insights thus
undergo a 'functional transmutation', a kind of genuine *growth of the
human mind* takes place both in the life of the individual and collectively
over the course of history (not by heredity but via tradition), and this
growth is *utterly different* from all aptitudes acquired and as it were inherited
merely through influences at work on the human organism and its sensory
zones; it is equally distinct from any genesis which may be explicable in
merely psychological terms (*e.g.* by rules of association, habit or psycho-
biological function).

The *functionalization of essential insight* enables us to understand that there
can be an *evolution and growth of reason itself*—growth, 'that is to say, of its
property in a-priori rules of selection and function. And at the same time
we can see the *delusory* nature of Kant's famous assumption that human
reason possesses absolutely original, absolutely immutable, inaugmentable,
undiminishable functional laws—basic principles, categorical functions
and the like—whereby it synthetically constructs the cohesive empirical
world out of a chaos of data, while an absolutely unknowable '*Ding an
sich*' lurks behind the façade of this fantasmal edifice. We on the contrary
maintain that all functional laws derive from original experience of
objects (through experience or intuition of their *essence*), but that this type
of experience is in nature and basis different from any 'experience' of
contingent facts—which is always in principle sensory experience. And so
we also *contest* Kant's principle of the *logical identity*[1] of the rational mind
in all communities (races, peoples, civilizations, etc.), in so far as it is
applied to more than the purely formal mental functions or laws—and
even *their* identity is conceivable only in the light of the identity of those
formal essences of the object which are given in the simplest and basic
essential insights. For since the milieu of 'matters of fact' is different for
all men and all groups of men, the *sets of essential insights* enjoyed by
different subjects (peoples, races, etc.) may also *differ* one from another
without prejudice to the self-evident and a-priori nature of the insights, or
to their indestructible validity. Not a jot of their validity is lost, nor the
a-priori *nature* of their validity in any degree harmed, nor their strictly
objective character diminished.* For even if there exist a *realm of essences*

[1] Still more emphatically would we reject the doctrine, taking shape in Fichte
and explicit in Hegel, of a *real* identity of reason (world-reason) in all men, a
doctrine in which the pantheistic Averroism already sketched in Kant came to its
full embodiment. To such doctrines we would oppose a pluralistic view of even the
original properties and equipment of the rational human mind.

which offers a constitutional model for all possible worlds and realities made from matters of fact (not only for our world of possible human milieux), we may still expect—considering that every man and more especially every large group of humanity has a *different* path of access from contingent facts to that realm—that mental functions and their laws, which have come into being through the functionalization of essential insights, will show differences in everything which goes beyond the purely formal determinations of objects as such. No less than the logical (or for that matter real) identity of rational functions in all contemporary communities we *contest* what may be called the *eternal stability* of human reason (truly a property of divine reason alone), which Kant presupposes in his attempt genuinely to *exhaust* this reason (in a direct theoretical manner) with the doctrines of transcendental aesthetics and transcendental analysis (table of categories and doctrine of the deduction of basic principles). Not only do we envisage the whole domain of contingent experience as in continuous growth, but we maintain that the rational human *mind itself*, as the embodiment of all rational laws and functions of an a-priori kind of validity, *grows and develops*—in such a way, of course, that its former stages of growth are in no way depreciated by the new. For a depreciation of this kind would take place only if this growth were consequent not upon ever-renewed acquisitions of essential knowledge, and thereafter functionalization on a basis of the mind's intrinsic orientation to the eternal and divine, but upon mere adjustment and 'adaptation' to man's natural and positive historical milieu (as taught by Herbert Spencer).

Since the human mind, both in the individual and in the species, thus grows not only in its knowledge but also in its *functions* and its powers of gathering knowledge, not only in its work and achievement (*e.g.* art and moral guidance) but also in its artistic and moral *capabilities*, the rational human mind cannot at any point in history be *completely* defined; philosophically—in *all* noetic fields—its definition is always markedly incomplete. Moreover, this growth of the mind through the functionalization of essential insights is in no way conditioned by change in the natural human organism in its physical aspect (as including the cerebral and nervous systems), which, on the hypothesis of inherited aptitudes, was the theory of Albert Lange and Herbert Spencer. On the contrary it may be demonstrated—though this is not the place—that *one* catalytic cause of the human mind's (=reason's) independent, autonomous development *qua* mind (as distinct from psychic existence directly conditioned by the body) lies precisely in the eminent *biological fixity* of the human, as the most differentiated, animal organism. There is a universal biological law that capacity for evolution (or self-restitution) decreases as the organism rises in the scale of evolution; precisely because man is by this law the most 'fixed' type of animal from the viewpoint of evolution, he is subjectively driven to allow his mind's unbounded capacity for objective development to come into play via functionalization of his essential insights. By thus developing, as a mental creature, in a direction and manner both utterly different from the biological, he finds in his higher supernatural organization a far superior compensation for what he has lost in terms of actual development and evolutionary capacity as a natural earthly creature.*

I need hardly say how fundamentally the above view of man's development differs not only—as we have shown—from the Kantian doctrine of the identity and constancy of human reason but also from theories rejecting this constancy and representing therefore a theory of growth and development. Under this heading come the relevant teachings of Herbert Spencer and his school, based on a *positivist*-sensualist epistemology, and of Hegel, based on an extreme development of a *rationalist*-constructive theory of mind and reason.

Spencer saw clearly enough that the old doctrine of innate ideas directly implanted by God could not answer our questions, and that neither common individualistic empiricism, which holds that all principles and thought-forms are derived by individuals through induction (whether mechanically associational or consciously methodic), nor Kant's doctrine, which has no place for a theory of mental evolution, is feasible. But since Spencer knew no difference between contingent sensory experience and perception of essences, or even between contingent facts and eternal essences, since he acknowledged only a difference of degree where there is truly a difference in kind, he still clung to the old fallacious identification of a-priori knowledge and innate (potential) knowledge. What the species has slowly acquired he supposes innate in the individual, and the processes of reason's evolution he supposes explicable in terms of the here quite inappropriate theory of 'organic adaptation to environment'. He fails to notice that he *takes for granted* the present maximal development and validity of reason and its highest principles in all fields— including practical ethics—in that he already conceives in *terms* of those principles the object towards which adaptation is directed. Neither does he observe that we may conceive an ideally perfect adaptation to environment of the human organism's reactions and practical conduct without the necessary acquisition of an iota of *knowledge* concerning the object of that adaptation; nor conversely does he see that *mere* knowledge (like mere good will or personal moral goodness) is of no use at all as a measure of the adaptation.

Hegel's error is almost diametrically the reverse. He failed to understand that the acquisition of essential insight is a matter equally of intuition and of experience (though experience of a basically different *kind* from the sensory and inductive), and that one cannot therefore seriously talk of a unitary process, permeating all forms of consciousness, in which the 'idea' is developed solely in accordance with a dialectical law whereby the idea's pre-existing 'intrinsic' content is merely unfolded and brought to light.

Neither thinker supposes original, distinctive reason-moulding processes of direct essential perception; neither proposes any true growth (or decrease) of the rational mind itself (as distinct from its mere employment and exercise in cognition of the world). The reason for this lies in the fact that both, in their view of the history of philosophy and their sociological theories—*i.e.* in their application of their theory of mind—keep strictly within the narrowest bounds of what I have elsewhere called 'Europeanism'.[1]

In opposition to these points of view we would assert a development of reason through the functionalization of essential insights, a development of such a nature that beyond the most formal content of these insights it has produced different mental structures within the different main *groups* of humanity, and furthermore can lead—as it has in fact led—to genuine growth (and genuine diminution) of man's higher spiritual powers. Since—to speak figuratively—the human mind has not only been looking into different parts of the one 'real' contingent world, giving them rational shape and cohesion, but has also from the beginning been looking into different parts of the one world of essences, its 'a-priori' functional laws, valid in their own right, have necessarily, through the functionalization of different sets of things 'beheld' or intuited, undergone differentiation. But this in no way prevents each one of these insights into or through the essential sphere of possible knowledge from being manifest, true and valid in its own right. Here the one lesson to be drawn is that, cognitively, great human civilizations and systems of knowledge may not —even at the level of a-priori knowledge—*deputize* or be compatibly *substituted* one for another. Consequently the possibility of a *comprehensive* knowledge of the essential world does not lie with historical contingencies or the chances of blood and racial predispositions—still less with any division of labour—but, in the nature of reason and knowledge *themselves*, it depends solely on a *fraternal comparison* of cognitive notes—a *collaboration* of mankind in all the highest mental activities, including decision on what

[1] Cf. the section entitled '*Die geistige Einheit Europas*' in *Der Genius des Krieges*. Cf. also H. Gomperz, *Weltanschauungslehre*, Jena 1905.

may be the ideally correct manner of their application. It is true that in principle peoples, races and other groups (and individuals in the last resort) can 'deputize' one for another in all applications of similar *a-priori* principles to the cognition of the world's contingent reality; in this sphere it is also true that marked differences of 'talents' and 'predispositions' (*i.e.* psycho-physical idiosyncrasies), together with differing degrees of access to this or that sector of the real world, necessitate mutual complementation of knowledge (and here the purely technical fruitfulness of the division of labour appears to prescribe just such a complementary co-operation as we have mentioned). Nevertheless, the sphere of *essences* is in quite another case: here the *impossibility* of substituting one man or group for another is an absolutely basic principle—*i.e.* one not merely relative—and for that very reason collaboration and complementation become a pure and absolute objective prescription—an objective prescription entrenched in the very nature of this basic type of cognition.

As a further consequence of our doctrine of mind it follows that we must acknowledge the possibility of genuine evolution and growth, likewise genuine retrogression and diminution, of the rational human mind *in history*—phenomena quite distinct from the development and unfolding of any assemblage of positive ideas and from any mere adaptation, differentiation, variation of practice, etc. For not only may knowledge 'about' the essential world (or the functionalization of such knowledge) increase and decrease in history, but any locus in the unique and irrevocable flux of concrete events may serve from its inception as a springboard for essential insights to which no other one locus of the world-process can assist the mind. And this implies that the *purely* rational mind itself, independently of all inductions and all accession of new sense-data, may also grow or diminish through functionalization of insights thereby acquired—or may expand in certain of its essential functions and contract in others. And it further follows that the epochs and ages of man's history (as part of the history of the universe) are in principle just as mutually *unsubstitutable*, in reference to the essential knowledge that may be acquired through them, as are individuals, peoples and all other groups. It is true that the history of knowledge is attended by a mounting accumulation of inductive material and an intensification of its logical treatment (as positivism maintains, while setting up rules for the method of accumulation). Notwithstanding, Hegel and Hermann Cohen (with his school) were wrong to teach that this history forms a process of logical unfolding in which the 'foundations' of empirical knowledge were 'laid' one after the other. But this is not all. The rational mind itself, as the sum and substance of acts, functions and powers, *grows and diminishes*, 'evolves' and

'regresses', because certain of the essential insights by whose functionalization its progress is controlled are attached to this or that particular locus
in the concrete world-process and possible only at those points. Progress
and recession in the dimensions merely of inductive accumulation and
logical deduction (or reduction) are on the other hand solely a matter of
applying particular essential insights (through their functionalization)
to the contingent real world. Here, moreover, progress only takes place
where, on the whole, knowledge of the contingent real world has become
the principal object of cognition (*i.e.* pre-eminently in Europe, as it
happens), and takes the form of a continuous process only over the
stretch of history represented by one era constant in its system of essential
insights (and its corresponding 'rational system').

And so it may very well be (*i.e.* the general theory of mind has nothing
against it[1]) that one period of humanity or of part of humanity might
penetrate the realm of essences in a manner which *any* other age is
precluded even from attempting, and that succeeding ages are therefore,
in the very nature of human knowledge and its *object* (thus not from
considerations of predispositions, aptitudes, division of labour and so on),
under an *obligation* to *preserve* as an eternally valid store of knowledge whatever they themselves have not wit enough to know first-hand. As guardians
of the treasured store they need but *apply* it to contingent reality. Thus
co-operation among the succeeding ages of humanity through the medium
of tradition—the handing down of things which the 'reason' of the
current age could in no way discover, even if it were applied in an ideally
perfect manner—belongs to the very *nature* of this type of (a-prioristic)
knowledge and its functionalization, for the functionalization depends
on the possession of *items* of knowledge to which in this case tradition alone
can provide an access. Far from its being the case that every newcomer
stands on the shoulders of his predecessor and is equipped with the *same*
mental powers as he, to see and to know, the circumstances are quite
otherwise: he simply does not possess the same powers, or not all of
them, that his predecessor enjoyed. Thus in *any* question of genuinely
philosophical reference—that is, questions of essential knowledge—and
not only in the highest philosophical questions, all philosophers throughout
history have to discuss their problem, so to speak, *in common* (*i.e.* by specific
consultation of predecessors and contemporaries in their cognitive inquiry). This is in flagrant contrast to all 'positive' science, where only
the immediate predecessors are capable of exciting interest—provided
they have not simply forgotten or failed to appreciate some earlier

[1] It is for positive examination of historical material to decide whether this
possibility has been realized.

discovery. The philosophers must all, in 'co-operation' (not working against one another or taking their stand merely on 'results', as in the positive sciences), add their brick to the edifice of the *one 'philosophia perennis'*— always bearing in mind the rules of the historical distribution of the *cognitive powers themselves*, to discover which rules is itself a highly important task for any epistemology wishing to treat exhaustively the cognitive powers of man.[1] While the philosopher takes his stand on this theory— which does not spring from tradition but from his own perceptions— he is in no way obliged to accept items of traditional knowledge, in which may lie the essential insights of other ages, without testing their content. But he has always to reckon with the possibility not only of in fact missing, but of being *unable* to see, what other ages have seen.

Thus it is in the very nature of the realm of essences and man's path of access to it that all philosophy, and even reflexive knowledge of the idea of the divine received in the religious act, is in general only possible through the *concert of peoples and ages* in the transactions of philosophy—whatever form is taken by the special positive rules according to which reason has in fact evolved and regressed, grown and decreased, on earth among men. To these rules we shall have occasion to return, likewise to the real forces and driving factors of man's history, whose own rules, in conjunction with those positive rules, would enable us to understand the actual history of philosophy and of natural religion. Here only one thing is important: what consequences follow from the foregoing for the *natural knowledge of God*.[2]

The following consequence is salient and emphatically true: the nearer perfection an essence is in its essential content, and the more remote it is from the general possibility that the human mind (as human) may adequately apprehend it, the more urgent is that collaboration in inquiry of which we have spoken, if that essence is to be known in the most adequate way possible. Therefore the urgency is at its peak when we study the essence of all essences—God.

If we may and should ascribe to God a rational mentality (but, as we

---

[1] . . . and therefore in strict contrast and conscious opposition to an epistemological method like that of Kant, who undertook not only to determine but exhaustively to define the nature of human reason (and thus its limits also) merely by answering the question of how such a thing as 'learning' is 'possible', though by 'learning' he envisages the specifically West European (and even then *recent* West European) variety—indeed it is something narrower still, mathematical natural science, or *much* narrower still: the mathematical natural science of Newton, which today the theory of relativity and the quantum-theory have already transformed to something different not only in its results but in its *principles*.

[2] Cf. the final section, 'Why no new religion?'. We intend shortly to devote a special systematic study to this branch of a 'pure sociology and historical philosophy of cognition'.*

have seen, only by analogy), it is to be expected, after the foregoing, that only *part* of the fulness of his mentality should be accessible to any one man, one group, one people, since the capacity for spontaneous metaphysical cognition belonging to each of these cognitive subjects is different according to the manner in which they functionalize acquired or traditional essential insights. It is, again, only to be expected that this mentality should be the object of widely differing conceptions within the *ideas* of God promulgated by positive religions, that the various mental functions (will, intelligence, love, power, wisdom, etc.), should enter into the idea of God in widely varying proportions and with a widely differing order of importance, and that the traits characteristic of the mental make-up of particular groups and persons should seldom be absent from the idea of God's 'mind'. This disparity might—but certainly need not—be attributed to the peculiar limitation imposed on a single rational *model* of mind (with uniform a-prioristic functional laws) by natural predispositions, passions, history—that single rational model known to Kant and the rationalists, but whose very existence we contest. Yet the different ideas of the mind of God *may* even all be *true*—though inadequate in differing *senses*. The disparity does not have to lie in the limitations of man—it may derive from the inexpressible *richness* of the divine mind, and its infinite, even qualitative perfection.

There is simply this one necessary consequence: it is of the essence of natural religion and knowledge of God, as much as worship and veneration, that in contrast to all knowledge of positive science they must be *communal and co-operative*. In these circumstances the idea of the Church as a somehow-organized communal knowing and honouring of God, and likewise the idea (given the premises of monotheism) of a world-embracing Church, are not learned from positive experience but follow as a postulate from the very nature of the knowledge of *God*. Knowledge of God, as knowledge and grasp of the divine *mind*, is knowledge which, being natural, must *necessarily* remain incomplete (even within the limits of what is here accessible to man) until *everyone* of the human groups we may distinguish—indeed every individual—has delivered its (or his) contribution, the contribution possible to that group or that man alone, and until each contribution is grasped by all other groups and individuals, included in their own relationship to God and made fruitful for it. Religious 'singularism' is therefore intrinsically nonsensical, since it denies the essential relation subsisting eternally between knowledge of God and communal knowledge. And—however paradoxical it may sound—it is precisely the essential individualism of knowledge of God, the permanent impossibility of substituting one cognitive subject for another, taken with the universal obligation to seek such knowledge, which renders the communal *from* of cognition *necessary* in a sense applicable to no other kind of knowledge.[1]

Just as necessary is the *historicality* of even the natural knowledge of God—a principle which all rational theology, in the radical sense of the philosophy and theology of the Enlightenment, but Kant as well, completely misunderstood. Since any particular rational organization *evolves* or grows (and diminishes), by the transmutation of essential insights into functional laws, it is true to say that the full and pure sense of the proposition 'God is mind' (itself of merely analogical force) can only be revealed gradually, as the human mind develops in history, in each never-returning conjunction ʿof circumstances. This proposition that knowledge of God is necessarily historical is, however, falsified (and is then thoroughly false) when it is taken to mean that God's mind, like a natural force in process of self-exhaustion, is *working itself out* in objectively different ways in the different phases of world-history, and that every age must therefore have its own special idea of the mind of God. That would be a pantheistic, Hegelian thought. If it were true, not only philosophy but also natural theology would be no more than 'the *Zeitgeist* reduced to ideas and concepts'—a relativistic assertion which is utterly mistaken. God is not a force which to become explicit must spend itself within the dimension of time and history: he is an absolutely self-sufficient subject (*absolut aktuales Sein*). What is imprisoned in the historical process is only our cognitive exhaustion of his mental nature—assisted of course not only by increasing knowledge of the human mind as an inadequate, finite, analogical model of the divine but also by expansion of finite reason itself. And it is the ability to understand historically not merely the *works* of the mind but *mental structures* which deviate from those 'current' (the subjective categorical systems of reason, at their various stages of evolution) which enables us to overcome the defects of misplaced emphasis in the present stage of rational evolution by integrating into our own conceptions those of earlier stages—that is, by turning what the course of history has differentiated into a single collective power of reason. If therefore we wish to enjoy exhaustive knowledge and experience of the mind of God—even in a merely analogical way—we must *not* be content to follow the rational structure of our age alone, we should not seek to

---

[1] By the principle of the primacy of love over knowledge this purely epistemological principle about community may also be argued in the following way, that love for God as a condition of knowing him *necessarily* implies love for one's 'brothers' in their united reference to God—and primarily a loving concern for the *salvation* of one's fellows. Thus any person who does not follow *this path* to his knowledge of God is *necessarily in error*. This is the basis of the concept of 'heresy'.

construct any 'philosophy of the times', but we must also accept into our idea of the divine mind all that the mental structure of other ages enabled them to understand and express of the 'mind' of God. However wrong Hegel was to teach as an article of his pantheism that God was the '(mind or) spirit of the world', the fact remains that only the complete '*mind of man*', naturally, knows God completely as the sum and epitome of all the rational structures which have taken shape or will take shape through functionalization and defunctionalization. Thus construction of even natural knowledge of the divine mind, to the extent of its general accessibility to man, is *necessarily* also dependent on the *co-operation* of human societies *in their chronological succession, on a basis of tradition*. Indeed, even if there were quite other reasons for assuming that certain outstanding ages have represented conjunctures in history whose constituents equipped them in some special way for expanding the race's knowledge of God, or that the specific mental functions which come into play in acquiring such knowledge have in the course of history suffered a retrogression rather than grown and moved forward, the one thing prescribed to us would still be the duty of preserving the once adequately known, which we for our part can attain only with a degree of insufficiency.

Let me explain more closely what I understand by '*functionalization*' *of essential insight*:

1. To see essences *as essences* is something other than to know *contingent facts* (to perceive, adjudge, etc.), in conformity with the guidance of previously intuited essences. In the latter action the essence does not come to separate consciousness. It is only a case of the *functioning* of essential knowledge—as a selection-process, not as a synthetic act of combining or connecting—without its being given to our conscious self. It renders supraliminal for the knowledge of contingent existence everything which accords with the intuited essence or is possibly a case where foreknown essential principles of interrelation or essential structures apply. In this way the originally objective a-priori *becomes* the subjective a-priori; the thing thought becomes a 'form' or pattern of thinking, the thing liked becomes a 'form' and manner of liking.

2. Self-evidently, the initial 'catching sight' of an essence is unreflective: it is not a vision based on a *judgment*, in which the 'idea' corresponding to the essence, or the ideal interrelation corresponding to the essential interrelation, is grasped as true.

3. All the subjective a-priori in Kant's transcendental sense—that is, all laws of experience which are also laws of empirical objects *because* they are laws of experience—is not an original but an evolved component, varying according to the vehicle of experience, the empirical subject.

On no occasion and in no sphere of mental activity does the subjective a-priori function by means of spontaneous connection or combination (in accordance with some basic principle) of originally isolated and amorphous data (Kant's 'sensations') nor by any positive 'construction', 'assembly' or 'formation'. Its mode of operation is exactly the reverse. It is a negation, suppression and disregard, definitively governed in accordance with previously known essences or essential interrelations, of all contingent elements in the existent object which perform no function of fulfilment or confirmation in respect of the aforesaid essentials. Thus the subjective a-priori does not produce, but suppresses, destroys, distorts— for possible knowledge of the world—all parts and aspects of the world which have no reference of applicability or fulfilment to already known essences and essential structures. All subjective a-priori is therefore not a particular kind of shaping and connecting, but a particular form of selection. The 'relation' in its widest sense (leaving out of account that kind of relation exemplified by union, similarity, causality, etc.), is by nature no positive thing which our mind confers on a relation-free datum (a mental 'bond' derived by synthesis and combination), but is only the residuum which remains after the exercise of selective disregard upon the datum's self-constituting world-significance, which itself is positive in the round. In every case the relation, as intuitive and as thought, is the by-product of a definitely *controlled* development of perception and thought. It is therefore not of positive but of negative character. It is not the product of synthesis but the residuum of analysis—what is left on one side in the assimilation of the object. How strange it is that many thinkers permit an astonishing interweaving of the two mutually exclusive views, when they come to characterize the origin and function of the subjective *a-priori*! Windelband is a notable example.[1]

Certainly, what Kant calls the transcendental reference, experience and object of experience are in a sense present in both opposed views of the nature of the subjective a-priori. In both cases the object must 'order itself' according to the rules of the knowing mind or its functions, irrespective of whether the specific function of cognition is based on a systematic construction, synthetization, formation of the object from 'given' sensational material or on a methodical selection-process (suppression, abstraction, disregard) imposed on a self-constituting object. For if the order of selection in which the fulness of the world, as it is in ipseity, reaches man (or a particular kind of man, *e.g.* a type of racial or cultural unity) is so governed that an object of essence B is only given when an object of essence A has already been given (if, that is to say, A has datum-priority

[1] Cf. *Einleitung in die Philosophie* (1914), pp. 235 *et seq.*

over *B* in order of time—not necessarily in direct succession), then if an object *X* is simultaneously of essence *A* and *B*, everything which is true of *A* must necessarily be true of *X*—not vice versa. For example, if spatiality and extensity have strict perceptual priority over all essential properties of matter and corporeality, geometry must be strictly valid for all possible bodies. But the same principle, the applicability of geometry to all bodies without exception, would still hold good if Kant's doctrine were true— though it denies the very reality of extension and space, and explains the spatial form as merely a subjective aspect of the datum. Thus in both cases the transcendental validity of the so-called *a-priori*, even for the objects of experience, would persist, so that in itself it offers us *no* criterion of choice between one or other *hypothesis*—that which supposes a synthetic addition of the form on the part of the spontaneous mind, or the other, which postulates an ordered selection in conformity with foreknown essences.

Notwithstanding these considerations, the two theories of the *subjective a-priori* remain divided by an abyss—both in themselves and in their consequences for metaphysical knowledge.

In our hypothesis what coincides in the datum with the nature of world-reality is self-constituting, already formed. Out of the vast range of these forms and figures, which have their being in themselves and are un-equivocally bound up with their specific, individual contents, our mind takes up, according to a particular order of selection, some only, while as it were negating and suppressing the others. It analyses the world according to a determined and—by virtue of the history of cognition, indeed of essential cognition—predetermined order. The statuary of experience is present in the world, just as the statue can be said to be present in the marble and the sculptor regarded as merely liberating and revealing it with appropriate blows of his hammer. In Kant's teaching, on the other hand, the mind is a power of synthetic combination according to laws and models which are basically its own, which may be neither derived nor explained—which dwell in it, and are its fate.

Attributes of the divine mind

Once God's mentality and all-causality are sufficiently known on other grounds, the attributes of his mind are discovered by two methods, each proceeding in independence of the other, but which by reason of the essential connection between the type of act and the type of object *must* lead to the same results—always provided they are correctly used. The first method proceeds from the essential structure which is realized in the *actual* world and to which those attributes of the divine mind must correspond whi ' *can* be known to us from God's relation to the world, if he is really its cause (as personal mind and as creator). The second method proceeds from the essential structure of the human mind (thus not from empirical psychological facts) in that it indicates the nature of God's mind by analogy with those essential features (imagined absolute and infinite) and that essential network (*i.e.* the underlying order of types of mental act) which are discovered in studying the nature of the mind of man. Throughout this second method we must have recourse to extrapolatory, terminal concepts such as we may form for ourselves of the pure mental component in the soul of man by ascertaining what is left of the mind when we observe it at levels of decreasing dependence on the body and its modifications (levels which we uncover progressively in the course of the experiment). In this kind of observation we at least obtain the directions of the lines which, imagined as produced to the ideal limit of independence of the body, communicate to us the terminal concepts of a body-free mind—as which alone we may designate God, albeit by analogy. Indeed we obtain thereby, in progressive stages, a series of ideas of possible minds divested of internal contradictions yet corresponding to the material regularity of the human mind: in the mind of God this progressive series does but find its highest terminus, its pinnacle and crown.

Of these two methods the Middle Ages preferred the first, at least in the era of high Scholasticism, and modern philosophy, where it has followed the right path, has preferred the second. In fact, *both* methods are necessary and prescribed, since both the ideal-objective system of the universe, as God's highest creation and most direct of mirrors, and the intellectual soul of man point to the divine mind's attributes in equal measure.

Moreover, both methods lead only to analogical definitions. That much is known as soon as we have performed the necessary transference to the divine mind of God's formal attributes, *simplicity* and *indivisibility*. The divine mind has no special 'abilities' (intellect, will, capacity for love, etc.), not only because it is everything that it is *actu* (the *actus* necessarily preceding potency in all cases, as Aristotle long ago recognized), but also because every 'real' partition, or merely relatively independent capacity for action, of abilities and functions as they are found in the human mind, is a *sign of imperfection*. Already we consider the soul of man as something relatively more perfect because it enters into every *actus* as something relatively *simple* and *whole*—so that intellect, will, love, all manner of 'feelings of . . .', etc., seem to be nourished by *one* indivisible stream of mental activity. But God is absolutely simple. Nevertheless, the attributive definitions of the divine mind as love, will, reason, have a sound and justified *meaning*, in that they are only intended to express that the divine mind must in fact contain powers of *this* essential kind and tendency, without of course our being able to know and give an account of the *continuous intermediate stages* and components which in the divine mind fasten these powers together into one absolutely unitary and simple efficacy. And so the attributive expressions ascribe neither real nor 'abstract' parts to the divine mind but convey only the meaning that God's mind *resembles* in this or that respect what we call love, will or intellect in the human mind.

The same is true for the basic ordering, as between intellect and will, will and love, etc., which we may likewise discern in the human mind as the internal regularity of a mind as a whole. Without importing into the very idea of God a presupposition of an order of functional priority— and thus these abilities which differ even though they function as a unit— we must yet accept that within God's mind there is an *analogy* even to this order. Thus, if investigation of the human mind led us for example to a doctrine of the primacy of intellect over will, but at the same time to a basic view according to which love enjoyed absolute priority over both will and intellect,* we would also have to assume that an analogy to this hierarchy exists in God.

A succession of metaphysical systems (by Plotinus, Spinoza, Hegel, *inter alios*) have erred by understanding the mind of God solely in its logical aspect. In that philosophy shows us by the example of this real world the essences and essential structures which are in every possible world and whose concomitant truths hold good for any world, philosophy lifts itself by its own efforts out of thraldom to this world. But purely of itself it would lack inducement to venture beyond the environing sphere of the logos thus immanent in the world, which sphere it might regard as the sum of all essentials, if the formal existence and essence of God were not already established. However, when this as yet purely impersonal logos is seen in the light of the idea of God, it is invested with a personal, living subject, a subject who 'sees'[1] and thinks in a manner consonant with known essences—in such a way that the powers of insight[2] and thought,

---

[1] *Anschaut:* 'views' and 'intuits'. See next note (*Translator*).

[2] *Anschauung*. It is apparent from two phrases in the text (bracketed, p. 217) that Scheler regards *Anschauung* and *anschaulich* as interchangeable with *Intuition* and *intuitiv* (of course the root-sense of *anschauen* is to 'look at'). However, it has not been thought advisable to translate accordingly. Apart from the various unrespectable associations of 'intuition' (*e.g.* the 'lucky hunch' connotation), to say at this point that God 'intuits' would be infelicitous, since one intuits from a prior ignorance. On the other hand one may 'see' or exercise 'insight' when one cares to do so, and one's prior state may be no more disgraceful than a voluntary disregard; this is much more in accord with God's freedom and omniscience— and in fact when Scheler says *Anschauung* he means something which differs in

an important way from the 'mental instinct' or willy-nilly impulsion which most of us feel in the word intuition. The difference is clearly that anything analogous to instinct, even if it has no sensual connotation, must at least be innate and involuntary, whereas Scheler's *Anschauung* is voluntary (in a roundabout way) and has a minimal hereditary component. This is not to say that it is not a mental *habit*: on the contrary, it is *the* mental habit, shaped in Scheler's view by the selective 'functionalization of essential insights'—'insight' in this concrete, objective sense being quite literally *Einsicht* in the same metaphorical framework (cf. remark about the Greeks, p. 136 l. 10).

Anschauung, then, is the exercise of that direct mental contact which Scheler mentions on p. 199, where he outlines a process of which 'intuition' would be an unfair description. In connection with that passage it may be remarked that Scheler's understanding of perception as a whole will become clearer if this page is collated with others on the same theme, notably pp. 249 and 291. The key to his view lies in his doctrine of the pre-sensory 'intentional unity' (in the strict epistemological sense) to which he *also* gives the general name, in concrete uses, of *Anschauung*; in this sense *Anschauung* is not only the provider of 'essential insights' (which is its analytic function) but the sole furnisher of material to consciousness, since all other data-supplying agencies must deal through this 'middleman'— though the chronology of commercial transaction is misleading here. Indeed, *Anschauung* and ratiocination (*Denken*) appear to Scheler to make up the whole of cognition. It is important to understand that when Scheler says that direct mental contact is 'unmediated' (*unvermittelt*) by the sensory organism, he does not mean that the senses do not bring sensual objects to consciousness; he means they do not convey them *as objects* to the *mind*: they fail to convey what the object 'conveys'— in the first place its concrete thinghood, the apprehension of which is purely mental, the business of *Anschauung*. Without any guiding *intention*, which must be mental, the senses are incapable of the *kind* of value-analysis that *Anschauung* can perform: they merely present a kaleidoscope which *Anschauung* seizes as a meaningful *whole* (the intentional unity) before the process of analysis. (These remarks are only concerned with sensual objects.)

Thus *Anschauung* is used in three senses: 1. the habit of mind formed by the functionalization of essential insights (in group-senses this becomes *Weltanschauung*); 2. the activation of 1. in direct mental perception, including the act of cognitive intention; 3. non-inferential grasp of essentials, simultaneous with 2. and providing —sometimes—new essential insights.

As can be seen, it is only in the *whence* of these processes that the 'pure gift' connotation of 'intuition' could be appropriate. But *Anschauung* is not the gratuity or psychic phantom we often seek to designate by 'intuition'. Though it is not spontaneous in the sense in which that word is associated in the text with rational method (*i.e.* not deliberate and self-conscious), its quality depends, as 'functionalization' ultimately depends, on a mental readiness (expressed in 'intentions') and an *anti*-subjectivist moral alertness with a substratum of self-discipline. It is in this roundabout ethical way that *Anschauung* is voluntary and deserves a more honourable name.

In certain senses (not necessarily for *Anschauung*) 'intuition' and 'intuitive' have been sparingly used. For the rest the following equivalences apply: *Anschauung* the general function = insight, direct or mental perception; an act (or content) of *Anschauung* = perception, overall or unitary perception; a truth got by *Anschauung*, an *Einsicht* = an insight, axiom; reason from a basis of essential insights = percipient reason. The context should suffice to distinguish these uses from sensory perception.

Ultimately, Scheler's understanding of *Anschauung* is the crux of his own 'essential insight'—that to love is to know (*Translator*).

which function separately in the body-laden mind, are completely inter-penetrative, forming one living unity. Human epistemology teaches us that the bodily-conditioned senses do not supply the positive content of our perceptions of the world but merely appropriate it teleologically for the organism. There is therefore no reason why insight should not be as genuinely proper to the asensual logos of God as so-called rational thought. On the other hand human thought, with its typical tripartion into abstraction, judgment, inference, and its discursive nature, may be transferred analogically to the mind of God only in so far as it is thinking in the sense of grasp of meaning, not in so far as it possesses the inferential form and unfolds in stepwise succession. For just as the sensory perception is not the concrete mental perception but only a bio-economic way of evaluating it for the service of the organism, the process of abstraction, judgment and inference is only a bio-socially conditioned form of evaluat-ing and exploiting the grasp of meaning so that it may serve human ends. But the very division into insight and grasp of meaning represents a humanly conditioned form of cognition, a dichotomy, moreover, which whenever the cognitive effort has reached its goal is resolved into unitary knowledge of the thing or matter itself (in the self-evident overriding unity of what is signified and what is perceived). Insight is simply recogni-tion of the values inhering in objects, with respect to the objects them-selves; thought is simply the same mental recognition on the plane of general and collective reference. Thus insight is in no way, as Platonic rationalism believed, mere sensually clouded, muddled thinking, but is as purely and basically mental as thought in the sense of grasp of meaning. Conversely, and in contrast to the views of Mach, Avenarius, the English sensualists and others, thought is not merely the planned economy of insight, still less of sensory perception; it is not merely a technical means of husbanding the resources of insight. On the contrary, both, insight and thought, are differently oriented forms of evaluative 'exploitation' employed by the mind, which in its cognitive aspect is intrinsically unitary, and these forms may not be transferred to the divine mind as a dichotomy but must be ascribed to it, in an infinite mode of being, as a unity of 'percipient intellect' (*intuitiver Verstand*) or 'intellectual insight' (*intellektuale Anschauung*). And so it is the experience of the 'confluence' of insight and meaning in self-evident knowledge of things which alone provides us with the basic phenomenon from which we must construct for ourselves the idea of a 'divine intellect' as the subject-correlate of the essences realized in the world.

But the divine mind is not only intellectual insight, as the above thinkers believed. It is also of an originally *volitional* nature.

We know the volitional nature of the divine mind from the basic character of the world, which, in conjunction with a series of essential insights, impels us to assume it. The world is not *only* an assemblage of essences in a peculiar interrelation: it also exists *as* this world—in other words, it has as *a whole* the character of concrete, contingent reality. That it is 'a' real world (not simply a world-shaped collection of essences) is itself one more essential characteristic of this world, but it is a fact which we should distinguish from the positive contingency of its real content, even though the fact of 'a' real world necessarily entails the contingency of its content.[1]

Now the realness of a thing requires in the first place an effecting action and an effecting agent 'through which' it 'is' rather than is not, and within the scope of the principles governing its quality and character it further requires an effecting action creating it thus-and-thus and not otherwise. The principle here postulated alone deserves the name of *general causal principle*—in sharp contradistinction from *special* principles, which represent more or less direct application of the causal principle to particular existential forms in the universe. Such for example is the principle that any state of affairs or alteration (even if it is unique or unrepeated) is the consequence of the action of a thing A on a thing B—which represents the causal principle at work in the *time*-aspect and continuum of existence. Such again is the principle that any effect is a reciprocal effect (A affects B, but B must at the same time affect A), which is concerned solely with *spatially simultaneous* things. And of even more special application is the principle that if a state of affairs should recur (or appear) in *identical* form in time and space, supposing the *uniformity of existence* and laws of eventuality, identical effect E will follow from identical cause C. Within this proposition there lie not only the causal principle but no less than three special conditions of its application: 1. spatio-temporal existence, 2. the uniformity of being and happening in space and time, 3. the proposition that like causes have like effects—consequent upon the causal principle combined with an extended identity-principle, 4. the principle, restricted to mathematical quantities, of the inter-dependence of all variations of objects—that is, the principle which endows the theory of functions with the unity of a science. None of these four propositions forms part of the *most general causal principle*; neither, it goes without saying, does the causal principle of spatio-temporal contact, which—as may be shown—is embedded as a logical component in the

---

[1] Everything real is contingent, but not vice versa. Contingency, in the sense of gratuitous, relative existence, is also to be found in the sphere of irreality, *e.g.* mathematical constructs.

above four propositions when taken *together* and excludes all remote effects in space as well as all purposive or final causes in time. This last-mentioned principle, as need not here be shown, may *not* be validly applied to intramundane biological causality, much less (for different reasons) to psychical and historical causality. Neither does the general causal principle contain any trace of the distinctions implied in the concepts *causa efficiens* and *causa finalis,* or the others designated by *causa immanens* and *causa transiens.*

It is directly on the basis of the general causal principle, and *solely* on that basis, that the world, as a real and therefore contingent world, demands an effecting action and an effecting agent to posit it as real—something which either calls it from not-being into existence or is eternally 'calling' it and sustaining it in existence. Here as yet we are not referring to a temporally 'first' cause; the requirement that the world's existence should have a cause would be no less valid if the world had 'always' been and had endured from everlasting, *i.e.* if the world were sempiternal. The world would *not* in that case be also 'eternal', since an entity whose existence, if it does exist, does not follow from its essence can never be 'eternal'.

Meanwhile, the causal principle *alone* does not lead us forthwith to a supreme cause (in the non-temporal sense), since the cause of 'a' real world, though undeniably required, could also have a cause in a second real world and this be caused by a third. The infinite regress (always in a non-temporal sense) which the causal principle in itself would impose cannot be arrested unless we already *know* that there is in reality an *ens a se et per se,* which may be invoked as the cause of the world, and unless we further posit the unity and singularity of the world which is 'a' real world. *If* unity and singularity are *a priori* certain truths of anything, they are certain only of the *ens a se*—not of the world. Again, the insight that the cause of the world has not an immanent but a transcendent character presupposes the insight that there is an *ens a se* and that all contingent things are dependent on it. Taken by itself, the causal principle could be satisfied by a dynamic pantheism—but not by a merely logical pantheism, such as those of Spinoza and Hegel.

Now we already know not only that there is an *ens a se* on which all things are dependent, but also that we may legitimately term this *ens a se,* analogically, 'mind'. Hence we now acquire the logical right to infer that the cause of the world's realness is 1. a unique and supreme cause (this follows from the *ens a se* 'as' cause), 2. a cause of a volitional nature. For volition is the only 'case' known to us of a mental function through which we see a merely ideal quiddity *pass over* into reality, see it 'become' a real thing.

If we leave on one side two questions which must be sharply distinguished, 'What is the nature of realness?' *and* 'Under what circumstances, in the presence of what criteria, may we and should we call an intentional object real, *i.e.* judge it to fulfil the requirements of the essence "real"?', there still remain two other questions, 'In what acts is something of the nature of realness "given"?' and 'How must we understand the process of *"becoming"* real?' But we are provided with an answer to these questions by *two general principles* which, in conjunction with the causal principle, with the assurance that the world is 'a' real one and with our premises of God (*ens a se* and mind), must necessarily lead us to the proposition that the world was created and is upheld *by* the will of God. Only this proposition allows us to glimpse the possibility of strictly refuting *other* highly esteemed metaphysical doctrines of God and the world, teachings, for example, that the world is eternal, that the world has *necessarily* proceeded from God, or is necessarily proceeding from God— whether in the manner envisaged by Spinoza, or that of Plotinus and Hegel, *i.e.* by emanation, not creation—; or teachings that the reality of the world is a subjective illusion, since it is the mere wish-fulfilment in man (as Buddhism believes) of 'originally' unreal components, or that the world (as a permanent process of evolution into cosmos) is the 'creative evolution' and 'growth' of a God freely 'making' himself—'*un dieu qui se fait*' (Bergson).

These general principles are as follows. Firstly, the *realness of a thing* would necessarily be concealed from a mental being that was only logos, or only logos and love; it is only given in the intentional experience of the possible *resistance* of an object against a mental function of the type volition *qua* willing (not, that is, *qua* 'wishing to do' or actually doing, and, of course, irrespective of the corporeality of the volitional subject, or the relation of volition to the body and of the body to the corporeal world).*

Objectively there would be no impediment to the realness of a complete fairy world, in which whatever we wanted appeared as soon as the wish for it, but its realness could never be *given* to us: we would have no standard of difference between the ideal and the real object (however independent or even transcendent of consciousness this object may be in fact and as perceived). But resistance cannot be 'grasped' in any other way than as an *action* of resistance impinging on our volition, though we do not experience any 'sense (*Gefühl*) of resistance' (a common 'psychological' misnomer) but simply perceive in the empirical resistance of 'something' (let it be mere *x* or, with utter generality, the 'resistance of the world') the *effect* or action of something which is resisting—in just the same way as we experience in the most elementary perception an object of perceiving and a 'provenance from it' of the ideal content of the perception. Remove *this* effect, and the interaction of things which we interpret in its light, from our consciousness of the world, and though you leave intact the chronological subsistence of the world's content, all its dependencies of being and becoming which underlie the assumption of a basis, all natural, all psychic regularity—the force of the world as a fact, the world-*reality*, has vanished from experience.

The *second* general principle is the essential connection between the *original* becoming real and the having been willed. All other kinds of becoming, however disparate, whether in the natural, psychical or historical worlds, mathematical procedures, physical processes, biological change—change, growth, unfolding of all kinds—are alike in this limitation: when we study them phenomenologically they never show us the becoming real of anything *originally altogether unreal*, but only all kinds of reshaping of real things into other things different in content; it may be that the new thing represents genuine growth, but it may also represent an ideal quantum no greater than the original. It is only when we experience the congruence of a thing that was willed with the process of its realization and final realness 'through' volition, only when we have disengaged this experience from the various modes of psycho-physical and biological causality which accompany the volitional acts of a mind imprisoned in a body, that we have an instance of 'seeing' something originally non-real (the 'projectum' given in the willing) *become truly real* 'there outside' in the world (or 'there inside' in the psyche, in the case of an act of will with reflexive intention). Needless to say, the concrete fact of this irreducible phenomenon is self-evident in a way quite unaffected by questions such as 'Does my will act on the body and if so how?—and by what anatomical or psycho-physiological intermediaries?' No matter what hypotheses and theories are formulated in answer to these questions, the primary phenomenon, in the sense of Democritus' σώζειν τὰ φαινόμενα, must remain intact and aloof. For it towers in self-evidence above all hypotheses of the psycho-physical mechanism of volition. And in spite of the fact that, empirically, human volition can 'create' nothing in the absolute sense but always exercises itself upon what is already given as real, it is not the 'choice' of the will as such in human volition which confines the original creative intention contained in all will to (in fact) a mere reshaping of the world, but the force of the resistance to volition which first arises when we attempt to enact a project of the will, and of which *experience* increasingly informs us through, ultimately, the resistance of our bodies as well as the external world of nature and the historical continuum.* For it is this force of resistance which, by restricting the possible *contents* of will, sets bounds to the goals, plans and resolutions we may form. Originally man wills even the impossible; the contents of his will are never *exclusively* derived from experience of what is and what has been. Habitual or instinctive impulses do not unequivocally determine the quality or positive content of the volitional project but only precipitate the here-and-now volition or dictate the range of volitional activity by curbing the original scope of choices.

Only these considerations enable us to understand that all human volition takes place on some rung of a ladder stretching from mechanical *application* to *creating*, a height which it never quite attains.* (Only creation-from-nothing[1] is essentially withheld from human will, not as human but as finite.) For the more the material in which the content of both the initial will and the finished work is apparent *fades* in significance for the meaning, value and importance of the whole, and the more 'original' is the realized project (hence unpredictable and not deducible from previous data), and the more adequate is the congruence of project and work—the more the realizing of the will was 'creation'. It is in the volition of the would-be holy man, the saint, that we may best find epitomized the nature of the phenomenon, since he most nearly approaches true creation; in no other medium than the one constantly 'given' and accessible, his own soul —and indirectly the souls of others, through example and emulation—he creates 'himself' as a 'most perfect good possible' in accordance with an ideal value-image which he has gradually acquired in the act of loving himself only 'in God'. The *saint* is the person most independent of extrinsic material, in that his 'work' is none other than 'himself' or the souls of other men, who in voluntary emulation reproduce afresh his work's ideal content of meaning and value—that is, his own spiritual pattern and figure. Next most near to the phenomenon of true creation is creation on the part of the *genius*, who creates a unique and unexampled original from extrinsic material. Next below stands the kind of human being we may summarize as the *hero*; he forges his value-personality neither in the medium of himself and other souls nor in works that lead a separate, concrete existence; at his level a man is already more utterly dependent on the *historical* material wrought by societies, peoples, states and other groups, and these, within their *given* potentialities, he leads onward through irreplaceable deeds—which, however, as not in the case of genius, could conceivably have been performed by someone else.*

Given these principles it is clear that the general resistance which informs us of the realness of the world as a unit (and tells us also of *a*

---

[1] *Erschaffen* as distinct from *Schaffen*, relative creation or simply making (*Translator*).

resistant action) is in the last resort only comprehensible through a willing of the world by God—not, then, in terms of merely natural forces, which we assume between substances when there is phenomenal repetition and regularity of interaction. The phenomenon of the as yet undifferentiated world-resistance as such is given to us far more originally than any individual or special resistant (or non-resistant). In thinking, the fact that objects belong to the world is given in the particular object, while in sensory perception the existence and structure of the environmental world is given *before* any particular object. Likewise when we notice a psychic process in ourselves we are conscious of the looming whole of the psychic unity-in-complexity from which it emerges, while in the single soul we are given the category of the psychic to which it belongs and see that this category has the character of a unitary group. Therefore the various dynamic agencies which we posit *within* the world as effective '*causae secundae*' ('forces', 'energies', teleological urges, etc.) presuppose, both objectively and for the sake of their comprehensibility, some understanding of the resistance of the world and its reality as a *whole*—an understanding which must needs be based on the only model we have for the becoming real of the unreal, namely creation from volition. The bare 'sum' of *causae secundae* would be no more able to explain to us the *irreducible phenomenon of world-resistance* than the assumption of a *single* world-force or world-energy.

Creation is a process of which we have at all events a definite 'idea', which is clearly distinguished from our ideas of all other ways of becoming real, such as transposition, modification, growth, breeding, etc., etc. Now if we consider the ladder of the phenomena wherein man as a volitional agent approaches creation, and if at the same time we look into the limitational reasons why 'perfect creation' is always withheld from us, we need only 'produce' the ladder and think away the limitations in order to obtain the idea of 'perfect creation' (*vollkommenes Schaffen*). The idea of perfect creation arises from the idea of a mental volition to which the 'material' in which it enshrines its project must be, so to speak, utterly obedient, without any resistance stemming from the laws of its composition, a volition, moreover, which took none of the ingredients of its project from the material itself. A god who 'created perfectly' in this sense would nevertheless be no more than a demiurge, not the God of theism. He would still be no more than a finite world-architect; not the final sustainer and disposer of the world but only its fabricator and director. He would be an artist-god, a genius-god, but not the God of the saints. No, if we would find the closest analogy to God's real basic relation to the world we must raise our idea of volition to the higher power commensurate with an infinite mind *a se et per se* and therefore add to our 'perfect creation' the fundamentally different idea of '*absolute* creation' (*Erschaffen*). When a real thing is absolutely created it is made by a volition which, employing no given material (either from itself or from elsewhere), creates perfectly 'out of nothing'—an analogical way of speaking which no more than formulates the liminal observation which is the origin of theistic doctrine.

But even now the road of knowledge which leads to the Creator God is not entirely complete. For the idea of the Creator God implies not only the proposition that an infinite mind once brought or enduringly brings the world into being but also this other proposition, that what brings into being is, originally, a *freely choosing personal will*. Only this stipulation excludes the following ideas: 1. that the will which caused (or causes) the world was (or is) somehow *determined*, not free; 2. that the world's proceeding from God was *necessary*; 3. that an absolutely fortuitous, blind and irrational impulse of will called the world-idea into existence; 4. Aristotle's notion of a mere eternal and unmoved 'mover' of the world, in the sense of a divine reality attracting the movements of the world towards it; 5. the Bergsonian conception of a world which is purely thought-projected in time, a world which unfolds creatively out of a deity '*qui se fait*'.

A god who was *only* a will eternally *predetermined* 'out of itself', a god who was not also something else (*e.g.* love, logos) or who was even *primarily* such a will (so that the essential principles and ideas inherent in the world also rested on his eternally predetermined decisions of will) would be indistinguishable from a universal force of *destiny*. The Greek *heimarmene*, the Mohammedan doctrine of God and the fearful errors of Calvin often come near to this over-tension of the sovereign power of the divine will. God's analogical will is not necessary *ex se*, but is necessary only in so far as he freely follows, in the sense of realizing maximal value, the essential law that the self-evident value-insight necessarily determines the content of volition and only leaves free the *willing* of the contents thus determined. In other terms, it is only the willing of the maximal value which is absolutely 'free', not the contents of volition, which are *necessarily* predetermined, *before* the act of will, by love, goodness and wisdom.

Any doctrine of a primacy of will in God is therefore as fallacious as any doctrine of a primacy of will in the mind of man. No less fallacious is any doctrine ascribing to God only the mental attributes of volition and intellect while denying him goodness, love and wisdom (such a one as the doctrine of Eduard von Hartmann). If we look rather more closely at the analogical basis of the types of mental act, as we must transfer them to God from knowledge of the human mind, we see that the most original root of all 'mind' in God as in man is *love*.[1] Love alone it is which founds the unity of will and intellect, which but for love would fall dualistically apart.

The first thing which is derived from God's love is his *objective goodness*, and this we must distinguish from its consequence, the goodness of his will. God is the *summum bonum*, which when personal is the quality of absolute objective goodness. But in content, in accordance with the axioms of ethical value whereby the highest value in respect of acts accrues to love, God's absolute goodness is nothing other than love. The specific goodness of God's will is already a consequence of the fact that his will is eternally one and coincident with what he loves. God does not love what he wills, loving it because he wills it, but wills eternally what he loves and affirms in love as value.

However, not only God's love but also God's intellect is set over his volition and directs it, guides it. 'In the beginning' was not the *deed*, but the love-guided logos. The intellect is directly set over the will, not as knowledge of all things but as *wisdom in all things*. Yet wisdom is knowing the proper objective hierarchy of value-units and value-qualities. And since we cannot know and grasp the being of anything which we have not originally perceived as a value-unit, the supreme wisdom of God must precede his omniscience. But both the wisdom *and* its dependent omniscience precede the volition. Wisdom is not a *post facto* assessment of already-won ontological knowledge, so that it may be pressed into the service of the highest value-ends. Rather is it a capacity for originally conceiving and disposing the thing to be done or made in such a way that any possible knowledge of it can be a knowledge worth acquiring. Thus wisdom takes its place between love and the pensive 'seeing' of the ideas which must be realized through volition. The very idea of a creator-god implies love—not knowledge—as the nucleus of the divine mind. If the Aristotelian idea of God does not share with the Christian the essential characteristic of creative power, it is because its object lacks the attribute of love. Moreover, it is only the love of God which renders it comprehensible that he should exercise his volition in the sense of creation rather than confine it within himself in eternal inertia. I have already shown[2] how the specifically and positively Christian predicates of God, as one who imparts himself in revelation and condescends to man in the Incarnation, can only be understood as corresponding to the idea of a divine mind in which love, not intellect or will, is posited as the underlying attribute.

[1] See my study of 'Love and knowledge' in *Krieg und Aufbau*; see also the third volume of the present work.*

[2] Cf. the article '*Das Ressentiment im Aufbau der Moralen*' in *Vom Umsturz der Werte*.

Just as act and object coalesce in the being of God, so the definition of God as *summum bonum* (the infinite, positive, holy, absolute good) coincides and merges with God as an infinite *activity* of love. For this reason alone the mystic, contemplative love for God as the highest good must necessarily lead to participation in, and emulation of, God's infinite *action* of love towards himself and his creatures—so that the conduct of us men towards our fellow-creatures is analogous to that of God towards us. Conversely, love '*in*' God, which is the active insertion of the *nucleus* of mental personality into the core of the divine person, and a loving of all things with the love of God, must of its own accord revert to God as the highest object of love and thus perfect itself mystically, contemplatively, in the *amare Deum in Deo*. Greek piety found room only for the contemplative love of God, ignoring the love 'in' God to which anti-mystical Lutheranism devoted as one-sided an attention. But if we follow their examples, cultivating one heart-felt impulse of love at the expense of the other, with its different orientation, we are bound to be led into grave errors.

To summarize, then: since God himself eternally and necessarily establishes his own existence in conformity with his essence, his own free will-power is enclosed within the bounds of his eternal mental essence: God is free by an 'essential necessity', and wills himself—his *essence*, that is—free as a fact eternally necessary.

Thus any teaching is erroneous which supposes that the elements of God's mind corresponding analogically to reason and love are wholly overborne by his analogical 'will'. But no less mistaken is the teaching, variously recurrent from Plotinus onward and most cogently expressed by Spinoza and Hegel, that the world *necessarily* proceeds from God's essence, whether in a non-temporal, logical manner, or in the dynamic form of a non-temporal becoming, or even in the form of chronological evolution. This doctrine is inextricably tied, by a necessity of principle, to an extreme *intellectualism* in the theory of mind (the human included) and to some form of *pantheism*. Moreover, this pantheism is invariably of the acosmic variety —that is to say, it begins with a radical misconception of the world's contingency and realness and of the non-derivability of its things and processes from the essential correlations and qualities which are realized in the world. Only one who fails to see the *reality* of this world can pledge allegiance to such an outlook. And only one who in spite of seeing this reality misunderstands the essential connection between realness and the having-been-willed could ascribe the world's existence to a *purely* intellectual mind. If—as in the pantheistic view—God were related to the world only as the whole to its parts or the essence to its phenomenon or the substance to the modes of its attributes, finite minds would be left with only *one* task, to 'think' the world rightly and know it truly. No longer would they have the task of *reshaping* the world, of *freely* making a better world in accordance with a *plan*, under the dominance of norms and ideas of value (which are not abstracted from the world's existence). The *moral* task of life would be resolved and submerged in the contemplative. This shows clearly enough how our idea of God is also drawn, inevitably, into the gravest errors if we neglect to find a place for man's experience of will, as a world-factor, in our philosophical conception of the world, in our comprehension of reality and explanation of man's constant inner sense of the world's resistance. The world postulates a volitional *cause* only because it is real and contingent and in so far as it is real and contingent—only because the essential correlations which are in the nature of things do not unequivocally effect and determine what is real, though they do indeed frame the limits of the world's ideal 'possibilities'. Though God's freedom is not free to be independent of or opposed to his eternal essence, but is included in it, this component of his essence is nevertheless *free-will*.

Epistemologically, therefore, a fallacious, hyper-realistic Platonism is involved in the doctrine of the world's necessary emanation. The whole realm of 'contingent facts' and 'second causes' is disregarded, and the legitimacy of empirical induction in the field of extra-essential phenomena is denied. Logically the positive sciences must then merge with philosophy, while religion for its part—the positive kind being assimilated by the natural—is reduced to philosophical gnosis. If the nature of the personality and freedom of God-the-mind is misconceived, our understanding of the finite creature's person and freedom must needs be perverted. They become mere modes of a divine attribute known as 'thought', or simply relay-points for the passage of some logical or dynamic process—at best mere functional units of the mind of God. On this assumption error and sin necessarily appear to proceed directly from finitude and corporeality— not from free acts of a personal, mental will—or, as in Hegel's historicizing pantheism, they become necessary stimuli of historical development, illustrating the basically fallacious 'dialectic' doctrine of the creative power of negation (*omnis determinatio est negatio*), a view which ever since Nicolaus von Cues has been growing into one of the most questionable elements of the German mind. The distinction between the evolution of the world and the world-process (or the world's conservation and governance) is blurred. The world is either eternal like God himself, since it is a necessary consequence of his eternal essence (*sic* Spinoza), or, as in Hegel's view, God himself is drawn into the becoming of the world.

Now the mistake of this doctrine does *not* lie in teaching the *immanentia Dei in mundo,* the omnipresence of God in all entia, God's collaboration (*concursus*) in the effects of all second causes, the necessary predisposition of God's will by ante-volitional *ideas,* and love borne to the world not merely in respect of specific contents but in respect of the total world-entity. Neither does it err in (apparently) intensifying the human sense of the soul's 'utter' dependency on God, or in seeing the contemplative life as something superior in status to the life of practical activity. The criticisms levelled at intellectual pantheism by north-German Protestant philosophy, with its attachment to will, power, work and '*Kultur*', its strictly correlative false religious supernaturalism (as evinced in the interpretation of 'My kingdom is not of this world' to mean it is either outside or simply 'above' the world)—these criticisms have always fallen *very* wide of the mark. No, the pantheist doctrine has fallen into other errors, no less deep-seated, to be sure, than those features to which we have alluded. In comparison with Protestant theism, pantheism enshrines a profound *truth.* It has always *tended to counteract* the danger inherent in theism, that of lapsing into henotheism. Where it goes astray is in seeing God himself in the very *substance* of the world and thus properly teaching an immanence not of God in the world but *mundi in Deo;* it errs in making a somehow sensorily perceptible indwelling of God in the finite *ens* out of the ontic omnipresence of God in all entities—which of course we too conceive as something quite other than God's *omniscience* and *omnipotence* concerning the entity, as we see in it a *condition* of that very omniscience, that very omnipotence. Pantheism is again mistaken when the *concursus Dei* in all finite action of second causes is magnified into an exclusion and denial of the efficacy of second causes, with a consequent doctrine of divine *omni-causation;* it is wrong when it maintains not only that the *disposition* of volition is determined by ideas, but that volition is in final dependence on a 'fiat' of ideas which *exclusively* determine it; it is wrong in supposing that love of the world 'in' God, for the sake of its divine creator and highest end, a love which is necessarily prescribed and well-justified, is also love 'of' God, while the *amare Deum in Deo* is yet not seen as the highest plane of love, which must of necessity comprehend love both of God and world.

The Protestant philosophy of will rejects the superiority of the contemplative life. But the superiority of the contemplative over the practical life as such is no fallacy. In spite of all that may be said to the contrary, this belief is certainly no mere 'Christian intellectualism': it is one of the *eternal* truths which Christian philosophy has discovered. It is disregard of the essential facts about the operation of the will, together with the attempt here in evidence to resolve volition in terms of intellect (in man as in God), which leads into a false intellectualism. For it is *this* which fosters incomprehension of the heuristic necessity of ethical cognition, of the moral practical life, as stepping-stones to the extra-ethical, philosophical contemplation of essences,[1] and it is natural that in consequence there should be a failure to understand that this contemplation itself, no matter what its own intrinsic worth, is *in turn* a stepping-stone to the *purely religious* intimacy in God of the *amare Deum in Deo*.

Finally, the functional *primacy of loving* over knowing (which is closely linked with our principle that intellect enjoys a value-primacy over will) is obliterated in intellectual pantheism. To give an example, Spinoza's *amor Dei intellectualis* is not a spontaneous act of intention which is a condition of fully adequate and clear essential cognition, but represents merely the *terminus* of the cognitive process: 'perfect union with the object itself', or the mere emotional effect of this union. In particular, the idea that love of God is a condition, not a consequence, of any (love-free) knowledge of God, is in this way distorted into its opposite. From Spinoza to Schopenhauer, Hegel and Hartmann, the pantheistic theory of love, erring even in its phenomenological premises, has taught that *A*'s love of *B* is itself only a form of vague knowledge, witnessing the *unity* of the world-basis and the non-existence *qua persons* of those who love (in other words, their merely modal or functional existence *vis-à-vis* God). This, though in the last resort the metaphysical starting-point of every false *sociological communism*, is also a necessary consequence of pantheism's erroneous premises. All genuine 'love' affirms and attests its object in respect of the final realization of the value-essence proper to the *object;* it loves *in spite of* the object's existential separation from the loving subject, in spite of its otherness, even while fully conscious of both separation and otherness. If I 'loved' God only because I am a mode or a function of God, and other creatures only because they too are such—being thus in substance not different from myself—my action could not be accounted love. It would be nothing more than a petty egoism, and that in turn would be no more than a part of the great cosmic egoism of a god, similarly devoid of any distinctive personality, engaged in a sterile love of himself. And that is in fact how Spinoza sees it: our love of God, in his view, is only a *part* of the love with which God loves himself. And so the soul's dependence on God is here, in the last analysis, not a *religious* dependence. If the soul necessarily proceeds from God as a function of the divine mind, in such a way that it remains wholly immanent within him, or if it is only the 'idea of an idea in the thought of God'—Spinoza's phrase—all the religious significance

[1] The view expounded and justified in the chapter entitled 'The Nature of Philosophy', *q.v.* (*Translator*).

and value which its dependence can have is lacking, because the free and moral *character* of that dependence is absent. It is not, as it were, the dependence of child on father but that of the slave on his master. Well, then, may Spinoza say 'We are servants, yea slaves, of God', in his treatise on theology and politics. If God himself thinks, wills, etc., in me, if religion is, as Hegel maintains, no more than God's consciousness of himself *in man*, or his growing self-awareness (Hartmann), then there is not even any such thing as *obedience* to the divine will (let alone freely borne love), since even obedience[1] is a positive autonomous act of the human person (in contrast to compulsive suggestion, in which there is no consciousness of a commanding alien will as alien).* Still less can there be any *'velle in Deo'* in the sense of free volition; we are 'slaves' with a vengeance, in the strictest sense of Aristotle's dictum: 'The will of the slave is *in* his lord.'

Certain metaphysicians of modern times have made strongly individual pronouncements concerning the relationship of the real world to possible worlds, with reference to *the world's goodness or badness*. Leibniz asserted his ability to demonstrate that the world is not only good and perfect but—in the form in which it first proceeded from the hands of the Creator—the best and most perfect of all possible worlds. Schopenhauer attempted to prove that on the contrary it is the worst of all possible worlds, and that if it had been just a little worse—it would not have been possible, or its parts would not have been compossible. E. von Hartmann's contention was that the existence of any world is in itself bad and senseless, but that of all worlds which could possibly exist the *de facto* world is nevertheless relatively the best and most reasonable.

But these theories lack a proper understanding of the freedom of the divine creative will. They fail to see that although the positive essences and essential structures which philosophy recognizes as ideal possibilities for any real world do indeed hold good for all other worlds that could possibly be real, we cannot know all possible essences which lie in the thought of God, but only those which are realized in our own *de facto* world. These, however, must be known, if we are to dare any assertion of the above kind.

All the more important for us is the question of how, in the light of the foregoing, *i.e.* with our present acquisitions in the study of God, we must understand the *origin of evil and wickedness*.

Since we have not inferred God's existence and essence from the

[1] See my article '*Zur Idee des Menschen*' in *Vom Umsturz der Werte* for an apposite criticism of pantheist objections to theism. In the same article I seek to demonstrate how the Kantian concept of the autonomy of reason (not of the person, as it is often misquoted) leads in like manner to rational pantheism, as illustrated by the doctrines of Fichte and Hegel.*

existence and properties of the world, but have concluded, after independent knowledge of God's existence and most formal essence *and* knowledge of the world's existence, that God is the world's prime cause, we may legitimately ask, and must in duty ask, in what way the real world we empirically know is related to *the* world which we might expect as the creation of a supremely good and loving god. Since, indisputably, we would not expect a world made by a creator equipped with the attributes of love and infinite reason to be anything other than a perfectly good and reasonable world, whereas the world we know confronts us at every turn with a stark reality of imperfection, evil and wickedness, we can but draw the inescapable rational conclusion—which is quite independent of revelation—that after the world's creation it was drawn by some free mental cause into a condition basically different from that which it enjoyed immediately upon leaving the creator's hands. The real world known to us is far worse than what accords with its basis. So the free action of some mind superior to human strength, an action whereby the world has fallen into its present condition, becomes an assured truth of reason. The 'fall' is thus a truth of reason inseparable from theism: it is no mere proposition from revelation.

Within German philosophy it was a decisive advance on the rational pantheism of the classic Kantians when Schelling and Schopenhauer came newly face to face with the Christian doctrine of the 'fall' in all its truth and profundity. Schopenhauer in particular saw 'Christianity's deepest truths' in the doctrines of the Fall and inherited sin. But in his own philosophy he converts even these truths to falsehood, in that he lays the 'original blame' on existence itself and the will that posited existence.

By what deeper philosophical reason was Schopenhauer led to his proposition? There are in fact two pre-eminent reasons.

1. Schopenhauer does not take up into his 'world-basis' the three attributes of *reason*, *love* and *goodness*. 'Reason' as a capacity for essential insight is unknown to him; for him reason does not reach beyond the discursive intellectual activity of inductive concept-formation, inference and conclusion—which, it is true to say, in the absence of higher guidance from a positive spiritual love, and in the absence of direct essential insight (*i.e.* percipient reason), can only lead to something which is to men as is a wooden hive to bees, a mere technical *Ersatz* permitting the satisfaction of dark instinctive urges. But it would remain inconceivable that even this technical intellect should originate in a blind life-will: the blind life-force can kindle no 'torch' for itself, so where can the light be by which the value of the torch may be seen? Intellect is only comprehensible as the servant of percipient reason. Love Schopenhauer falsely reduces to

pity, and pity to emotional infection, or to a vague, instinctive recognition of the all-and-one.* Goodness he does not know, knowing no 'good will'.

2. Even Schopenhauer rightly assigns the attribute of *volition* to the world-basis. But in *his* case volition is no more than the sum and symbol of the will-to-life's dark boundless drive, not a rational volition centripetally counteracting the vital urge and accompanied by love. Knowing, then, that *reality* or *effective* existence is a category not of logic but of the will, but repudiating the notion of a will accompanied by love and ideas, he sees in the world as a *reality* only the *object of a blind desire*. The consequence is that he must regard the very *realness* of the idealities realized in the world as blind and bad *as such*. (Together with Schelling he adopted this view from Indian sources and was followed therein by Hartmann.) The *meaning* of life according to this teaching can only reside, therefore, in a systematic *irrealization* of the world—that is, in the attempt to turn it into an objective ideal image: in saying 'no' to the will-to-life, which is the same blind urge in all things. This 'no' is alleged to be the common fount of all the highest forms of humanity (the genius, the philosopher, the holy man). Yet it is still impossible to grasp *what* it is in us which says 'no' to life, if we are nothing but a grim vital urge in the very roots of our existence. And bare negation can bring forth nothing of positive value. For the sake of what higher good, moreover, do we say 'no' to life? Even peace, rest, stillness, blissful repose in aesthetic contemplation of the contents of the All, are positive conditions of mind, not merely absence of the vital urge. But Schopenhauer requires that the higher good should spring exclusively from repudiation of the lower. The consequence is a negative ascesis of spleen. Schopenhauer's metaphysics is false, because it cannot point to the origin of good, of spiritual light, of *reason, love, self-sacrifice*, of justice and true pity in the world.

But Schopenhauer was also mistaken in this, that he deformed the *vital* urge into a 'blind', a 'bad' and 'evil' thing. Evil has its seat in the *mind*, in hatred and wilfulness—not in the life of instinct. To be sure, the vital urge is not morally good, but neither is it bad and blind. It is a *means to an end* in all its stirrings—even though intelligence and concepts be absent—and the goal towards which it is aimed is not preservation but evolution (generation, growth, the formation of higher and higher organisms). Certainly it is not, purely in itself, guided by love and reason; we may therefore call it *demonic*, but not evil. What is evil is only the personal mind's concurrence in its tendencies, in so far as they are consciously known to be inimical to a known and loved good.

While Schopenhauer rejects the idea of God (in both theistic and pantheistic senses) and reduces religion to a technique of personal salvation prescribing steps on the path to denial of the will-to-life, Hartmann, and Schelling in his later years, hold fast to the idea of God. Moreover, they hold fast to the idea of a world-reason, but they locate the origin of what is bad and evil in the *origin of things themselves*, in the very fact that God *did not only think* the world but in addition *realized* it. Since this 'volition' of God is in itself a blind and absolutely random velleity (even if, according to Hartmann, within the *bounds of his rationality*, so that if God willed the world, he had to will the relatively most reasonable), the factual realness of the world, or of any *possible* world, is bad in all cases and any circumstances. Here then we have a quasi-coincidence of creation and fall. That it should have *become real*, that is the 'fall' of the world-idea which merely as such is good and reasonable—it is a 'fall' into reality. In this case, too, the way of salvation is active self-redemption out of this reality—the way of irrealization. For Schopenhauer this is a conversion which happens suddenly and sporadically in this or that great individual; Hartmann believes it operates through the gradual salvation of human history. But this 'redemption' is *self*-redemption and, in a further analysis, redemption of God through man the knower, the moral agent, the deployer of will and constructive artist. In that God, the absolutely unconscious mind, becomes more and more clearly *conscious* in man of his blind *misdeed*—that he should have realized the world instead of merely thinking it—this blind, aimless act of will is to be retracted at the end of world-history, and the world will then revert to the good and blissful state of 'irreality', of existence *purely as a thought and ideal image*.

From the historical aspect these doctrines are thoroughly understandable. In the first place they represent a very healthy reaction against the childish *optimistic pantheism* of Fichte's and Hegel's time. If we must at all costs have pantheism and not theism, then it is only logical to locate even evil and wickedness in the world-basis *itself*. (The whole history of pantheism goes to show this.) Only theism can make sense of evil—without assigning it to the world-basis. For it is senseless to blame evil and wickedness on our defective and fragmentary acquaintance with the world (thus Spinoza)—as if behind the known fragments everything were united in a meaningful and harmonious whole. And it is senseless, not to say fundamentally criminal, to see with Hegel in all moral evil only the spur and stimulus of *new and positive developments*, the so-called 'creative negation'. There is no creative negation. The proposition *omnis determinatio est negatio* is false and misleading. It is rooted in the persistent romantic delusion that 'creation is the fruit of contradiction'.

But these doctrines (of Schopenhauer and Hartmann) are none the less also a healthy reaction against what I call 'theism without the fall'—whether the fall is denied outright or presented as merely an article of positive revelation. As we have already said, the scandalous contrast between *this* world and a world created *good* by God must lead us *of necessity* to assume the fall. Even if the fall is granted, it is not sufficient, even for natural theology, that it should be admitted *only in regard to man*. That man should 'fall' exclusively from his own free-will—without temptation by any higher and mightier element of evil above him—is unthinkable for the *god-created* image of God, even if we attribute to him a genuine personal freedom, a genuine freedom of choice. Freedom, being intrinsically a positive good, is *ceteris paribus* freedom for good rather than freedom for evil. The activation of freedom in the sense of a real choice of evil therefore requires a stimulus outside and above man. A correct axiology, moreover, must retain the principle that even all *world-evil* is grounded in a concentrated power of *wickedness* and, since 'wickedness' can only be the attribute of a person, in a wicked person. Wickedness is not merely an evil, or something necessarily arising from evil, as is taught by all naturalistic doctrines which regard it as only natural 'imperfection', 'an evolutionary impediment', 'atavism' or sickness (Leibniz and Spencer, *inter alios*).[1] It is through and through a predicate of free mental acts, thus a free and conscious insurrection against a power and reality grasped unequivocally as good. Evil, pernicious frustration of good ends, is and can only be its *consequence*—for any view which assumes the world has a *mental* basis. But if one considers the proposition that *wickedness is also the fount of evil* regarded as the summary of negative extra-moral values in so far as they inhere in extra-mental conditions (such as sickness and death), it is impossible to derive the *world-evil* known to us exclusively from the wickedness of man. For the world-evil is a necessary constituent in the world we empirically know, and is also necessarily *bound to the world's good* by a transparent natural law of *causality*. Indeed, the very ground of all individual evil is this necessary bond between good and evil, even the good and evil of human nature; it is a bond of which we are conscious with an impression of something fatefully *tragic*. The truth that everyone has the virtues of his faults and the faults of his virtues, that the faults and virtues of every person and every people clearly rise and flow from one source of character in each case—that is what makes the *tragic nature of existence*.[2] The phenomenon of the *tragic* is itself a proof that not only pantheism and 'theism without the fall' but even assignment of the origin of evil to the

---

[1] See *Formalismus in der Ethik*, where these doctrines are refuted in detail.

[2] Cf. the section entitled '*Zum Phänomen des Tragischen*' in *Vom Umsturz der Werte*.

world-basis are fallacious. It is the *tragic* necessity lying in the bond of good and evil, good and wickedness, in the world we know, which precludes us from seeking the origin of evil only in human wickedness. This tragic bond is itself the *greatest evil*. It is the constitutionally fragmentary character of everything of positive worth in this world, and to attribute this to the mere 'under-development' of the world, to believe it may be overcome by 'progress', that is the great puerility of 'liberalism' and all its spiritual progeny. As Kant so profoundly remarked, man is indeed 'made of timber so crooked that nothing wholly true and straight can ever be carpentered out of him'. In general terms, and objectively speaking, the *world-evil* is doubtless the consequence of wickedness (such it can only be, *if* it is mind which controls the world), but it is nevertheless, *antecedent* to human wickedness and man's permanent, great temptation to wickedness in character and conduct.

Metaphysics is unable to *tell tales*, to narrate any incident occurring in the personal realms subsisting between God on the one hand and man on the other. Nevertheless, taking into account the positions implied by the foregoing essential truths, it may conclude as follows from our present position.[1]

The origin of the *wickedness which is the ultimate basis* of this world's evil and also the cause of direct temptations to human wickedness, can lie neither in the world-basis itself nor, solely, in man. It must reside in a metaphysical zone lying intermediate between the two, in a free insurrection against God instigated by a person having power over the world. But for the same reason the need for the *redemption* of the world, and of man in the first place (man being the microcosm in which all the elements and forces of the world are concentrated), is a metaphysical truth. Man cannot come to his salvation save through *redemption*. It is not this hypothetical necessity, but only the *fact of redemption* rooted in God's free act of will, which belongs to *positive* theology. To that extent one must say with Newman, 'The world has fallen away from its creator: it is not constitutively in accord with him. This is a truth *as certain as my own and God's existence*'.[2] The world needs redemption and sighs to *be* redeemed. The concept of 'self-redemption' is on the other hand wholly self-contradictory—a *contradictio in adjecʋo*. Whatever we can achieve by our own spontaneous effort is *ipso facto* no redemption. But Hartmann's notion of a 'redemption of God by man' is more senseless still. For—

[1] Cf. J. H. Newman, *Apologia pro vita sua.*

[2] A literal translation of the German words. Newman's own words are rather less succinct and emphatic, and may be found quoted in the chapter on Repentance, p. 62 of this book (*Translator*).

1. What underlies this idea is not an experience pregnant with religious meaning, but merely a dialectical *trouvaille*.

2. But it is also nonsense to suggest that the *derivatum* could redeem the *basis*, or that man, who *cannot* possess any positive forces that do not lie in the origin of his mind and person, could redeem that origin. This is as senseless as repudiating the will-to-life, when man is thought to have no other original content than blind will.

Those doctrines which locate the origin of evil in the world-basis may also be accounted for by a one-sidedly aesthetic or merely *speculative* attitude to existence and to life, derived likewise from the spirit of romanticism. In Schopenhauer and Schelling it is more the aesthetic, in Hartmann the one-sidedly speculative attitude which lead to seeing *evil in itself* in volition and its correlate, reality. Jakob Burckhardt, who was strongly influenced by Schopenhauer, expressed a very similar feeling when he said that power was 'evil by nature'. To Schopenhauer 'suffering' and 'reality' are one and the same vital sensation, one and the same thought, and only the *flight from reality*, into the *repose* which luminously reveals the world as an *aesthetic* image, is the intrinsic *good*. For Hartmann, life in the *ideal* and unrealized is already the intrinsic good.

Yet in the one-sidedly aesthetic attitude to existence the very attitude itself, its correlative field of aesthetic values, and at length the metaphysical sense of art and the aesthetic phenomenon, are misunderstood. The aesthetic attitude is not exhausted by the negative circumstance of 'disinterested non-conceptual intuition' or—as Schopenhauer sees it—by stillness, repose and peace, such as accompany the cessation of the vital urge. It is also guided by a kind of positive love of the absolute in its purely intuitive aspect, and its attendant happy enjoyment is not only peace but also a positive bliss. Moreover, art is not, as Schopenhauer interprets it, a means of contemplative flight from reality, but a spiritually victorious penetration, through the *process* of representation,* into the world's intuited inner value and nature, the positive attempt to re-create in the 'image' a world such as godly eyes beheld in radiance before the 'fall', the attempt to restore to it in the image the freshness and virginity, the perfection, which it lost by the fall. It is more an earnest of possible redemption from the consequences of the fall than a mere flight from reality.

I have said that the 'fall' is a truth of a metaphysical order, or rather that it is *also* such a truth. For that reason it is not only a historical event, a singular consequence of one positive deed, but an ever-present and ubiquitous tendency in the being and eventuality of the world. A world left to itself would, to the extent to which it was left to itself, constantly decrease in positive total value. *Qua* world, the world given to us is always 'falling'. This tendency of constant 'falling' forms so ingrained a characteristic of its existence that it pervades all that we know, all domains of reality—from inanimate nature to the highest exemplars of humanity. If one wished to infer the nature of the world's cause purely from the teleology immanent in the world, one would most probably come to assume a god, but a god constantly letting slip from his hands the reins of command over his creature—a god who is ageing and one day will die. Only if it is not from the world of evil and suffering, not from the fallen world, that we infer God's essence and existence, may we and should we believe and hope that God's purposes will be carried through in the teeth of this universal tendency to decline and depreciate. But—by *one* means alone, *redemption.* For every force of decline in the great order of forces, a superior force must be imagined which can reach out from itself to take command and stem the immanent fall, a force whose highest starting-point is the strength of God himself. No *laisser-aller*, but only ever-renewed positive *deeds* of redemption on the part of God—according to a determinate order of redemption—can bring the world-drama to a positively meaningful and valuable conclusion.

And so those who completely deny an immanent teleology are as wrong as those who ascribe to it a power for immanent growth in positive value, and thus must hold that the world is able to 'evolve' toward ever more worthy forms of existence by means of the forces latent in its own elements. The former are so engrossed with the fallen world, and in particular its further tendency to fall, that they can no longer grasp the idea of the world which has not fallen, and moreover, quite overlook the positive strivings and purposive activities, whose collective influence is admittedly under continual erosion from strivings to negative ends. The latter— among whom we must include all those who make Aristotelian metaphysics (that of a self-enclosed and perfect world not in need of redemption) the basis of their account of the world—fail to notice the forces that strive toward negative ends and believe that a world which is metaphysically fallen, and is thence in a continual physical decline, is the world which God originally made. But both misconstrue the world's constitutional need for redemption. Christianity is a religion which starts from the premise of the world's need for redemption—it is the religion of a world which in *all* its motions sighs for redemption. It is not possible to impose redemption from without upon a self-enclosed, rationally ordered world. For the idea of redemption to reveal its full profundity, develop its full momentum, the fate of the world must at bottom be staked on redemption: it must, that is to say, depend on the world's ultimate possession by a force welling not from it, but from a superior order of existence.

There is a widespread method of employing the so-called 'teleological proof' which overlooks this central point. It fails to see that power and value, durability and viability are in inverse proportion to the 'height' or superiority of the existential form, in the world left to itself. It fails to see that all 'advances', 'higher developments' and universal forms of growth in value are only 'stopgap measures' unable to call a halt to the constant universal tendency, resulting from the fall, for values to depreciate.

That the world possesses this fundamental aspect is not hard to see even at a superficial glance, and has even been scientifically demonstrated in many separate fields; all that is lacking is a general view of these results of recent research, gathered under one metaphysical viewpoint.[1]

1. For Aquinas, the finite nature of the world, in space, time, mass and energy, was a truth of positive theology. One may say that it has now become a *natural* truth. The theory of relativity has confuted a basic dogma of all freethinkers and optimistic metaphysicians. According to this theory all world-reality is embedded in a finite, even if unbounded, four-dimensional spatio-temporal system. If it were possible for the world to be 'infinite' in its basic forms, we could no longer assert it to be, in its essence, in need of redemption. All positive values that might be sought in vain in finite space and finite time could accede to the world in an infinite process; all negative values could in the frame of an infinite world be reduced and blended with the other constituents of a harmonious picture. But that is not how things stand. In all seasons and places the world must husband finite and exhaustible resources. There is a beginning and an end to the world: the world will have a death. A once-and-for-all process, a sand running down in the hour-glass: this we call 'world'.

If an essentially finite world has a divine cause, it must be concluded that the preservation of such a world costs no less than its creation, its creation no more than its preservation. For if the world could of itself and unassisted prolong its existence for but one moment, it must, other things being equal, have the ability to exist for an *infinite* length of time. Since it has not this ability, it cannot exist of itself for even one *moment*. If it is not, so to speak, constantly preserved anew by God's positive action, it needs must relapse into the void. God must for ever be checking its plunge into nothingness.

2. Within the inorganic world there reigns the law of the constant

---

[1] The following passages must needs dispense with their deeper foundation until my recent lectures on metaphysics, delivered in the University of Cologne, receive publication.

dissipation of motion. There is a continual transmutation of molar move-ment, with a capacity for work and a steady direction, into random molecular movement, incapable of performing work. If we range forms of energy according to their working capacity, we may say that given a constant quantity of energy there is a continual decline into the more worthless forms—into heat-energy, in the final stage. The death which is heat is the goal toward which the world-process asymptotically strives. Here let us leave on one side the metaphysical interpretation of these three laws. Here we are only concerned to show that the law of universal depreciation obtains also in the inorganic sphere. Note that these laws do not permit one to forecast any future entry of a new factor. In fact they only hold good under the hypothesis, which is contrary to the facts, that the world contains nothing but inorganic matter—implying a conscious disregard of life, mind and God. If, in Maxwell's sense, organic life were able to turn back the fearful downrush of the dead world, or if its exertions could restore to energy its capacity for work, which these laws declare to be trickling to waste, their pronouncements could not be accepted as indicative of reality. The same would be true if a metaphysical action of the world-basis were going to make a general retraction of the world's existence before it reached the hypothetical final stage. And so it is only tendencies which these laws express. Among others, Auerbach and Bergson[1] have laid great stress on the power of the organic, in order to lay the foundations of an optimistic metaphysics. Life, as a 'tendency to the improbable', so the theory runs, successfully works to counteract the tendency to the 'probable stage' evinced by the dispersal of energy (accord-ing to Boltzmann's mechanistic interpretation of the second law of thermo-dynamics). But even if this conception of organic movement is correct, it is still not shown that organic life can of itself accomplish more than a delay of that depreciation of energy, accompanied by a simultaneous adaptation to ever smaller differences of energetic tension. Both this adaptation, which has received attention from W. Stern, and that delay have narrow limits. Moreover, adaptation and delay work one against the other in such a way that the higher one's estimation of life's own activity in the direction of adapting the inanimate to itself, and the lower one must then estimate the capacity of life for adaptation to the diminishing differences in tension, the greater indeed is the delay in the levelling down of energy, but the greater too is the threat to the general existence of life. If one puts the adaptability of life as high as W. Stern,[2] who regards *differences* of energy

[1] F. Auerbach, *Die Weltherrin und ihre Schatten*, Jena 1902; H. Bergson, *L'Évolu-tion créatrice*, 1907.

[2] See W. Stern, *Person und Sache.*

in the environmental stimuli, and in no way absolute quantities of energy, as *conditiones sine quibus non* for the existence of organic life, then one cannot expect life to have even a delaying effect on the trend of the dead world, still less any power of reversal.

And so in this fight between the living and the dead, God and mind apart, it is not life but death which is inevitably the victor.

Seen only from the point of view of nature, the whole universal life of organic structures remains an *interlude in the world-process*—an uproarious holiday in the course of the world—but a venture attempted with unsuitable means.

Only if 'life', meaning the aggregate of all structural and formative forces not reducible in terms of the inorganic's laws and elements, possessed another possible 'way', quite different from the way of *fighting with the dead*, shaping and materially altering it, would there open before it prospects of rescue from its fate in nature.

Such a way there is: *it is the way of the spiritualization of life*—the harnessing of its power-factors to the 'acts' of the mind, which in themselves are powerless. It is a raising-up, a salvage and rescue of life from the engulfing whirlpool of those nether forces and elements with which it is contending (in its higher form as civilization's technical science), waging by work, by deed, by man's reshaping of the inanimate world, a war which in principle must be without issue.

Is this 'way' possible with the resources of the human mind itself? Doubtless it is possible, but alone the mind can no more lead to final success than can life's animation of dead matter. It is impossible that the human mind, left to itself, could successfully pursue the way. Always life, even in man, will have to spend the greater part of its strength in the ultimately hopeless fight against things dead, whereby alone it can maintain its existence in some form of the very organism which binds it to the dead world in a debt of fundamental obligation. Always—even when the best use of human freedom is made in the spiritualization of life —the sector of vital forces open to spiritualization will always be smaller than the rest; in fact, as the difficulty of the conflict increases step by step with the superiority of the organism, it is bound to grow smaller and smaller. In other words, life in the end would 'conquer' mind, and all mental activity would be an attempt with *unsuitable means* to rescue life in its spiritual cosmos from the dead clutch of inanimate nature. This trend could only be reversed if the human mind were replenished by a continual flow of strength from God.

In brief, then, we have this picture of a world left to itself: things dead relapse into nothingness; where they could perform work they lose that capacity; life relapses into the dead; mind topples into the whirlpool of life, is overwhelmed by passion and instinct.

An incessant drift from the superior to the inferior value is the reigning *tendency* of this fallen world—a fount of growing evil and of intensifying temptation for beings of mind and spirit.

3. Can the lesson we learn from the evolution of life in its organic forms be any other than this? Only while we refrain from probing the meaning of 'higher' organization can it appear otherwise. And it is only while we are attentive solely to the order of origin of life's forms, types and species, ignoring their order of death and decay, that this appearance can be supported by new seeming truths. The very fact that the animate, both as kind and individual, pays for its superiority in value over the inanimate with that absolute cessation and removal from the scene which is unknown to the inanimate's laws of mere conservation—pays, that is, with *death*—that very fact, so simple and momentous, is evidence that durability and superiority-in-value are distributed to the constituents of the world in inverse proportion. Why, one may even define a living creature outright, in the manner of E. von Bär, as a 'thing which dies', as a force which undergoes genuine exhaustion—*i.e.* is not conserved like all inanimate forces, which are merely transmuted.

But what is true of universal life as a whole in relation to dead nature— that it is a mere episode in the world-process, a thing which once was not and one day will not be—that is also true by analogy of the relationship of the higher organisms to life's inferior and simpler structures. Thus in its turn the existence of the higher organisms is but an episode of this world-episode which is the history of universal life. Last evolved, the higher organisms will all the more early—the higher the earlier—fall victim to the death of the species in the universal order of demise. Death, as Minot has said, must be envisaged as by nature the price life pays for its more differentiated and integrated organization or, we would add, as the price of the mounting richness and complexity of life's engagement in inorganic nature. The more its *radius of action* expands, as organization reaches newer heights, the more life becomes entangled in the increasingly intricate systems and machinery which it constructs as means to its ends. It is clear that capacities for development and organic restitution, as well as the degree of plasticity, decrease continually as the organism is refined. The greater and the more complex the dead baggage which the living creature has to carry when it pits itself against its environment, the more its existence is in peril. Generally speaking, the increasing duration of the individual life is paid for by the diminishing viability of the species. The evolutionism of the nineteenth century, in so far as it held out to the human mind an unlimited prospect of the higher and higher organization of life's evolution, was a gross mistake. No less mistaken was the doctrine that the victorious organism in the conflict with the remaining forms of life, or in adaptation to inanimate environment, is the 'higher'. In the so-called 'struggle for existence'—a thoroughly ruinous, not a constructive principle —the minority of higher organizational forms succumbs to the majority of lower. In this 'war' victory goes not to the high and noble, but to the mass of the petty. Moreover, the characteristics of adaptability are utterly different from the characteristics of organization.

If one surveys the trend of biological evolution, the same picture emerges: it is all an attempt with unsuitable means—a venture which, measured purely by the standards of life, is, all in all, *not* worth while.

It is only as a precondition for the realization of the *mental-spiritual* forces of the *rational* consciousness, or rather a condition of their attachment to living forms of existence, that evolution acquires an (in principle) positive meaning.

4. But the mind of man—existing as an episode in the episode of animal evolution, as a thing which, measured against the values of life, appears such a sickness as to prompt the unhesitating definition of man as, biologically, the 'animal grown sick'—has this human mind within itself alone the power to reverse the great downward trend pervading the universe?

The answer to this question is provided by certain laws of human history and society which are firmly implanted in the nature of man.

The philosophy of the nineteenth century has instilled in us the conviction that the history of man exhibits a steady progress and a constant growth in all kinds of spiritual and material goods produced by the agency of man. But the picture changes if we press more deeply into the question of what it means 'to progress' and by the application of what fundamental standards we are to decide whether something in history has 'progressed' or not. A law is at once revealed to us which I have demonstrated elsewhere in greater detail* and which is given to us in the essence of human nature as we know it. It is as follows: since man's capacity for deliberate and planned production of the varieties of good which he brings forth and passes on to succeeding generations is higher when the value-modality of those goods is *lower*, since on the other hand he must wait the more on grace, hoping it will be granted to him without his activity, when their value-modality is *higher*, it follows that the principle of the slackening of regular progress, accompanying the rise in value, applies also to these goods produced. The one thing which is really in constant progress is the apparatus for producing pleasant and useful articles—the 'international' cosmos we are wont to call civilized society.

The same can in no way be said of cultural and spiritual goods. To be sure, we have a growing supply of them—while they do not fall prey to destruction by natural catastrophes, wars and barbaric reversions—but that cannot be held to mean that their value is constantly increasing. Still less is the capacity for producing such goods increasing. Only at rare and meteoric intervals are we favoured with a creative epoch and the genius at work in such a time. The forces active in that kind of period do not travel and strike root beyond national frontiers—they are the virtue of certain specific moments in the history of one particular people or one particular class. Be that as it may, within humanity's highest forms and goods, belonging to the sphere of the religious, the holy, I believe one can descry at least a tendency for a steady, natural waning of the power to discern and produce these goods.[1] Hence the form of slogan invariably adopted by any major religious ferment is 'Back to first principles!', not the cry of progress. Every form of religious movement has an enthusiastic phase, mostly short-lived, followed by relapse into a more leisurely and ordinary phase of rationalizing 'adaptation to the world'. The great men of religion, on whose irruption there hangs the whole history of religion, belong to the types of man who can least of all be manufactured by education, politics and organization—in short by any of the things one can systematically 'do' to produce this or that type of humanity. They can scarcely be sought. Their existence is more than any other phenomenon a grace of history, least of all phenomena a product of history.

Sociologically (says Tönnies), known history exhibits a transition from the 'community' to the 'society'. In other words, it proceeds from an internal, organic nexus to an external, mechanical network—or, in the last analysis, in the direction of a human mass, characterized by the constant levelling of qualities, which is more and more vehemently preoccupied with bending its mental powers to the organized satisfaction of its relatively lowest needs. Thus it can less and less apply these powers to truly mental, to spiritual ends. Moreover, the possibilities of world-events in history are successively diminishing as racial tensions are lowered by gradual miscegenation.* The course of history *is becoming* more even and gradual, and the personal mind's freedom of scope to determine its course is decreasing in comparison with automatic and inexorable collective forces. The growth of humanity is disproportionate to the increase in food-producing areas. In essentials Malthus was right. Whatever technological civilization can contribute to the liberation of man's spiritual powers, through easing the burden of work (future possibilities of which, by the way, are much smaller than is generally believed) and shifting the task to

[1] See the conclusion of this study.

natural forces, whether organic or inorganic, this is not only equalled by the rapid rise of population, but over-compensated. Seen as a whole, the rising civilization also appears to be producing more illnesses than it can contain with advances in prophylaxis and medical skill.

Plainest of all is the diminution, and still more the levelling, of human happiness over the course of history. In this particular, Rousseau and Kant were right. Those same great revolutionary upheavals, which everywhere bring about the downfall and eclipse of the nobly-born minority, also *level* the condition of happiness. What Talleyrand remarked after the French Revolution, that nobody who lived after 1789 had tasted the sweetness of life—can we not, relatively, say it again of 1914? The 'democratic' centuries to come can never again produce the arts and the formal manners of nobility as they were known to aristocratic ages and monarchic forms of government. This much is certain: every quantitative increase in the pleasure of the masses, or in the alleviation of their rawest forms of distress, is attended by an eternally irreversible reduction toward mediocrity of the emotions of happiness and grief.[1]

In knowledge there is manifest a similar fatality. Man's theoretical knowledge is still our best example of continuous progress. But this progress is limited to the kind of knowledge which is technically practicable and at the same time singles out for our picture of the world the points and parts of the world amenable to human control, summarizing them in abstract symbols and laws. All this knowledge is thus knowledge about objects existentially relative to 'vital' values[2]—for such is mastery of the world—and human organization. The less, in a given field, the objects of knowledge are relative to the various levels of human organization, the less evidence there is in that field of constant and international progress. Even in positive science we are discovering biology and the sciences of the mind to be more desultory in progress, and more dependent on personal and national character, than the sciences of the measurable and mechanistic. Metaphysics itself, seeking truth about the very being of things, and striving to free itself from the symbolic apparatus of thought, shows no sign of constant progress. Here only penetration into the different metaphysical essays of all ages, with a subsequent endeavour to supply their deficiencies, seems to promise a further advance. Finally, the religious sense, the soul's capacity for entering into clairvoyant, emotional contact with divinity, shows in the course of history less an increase than a diminution.

[1] On the subject of profound emotions *versus* superficial feelings, see *Der Formalismus in der Ethik*, Section 5, ch. 7.

[2] *Lebenswerte, i.e.* values whose standard of reference is the material preservation and well-being of human society (*Translator*).

The same picture is observable in both theoretic and practical civilization: mankind seems to be entangling itself in an increasingly complicated embroilment with nature and with itself and, ever more deeply, in a universe of means, which it is less and less able to control and direct for spiritual ends—which ever more deeply controls mankind itself and the life of mankind. Man's handiwork is gradually becoming his master.

But this tendency for mankind as a species is none other than that which in the individual organism we would call ageing and decay. For the gradual overwhelming of the living organism by the regularity of processes proper to the dead materials and forces which it annexed for its evolution is among the basic phenomena of senescence and extinction. Even if the various parts of mankind—races, peoples, civilizations—exist in different stages and phases of the process, the vital law of withering and death still holds good for mankind as a whole, as well as for the individual.

The idea of boundless progress in all fields of value will therefore have to be replaced by quite different ideas. In the first place, the meaning of history cannot reside in some goal, lying in the future, which mankind has to attain. It resides in the whole portrait of manifold humanity drawn and painted by history, presenting the idea of man in temporal form. And if there is some order to be remarked in the inflection of the images which present man and the human in ever-changing aspects, it is certainly not the order of a steady rise in value. The growth in value of the lower fields of value is offset by decreasing value in the higher fields of value (or such is the trend), and it is only if we ascribe to history as the stream of time the following meaning: that this latter-day, older and cleverer humanity has but to imprint into the intractable stuff of the world, and to preserve, the values which an earlier, younger, more spiritually alive humanity saw and sensed—it is only then that we do not forfeit the whole of its meaning.

The foregoing shows above all that the world's object is not the development of its own forces in the sense of a constant enhancement of value. If it is not raised up by redemption, if higher powers do not freely condescend to it, to raise it ever anew, then—it falls into the void. Constant danger of death—and the possibility of rebirth dependent on redemption; constant sinking to his knees for weakness—walking only by virtue of a power descending in compassion to raise him ever and again: this I believe to be a far truer picture of man in his passage through history than that of the merry jackanapes bounding with a spontaneous vigour of limb into a land of increasing splendour and limitless horizons.

THE RELIGIOUS ACT

That certain intentions of the human mind can be characterized as purely immanent is insufficient to distinguish them as 'religious'. For this purpose, the first criterion of their collective unity is rather their inherent reference to *God*. To that extent they suppose the *idea* of God. Therefore there is no sense whatever in such attempts as have been made by Georg Simmel and others to regard the 'religious' orientation to life as merely a subjective and enthusiastic *manner* of envisaging *any* general object (be it God, humanity, one's country or one's self, etc.), implying that the idea of God can be treated as just one among many possible 'objectivizations'— one from whose 'formulation' the religious experience turns back once more into itself and its psychic stream, as if God were no more than a circuitous 'détour' method of intensifying the religious life *within itself*. Even if this 'philosophy of life' (in Simmel's sense[1]) were in other respects correct; even if all 'objects' apart from God were merely transient 'objectivizations' of a 'life' emanating continuously from itself, momentary object-forces wherein life achieves intensity and differentiation, only to withdraw and re-discharge them into the *movement* of life itself, once they have served their purpose,—this 'metaphysics of life' would still have to renounce the inclusion of *God* in the scheme if he is the *absolute* reality. But if (as in Simmel, who here embraces Bergsonian doctrines I have elsewhere taken to task*) God is identified with this self-creating life, then the 'détour' via an idea of God which religious life has somehow to form as an immanent process—*necessarily* so, even according to Simmel—is both unnecessary and inconceivable. If religious life, as an ontic orientation of the soul, resides in itself, and if its final meaning does not lie outside its own activity—even in what it receives into itself from *God*—but lies in itself alone and its own activity, then it is inconceivable it should show this predilection for circular excursions and stray so far from the truth as to regard the 'détour' as the destination. It is just as nonsensical to entertain the notion that God might be simultaneously regarded *as* God *and* as the 'way' to some other goal. In envisaging a 'way' one is not envisaging God; if on the other hand one has God in mind, one has in mind no 'way'—but an absolute goal. Just as love of *A* is not genuine love of *A* if it regards *A* as a mere 'point of transit' whence it may return in ultimate intention to the self of the lover (this is the case of Spinoza's God), so *belief* in God cannot be considered truly belief in God if it is reflected back to the being of the subject. In the first instance there is a form of auto-eroticism, veiled

---

[1] See Georg Simmel, *Lebensanschauung: Vier metaphysische Kapitel*, Munich 1918, especially the chapter entitled '*Die Transzendenz des Lebens*'.

by the mere *appearance* of love for another; in the second there is self-worship, veiled by the mere appearance of worshipping God.

But we mention this rather curious view of Simmel's only in order to show, from what is probably the extremest form of religious subjectivism, how *absolutely* false it is to seek to ascribe a purely 'immanent' basic character to the religious act. One has merely (with Luther) to give precedence to religious *certainty* of faith and *assurance* of salvation over religious *truth* of faith and salvation[1] in order to start a train of thought which can only lead to making faith its own object. It is for example plainly a circular argument to stake the *truth* of Christ's self-sacrifice in dying to bear our sins on the individual act of faith in accepting the word of the gospel, and then to make personal assurance that Christ died 'for me' exclusively dependent on firm belief in an already believed *truth* of salvation. That is faith in faith—a reflexive exercise that can be prolonged at will. Faith-faith is no more faith than the velleity of willing to will an object is willing that object.

The immanent aspects of the religious act

Nevertheless, it is necessary to characterize the religious act *in so far* as it is immanent. Such a description is *more* than psychological if the religious act does not represent a random nexus of extra-religious intentions (feeling, volition or thought), if it has on the contrary its own genuine *essence*, corresponding to its object as the essential form of apprehending it, and if it does not only in fact occur 'in all men' but belongs to the *constitution* of the human, and indeed any finite consciousness—the latter at least in accordance with its formal character and meaning. It is, finally, more than psychological if, as we have already maintained, religious acts, in their formation and elaboration, take on a *consistency of significance* derivable from no other such consistency, plus strict and formulable conditions of *self-evident* fulfilment or non-fulfilment.

That this is so, that is our thesis.

Let us be perfectly clear about the meaning of this question. Man possesses innumerable wishes, needs and desires for things, whose psychological existence does not offer the remotest *guarantee* that somewhere something must exist which might satisfy these wishes, needs and desires. That is why any theology or metaphysics inferring from need or desire is so utterly absurd.

But quite a different state of affairs would be represented by man's possession of an *essential class of acts* of which the following could be demonstrated:

[1] Luther was only doing for religion what Descartes was to do for philosophy.

1. In essence these acts are of a kind which is as *constitutive* a part of human consciousness as thought, judgment, perception and memory.

2. They do not belong to this consciousness because it is 'human', in the sense in which certain inductive, empirical phenomena and psychical processes are specifically human, but because, more primarily, it is a *finite* consciousness.

3. Religious acts therefore cannot be identified or equated with mere wishes, needs or desires of any kind, since they intentionally regard a wholly different *realm of essences* from that comprised by types of empirical and 'ideal' objects. For all wishes, needs and desires envisage only empirical *types* of object—even if they are often types which do not exist or could not exist, for such are nevertheless constructed, like all *ficta*, from the materials and characteristics of empirical objects.[1]

4. Religious acts can neither be derived from psychological causality *nor* teleologically regarded as fulfilling some purpose in the life-process; only if one accepts the reality of the *kinds* of object which they envisage can one properly grasp their existence. Thus they show the human mind as adjusted and directed toward a *super*natural reality—that is, one different *in essence* from empirical, natural reality, no matter how the particular constituents of what men *accept as real* in either domain may change in the course of history.[2]

5. Religious acts conform to an *internal regularity* which is autonomous for them and which therefore—no matter whether the acts arose from particular conjunctures in the empirical life of the soul, or from specific external circumstances—*cannot* be grasped from a knowledge of empirical psychic causality. This regularity is of a noetic, not a psychological kind. In this respect religious acts are also distinct *in essence* from all human needs that induce a fantasy-creation of fictitious things.

6. Just as religious acts are not psychic phenomena which form and disintegrate within us according to natural psychic laws (thus at best obeying, in their evolution and dissolution, the dictates of some biological or sociological purpose), so they are not a mere subdivision or combination of *other* groups of noetic intentional acts, such as logical, ethical, aesthetic acts, etc. Certainly, the content of meaning 'given' in religious acts can

[1] Should anyone wish also to speak of (in the strict sense) 'religious' needs, wishes, desires, he is of course perfectly entitled to do so. But he is in that case presupposing the *religious act* through which we receive the *idea of the good* for which we feel a need. For the need is 'religious' only by virtue of its reference to the object of the religious act. This is quite another matter than the converse reduction of the religious act to a need that is not itself 'religious' but arose in the same way as any other needs.*

[2] Men's views on God have perhaps differed considerably less than their views on the earth and the sun.

itself become material for the formation of logical concepts, for judgment and inference, and also for ethical and aesthetic appraisal, estimation and valuation. But this does not imply that the full meaning of religious acts 'proceeds' from the potential meaning of these other groups of noetic acts. No, in relation to them it is, if anything, '*given*' material.

If, as I said, this can be shown to be true, we obtain both a *measure* and a *norm*, created from the very *nature* of religion and not from any extra- or sub-religious set of norms, for all empirically encountered cases of the religious orientation of life. For if we compare the regularities recurring in the activity of this 'pure' religious consciousness, which is freed of involvement in all other kinds of mental activity or in the biophysical life-course of man, with what is empirically discernible in ostensibly religious orientations, we can discover *laws of right and wrong*—but laws applying exclusively to *religious* right and wrong.[1]

Now, as I believe, this is indeed what may be demonstrated by an analysis of the nature of the religious act.

And so anyone who, in studying the nature of that act, first looks for a 'psychic aptitude' (*e.g.* thinking, feeling, trying and willing) under the heading of which to range it, is taking the wrong direction. For religion is as fundamentally religious cognition and thought as it is also a special kind of (value-)feeling, of (regulated) expression (in religious language, prayer and liturgy) and of volition and conduct (in the service of God and religious morality). Moreover, anybody who sets out from supposed elementary psychic facts falls into error. Needless to say, a number of different elementary phenomena are in evidence in all acts of an intentional nature (not only religious acts): for example, in any normal perception there are sensational elements, forms, value-qualities, factors of meaning and reality, or, on the subjective side, sensation, feeling, interest and attention, judgment, etc. But intentional *unity*, as a unity of experience, is entirely *unaffected* by the division of the psychic into 'elementary phenomena', which is a matter quite distinct. Here the position is comparable to that prevailing in the living organism, where within unities of a morphological or functional, physiological kind quite distinct chemical ingredients or elementary chemical processes can exist

---

[1] Thus the laws of the 'pure' religious consciousness function *also* as norms of right and wrong for the empirical religious consciousness, without possessing the inherent character of empirical norms. However, the correctness of the performance of religious acts itself proves nothing about the real and material truth of the intentional object of religious consciousness, any more than the truth of a thing thought is proved by correctness in thinking (*e.g.* correct inference). In both cases correctness is only a *sine qua non* for the evidence of truth, not such evidence itself —let alone the actual truth.

side by side. And just as anyone approaching the organism only as a chemist would be unable to discover its morphological and functional unities, its life-process, so no one who sought only psychic elements would ever discover the 'intentional' unities. The religious act, taken with its implicit correlate, which belongs to it as its 'fulfilment', forms a unity in itself: *e.g.* prayer, in conjunction with the personality of God; worship, in conjunction with the *summum bonum*.

Thus the distinction between religious and non-religious, as a method of classifying acts, cuts across all classifications derived from reference to 'psychic aptitudes' or elementary psychic phenomena. It likewise cuts across any classification derived from the important opposition of social and reflexive acts (self-regarding acts).* Religious self-absorption, pondering one's own salvation, repentance are examples of reflexive religious acts. Religious petition, thanks, praise, wonder, veneration, obedience, and the exercise of religious authority are social religious acts.

Religious acts are a law unto themselves

Before a more detailed examination of the essential components of the religious act, we may begin with three unmistakable characteristics, which do not exhaust the religious act but at all events have *diagnostic* value for its distinction from all other types of act: 1. the world-transcending character of its *intention*, 2. the fact that only the '*divine*' can fulfil its intention, 3. the fact that it can only be fulfilled via the acceptance of a divine kind of *entity* which is *self*-revealing and gives or *devotes itself to man* (natural revelation of the divine). In other words, the basic principle of all religious cognition holds good: 'all knowledge of God is knowledge *from* God'.

1. The first thing peculiar to any religious act is that not only the things and facts experienced by the person, but also all things of a finite and contingent kind, are gathered together in a single whole, which includes the subject's own person, and are joined in the idea of 'the world'. Without this preparatory operation a religious act cannot take place. The second thing proper to the religious act is that in its intention this 'world' is overlapped or *transcended*. It is not a question of this particular transitory world that 'happens' to exist, but a question of everything partaking of the *nature* of 'world' in general—that is, a world in which there is somehow or other realized an embodiment of the essences realized in the world which I know. Transcendence in general is a peculiarity of every conscious intention, for in every one there is present an intending-above-and-beyond its own empirical standpoint, together with the simultaneous awareness that the being of the object

reaches out beyond the empirical content of the intention. But only where the thing thus transcended is the *world* as a whole (including the subject's own person) are we entitled to speak of a *religious act*. Though, to be sure, one isolated thing, some specific experience of the life of the cosmos or of one's own life, may precipitate the religious act, this act may only come into being when the experience has been related in a quite special manner to the *whole*, and the whole appears symbolized in it.

2. The most conclusive, though merely negative, sign of a religious act, as distinct from all other acts of mind or spirit, is an attendant insight into the fact that *of its essence it cannot be fulfilled* by any finite object belonging to, or itself forming, the 'world'. In this sense Augustine's dictum, *Inquietum cor nostrum, donec requiescat in te*, is a basic formula for all religious acts. Even pantheism does not refute but complies with this essential law. For there never yet has been a pantheism which dared to make a *finite* world the object of religious devotion. It evens seeks to concord with the law by declaring the world *itself* to be infinite.

It was, as I indicated, *manifest* that the religious act could not be fulfilled from within the world. The implication is that the religious act is not constituted when an individual tells himself that his intention (whether it be theoretical, whether a particular kind of love, a striving for happiness and perfection, whether gratitude, hope, awe or fear) has only *hitherto* found no adequate fulfilment, by reason of his own limited experience or that of times and peoples, but that it is *possible* that some finite fulfilment should appear 'one day'. No; it is characteristic of the religious act to be dominated by the intuition that there could be absolutely *no* thing of a finite kind, no good of a finite kind, no loved object of a finite kind, which might fulfil the intention that is present in it. All tests of experience, though they confirm this intuition, do not function as negative proof (via inductive inference) that this act cannot be fulfilled by things finite, but simply offer examples wherein that essential insight is acquired. It is imagination which can come to our aid and show this insight in a clearer light. The epistemologist ascertains the a-priori nature of a proposition, *i.e.* its unprovability and invincibility, by attempting possible observations of some kind; that is, he asks himself whether he can even *imagine* possible observations which would decide him to abandon his proposition. Similarly we can try as it were to confront the intention of the religious act with an imaginary finite good, an imaginary condition of the world, an imaginary perfection of society or human civilization. And only if we are then aware of the imaginary object's patent *in*adequacy to match the intention of the act can we be sure of that act's *genuinely* religious character. In the religious act we envisage a being which is *different* from any finite being and also from any being which is non-finite or infinite in some specific *way* (such as infinite time, infinite space, infinite number, etc.); we find ourselves directed toward something whose place cannot be taken by any finite good, however worthy of love, since religious love transcends the essential nature of all such goods. In the religious act we are seeking a felicity concerning which we are perfectly clear that no progress of humanity, no perfection of society and no kind of multiplication of the internal and external causes of human happiness can bring it to pass. In the religious act we experience a fear, an awe, which we are unable to refer to a specific, definite peril whose nature, if nothing else, is known to us, or to something menacing, while worthy of respect, of which examples are present to us from our experience. 'Religious' fear, viewed thus empirically, is *groundless* and *aimless*. In 'religious' hope we hope for something we have never experienced and of which we know that we *could* never have experienced it, and we fervently hope what we hope, though there is within us no well-grounded confidence, founded in our calculation of earthly chance or prompted merely by an instinctive blind trust in life, that events will supply the substance of our hopes. In 'religious' thanksgiving, with which we overflow at the glimpse of some exceptionally pregnant aspect of nature, or as a result of some experience through which we have acquired a particular success or good, we give thanks for 'something' in relation to which what we have acquired is only a sign, indication or symbol, and not the proper object of the thanks; and for that 'something' we render thanks to a giving and bestowing subject for which we cannot, even in imagination, substitute any earthly power, any earthly person, however great, worthy and mighty. When, again, we adopt a religious attitude in the act of repentance, we know invincibly that to our self-indictment there belongs an 'ear' to hear it, to every 'judgment' a law whereby sentence is passed and a judge who judges; we know that to forgiveness belongs a forgiver that *can* only be such a being as decreed the very law from whose rigours the forgiveness absolves; but although we experience all these intentions and fulfilments of intentions, we find *nothing* to which we can ascribe them in the whole range of experience known to us in the finite world. *Before whom* do we then indict ourselves, when our lips keep silence? By what law is there judgment, when we cannot say we have received this law from other men or through ourselves? And who then judges when we know ourselves judged, and who is then to forgive when we seek forgiveness, and who then gave it when we believed we had received it? Our mind casts about in all the world we know, and finds, not only in the parts familiar to us, but in any part that may resemble them, *no* definite answer to these questions. Thus, in every one of these acts—praise, thanks, fear, hope, love, endeavour, striving for perfection, indictment, judgment, forgiveness, wonder, veneration, petition, worship—our mind *oversteps* the bounds not only of this or that one finite thing, but of the very sum and substance of all finite things.

And so the religious act is always *negatively* characterized by its being *empirically* as *groundless* as it is *aimless*, however much it may be empirically occasioned, and however the ideas we subsequently form of its object may be coloured by our experiences and still bear, as it were, the traces of the subjective recollections in which they originated. This implies that no goods which can conceivably be *produced* by our own efforts or by the united forces of mankind can *ever* lead of themselves in the direction of a specifically *religious* kind of intentional object. Hence, what the religious act mentally envisages is no mere ideal perfecting of all goods which we find in our experience either as factual or possible, for it comprises a definite and clear awareness that if finite goods and entities are *unable* to fulfil the religious act, it is not because they have these or those secondary qualities but because of the very nature and essence of the finite in general. Both mind and heart, our temperament as much as our will, find themselves directed in the religious act toward some thing which 'is' and has value, something which hovers before our mind over against all possible world-experience as the 'totally other', 'essentially incomparable' thing, which the former can in no wise contain.

To be sure, this description does not allocate, as it appears, any other than a purely *negative* fulfilment to the religious act. Nevertheless, the meaning of this kind of negation must be sharply distinguished from merely negative theoretical judgments, for the only purpose which this kind here subserves is to segregate religious from all non-religious acts. Admittedly it does not state *what* is given *in* the religious act, but inasmuch as it attempts, in such words as 'indescribable', 'inexpressible', 'infinite', 'immeasurable', to describe the content of the religious object, it is of negative significance only in the composition of the words, not in a truly semantic sense. When we make these characteristic negations as considered statements, it does not alter the fact that what *resides* in the religious act is always a 'positive' or substantial religious *content*.

3. The religious act—herein differing from all other kinds of cognitive act, including even metaphysics—demands an answer, an *act of reciprocity* on the part of that very object to which its intention is directed. And this implies that one may only speak of 'religion' where the object bears a *divine personal form* and where revelation (in the widest sense) on the part of this personal object is what fulfils the religious act and its intention. While for metaphysics the personality of the divine forms a

never-attainable boundary of cognition, for religion this personality is the alpha and omega. Where it does not stand before the mental eye, where it is not thought, believed and inwardly received, there can be no question of *religion* in the strict sense. For all these factors are essentially inseparable. The religious act is unable from its own resources, or with the help of thought, to *construct* what hovers as an objective idea, notion or intuition before the human performer of the act. He must somehow *receive* the truth he 'intends', the salvation and felicity he 'seeks'—and receive it via the very being he seeks. To that extent he is in his primary intention already disposed for and concerned with a possible *reception*, however much a multifarious internal and external spontaneous *activity* may be a prerequisite of his reaching the threshold where the reception begins. Where the soul does not—however indirectly—touch God, and touch him in knowing and feeling itself touched *by* God, no *religious* relationship can subsist—not even a relation of 'natural' religion. Positive and natural religion are *not* divided by the former's resting on revelation, the latter on spontaneous rational knowledge—quite independently of the religious act. Emphatically, metaphysics is *not* religion—not even 'natural religion', however it may lead in part to conclusions identical with some to which natural religion *also* leads in its own way. No; the essential difference between natural and positive religion lies in the *nature and manner* of revelation. It depends, that is, on whether the revelation in question is one which is general, symbolically mediated through the essential constants of the internal and external worlds, of history and of nature, one everywhere and at every time *accessible to everybody* through the religious act, *or* is one transmitted by the exceptional and sublime link with God enjoyed by certain *persons*, their being, work, doctrine, message (including the tradition of their message), and thereafter mediated by belief 'in' these persons. *Necessary and universally valid* knowledge is far from identical or coincident with spontaneous rational or sensory knowledge: it is just as likely to be yielded by the natural revelation always and everywhere accessible to any man—provided he is religious in his subjective approach to the world. For that reason it is impermissible to equate revelation in general with 'positive' and handed-down revelation through *persons*. *Revelation as such—in the widest sense of the term—is simply the manner, strictly correlative to the nature of the religious act, in which a reality of the divine character is given to human consciousness.* As such it extends over the *whole* area covered by religion of *any* kind, and it therefore includes both sides of the antithesis (based on quite separate criteria) of true and false religion.

So much should go without saying. Just as, in both introspection and external observation, we may fall a prey to the most manifold sources of delusion and, in making inferences from our observations, to the no less numerous sources of error, so we may here—indeed to a much greater degree—be the victim of errors and delusions. The particular sources of religious delusion require special investigation. But just as no one has the right to claim the risk of error as a reason for rejecting outright, as a source of knowledge, all internal and external perception, so no one is entitled to cast doubts upon revelation as the appointed response to the religious act.

Can the *existence of God* be *inferred* from the existence of religious acts, or the 'religious proclivities' of man?

If the divine, and everything essentially connected with it, is 'given' only in acts of a religious nature, then the existence of a supernatural sphere of being cannot in the first place be demonstrated by 'proofs' derived from facts of extra-religious experience, but only by the stimulation and activation of religious acts in the human mind itself. This must be followed by either a drawing of the attention to the *demonstrandum* as to a thing present and existent or—if the attention has already seized upon this object—a *post facto* indication of the *demonstratum*'s essential content, as it is intuited in religious acts.[1]

Unfortunately the truth of this observation is at the present time obscured for many thinkers by the persistence of two hidebound philosophical prejudices.

The first is that only what rests on experience (if at all possible, on sensual experience) may be regarded as 'given' or, to be precise, as originally given, *i.e.* primary data. However, it can be no less true to say that to every kind of primary data there must correspond a manner of experiencing which is such that data of the kind in question can be given through it. Let us concede that everything which 'is' owes an account of itself to experience. But conversely everything that is experienced has a claim to be posited as in *some* way existent. In this context nothing could be more disastrous for epistemology than to set up at the beginning of one's methodical procedure *too narrowly exclusive a concept of 'experience'*—to equate the whole of experience with one particular kind of experience (sanctioning only that mental attitude which is conducive to it) and then refuse to

[1] Scheler plays upon the meanings of three German words: *Beweis* (proof conclusive), *Aufweis* (a 'pointing to' a truth which should thereupon be evident to a second person, *i.e.* literal 'demonstration') and *Nachweis* (a consolidation or recapitulation of an established or provisionally accepted point). The distinction between one and another of these three terms is developed in the succeeding pages. The sentence to which this note is attached is a paraphrase rather than a direct translation (*Translator*).

recognize as primary data anything which cannot be reduced to *this* one variety. And yet what comes under the heading of sensual phenomena in empirical data, and which sensory functions or organs we must assume or seek, if we are to understand the 'given-ness' of given sensual phenomena, that is a complex of questions which only becomes meaningful when we have *first* diagnosed and analysed the sense of 'the given' in general.

The second prejudice lies in ignorance of the limits of *provable* knowledge and cognition. Every judgment admittedly requires justification: it must present its title to pronouncement. But this potential justification is 'proof' only within limits which must be clearly ascertained. There are other kinds of justification which differ from proof (*Beweis*), such as *Aufweis* (properly *demonstratio*), *Nachweis*,[1] construction, verification and so on.

As for the first prejudice, when we today consider the common lessons of phenomenology, epistemology and experimental psychology,[2] there is scarcely anything we *know* with greater certainty than this: *the given is infinitely richer* than the part of it which strictly corresponds to sensual experience. Moreover, sensual experience is neither the only experience there is nor, in order of origin, *i.e.* the chronological sequence of experience, the most primary. It is more true to say that to every living creature the structural contents of its habitat are 'given', and to every intelligent creature the structural contents of its world are 'given', *before* all sensation, and that nothing can possibly *become* sensation unless it is of a nature to 'vitalize' a creature's environment, its peculiar regularities and uniformities. No principle is now so thoroughly discredited, therefore, as the old philosophical tag: *nihil est in intellectu quod non fuerit in sensu.* The sole significance of sensation and the whole sensory apparatus of organisms is that of a system of signs and signals enabling the organism to react to its environment in a manner favourable to the ends of life.* Emphatically, they exercise *no* genuine cognitive function. They do not produce perception and experience: they merely *analyse* them. Moreover, they analyse in accordance with but *one* point of view: the *practical* distinction between what is beneficial or harmful for the unitary creature, as opposed to the species.

With the rich inflow of new insights attendant upon these general propositions, insights it would not be pertinent to enumerate here, we consider that two types of theoretical philosophy, which in our view are the greatest obstacles in the way of a philosophy of religion, are disproved

---

[1] See preceding note (*Translator*).

[2] A general survey and theoretical appraisal of the relevant discoveries of experimental psychology are to be found in Wolfgang Köhler's *Die physischen Gestalten in Ruhe und im stationären Zustand*, Brunswick 1920.

root and branch: sensualist empiricism and positivism, for the first, and secondly the system of Immanuel Kant. The former undertook the quite impossible task, inconceivable with any but a wholly primitive phenomenology of the given, of tracing the genesis of all contents of experience back to sense-data and derivatives thereof. Accordingly its form of logic demanded an inductive proof for every judgment whose statement did not refer to sensible phenomena. Kant on the other hand, having uncritically adopted from the English and French sensualists the pre-judice that only sensation is 'given' (the so-called 'chaos' of sensations), concluded that any asensual or hypersensual component of experience is never the primary datum but must be regarded as the product of an autonomous and rational activity of the synthetizing intellect. Today we know that data such as reference, order, substantive category, effect, motion, forms, shapes, realness, materiality, space, time, number, quantity, value-qualities, unity of the self, unity of the world, of material environment, etc., are true and genuine data, not elements either consciously or unconsciously constructed, produced or engendered by the intellect. At the same time we know that they are none the less asensual data which in their particular category are independent and are present *before* the 'sensations' transmitted via the senses of a living being.

If then there should prove to be primary data of a religious nature, and *if* they were to include the quality of divinity and its whole sphere of essences (whether it be a primordial or an evolved category, whether it be really or only ostensibly divine), this would be nothing mysterious *in the framework of a philosophy with a phenomenological basis*. The ascertainment and recognition of what is real within an irreducible sphere of data (or of what propositions are true concerning real things in this sphere) is of course invariably a later operation, subject to the fuller development of knowledge. It may never, never be given precedence over the demonstration of the self-contained existence and true essential nature of a substantial sphere of being. Thus we ought not to regard the existence of an external world, or the fact that 'something real' is present at every point of the external world which I examine, as a hypothesis of thought, as a logically required assumption, for what is a hypothesis is only what this real thing may be, or whether a real thing corresponds to this or that phenomenal component in the sphere of the external world. A similar statement may be made about the self as the unitary form of the so-called 'internal world'.

But precisely in the same sense as the self and its various worlds, the external, internal and environmental, or as the contemporary historical context of the self (in which it associates with other selves and which also possesses internal as well as external components), the sphere of the

I

phenomena disclosed to the mind in the religious act, the *sphere of divinity* and of the general reality it contains, is a *primary datum* which it is impossible to derive from anything else.

Furthermore, just as 'the' (individual) consciousness, with its essentially finite constitution, invariably and necessarily has as its correlates *ab origine* the spheres of the external world, of the 'I' and of the 'We'—without the possibility of reducing any one of these given spheres to any other—so in the religious act it also looks into the sphere of divine, supersensual facts and phenomena, a sphere which is just as much *ab origine* its correlate. Evidently it may fall into any number of errors in deciding which things are real in any of these spheres, but that does not in itself cast doubt upon the original existence of the *sphere*.

Hence, there can be no question of 'proving' the existence of the entire religious sphere by inference from other facts of the world, as little question as there is of 'proving' the existence of the external world, of the self or of one's fellow-creatures.* To insist on such proofs is to misconceive in principle the limitations of 'proofs' and the extent of their validity.

Let us establish some of these limitations, in so far as they apply to the proof of the existence of a thing. For it is only when it is recognized that religious objects offer in this respect no special case and that the religious domain of knowledge merely conforms to the general principles of what is provable and what is not, that men will cease to demand concerning the existence of God what it does not enter their heads to demand concerning other domains of existence.

The notion of 'proving' reality or existence is absurd. All that is provable is *propositions* about the real, not the real itself. We know with a knowledge *antecedent* to all possible proofs of existence that in general terms 'a' reality underlies all phenomena and that different realities underlie essentially different phenomena. In this respect the only thing which can be the object of a proof is whether a given phenomenon may properly be accredited with the predicate 'real', and of that the only touchstone is the content of the typical reality-experience, the establishment of which is the business of the phenomenological analysis of consciousness. Moreover, the following principle applies to the relation of truth and proof: only the *true* is provable. The converse, that only the provable is true, is invalid, nor may we say that the truth of a proposition consists in its provability. It is clear that on the contrary one and the same proposition—one and the same true proposition—is susceptible of different kinds of proof, *e.g.* direct or indirect, simple or complex. Its trueness does not assume as many guises as there are kinds of proof for it. But the proof, of whatever kind, invariably leans on other true propositions, which are not themselves provable but are 'manifest' in some other way. And in the case of proofs of the existence of a particular object already given as a phenomenal something there are always in addition the following two presuppositions: 1. other definite existence in the same material sphere of existence, 2. principles, external to those principles of formal logic ruling proof in general (*e.g.* the laws of syllogism), which state solely the internal conditions of the particular sphere of existence. Thus, for example we could never infer or 'prove' the existence of a living being, albeit the simplest and most primitive, from knowledge of the dead world, however complete our understanding of that world. Only if we presuppose knowledge of the essence of living things, together with the essential relations and conditions prevailing in the living world, can we prove the existence of other living beings or phenomena of life from the existence of given examples. But never and nowhere, with respect neither to the essence nor to the existence of a given object, can there be a bridge of pure analysis from one sphere of essences to another. How could one seriously expect not merely that the existence of a particular religious object should be provable, by laws relating solely to religious being and consciousness, from the preposited existence of other religious objects—but that the existence of *the* religious object itself should be similarly provable? God's existence—so the demand runs—should be 'provable', without the assistance of any informative insight into the nature of divinity, without the aid of any exclusively religious dialectic, solely from domains of essence and existence which are entirely different in character, by the sole employment of formal logic. Yet it is undeniably impossible for anyone to prove the existence of a living creature unless he has at least derived from another living creature a notion of the essence of living form, living movement, etc. How should we expect to succeed, where the void between category and category demands the greatest leap, in accomplishing what we cannot achieve where that demand is at its least?

Again, only a proposition already *discovered* is susceptible of proof. This applies wherever the object to be 'proved' does not arise in, and regularly from, the deductive process itself, which is for example the way it arises over wide areas of mathematics. Here indeed, but *only* here, the deductive course of so-called proof does coincide with the construction of the object, *i.e.* with its coming into ideal existence. But nothing is clearer than that this case of coincident proof and construction is *least of all* applicable to the religious sphere of knowledge. Neither God himself nor the idea of God can be 'constructed'. The human mind's power of construction with reference to an object is in proportion to the extent to which the *existence* of that object is *relative* to human consciousness. In respect of the absolute being which is itself independent of everything while everything is dependent on it, that power is therefore *nil*.

However, to teach the way to *discover* God is something basically other and higher than to prove his existence. Only one who has *found* God can grow aware of a need to prove his existence. Again, the logic of discovery (*logique de l'invention, ars inveniendi et investigandi*) is a thing distinct from the logic of proof (*logique de la démonstration, ars demonstrandi*). What the Fathers of the Church taught, with Augustine at their head, was how to *find* God. Their proofs of God are in reality accounts of how the religious consciousness *proceeds* when on its way to God, and of *how* it reaches its goal along this way. Certainly this task, that of discovering the rules pertaining to the course of the religious consciousness, what one might call the dialectic (*Sinnlogik*) of the religious act, is not the only task of a natural theology. It is no less necessary to establish logical connections between religious truths (here as always we refer only to those of natural religion) and truths about the world and its parts. But in the first place this is always the *secondary, posterior task*, and in the second, which is more important, it may not be regarded as a substitute for the other, primary task. The logical concatenation of religious truths, or their linkage with mundane truths, is no 'proof' of their truth. At the most it offers a mere 'verification' in the sense of that word whereby mathematicians sharply distinguish it from proof.

By *Nachweis* as distinct from *Beweis* we understand learning to rediscover by rules a thing which has previously been discovered. By *Aufweis* or 'disclosure' we understand a preliminary indication of a thing which has yet to be discovered. Thus the *Nachweis* supposes the *Aufweis*. Of course an *Aufweis* can be of such a nature as to include in its mental midwifery various kinds of inferential operation. But the whole of the process called *Aufweis* has only the significance of a pointer with which we may draw attention to a thing, or render it visible, so that a second person may the better see it or see it for the first time.[1]

In natural theology the *Aufweis* must *precede* the *Nachweis* and the *Nachweis* the verifications of religious truths.

The nature and existence of God are susceptible of *Aufweis* and *Nachweis*, but not of proof in the strict sense (*Beweis*) from truths which are solely of this world.

Having made these preliminary remarks we once more take up the thread of the question: how far may the *existence of God* be *inferred* from the existence of religious acts within the mind of man? If we do not merely investigate religious acts with attention to their essence, in isolation from

[1] See note to page 255 (*Translator*).

their existence, and their internal economy, but proceed with their existence in man as our starting-point, not only may we ask questions about
the objects of these acts (in which the religious consciousness dwells as in
its natural element) but, with their existence in the foreground of our
thoughts, we must inevitably ask what is their cause. To this question the
following is the only meaningful answer: Only a real being with the essential character of divinity can be the cause of man's religious propensity,
that is, the propensity to execute in a real sense acts of that class whose
acts, though finite experience cannot fulfil them, nevertheless demand
fulfilment. The *object* of religious acts is at the same time the *cause* of their
existence. In other words, all knowledge of God is necessarily knowledge
from God.

The reproach of being a circular proof has often been levelled against
this conclusion. I can think of two cases where a circle is present. It is
present for example if, like Descartes, one does not start from specific
religious acts and demonstrate in detail their essential characteristics, but
first derives from the *veracitas Dei* (God being the cause of finite reason) a
confidence that reason will in principle lead one to the discovery of truth—
not into systematic error—and then proceeds to base the fundamental
truth of religion upon the same acts of reason which serve to advance the
sciences of the finite. This is the notorious error of Descartes and of many
'ontologists'. They are correct in this, that belief in the systematic whole of
reason (*with* all its manifest truths)—*i.e.* the belief that there is active in
man a mental principle which is and could only be determined in
accordance with the object, and not by any psychic or physiological
factors—that this postulates belief in God as the cause of finite reason. To
that extent we may say that only if God exists is there any attainable
truth.[1] For however self-evident a rational insight may be, it is self-
evident only *for* reason, which as a *whole* could still be supplying no more
than a purposeful illusion, subserving, say, the ends of biology. Nietzsche
was right to maintain that the assumption of the idea of truth is bound
with belief in God and that for the sake of his atheism he would have to
sacrifice even the idea of truth. If we suppose that an irrational principle
underlies the existence and essence of the world, reason itself cannot be
what humanity has always considered it. The very *possibility* of a self-
evident objective good and objective truth is essentially connected to the
fact of a good and rational world-principle. This assertion of mine has
been contested by a sharp-witted critic,[2] with immediate reference to the

---

[1] This is true also for the special case of the objective validity of the causal
principle.
[2] See D. H. Kerler, *Max Scheler und die impersonalistische Lebensanschauung*, 1917.

idea of good. This critic held that one had a right to take more or less the following attitude: 'Let me but see what is good and I will acknowledge and will this good, no matter what form the world basis may take. Let it crush me and crush my will and bring the good (mine and every other good) to perdition. Then I shall say: So much the worse for the basis of the world! I will not acknowledge it though its might be infinite. I shall stand my ground in ultimate metaphysical defiance, upheld by my moral self-evidence, and hold the world-basis in the utmost possible comtempt.' And, with respect to truth, one could equally believe oneself entitled to hold fast to the theoretical self-evidence of truth in the teeth of the blindness of the world-basis. To this inspirited author his standpoint seems one of wellnigh dizzying grandeur and sublimity. But the more deeply I try to live into it, the more untenable it appears to me. However much I concede one may ascribe neither the good nor the true, neither the logical nor the ethical insights, to the bare fiat of the almighty will, however much I agree that a self-contained, autonomous, rational self-evidence is the basis, not the consequence, of belief in God, I find the following intuition no whit less compelling: If the world-basis were blind and wicked, then the alleged self-evidence of the good and the true would be no more than a very remote and derivative consequence of the blind and wicked world-basis—and could therefore *not* be what it appears to be. Clinging to the good and true as lodestars of my life would be a blind velleity and a senseless gesture against the very nature of existence. This ontic truth need not, I feel, fear comparison with any of the insights yielded by epistemology or axiology.

Where Descartes was wrong was in thinking that God's existence could be known without special religious acts and through operations identical with those for which he based the necessary confidence on God's existence and veracity. But the religious acts *precede* the remaining acts of finite reason; the latter take root in the former as in the person's most immediate and profound acts.

One also encounters the following argument: Could not the religious propensity of man (by which is meant his property in acts of thinking, willing, feeling, which are plainly unadjusted to a finite environment and find no fulfilment in any possible kind of finite experience)—could not this religious propensity be a snare and a delusion even if it were more than a historical phenomenon and belonged to the essence of human nature? Only if we know on other rational grounds that God exists, and is thus the cause of that propensity, shall we feel immune from this doubt.

If this doubt is a weapon to demolish the theology of inference from need, it is wholly in the right. Man may possess unlimited wishes, cravings, needs, for which there is no fulfilment on this earth or elsewhere.

But are we talking of such things when we talk of religious acts? Wishes, cravings and needs are either religious or extra-religious—not infrequently they are extra-religious masquerading as religious. But whatever they may be, they always require an explanation and moreover an explanation which must presuppose the nature or category of the objects which the wishes, cravings or needs envisage. Be they ever so incapable of fulfilment, they still, empirically, require this explanation. But *we* did not take as our starting-point any generally broadcast propensity to actual needs, wishes, etc., but an *essential class of mental acts* and their correlates, concerning which it is in itself a matter of indifference whether they are to be found in all men or in one man alone. And it was only at a secondary stage that we also discovered through induction a universal propensity to acts of that kind. It is self-evident that specifically religious 'needs' could only arise from given religious objects or knowledge of such objects and could not therefore form an explanation of the objects themselves. Hence religious objects must already have been given through and in religious acts, if they are to give rise to felt needs with which to concern oneself, or wishes and cravings of a religious kind. Needs are always objects of an explanation; they themselves can explain nothing.[1]

But if the concept of the insight-providing religious act is correctly understood and not confused with such derivative things as religious needs, it becomes impossible to contend that God's existence must 'first' be known —*e.g.* through inference from the nature and existence of the world—before religious acts may be accorded more than a fictional significance. For how could that be, if God, by his very nature, is revealed only in and through these acts, and is simultaneously revealed, in a basic, indestructible experience, as the effective cause which moved the subject to perform them? Such a contention would be tantamount to requiring that before colours are seen, or sounds heard, their existence must be rationally authenticated.

Thus everything hinges on the proper characterization of the nature of religious acts. Once we have been able to show with clearness and precision that the human mind performs certain intentional acts which differ from all possible syntheses of finite mundane experience, we have shown that it is *not* entirely subordinated to the world of the finite but possesses a *surplus* of powers and aptitudes which can as little find employment in this world's work and knowledge as be *explained* by experience of the world and adaptation to it. As a system these acts thus clearly demonstrate that the soul's design points infinitely beyond this life, that of its nature it

[1] Cf. my *Der Formalismus in der Ethik und die materiale Wertethik*, where this is also shown with respect to *e.g.* economic needs.*

participates in a supersensual realm of being and value whose contents and objects cannot stem from experience of finite things. And so there is a *power* which soars above any employment it can find in this world, there is a *surplus* of both spiritual powers and spiritual requirements, incomprehensible from the viewpoint of even the most perfect conceivable adaptation to the world, which require to be understood and explained. It would be wholly irrational if these things should be and there be *no* corresponding sphere of real objects wherein is fully realized what we now but dimly see, because of the downward drag of the vital drive, what we now will, love, think, hope or fear. At all events there remains the task of making religion comprehensible. If the genesis and intentional aspect of religion can be explained in terms of extra- and pre-religious facts, if its object is to be regarded as a fiction or a synthesis derived from phantasmagorical distortions of mundane experience, then the truth of religion is a lost cause. If it is *not* susceptible of such explanations, then we are obliged to assume a domain of reality corresponding to religious acts with exactly the same right as that with which we posit the external and internal worlds, and the consciousness in fellowmen, as spheres of existence.

Moreover, it is in this way that religious acts lead us to certainty of the existence of God and a realm of divinity. If by nothing else, God's existence would be proved by the impossibility of deriving man's religious proclivities from anything but God, who through them takes a natural way of making himself knowable to man.

The religious act in its internal and external, individual and social aspects

Briefly, it is in the nature of the religious act not to confine itself within the human interior but to manifest itself to the outside world in two ways through the medium of the body: purposive conduct and expressive action. For that reason there belong to every religion a form of *ethos* and moral practice determined by the religion's character, and a self-presentation, regulated in some way, of the religious consciousness in *forms of worship*.

Schleiermacher's attempts to define the nature of religion fell into grave errors because he maintained that it is only a chance connection which attaches a particular ethos to a particular religion, while the specifically religious extends no further than the outward *expression* of itself in forms of worship. But no less mistaken are those who one-sidedly refer religion to moral values alone and regard the liturgical worship of the divine as no more than an accidental by-product of religion or as something whose sole function is to symbolize externally and make known to others an element which is already complete within the internal consciousness.

Since the apprehension of moral value (of God as the good) enters into every religious act and since all moral cognition, to the degree of its immediacy and adequacy, *necessarily* determines not the existence, to be sure, but the quality of the act of will,[1] therefore, every time the supreme good is conjured up in a concrete vision a supreme concrete *model* of morality is proposed to the volition, a model which both precedes and determines everything we call by such names as rule of conduct, moral law. Nay more. Morally good volition and conduct, conforming to whatever image of divinity hovers before the mind, necessarily *govern* as a *sine qua non* the possibility of cognitive advance into the full breadth and depth of deity. For, of all kinds of cognition, knowledge of God is the most inseparable from moral progress.[2] Thus moral volition and conduct are not mere *consequences*, as Luther thought, of religious faith, but an identical component of value-cognition is present in both moral and religious acts, so that a moral act is partly implicated in the performance of any religious act, and vice versa. Just as a person's true moral intent (for good or evil) first declares itself in his readiness to perform a certain deed,* so genuine faith declares itself in readiness to give effect to the ethos contained in a religion. Good will and conduct do more than reflect religious awareness: at every step they widen and *deepen* one's concrete knowledge of God. They form a genuine penetration of his volitional aspect, a heightened *participation* of the person in his internal dynamic, even where there is no conscious reflexion that such is the nature of the process. And since knowledge of values is the foundation for knowledge of being, this kind of penetration is also a *precondition* of knowing God's being.

There are similar things to be said of liturgy and forms of worship. Religious knowledge is not wholly present *before* liturgical expression; ritual is an essential *vehicle* of its growth. Thus while the religious act is certainly rooted in the mind and spirit, in execution it invariably takes the form of a psycho-physical rather than purely psychic unit. In this respect religious cognition is far closer to artistic apprehension of the world than to science and metaphysics. In so far as the artist 'knows', he does not know *before* the process of representation but, as Fiedler was the first to discern,[3] in the very course of it. Representation is the artist's way of penetrating the world—and no science can ever be its substitute.* It is as if the mind's eye were fixed to the tip of the drawing crayon or painting brush and saw for the *first time* that part of the total project which the brush or crayon was on the point of representing. Similarly, the religious experience is not rounded and complete until it is expressed in forms of worship and

---

[1] Cf. the proof of this Socratic axiom in my *Der Formalismus in der Ethik, etc.**
[2] Cf. the chapter on 'The Nature of Philosophy'.
[3] See C. Fiedler, *Der Ursprung der künstlerischen Tätigkeit,* 1887.

receives ritual representation. For that reason it is a strict law of the history of religion that ritual and the concrete idea of the religious object are *mutually* interdependent variables. It is for example impossible that the ancient Roman, who in the act of prayer covers his eyes in a mood rather of submersion than expansion, should have the same concrete *idea* of God as the Greek who opens both eyes and arms to the deity. Everywhere, as Usener has convincingly shown, the history of religion attests this law— but attests, not proves. They who pray kneeling have not seen God in the same light as they who pray standing. Since religion is just as much practice as theoretical knowledge, and since theory and practice are here inseparable, it would be ridiculous to say to a man who has made some approach to a given religion or Church, 'While you have still not accepted every one of this religion's tenets of divinity, you may not, for conscience' sake, perform any act of worship which this religion prescribes'. One might as well tell a painter that before he begins to paint, *before* the process of representation, he must see a landscape in the *same* way as that in which he gradually learns to see it as his picture takes shape. No! Pascal was right when he said, 'Do thou but kneel, and faith will come.' And so we should thus advise our man: 'Try to perform the moral acts and ritual which this religion lays down, then see whether or how far you have grown in religious understanding.'

Finally, every religious act is simultaneously an *individual* and a *social* act. In a generalized sense, the saying *Unus Christianus, nullus Christianus* applies to all religion. It is a general principle that one cannot have *God* as the object of one's thought without thinking of him as bearing the same relation to all men as he does to oneself. The thought of God, even in the solitary hermit of the wilderness, must always lead to thoughts of the *community* of men. One can make a work of art purely 'for oneself', enjoy a thing purely for oneself, know a thing purely for oneself or merely know a thing objectively without intending it 'for' anyone in particular or being conscious of any need to communicate it. But one cannot in the same sense believe in or pray to God 'for oneself'. Even if *all* promptings to communal life were dead in a man, even if he had ceased ever to give a thought to his neighbour, the religious act which leads him to God would suffice to lead him back, at least in *spirit*, among his brethren. I have elsewhere[1] shown with respect to the 'sociological proof[2] of God' that the mere idea of a human community postulates the idea of the kingdom of God as its

[1] See the later chapter on the Christian idea of love and community.

[2] In this case, *Erweis*, proof as the most cogent inference from the results of extended trial (cf. 'to prove oneself'), as in a legal or practical sense, or that of 'satisfying the examiners' (*Translator*).

condition and its background. Thus it also postulates the very idea of God. The knowledge that each person does not exist only for his own sake, but is also a *member* of an immeasurable whole composed of spiritual beings, is not something we learn by chance but is implanted in the very nature of the mind.[1]

But there is more to be said. In knowledge of God, conceived as ideally adequate, no man or group of men can act as substitute for any other man or group. Precisely because the religious is man's most personal and individual act, it is necessarily one which can *fully* attain its object only in the form of the general concert of men. Hence, in contrast to any other form of cognition, religious knowledge has the *community of love and salvation* as an essential *constituent*. Since every soul has *individuality* as an idea of God, and is no mere stereotype, it is characterized by one peculiar accession of knowledge within the fulness of divinity. For that reason there belongs to every positive religion a positive idea of community which is *necessarily* connected with the idea of its supreme object. This fact must be regarded as a major premise in the comparative history of religions.

No man can avoid the religious act

Since the religious act is an essential endowment of the human mind and soul, there can be no question of whether this or that man performs it. The question can only be of whether he finds its *adequate* object, the correlative idea to which it essentially *belongs*, or whether he envisages an object, acclaiming it as divine, as holy, as the absolute good, while it yet *conflicts* with the nature of the religious act because it belongs to the sphere of finite and contingent goods.

This law stands: every finite spirit believes either in God or in idols. And from it there follows this pedagogic rule of religion: the correct way of dispelling 'unbelief' is not that of guiding a man to the idea and reality of God by arguments external to his personal condition (whether by 'proofs' or by persuasion), but that of showing him invincibly, as may certainly be done from any individual life or life typical of any class of men, that he has installed a finite good in place of God, *i.e.* that within the objective sphere of the absolute, which he 'has' at all events as a sphere, he has, in our sense, 'deified' a particular good—or 'become enamoured' of it, as the ancient mystics would have said. In thus bringing a man to *disillusion* with his idol, once we have exposed it in analysing his life, we bring him *of his own accord* to the idea and reality of God. Hence, what I have called the 'shattering of idols' is the principal (and only) way to prepare the religious

[1] J. Volkelt also makes this point in his recent book, *Das ästhetische Bewusstsein*, Munich 1920.

development of the personality. For though belief in God (orientation of the person's spiritual nucleus to the infinite being and good in faith, hope, love, etc.) has no specific, positive cause in the psychic history of a man, such a cause certainly underlies disbelief in God, or rather the permanent self-delusion of putting a finite good (*e.g.* the State, art, a woman, money, knowledge) in the place of God, or of *treating* it 'as if' it were God. Once this cause is uncovered, once the veil is removed which concealed the idea of God from the soul of a man, once his idol is shattered, which he has *interposed* between himself and God, once he is restored to a correct vision, from the jumbled or inverted order of things with which he bedevilled his mind's eye or from the order of values that enslaved his heart, *then* it is that the religious act turns from its whoremongering in spontaneous quest of its proper object, the idea of God.

Thus the right method for all religious initiation, the method which must precede any kind of instruction concerned with religion, is not 'proof', but the awakening and activation of the religious act, the guiding of it to its proper object and objective good. This principle is no more than strictly consequent upon our theory of religion.

I have been describing some of the important consequences of the idea that finite consciousness by nature possesses a correlative sphere of absolute entities and values, which it fills with one kind of content if not another. This content is the good on which the person in question pins his faith. It stands in that unique relationship with him which is founded by the spiritual act we call *faith* (belief *in* a thing) as opposed to *belief* that a thing exists, happens or has happened.[1]* This act is *sui generis* and cannot be classified under the heading of either intellectual or volitional acts. If I am to describe it, an internal distinction will have to be made between the act which initially supplies the object and the concentric act of unconditionally upholding and adhering to the object of faith. The former act, by nature, is a glimpse 'through a glass darkly' which both needs and can acquire the completion of direct intuitive perception. The latter act is best envisaged on the model of what we mean by the phrase 'self-identification' with an object. The personality senses that the very nucleus of its existence and value is bound so closely to the object of faith that it is 'pledged' to that object, identified with it, as we say. 'I shall exist and have worth, and *wish* to exist and have worth, only in so far as thou, object of faith, art and hast worth' or 'we two stand and fall together'—these expressions render into words the relationship in which the person feels that it stands to the

[1] Scheler employs the English words *faith* and *belief* to distinguish two senses of the German *Glaube* (*Translator*).

object of its faith. Essential to the act of faith is the *un*conditionality with which faith is pledged, and this of is course in accordance with the object's location in the sphere of the absolute.

In this sense every man must *needs* have an 'object of faith', and every man performs the act of faith. Everybody *has* a particular something, an object bearing (for him) the hallmarks of the supremely valuable, to which he knowingly, or by the unconscious test of practical conduct, accords precedence over all else. This object is for the leading minority in this capitalist age, to give an example, the maximal acquisition of economic goods, or of their measure—money (mammonism). For the nationalist it is his nation, for the Faustian limitless knowledge, for the Don Juan repeated conquests of woman. In principle any finite good may enter the absolute sphere of being and values in any concrete mind, and thereafter be striven for with 'unending endeavour'. In such a case the good invariably becomes a false god. The finite good is torn from its harmonious context in the world of goods: it is loved and pursued with a total lack of compromise wholly out of proportion with its objective significance; the human being seems magically enchained to its idol, and behaves 'as if' it were God himself.

You cannot choose between having and not having a good of this kind. You can only choose whether your absolute sphere will be inhabited by God, as the one good *commensurate* with the religious act, *or* by an idol.

This applies even to men who call themselves 'indifferent' in matters of religion, even to theoretical 'agnostics'.

So-called religious *agnosticism* is not a psychological fact, it is pure self-deception. The agnostic maintains he can refrain from the act of faith, claims that he does not believe. Did he but look more closely into his state of mind, he would notice that he is deceiving himself. He too has an absolute sphere to his consciousness, one filled with some positive phenomenon. He is not without any such sphere, neither is that he has empty. But this positive phenomenon is the phenomenon of the '*void*', or of nothingness (in respect of value). Thus the agnostic is not in fact an unbeliever but a believer *in* nothingness—he is a metaphysical nihilist. Belief in 'nothingness' is quite different from non-belief. As is witnessed by the strong emotion with which the thought of 'nothingness' disturbs our soul, it is an intensely positive state of mind. But *absolute* nothingness must be sharply distinguished as a phenomenon from any form of merely relative nothing. Absolute nothing is the conjunction of non-existence and the not being anything, in downright unity[1] and simplicity. It is the

---

[1] This is what distinguishes absolute nothing from the Buddhist idea of Nirvana, since by that is meant liberation and redemption from reality, while leaving the positive idea and value of the entity intact.*

diametrically contrary—not contradictory—antithesis of God, *i.e.* of him who is what he is ('I am what I am'). Even within the soul of the religious nihilist something is at work which causes the soul to grope secretly for the *ens a se*, for the subsistent entity itself which lies above and behind the kaleidoscope of sensual images as they impinge on the self and recoil. It is not simply a non-performance of the religious act which underlies this mentality, but a positive, *active resistance* of the will against this covert foreknowledge and quest of the *ens a se*, a resistance which will not even permit the mind to form and judge the question of God's existence. This active resistance is accompanied by a factitious clinging to the appearance of things, their superficial aspect. The two attitudes are complementary; each looks for support to the other. The metaphysical *disquiet* and religious *dread* experienced in the presence of that absolute nothing which here fills the sphere of the absolute have the effect of intensifying and stabilizing the energy expended on clinging to the motley assemblage of appearances. But such clinging, such vain love of the world, in turn restores the void to the absolute region of consciousness. This is the tragic round of the mind indifferent in matters of religion.

For the present I do not wish to take any further the analysis of the nature of the religious act. Its full importance would not be apparent until we had proceeded to analyse in detail the most important religious acts in illustration of what we have had to say. But here and now that lies outside our scope.[1]

The way we have hitherto followed in laying a theoretical foundation for religion has deviated in some respects from the ways which philosophy and theology are currently wont to follow. This gives us cause to turn our attention to certian types of theoretical foundation for religion which still command a following in our country and, more generally, in the ambit of European and American civilization. This will make clear in what ways the views we have advanced are related to these types.

SOME RECENT BASIC THEORIES OF NATURAL RELIGION

To affirm the existence and legitimacy of a natural knowledge of God is not at all the same thing as to suppose there are rational proofs of God—though even today this supposition is accepted by many as the basis of all theology. Moreover, the doctrine, which has appeared in various guises since the time of Augustine, that there is a *direct* factor in knowledge of God (*i.e.* one independent of inference and proof), is in no way incompatible

---

[1] It is my intention to devote special studies to this task. They are to appear separately as *'Religionsphänomenologische Analysen'*.*

with belief in the existence of a knowledge of God from nature. Even a view divergent from both methods of natural theology—the view I am here propounding—may also claim to uphold the natural knowledge of God as something distinct from whatever rests on positive revelation.

We must distinguish between *natural religion* and *natural theology*. Natural religion is the artless knowledge of God which every man endowed with reason—quite apart from the kind or degree of scientific method in his make-up—can acquire, and indeed acquire in such a way that he does not necessarily bring to conscious reflection the way in which he acquired this knowledge. Even the upholder of a natural theology based on indirect proofs of God must concede that men wholly ignorant of methodical proofs do not derive their knowledge of God *purely* from tradition and revelation. Admittedly *his* particular theory for this kind of natural religion requires the assumption that even this natural layman's knowledge is based on the very conclusions which he as theologian reaches by scientific method. He can only say that these conclusions (for example, the causal inference of a supreme, eternal world-cause) are unconsciously and unmethodically drawn by the man unschooled in 'proofs of God'. But it is my opinion that this assumption of *'unconscious inference'* has no right of passage in any field of philosophy. In the different forms which *inter alios* Schopenhauer and Helmholtz gave to this doctrine in their treatment of the problem of perception, this assumption has led into nothing but fallacies. This is no less true where it has been supposed to support the assumption of an external world independent of consciousness, and to justify the natural assumption that other minds exist.[1] To ascribe such unconscious inferences to the untaught religious mind is no more justified than the corresponding assumptions in these questions. And it is doubly unjustified when the inference, even as reached by regular method, falls short in fact of what it ostensibly attains—a single, supreme and creative world-cause.

But it is also hard to imagine how natural religion could be only an unmeditated, or relatively unmeditated, unmethodical theology, since *qua* religion it shows not the slightest trace of any *organized* lore—not even, that is, any primitive theory or theology.

If there is any independent subjective realm of religious knowledge we should rather assume that natural theology, as rational theory of God, must look for *support* to natural religion, as to an authentic and characteristic *source of experience and insight*—however much it may be entitled as a science to submit its sources and the insights they supply to

---

[1] On this point cf. the appendix of my *Zur Phänomenologie und Theorie der Sympathiegefühle.**

purification and criticism, as well as to re-interpret data by due process of thought.

In other words, natural theology must first and foremost base itself on natural religion, just as the sciences of the material world must start from the categories, *i.e.* forms of being, to be found in the natural Weltanschauung.

Natural religion, however, must first of all be studied phenomenologically in its constituent acts and objects. Once this has been done natural theology can and should forge a link between the known ingredients of the natural religious outlook, on the one hand, and secular knowledge on the other, or (more specifically) philosophical metaphysics as the culmination of such knowledge. This connection must be made in a rational way which will yield some kind of theory of God's existence and relation to the world.

In this way we obtain a natural knowledge of God and also remain in strictest accord with Paul's dictum that we may know the craftsman from his work. It was not for very many years that this saying was narrowed to the assertion of a scientifically rational knowledge of God, and it was much later still when it was confined to the very special contention that there are absolutely self-evident causal inferences which lead us to God.[1] But the propositions that the whole of nature bears 'traces' of its divine creator or 'signposts to God', that its constructs everywhere declare it the 'work' of a rational mind, that an intelligent power 'expresses' and 'proclaims' itself in its processes, that we can never, never explain the essence and existence (as distinct from being thus-and-thus here and now) of *any* natural structure or process by reference to any other contingent being, that in fact it bears the stamp of origination from a being which 'is' through itself and by reason of its own essence—these propositions are indubitably part of natural religion itself. Yet they are adequately confirmed solely in the intuitive apprehensions which the *religious* conception of the world adds as completely new positive phenomena to the facts of extra-religious observation. Thus they can only be wholly misunderstood if the intuitive references of words like 'trace', 'signpost', 'work', 'express', 'proclaim' are replaced by a putative causal inference from the *pre-religious* data of secular observation.

It is not every observation of nature which yields these phenomena, these symbolic and intuitively grasped references of natural things to God; they are yielded in *religious* observation alone, and this indeed is (historically speaking) the primordial and 'most natural' way of regarding

[1] On the point that these doctrines are absent from patristic literature cf. Möhler, *Die Einheit in der Kirche*, Tübingen 1825.

nature. By comparison all 'scientific' observation is artificial, since one by one it strips the original natural datum of the phenomena which have no bearing on its particular purpose of producing a picture of the world that may prove useful in controlling nature. *First and foremost these are the phenomena observed by natural religion.* To give an example, natural science cannot, and even should not, take any interest in the factor of 'effectedness' or creatureliness, or in the essence, the pure quiddity (or idea) of a natural object, since these two aspects are in any case unalterable *a priori*, which nullifies their significance for the control of nature; they are metaphysico-religious constants which do not concern science in the least. For similar reasons it has to set aside, by an artificial abstraction, the final purpose and destination of natural objects, their values, and in the long run—if it be possible—their very qualities. And since it limits itself to grasping them only in so far as they unequivocally determine one another, it does right, from a methodological point of view, to disregard nature's author, lord and supreme controller.

But is it not surely perverse to *employ* science to belittle our a-rational insight into nature, to remove from consideration its components' symbolic reference to God, and *then* to go on maintaining that God's existence can be inferred from purely objective, logical, causal arguments? First one bludgeons nature into a corpse, and then one claims to have just discovered the innermost secret of its life.

On this point the *fundamental* error of traditional theology has always been the same. One presumes to have inferred what one already knows in its very thatness from an entirely different source of knowledge. *Within* the world of religious insight one—quite rightly—draws conclusions, but presumes to have inferred the material of that world from pre-religious facts. This mistake is similar to that which many thinkers make when they believe that one can 'infer' a real state of bygone experience simply from a present self, a real external world from the pure contents of consciousness, another mind from the datum of another body—errors which I have refuted elsewhere.* What one truly may infer—once one possesses in *direct* apprehension the spheres of 'past life', 'external world', 'other minds'—is at most the particular properties, qualities and characteristics which real things possess in those spheres.

Let us take as an example the well-known 'causal inference', which is supposed to bear the whole weight of natural theology. Its sense is fully justified provided that it is understood to rest on two quite non-inferable, intuitively evident factors which are integral elements in any religious observation of the world: 1. the apprehension of a being absolute by reason of its very essence (this is given whenever the factor of contingency is grasped in *any* natural or psychic object), 2. the 'work'-character or creatureliness of every natural object, together with the symbolic 'import' latent in the thing itself, *i.e.* the 'signpost' to its creator; by these I am led to the *ens a se* of which I am already aware. This factor of the 'created work' is salient, necessarily salient, in any natural object when I mentally project it as a 'case' against the background of a *generally contingent world* and then pay attention to its pure *quid-est*. There it stands (this tree, say), as if lifted out of all its context of contingencies, whether real or ideal, and exposed in the isolation of an irreducible phenomenon which is what it is —as if nothing existed but itself. And it is as such that it takes on a secret power of speech, and tells unasked of its author, of that whereby it is, and is not *not* in being, that whereby it is what it is and not a mere exemplar or another thing altogether. This effectedness, this state of being 'the work' of *X*, is not itself inferred but is an intuitively evident factor, just as— in extra-religious observation—I do not *infer* by rational process that this table is the work of a man but *see* from it that it is an artefact. Certainly this factor may very well play a part in a causal inference—but only through its inclusion in the material premises. *If* natural objects exhibit this feature and *if* I know there is an *ens a se*, then I may infer that they are the work of the *ens a se*.

It is possible to analyse the quality of creatureliness in greater detail. If I do so, I discover that it is only at *one* point in all my experience of the world that the provenance, the process of 'realization', of a pure quiddity is given to me in its essence. It is where I witness how a hitherto imaginary thing comes into being as an empirical result of, under the sensed influence of, my own volition—as for example when I paint a picture, making certain motions with my arms or hands just as I wish, and because I wish to do so. In every such case I 'see' once and for all the following essential state of affairs: a thing is real only through an effecting cause which brings it into real being,[1] and the only truly 'free' *volitional* causation of things is direct effecting which is not itself a caused effect. It is out of the question that I am here by mere analogy transferring an adventitious human experience of causation to a realization and causation which is of an extra-human order, thus explaining the existence of natural phenomena in an 'anthropomorphic' manner. On the contrary, my experience of human volition and causation is the *only* place in the whole of all possible experience of the cosmos where I actually grasp in a contingent fact the nature of realness (= the possibility of offering resistance to volition), the nature of coming-into-being (= being realized in

[1] Literally, and more cogently: 'A thing is effect-ive (*wirklich*) only through an effecting (*Wirken*) which effects (*erwirkt*) it' (*Translator*).

and through volition) and the nature of direct and primary effectedness. And for that reason I need not 'transfer' anything, project anything specifically human into things in general; I see things once for all in the essential character of *having been willed and effected by a creative volition*, see them as work and creature—that is in so far as I regard them solely from a religious viewpoint, *i.e.* not in their interdependence within the spatio-temporal system, but with regard to their 'eternal' thatness, their existence 'in their own right'.

When therefore the language of religion 'glorifies the works of the Eternal', when it finds that the concrete forms of nature 'express' or 'proclaim' a creative will, eternal reason and goodness, etc., or that all things show traces and footprints of God, it does no more than reproduce the objective speech of things themselves, their meaning hint, their significant pointing beyond their contingency. This 'meaning', this 'signifying', inhabits them, inhabits *things*, phenomenally; before it man feels humble and knows that his mind can hear, understand, re-echo but miserable fragments of this glorious discourse. He knows, then, that this language, and the meaning of 'divine words' in things, is infinitely richer, greater and more manifold than the possible extent to which man can *understand* and transcribe it. What scientific concepts, categories and designations select for *their* purposes from this meaning of things is only a minimal part of the whole—that part by which things indicate the degree of their interchangeability for the related technical ends of displacement and alteration.

But if this speech is objective, if its 'meanings' are, as we say, far from projections of the human mind (and after all, as given they evidently transcend *all* human understanding), to that extent this prodigious telling of the works of its creator already *postulates* the *religious* way of looking at nature; and it is evidently absurd to think one can use logical processes to pass from a *non*-religious to a religious frame of mind or form of comprehension.

And yet I find it very understandable that so many should take exception to this thesis and feel themselves driven back to the rational kind of natural theology which has become traditional. There are two things which they ignore.

In the first place they fail to see the *essential historical difference* between the age which gave rise to rational theology and our own age, in respect of the former's unquestioning acceptance of the religious outlook on the world, which is now *no longer* taken for granted. Secondly they believe that if one says there is a specifically religious, as distinct from scientific, way of observing the world, one has implied a further metaphysical assertion, namely that the religious is 'only' *subjective*, whereas the scientific is *objective and unquestionable*.

The meaning of my first point is clear. Man, while he breathes normally and the air is calm, knows nothing of the atmosphere in which he lives. Only in a storm, only when he notices the thinness of mountain-air, does he understand that he has always lived in this atmosphere. The theology of rational deduction was able to arise in the line of tradition and to retain validity in an age which so took the religious outlook for *granted* that it was totally *unaware* of it 'as' a religious outlook: there was *no chance* that it should stand out in sharp distinction from other forms of outlook. For while, taken as a whole, the forms of observation possess as forms of the finite mind a store of essential features which are 'eternal' and immutable, the actual *vital emphasis* which they are given, in comparison one with another, varies according to the spirit of the age. And there is always one particular outlook which enjoys the primacy of 'going without saying'— and has an apparent natural right to do so. In the capitalist age of the bourgeois, an age of systematic rationalism which, blind to the *narrow* conditions its attitudes impose on its *status*, *will* and *expansion*, has mistaken its *technical blueprints* for an authentic metaphysics, the religious outlook no longer 'goes without saying'. We may find this deplorable from a religious point of view, but for our knowledge of religion it affords one advantage: it deepens our comprehension of the religious outlook and the essential *uniqueness* of religious cognition; it shows us the limitations of rational method in this domain.

For, however they regard the logical validity of their proofs of God, there is one question which all supporters of orthodox natural theology must surely ask themselves: How is it that these proofs, really not complex or hard to follow—Pythagoras being much more difficult in this respect— are totally devoid of power to *convince* modern man or any man who has not already derived a belief in God from tradition, faith or some other religious way of knowing? If these so simple proofs (from motion, from world-cause, etc.) are as clear, self-evident, certain as they are given out to be (for that matter, in contradiction of *e.g.* so great an authority as Newman, who never concealed his mistrust of *this* natural theology), how is it that on all counts they incur the rejection of modern man—or rather of all those who have not been brought up in this theological tradition? Is it not remarkably anomalous that such simple proofs, which are supposedly hinged on a reason common to all men, wholly free of religious assumptions, should in psychological fact work only when assisted by the *tradition* of one narrow school of thought? One appeals to reason, and tradition does the work! But is not 'traditionalism', which we ourselves find utterly wrong, precisely what 'natural' theology ought to avoid?

For my part, I know of but one answer available to the 'traditionalists'. It is quite insufficient to answer that one ought to regard the psychogenesis of religious conviction as wholly separate from its logical justification, that we were asking something of the proofs which they were never intended to supply. For we may make the same distinction with regard to *all* judgments and convictions—even mathematic and scientific. Yet in these spheres proofs also carry psychological conviction. Furthermore, one's pleasure in having made the distinction should not blind one to its very definite limitations. Everything in the world is and takes place 'in accordance with' the self-evident laws which apply to objects simply because they are objects: the being of a stone and its fall correspond to the laws of identity and sufficient cause as much as human thought (both true and false). But where the human mind is concerned laws have an additional meaning; they are 'also' in some way psychological; they also move and determine its thinking, if it thinks correctly. In their ideal acceptation they are realized in a man not only in the same way as in the falling stone (where the fall may be regarded as the *conclusion* to the major premise of gravitation and the minor of the stone's distance from the earth) but also in that he takes note of them in his thinking and consciously fulfils them. How is it that this kind of realization in thought is missing from the proofs of God? How is it that when the modern man unschooled in tradition is confronted with these proofs, these simple proofs, his *brainpower*—which is not altogether negligible—cannot apparently rise to the occasion?

There is only one reasonable answer, and it is the one which is given by upholders of this kind of natural theology, if they are consistent in their reasoning. It is this: the proofs are simple, fully clear and self-evident, but the *will* of modern man—the 'sinful' will, the will with an interest in God's non-existence or the absence of any sure knowledge of his existence—fights shy of accepting their clear and plentiful enlightenment. Far be it from me to decry the force of this argument: it is one whose significance for the understanding of moral self-deceptions, among other things, I myself have broadly developed.[1] But here, in my opinion, its force is of no avail. For in the first place it is simply untrue that if these proofs are unconvincing it is only in the case of minds already inclined to atheism or pantheism, or those in whom this interest in rejection can somehow be detected. Those who are filled with the deepest love of God, and believe as much in his existence as in the possibility of acquiring a sure knowledge of it, find them just as unconvincing, if not more. One should therefore

[1] See section entitled '*Idole der Selbsterkenntnis*' in *Vom Umsturz der Werte*.

treat with circumspection this dangerous and even morally dubious *argumentum ad hominem*, whose tendency is to reduce the breadth of catholicity to the tradition of one narrow school. To accuse the atheist of a sinful will, save when the case rests on verifiable known facts and takes a form which can be settled exclusively by reason, is not far removed from irresponsible calumny. Sometimes this accusation, as the required psychological explanation of the ineffectiveness of logically clear and simple proofs, is not levelled against individuals as such; the inability to convince is blamed on a perverted modern habit of thought, at whose *origin* there stands a sinful will, while the man of today has grown up within it, remaining *personally* guiltless. The culprit is, in other words, a kind of partial original sin; but even in this reading the accusation is unjustified. For however correctly this theory may explain the general lack of interest shown in natural theology by the 'scientific' philosophy of the period 1850-1900 (in glaring contrast to the far more genuine 'scientific' philosophy of, for example, the seventeenth and eighteenth centuries, which was 'scientific' in the proper sense), it is quite inapplicable to the deficiencies of this particular *form* of natural theology.

We are left with the riddle. Why, out of all methods of justification and foundation, should these proofs have so little power to found and justify—save where tradition renders them otiose?

My answer is not that of Kant, who cast groundless doubt on the objective validity of the causal principle and, as I shall not pause to show, erroneously believed he had logically refuted the proofs of God. In spite of Kant, these proofs retain their legitimacy and *profundity* of meaning, in so far as they refer to *attributes* of God. The causal principle—which Kant confuses with the principle that phenomena eventuate according to regular chronological *rules*—is a universally, objectively valid and *self-evident* principle as applied to the coming into being (even when timeless) of any real thing whose existence does not (objectively) *follow* from its essence.[1] I would only insist that the fact and the validity of these proofs *postulate* something in addition to the formal laws of logic, the causal principle and the *facts of experience* in the inductive sense: they postulate that this mode of probative thought is essentially one embraced by the *religious outlook* on the world and the facts and conditions peculiarly—and

---

[1] A wholly untenable position is maintained by those neo-scholastics who seek to prove that the causal principle is, directly or indirectly, a principle (demonstrably) 'necessary to thought'; they reduce the validity of such principles for the extra-mental *entity* to the statement that God ordained being and thought for each other (the preformation-system). But they *nevertheless* wish to prove the existence of God by reference to the causal principle. It need hardly be said that here we have a blatant *circular proof*.

only—'given' in this form of observation. In fact I would go so far as the following general contention: To every essential region of being there correspond (*a priori*) certain perspicuous material conditions and internal relationships, standing over against all positive inductive experience, together with a class of acts that is inseparable from the form of insight proper to that region; unless these elements are added to the laws of 'pure' logic, the logic and substantial ontology of the realm in question remain incomplete. Thus there are also objectively valid axioms and categories for the religious form of perception and knowledge—though they cannot become perspicuous until we actualize within ourselves the eternal nature of that attitude, until we awaken the 'religious *act*' and *train* ourselves to conceive the world in a religious manner. To that extent there is thus an objective logic of religious thought, which of course, like any other special logic, comprises purely formal logic and dialectic, but which, above and beyond their general principles, rests simultaneously on ontic insights that are wholly peculiar to the religious sphere of being. Hence when, for example, a natural object is envisaged *as* a concrete instance of contingency, *as* generally existing, being 'something' in particular, *as* a 'real-ized' thing—a 'creature'—and *as* signifying something aloof from meanings purely relative to men and other contingent things, yet related to its own and the world's 'grand design', *then* for the first time are disengaged those phenomena which, as against merely formal laws of logic and ontic truths, represent the *material*[1] premises, the specifically *religious* laws of sense and thought, in whose light the proofs of God first become meaningful and carry conviction. And what raises that mysterious barrier, in the stranger to the narrow school of theology, between their proofs and his reason is not his lack of brainpower, nor is it his 'sinful will', nor the inheritance of a way of thought; it is his complete overlooking of the *onotological* domain of the holy and absolute—his non-possession of the needful *bridge* between religion and rational knowledge of other kinds, the necessary basis of all religious understanding.

From this we may extract a simple pedagogic rule for the power of conviction of 'proofs of God'. The conditions of the power are 1. a bringing to light of the *primary phenomena* of religion, which are irreducible in terms of any other class, 2. the deliberate training of modern man in the

---

[1] *I.e.* constituting the supra-formal, 'substantial' component of the essential; pertaining to the effective individuality of things, their ideal hypostasis *sub specie aeternitatis*—as in the title of Scheler's book, *Der Formalismus in der Ethik und die materiale Wertethik*, wherein are propounded concrete, non-formal and objective values which inhere in things as their value-*qualities*. This Platonistic doctrine, it will have been noted, colours the present work throughout (*Translator*).

religious conception of the world, which is an essential part of consciousness and has only in modern times been obfuscated; this training must be
based on the most precise delineation of the types of religious act through
which alone this conception is operative. In my experience, this is the only
method which holds out any hope of spanning the chasm which yawns
between modern civilization and knowledge of God. Moreover, only this
theory of the nature of religion offers a *psychological* explanation—though
it was neither sought nor found for the sake of this explanation—of the
inefficacy of established forms of religious foundation-laying.

It is significant that so new a form of natural theology, taking its stand
on natural religion itself, not presuming to regard it as a merely 'simple-
minded' theology, is held to be 'unsure' by not a few followers of the old
tradition, who think it a 'shifting foundation' on which to build a sure
knowledge of divinity. Can religion then, which even subjectively is the
most deep-rooted of spiritual instincts and aptitudes, stand on any firmer
basis than *itself*, its very *nature*? Can specific items of religious knowledge
be more firmly based than on the nature of *religious* and no other kind of
knowledge? We have already[1] shown how essentially and historically
absurd it is to rank philosophy, the queen of sciences, *among* the sciences
themselves. Why then should not religion take its stand on the eternal and
incomparable nature of religion? How strange is this mistrust of the self-
sufficient force and compulsion of religious awareness! It betrays itself
whenever a thinker forsakes the very content of religious objects to seek
elsewhere a basis for the most cogent and primary promptings of religion.
Are we then to base the more fundamental on the less? No, such an
attempt, proceeding from already present mistrust and misconception of
religion, contributes nothing; what is needed is a psychological and historical demonstration of the fact (which no more than corresponds—
subjectively also—to religion's true place in the human mind) that all
primary changes in Weltanschauungen, philosophical trends, ways of life
and work, even ethical, political, economic systems, are *rooted*—whether
they tend to the true or the false—in antecedent religious changes, changes
governed by the internal principles of religious evolution. Precisely because religious acts are the most deep-rooted, simple, personal and
undifferentiated basic acts of the human mind, while the divinity forming
their intentional object is the foundation of all other being, any variations
within this focus of man must at least have the effect of demarcating a new
scope for all other forms of human knowledge, work and culture, according
to what is possible within the current orbit of religious Weltanschauung.

Hence, we find it easily conceivable that the intellectual leaders of the

[1] See chapter on 'The Nature of Philosophy'.

thirteenth-century Church could believe that the rational theology which they had developed provided a sure foundation for natural religion. That age of rising bourgeois rationalism, represented by an awakened European urban middle class with a will to *set about* the world, demanded a justification of natural religion. The ultimate bases of our knowledge of God had to be demonstrated in a manner which was 'also' valid for reason, even if reason was not to be the sole instrument of the demonstration. In its new Thomist theology the Church bowed to the new form of intellectual awareness exhibited by the age, the age of a young rising middle class; it acquiesced by departing from patristic forms and espousing Thomism's new *way* of line-drawing between *reason and grace*, between the *natural* order and the order of *revelation* (—new *way*, because the dichotomy itself is an essential constituent of the Christian Church and was also present in patristic times). Well might the Church acquiesce, for the ethos and rationalism of the burghers were still firmly embedded in the generally religious *way* of looking at the world, still deeply nourished by the forces of an overtoweringly universal Christian tradition. But today—how *utterly* different! As a whole the modern world is *not* thus firmly embedded —it is not embedded at all. Moreover, the type of man that corresponded to that old awareness, his ideals, institutions, ways of life, are not even any longer ascendant; they are descending *slowly to the grave*. We have come to take for granted—as nearly automatic habits—the things which, back in the years of Europe's education in reason, seemed something *new*, as yet untried: proper inference, proving, deduction and calculation. On the other hand, what was then taken for granted is ever more remote from us: the sense of religious, not to say absolute, existence and values, the felt presence of an objective order of things with a perspicuous order of values. If the traditional proofs of God do not impose themselves on modern man, it is not because he is deficient in powers of thought and inference; it is because the requirements he imposes on a proof are more subtle than proofs had been wont to encounter, and because he lacks the intuitive moulds and *materials* which used—covertly—to support those proofs.

But, as I have said, there is one further consideration which underlies the stand some take on the natural theology of tradition. They consider that the original assumption of a peculiar religious class of cognitive acts and peculiar religious outlook on the world is a concession to *subjectivism*, and they infer that any natural theology derived from a theory of such acts must be unstable and indeterminate, since its theses and propositions are not rigorously grounded in *objective fact*.

Now in principle this argument would be correct and unassailable, if its tacit supposition were true. The supposition is that in all its specific forms the religious act is an occurrence with only a subjective aspect, that it has no *permanently* corresponding raw material within an independent and self-contained circle of objects, existing on the plane of the absolute—not to mention the *only* object whose existence is in no way dependent on that of a subject but which is *absolute* in existence and value. We of course uphold what that supposition denies. The essential conditions pertaining and giving shape to any *object* of a religious act are in no way 'already' contained within the field of non-religious 'experience'. They are not in some way 'extracted' or 'abstracted' therefrom, nor constructed from its elements by process of manipulation and synthesis. We are, therefore not dealing with a *form* of knowing or regarding, in the sense that the same material or basic phenomena might just as well enter into some *other*, hence non-religious, form, that they could change the mere *form* while the content remained identical—or that the materials of the religious act could be extracted from the content of pre-religious forms of observation. On the contrary, even the most rudimentary religious act enables man to glimpse a plane of objective being and bestows essential insights, only accessible on that plane, which otherwise are wholly—and necessarily—concealed from him, just as the nature of sound and colour, together with the whole tonal and chromatic world, whether 'real' or imaginary, must be eternally hidden from a creature devoid of sight and hearing. There is therefore an essential, immutable *connection* between religious *act* and religious sphere of *objects;* it is not that there is any kind of dependence of the object on the religious act, either objectively or functionally, but that the specific natures of act and object are interconnected and belong together. It need scarcely be said that connections of this kind are no exception, for they obtain—witness the findings of phenomenology—over the *entire* realm of our cognition, feeling and volition—with their correlative objects. Quite apart, for example, from all man's positive sensory equipment (or that of beasts), it belongs to the nature of colour, even imaginary colour, to be given in the function of seeing, and it is of the essence of sound to be 'heard', but a 'danger' must also be 'feared', and a value apprehended via a certain type of emotional reaction. And in all such cases it is fallacious to conclude that the *existence* of the datum depends on the act through which it is given. Thus it is that the absoluteness of an object, or its rootedness in the absolute sphere of existence, or the value 'holy' with all its plenitude of factors and subdivisions, is given to us, offered to us, in the religious act alone.

But it is not merely wrong to attach the idea of a *dependent* religious object to the idea of a specifically religious outlook on the world: it is to reverse the truth. It is the very property of the religious act—and also in the last resort of the act of religious cognition (and no other cognitive act) —to find satisfaction (*i.e.* to be capable of 'fulfilment' in accordance with its essential intention) only in a being and a value which exist independently of any other entity or valuate object, and on which every other thing, including the existence of the subject as vehicle of the religious act, is dependent. There are many degrees of existential dependence of knowable objects on the particular organization of the cognitive subject—not fewer but *more* than Kant accepted when he divided objects into three strata: subjective being, objective phenomenal reality and the thing-in-itself. It is the task of epistemology to distinguish among these degrees, and the *correct* performance of this task is one of the most important services it can render. But the absolute sphere of existence is exclusively the province of the religious act. And so the religious class of acts is the only essential category in which the performance of an act is, and knows itself to be, dependent on the *intentional* object. 'All knowledge of God is knowledge through God'—the axiom is part and parcel of the religious act.

For these very reasons the danger of *subjectivism* is here entirely precluded. It would be far more profoundly menacing if knowledge of God depended in the last resort on the mere *option* of drawing or not drawing certain *conclusions*.

How was it possible to misunderstand this position? The only *reasonable* answer is that the philosophers and theologians who in the course of the nineteenth century developed theories of the religious act, as a specific source of experience and knowledge, clothed their ideas with a philosophy that was already *subjectivist in general trend*, and that there has been a failure to separate this 'clothing', that is their *philosophical* standpoint (which is generally false, and not only for religion), from the kernel of relative truth which their teachings provide, in particular for religion.

Historically viewed, this universal *subjectivism* is a child of Protestantism; but the same is by no means true of the doctrine of the *religious act* as a special source of material for natural religious knowledge. For we find that this doctrine—as yet free from the errors of modern subjectivism—is copiously and broadly developed in very many Fathers of the Church, especially the *Greek* Fathers, under the name of the 'religious sense', by which is given to understand that in addition to positive revelation there is a specific conceptual and expressive organ of the human soul whereby it has a living contact with God, and can reflectively *know*, under appropriate conditions of life, that it has this contact; only subsequently does it exercise *reason* on the material received through this contact in order to reach definite *judgments* concerning God's existence and attributes.

In modern times the French Oratorian Gratry has most meritoriously collated the relevant passages from the Greek Fathers.[1] The same doctrine is most exhaustively treated in the great theological work of that outstanding writer, Thomassin, on whose great scholarship Gratry also leans. Moreover the whole Augustinian trend of mediaeval and modern philosophy and theology, up to Newman (who certainly stands on this side in this question), has always clung to the principle that the soul, in so far as it is able to know and love all things *in lumine Dei*, possesses a potentially conscious, direct and unmediated contact with the light of all creation. It was Aquinas who first thought it decidedly permissible to read this *in lumine* as no more than *per lumen* in an objective causal sense. Thereby he paved the way for the proof of God now typical of natural theology.

We shall elsewhere closely examine the sense and historical evolution of these doctrines, so different in their conformation. We further hope to be able to show that even in Aquinas there are far more numerous traces of concessions to the older trend of theology in this respect than are admitted by modern Thomists. Our present concern has been merely to show that even a natural theology in our sense can quite legitimately claim the support of a truly not inconsiderable current in a great intellectual tradition.

Meanwhile attempts to demonstrate a special source of religious insight, where they have been inspired by *modern* philosophy, are to be seen in quite a different light. Having sprung—in essentials—from Protestant cultural soil, and having been undertaken by Protestant philosophers and theologians, they have also been nourished by the residuum of the more or less *subjectivist philosophy* which flourished in the same soil.

In this respect there is nobody who—in spite of otherwise considerable philosophical merits—brought this doctrine (and its corresponding apologetics and evangelizing praxis) so much into *discredit*, both for the Catholic world and, as we believe, in respect of its *objective* sense and value, as *Schleiermacher* and all the currents deriving from his thought, which at length have noticeably intermingled with Kantian preconceptions.

Here is not the place for a comprehensive criticism of his theory of religion, as developed first in his discourses and later in his dogmatic writing.[2] Suffice it to point out the chief among the relevant errors which

---

[1] See his *La Connaissance de l'âme*, 1857, vol. 1: I commend this work to the reader's attention.

[2] F. E. D. Schleiermacher, *Über die Religion, Reden an die Gebildeten unter ihren Verächtern*, Berlin 1799; *Der christliche Glaube*, vol. 2, Berlin 1821-2.

he so insidiously wove into his thesis of religion's self-contained *independence* of ethics, science or philosophy—a thesis which at the core is just and true.

1. Schleiermacher's principal and profoundest error lies in his being unable to allocate any other *object* to 'intuition and feeling' (*Anschauung und Gefühl*)—his source for knowledge of the eternal—than '*the universe*': the universe which, grasped as a totality, produces in man a '*feeling of utter dependence*'. But even in the most primitive religions the specific objective domain of the religious consciousness has ever and always been *peculiar and self-contained*, one different in essence from the 'universe' and all its content: it has been the domain of *divine* and *holy* being and value, which is brought into some kind of causal or symbolic rapprochement with the world only at a secondary stage. From the outset Schleiermacher overlooks the non-inferred *essential insight*, from every instance of a contingent entity, that there is also an *ens a se = ens a nihilo*, an existent, moreover, whose existence rises from its essence, and that this existent is a thing *distinct* from the world. This he overlooks, together with the specific type of value which 'holiness' represents and its irreducibility in terms of other kinds of value. Already we may say that Schleiermacher's theory is as deplorably interwoven with pantheism (deification of the world) as with subjectivism, inasmuch as he attributes no primary ontic domain (God) to religion, but casts it only in the rôle of a subjective attitude to the very *same* facts (of the 'universe') which are also objects of extra-religious cognition.

2. His second error is to connect the object of religion to the 'feeling of utter dependence' not in an intentional or cognitive but in a merely *causal* relationship. In his book *Das Heilige*,[1] which strikes very deep in its descriptive section and is of the highest importance for all questions of natural theology, Rudolf Otto makes the following judgment, which is perfectly correct: 'We have now to note a second defect in the formulation of Schleiermacher's principle. The religious category discovered by him, by whose means he professes to determine the real content of religious emotion, is merely a category of *self*-valuation, in the sense of self-depreciation. According to him the religious emotion would be directly and primarily a sort of *self*-consciousness, a feeling concerning one's self in a special, determined relation, viz. one's dependence. Thus, according to Schleiermacher, I can only come upon the very fact of God as the result of an inference, that is, by reasoning to a cause beyond myself to account for my "feeling of dependence". But this is entirely opposed to the

[1] See p. 10 of the First Edition, Breslau 1917 [E.T. 1923 ed. p. 10, 1959 ed. p. 24].

psychological facts of the case. Rather, the "creature-feeling" is itself a first subjective concomitant and effect of another feeling-element, which casts it like a shadow, but which in itself indubitably has immediate and primary reference to an object outside the self. In these words Otto has succeeded in touching *one* nerve of Schleiermacher's false subjectivism. Reading his profound and beautiful book, representing years of serious and fruitful devotion to the phenomenology of religion, I marvelled to learn how investigations undertaken quite independently—his and mine —cannot but reach precisely *similar* results if only the investigators, as open-mindedly as possible and as untroubled as possible by traditional academic theories, will trust themselves to the guidance of the *matter in hand.* It is only with chapter 19, where Otto exerts himself to demonstrate that the holy is, in Kant's sense, an *a priori* category, that he begins to burden his fine study with a theory which we must consider false and discredited—not only in this connection but *wherever* it is adduced in explanation of extra- and super-sensory phenomena in the field of object-perception. Even apart from his misguided insertion of his findings into the frame of a false philosophy, which maintains that anything it fails to find in the content of 'sensation' is added to sense-data by mental synthesis, Otto fails to shake off Schleiermacher's methodic error of wishing to isolate *in concreto* the basic phenomena of direct religious apprehension, which furnish all constructive theology and religious speculation with their irreducible material, but *only* their material. He seeks, that is, to isolate them from the complexes into which they enter with all the other *activities* and contents of the mind. Schleiermacher thought himself entitled to trace religion back to isolated 'intuitions', 'visions' and 'emotional experiences' in the 'pious', without regard for the essentially collective and *communal* character of religious experience. This led him to believe that every system, every dogma indeed and every kind of theoretic formulation must be regarded as a 'deformation' of those *primary elements.* Likewise, having disintegrated the bases of christological dogma into 'intuitions', notably the presentiment of Christ as the 'shielding and atoning mediator', Otto voices the following opinion: 'We are not, then, to deplore the fact that intuitions of this kind find a place in the doctrines of the Christian faith: they do so of necessity. What we must deplore is, that their free character, as springing from "divination", is so generally misinterpreted; that too commonly we dogmatize and theorize about them, deducing them from "necessary truths" of exegesis or dogma (which are in fact always dubious), and so failing to recognize them for what they are, free-floating utterances and trial flights at expression of the numinous feeling; and that too often we give them an emphasis which puts them unwarrantably at the centre of our religious interest, a place which nothing but the experience itself of God ought to occupy' [E.T. 1923 ed. pp. 175f., 1959 ed. p. 188]. Here we must firmly part company with Otto: we scarcely understand how, after so clear a recognition of the errors in Schleiermacher's subjectivism, he can talk of 'vaguely floating utterances'—as if these intuitions did not uncover (merely uncover, not form or construct) the *ontic features of absolute holiness* which are firmly established in Christ's person and there discovered. We are also at a loss to see why these 'intuitions', which are the only transmitters of our pure and direct apprehension of religious fact, should be exempt from the *rational* and *systematic* treatment, hence formulation in theory and dogma, which *any* kind of imaginative apprehension has to undergo, for example in the 'sciences'. Suppose one were to insist that astronomy ought to renounce its systematic edifice of centuries, its reasoned picture of a cosmos modelled with fixed constants in accord with strict laws, in favour of uncollated observation of the heavens, the mere registrations of the measuring instrument that supplied material for the creation of the picture.... What would Otto say? What nonsense! Otto, like others unmentioned, has fallen into Schleiermacher's error of making a concrete religion, supposedly existing *per se*, from the result of a *theoretic* attempt to get at the irreducible, primary data (the first in order of being 'given') of directly intuited religious objects (here positive and Christian) by a process of reduction which begins with an analysis of the ready-formed and theorized dogmas to hand. He further believes, in a thoroughly Lutheran manner, that the genetically earlier (primitive Christianity) must here be the superior, better, more nearly perfect; and he will have it that the *intuitive*—not intuited—substantial and pre-logical components of dogma, which as such are certainly *objective* materials for communal articles of faith, are simply the conscious, subjective reactions of individuals, reactions of which it has become impossible to say that they are reactions to 'this' rather than to 'that', or that they are reactions for 'this' reason and not another. For the concrete article of faith, that objective entity in respect of which alone these reactions are possible, is absolished in Otto's treatment, inasmuch as it (presumably) is entirely derived from these subjective reactions as their objectively vacant goal-point X.

3. Schleiermacher's third error (which in large measure is also Otto's) is to lay an utterly disproportionate emphasis on *emotion* in his definition of the religious *act*, which he even conceives as preponderantly a passive emotion brought into being by the effect of the universe. In this way the true state of affairs is flouted; the acts of a directly percipient reason, which are part of and even *direct* the religious act, are excluded in favour of

value-oriented emotional acts—which the religious act *in concreto* also contains—and that on the false philosophical presumption that the only reason to exist is the kind which draws indirect conclusions, though Aristotle had already taught, even if with insufficient foundation, that there is also a reason which *directly apprehends the essence of things.* This withholds due recognition from the rational idea of an *infinite being*— as already posited in the *ens a se*—and indeed imparts to the whole natural theology founded on this doctrine the character of a false irrationalism or *a-rationality.* But this must also be understood in the light of history. Schleiermacher—here at one with romanticism—was above all critical of the *Enlightenment's* theory of religion, yet he shared the rationalists' ignorance of the whole sphere of direct thought and *intuitio* and can be said to have postulated the equation 'all thought' = indirect, inferential thought. He was, therefore quite unable to see that the religious consciousness is rooted, in fact primarily rooted, in a reason which remains free of the technical goal-fixing that typifies 'science'.

4. The third is immediately attended by a fourth error. This is the equation of the value-cognitive emotional acts, in their original and *intentional* (thus not causal) reference to the value-aspect of the divine— to the holy, that is—with 'the emotions' (or a particular kind of emotion), *i.e.* with states of consciousness in the subject that by nature are not acts, are not primarily directed to an intentional object and, finally, have no cognitive significance.* Religious 'emotions' are only retrospective *reactions* released by vital contact with the sphere where the objects of religion are *truly objective,* as it is ultimately embodied in the dogmatic form of *fides quae creditur.* But this fourth error results in a total failure to grasp this most important and basic insight of religious objectivity, which indeed it distorts into the very opposite. It is the opposite which we find expressed in Schleiermacher's gravely erroneous dictum that religious dogmas are in general no more than retrospective 'descriptions of pious emotional conditions'. Against that we know nothing more certainly than that *reflection* on 'pious emotions' has nothing to do with living religion,[1] that even artless and simply felt emotions of piety can flower and flourish in the depth of the heart only when they receive nourishment and renewal from their interchange of prayer and knowledge with the objective sphere of faith and grace. Even the specifically religious emotional acts, which give access, when objectively directed, to the value-aspect of the divine, are different in essence from everything which Schleiermacher labels 'pious emotions'. These last are at the most the

[1] Concentrated reflection on religious emotions tends to blunt them and in the long run even kill them.

posterior effects of their objects. The above emotional acts are no less different in essence from all *volition* and *conation*, with which the neo-Thomists, who are here very backward in their psychology and axiology, still confuse them. Love or fear of God, veneration, holy awe, etc., are not simply emotions causally aroused by the idea of God (or 'universe', *pace* Schleiermacher), but acts of the emotional focus in which a divine and holy object is grasped and *given*; that is, it discloses itself to us, and in the absence of these emotional acts we could as little perceive it as a blind man colour, but it is only at a secondary stage that they may lead the subject to 'pious emotions'.

From the above it is easy to see why Schleiermacher's school of religious theory has been rightly called 'emotional theology' and for that reason rejected outright by every upholder of philosophical and theological objectivism. Yet it would be monstrous to pretend that the vagaries of this 'emotional theology' (with its pietist subjectivism of Herrnhuter provenance) are endemic in *any* doctrine which postulates some other necessary basis for natural theology in addition to the 'causal inference' from the world's existence: some kind of insight supplying data about the *object* of religion by means of a directly percipient reason and intentional acts of an emotional nature.

5. The last of Schleiermacher's basic errors in this context finds him over-reacting against *Kant's mistaken ethicalism* in a manner which parallels his over-reaction, as an emotional theologian, against the Enlightenment's rational theology. It is that he ignored the active side of religious consciousness, in particular the possibility that the human *will* might be directly or indirectly united to the will of God through religious acts of knowledge and love; thereby, like Luther, he introduced a most *harmful schism between religion and morality*. Here again we witness in Schleiermacher the activity of that spurious consciousness of superiority over right and morality which is typically 'romantic'. It is there to assist his all-important reaction against Kant's ethicalism, which is admittedly philistine. It was an untenable attempt of Kant's to found the existence of God—whose nature, unlike Schleiermacher, he regarded as given in the form of a pure rational idea—on a *postulate* of *practical reason* which at bottom would only lead, on the basis of a previously given and valid moral law, to a being X that settles somewhere between bliss and virtue— hence to a *guarantee of justice and retribution.** A being so discovered would be neither *omnipotent*, nor omniscient, nor supremely wise, good and loving. In so far as the question is of natural religion, Schleiermacher would merely substitute a purely *pantheistic but omnipotent* God, as a correlate of that feeling of 'utter dependence' to which he gives so undue a prominence.

K

In his opinion all the other positive attributes of divinity are divulged only in experience of the historical person of Christ. Thus neither in his case nor in that of Kant is there any question of a comprehensive theory of God, establishing a proper hierarchy and equilibrium of attributes. In neither of their doctrines is there even any construction of the essential personality of God as the object of natural theology, though merely as such it would entail nothing so positive as the question of single and threefold personality. For it is not in any way a rational necessity that a merely 'retributive' principle of justice should be also *personal* (since a metaphysical law of the cosmos, a mere 'moral order', would equally suffice, and plainly should suffice according to Fichte's early Kant-inspired teachings), neither does the feeling of 'utter dependence' require the correlate of a personal God. But we have observed that 1. the personal form of existence is essential to a *concrete* mind or spirit (—only what is concrete can be 'real'—), and 2. irrespective of any religious considerations, *personal value* is self-evidently superior to the values of impersonal things, acts, states, etc. Only when these insights have been accepted and digested are we led to infer that an *ens a se*, distinct from the world, must as a *mind or spirit* also be *personal*, and that a *summum bonum* (as an essential axiom of objective axiology) must likewise be not an impersonal good but a *personal value*, or rather a *valuate person*.[1]

Thus theories of the religious act and the autonomy of religion lead to subjectivism and uncertainty only—as shown—if the thinker fails to proceed from the relevant *essential ontology* when constructing these theories as a precondition of natural theology, regarded as real knowledge of God. The *first* object of natural theology is God in his natural essence; an essence-less, indeterminate God-reality is an absurdity. The *second* is our relationship to God, hence also the types of act through which a deity becomes apprehensible, knowable, plus the study of the *religious act* and form of consciousness. For this study our source of information is concentrated reflection on the ways and forms of human participation in the being of God, *knowledge* of God here representing only one of the ways.

If natural theology is constructed in this way—we offer but a signpost— the doctrine of a *material*[2] source of knowledge accessible to natural theology, hence one over and above mere inferences and data derived from the pre-religious empirical world, is entirely purged of the *general* errors of a subjectivist philosophy. For of course what is to be found in Schleiermacher is not an error confined exclusively to the philosophy of

---

[1] I have reasoned these propositions exhaustively in *Der Formalismus in der Ethik und die materiale Wertethik.*

[2] Cf. note to p. 279 (*Translator*).

religion, but the generally fallacious proposition, refuted by phenomeno-logy, that everything in the datum of intuition, perception and experience which transcends 'sensational' or 'sense'-data ('sensation' here being mis-conceived) may be 'reduced' either to a derivative of sensation or to a constructed adjunct—the product of mental synthesis. By this reasoning there simply *cannot exist* any asensual or suprasensual, and at the same time primary 'datum', or any positive realities and essential struc-tures akin to this datum, such as might rise above all contingent existence in the here-and-now and dictate the range of its ontic possibilities. But we know today that this hoary prejudice is not even true of the simplest facts in natural sensory perception, so-called. It is not true of the element of meaning, the quality of reality, shapes and other formal elements, phenomena of objective relevance, value-qualities and the phenomenal modes of sensual qualities when subsumed under that heading, the quality of concrete and homogeneous entity which we designate with the term 'thing' (together with its essential component factors), materiality and, when such is the case, cause-effect relation to other perceptual objects or to ourselves (*e.g.* the phenomenon of 'feeling', which is not itself felt). Again it is untrue of spatial or temporal extension and of plurality, untrue of the simplest phenomena of motion, alteration, substitution, etc. Everything in which we intuitively embody the sense of those words is essentially *extrasensual* and yet is truly '*given*', not 'produced' or 'added' by the mind. Why then should we not explore, legitimately explore and without pre-conceptions (unlike all genetic and other 'epistemological' theories), the essential primary data of the natural religious consciousness with all their ontic elements, just as we have at last learnt to explore the field of pre-religious extrasensual phenomena? The *supra*sensual datum (the very basis of the 'supernatural') takes its place alongside the sphere of the asensual and extrasensual as an object of phenomenological study.

But, one may protest, here is surely a limitless number of phenomena to study, which rather confuse than enlighten our mental vision? Admittedly this danger has not been absent from one current in the philosophy of religion. I am thinking of William James's famous work, *Varieties of Religious Experience*, which has been translated into German and made a strong impression in this country, also of similar essays, including that of Starbuck. However valuable, in James's work especially, are the vivid descriptions of religious states of consciousness, this undertaking has nothing in common with our present outline of an endeavour to improve the conduct of natural theology. For *our* attention is not turned toward the chaotic and random world of individual religious experiences, but in the first place to the *nature* and *essential structures* of their objects, and next to the forms of religious act appropriate to those experiences. For our purposes descriptions of this kind are only useful as illustrative experiments (as in mathematics or mechanics), not for inductive generalization and abstraction. Moreover, this 'philosophy of religion' lacks any specifically religious theoretical criteria of *evidence*, in the light of which one might chart the chaos of 'cases' adduced, by making distinctions of the following order: objectively based *versus* illusionary, genuine *v.* non-genuine, adequate *v.* inadequate, normal (in the ideal sense) *v.* abnormal, perfect *v.* imperfect. For such criteria it seeks to substitute an utterly worm-eaten pragmatism forming a quasi-biological if not downright utilitarian touchstone: the happy issue of convictions in practical life. As there is no occasion here for a general criticism of this trend of thought, I pass over its other deficiencies: neglect of divine ontology (which is the necessary preparation of all religious theory), almost total ignorance of the collective form that is peculiarly needful to religious knowledge, and of the communal form of religious act; an unhealthy penchant for the pathological and coarsely 'sensational'.

Are there then, one may ask, any such criteria for a natural theology in our sense, any norms of religious truth and value? If we are to gauge the truth or falsity of religion's natural forms, must we not have recourse to the criteria offered by some extra-religious principle, or to a general apparatus of logical and ontological propositions such as the old, purely rational, natural theology possessed in the causal principle? Failing that, must we not, like Kant, employ a pre-religious moral norm, the satisfaction of which is the test of religion, unless it be—with a merely 'transcendental' presumption of its positive theses—religion's capacity for the greatest concentration and development of all spiritual civilization, and realization of its fundamental values? In my opinion all these attempts to find extra-religious yardsticks for the truth of religion are misguided in principle. Even the significance of religion in relation to extra-religious values (science, ethics, government, law, art) is illusory unless religion is countenanced and practised not for the *sake* of that significance but by reason of what it manifestly testifies in *itself*. Of course no religious thesis may *contradict* any manifest ontological, logical, moral or aesthetic truths. But it does not follow that in this direction there lies any finding for the *positive* truth of religion beyond the 'not-false'. What does follow is that the norms of religion's truth, or of its cognitive value in other respects, can be found only within the nature of religion, and cannot be imported from any extra-religious sphere. Needless to say, a statement of this kind is not exclusively applicable to religion. If it were not for a peculiar 'self-evidence', reducible in terms of nothing else, whereby their relevant values are unambiguously self-proclaimed, the whole of ethics and the whole of aesthetics would be moonshine and quackery, no matter how many inductions one made, no matter how many applications of ontic and logical axioms.*

Likewise religion possesses in the self-given quality of the object to which the religious act is directed (God, that is, in the final analysis), and in the self-evidence with which that quality is disclosed to consciousness, its supreme and ultimate cognitive norm; to find that 'insufficient' is to seek to base the firmest on what is less firm. Here, as invariably, all 'critical' judgments, all questions of the right to judge what one 'sees' or 'believes' are what Meinong has strikingly called '*Nachurteile*'[1] and furthermore themselves require the support of *self-evident* principles. It is not our present intention to elaborate the nature of belief as a basic act of all, including natural religion, and to distinguish it in detail from extra-religious knowing, supposing and 'believing', from all mere acts of will and from the 'seeing' of the religious object. But manifestly all 'believing'— objectively speaking—is founded in a 'seeing'; by *objectively* I mean to indicate that both acts do not necessarily have to occur in the same subjective consciousness. Thus, in the last resort all Christian belief is founded on what it was given to Christ to know about God and himself, in the form not of belief but of seeing—or on what he thought fit to impart of it to his Church.

But from this it does not follow that whatever entity or quality appears self-evident in a hypothetical act of mental vision—of 'seeing'—*directed to that entity or quality* must, solely by virtue of this kind of self-evidence, be accepted as a certainty. Genetically the first norm of all religious knowledge, that it should be self-given and self-evident, stands not at the beginning but at the *end* of the religious cognitive *process*, and we may very well need a complex apparatus of indirect thought in our approach to this self-evidence. And so the application of this norm follows such a course that from the very essence of the divine is developed a complete *axiomatic lore* of the being and value of the religious object, an uncommonly rich seam as yet almost unmined. In this axiomatic lore we have a serious, ideal criterion, peculiar to the religious domain, of all actual crystallizations of religion, whether positive or natural; we have a specifically religious yardstick to *add* as a positive standard of religious cognition to the universal ontological, logical, ethical and aesthetic insights which form criteria not of truth, but of falsity—that is to say, they are criteria only inasmuch as a religious thesis must be compatible with them.

Meanwhile it is insufficient to be aware of this yardstick's potential

---

[1] See A. Meinong, *Über Möglichkeit und Wahrscheinlichkeit*, A. Barth, Leipzig 1915. (The literal meaning of *Nachurteile* is 'posterior judgments'—*Translator.*)

significance; one must also have a precise notion of its limitations.

It is, like self-evidence generally in every field, a measure of the cognitive value of the prelogical factors in our knowledge. Self-evidence is a norm of truth only in so far as the intrinsic *verum* of things, as indicated in the adage '*omne ens est verum*', comes under observation, but in this context the 'true' is to be understood as when we speak of 'true coin' against counterfeit or the 'true God' who is not a false god. When on the other hand we speak of the 'true' and 'false' which apply to *statements* and *judgments*, self-evidence offers no guarantee of truth. These two senses must be clearly distinguished.[1] 'True' in the first examples (or 'genuine', with a connotation of value) indicates that an object is precisely what it 'means' in the sense of 'purports' (not what *we* mean in intentional references to it or designations of it). What stands in opposition to this kind of 'trueness' is therefore *not* false*hood* (which exists only with reference to statements and judgments) but the falsity of *illusion* (and of its vehicle, the phantasm), which is present whenever an object is not what it purports to be, what corresponds to the meaning immanently postulated. On the subjective side, what corresponds to illusion is not error, which corresponds only to 'false' judgment, but *delusion*, which thus also lies in the *pre*logical sphere of cognition and can *never* be overcome by true judgment (congruence with the designated perceptual data) or correct judgment (immanence of the predicate in the subject.)[2] The path from illusion to what is right and true lies always through the removal of delusion, which we call disillusion, a process which plays a far greater and more penetrating rôle than true or correct judgment in the soul's adventures on its cognitive way to the 'true God'. The way to the true God leads far beyond disillusion, but disillusion has already taken the soul out of reach of a thousand false gods and idols.

Hence the full truth of a judgment (including religious judgments) is not only bound up with its congruence with the object and correctness of judgment (or inference, when judgments are inferred) but is dependent on the *genuine* nature of the object with which the judgment is in accord, an object which must not be illusory or a religious phantasm. And it is this prelogical sphere of insight and delusion, truth and sham, in religious objects *themselves* (not truth and falsehood in judgments about them, or in the method of coming to these judgments) in respect of which we must lay claim to a norm of religious self-evidence and the special axiomatic lore of the religious realm of being and value.

[1] The distinction is less crucial in English. If I am not mistaken, *true* in the sense of 'true coin' or 'true Blue' is generally avoided in technical uses (*Translator*).

[2] See my essay on '*Idole der Selbsterkenntnis*' in *Vom Umsturz der Werte*.

It follows that it would be utterly wrong to suppose, as will an over-dogmatic method, which invariably has a rationalistic bias, that the truth of religious or theological statements and judgments can be sufficiently attested by their compatibility with as unified and consistent a system as possible. Whatever the degree of internal concordance among propositions, however much they may all be derived from the same few basic principles, there is no guarantee that the system as a whole is true (in the first sense). A self-contained system is also possible in a realm of pure phantasmagoria. For that reason natural theology, and positive theology no less, must not only test its propositions continually against the findings of religious experience and *direct insight,* findings which underlie those propositions: it has also continually to test those very findings with regard to the *genuine* or illusory character of their objects. If natural theology (which alone is the object of our present inquiry) disregards these distinctive cognitive norms of religious truth and value, accepting only those which apply to the *judicative* aspect of religion and theology, there is no occasion for surprise if it remains without effect or awakens no response where response and effect are supremely desirable—while it is heeded only where it is otiose.

The *rational truth of judgment* about the religious object does not take on decisive importance until the bases in direct insight of natural theology's judgments and conclusions have been ascertained in the course of elaborating the primary religious phenomena, with their essences and interconnections. But once this foundation is assured it would be quite wrong to *refrain* from connecting these truths in a rational manner. Moreover, the traditional proofs of God come into their own and are seen in their correct light as the basis of a far subtler and more highly differentiated edifice if they themselves are based from the beginning on religious axiomatics, if they discard all pretention to *construct* the primary phenomena of religion, supposedly deriving them *per analogiam* from pre-religious facts and findings, and rest content with having organized them, or judgments about them, into a rational, systematic unity, correlating those judgments with given extra-religious knowledge of world-reality.

Here it should be explained that it is not the propositions of 'science' (which does not exist, there being only *sciences*[1]) with which natural theology must bring religious objects into rational unity, but those of *philosophy* or pre-eminently *metaphysics*, which is itself based on 1. the manifest connection among the essential ideas of contingent world-reality, and 2. the day-to-day findings of the positive sciences. Just as philosophy alone may mediate between theology and the sciences, direct

[1] See chapter on 'The Nature of Philosophy'.

communication being unthinkable without this mediation, the interval
between secular knowledge and knowledge of things divine must be
bridged by *natural theology*, when the approach is from the religious side,
or, when it is from the philosophical, by *metaphysics*, as philosophical
knowledge of the real world-basis. As such, metaphysics, the ontological
eidetics of all data presented by both internal and external worlds,
reveals the eternal λόγος dynamically realized in this contingent world-
reality as the consummation of all essential qualities, structures and
interrelations. It thus furnishes a series of truths which though found from
this one casual world are valid for any possible world, hence also for that
part of reality which *transcends* the possible bounds of our merely random
and inductive experience. These truths, or the aptitude for learning them,
are neither 'innate' nor simply the expression of our mind's subjective
functional laws, allegedly valid (*sic* Kant) for the objects of experience
because they are valid for the process of experiencing them. They are
discovered in the casual empirical object by penetration into the ideas and
ideal relations therein realized, but they hold good for all empirical objects
of the same nature. For, *a-priori*, what is valid for the essences of an object
is also valid for *all objects of the same nature*—irrespective of whether those
objects are potential objects of our *casual experience*. It is in the consummation of the substantive *a-priori*, the sum and epitome of all ontic essences
both in themselves and as gathered up in a concrete world of essences, that
metaphysics has its foundation—that is, what we may call its major and
overriding premise. In contrast with the principles of formal logic these
propositions are collectively synthetic *a priori* truths (provided that by
'synthetic' is not understood 'created by acts of synthesis' but 'beyond the
bounds of all that follows from the principles of identity and
contradiction'). For they are based on seeing the self-evident *quid*dity of
objects themselves, not on contingent perception and observation, which
by nature is as inconclusive for a given object as direct insight is final and
complete—quite apart from the fact that the latter, too, is naturally
capable of delusion and may have varying degrees of adequacy. And so
the metaphysician knows *a priori* and self-evidently that even in all parts of
world-reality (including the real world-basis) which have no direct or
indirect causal connection with the vehicles of perception in our human
psycho-physical organism, the same essences are realized, the same
rapports prevail, the same structure of a world of essences and values is
clothed with reality as is realized in that part to which we have potential
access through perception and observation. I can therefore very well
know the nature of a contingent reality with which I am not acquainted
as a reality, and which indeed I cannot know as such on account of the

limitations peculiar to my organism. It is precisely on this possibility that the *possibility of a metaphysics* rests. For since we on the one hand know that only a part of contingent reality has a causal connection with our organism (briefly, only that part which impinges on our senses and is 'of consequence' for the furtherance or hindrance of our life), and since we on the other hand know that the axioms of causality and the universal interdependence of entities also rest on essential insights which hold good, beyond the real we casually encounter, for everything sharing the real mode of existence—since we know this, we are fully entitled to construct a mental image of the real world *in general* and the basis of its existence, employing as major premise those insights and as minor whatever contingent realities are uncovered by positive science in its essentially endless progress.[1] Yet we must be clear that such a metaphysic can never be more than hypothetical in character and communicates a merely probable knowledge; this is by reason not of the major but of the minor premise. For this very reason it can never be a substitute even for natural religion and the natural theology derived from it—not even in its ideal perfection. For it is of the nature of every religious conviction that it knows its content to be legitimately absolute, not relatively certain. For that reason—and that reason alone—faith and its 'gamble' must take over in religion where there is no direct sight of the religious object.

If we are to apply the principle that metaphysics and natural theology (not to mention religion itself) are essentially different right down to the ultimate roots of theology, if accordingly we must reject the doctrine that the supreme bases of metaphysics are at the same time fundamentals of theology, we must be all the more careful to recognize that religion and theology *without* metaphysics would lack all those points of contact and communication with secular knowledge and practice that they require for their own subsistence. The mistaken and groundless skeptical bias against metaphysics, engendered by positivist sensual epistemology and that of Kant (which is only the former in another guise), has appeared to a

[1] All essences, and relations among such, which are found from the contingent world-reality accessible to our organism are to be assumed as somehow realized in the inaccessible world-reality, if it has been shown that we could not ascertain their reality *even* if it subsisted. Only in a case where it has been shown that, if a hypothetical reality *were* in fact real, it would be within the compass of our organism to establish the fact may we legitimately assert (where appropriate) the non-realization of the essence within the realm of contingent reality. In consequence, ultimately, of the principle that the *ens a se* as basis of the world exists by virtue of its very essence, the onus of proof lies on whoever would assert the *non*-reality—beyond known cases of realization—of any known essence. There is no onus to prove its reality. Of course these theses do not entail the contention that in the sensorily unknowable parts of reality *only* those essences are realized which we may abstract from the known parts.

whole school of Protestant theology—without any deeper epistemological inquiry—as the welcome means of setting up an irrationalism of faith by the supposed stabilization of an utter *dualism of faith and knowledge*. This, in the opinion of these theologians, restores true freedom and independence to faith and religion. Thus in particular the neo-Lutheran theology of Albert Ritschl's school, not content with rejecting metaphysics as epistemologically impossible—here showing epigonic leanings to either sensualism[1] or Kant[2]—has also dismissed it as a *noxious parasite* on religion. In their view the renunciation of reason and rational knowledge (that 'whore, reason', as Luther was wont to remark) clears the stage for henceforth unhampered, massive and subjective religious 'judgments'— 'judgments of faith' concerning things of this world. By-passing as far as possible all experience of the world or of nature, ignoring the historical development of religion, culture and civilization, these judgments are purported to focus on the isolated person of Christ. Here I shall refrain from speaking of the monstrous mendacity to which this division of spheres of influence has led; however, let it be remarked that it not only severs faith from knowledge but also divides the pastor from the theologian. Here we are only concerned that the following should be clearly seen: it is a division which grievously *shatters* the personal fabric of spiritual *unity* and *harmony* in the mind of man. This is the picture of man conjured up by this singular theology: with regard to all worldly matters, whether theory or practice, he is a crawling worm, pent in the confines of his organism and immediate environment, but suddenly, straightway, with the 'fiat' of a judgment from faith, he is able to transport himself into the profundities of the godhead. Now, that is impossible, senseless—from the point of view of good taste, let alone logic. Unless a man already looks on the things of this world *sub specie aeternitatis*, with that Platonic love of the ideal and the absolutely-real which is the eternal motive of philosophy and whose questing alone can *open* his mental eye to the λόγος realized in the world, he is too aphilosophical, too 'amusical' ever to possess the *predisposition*, the mental attitude, wherein the realm of religious objects can disclose itself to him.

Even if metaphysics is not logically and objectively necessary to the foundation of religion, from the pedagogic standpoint—and quite apart from its internal theoretic legitimacy—it is not a contingent but an essentially *necessary* preliminary of all religious knowledge and self-perfection. For Auguste Comte was quite wrong to teach that the aims and motivation of religious, metaphysical and scientific cognition correspond

[1] Especially J. Kaftan in his *Philosophie des Protestantismus*, Tübingen 1917.
[2] Especially W. Hermann, *Der Verkehr des Christen mit Gott*.

to separate stages of historical development or so-called 'ages'; on the contrary, they correspond to a *permanent constitution* of the human mind, to a quite definite constitutional construction, wherein the lower forms a necessary preliminary to the higher—that is to say, it forms a stairboard which cannot be overstepped without a disastrous stumble.

It is thus a religious *impossibility* that either an entire culture or a single 'cultivated' person should come into being *without* the intervention of metaphysics. Should the attempt be made to dispense with its assistance, the inevitable and frightful consequence is that individual sciences advance *metaphysical pretentions*, which results in bad, disunified, anarchic metaphysics. For the metaphysical incentive demands satisfaction as *necessarily* as that of faith. And just as the latter offers man the one choice between God and idols, the former will have him *choose* between a conscious metaphysic with a view over the whole world (as an edifice of ideas and essences) and a semi- or unconscious metaphysical *hypostatization* of some technical working-concept in one of the many positive sciences. 'Scientism' (neo-Kantian), energetics, sensational monism, 'panpsychism', historical materialism, philological paganism, biologism, etc., etc., are *pseudo-metaphysics* of this order, exactly corresponding to the various forms of idol-worship such as mammonism, state-fetishism, nationalism and the like. The sociological picture presented by a society in which metaphysics is lacking as a cultural and civilizing function is that of an unbounded, unbridled *anarchy of specialization*, devoid, even in the 'University', of all universality of spirit in its knowledge and characteristic outlook, and trying to forge *keys* to the secret of the universe out of its departmental interests and technical concepts.[1] The universe accordingly becomes the *X*, the supposed 'ward'[2] for which the expert has made himself a key; thus 'at bottom' it is turn-and-turn-about 'life', 'soul', 'energy', 'sensation', 'economics', etc., etc. If anyone deny the possibility of metaphysics, one must first show him before proceeding to theoretic refutation— and here one may be confident of the outcome—that he already *has* metaphysics, *i.e.* ideas, representations, judgments in his mind which impinge on the metaphysical sphere of being, and that these judgments are merely bad and partial quasi-judgments. The position here is thus exactly parallel to that obtaining in religious pedagogics. If anyone deny God he must be shown, before God's existence is vindicated, that on the very evidence of his life-history he *possesses* at any given moment a good, some

---

[1] That today's all-important specialist is also capable of another way of thinking has been brought home to me by a book that comes to mind—Karl Jellinek, *Das Weltgeheimnis*, Stuttgart 1921, in which this physical chemist most admirably undertakes a genuinely philosophical synthesis of our present state of knowledge.

[2] *Das Schloss*, 'the lock' or (as in Kafka's *roman à clé*) 'the castle' (*Translator*).

thing, which he in fact treats 'as if it were a God' or a thing of divine nature. He must be brought to a full awareness of this object and made to see, by the way of *disillusion*, that it is an idol.

As metaphysics introduces the possibility of replacing sociologically an assemblage of specializations with a *unity* of spiritual culture, it alone also provides the *common intellectual platform*, an atmosphere in which adherents of different positive religions and Churches can confer together, or with skeptics, and try to win the other party over to their cause. Thus it is no exaggeration to say that the indefatigable endeavour to create *one* Church of God from out the present multiplicity of positive religions and 'Churches',[1] an attempt prescribed by absolute dictates of reason and morality, is totally dependent on the existence and recognition of a metaphysic. If it is denied, an '*incapsulation*' of Churches and other religious communities—a departmentalization which is contrary to moral and religious sense, to the principle of solidarity in salvation, to the commandment to love the salvation of one's brother—is inevitable. I have, moreover, shown from the example of the German nation[2] that such a fragmentation gravely endangers the spiritual unity of aims and aspiration in a people or nation, leading to an anarchy of contending factions; in such a situation no amount of co-operation for merely technical and utilitarian ends will restore unity—on the contrary it but tends to increase the tension and danger.

Finally metaphysics is the necessary medium through which *nations* may come to understand one another in the world of knowledge. For as the deepest concentration of all pure theory (*i.e.* not restricted technical knowledge) metaphysics is *cosmopolitan* in its sociological implications (not 'international' like science) and expressive of national mentality in its psychological roots—not merely vaguely human, like science.* It is only in the interaction of metaphysical ideas, their fruition, mutual *approfondissement*, that the high converse of national temperaments is engaged and ravelled out. Religion and Church are in the nature of things above nations and independent of them. Conversely the sciences *qua* sciences are *inferior* to the plane of the national mind, and for that reason their disciples are in principle able, no matter what their nationality, to 'stand in' for one another *ad infinitum*, without necessarily ever raising the question of nationality or touching upon specifically *cultural* values in the pure sense of the word. In default of metaphysics, therefore, the highest spiritual

[1] I have already shown, in Part 2 of *Formalismus in der Ethik* . . ., that self-evidently the Church, as instituted for the salvation of mankind collectively, is essentially *one* by reason of the indivisibility of merit.*

[2] Cf. in this work, 'Christian Love and the Twentieth Century'. See also my essay entitled *Der Friede unter den Konfessionen* (1920).*

commerce of nations in a common forum is paralysed and the unity of mankind's spiritual civilization becomes a lost cause. Even the religious and ecclesiastical authority which has an aboriginal and natural superiority over all nations may no longer influence or be generally comprehensible to nations that have thus renounced a common field of intellectual inquiry and ambition. Thus the lapse of metaphysics threatens the supranational efficacy of the Church, and through it, indirectly, religion itself.

Nevertheless, in spite of this considerable indirect importance which metaphysics possesses for religion, and always will possess for reasons that lie deep in human nature, religion must maintain its *independence*, not only at the level of positive revelation but at the more primary stage of *natural* religion, which is the necessary rational basis of the revealed. Religious knowledge is separate from and—objectively—independent of metaphysical knowledge.

However, it is not only permissible but must even be stipulated that acquired religious truth and knowledge should illumine metaphysical knowledge and lend it a final religious *interpretation* of which it is not itself capable.

Let me illustrate this from one *crucial point*: the religious interpretation of *world-systematology*, which, as shown above, forms the springboard to metaphysics as knowledge of that part of contingent existence which lies beyond the reach of human experience.

If we have reduced all given entities to their pure essence and reduced all actually experienced and performed acts, through and in which these entities are given, to their essence and basic structure—if we by this means have unveiled the all-pervading λόγος, there is *no* metaphysical consideration which either obliges or empowers us to seek a further derivation for these essences or a subject in which they might inhere. Metaphysics, with its precondition, essential phenomenology, is and remains an autonomous form of cognition which does *not* hold its peculiar *evidence*, truth and value in fee from religion.

But if by means of the internal and independent evidence of religious acts we have acquired a knowledge of God's nature and affirmed his existence, or the existence of such a one as he, by the (natural) act of faith, then the case is *altered*. From our newly-won position of faith we may and we should attach to the glimpsed essences the meaning of an ideal, eternal model in *accordance* with which God—who if he exists is not only the world's *one* and *final* cause but also its *free, personal creator and preserver*—created and now preserves the world. For though we have no right to make a causal inference from the existence of the world to *God* as its creator, we have a perfect right—*given* God's existence and that of the world—to infer that God is the cause of the world and its *free*, personal creator. And only from *that* position can we see the known essences (*i.e.* fragments of the world's indwelling λόγος) as *ideas* of God, and their ideal systematic relationships as the *veritates aeternae* (or an accessible cross-section of them) in accordance with which God made and sustains the real world.

Even the meaning of the *cognitive process* by which we know the essential structure of the universe changes with its religious interpretation. We now recognize that if ever we have 'seen' an essence we have in an inadequate way seen something of the idea which *God himself* has of the thing in question, the idea in accordance with which he acts upon it in a creative or preservative fashion (irrespective of the *causae secundae*, which only concern its relative thusness or otherness or other-becoming in relation to the here-and-now). Nevertheless, we are in *no* way contending—as Malebranche maintained—that we know all ideas 'in God'. God is not the 'locus of ideas', not the mere subject X of ideas.[1] No, it is *in and from things themselves* that we know their essences, but from a position of *faith* (which is certainly not attained through metaphysics, as Malebranche assumed in attempting to *define* God as the mere 'locus of ideas') we can and should *subsequently interpret* our knowledge of essences as knowledge of *ideas of things in the mind of God*. Moreover, in the light of faith our very knowledge—rational knowledge—of the essential structure of the universe, not only the object of that knowledge, acquires a new meaning which is certainly not originally inherent in it. Self-evidence, the *perspicuity of the essence* wherein it presents itself as *self*-given, takes on the character of a 'natural revelation of God' by which he actively *instructs* man's cognizant mind concerning the nature and sense of his created work. Essences with their interrelations become 'words in God's natural discourse' as implanted in things and addressed to man, words whereby he 'answers' man's 'questions' through the medium of the 'light of nature'. Similarly, the *first precondition* of all philosophy, which appears to the pre-religious state as the mind's spontaneous love of the absolutely-real in all things, reveals itself to the religious interpretation as something new and different, as a *reciprocation* of God's own spontaneous and antecedent love, whereby he actively *discloses* the nature of his creation, causing it to shine through into the mind of man. Therefore the position is not as envisaged by Augustine and his followers, that the subsistence and validity of eternal truth (and of principles whereby it may be known) themselves constitute a 'proof of God'. One cannot identify 'truth' with God in the manner attempted by Augustine without abandoning the idea of a *personal* God in favour of a

[1] See Malebranche, *La Recherche de la vérité*, vol. 2.

mere Platonism.[1] Neither is it tenable to say that in the performance of a cognitive act relating to the essence of a thing we already have a clear sense or simultaneous awareness that this act is caused by eternal reason, as implied by the meaning of Augustine's '*omnia cognoscere in lumine Dei*'. It is on the contrary a question not of any empirical sense but of a retrospective interpretation of the cognitive act, and moreover it is not an interpretation such as might lead us to a new-found knowledge of God, but one whose internal legitimacy depends on the autonomous self-evidence of the religious act of faith and insight. This act indeed must vouch for the interpretation—which thus presupposes that *conviction* of God's nature and existence is already based elsewhere than on philosophical perceptions.

Finally, *knowledge* of all possible truth, which in itself is an absolute value for philosophy and science (in the latter case, within the limitations imposed by technical aims), takes on a new axiological meaning. It is now *subordinated* to the values and final purpose of an *ontic* process, a *becoming*, which far transcends all knowledge, namely to *the* value and end of the projection of human *personality* into God's personality. At the same time it is subsidiary in the cognition of objects to an extension which is to be coeffected in the cognitive act: here I refer to the extrapolation from known things of their ultimate *determination* or destiny, which is an *ontic* participation in God and can be apprehended when we share some part of the *idea* which God has of them. Indeed, at this stage knowledge is *no longer immaterial* for things. We may now say that things are in some way *affected* by the knowledge man acquires of them. Without undergoing a strictly real alteration (such as is possible through volition, re-conception and action) or being in whole or part constructed (Kantian fashion) by the human mind—without deriving their nature and substance via the cognitive act, since these they possess independently of man through God's idea of them—the 'determination' and 'meaning' of things are here *realized* by man for the very first time in the cognitive act. Things acquire *ontically* the part of their determination and meaning which ideally they already possess: they are led, *raised, restored* to God as the root of all things, the underlying concept and consummation of all essences.[2]

Thus in the light of faith, be it only natural faith, all knowledge represents a greater quantity and a higher thing than knowledge without faith. So far cognition has stood over against all being and processes of being and

---

[1] See M. Grabmann's recent *Grundgedanken des heiligen Augustinus über Gott und Seele* (Cologne 1916) for a lucid and subtle critique of this Augustinian 'proof'.

[2] Or we may say: in and through man reality becomes conscious of its meaning, significance and worth.

therefore, when it has not been misconstrued by pragmatists as real alteration of things or a *means* to that end, or by Kantians as synthetic construction, it has probably been misconstrued as simply an *ideal duplication* of things in being or process of becoming, a duplication whose sense and purpose is at bottom incomprehensible. But now it takes on the form of a merely *constituent* process within an *ontic process of the cosmos* which —so to speak—pursues its way through the cognitive human mind, availing itself of the cognitive process only as a means to *its own end*. If we must give this process a name it must surely be called the *interdependent restitution* in man of all things to God.

In fact the intellectual person of man, which in philosophy sets itself the goal of truth and essential knowledge as an absolute objective value, without however postulating them as personal, finds *redemption* in the light of religious faith, in that it does no less than devote itself to essentials in loving contemplation and in that devotion wins its portion of the light of God. Or rather, which embraces this, it comes to know itself *in process of redemption from* the confinement and particularity of its psycho-physical organism when it begins to see its love of absolute reality as the response to God's cosmic love and his love-moved acts of natural *revelation*. But simultaneously it understands that it is actively *assisting in the redemption* of things themselves—the things it knows—understands that it is bearing them ever higher toward *their* eternal meaning and *design*ation, which is to say their *destination* in God who thus determined them.

As we have seen, we can make no causal inference to God, as the one free creator of the world, from a still non-religiously envisaged world-reality, neither can we use *purely* philosophical means to pass from theory and ideas to the reality of God as the personal light of the world who in our knowing of it speaks to us the language of nature. Nevertheless we have in either case the full right to interpret religiously, in this sense, the given relations of world and world-basis, knowledge and essences, *provided* we have already grasped the independent truth of faith and religious insight. And it is only when we make use of that right that the totality of our spiritual relationship with ontic reality receives its *ultimate unity, ultimate harmony, ultimate meaning*.

The above in no way prejudges the content of an authentic metaphysic, but this and kindred questions I reserve for treatment in a special work on metaphysics. This much is, however, clear: whatever appearance is presented by the content of a metaphysic, we know *a priori* that *metaphysical* propositions remain permanently hypothetical and can be no more than probable. This, if for no other reason, is due to the character of the 'minor premise' above discussed—that is, the essential contribution of positive scientific knowledge of contingent facts. And we may also be sure of the following: metaphysics can mount the ladder of decreasing existential relativity until it comes to the confines of the absolute existent, but the nearer its approach to that absolute entity the greater the element of hypothesis and the less that of probability. With respect to the absolute entity itself, the *ens a se*, the probability enjoyed by metaphysical statements is nil beyond wholly formal ontological and axiological definitions (*e.g.* the *ens* is an *ens a se*, an *ens* of supreme value—though not necessarily good—etc.). In other words, although there is a merely *formal*, there is no *substantial* metaphysic of the absolute.

At this farthest reach of all metaphysics, however correct, the religious object begins and the religious act through which alone it can be given comes unaided into its own. Here where the highest attainable knowledge of philosophy and metaphysics loses all force of probability religion offers an absolute and rocklike assurance. Unlike the metaphysical act of cognition it does not approach the absolute, with the aid of conclusions from essential premises and contingent propositions culled from empirical knowledge, as merely the 'basis of the world'; as the religious act it transports the subject directly into a sphere of existence and of values to which it alone holds the key, and this sphere is the positive *substance* of the world-basis—a definite *religious* hypostasis. Within this sphere the subject may, by the light of religious assurance, apprehend and comprehend all other entities.

Thus religious knowledge retains its independence and autonomy in relation to metaphysics. This principle becomes all the clearer in sense and validity when we contrast it with a series of modern attempts to *found* religion on extra-religious knowledge, values and axioms. These attempts, be it noted, also reject the authenticity of metaphysics even within its limitations.

An early attempt of this kind was Kant's endeavour to build religion on the *moral law*.

To ethical values there corresponds an ethical self-evidence whereby for example a value is given as preferable to another with which it may be compared. This preferable value we call the 'higher'. Thus it is with reference to this self-evidence that a thing or act is morally good if, in respect of personal value or personal attitudes, volition and conduct, it stands for the realization of a 'higher' value than would have accrued to the world if *ceteris paribus* that person had not existed, that conduct not arisen, etc. But ethical values and self-evidence only give access to the religious sphere *once* we have taken up into the *objective hierarchy* of values the specifically religious value of the '*holy*', of personal salvation and its correlate of bliss.[1] If it is so taken up it must be as the self-evidently *highest* value, and then it goes without saying that its realization in a person is also what is morally the 'best'. Should it *not* be taken up it is out of the question to derive the value of holiness from other values or to construe it as the 'necessary complement' to these, *e.g.* spiritual, intellectual, vital,[2] utilitarian or amenity values, or however one feels inclined to categorize. That the value of holiness is certainly no mere component of the perfect moral good or of total knowledge, etc., etc., but is quite simply something new and distinct in value-quality, has recently been admirably shown by Rudolf Otto. He has all the more convincingly verified my own contention in my book on formalism in ethics. Admittedly it is *possible* and, from the religious viewpoint, necessary to 'sanction' certain non-religious goods; thus we must characterize moral goods as 'holy' and things which are wicked, which depart from moral norms, as 'sinful'. But to do so invariably presupposes that we are already in possession of the specifically religious values. A 'moral law' becomes 'holy' only by reflection from the worth of a holy lawgiver who is also a perfect *person*—and it is impossible to follow Kant in constructing the personal lawgiver by 'postulates' from a given categorical imperative. The postulate of a lawgiver *X*, or of a moral disposer of the world who satisfies the exigency of retribution, is a mere shot in the dark unless the place of this *X* has *already* been filled by a *given* positive and substantial (*religiously* substantial) idea of God—and a reality corresponding to the object of that idea.

But there is a yet more basic tendency in which Kant's definition of the relation between religion and morality is not merely wrong but nonsensical. To us it appears obvious that if there is a God an absolute autonomy of practical reason is absurd and therefore *impossible*, with the corollary of a *self-evident theonomy*. But how then can acceptance of the existence of God be based on a finding that practical reason is autonomous, since that is a supposition whose sense, if it is true, makes nonsense alike of its truth and sense!? *If* God exists, a practical reason could only be autonomous if it coincided with divine reason itself. And in fact Kant's successors, above all Fichte and Hegel, did tread the path of this identification. This however led, under the auspices of a rational pantheism, to an extreme *heteronomy* of the human mind and personality, which by reason of the assumed identification had to be regarded as a mere function of this autonomous primal reason, if not as one of its

[1] Cf. *Formalismus in der Ethik, etc.*

[2] By *Vitalwerte* Scheler means values relative to the day-to-day subsistence and contentment of race or individual—the values with which materialistic humanism is preoccupied (*Translator*).

points of transit or paths of conduction.[1] But if conversely autonomy is attributed not to reason *qua* reason but to the *person qua person*, this autonomy is no longer compossible with the assumption of the existence of God. It is thus impossible to base acceptance of God's existence on a postulate which is either identical with that acceptance (rational pantheism) or plainly nonsensical *if* that assumption is true. The position is no different when Kant explains that the idea of God held by a person must first be compared with the content of the *autonomous moral law* so that the person may decide whether this idea is indeed the idea of *God* and of nothing else. It is obvious that God, if he exists, cannot be measured against a *human* moral law, that he cannot be put under the—so to speak—*a priori* obligation either to concord with it or remain unacknowledged. If he could, the proposition that 'God is good', which is synthetic, would become not only analytical but tautological. For if he is originally defined and conceived as merely the 'giver' of the moral law, it is self-evident that his will must be congruent with that law. But that the 'Lord' of all being (the religiously formulated *ens a se et per se*) is *good*—that is not a thing which goes without saying,[2] and to oblige him, as it were, from the human point of view, to be good by sheer definition, on pain of our refusing to acknowledge his sovereignty, would remove in advance both freedom and autonomy from his possible goodness—though these are essential properties of divine, if of *any*, goodness.

Of course by dismissing Kant's 'ethico-theology' I have not the slightest intention of supporting the only alternative course he recognized, that we should properly define as good what corresponds to the content of the divine *will* (heteronomy). For it is generally wrong to define the good as a content of a previously given *volition*—whether it be God's or that of a practical reason. 'Good' is primarily a value-quality, but moral good is a personal quality and any volition—hence the volition which in the hypothesis determines *what* is good and *that* a thing *is* good—must *be* good in the first place in order so to determine. In reference to God, good is thus an *essential predicate* of the divine person *qua person*.[3]

---

[1] Cf. my thorough analyses of the concept of autonomy in *Formalismus in der Ethik, etc.*, Part 2, Section VI.

[2] This proposition is, moreover, not analytic in the sense of the Thomists, who wish to employ the intermediary concept of perfection (completion) to translate the good in terms of degrees of being, in accordance with *omne ens est bonum.* Cf. my refutation of this attempt in *Formalismus, etc.* . . .* I recognize the truth and cogency of *omne ens est bonum*, if we may take *bonum* to mean 'partaking of value', not value-neuter, but this meaning fails to identify it with the first member of the dichotomy of 'good' and 'bad'—not to mention (moral) 'good' and 'evil'.

[3] On this point we agree with Aquinas as against the Scotists. Even Kant was here a 'Scotist'.*

This insight provides us with the means of escaping from the other false alternative which Kant proposes in his definition of the relations of religion and morality. Moral volition, he says, must either arise without any reference to God, *or* it is *necessarily* (=heteronomously) determined by fear of punishment and hope of reward. It is this *alternative* which is false, not the intrinsically correct proposition of Kant's, that *in concreto* volition and conduct in the latter sense are not (perfectly) good.

In the first place, a (perfect) moral volition without reference to God is an *objective* impossibility. For ideally conceived, the most perfect moral volition is the volition of the person who embodies in the form of personal value (more or less adequately) the evidently highest among values, which is holiness. But the holy person is at the same time he who feels and knows that to the extent of his 'holiness' he is manifestly 'united' in part—not *realiter,*[1] but by the nature of his inner seat of responsible action (hence of his moral deeds)—to the highest good, which as 'highest' is itself holy in an infinite and absolute form and is itself a valuate *person.*[2]

Even so, a (perfect) religious way of life, though it cannot be defined in terms of moral conduct or by the use of 'proofs' and 'postulates' of ethical provenance, is plainly impossible unless it *embraces* perfect moral conduct. For the human person is not perfectly religious, does not behave in a *perfectly* religious way unless the *summum bonum* is present in the mind's regard both during the cognitive act of preference *and* during the execution of the act of will which attempts to actualize the preferred value. Here of course the *summum bonum*, in the light of religious ontology and axiology, is the absolutely holy personal God whom the act of preference envisages as the Lord of all being. But there is in our example a further condition of perfection: the human person must itself will and seek to actualize 'from out' the will of God (*velle in Deo*), not simply yield obedience to God's will as if to a commandment or 'law'.

There is one point alone in which Kant is entirely in the right: the *objective axiology of ethics* is not only applicable in the philosophy of religion but offers *positive material* for the construction of a true *concept* of God. And yet he is still in error, for he is entirely *unaware* of any *objectively* axiomatic and material[3] ethical values, preferring (like the Scotists before him, only reading 'man' for 'God') to define the good as content of a pre-given

[1] That as holy the human person enjoys real union, is a part or function of the person of God, is the *erroneous* contention of high-flown mysticism and of pantheists such as Spinoza, Fichte and von Hartmann.

[2] Personal value is *self-evidently* higher than the values pertaining to things, acts, functions. Hence a *summum bonum* would not be *summum* unless it were a personal value and in fact a valuate person. In this connection, see *Formalismus in der Ethik, etc.*, Part I.*

[3] See note to p. 279 (*Translator*).

volition, and he furthermore was unable in consequence—and for other reasons too—to see either the peculiarity of the *value* 'holy', as it also underlies ethics, or the preferability of *personal* value over impersonal and functional values (including those of reason or of any 'law' there may be). *Of themselves* religious and ethical axiologies, though separately derived, coincide in the idea of the Lord of all being, who is at once holy and perfectly good.

In this we discover a basic principle of the relation between religion and morality which can be expressed as follows: in *perfection* religion and morality are not independent but *essentially interdependent*; in no sense can this be taken to imply that they are identical, whether from the religious standpoint, as Luther thought, or from the ethical, as Kant wrongly believed. They become *in*dependent of one another as soon as either morality or religion or both are *imperfect*, and the divorce increases in proportion to the imperfection. But here is not the place to analyse the principles in accordance with which moral and religious demands on man are to be reconciled or adjusted on the varying levels of imperfection.

Other kinds of attempt to cast doubt on the self-sufficiency of religious self-evidence and truth have been made by—among others—Wilhelm Windelband, Jonas Cohn and Paul Natorp,[1] but the saddest, most wrong-headed attempt of all was made by William James and his pragmatical disciples—some following him consciously but by far the greater number semi- or unconsciously. Here I shall merely sketch the main ideas as a basis for criticism.

Windelband's 'absolute and real normal consciousness', which he calls 'the holy' and supposes to reveal itself in the experience of obligation in the various fields of logical, ethical and aesthetic prescription, is on the showing of his own elementary axiological principles a totally unjustified 'hypostatization' of the concept *'general consciousness'* (*i.e.* not concrete), which—into the bargain—is itself in substance *nonsensical*. Apart from his partly deficient, partly erroneous foundation of the *existence* of any such normal consciousness, it is the fundamental mistake of this attempt, from the viewpoint of religious theory, that it fails to acknowledge the peculiarity either of the objective dimension of the 'divine' or (in respect of actual content) the value-dimension of the 'holy'. Instead it endeavours to reduce God's existence to an *imperative* (*ein Sollsein*), which for the rest is confused with an obligation 'to be' (*Seinsollen*), whereas the

---

[1] See Windelband, *'Das Heilige'* (in *Präludien*); Cohn, *Der Sinn der gegenwärtigen Kultur*; Natorp, *Religion innerhalb der Grenzen der Humanität*. R. Eucken's book, *Der Wahrheitsgehalt der Religion*, must also be ranged among these attempts.

value-modality of holiness, though it has its own substantial identity, is reduced to the mere summary or totality of the spiritual values 'good', 'beautiful' and 'true'.

1. According to his own first philosophical principles Windelband's attempt is impossible, because—once one has *divided* being and obligation, even in the very sphere of the absolute, by the deep abyss which this school prescribes—it is impossible to extract from 'obligation' alone the kind of real existence which Windelband imputes to the religious consciousness. If that division were correct (and, with it, the basing of axiology on a *theory of norms*, a procedure I emphatically contest[1]), and if nevertheless the religious consciousness were to hypostatize this inchoate 'obligation' into a real essence, this 'religious consciousness' would be no better than a *source of delusion, error and vain figments*—and the most dangerous to boot. For it would present what we men have yet to make real in the specious light of a thing realized, thus falsifying the sense of our task and withdrawing our strength to carry it out, to actualize the 'imperative'. The only correct logical and practical *consequence* of these suppositions would be every possible form of *fight* against religion and the religious consciousness. One would be fully justified in echoing Kant's words, '*If* there were gods (or God), I would have no *duty*; therefore there is no god'. But Windelband's suppositions are *entirely false*. As had already been seen by the profoundest thinker of this neo-Fichtean school, the brilliant young Emil Lask,[2] whose death in the War we must all lament, the concept of value can in no way be reduced to the concepts of obligation or the norm. On the contrary all obligation must be based on given values, normative ethics on pure ethics of value, normative logic on pure objective logic.[3]

Furthermore (as Lask had not yet seen) there is a concept of 'being' which covers (objective) *valuate* being and (value-neuter) *existing* as subordinate categories, and which inheres in the idea of the *ens a se*. It is this concept which bestows supreme and ultimate *unity* on the two spheres of *existence and value-possession*, which the philosophy under discussion[4] places in the false position wherein the existential principle is reduced to the 'validity' of a truth-value (or the *judgment* of existence to the subjective recognition of that validity). It is this unity which makes it understandable that there are ultimate formal axioms which *govern* the ontic relationship of existence and value. I hope I need not mention them all here, or bring

[1] See *Formalismus, etc.*, Part 2, Section IV, 2: '*Wert und Sollen*'.
[2] Lask, *Die Logik der Philosophie und die Kategorienlehre*, Tübingen 1911.
[3] Thus also Husserl in the first volume of *Logische Untersuchungen*.
[4] Regarding what follows, cf. H. Rickert, *Der Gegenstand der Erkenntnis*, 3rd edition, Tübingen 1915.

them all to light.[1] Let me but name a few. One is the proposition already known to the Schoolmen but misapplied in the philosophy under review: *omne ens est bonum* (*i.e.* essentially a thing of value). The truth of this proposition is quite independent of the extent to which we as men are able to feel and grasp the worth of the existent. Another such axiom is enshrined in the propositions I have elaborated in my ethics: the existence of every value is itself a value (that of positive value itself a positive value, that of a disvalue a disvalue); the non-existence of a positive value is a disvalue; the non-existence of a disvalue is a positive value. Again, every value (as a quality) is the property of an existent subject—whether or not that subject is known. It might be thought that these propositions could give rise to a proof of the existence of God similar to the ontological proof, but this is not so. However, it does follow from them that if there is a 'highest' value we must attribute *existence* to its thereby postulated real possessor. And it also follows that if there is an *ens a se*, in the sense of an existent whose existence is a consequence of its own essence, this existent must also be the possessor of an *absolute intrinsic and self-sufficient value*. (It is of course impermissible at this stage to introduce the value of moral 'good' into these strictly formal ontological and axiological definitions.) And to these objective axioms there correspond on the subjective side of mental activity the basic laws that 1. no existent can be first known (whether by thought or direct apprehension) by any consciousness unless it has been the intentional object of *interest-taking* acts, which must come first in the sequence of perception, and has thus been envisaged as a valuate object of definite value-quality, whether it was loved or hated; 2. the *same* order of succession obtains between interest-taking acts and acts of volition—that is, the former must precede the latter, just as value-apprehension must precede knowledge. As I have elsewhere* shown, that is the astonishing thing about the *act of loving*, which is attributable to neither cognition nor volition; it grasps its object on a plane of 'being' where the object's *quality*, whether the peculiarities of its existential being or the quality of its valuate being, is as yet indeterminate. In consequence, one can still *determine* through this class of act both the unequivocal result of its adequate cognition and the possibility of its transformation by volition and action. This level of being is the as yet *indifferent stratum*, with respect to the dichotomy of valuate or existential being, and it is at this level alone that the finite object is still bound to the *ens a se* in the state of utter dependence. For that reason we must necessarily impute to all mere 'finished' existence—'finished' as envisaged by the pure theory of the objective sciences, which expressly disregards the values that an existent must needs have—a factor of love

[1] But see Part 1 of *Formalismus, etc.*

which has co-determined the existence of *this* qualitative *ens* or the quality of *this* existent, a factor without which it would not *be*, or would not be what it is. On the objective side this factor is the universal, loving confirmation by God of the essence and existence of the finite object; it is by virtue solely of this confirmation that the object is in being (is as it were saved from the infinite sea of nothingness and non-existence); on the subjective side this factor is the stirrings of love and hate in the cognizant subject, stirrings which *co-determine* whether *knowledge* will be acquired and what will be its particular content.

2. Quite apart from the vagaries we have witnessed in Windelband's attempt to found religion, his concept of *'general consciousness'* is *intrinsically nonsensical* and incompatible with the nature of things. If one successively removes all so-called empirical elements from the consciousness of something (the physical, psycho-physical and purely psychological content), all that remains is the *concept of a knowing or evaluating subject—evaluating*, if one makes the mistake of equating cognition with judgment and of regarding judgment as acknowledgment or repudiation of the truth-*value*, while 'reducing' 'existing' to the validity of a true affirmative proposition about an object.[1] That it is absolutely absurd to hypostatize this concept into a reality is now seen even by the school of philosophy descended from Windelband. Now, that is already sufficient to condemn Windelband's endeavour to produce a philosophy of religion. But here we have to go further and to show not that this concept is 'self-contradictory' (without the help of material, *i.e.* supraformal, logical axioms), but that it is *nonsensical.* If we do not use the word 'subject' as it was commonly used until the end of the eighteenth century, that is, as a general word for 'object'[2] (as is still the case with the French *sujet* and the Latin *subiectum*), but, as in modern usage, to mean the so-called '*I*', then the following is essentially and necessarily true of every entity to which this concept can possibly be applied. 1. Every *I* is necessarily an *individual I*; 2. Over against every entity which is an *I* there stands a possible *Thou*; 3. Over against every entity which is an *I* there stands an *external world* independent of the being of the *I*, and given to the *I* as thus independent; 4. Every *I* falls into two parts, a corporeal self always given as here-and-now and possessing an *environment*, and a psychic self possessing a correlative stream of empirical factors which, once they have been given as *units*, are secondarily divisible in different directions.* But every one of these propositions, which are independent of inductive experience, is flouted by the bare concept of a

---

[1] . . . and therefore also the *possibility* of a judicative grasp of the positive or negative condition of the object, with a subsequent affirmation or negation of it.

[2] On this point cf. R. Eucken, *Geschichte der philosophischen Terminologie*, 1879.

'general consciousness' in the sense of a 'general subject'—and flouted even before any hypostatization of the concept, which is not even a *viable abstraction*. For one has every right to abstract by progressive elimination of an existent's contingent features, but it is quite impermissible to perform a similar operation on what belongs to the essence of a thing, irrespective of the contingent existent which embodies it. For this would amount to removing the thing itself, in so far as it *can* possess meaning and identity— and this is the very opposite of what is meant by forming a *concept* of a thing. But the very sense which the term 'general subject' is meant to convey is a contravention of all the above propositions. The general subject or consciousness, as general, must be 'super-individual'—chalk which is yet cheese! For there is, to be sure, a supra-*singular* collective consciousness (*e.g.* of corporate personalities, the people, the state) but there is no 'super-individual' consciousness. I mean not only that no such thing actually exists but that in the nature of things it is an impossibility. In the same sense there is no *I* transcending the *I-Thou* dichotomy. For it is an *essential* of every *I*, not merely an optional accessory, to form, potentially, a member—a *part*, that is—of a collective entity. Thus though we may disregard the particular character of the *Thou* which must of necessity stand over against any given *I*, we may never discount the *Thou* in general. Likewise in thought we may abstract the particular characteristics and content of the external sphere which is given to every *I* as 'transcending' any *possible* content of its own consciousness, but we eliminate the *general fact* of that sphere only at the certain risk of removing the very essence of the *I*. Even the body is certainly no mere group of the *contents* of consciousness (of closely associated external and internal sense-data relating to it, as this theory unwarrantedly assumes); it is a sphere of existence possessing its own specific, formal, quantitative, qualitative and homogeneous character, a sphere which is sharply divisible from all purely psychic or extraneous elements, and would remain so even if we were to 'abstract' every separate content of organic sensation.* There is of course room for doubt as to *which* sphere is inhabited by this or that datum of experience (whether the purely psychic, the corporeal or the external world), but we can surely be in no doubt of the essential difference of the spheres themselves. To 'abstract' them in entirety—not simply their particular content —*cannot* have the result of leaving a *'pure I'* as remainder: it can only *remove and destroy the essence of the 'I'*.

There is one last flaw in the process of abstraction which is supposed to reveal a 'general consciousness'. The purely psychic contains a multiplicity of elements whose phenomenal point of unity is not any specific act or component but only a *focus* of momentary value. Any act can acquire this focal value if at a given moment it occupies the spearhead of consciousness where the *I* is located, but there is no *I*-element or *I*-act which differs from all the remaining acts and contents of consciousness, and in relation to which *every* remaining datum is simply phenomenal matter or envisaged object. Thus if we follow the requirements of Windelband's method and remove *all* the (purely psychic) contents and acts of the consciousness, we are admittedly left with the shell and form of the purely psychic being, built on monarchic constitutional lines, but where is the monarch to inhabit it? Where is *a* monarch, any so-called '*I*'? Here we have the very hypostatization of a *focal point*, of the culminating 'tip' wherein are gathered all acts to do with the consciousness of a thing. We are to suppose that this is an act identical in all individual consciousnesses, and even that it is a performer of acts. Windelband's 'normal consciousness', which he unhesitatingly posits as fairly and squarely real, and makes into a kind of God-surrogate, is merely the most unblushing form of this hypostasis, of which we must however also accuse the subtler forms in which this doctrine has been expressed by Rickert and others. The formal law of the purely psychic consciousness, whereby one act, subject to no matter what modulation, must arise from its complexities to take up the focal *I*-position at any given instant, this being of the essence of the case, is here wrongly hypostatized into the existence of one definite, absolute *I*-act. Once this mistake has been made it is understandable that one should think it possible to derive an 'epistemological subject', a '*general I*', existing absolutely and identical in all individual *I*'s, by the successive abstraction of the so-called contents of consciousness. But what one in fact is left with is not an 'absolute subject', not a 'normal consciousness' and not a God, but pure *nothing*—or a concept which contradicts the eternal nature of things. For what else but nothing could be the result of this purely negative abstraction of all things? All negative abstraction supposes that I have already beheld that positive thing which I wish to purify (by the removal of the foreign matter with which it is somehow intermingled) and which I wish to make *visible* to those who have not yet beheld it. The abstraction of pure negation never has the effect of 'creating' the positive content of a concept. Are we to suppose that by abstracting all the empirical contents of consciousness we but purge the 'epistemological' *I* of the subjective limitations, the obscurities, stumbling-blocks, delusions and errors of human cognitive subjects? . . . that nevertheless the general epistemological subject retains the correlate of the world-totality at its purest, richest, most objective, so that true and adequate human cognition of an object would amount to becoming its 'epistemological subject', or the metamorphosis of the individual into the 'normal' consciousness? To cherish so singular an opinion would be the *perversest* self-deception conceivable. By 'abstracting' all 'content', by taking abstraction to extremes, one 'abstracts' all that part of empirical data which has any kind of *truth or cognitive value;* what then 'remains' is not the fulness of the world freed from the contamination of the individual subject, but absolute nothing—the void.

Make no mistake: behind errors of thought so profound as these lie *wrongful* ways of life. For this theory is ideally designed to enable the thinker to puff up his own precious *I*, like Fichte, into a consciousness both cosmic and divine, and to forget, in the moment of exercising his wisdom, the subtle—but *in practice* impossible—distinctions he has made on paper between his own little self and the 'general consciousness'. Merely to read the works of this philosophical school is to find confirmation of the sad inner fate to which all thinking of their kind is doomed—to snatch at holiness and grasp the inane. It is their inexorable lot to circle endlessly and dizzily round an ever more vacuous self; to stereotype endlessly and monotonously the same few wearisome ideas; to lose all capacity for devotion to a being, immersion in a cause. And the way of life which accompanies these ideas, that empty, inflated ego-sovereignty which abolishes all connection with objective fact and reality, and spurns the humility which beseems man in the presence of holiness, is worthy of the strongest condemnation.

Thus the idea of God and the grasp of his existence cannot be based on a 'normal' or 'general' consciousness or 'general *I*' and suchlike. On the contrary, the divine being, superior to *every I*, and the peculiar nature of the subject and vehicle of all universal norms must already *have been given* in quite another way, if we are to accredit that being with the character of a logical, aesthetic and moral lawgiver.

3. But what is true of the general philosophical basis of this theory of religion is *mutatis mutandis* no less true of its specifically religious self-deception, by reason of which it ignores the special *modality* of all values in the sphere of holiness. It would scarcely be an exaggeration to say that Otto's splendid book, *Das Heilige*, was written with the purpose of refuting the idea that the holy is no more than a blanket-conception covering 'the good, the true and the beautiful'. Indeed it pays special attention to the 'irrational elements' in the holy, and thereby to everything wherein the holy differs from those three values. The fact that they too, at a certain stage of religion, are 'sanctioned' or sanctified, that they are recognized and confirmed with the force of religious prescription, ought not to blind us to the unique and incomparable character of the value of holiness. In fact its special nature is but freshly demonstrated by the very necessity

and possibility of 'sanctioning' other values. But a theory, be it ever so true, a work of art, be it ever so glorious, or moral conduct, be it ever so admirable—none of these can in any way produce the characteristic impression of *holiness*. The emotional acts through which the holy is grasped as 'holy', and the emotional reactions which release the sense of the holy, are divided by an abyss from similar feelings and emotions which stem from good conduct, knowledge, art or the naturally beautiful. An object from the latter sphere, if it plays a part in the act of worship, (a 'holy' picture or a consecrated vessel) appears to consciousness with quite other value-qualities than those of the loveliest work of art. 'Miracle-working pictures are bad paintings for the most part,' said Goethe. Holy fear, awe and reverence, the unconditional sense of reluctance to touch the object save for liturgical purposes (a reluctance yet accompanied by an equal power of attraction exerted on the emotions), these have nothing in common with *aesthetic* pleasure and enjoyment. The same is true if we seek the 'holy' in its highest form of this-worldly existence, the personality of man. The saint is no mere raising to a higher power of the artist of genius, the wise man, the good man, the righteous—nor any super-philanthropist or legislator. If a man were all these in one, he still would not create the impression of holiness.

Therefore we must reject any theory of religion if, resting on these false assumptions, it regards the religious object-world as merely *complementary* to the spiritual values and goods of civilization (*sic* Jonas Cohn) and religion itself as the hitherto undifferentiated overall consciousness of the unity and interdependence of the spiritual forces which create culture and civilization; such a theory, moreover, tends in consequence to see a yardstick of a positive religion's truth in the extent to which it has prepared, furthered or developed 'civilization'.[1]

The defensive position taken up by adherents of the positive religions in the face of attacks from the ranks of *Kultur* has had the unfortunate result that the thinking of the believers has been consciously or unconsciously undermined by an *adaptation* to the basic values of the irreligious, so that this reputed method of *verifying* religion has been in fact espoused where *in abstracto* it has been ruled out of court. There is a tendency to regard the philosophy of religion as a mere branch of '*Kulturphilosophie*', so-called— even the abominable term of 'religious culture' has gained currency in extensive circles. As distinct from questions of what religion in general, or in specific examples, has contributed to the 'education of humanity', what it means as a spiritual cement and a creative force in the character-

---

[1] Rudolf Eucken also follows the path of religious theory rejected below. See in particular his *Der Wahrheitsgehalt der Religion*.

formation of communities,[1] what use it is as a weapon in the conflict of communities, what it has meant and done for the state, for the structure of the economy, for art and science, public education, etc.—questions about which many learned and often valuable works appear every year— *the independent claim to truth of the basic religious theses escapes our age in a manner almost grotesque.* The preponderance of these questions over that of religion's own claim to truth is indeed the most characteristic factor in the attitude to religion typical of the second half of the nineteenth century. And this *convention* in the treatment of religion is perhaps yet more dangerous for its true nature than the openly expressed theory that would measure religion against its power to complement cultural values or to further and uphold them.

Let us, however, pause for one moment to become quite clear about the *senselessness of the foundation* for any such utterance if it is intended to do more than give mere descriptions of historical situations—if it is intended to make some assertion for or against religion *on the basis of that yardstick.*

1. *If* there is an eternal being and supreme good which is raised above all the contingent existence of worldly things, *if* there is a whole 'kingdom' of God, whose possession can and should stand before the soul of man as the most central and the highest of all expectations, then nothing is clearer than that all possible human culture—not merely civilization as it actually is—sinks to an incident on the *periphery* of existence. In relation to God's eternal perfection the works of human culture appear as a flux of unstable, ephemeral patterns, confined in a narrowly bounded Time. Like the sunbeam in the fleeting wave, the eternal values made real and one in God's eternal perfection are from time to time reflected imperfectly in the distorting mirror of human endeavour. It is impossible even to think of God without seeing that *this* is all that the works of man can mean. Yet we are told to justify our belief in God by the fact that it assists the progress and varied fortunes of *cultures*! For sure!—to the man, snared and tangled in the grim passions of earthly life and temporal ambition, who looks on the goods of civilization, they appear to stand at the *centre* of all existence, the focus of all values. For even *nature,* active outside man and within him also as the unresting drive to preserve and re-create existence —even nature, though it is so superior to those goods in power and solid existential basis, has only blossomed and flourished to the best advantage in the history of culture (here *cultivation*), science and technology, *i.e.* under the impact of human knowledge. To that extent it is thus dependent on acknowledgment by acts of the *mind*, which themselves may be thought

[1] Thus in particular the French 'traditionalists', whose latest representative is Maurice Barrès.

of as 'cultural' acts. Even if, measured by its psychic existence, the thought
of man is no more than a sudden flare in the overwhelming engine of
existence (which runs as darkly and quietly after as before), measured by
the sense and content of human thought, the very process of that engine
is but a tiny part of the meaning within that incidental spark, no more than
the correlate of that little part we call 'science of nature'. That very
science is but one branch of *culture*. Thus, provided he pays no attention
to God, man *may* rightly consider himself the source and nurturer of all
cultural activity, and the very mid-point of the world. He may think
himself superior to all the elements and forces of nature, which so often,
like children at play who unknowingly shatter a priceless vase, destroy the
works of man with fire and flood, if not the corruption of rust and moth.

How great the change, when the *thought of God* possesses the mind and
heart! Well may man's thought 'prescribe laws' to the rest of existence
through the science with which he comprehends it; in reference to the
absolute being and the eternal good the very thought is at once absurd and
sinful. How impossible and senseless an idea it is, to base God's right to
recognition on something which could occupy the centre of things *only if
God did not exist*! *If* he exists, its metaphysical position must be relegated to
the 'periphery of existence', where, comparatively, it enjoys no more than
insignificant and ephemeral value. What kind of 'ground' or reason is it,
which only firmly 'grounds' while one refrains from asserting what it is said
to have founded, what kind of basis, which sways and totters so soon as
one affirms what it is said to support? Clearly the very sense of the
proposition that 'there is a God' radically precludes our basing it on the
possibility of culture. Here we have a unique and unrepeated relationship
between, on the one hand, the content of the thesis to be established, and
on the other, the possible way of establishing it. Only if the source of
'culture' stood at the centre of things could one establish God's existence
from it. But if *God* exists, the source cannot occupy the centre. Thus the
thing founded would remove the justice of the foundation. Here then is a
way which only leads to the goal if it fails to reach the goal—the existence
of God. Moreover, it would always have been the wrong way if it *did*
lead to the goal. The very thing to be established disqualifies the establishing reason, and solely by virtue of their interlinked significations. It is
incorrect to think that in this case the following distinction provides an
answer: God is the basis of culture's existence and value, as well as of the
act which produces culture; on the other hand both act and culture offer
the reason for *knowing* and believing that God exists. For, as I have said,
it is the very *sense* of the proposition 'there is a God' which makes *nonsense*
of this method of founding it, in that it is sufficient in itself to disqualify

the basis, even if it be a basis for mere knowing, on which the relevant proposition of existence is to be based. If a God were assumed not merely to exist, but to be of a certain essence, for the sake of culture, he would be no God in the true sense. *If* one has God, the foundation of his existence on culture—as value and cultural act—is ridiculous. If God is not already present in the mind, he cannot be reached in this way without removing the sense and value of the premise from which one wishes to argue his existence.

But it can be seen how this method is ruled out by the religious way of life and the laws governing the reaction of the whole man to the various kinds of good. If the heart is set on the supreme eternal good, or even on the mere *idea* of such a good, it inhabits a sphere, a culminating plane, from which human civilization appears more and more vain, vacuous and fragmentary. How then shall the heart affirm the existence of that highest good not for its own sake but for the sake of that which is so vain and empty? As may be seen, it is not mere logic-chopping to unmask the error in this method of founding religion. It is as much a question of religious probity, of looking the religious facts in the face. In the last resort this type of foundation, so dear to our age, has its root in a moral deficit, in improbity and a kind of mental squint in matters of religion. The upraising of the mind and spirit, their self-elevation to the idea of God, though it is this which prepares the way to all understanding of culture, is no longer resolutely carried into effect. We cling to the cultural goods of this world, setting them at a premium which we refuse to abandon even in looking up to God, though his very existence renders it meaningless. It is even by this premium that we seek to justify his existence. And so religion's endless 'meanings relative' to X, Y and Z are allowed to stifle its essence and obscure the simple 'all or nothing' which alone is of the essence of the religious thesis. One can relatively esteem what is relative, but one cannot so prize the absolute. The absolute must be *absolutely* prized: unless one esteems absolutely it is not the absolute one prizes. In the end the way of thinking which we are repudiating relegates God to a mere viewpoint, the still-sought and unknown focal X of all 'meanings relative'. Thus the state has an X-reference, and economy, art and science can all be referred to the one X-co-ordinate. But it is the *content* of this X in whose fulness true religion has its being and life, this *content* which to understand and serve is the only key to all relativities.

2. For that reason there can be no question of regarding religion as merely the vital, as yet undifferentiated unity of the spirit informing culture and civilization. Neither can we see in the realm of religious objects and values no more than an 'ideal complement' of the world of

cultural goods and values. If for no other reason the first hypothesis is false because religion, if it were indeed such a unity of the cultural spirit, would decay in proportion to the advance of differentiation, as the spirit extended its spheres of action and created new realms of value. Of that we see no trace in history. Rather do we find that religion itself, with its goods and values, undergoes differentiation just as art, government and science do for their part, and that this happens on the specific ground of religious values as such, these forming a world that is in no sense a 'combined version' or undifferentiated unity of other spheres of value. If there is a stage of conceptual thought where, relatively, differentiation has not yet taken place, and if it has any corresponding specific 'world',[1] then it is not given in religion and the religious act but in *mythical* thought and feeling and the object-world of the myth. The myth—psychologically seen as the collective waking or half-waking dream of the peoples[2]— is not a mental activity directed to specific domains of objects and values, it is only a *psychic* perceptual and conceptual modality which may be possessed, and on certain levels of development is possessed, by all essential types of mental act and acts pertinent to all kinds of goods and objects. It is not an ethical or axiological but a psychological category. Legal, economic, artistic, scientific, political, ethical and—*it may be*— 'religious' thought and estimation, valuing and preference may be seen tightly interwoven in the myth on these levels. Furthermore, even when, with increasing *wakefulness* of the group-consciousness, the active and objective realms of the mind have disengaged themselves from myth and stand opposed to it, the myth remains as a colouring and co-determining psychic influence. But religion disengages itself no less energetically than the various cultural fields from the mythical stage of consciousness, and in principle the manner of its disengagement is not different from theirs. We may therefore conclude that to equate religion with the undifferentiated or less differentiated spirit of culture is to confuse it with myth, and —into the bargain—to equate a noetic with a psychological category.[3]

But this by no means implies that it is not religion which gives, and everywhere has given, the final unity and meaning to civilizing and cultural activities; I have wished to show only that it *is* not that mere unity. For it *bestows* that unity, precisely, and only can bestow it, from the bedrock of

---

[1] The German has 'work' (*Werk* = *opus* rather than *labor*), but 'world' (*Welt*) seems imposed by symmetry of meaning (*Translator*).

[2] The myth is subject to the same rules and laws of formation as the waking dream or fantasy—however, it would not be of present relevance to demonstrate this.

[3] The confusion of myth and religion is particularly common within the romantic philosophy of religion (F. von Schlegel, Schelling) and traditionalism.

its own peculiar nature and *by virtue of* its own specific goods and values. And this is of special application from a sociological point of view. Mythology is divided among peoples and nations, and its content depends on the factors which in the early histories of peoples (since as with individuals their minds are most plastic and impressionable in youth) make the deepest impression and pass into *traditions*, where they are subjected to the most varied treatment by the national fantasy-shaping consciousness. Religion on the contrary merely *uses* the natural-historical division of mankind into nations in order to found specifically religious and ecclesiastical communities with the material to hand, though as to character they stem from religion itself and its own values. These societies, as so formed, are not anchored in the semiconscious phantasma of mythology but in dogma, articles of faith and acts of worship which in turn are not transmitted by bare tradition, emotional infection and the reflex of involuntary emulation, but by *conscious* doctrine and instruction from generation unto generation.

3. Similar criticism must be levelled against the theory that (objectively) religion is the 'completion' of the world of cultural values. I would ask what direction we are to imagine this 'completion' as destined to follow, if we have not already been given something divine and holy to indicate the goal, the direction and manner of it. If such a thing is *given*, on the other hand, why must we seek this complement before we can attain it? This theory, as adroitly argued by Cohn and others, is in the same position as all those philosophical doctrines which attempt to derive conceptual objects from processes, whether of progressive limitation, idealization or completion. To me it is unthinkable that the concept of a straight line should result from my saying 'Let us take this line and set aside its thickness, its colour, its length and any bends it may have by virtue of which this or that part of it can only be an arc of a circle of any requisite diameter —therefore not strictly "straight"'. For such abstraction does not lead to a straight line but to *nothing*, unless I already know somehow, and have clearly seen, when and where I should call a halt in the process. Likewise an 'idealization' presupposes my having seen the *goal* toward which I wish to idealize. Again, 'completion' presupposes at least a given model of the *entirety* prescribing the manner of completion. Thus, if we are to proceed with idealizations and completions which pass from a given culture to religion or the religious object, we must *pre*suppose the idea of God.

4. There is a further objection to be brought against this way of thinking, that a theory of completion leaves unexplained the place which religion occupies in the history of humanity, as well as the sociological institutions which are its outward form. Religion is a phenomenon which is wholly

L

independent of the existence of a higher civilization. While the latter is a very infrequent phenomenon in the history of peoples, religion is universally human. Even primitive tribes and semi-civilized peoples have their own forms of religious consciousness. But even where intellectual civilization shows signs of maturity and a higher degree of perfection, religion is so far from being its 'complement' or cope-stone that historically it is the rule for religion to *lead the way* in its characteristic form and to dictate the basic form and tendency of the new cultural alignment. While we have no recorded case of a civilization initially independent of religion which led of itself to a new formation of the religious consciousness, it is often the case that in the name of a new religious awareness, and by means of its energy, an existing and often highly evolved civilization has been cut off in its prime and *destroyed*, and a fresh start made with the building of culture. Indeed, at periods when the higher culture has disintegrated it is always to the religious consciousness that men look in order under its guidance to found a new culture. Like pantheism—the form they mostly take—the so-called 'cultural religions' are always frail and derivative, intellectual institutions which, moreover, do not derive whatever religious elements they still possess from culture but from the more *vigorous*, intuitive and first-hand organisms found in the *positive religions* of peoples. They scarcely ever find the strength to free themselves from such traditions—as is illustrated by the thousand-and-one religious sects of Hellenism. Again, while the *nation* and *nationality* represent the typical sociological forms of culture, every religion at least claims to be striving after distinctive sociological institutions, such as the sect, the Church, the Order, the school, which rise superior, in their mission, to national division.* Where we find a superior culture it is always the concern of an *élite*, whereas religion, though it claim to speak of the meaning of existence, must present itself to *all* as the way of salvation.

5. But if it is right that we should reject this theory of religion, it is not only on account of the independence of religion's nature and source of truth but also for the sake of the relative independence and special nature of *cultural* values. If by the word 'culture' we understand the existing empirical products and values of civilization, together with their prevalent forms—styles, methods, etc.—this 'culture' certainly requires the most diverse forms of *completion*, however perfect it may be. But it is difficult to see why this 'complement' should be found in religion, and not within the purview of culture itself, whether in the ideal of itself which every culture carries at its heart as a permanent striving for the highest ends derivable from its particular structure, or, in the wider sense, in the universal spiritual values whose characteristic system every culture endows with

one particular structure and distinctive world of cultural goods. The *completion* which culture needs and which it seeks within its own resources is therefore grounded not on religion but on its own *ideality*. In the nature of its own cognitive act, science for example is an endless process of the precise determination and ordering of observations which are interminable even in respect of a single object of perception. It is difficult to see where and when a halt should be called so that a transition might be made to its completion in the alien dimension of religion. The same applies to the growth of art, philosophy, technology, social and judicial institutions. In all these cases the 'completions' are prescribed by the ideal intentions and trends possessed by the sphere in question above and beyond its actual empirical existence. These can be prognosticated from existing manifestations in the empirical world, and while this or that activity may fall short of its ideal in varying measure, it is not necessary, in order to pronounce on this, to call in values, norms and ideals from outside, to introduce criteria not derived from the sphere itself. There is no work of art which apart from what it actually yields to observation and enjoyment does not at the same time betray what it *should and would have wished to yield*, hence in what way it has fallen short of this focus of its radiating values. The 'spirit', in the work as in the person, has always the property of transcending its own real manifestation, so that it not only presents the evidence of its empirical creation but also divulges the goal and aspirational forms which it failed to reach and from which it was in fact diverted by a thousand checks to its self-expression, a thousand limitations and compromises. In examining any personality, nation or separate group we do more than recognize in its actual spiritual condition the 'character' it has forged from the contingencies of history; we are also able to divine its unique and ideal *character-designate*,* against which we can measure the empirical character and which gives us the key to every speech and written sentence from the source in question. Thus in all the vital utterances of the spirit we not only grasp what is said and done but may see what *ought* to have been said and done according to the guiding intention. In this way, precisely, all the works of culture not only demonstrate what they *are* but intimate an ideal beyond their empirical existence and express an ideal of *yearning* aspiration. And since in every part of historical culture, in its personalities and works, be they legal institutions, works of art, sciences or philosophies, we are able to grasp the internal ideals of culture as complementary to their empirical existence, we need *no religion* to diagnose the normative elements that lay down the lines of their 'completion'.

We naturally have not been intending to deny that—in an utterly different sense—religion lends the finishing touch to all things cultural, however perfect or ideal. But a completion of this kind follows *from religion itself*; its underlying considerations are religious insights, values and ideals, and indeed culture's need of completion, in this sense, becomes apparent only from the independent viewpoint of religious awareness. *Only* if in the centre of my mind and heart a love is at work, and a yearning based thereon, which respond to cultural perfections, to every proposed cultural fulfilment, with 'No, not this, but only something quite *different*, can bring me fulfilment'—only then will culture's *need* of supplementation stand revealed, and the religious consciousness 'open' to receive the goods of salvation. It is only from the viewpoint of the idea of God that we see culture and civilization as no longer self-sufficient. Only when I have attained that idea, moreover, does the dark, anfractuous way of man's spiritual development, all his culture withal, appear to me in retrospect a stairway of man to God. But the steps therein are not even recognizable *as* steps until the climber stands on the topmost; therefore not in objective foundation of our knowledge of God but only *pedagogically* may we use them to trace our way to him.

6. Finally this theory of religion is the very last to satisfy our understanding of all *religious ethics*. I have elsewhere offered a thoroughgoing refutation of the hypothesis that moral values and norms are in origin subsidiary components and *ad hoc* instruments of cultural evolution.[1] Advanced and climactic civilizations are known in history which were attached to relatively valueless forms of ethos, objectively speaking, and even more to the most defective morality. If further proof were needed the Great War must have provided it in no small measure. Elaborate civilization, though it include the highest moral sophistication, by which I mean acute sensitivity to all the wide range of subtle qualities inherent in values of ethical significance, is something very, very different from moral goodness of human will and conduct. Moreover, every ethic expressive of a particular civilization is as such debarred from validity in the objective sense or even as an ethic of success.* Thus the Egyptians, Babylonians, Aztecs all went to the wall, and their ethics with them, but they would have laughed out of court any suggestion that they should have bridled their passions for the sake of, say, the European culture of today. But even if we pass over the other errors of this ethical trend, the endeavour to regard the religious ethic, which for centuries was—and covertly still is— the only living ethic of mankind, as a mere 'completion' of pre-, sub-, extra-religious ethics remains an undertaking perverse from the beginning.

---

[1] See my article '*Ethik, ein Bericht*', in the Frischeisen-Köhler *Jahrbücher der Philosophie*, No. 2, and also *Formalismus in der Ethik, etc.* Viktor Cathrein, in his *Moralphilosophie*, also has some extremely apposite observations.

However many moral prescriptions and norms which have proved their validity are 'sanctioned' by religion, this is never *all* that religion does. Indeed, wherever religion is at work it produces its *own* contexture of values, norms, *ideals* of life which are morally binding, and where these are not alone considered viable they overlay as a higher stratum all those norms and values which are merely sanctioned by religion. Such at least are duties owed to God and the values pertinent to man's salvation, whether that of the individual or the race—that is, *solidary* salvation. By these values I mean those which only the man with a religious awareness, one relating himself and his destiny to that of the world and to the sphere of the absolute, is able to behold. No matter how much the actual acceptation of these values may have changed according to the prevailing positive religion, they have always (at least in intention) occupied a place apart in the collections of norms and values under whose dispensation men have lived. And for that reason natural morality and natural religion have always been cemented indissolubly together by the *values of salvation* and their own particular modal character. They cannot be derived either from the category of intellectual, cultural values or from that of vital values.[1] Once a man is conscious of them they relegate all other kinds of value to the sphere of the relative: only in their absence can any other group appear the 'highest'. However often it may *in practice* be contravened, it is an invulnerable axiological principle to prefer unconditionally the values of salvation, wherever they make their appearance, above all others and to sacrifice to their realization all goods which they do not comprehend. But even when religion no more than *sanctions* in retrospect certain values of extra-religious provenance, it does so autonomously *ex cathedra*, and it happens as often as not that values inspected are values rejected: despite their secular validity they remain unhallowed, or even are combated as inimical to religion. If the religious ethos were no more than 'complementary' to the moral consciousness in its pre-religious and unsanctioned condition, this would all be senseless and incomprehensible.

There is therefore no doubt that to deny in *this* way the existence of a self-sufficient and primary realm of religious objects and values is as untenable as any other such denial, and should be avoided by any philosophy of religion which lays claim to sense.

At the present time it is peculiarly apposite to insist on this requirement. If religion is once again to become the true guide and leading spirit of civilized humanity, if it is to deploy those deeper unifying powers which it alone possesses (powers without whose assistance all expectations of

[1] *Lebenswerte*: Scheler presumably means what he elsewhere calls *Vitalwerte*— see my note to p. 306 (*Translator*).

human unity 'from below upward', out of self-interest, must by an eternal decree[1] ever suffer frustration), then it is first and foremost on condition that it become aware of its *autonomy*; the religious consciousness must extricate itself from dense entanglement with the values and norms of secular 'culture', which the Great War rendered all too questionable. But the delivery of religion from its servitude, from the thousand-and-one unworthy offices it performs for the nation, the state and who knows how many 'organizations' at the risk of its own extinction, will only be possible and soundly based if we banish from the basic doctrines of religious theory the idea that religion is *complementary*. This 'theory' is nothing more than a logical formulation, in the purest imaginable form, of the practical historical situation. It sees religion as a mere point of intersection of civilized energies, or objectively as a mere overall unity and omnibus-version of the highest cultural values. Here we have the precise formula for that way of thinking which ends by presenting God himself as the vacuous goal X of an unappeased cultural appetite, a blank to be filled in at will by the whim of each and every group or nation. How then is religion to make a stand, say, against nationalism?—how contain and moderate nationalistic passions with that absolute universalism which only men's common attention to God can give, if it must perforce be no more than a completion of a culture that in essence and of necessity is of *national* fabrication?

Here let us note a remarkable rule: religion can only perform the sublime and practically inexhaustible services which it alone and its organs are fitted and destined to render to all civilization *if* it does not base on their utility its claim to truth and worth, for that utility disappears unless religion takes its stand exclusively on *itself* and its own manifest invincibility. Its service is the *freest* imaginable; to place its truth and value in fee to that service is to deprive religion of its freedom and therewith all capacity to render *true and valuable* services to civilization.

The aim, then, that we prescribe is to uphold the independence of religion, but this is by no means to wish to *isolate* it from the cultural contexts into which it has entered of its own accord and by reason of the unity and interpenetration of all historical elements. It can scarcely be disputed that the *ideal* state of affairs is not one in which religion stands in aloof isolation or presents a front of rude hostility to culture, but one where the deepest and richest possible *harmony* reigns between religion and intellectual, spiritual civilization. Yet this harmony must never be striven

---

[1] I discuss this aspect of self-interest in *Krieg und Aufbau*, in the essay entitled '*Soziologische Neuorientierung und die Aufgabe der deutschen Katholiken nach dem Kriege*'. The 'eternal decree' is imposed by the laws governing the divisibility and transmissibility of values: these I develop in Section II, B3, of *Formalismus, etc.*

for at religion's cost, as lies in the spirit of the theory we have been seeking to combat. Ages which exhibit this harmony—for example thirteenth-century Christendom or the seventeenth century in France—have brought this ideal situation to such a pitch of reality that attunement to *their* theories of religion will easily conceal the ultimate *essential* independence—one from the other—of man's two great preoccupations. Hence it is most dangerous to apply the theories of such ages too directly to other ages which fail to exhibit a similar harmony. For then what once was understandable and meaningful reappears as a specious gloss. However, there have been few ages in history which realized the ideal concord so little as our own; few in which religious values were more generally rejected—and with more unconcern—by the prevailing trends of culture. Few ages have had a keener presentiment of a *turning-point* at hand in the history of civilization: few such a sense that some kind of break with the outworn is needed, or—to put it plainly—a *radical* break with a culture hostile to religion at the core. It is no wonder that religion's essential independence of civilization, which at bottom is an ever-present factor, should be growing more obvious now than in periods of harmony. No wonder that when all the traditional props of secular culture are rotten and worn only that *point d'appui* of man's heart and mind which of its nature *endures*—a stand taken on God—can supply the hope and strength to approach once more the ideal of concord, on the basis of a *new and different manner of cultivating the spirit*. Thus at a time when the prevailing culture is largely the product of forces hostile or indifferent to religion, when compromise therefore is at its most dangerous for the purity of religion, the theory we oppose could not fail to produce a wrongful falling into line with a secular culture in senile decay. For harmony of religion and culture is not automatically the perfect state of spiritual life in society. Perfection is not achieved until the independence of a religion is respected while it is yet recognized as the highest and foremost of human activities, until on the other hand it *involuntarily* so inspires all fields of culture, wishing neither to dominate them with high-handed encroachments nor to rob them of their peculiar rules and values, that the breath of eternity sweeps spontaneously through all man's creative work.

Again, our thesis in no way denies or questions the possibility that even today a man, no matter what the form of his subjective evolution, may begin with a searching preoccupation with one branch of culture and may journey so far toward the threshold of religion that he can grasp religious values in an act of faith still *free and independent* of positive doctrine.

There are two typical paths of 'conversion', each legitimate in its way: the direct and the indirect. The first and more personal consists in a preponderantly sudden or spasmodic manner of coming to the conviction that only in devotion to God and surrender to the divine power can the substance of the person find the full meaning of its existence, its deepest expression, its salvation. Profoundly affecting *personal* experiences are the supreme vehicle of this kind of conversion. Heedless of the aftermath of consequences and obligations in civilized life, which religion—like irreligion—brings in its train, unaided by the guiding-lines wherewith religion is ramified through civilization, the individual *leaps* as it were directly from his pre-religious state into the *centre* of religion. Such are the conversions which pietism, methodism and similar strains of devotion strive to precipitate—the leap from profound sin through blinding revelation into the plenitude of grace under the sheltering wings of Christ.[1] The *indirect* path is quite different. It begins with the content of religious inspiration to be found in some cultural field—say art, philosophy, science, education, government, law, ethics. Allowing himself to be guided by the 'inspirational' values of his chosen field, the thinker is immediately concerned, in a gradual, methodical way, only with what he regards as the 'religious assumptions' operative therein, yet having found and inspected these 'assumptions' he discovers they must represent *more* for him than mere theoretical premises: they impose themselves as supreme truths and values in their own right. From working-assumptions they become the main propositions. Simultaneously (if he gets thus far) the concrete *whole* of the religious world comprising the values of salvation, of which he has hitherto enjoyed but a glimpse from one particular viewpoint, will stand revealed to his survey. Thereupon he will abandon the attempt to devote to these values no more than his individual function in society (as artist, educator, etc.), and yield himself to them in his very being and substance. There may be many stations on this road, and at each of them development may be arrested for a time or for ever; as a rule it is a process which undergoes a slow and gradual completion. But however the goal is reached, it would always be erroneous to suggest that this path of conversion could lead to religion if the thinker did not perceive, however vaguely, that religion is by nature something more than a working-assumption which assists the exercise of cultural functions. Indeed we are offered quite a contrary indication in the fact that as the process unfolds it is usual for more and more, richer and richer prospects to open out, new lights on things and realities, goods and values, which the subject could not expect *nor foresee*, even though he exercised an ideal foresight and drew all possible conclusions; though these new perspectives *also*

---

[1] In *Varieties of Religious Experience* William James offers most penetrating descriptions of this type of conversion.

represent the ends in the divine of those guiding-threads which led away from the 'inspirational values' he observed at the outset of his quest, it is quite impossible for him to see them as such 'ends' without at the same time beholding much *more* than the terminal points—without seeing *the full range of natural divinity*. We may compare this journey of the soul to the adventure of a wayfarer who, attracted by a landscape of homely charm, strikes out in a certain direction. But before he quite reaches the goal he has set himself as the *only* goal, there unfold new wonders of nature, the like of which he never saw, and under their enchantment, with the prospect opening ever more gloriously before him, he appears to forget the goal which was all his original concern. Thus described, this heuristic path to religion is in full accord with the doctrine of religion's self-sufficiency. Far from corroborating the theory that religion is a working-supposition of civilization, it flatly contradicts it. For this theory would lead us to expect *not* what we in fact discover—a process of evolution continually drawing enrichment from unforeseeable religious insights, with a constant conversion of means into objective values—but at most a purely *analytical* enhancement of religious material by the provision of new points of approach in the domain of cultural values.

Furthermore it is important, in this region of pure religious heuristics, to distinguish between on the one hand the *typology of the subjective ways* in which representative men in general, or typical men of different cultural epochs, arrive at religion and, on the other hand, an order implanted within the process itself, an order which is independent of the varying subjectivities of individual types and which we may relate to the ladder of objective values and goods. The objective hierarchy of being and values prescribes this order as a scope or range of possibilities to every case of subjective questing for God.

There is, as it were, an *educational path* to God, divorced from the purely objective establishment of the idea of God and the conviction of his existence. It is prefigured in the objective ordering of the world of values and in the perfection and self-sufficiency of things in themselves; indeed in this regard we may say that—quite irrespective of the human subject— the axiological order of the world is one great *signpost to God*, a signpost divided into a multitude of minor indices which do not become wholly comprehensible until they are seen in the *ensemble* of their mutually supporting indications—their chorus of pointers to the One Divine.

If we lay aside image and metaphor, we may resume our meaning in one simple rule. Goethe was near the mark with his simple pronouncement: '*Everything which is perfect of its kind also transcends its kind.*' Yes; it breaks through into a *higher* kind of value.

There is in fact a law of *continuity between goods*, though as such it does nothing to alter the discrete and 'quantum' character of *values* themselves.[1] By this law the *perfect* embodiment of the goods appropriate to any basic category of values (value-modalities and their subordinate value-qualities) automatically passes over into the next higher category, which is modally, or qualitatively, different.

And because the goods of salvation, representing the modally highest kind of value, are the goods possessing the highest form of value-modality, it is true objectively and true in practice that if the continuity of goods is pursued to its rigorous conclusion—passing from the less to the more perfect good in each category, and from the lower category to the higher —the end must finally be God, as the absolutely holy and therefore 'highest' good.

It is these two axiological laws which impart to the kind of conversion we called 'indirect' an objective justification beyond the fortuitous success of attaining the goal—that is, winning through to God. This is because the indirect conversion takes its stand on the objective indices to the divine which are implanted not merely in the nature of man but in the comparative axiology of the world as a whole.

In all fields of value we find confirmation of these laws. Where the exercise of a craft that still lies within the bounds of utilitarian activity achieves a perfection of its kind, it achieves at the same time something *more* than the merely useful—a minor work of art possessing at least an accessory beauty. The useful itself acquires beauty when its utility is perfect.

When the worker in any positive science plumbs the ultimate bases of his knowledge or the deepest, hence the most fruitful, principles of his research, he can scarcely avoid violating the frontiers of the higher species of human knowledge which we call philosophical. His highest 'assumptions' must always be *also* essential truths. For though he may recognize in the essential content of his defining concepts certain 'assumptions', which to him are *mere* assumptions even if they are also basic, to the philosopher they are *already* an object of study. Furthermore, the philosopher, provided he works out the consequences of his essential knowledge to their utmost implication, must glean a knowledge of what the true 'assumptions' of science mean—without for that reason acquiring them

[1] Scheler's theory of values being very much his personal property, I would not wish to thrust the expression of 'quantum' into it without due warning. The author's phrase here is *Diskretion und Sprunghaftigkeit*, the sense of the second noun being literally 'jumplike character', hence spasmodicity, discontinuity, discreteness. Readers will recognize the Schelerian insistence on the stable identity of the individual value (*Translator*).

only 'as' assumptions, which is the habit of the bad, unphilosophical 'philosophy' that is the mere handmaiden of science. Despite the essentially different kinds of knowledge which the philosopher and the scientist are striving to attain, philosophy and science pass smoothly over into one another to the extent that both are *perfect*. They diverge only in their imperfection, their *debasement*. In creative men, in creative times, they are contiguous: no party-wall comes between them. Only in the uncreative does each go its own way.

And must not a *perfect* hero needs become a genius: an Alexander, Caesar, Napoleon, Frederick the Great, a Prince Eugene—as opposed to 'just another hero': a Blücher for example? The higher the spheres of endeavour (as embodying and realizing intentional values), the more they are subjectively of mutual assistance—the more indeed they *require* and enhance each other. Can an artist be perfect without being morally good? I must categorically deny that he can, though I am naturally not unmindful of the 'cases' that can be held against me from history and the experience of life. But unless one confuses technique (on *both* sides, for morality also has its technique) with artistic worth and moral goodness, and unless one wrongly measures these *intuitively* evident principles against empirical 'realities' (instead of using them to establish the true facts by *correct* analysis of experience), one may easily dispose of these alleged 'facts' and 'cases'.

Can one be a perfect 'leader of men' other than by being *more* than a leader? Must not the perfect leader be a spiritual figure devoid of personal ambition who as an involuntary exemplar, with no intentions of leadership, attracts a following? Does not the value of such a man appear to lie not in his leadership but in the simple fact that 'such a one is in the world'?

This law enables us to understand that in the very nature of cultural values man must be able to reach the religious attitude, and therein attain to God, from *every* sphere of values, be it economics, law, government, art or science. But this heuristic law does not imply that one could establish religion on the answer to the question *Why is civilization possible?* Religion and its values will ever be a *supracultural* realm, though admittedly one which bestows on cultural values, if they are comprehended in the religious cognitive act, their ultimate meaning and purpose, permitting us retrospectively to look on the production of cultural goods as stages in the ascent to God.

And so we feel unable to say that recent attempts to lay the foundation of natural religion, attempts mostly within the philosophical ambit of Protestant culture, are likely to be crowned with success. However valuable this or that attempt may be, only the method we have sketched appears to us to comprehend what is valuable and permit it to be used correctly.

But this investigation would be incomplete if it were to take into account only attempts to underpin religious contentions which are already accepted. For, as the reader will be aware, there are large circles today which understand the renewal of religion to imply that one should look for the advent of a *new religion*, if not 'invent' one. The ranks of religion-founders, all of whom find some kind of following, are regularly swelling.[1]

What then are the prospects of a new religion—one not 'founded' but *invented*, if I may use the term?

3. WHY NO NEW RELIGION?

There can be no doubt that it is the force of custom and not of insight which moves the majority of believers to lead their religious lives within the traditional forms of belief and worship. Of course that is not saying much. For all possible kinds of alienation from religion, from denial of God to indifference, have also long ceased to be the revolutionary discovery or novel adoption of skeptical minds. They too have become *traditional* over wide areas of the European population and are part of the baggage of thought transmitted from generation to generation. No longer is any high-souled individual tempted by love of heroism to oppose the Churches, for such heroism, which purely as such must have attracted rather than repelled the stout-hearted *esprit fort*, is no longer necessary. For a long time now such men have been finding a more rewarding field in the economic or political worlds. Indeed, before the War any kind of atheism could find its niche in our *Hochschulen*, but woe betide the scholar of Marxist or republican leanings! Thus, broadly speaking, freedom from preconception has become a more urgent cause in the field of national economy than in that of philosophy. Nevertheless, the very fact of religious traditionalism is incentive enough for certain more lively religious groups to hold that religious renewal, in the sense of a 'new religion', is desirable. It is to such groups in particular that the following is addressed.

There is a question which is seldom asked, and I would put it thus:

Setting aside the question of ingrained and traditional beliefs, must not a strictly philosophical perusal of the situation lead us to conclude that

---

[1] To mention but a few, there are Christian Science, theosophy, the efforts of Johannes Müller and the young circles of religious enthusiasts gathered under the banner of Eugen Diederichs's periodical, *Die Tat*.

there are *grounds*, lying in the very nature of religion and of the possible origin of religions, for assuming that a 'new' religion is no longer to be expected—certainly not in *Europe*?

If there were any such grounds, existing independently of the motive of custom, how deeply mistaken would be those who count on the possibility or likelihood of a new religion only because they observe the reaction against beliefs of habit, or have vague ideas about the necessity of 'progress' in all that men hold valuable! Awaiting what is 'better' or 'nearer perfection', they would all this time have been eschewing the *good* pure and simple. If there are such grounds, only one attitude to religion is open to us—desire to *preserve* the religious benefits we *have*, and care to increase their fruitfulness, to ensure their full activity in the souls of men.

It appears to me that there *are* such grounds, grounds of principle which lie in the nature of religion and its relation to history, and I have often thought it remarkable that (with a few exceptions) so little has hitherto been done to set forth these reasons systematically.

The grounds are of different kinds and varying importance. There are 1. metaphysico-theological grounds, lying in the nature of the idea of God, and 2. grounds lying in the evolutionary trend of the human mind.

They are wholly independent of the confessional viewpoint, and are rationally acceptable.

Only when they have been digested and understood may one further ask what place Christianity occupies among religions. Only then may one seek out the reasons for or against its 'absoluteness'—those, that is to say, which support or weaken its claim to be not only the *so far* highest, purest, 'most perfect' religion but 'the' utterly true or absolute religion.

THE IDEA OF A PERSONAL GOD CONFLICTS WITH THE EXPECTATION OF A NEW RELIGION

The first ground lies in the nature of the divine itself, in so far as it is conceived as personal—hence, at a more primary level than the positing of the reality of any particular doctrinal form of that nature.

If we were able to contemplate or imagine the idea of God without importing into it the idea of a personal form of being—if, for example, we could envisage it as the idea of an impersonal cosmic spirit, a mere world-order, an all-pervasive life, as a substance, thing or idea devoid of personality, then it would certainly be an intrinsic *possibility* (in the nature, that is, of the cognitive object) that an unlimited number of new religions should make their appearance in the course of history, each one a steady improvement and advance toward total knowledge of God. Why not? To take an example, has not astronomy progressed in this way throughout the history of knowledge, not only by making small gains but by changes of *system* in the manner of regarding the heavens (*e.g.* ancient biomorphism, modern mechanicalism, heliocentricity, geocentricity)? There are similar possibilities wherever knowledge of entities, cognitive participation in their nature, is effected solely by *spontaneous* acts of the human mind.

This proposition is also applicable to the divine basis of the world—for so long as it is regarded as impersonal. With that proviso, there is no reason why in this field of natural, spontaneous knowledge of the divine world-basis, its essence and existence, the work of cognition should not accumulate in the course of history, so that every disciple stood on the shoulders of his teacher.

But what a change we see if—following the ethically derived axiom oi the superiority of personal over impersonal values—we regard personality as an essential feature of the *summum bonum*! For though reason may have shown to our satisfaction that the world-basis exists with such and such metaphysical predicates, the means whereby we come to know it as also personal can scarcely be described as a spontaneous cognitive act. Indeed it is precisely because we perceive the necessity of ascribing personality to the *summum bonum* that we encounter the following manifest truth: *if* God is in some way personal, it is of the very *essence* of God that the peculiarly personal sector of him can never—evidently—be brought to our knowledge *solely* by our own spontaneous cognitive acts. On the contrary, if such knowledge is to come into being *at all*, it must originate *in* God with *his* free and sovereign condescension to us; it must begin with some act whereby he discloses and imparts himself to us, reveals himself as a person. But we have a name for this kind of communication: 'revelation'. We therefore know that a personal God—if he exists, and in respect of his personality—could *only* be known through revelation (or grace and illumination).[1]

It is not through any supposed deficiencies in 'our' cognitive power, or any natural limitations we may suffer in that direction, but it is rather an essential consequence of the *object* of which we wish to acquire knowledge, that God's personal essence—or indeed his existence *qua* personal—can never be known to us through our own *spontaneous acts*, but must be vouchsafed by a free act of self-revelation on the part of the divine person. To that extent the unprovability of God as an existent *person* is *axiomatic*—here, if one should require it, is a 'proof of the unprovability of God as a person'.

---

[1] For all that rational insight (without the light of revelation) can uncover the existence of God to the extent of the definitions *ens a se, res infinita, summum bonum,* pure spirituality—and can even firmly establish the fact that if there is a highest good it must have the attribute of personality—the proposition that 'the existing God is a person' must always transcend *all* rational knowledge.

For let us clearly understand how, in the nature of things, it is possible for us to know the existence and substantial content of an object of personal character. I become aware of a man via all the sensory impressions, all the perceptual and representational data concerning him which are accessible to me. If I seek to know him, it is with the aid of all the inferences which I am able to draw from, or build upon, these empirical data. Can I then know *what* specifically he is thinking, how he is judging, whom he loves or hates—unless he freely invites me to know these facts by speech, writing, self-expression of all kinds? I cannot. *A man can be silent. Only a person* can in this sense 'be silent', be 'unforthcoming'. For it is of the essence of a person—as distinct from a merely animate organism, a bundle of vital processes signalling an *automatic* self-expression to the outer world—that it can make knowledge by others of what it thinks, wills, judges, dependent on its *free discretion*. A spiritual person is known only in self-revelation. A person can lie, dissemble, hide itself. *Only* a person; the stone cannot, neither can the animate organism, the plant, or the animal. Admittedly, man, since he is not *all* spirit but is partly an animate creature, since he is not a perfect but an imperfect person—one, that is, whose acts (and the constant self-fulfilment of whose existence in acts) are bound to the organs and vital processes of a body—is unable to hide his mere *existence* as a person, by reason of the natural inseparability in him of vitality and spirituality, corporeality and personality. For if it happens to be a human *body*—or certain traces of it—which draws our attention, we inevitably apprehend it in such a way as to tell us that here also is a personal being. This is because there is an intuitively evident and essential *rapport* between human body and human personality.[1] Even if a man's personal existence is never *directly* given to perception, it is given in an inseparability of significance by reason of that essential *rapport*, which is embedded in the pure substance of human corporeality and personality; at the very least it is clear to us from our self-experience, *i.e.* irrespective of the number of cases in which we encounter it. *Man*, then, can withhold only what he thinks, loves, judges, all of which are components of his personality, but his very *existence* as a person he cannot conceal.

What of an incorporeal, invisible, perfect, infinite and absolutely free person? It is clear that *its* nature does not preclude the *possibility* of its concealing not only its spiritual content but also its very *existence*.

Few have gone to the extreme of imagining the immeasurably deep, the fearful idea of a God who *exists*, who is a person and who is yet silent, a God who conceals himself as a person may. Few have confronted the

[1] On this point, cf. the appendix of my book, *Zur Phänomenologie und Theorie der Sympathiegefühle.**

idea of a world and a universal history of finite rational beings over which there presides in glory a God who does *not* make himself known, a God who will not permit himself to be known; a world, this would be, whose inhabitants could know nothing of God's existence as a person, not on account of their own guilt or shortcomings but because it pleases God that it should be so. And yet the nature of God as a perfect person permits, *a priori*, the possibility that two worlds, two histories, in one of which there was a God and in the other none, could be totally *indistinguishable* by the cognitive powers of men, for the reason that God did not reveal himself in the former.

Clearly, the greater the disparity in perfection and sovereignty between two spiritual beings, the more any knowing of the more perfect by the less is dependent on the former's *spontaneous* initiation of a self-disclosure.

If the idea of the silent God has so seldom been brought into sharp focus, the reason is surely this. The *idea* of God comprises predicates, such as his *loving kindness*, his total *goodness*, and perfect *veracity*, which 'forbid' him to exercise the freedom of self-concealment which he enjoys as an absolutely free, sovereign and perfect person. Once we are clear that *love*, as the highest active value, is as essential a component of the idea of God as personality, love which, as we have shown, underlies volition and cognition in all minds, but in God's also wisdom and creation—the idea of a silent God who conceals his very existence is shown for what it is, the notion of a frightful spectre that *cannot* exist: as self-contradiction cannot exist.

And so a God already possessing those predicates which must be ascribed to him by virtue of the invincible *ethical* axioms must also comprise in his nature a *freely* chosen self-revelation, which we know as a constant whispering in the deep personal nucleus of every finite, rational being, the enduring shining of the eternal light into finite minds, and their gathering together to one solidary whole in the unity of this love and light.

For this reason alone ignorance of God, if he exists as a person, must of necessity be accounted a *fault* in man. The fault lies in his giving no heed to the whispering and no welcome to the light, because he fails to loosen his ties with the objects and images of finite existence. On the other hand, ignorance of an impersonal God could never be a fault but could only be an error. And so it is not a failure in adequacy of a spontaneous cognitive act which constitutes the nature of the fault, but the obstinate shutting of the self against the light of natural revelation and salvation, a light which shines before any stirring of response. The fault is motivated, but not determined, by infatuation with objects of finite experience.

To resume, it is in the nature of a personal God that knowledge of his existence is only possible by grace of this *fundamental* act of self-disclosure, his allowing himself to breathe and shine through the whole of the meaning of the world, which is centred in God and comes to our knowledge through his all-embracing love and the revelation it inspires.

It is in love of the divine and holy, a love which has to move toward its goal before it recognizes itself as the response to a *pre-existent* love directed toward the loving soul, that God has located, in the final analysis, that mysterious driving-wheel which sets in motion all our cognitive knowledge of him as a person.

There now comes into view, unexpectedly, a link attaching the question of a 'new' religion to the very idea of God.

Let us for a moment imagine a personal God bearing some resemblance to the marginal notion of a self-concealing God. Imagine a God who has fettered what (if there is a God at all) can alone be the highest end of rational creatures, namely to love and know him, to a *'law of historical progress'* in knowledge of God, and has in turn bound progress in this knowledge to the existence and activity of an *educated minority* in the groups of finite minds we call nations. What are we to think of so 'thrifty' and 'miserly' a God—one so sparing and stingy of his love, so anxious to husband his secrets? I can understand—in fact I think it necessary—that pantheism, and any kind of impersonal conception of God, should rest content with this picture of 'knowledge of God progressing through educated minorities'. For if knowledge of God is *only* a matter of human initiative and accumulative research one cannot deny that in time the more advanced nations, ages or generations, and at the same time the intellectually more gifted people, the 'wise', the 'scholars' and the men of parts, must come to know God best. To that extent pantheism, viewed as a product of society and history, must be a way of thinking in which theoretic religious progress is virtually synonymous with an *aristocracy of the intelligentsia*. It is therefore no mere historical induction which teaches us (for *all* peoples) that pantheism has always been a 'cultural religion' and has everywhere distinguished (in Spinoza's terms) a 'religion of the masses' and a 'religion for thinkers'. No, behind this induction lies dormant the *essential* ideal connection between pantheism and intellectual aristocracy, the discovery of which provides us with the key to that induction.

But what are we to think of a personal God who from loving-kindness must freely give himself, and who has yet given himself to his children only in such a way that the giving, or the giving again, is dependent on the chance that a man or people might belong to a 'more' rather than 'less advanced phase of history', or that a man might have satisfied all the necessary requirements to become wise and scholarly? The very question shows that the idea of such a God can have no real correlative object, and cannot be true: it is against all reason. An alleged 'personal God' of this kind might be anything—but a God. Until it is proved that it is sinful for a man to appear in the world earlier than another, a deficiency in knowledge of God could not be what it *must* be on theistic premises—blameworthy. That also expresses an essential connection between the content of the idea of God and the history of possible knowledge of God. *Can* a loving God set his children at a disadvantage merely because they enter the world too soon or do not belong to 'learned circles'?

We understand well enough that in all fields of knowledge which are not necessary for *salvation*, however important they may be for welfare, utility, society, culture and all kinds of mastery over nature, their furtherance and degree of perfection is governed by the rule of progress and development, and that *advance* in those fields is dependent on minorities of scholars and scientists—men with specific gifts and the freedom from distraction which alone permits their exploitation. But a knowledge which is necessary for men *as* men 'pure and simple', and is furthermore necessary for *salvation*, a knowledge which can only be such because it does not concern objects whose existence is in some way and some degree relative to human organization, culture and social practice, but concerns absolute reality and the supreme goal of man, the very sense and *ratio* of his essence and existence—such a knowledge (if possible at all) cannot *a priori* be subject to *these* conditions. Either it is accessible to *all* or it is accessible to none. And having regard to its object and significance one would expect it to have been the earliest knowledge in history, one that it would have been the task of the successive generations simply to *preserve* rather than to *develop*. One would further expect that to show its utter dissimilarity from all other kinds of knowledge it would be brought to consummation where *fools* rather than the wise, where the simple and *untaught* rather than scholars—would be the first to receive it. Rather than on a throne or academic chair, one would expect it to have been born in an ass's stall—or something of like degree.

What wonder there is in the Christian mystery: the descent of God into that obscure and lowly prison—the body of the carpenter's wife! O marvellous birth of God in a stall! How utterly these Christian mysteries of faith are in accord with what our very reason *must* expect from God's deepest revelation of his nature!

Yet the Christian doctrine of Adam's primal state, that he failed to preserve his unclouded knowledge of God but lost it in part through sin and the Fall, also corresponds to the other expectation—that this knowledge, if at all possible, must have been the earliest.

Nevertheless, I am not directly concerned here with positive Christianity or with positive religions of any kind. For the principal error of those who demand a 'new religion' is not a mistaken belief but a rational error concerning the general nature of religion and the basic *idea* of God. They fail to understand the conditions of possible knowledge which are implicit in the nature of a personal being who is absolutely sovereign, free and almighty and at the same time infinitely loving. Either they consider God impersonal, hence a mere *summum bonum*, or they consider him, while personal, to be miserly and 'economical'.

If they truly understood those conditions they could not but see that their attitude toward a 'new religion', in expecting or demanding it, is in the sharpest contradiction to the attitude shared by all great and effective *homines religiosi* in history. This latter attitude never, never includes, even when these were men who genuinely 'renewed' religious life and knowledge, the expectation or demand that a 'new religion' should arise. In this respect they have solely the intention of *restoring* 'the' religion—the one true, absolute religion. The very thing which may perhaps be termed objective religious progress in history must of necessity represent the intention of '*back to X*' on the part of those who have brought it about.

In all fields of human endeavour where values are no matter of indifference the *homo rerum novarum* has his own very important justification. This, however, is with the exception of religion: here he is essentially an otiose and misleading phenomenon. *For 'back to X' is the essential form of religious renewal.*

In religion the *homo rerum novarum* is no less senseless an apparition than the typical 'heretic', by which is meant the man who 'prefers to differ' or (in other words) who forgets that the form of collective and solidary knowing, loving and believing, founded in the mutual love of all members of the moral world, is essential to knowledge of God—and in the strictest sense, the highest degree, *only* to knowledge of God.

Here let us lay down two very general rules, which can only find their full proof in a sociology of cognition based on epistemology.* The first is as follows: the nearer the objects of cognition to existentially absolute reality (*i.e.* the less they concern things whose existence is relative to the organization of the subject), hence, the more passively receptive (rather than 'dictatorial') our minds to win knowledge of the object in question, hence, the higher the objects in the hierarchy of values and scale of perfections—the less capacity there is for a continuous progress of knowledge; thus for example the spiritual values of culture make less progress, advancing by quite different laws, than the values inherent in materially constructive civilization. The second principle runs: the more absolute and nearer perfection the objects of cognition, the more the possibility of adequate knowledge is conditional on the most intensive and extensive possible form of *collective knowing* among the seekers of knowledge, and the more urgent it is that they should send roots down into as broad and deep a subsoil of historico-social connections as possible. In other words, the more we may say that the complete truth about the object is only attainable through the co-operation of group-individualities none of which is dispensable or can 'do duty' for another. In the last analysis this means that the *whole* of humanity is needed for the purpose. It is not difficult to see what these rules imply for knowledge of God.

The religious *homo rerum novarum* differs from the heretic in that his error does not *begin* with the assertion of *materially* false doctrine but begins at a more fundamental level. For his *formal* notion of God contradicts the very essence of divinity and therefore already precludes him from understanding the way God may be known. Even when, so far as we may rationally judge, his material assertions appear to be true, he is still on the path of falsehood. A false path *must* lead to false goals, however much the first steps upon it may appear to be taken toward the true goal.

But the very assumption that God is personal postulates the sole manner in which his personality may be successfully communicated to men, namely the mediation of *human persons*. All forms of theism must *essentially* include the basic conception that throughout its history religion but waxes and wanes, rises and declines, is purified and sullied in a rhythm of *personal* example and emulation, the leader and the following. They must therefore reject the belief, held by Hegel and Eduard von Hartmann, that any of the great turning-points in religious history, whether they arise from a 'spirit abroad among nations', from popular feeling or the impact of dawning ideas, can be thought to exemplify a definite law of evolution. Conversely, to maintain this belief is just as essential to pantheism in its historically dynamic forms, by which I refer not to a static, 'geometrical' pantheism like that of Spinoza, but to the doctrine of such thinkers as Hegel, Hartmann, Biedermann and A. Drews. These must needs hold that an *unfolding of ideas* is what lies at the heart of religion's history, which according to what they consider the nature of religion is first and foremost the gradual unfolding in the human mind of the divine self-consciousness. Any person, therefore, who demands a 'new religion' should note that *in that very demand* he is taking his stand on pantheistic ground. The theory of progress, the belief that God is impersonal ('religious impersonalism') and intellectual 'aristocratism' (epitomized by the false opposition of esoteric and exoteric religion) belong as irrevocably together as personalism, religious 'conservatism' and insistence on the universality of religion among mankind (or on the Church as an objective institution of salvation). These are not propositions which rest on observation and induction from history but eternal *bonds of meaning* between the content of the idea of God and the historical or sociological form of the human belief attached to this idea. They are propositions *in the light* of which we must understand the history of positive religion, distinguish its driving forces, disengage its manifold currents; they are not principles derived *from* these.

The mere assumption of this personal mediation of all possible revelation (implicit in a divine person of infinite love) rules out the notion of a law of progress as applied to religious truth. For the person is at bottom a non-derivative phenomenon of historical chance. This to be sure has an altogether special significance for the kind of man who may be regarded as the pattern of religious excellence, who combines holiness with outstanding intellect. This significance it can never have for exemplars in secular fields. For what then is a *homo religiosus*, a *saint*, by nature: what does the idea mean? Always on theistic premises (for on pantheistic there are only *teachers of salvation*), he is a person whose spiritual figure presents us to an extraordinary degree with a likeness, however inadequate, of God's own personality: this it does to such good effect that his utterances, pronouncements and deeds are no longer measured against a norm of common application to which our reason has already given assent but are accepted as divine, holy, good, true and beautiful, simply because *he* is their author.* In any other field of values—say in philosophy, science, art, government or law—it would be radically absurd to countenance a situation of that kind: every word, every deed of the leading spirits must submit to the test of the common norms which are recognized by reason. In contrast, the idea of a personal God implies that its 'truth' must also be represented in the *objective* spiritual figure of a person who, *as* a person, does not merely utter but *is* the truth—one who indeed utters it *only because* he is the truth. This, at least, is true in the case of perfect holiness, to which (in historical fact) Jesus alone has laid claim.

It follows that if the historical group of persons constituting the holy man's social environment are to advance in knowledge of religious truth—in the sense of factual truth—they must henceforth rely for their purpose on an *objective relationship* to him. It is a relationship created by inward self-modelling on the personal figure of the holy one, by 'following' him in the sense of taking his mould for one's life. Here then all positive religious knowledge *must be preceded* by a process of spiritual transformation, by self-conformation to the *pattern* of the holy exemplar, the model held out by the bearer of that 'charismatic' quality which demands unconditional faith. Necessarily, the continuous and vital reflection of the spiritual figure of the holy man in the material of the disciple's soul becomes the supreme and ultimate source for the *knowledge* of faith (*Glaubenserkenntnis*), by which I mean the knowledge and rational formulation of everything concerning God and things divine which was intuitively present in the mind of the saint. All other sources of such knowledge, including living tradition, 'holy' writ, the definitions of ecclesiastical dogma, which trace their institution to the 'original' man of God, are therefore in some way dependent on this *final* court of appeal and must be grasped, interpreted, applied in the 'spirit' which is re-created ever and again in reproduction of the holy one's spiritual pattern of being.

But however irrefutable it may be that the chain of *homines religiosi* descending from the original man of God forms (as it were) the living soul of any continuously meaningful history of Church or religion, however true that the crucial turning-points are characterized by the advent of a *new type* of surpassingly God-inspired man, we must observe one further consequence of what we have said in reference to the historico-sociological form of a personalistic religion. This is the essential necessity of an objective, all-embracing *institute of salvation with supreme, infallible authority*, for the preserving of the blessings of salvation and their transmission to men. Let us recall the principles with which our discussion concluded: in the nature of things, truth and knowledge of a personal God cannot be spontaneously excogitated—God himself must supply them. *Qua* person, no incorporeal spiritual person can even be known to exist, let alone known as of such-and-such a nature, unless through *free* self-revelation. But no absolutely good personal God 'can' refrain from revelation. And the 'man of God' (the holy man of the highest possible *type* through which God's self-revelation may be transmitted) must be the *absolute* '*author'ity of belief and salvation*—not in the *first* place by virtue of isolated conduct (such as miracles and moral example), nor by virtue of doctrines, which are not in themselves immune from external rational standards, nor on account of prophecies he may make, etc., etc., but *solely* by virtue of his *holy personage*. Holy acts, miracles and prophecies are no rational 'basis' for his original holiness or belief in it: they merely *prove* and *attest* it; they fasten and re-orient our spiritual attention, but within that re-orientation the nature of his holiness must then emerge 'in its own right' and become the object of our purest intuitive conviction.

Again, the original man of God, the holy man of the highest conceivable form (one, that is, in whom God's self-communication takes the form not of a mere imparting of will or knowledge but an essential, substantial, personal interpenetration of divine and human nature), he is also, even at the *ideal* stage, 'the only one'—*unique*. All that may be rationally doubted is whether there exists any reality correlative to the idea of him, or *who* this unique person may be. Thus there can be no *co-existence* and simultaneous acknowledgment of a plurality of *original* men of God as of secondary, derivative 'saints'—or heroes, for that matter, and men of genius. They would be mutually exclusive.

Whoever is not 'for' must be 'against' this holiest of holy men, and those who are 'for him' must be for him as the 'one and only'. For these reasons the truths he teaches are absolute not only in the sense in which all truths are absolute *qua* truths, even if they refer to the most relative of objects or fleeting of processes. They are absolute in a doubly intensified sense: they are absolute truths about absolute being, and they are 'the' truth (about God), *i.e.* the *whole, perfect, inaugmentable and undiminishable* truth. And so 'further development' can only be a question of *penetrating* deeper into this *totality* of truth, which is 'there' as a datum among men and is in a sense therefore 'known'. There can be no question of a general expansion in human knowledge of God. On the same grounds the mental acceptance of this truth must rest on a free, autonomous, self-subordination of the reason—in such a way, of course, that in all matters not concerning questions of salvation the reason not only retains its entire freedom of judgment but can even be said to have won, by its subjection to God, the perfect exercise of that freedom in relation to all that constitutes the 'world'.

We concluded earlier that it is in the nature of this knowledge and truth to be accessible to *all*—irrespective of nationality, education and all other such distinctions. But this implies that it is in the nature of the man of God to devise an arrangement enabling the supreme blessings of faith to be preserved and administered by virtue of an authority latent in it and transmissible by some kind of legitimate delegation—an arrangement for giving all men access to those blessings and procuring them for all. If this arrangement, known as 'ecclesiastical authority' in matters of salvation, is in essence so little understood, it is because there is a general failure to see its first premise in the very idea of a loving God, combined with the principle of the priority of love before knowledge—of God's redemptive will before the communication of truth. If, regardless of individual aptitudes, regardless of historico-social status by rank, class or nation, God unconditionally wanted out of love to impart to *all* men an absolute knowledge (in the sense above) about a thing, the most urgent for men, about his own nature and their final end and the world's—and he must have so wanted, in the nature of things—would not the holy man to whom he gave 'himself' (his *self*) *inevitably* have bequeathed an arrangement for formulating, preserving and procuring this knowledge for all time to come, in such a way that it will survive unharmed all the spiritual or intellectual currents of history, all the usurpations of reason by this or that ephemeral circle of pundits? Thus the *infallibility* of an all-embracing 'Church' *qua* Church in matters of salvation is a consequence of the fact that not primarily an infinite *wisdom*, nor an *omnipotence* nor a spirit of justice—but a *personal infinite love* of all men must be considered to inhabit the centre of things and wield the governance of the world. Wherever it is a question of relative values, of even the highest goods, those of spiritual culture, such an infallibility and authority would be radically *absurd*. No less absurd, however, would be the *lack* of infallible authority in matters touching salvation—in a world created and swayed by an utterly veracious God of infinite loving-kindness. In the case of spiritual cultural values the assumption of perfect truth and goodness streaming forth from a *unique* personage, and therefore to be preserved at all costs as absolute, would be altogether senseless. Only the absolute good and the truth requisite for salvation are of such a quality that—on the assumption of a personal God—they must be accessible *to all or to none*, that in all circumstances they either deserve to go *un*recognized or merit acknowledgment as absolute (not merely as the 'highest so far'), hence as valid for all future history and every nation, class or rank, etc. The essential choice between acceptance and rejection is no mere fortuitous imposition of history: it follows from the essence of the case begging acknowledgment, and is therefore ideally antecedent to the historical realization of that case. Here the *ways* in which faith acknowledges and acquires the truth are necessarily bound to the nature of the objects to which the acts of faith are applied. Not to believe *absolutely* is not to believe what *is* absolute. Not to believe in the idea of the all-embracing institute of salvation and its permanent possession of truth is not seriously to believe in *God's loving-kindness*. Not to consider one's religion the absolutely true religion, but only the relatively best that has hitherto appeared, is privately to believe that the object of one's faith is not *one* God—is not, though personal, a *God*. And so on. Unity and uniqueness, catholicity and absolute authority are therefore essential and inescapable features of the very *idea* of a 'Church', as the Church of *one* personal and loving God.

There is now an added relevance in the above-discovered principle that the way to God or to the man of God cannot be the way of the 'lonely soul' but must be the way of the *co-operation* of all men, all contemporaneous societies and temporally successive sections of humanity, in learning God's ways, believing in him, loving, worshipping and honouring him. And, since love must pave the way for knowledge, the condition and basis of all possible *knowing* and believing in this form is that those who feel drawn in one accord to know God must *love one another*. Any alleged 'knowledge of God' discovered in another way, with no reference to an envisaged solidarity, the responsibility of each for the salvation of all, and of all for that of each, can be anything—*but* true knowledge of *God*. It is from this principle (the least recognized among those who demand a 'new religion') that we necessarily derive the idea of the *good* of salvation, or blessing of salvation, which the Church—not as a sum of believers but as an institution—must preserve, administer and procure for souls. The acts in the mind of man which underlie the entity called 'authority'—and indeed constitute authority—are love and trust, trust which is manifestly placed in authority's higher and deeper insight by virtue of its *perceptible and sensible inner dignity*. This 'dignity' it does not possess through the individual personal qualities of its 'wielders' but because it was originally founded, with therefore all its 'offices', by the holy man of God. For this absolute trust, which distinguishes this authority from all other, merely relative kinds (*e.g.* that of the State) is simply the *continuation* of the attitude demanded by the very *existence* and *nature* (and only secondly by the works) of the man of God, the perfect *homo religiosus*. This is a readiness to believe solely because *he* speaks, who is *in persona* the truth made flesh. It is the transference of this attitude to his visible foundation, whose invisible Head he remains and in which he is mystically present, which alone explains and justifies the fact that this, and only this, authority may *demand* the highest and strictly most complete and noble sacrifice that is open to man, the *free sacrifice of his individual intellect*.

Now it seems to me that for a long time the idea of this sacrifice has been among the least understood, in the modern world, of all ideas belonging to the older body of religious doctrine. At its very mention, everything now circulating under such headings as 'autonomy of reason' or 'freedom of conscience' (mostly as the haziest of concepts in the vaguest of talk) seems to rear up in outcry. We have come to the point where the secular moral philosopher, the genealogist and historian of morals, has discovered a fascinating problem: how *could* the whole of Christendom have ever regarded this 'sacrifice' not as an action wrung from believers by the *force majeure* of need and fear (of earthly penalties, eternal pain), not as an action to which one might one day be driven, to avoid still greater hurts to oneself and mankind; in sum, *not* as a 'necessary evil'—but as an intrinsically meritorious and glorious action, of surpassing virtue in the sight of the Lord? Astounding!

How, indeed, could what the average educated European has come to regard as 'ignominious servility', 'childish submissiveness', 'contemptible abdication of reason', 'betrayal of the individual conscience' have originally been felt and experienced as exactly the reverse? How can one rank the voluntary subjection of the intellect with all the *other* sacrifices, for example of life, honour or property, which even modern man is prepared to admit, if need be, for the sake of one's private convictions and other forms of supreme good? Must one see it as a genuine free sacrifice like the others, only of a still *higher*, hence more meritorious kind? But how, in the end, is it possible that the value placed on a human action could undergo so radical a change?

Now it is my belief that in this regard the distance separating the *real* experience and sensibility of modern man from those of earlier Christendom is not so great as appears. For the immediate obstacle is a series of grave *misunderstandings*, which nowadays conceal from men the true significance of the older feeling toward the sacrifice of intellect, something that used to be valued at so high a level.

Firstly, it had to be a genuine *sacrifice*, which implies the *voluntary* (and in fact cheerful) yielding up of a thing which must be felt as of *high*, positive value. And indeed the act seemed supreme: it was superior to sacrifices of life or honour, for these the individual reason and conviction may even demand for the sake of their own self-preservation, and here was a free renunciation of that reason *itself*. Hence, the very idea of this sacrifice presupposes an extremely high valuation of the individual reason (as God's *lumen naturale* lighting every soul), a firm and lucid sense of possessing it and a deep confidence in its power. How else could the yielding of one's reason to authority have been a *sacrifice* and even, as a sacrifice, *supreme*? Thus, in spite of what modern thinkers 'take for granted' without benefit of proof, what underlay this idea and valuation was not exactly a depreciation of reason, a weak sense of possession, mistrust in it, stunted rational development, ignorance of its powers. Neither, then, were servile tractability, childish ductility and follow-my-leader sheepishness the ensuing frames of mind.

Furthermore the sacrifice of intellect was not designed to express a mere supremacy of the whole Church over the individual. For it is the individual, the individual person and soul, who is most ennobled— ennobles *himself*—in offering up his highest endowment. It is the consequence, not the subjective purpose, of this noble deed that it maintains the unity of the faith.

Secondly, the sacrifice was not—as assumed today—an *ad hoc* acquiescence whenever need arose, an opportunist subservience to authority at the price of betraying reason and conscience. Psychologically it is true that such compliance could result from authority's exercise of a power of suggestion, or a secret clinging to private convictions accompanied by false protestations or (among those who 'know better') ignominious silence on articles of faith.[1] Let us admit that such behaviour often skulks under the noble cloak of sacrifice; let us admit that adherents of the Church, dwelling in the thick of the modern fray (in Universities for example) and already infected with the current ethos of individual rational autonomy, all too easily succumb to such deplorable and loathsome equivocation, when they come into conflict with authority. But the *true* sacrifice is *utterly* different. It is impossible without the most vigorous independence of reason and conscience in all secular matters not touching salvation. It is systematic—that is to say, it is the *freely-chosen readiness*, regarding not the concrete, *ad hoc* rational act but reason as a *whole*, to submit the will to authority and its claim to interpret and formulate once for all, in the spirit of its founder, the supreme rules of belief and morality. In fact this voluntary readiness to obey is, as originally executed, *based* on the secular autonomy of rational choices, and further rests on the still *rational* conviction that knowledge of divinity cannot be won *at all* save by co-operation within the *ecclesia* of mankind (since rational knowledge of God must be preceded by his children's love of one another)—and by willing acceptance of the Church as an institute of collective salvation. The sacrifice of the intellect is therefore not conditional on a feeble, malleable or suggestible conscience, nor on a weakly submissive reason, but on a distinctive *content* of reason and conscience in respect of *possible roads* to things divine; in other words, on a religious epistemology which differs from modern theory.

Thirdly and lastly, there is no subjection or immolation of the *objective, ideal principles*, the forms and ideas of reason which represent the all-pervading, objective, ideal λόγος. All that is forsworn is the subjective, individual, humanly fallible *competence* to ascertain the λόγος for oneself. However, given the Fall, given original sin (*without* which, as we have seen, the whole of theism makes nonsense even from a purely rational viewpoint), the constant mindfulness of human fallibility must surely include an awareness of man's *propensity* to error and delusion—and it is clear that this tendency is aggravated in proportion to the perfection and value of the sphere engaging his attention.

---

[1] On this point cf. the relevant arguments which, in his short article '*Akademische Lehrfreiheit und kirchliches Lehramt*' (*Die Hochschule*, Nos. 11 & 12), Josef Mausbach employs against certain misconceptions of A. Messer in '*Über akademische Lehr- und Lernfreiheit*' (*Die Hochschule*, No. 7).

THE PROSPECTS OF A 'NEW RELIGION', SEEN IN THE LIGHT
OF THE SOCIO-HISTORICAL DISTRIBUTION OF COGNITIVE
APTITUDES

Up to this point I have rejected the expectation of—and demand for—
a 'new religion' on grounds presupposing theism and therewith postulating
revelation. For without revelation theism makes as little sense as without a
Fall.

As it happens, we consider it impossible to prove the existence of a
personal God, though we think it can be proved that God must be a person
if he is the *summun bonum*. Considering the possibility of knowing the
divine existence by natural lights as *summum bonum*, spirit, eternal reason,
etc., this latter proposition must at least *predispose* us to the possibility of
revelation. However, we are not obliged, for our present purpose, to
prove the bases of theism; there are reasons of a totally different kind for
declaring the idea of a new religion to be highly improbable, if not a pure
will-o'-the-wisp.

One train of reasons is derived from a tendency of the human mind to
evolve, a trend to which the history of peoples bears witness in all the
evolutionary processes that take place within it. Ultimately this tendency
is rooted in what I would call the *ageing of mankind as a species*.[1]

At present we have only the modest rudiments of a theory relating to the
cognition and experience of those objects which, conceived as a whole,
form the sphere of holiness. Properly speaking, most modern epistemology is mere theory of science, nevertheless it arrogates the right to define
and exhaust the *whole* of the cognitive mind by answering the question of
'what makes (scientific) learning possible'. At the same time the realm of
the a-priori, instead of being seen as the objective λόγος permeating *reality*
itself as the summing up of all essences and their interrelations, has been
interpreted as the unvarying structure of a subjective 'reason' and its
functions—hence, a reason which utterly precludes 1. any essential
difference between the representative of one great civilization and the
representative of another and 2. any true historical development, variation, contraction or expansion of the subjective cognitive aptitude. Given
this theory, it becomes quite nonsensical even to *ask* whether there might
not be distinct noetic-cognitive organs and functions, of different kinds
and aligned with different spheres of possible reality, which are irreducible
in terms of one another and which, despite the immutable fixity of the
λόγος (*qua* objective), may perhaps be distributed unevenly and in

[1] It has been hotly contested that species can be said, by analogy with individuals, to be born, age and die—from immanent causes, not external catastrophe. This is not, however, the place to offer a proof.

differing intensities among mankind 1. as divided in races and cultures, or 2. as divided by *phases* within civilizations. But for the prejudice in favour of a constant, subjective a-priori, it would be possible to imagine such a distribution of cognitive powers that each race, culture and historical phase would have some *specific*, distinctive contribution to make toward *total* knowledge of reality—a contribution which *no* other race, era, etc., could supply. Once a group had made a cognitive acquisition all groups thenceforth would be under an obligation to adopt and preserve it; they would not be entitled to reject. For if nothing less than the whole of mankind throughout history sufficed to contain or completely develop man's *full*, exhaustive capacity for knowing the *whole* of reality, it would be ludicrous for any single socio-historical part to set itself up as the decisive judge of the whole. This at least would apply to the *object*-world of knowledge—that is, once one had done with dictating the logical principles of admissibility (which for so long has detained epistemology) and turned to the materials of perception and the sources which supply those materials to perception, to 'experience' (in the broadest, non-sensual meanings of the words).

Thus the philosophy of the Enlightenment, with its subjective a-priorism, ossified the idea of the human mind into a 'reason' of ever-lasting sameness. But if one believes (as we do) that what now appears a 'frozen' functional law of thought, an assemblage of cognitive 'forms', was once in a state of flux, emerging at length from a more generalized cognitive function as the result of concentration on *practical* fields, there is no epistemology which would not have to include both an *evolutionary* theory and a *sociology of mental structures*—or automatically proceed to them after determining the most formal nature of the cognitive act.

We are therefore, I need hardly say, in no danger of falling into the errors typical of orthodox empiricism and sensualistic positivism, represented by Comte, Mill and Spencer. For of course their mistake was to suppress the general distinction—the most fundamental of all philosophy —between the a-priori=essential and the (inductive) a-posteriori= contingent. No form of 'mental adaptation' to *contingent* facts—facts from the sphere of inductive observation and generalization—can ever constitute a general functional law of the mind. Nevertheless it would be wrong to infer that such a functional law must have formed part of the mind's *primordial endowment*, for it could also have been acquired through the habit of intuitive contemplation—hence some form of passive *reception*. It need not therefore have entered the mind by spontaneous production (Kant) or as an inborn property (doctrine of innate ideas).

When we apply to our field of study these fundamentals of an epistemology whose bases we are not at present concerned to argue, we must ask the following questions: Is every mind in all times and places really endowed, as one is inclined to assume, with the same measure and proportion of functions and organs providing material for the knowing of objects in the sphere of *holiness*? (For the moment we make no distinction between 'true' and 'false' information.) Again: the organ of practical civilization, the intellect, wherewith the mechanically controllable is ordered and mastered in both external and internal worlds, was formed by certain selective processes; might these not have also been responsible for a slow *decline* in *other kinds* of cognitive and empirical organs, kinds no less qualified to lay bare reality, kinds—one might say—with no less important a cognitive 'mission'?

First let us remove a few preconceptions. The mere wish to prove that each and every kind of knowledge is marching relentlessly forward has often led thinkers to restrict the entire *sphere* of the knowable to all that actually exhibited continuous progress. The positivist theory of religion and all kinds of 'agnosticism' (even Kant's entirely theoretical variety) bear witness to this. The positivist theory (and general epistemology) did not, it is true, make the mistake of 'ossifying' the mind by assuming an 'eternally' valid subjective a-priori. Hence, its theory of knowledge has the closest ties with sociology and historical evolution. *Therein* it is preferable to Kantian epistemology. But since positivism, having begun with sensualistic notions, therefore restricted the sphere of the knowable to the fields of steady cognitive advance, it came to regard the religious tendencies of mankind as a mere *historical* category. Not content with denying that religious thirst could ever be quenched by knowledge of God, it saw in the very *thirst*—the very craving and quest for final, absolute knowledge of the world-basis—an atavism for the 'modern man' of the 'positive' era, that product of progress so different from man in the religious-theological and metaphysical ages.* But let us not jump to the conclusion that the fundamental error of positivism as a historical epistemology can be found where its opponents have often sought it: it does not lie in its assumption that the 'religious sense', the organ of religious cognition (and equally the sense of metaphysical curiosity, which is clearly distinct) has undergone a certain *recession* in the course of history—notably in Western Europe. Within strictly definable limits, that assumption is correct. No, this is what constitutes the gravest error: in the first place positivism considers that, like religious and metaphysical insatiability and 'problem'-anxiety, religious cravings—which in the final analysis are founded in love of God (still ideally indeterminate)—have diminished in just the same way as man's positive capacity to satisfy them by vital, percipient contact with transcendental being; secondly, from the mere *fact* that this capacity for knowing and making contact with the absolute has declined, positivism draws the wholly unwarranted conclusion that *nothing* of what an earlier humanity thought to have discovered by this then-more-active capacity for spontaneous apprehension of the transcendental—could in any way possess a *final*, objective validity, a truth and value independent of its discovery's time and place, and of later alterations in the human mental structure. A somewhat arrogant assumption! For, even if positivism rightly detected a decline (in European man) of the organ of religious cognition, one would still not be entitled to infer that religious knowledge is an illusion; if there are other grounds for believing that religious and meta-physical knowledge is *at all* possible and genuine, one should rather conclude the opposite—that the older and later humanity in whom these organs show a progressive decline should *preserve in faith* the transcendental realities which a younger humanity *saw* and *experienced*. One should further conclude that later humanity, by reason of its increasing mental adaptation to the merely relative, or more relative, levels of existence (which has the result of perfecting the intellectual organs of world-mastery) should take over the more *pedagogic and technical* tasks of mankind —this on account of its special aptitude for *incorporating* into the stubborn reality of the more relative levels all the values and truths which earlier humanity *beheld and won* through *its* leaning toward the absolute. It has not even entered the mind of positivists as a possible hypothesis that there could be any regular historical *division of functions* between earlier and later mankind, in respect of cognition, volition and discovery of values, based on the specific aptitudes of the great evolutionary phases for particular *kinds* and methods of cognition; in particular it has not occurred to them that the subjective knowability of real things may be trending, as humanity ages, from the absolute level to increasingly more relative levels of exis-tence. Moved and determined by the quite distinctively *European*—even *west*-European—frame of mind in which they received *every* historical fact; attuned, even in this limitation, to the *progressing* sectors of knowledge alone; entirely overlooking, moreover, whatever 'cognitive' functions* may lie outside the 'intellect', in the *emotional* nucleus of man—the positivists failed to wonder whether the *positive* evolutionary trend which *one* part of man's cognitive powers exhibits (in addition to the accumulation of results) might not be matched by the opposite tendency to *decadence* or recession of another part, in such a way that progress and decadence are aspects of *one and the same* mutation in the *whole* of the human mind.

The dogma of human progress, accepted without proof even in reference to metaphysics and religion, led positivism to a whole series of erroneous conceptions, of which I shall here mention only a few.

1. Failure to understand the peculiar nature of the specifically religious organs of cognition produced a misunderstanding in principle of the total significance of the world of religious categories (revelation, illumination, grace, divination, etc.). Ultimately this means looking on religion as a kind of primitive, imperfectly scientific explanation of world and nature, with the consequent assumption that every advance in the gradual perfecting of science must subtract a corresponding part of the religious consciousness.[1] Positivism took not the slightest heed of the fact that from the outset religion always centres on *one* object which is a closed book to the constitution of positive science; centres on an object which the unchanging category of *holiness* delimits in its *primarily* given value-aspect, and the category of absolute and infinite being in its existential aspect—an object to which there correspond quite definite *attitudes* of the emotional sensibility and cognitive faculties, attitudes that are inappropriate to all finite things and can at most be occasioned by them when they offer a means of representing or making contact with the divine. There was in consequence a failure to see the principle, fundamental to any theory of religious history, that *religious experience and its object form a closed and autonomous whole.*

2. Another fact which was left out of account is the following: even if we are unable to form mental images or ideas about things on the absolute level of existence, or even if our ideas are vague and clouded compared with the corresponding *value*-impressions, which are plain and clear—we *can* still have those very definite and characteristic value-experiences; at all events our emotional relationship with the transcendental *precedes* all our formation of ideas about it, and guides, governs that formation—in the nature of things our emotional sensibility has a less limited and more inclusive range of value-apprehension than our mental perception and intellect.

3. Positivism offers the following historical reconstruction of the development of religion: in the beginning came fetishism, animism, magic and shamanism, then different forms of polytheism 'developed' from them in various ways (*e.g.* 'animation' of realms of nature, ancestor-worship) and finally, by way of the gradual preponderance of one of the accredited gods, henotheism and monotheism came into being. The mere historical facts are sufficient to disprove this account.[2] It is scarcely more than a wishful attempt to read into the history of religion the same 'progress-

---

[1] See Vol. 1, Ch. 6 of Comte's *Sociologie.*

[2] Our present scientific knowledge of the religion of primitive peoples, notably the pygmies, which points to an original monotheism, utterly destroys the positivist thesis. See Andrew Lang, *The Making of Religion*, London 1898, and W. Schmidt, *Der Ursprung der Gottesidee*, Münster 1912.

pattern' which we observe in the exact science of western Europe. It is a construct making general use of two false principles. The first is that a Weltanschauung gradually coalesces by principles of association from the amassing of separate impressions (*i.e.* not that details of experience arise by analysis from original overall impressions). The second is that everything which transcends sensual elements in an impression of an entity must be embellishment due to human weakness. Both principles are untrue even of the simplest sensory perception.[1] Applied to religious experience, they become the grossest sources of error. The most primitive 'fetish' presents the irreducible nature of the divine, however clumsily, as a total sphere of absolute being that has all the attributes of holiness. Invariably this fetish is no more than a kind of window through which that *whole* of absolute holy being is envisaged, and (somehow) felt and seen, by the religious intention; it is not an isolated natural object into which the beholder has 'felt' or 'inlaid' some kind of psychic vitality.

Even with regard to these primitive religious constructs, the same 'facts' of research in ethnology and the history of religion take on—as cannot be shown here—an entirely different meaning, and for the first time a *religious meaning*. This happens when we proceed from the following assumption: that a *per se* identical, total natural revelation of absolute reality, invading (as it were) from all sides and through all kinds of media, is received often in utterly dissimilar ways by the different kinds of human association (peoples, races, etc.) and individual—is taken in, sifted, divided up and subsequently, by the rationalization and systematization of the isolated religious intuitions, united into a whole with the content of all other kinds of cognitive awareness relating to the world and the inner self. The *ladder of revelation* is not in the least called into question by the assumption of a *universal natural revelation* (as the lowest rung of all)— certainly not the knowledge, beginning in Judaism with the Old Testament, of the *content* of revelation as content of the *revelation* of a personal God. By this is meant knowledge of the specific *truth* of this revelation, as distinct from 1. merely 'presumptive' revelation and 2. the merely relative value for salvation of other revelations among peoples. The Christian Church must 'relativize' even the revelation of the Old Testament inasmuch as it must in the first place distinguish the pure revealed

[1] In support of this contention one should note the overwhelming lesson of the theoretic and experimental phenomenological and psychological investigations into perception which have been carried out by Husserl and his pupils, as well as by Külpe, Bühler, Wertheimer, Köhler, Koffka, Grünbaum, Jaensch, von Hornbostel, etc. A preliminary survey of the main results of this research is to be found in A. Messer's *Einleitung in die Psychologie* and in Koffka's series of articles on the '*Psychologie der Wahrnehmung*', in the periodical *Die Geisteswissenschaften*, 1914.

M

content of the Old Testament from the plane of the secular knowledge of nature and history also within it[1]—and in that it secondly must see the perfect and unsurpassable self-revelation of God exclusively in Christ as the *accomplisher* of the history of salvation. In the concept of *original revelation*, moreover, the Christian Church possesses a category which, rightly interpreted, leads of itself to our theory—provided that the immense amount of new material in the history of religion, which formerly lay hidden, is recognized. It is a question not of a new category, but of the application of given doctrinal categories. To assume there may be germs of true revelation in other religions, outside the religious-historical framework of Judaeo-Christian evolution, contradicts *no* essential idea of Christian doctrine. In fact it only strengthens the true 'catholicity' of the Church to whose principles it belongs never to reject the true merely because it is either *inadequately* true, or only true in reference to objects (*e.g.* popular deities) that, unbeknown to the men in question, are relative in existence; or merely because the particular object of which the truth in question is true is not yet clearly known (such as when the institution of God known as the moral world-order is taken to be God himself—*scil.* the 'heaven' of the Chinese). Least of all should the true be rejected only because it is often mingled with the false. Much has been given out as the content of revelation which is not that, and many a thing which—judged by its value for salvation—is a thing of genuine revelation appears embedded in false or imperfect secular knowledge. Supernaturalistic belief in the total 'exclusiveness' of the Judaeo-Christian revelation, which modern liberal theologians, for example Ernst Troeltsch, are inclined to treat as an essential ingredient of 'positive' theology (both Protestant and Catholic), is in spirit a feature solely of Protestant theology of Lutheran and Calvinistic provenance.[2] In so far as the conception may at times be found in 'Catholic scholarship', it is not grounded in the imperishable doctrine of the Church but in the narrowness of the historico-religious *material* with which one has been working for centuries.

4. No less grave is the positivist error concerning the evolution of the

[1] The highest principle applicable to this distinction is that of the unity and necessary harmony of, on one side, revelation and the truth of salvation and, on the other, rational secular wisdom. This principle is wrongly applied (in the sense of a false conservatism) if progressive secular knowledge is simply measured by what 'passed' up to then as unadulterated, 'pure' revealed knowledge. For the advance of secular knowledge has the *positive* significance, for this very purpose of refining the Bible's truth of salvation from the secular dross, of being a means of *reducing* all putative revelation to its pure substance.

[2] This is most apparent in the position which this theology takes up *vis-à-vis* the wisdom and religion of the ancients, which is an attitude of brusque dismissal, wholly unable to share Origen's and Clement's view of them as a heuristic *preparation* of Christian truths.

human mind and of religion as a part of its activity. This is a consequence of wrongful generalization, as to the past and future evolution of all mankind, from certain evolutionary trends of the *west-European capitalist age*. The positivist theory of world-history is only the historical self-projection of the west-European middle class, in which the 'spirit of capitalism' has automatically determined the ideals of knowledge and morality. It is more than the one-sided *'Europeanism'* of Hegel and Hartmann—more, that is, than a judgment and measurement of universal history against forms of ideal and assessment which are applicable only to Europe and need not in principle survive European civilization—: it is also the *class* philosophy of modern industrial enterprise, bent solely on the expansion of power, to which it subordinates all other values. The theory was born with the industrial bourgeoisie, and it will die with the ousting of that class from the conduct of nations and states. What then is but an episodic and—in the frame of world-history—*momentary diversion* of the merely European mind from its religious destiny, namely its exclusive concentration or the *savoir pour prévoir* required for technical world-control, is held by the positivist to be a universal human tendency, which will prolong itself into an indefinite future.

Just as history has shown that the increasing specialization and *dominance* of the merely technical intellect has led to a decline in human capacity for religious knowledge of transcendental forces, so the *social* conditions and forms of life requisite for the rise of new religions have been gradually dismantled by the very 'progress of civilization'. The transition from the organic community to social groupings based on coincident ambition or class, the path taken by all human associations,[1] precludes the sociological conditions in which alone a new religion could arise. It is for this reason, too, that all recent attempts, such as those of Comte, Hegel, von Hartmann, to set up new religious dogma and religious authority have so *utterly* failed. Here again the task of present and future humanity can only be to *preserve* the true and great, the all-embracing forms of community which religion created, and only could create, in earlier times—when it was possible to do so—: to preserve, vivify and reform them, and at best to *bind* them more tightly and deeply together, by striving for the union of Churches.

This insistence on the improbability of 'new religions' in the future history of mankind will astound, or fill with melancholy, only those unable to grasp the *essential* differences, set forth in this book, between

[1] This is made profoundly clear by F. Tönnies in *Gemeinschaft und Gesellschaft*, 2nd edition.

religious and philosophical, or religious and scientific knowledge. Or it will disconcert those who, like the positivists, attach each of the three permanent aptitudes inherent in the mind, one for each kind of cognition (aptitudes which may well lie hidden or submerged at times, but never replace each other), to *historical phases* of mankind; or those who gnostically expect religion to merge in a superior philosophy—ignoring the fact that religion has its *origin*, its own autonomous criterion, in a special type of personal humanity: the *homo religiosus*.

Another person whom these ideas are likely to bewilder and upset is the man who refuses to recognize the *functional division*, in the history of the mind, between the acquisition of the religious groundwork of life and the technical incorporation of acquired fundamentals into the earthly realities of this world—by a process of intellectual discovery.

To whoever avoids these errors, the task of preserving the store of religious blessings which exist as a vital force among us, of preserving them and procuring them in richer abundance for the souls of men—this task appears nobler and worthier than the misconceived urge to invent, where the watchword can only be—

> Long years ago the true was found,
> Long noble souls in league has bound:
> Cleave to the true, the old and tried.[1]

[1] *Das Wahre war schon längst gefunden,*
Hat edle Geisterschaft verbunden,
Das alte Wahre fass es an (Goethe).

CHRISTIAN LOVE AND
THE TWENTIETH CENTURY

CHRISTIAN LOVE AND
THE TWENTIETH CENTURY
An Address

I N every healthy human resides the ability to observe all world-events on different planes of attention. Even the barbarous spectacle of the war raging about us comes under this rule.[1] On what plane we were to concentrate when the war began, on what plane we still dwell day by day in our active share of its conduct, direct or indirect, in the field or at home —this was a decision in which our hearts allowed and allow us no choice. Before all else, our hearts spoke out clearly the one word—*Deutschland!* In fervent, ever newly welling thankfulness for what this dear land has daily given and gives to our bodies and our souls, we feel in the deepest roots of our being that we are the products of its soil and history. In all humility we recognize the good there is, likewise the necessary limitation, in the fact that God has inextricably woven our souls (which he directly made) into the history of this land and the destiny of Germany. So there may well be no time or peace for us in which to take up another attitude to world-events than the one which is summarized in the name of our home. Wherever a thousand compulsions turn the eyes of each one of us day after day: to the fortunes of our loved ones, our families, friends, relations, brothers in village, town or region; to the economic want of ourselves and others, now and in the future—all these ever-changing preoccupations of a lower plane are gathered in one bright, steady beam within our minds, a beam focused on Germany. And so it will, so it must remain until we come to an honourable peace. As yet we have no right, as *practically* active beings, to raise our attention to a plane which, apart from the alleviation of individual war-suffering,[2] would look out over the towering ramparts of the—thank God—still unharmed stronghold of Germany. As yet we have no right to care *practically* for the world in any sense.

[1] The date is 1917 (*Translator*).
[2] Perhaps Scheler is thinking of the internationalism of the Red Cross (*Translator*).

However that may be, in those still hours for which practical care for Germany still leaves us leisure, we may also think of the world: *the world*, in whose wholeness and unity the Creator who made both world and souls has set us down to love him, glorify him and obey him. We not only may but should think of the world. We should do it firstly for the sake of the *one* holy blood which flowed for this one world of solidary sin and guilt, flowed for the common tribulations, so marvellously interwoven, of all the children of Adam, of all creatures indeed. But we should also do it that we may illumine our minds and hearts and free them to perform in the *right* way our practical service to Germany; ultimately this means in a manner pleasing to God.

It is to such a quiet hour of recollection that I invite you today, an hour in which we should dare to project our minds beyond Germany to the world.

Before I begin, permit me one other observation, which perhaps may facilitate our understanding. Let us try for a while to break free from all wonted ways of thought and feeling, from all prejudices which party-feeling, daily conversation and the Press have instilled in us on the subject of the World War. Let us try to look on the spectacle about us with clear and uncommitted eyes—as if they belonged to a European of some bygone era, who enters our century as a guest and looks about him with amazement. Let us cast an exact, kindly and judicious eye, one yet religious and metaphysical—I was going to say *alienated*—enough to see everything around us not only as the individual, long-accustomed reality of the day (and perhaps our eye has grown all too used even to this slaughter and hatred), but as the *symbol* of the peculiar moral status of European man today.

At the *centre* of the moral way of life we call Christian stands the powerful commandment: Thou shalt love God with all thy heart and with all thy mind and thy neighbour as thyself. What feeling and what thought must imbue the man who, uninfluenced by history or by interpretation, looks on the miseries of our Europe from the viewpoint of this principle? The more seriously he takes the commandment, the more his feeling must be one of despair. And his thought?—the *bankruptcy of Christianity* or, as has also been heard, the 'abrogation of the Sermon on the Mount'. Let us not waste a moment in surprise that this verdict is passed as self-evident not only by Japanese, Chinese and Indians (as for example, quite recently, by the Indian poet Tagore in his Tokio address,[1] which is well worth reading)—but by many Europeans of all nations, whose views are entitled to respect. What else should be the verdict of an uncommitted

[1] Cf. in the book *Nationalismus*, Leipzig 1919.

mind? Write whole volumes for the defence, bring forth every possible argument—every plain man will answer:

'Black is not white. Whatever you tell me of the true sense of the commandment, or of the sections of European humanity which are supposed to bear the "guilt" of the event, what led up to it and how it came about—all that to me is a matter of *utter* indifference. What does it all matter to me? It merely serves to cloud my judgment: as you know, if anyone goes into the details of causes he usually succeeds only in confusing his clear sense of the value of the situation he is called upon to judge. The fact of the matter is simply this: Europe calls itself Christian and for nearly two thousand years it has been laying Christian principles before its children. And one of the results of almost two thousand years of Christian education is a wholesale atrocity the like of which the world had never seen, one to which the whole resources of the intellect, technology, industry, the written and spoken word, are devoted. *That* is the fact I'm interested in. I call that giving the lie to the Sermon on the Mount.'

That is the opinion of the impartial onlooker. Do we ourselves take any other attitude than his, when we enter a home where filth, disorder, the low talk of the children, everything under our eyes, testifies to a *total* condition of moral putrefaction? Such a condition is indivisible— irrespective of how it arose, whose 'fault' it is, whether the father's, the mother's, the great-grandfather's or anyone else. Every human experience of a deeper kind teaches that such group-guilt can never be wholly broken down into the guilt of individuals. Every attentively pondered experience teaches that the deeper we penetrate the moral interrelations of such a family, the more the unfathomable reciprocity of guilt is brought to light. The world of Christian ideas contains the important concepts of collective and hereditary guilt, which any deeply considered philosophy will confirm.[1] We ought to know them not only as the dogma of original sin, and not only in reference to the entire human race, but also in reference to specific ages, civilizations, nations. Thus the Christian will also have to regard the European anarchy of this war, or rather this *Kriegsrevolution*, as resting on a collective original sin of the last few centuries in European history.

But though the reproach of the 'bankruptcy of Christianity' is understandable, this much is no less so: Any person who has grasped the figure of Christ in faith as the sublimest model and exemplar of every human heart—*cannot* recognize as true the proposition that Christianity is bankrupt, once and for all, in Europe. What then should a man in that position do?

[1] See Part 2 of my *Formalismus in der Ethik, etc.**

Above all he should *not* acquiesce in facile and over-hasty 'explaining away', whether it comes from the ranks of unbelief or those of non-genuine sham faith. When radical unbelief speaks of Christian bankruptcy, it means the following: 'It is not the men, not the channels of Christian thought, which have gone bankrupt: it is Christian morality, the ideals themselves. The Christian ideal contradicts the very nature of man, demanding what he cannot perform; it should be replaced by another, more honest and more practicable one. Has not the deep-rooted tension between the demands of the Sermon on the Mount and the historical realities of politics, business and social relations always been with us? Is it not at most a merely quantitative difference which separates today from every yesterday in European history? So let us not try to change man, for that is impossible. Let us rather change our *moral standards* themselves; let us abandon this misleading, high-flown ideal; let us give it up for a new ideal—the greatest power, the greatest wellbeing, the highest cultural achievement' (or whatever else may represent these modern ideals).

In all circumstances this kind of argument must be condemned, with however many reasons it may be armed. For no matter how a man may envisage the content of the clear and manifest idea of good—whether it be Christian or not—tht idea must never be abandoned simply because men fail to make it a reality. The ideal must never be adjusted to reality and lowered to the plane of real conditions. The good must *be*, even if it never and nowhere comes into being, as Kant rightly said. This principle does not depend on the positive content imparted to the idea of good by the Christian commandment of love: it lies already in its formal nature.*
If the Christian ideal is a false teaching, this cannot be *because* man has fallen so far short of it or trodden it underfoot. Certainly there has always existed this *tension* between the earthly laws of political and social life and the great commandment. But tension is not the same thing as contradiction: the two are different in essence, not degree. That what exists is in this respect 'no more' than tension, but that tension *does* exist, is part and parcel of Christian doctrine, which moreover *explains* this very tension by the Fall, by sin and the need for redemption.

The tension is not meant to sunder the unity of our life into two separate halves, so that on the one hand we might as mere living creatures follow the urges to power and ambition, submitting ourselves and our nation to none but this-worldly 'rules of clean fighting', while as souls we remained open in faith (or in the 'depths of our hearts') to receive God and the blessings of salvation. The Christian explanation gives us no right to such a separation of spheres. It is a path of error—one which is the peculiar danger of the Germanic soul. It is the path of a wrongful division between God and world, soul and body, intention and deed, faith and works, *external freedom—political and social—and the 'inner' freedom of the mind: hence the divorce of politics from morality*.* Lutheran Protestantism, in contrast to the teaching and practice of Calvin's and Zwingli's foundations, has unhappily allowed this hereditary Germanic fault to penetrate deep into its dogmatic teaching, and no less into its ethical conceptions. It has powerfully contributed to the erection in the German nation of a false ideal, an exclusive *inwardness** recognized even where there is no express acknowledgment of Lutheranism. With it goes an *exclusive* ethic of private conviction[1] which, to preserve the purity of the inner world of the spirit, removes all political and public life from the jurisdiction of the Christian moral law, abandoning it to the cut and thrust of earthly powers, to Machiavellian *Machtpolitik*.[2] If, however, we refrain from sinfully abandoning the task, the task of incorporating the spirit of Christ into visible public life, into the reality of group-relations, we must offer the following reply to those unbelievers who put Christian morality *itself* in the dock: There still lies before us, for our task of incorporation, an immeasurable future; though, compared with other earthly institutions, Christianity is certainly old, it is still young and fresh to every person who has clearly grasped the meaning of endurance implicit in religious values when compared with cultural values in general.

But it is when we cling to Christian fundamentals, above all to the *commandment of love*, when we neither dilute them to the milk and water of welfare-morality nor show them the exit from all public life—it is then, precisely, that the other sense of Christian 'bankruptcy' strikes Europe the most forcefully. *If* this commandment is eternal, if it is absolute—however it may impinge on public life—then how much more fearful is the aberration of European history! And whose fault is the bankruptcy? Some say it should be laid at the door of the administrators of Christian law: that is, the Churches, who strayed from their duty, or their representatives—priests, preachers, teachers. Quite wrong! say others: one should blame the 'modern world's' falling-away from those Churches, or from a Church. Whatever the proportions of truth and falsity in either judgment, we are left with the clear *alternatives*: either Christianity *is* still in fact the leading spiritual force in Europe, or it is not. If it is still the leading spiritual force, still the substantial nucleus of the collective European mind, then

[1] Scheler's special terms here are *Nurinnerlichkeit* and *Nurgesinnungsethik*. *Gesinnung* means 'private attitude' or 'inviolable personal reaction' or 'inner consistency' (*Translator*).

[2] Books like that of O. Baumgarten, *Politik und Moral* (Tübingen 1916), exhibit this attitude to the point of caricature.

Christianity, at least in its representatives, its great representative bodies, is bankrupt. Only if it can be shown that Christianity has *lost* this leading rôle, has been forced to relinquish it to other, inimical spiritual forces, hence only to the extent that Christianity is suppressed, impotent, underground, *can* the reproach be logically and rightfully cast back as the opposite charge: that not Christianity but the hostile *modern spirit* is bankrupt. I put this choice to you bluntly. For I have the impression that there is a widespread attitude abroad, a lukewarm and insipid, not to say muddle-headed or dishonest way of thinking, which wishes to have the cake and eat it: to prove both that Christian moral principles *are* still Europe's leading spiritual force, still the *substratum* of the European mind, and that Christianity *nevertheless* is not bankrupt but thriving famously and waxing fat. Now that is taking the reproach (*e.g.* of all educated Asia) far too lightly and dismissing it at far too little cost. This fearful question is *not* concerned with the situation of France, Germany or any one European country, but that *fundamental trend* of modern *all*-European history which led to the War. Therefore, all those Europeans who, mocked and ridiculed by the whole of Asia, wish to place the responsibility fairly and squarely on the nation that fought their own, remain far *below* the problem's magnitude and gravity. The more it is wrong to saddle our nation or our government with a special responsibility for *common* European iniquities, the more it is wrong to ignore that *because* they are common to all Europe they include and do not exculpate Germany. On this point all the disputation of the belligerents must fall silent, if to the evident fact of Europe's falling-away from Christianity there is not to be added the grotesque and pitiful spectacle of professed Christian nations, the supposed members of a grand Christian Europe, squabbling away each other's claims to represent the faith.

Let us therefore beware of these wrongful ways of meeting the accusation of Christian bankruptcy. As I see it, we must before all else honestly admit to ourselves as to our accusers: the Christian ethos is no longer the leading spirit of Europe. However widely true Christian feeling may be spread among groups and individuals, however widely Christian *ethics*, the mere *theory* of the vital ethos, may be formally or intellectually acknowledged outside the Church and outside religion, the vital driving power which steers and leads the public and cultural life of Europe is *no longer* this moral force. This does not merely mean that its rules are, more or less, transgressed in practice. Such transgression has always taken place, even if the extent of it differed; that is not a matter of ethos but of practical morality.* No; it means that Christian norms and ideals *themselves*, where they influence the life of the soul in the 'stirrings of conscience', likewise the *principles* of value-judgment and preference (not merely as conscious but as divulged by practice), *no longer* inspire and guide that 'objective spirit' which has suffered defeat in works, forms, institutions, manners and customs. For the adherent of the Christian way of thought that is a fearful admission. But it is a necessary admission.

The second step of the Christian, shocked by this first admission, should be to attempt to trace the *causes* of Europe's demoralization—an enormous task which it is out of the question that I should seriously embark on here. For it concerns the genealogy of the whole mode of moral awareness which took over the reins of Europe from the Christian ethos, a mode which I would like to define by its historical period and social milieu as the *ethos of the modern bourgeois capitalist mind*. The third step would be to analyse carefully the prevailing trends of our age in all fields of value (culture, economics, law, government, etc.), and in different European nations, in order to discover which of them are favourable to the goal of raising the Christian ethos once more to the leadership of Europe's public affairs— and which are not. One would also seek to discover what the experience of the War—as a collective experience of Europe and indeed the world— can contribute to a change of heart and what guiding ideal emerges from comparison of actual conditions with the eternal aspirations of Christianity. *This*, it seems to me, not the biassed indictment or exculpation of the Christian Church, of separate Churches or their members, is the only way in which the bitter verdict of bankruptcy can be bravely met, and offers the only hope of alleviation in the deep torture of the Christian conscience when faced with the inner condition—*exposed*, not created, by the War—of Europe's ruling classes and cadres.

Today let us take just one of the central constituents of the Christian ethos, *the commandment of love*,[1] together with the ideas and norms of community which follow from it, hence the *Christian idea of community*, in order to show how, in a spiritual sense, the public reins of Europe have slipped from their grasp.

It is a coalition of the most heterogeneous spiritual forces which in the course of history have lent each other partial assistance from time to time and have at last combined in effect to defeat the Christian ethos and oust it from the place of European leadership. The most important of these forces, if we may characterize them in summary form, are the following:

1. Humanitarianism, taking the place of the Christian commandment of love;

[1] See my treatment of '*Das Ressentiment im Aufbau der Moralen*' in the collection of essays and articles entitled *Vom Umsturz der Werte*.

2. Doctrinaire individualism or socialism, inasmuch as both contravene the Christian idea of the moral solidarity of autonomous persons;

3. The 'absolute' and 'sovereign' State with an unbounded will to power and domination, the concept which shattered feudalism;

4. Modern political nationalism and its attendant exclusive cultural nationalism—the latter in opposition to the Christian idea that national cultures, though each irreplaceable, should be complementary members of an all-embracing world-culture;

5. The idea of the 'autonomy' of culture. This has supplanted the ideas and criteria of Christian cultural community, according to which art, philosophy and science should be integrated in the edifice of the ultimate, supreme and all-including human community: the visible and invisible Body of Christ, the Church and its spirit. No longer is the creative work of culture to proceed by the harmonious collaboration, in mutual sympathy, of contemporary peoples and successive generations. Instead it is to run its course in independence of such religious inspirations. Harmonious co-operation in the construction of *one* diversified edifice is replaced as incentive and driving-wheel by competition and rivalry among nations and generations. A group of phenomena results from this outlook: sometimes they appear as relativism, sometimes as historicism or skepticism. That is with regard to the chronological succession of generations; the consequence with regard to rivalry among contemporary nations is of course an increasing alienation of one culture from another, and the progressive dissolution of Europe's spiritual unity.

6. The replacement of organic communities and social groupings, joined in a living solidarity, by societies based merely on arbitrary legal contracts and closed for the attainment of sectional objectives, with a corresponding preponderance of human affiliation to *class* and grouping by property.

7. The bourgeois-capitalist economic ethos of unrestricted production and accumulation of capital (whether by individual, State or consortium) —of free competition working itself out in full, with State policy as the sole limiting factor. This has replaced the Christian economic ethos, the constant limiting factor of which is formed by the supreme principles of Christian conduct, and according to which all productive groups should be organized in solidarity of aim to supply the needs of the community.

It is on these points that we are now going to focus our attention.*

1. HUMANITARIANISM AND THE CHRISTIAN COMMANDMENT OF LOVE

Humanitarianism rebels against the first principle of the Christian commandment of love: 'Love God first above all things'—with the immediate corollary, 'Therefore love your neighbour *in* God, and always in reference to the highest good.' To one degree or another and in various ways it rebelled against the commandment in successive periods of classical renascence, in the age of 'humanism', and with special force during the Enlightenment. All these great movements worked to construct an ethos which *isolates* man from God and often indeed plays man off against God. Even where it leaves Christian values *in situ* there is a change in the emotion and spiritual act called love of man or love of one's neighbour. What is primarily envisaged by the new 'love of man' (of man alone) is no longer his invisible spirit, his soul and his salvation, solidarily included in the salvation of all children of God, with his bodily welfare taking an incidental place as a condition of his perfection and happiness. Moreover, humanity is its concern only in the contemporaneous sense of those who happen to be living at the time, not in the sense of men linked across history nor against the backcloth of a supernatural order embracing the souls of the dead. It envisages man the external phenomenon, his sensual well-being. And increasingly it envisages this well-being in isolation from the objective hierarchy of real and spiritual goods, which rises by degrees to the highest good. What is more, even in so far as love is still upheld as the deepest source of all good volition and conduct, and is not replaced, or intended to be replaced, by a purely rational, formal principle of righteousness (as also happened, for instance, in Kant), love *as* love, or as represented in the *sacrifice*, is no longer regarded as intrinsically the highest in value of all spiritual acts, one infinitely ennobling man and making him like to Christ. No; love now appears valuable only at second hand, as a means of promoting the welfare and sensual contentment of man or social groups. Of course, even in the Christian view we should on all occasions seek to further the welfare of our society, economically, socially, in respect of public health and so on. The very unity of existence and activity between body and soul puts that duty upon us, and it is no less enjoined by the insight of those who apply morality, that the lower the values in question the greater the *practical* possibility of perfecting men in that direction.* But in the final analysis we should promote welfare for the sake of the dignity of man's *spiritual* personality; within that dignity the crown and nucleus is the freest and purest readiness to love. It is in the way of humility, in free and loving service, that this very dignity must reach perfection. We should further the welfare of man so that he may become *ripe* to love and in loving sow the seed of all virtues.[1] But humanitarian love of man does not desire welfare for the sake of man's capacity for love—as corresponds to the parable of the widow's mite—but on the contrary demands love for the sake of welfare. Thereby the true concept of loving sacrifice is destroyed root and branch, and the Christian ethos of love is replaced by one of welfare on earth. Let us not be surprised, therefore, that the new kind of love of man or mankind is so eager to range itself against love of God, that it often in fact takes the form of a kind of suppressed hatred of God, a conscious insurrection against him and his order—against everything in human values, works, institutions which towers above those natural features in man which are *merely* common and generic, hence the substratum of *lowest values*.

This modern 'love of mankind'—an expression strictly absent from the Christian vocabulary—is a strongly revolutionary fervour and pre-eminently one which levels to uniformity all the objective value-differences between man and man. It is not a *spiritual act* of the soul but a seething, intemperate sensual pathos. As such it was especially active in Rousseau, and in its name the Robespierres and Marats were to storm and rage a few years later. Levelling brings in its train the habit of arranging men in inorganic units, of standardizing and centralizing—in other words, of obliterating the unique God-ordained character of each individual, class, race or nation in favour of a homogenized world-*purée* of mankind, the 'universal State' or world-republic, etc. From this it is no great step to the dangerous custom of pitting the merely larger unit against the smaller *as a proper object of love* (mankind *versus* homeland; nation and State *versus* regional loyalties, and so on).* No longer is it the higher *qualitative* value, the purer value-content, the value nearer to God as the supreme good, which a *well-ordered* love should prefer, but the mere greater number of men. An Englishman called Bentham was even simple enough to recommend the formula, 'the greatest happiness of the greatest number'.

We now see clearly the full significance, so fraught with consequence for men and the right ordering of their affairs, of the humanitarian erasure of the *first part of the commandment of love*. Once the common reference of all men to *God* is denied, and with it the final, deepest and most effective interconnection of souls, their link in and through God, it is *impossible* to go on assuming any *hierarchy* of values to which our love should be directed in varying measure according to definite laws of preference. At the same time we lose all firm basis for belief in a stable, integrated order of the

---

[1] In the sense of Augustine's *Ama et fac quod vis.*

communities appropriate to the preservation and attainment of the various kinds of good (Church, State, family, municipality, classes, professions, etc.). Therefore the new humanitarian love of man (and only man) is as much a principle of levelling and disintegration as the Christian commandment of love is one of edification and *organization*.

It is impossible to describe here in detail the great spiritual movements in Europe which have led to the displacement of the Christian commandment by humanitarianism. Allow me to give but a brief sketch of two phases in their history. One is the Reformation, the other the transition from the Enlightenment to the 'realistic' ideology of the nineteenth century.

Nothing was less in tune with the spirit of the *Reformers* (Luther especially) than humanitarianism. Quite the reverse prevailed in their teachings, where man, his will and works appear as little self-sufficient and as helpless as may be conceived; free-will is rejected in favour of a grace regarded as well-nigh forcibly imposed—though for all that it is not supposed that man, represented as wholly corrupted by the Fall, is well and truly rescued by grace from his passive state of sin, rescued and sanctified: grace is only assumed to bestow on man a pacific *awareness* that punishments are remitted by faith in Jesus' redeeming blood. Everywhere we see the spirit of the Reformation working in the strongest opposition to humanism, the Renaissance and their ideals of human cultivation nurtured by Greek or Roman poets and philosophers. Yet it was the movement of Reform which most contributed to the spread in Europe of the idea that *all* human associations and corporate entities should look for their final cement and cohesion to purely *secular* and natural psychic forces, absolved (as it were) from reference to God. For however profound and beautiful are for example Luther's dicta on the communal life of man, on marriage, family, the Church and the State, man's essential reference to God, essential indeed for *salvation*, was located wholly on one side, in the depth of the isolated *individual* soul and its faith. The entire group of psychic acts we may term *social*—love, promising, pardon, ruling, serving and the like—were no longer held to possess direct significance for salvation. 'The individual soul and its God'—in this sole interchange was to reside all the meaning of salvation. Only as a *consequence* of the forgiveness and justification reached through faith was it expected that living faith would generate love and community, so that each man would then be the Christ of the others. Though in this way all associations remained amenable to retrospective sanction they were withdrawn from the *primary control* and guidance of the *commandment of love for salvation's sake*. Can this be given any other name than capitulation to the forces, passions, instincts of the purely natural man? The immediate destruction was of course confined to one idea—the unitary concept of an invisible yet visible Church as God-ordained for collective salvation. But once the great principle of reciprocity was shattered at this *supreme* point in human life where it takes the form of solidary salvation, once love in the unity and community of one Church of God was considered a mere offshoot of the salvation won by each separate individual—no longer a true way to God and salvation, parallel to the other in necessity and original institution—, then the principle of solidarity, and men's sense of it, were doomed to crumble, beginning there at the crux, at the centre of the soul's life and strength, and spreading by degrees to *all* kinds of community. Government, industry, culture, research, creative activity—all of which are essentially communal occupations—were now to be separate and 'autonomous', each going its way or developing in accordance with laws that know no God. Exclusive—mark the adjective—*exclusive* individualism in religion gradually brought in its train political, cultural, at length economic individualism.

But this modification of the ethos had a quite special effect, which has prolonged itself into the present. When men are bound together in a society by common historical fate, territory, race or other elementary factor, what do they do if they can no longer unite in the supreme and ultimate object over which men can unite, namely their faith, their reference to the *basis and meaning of the world*? Imagine a marriage between two persons who are of disparate beliefs, though they are drawn together in deep love and in honest good will to live together, stay together and fight life's battle together. One day, for the first time, they fall out over some matter of conviction; overwhelmed, with pain-stricken hearts, they see that on this point they will never be able to think as one. Again it happens, then a third, a fourth time. Each occasion leaves a scar, a deeply painful *memory* of the conflict between their faiths and their wills to love. Each time there grows in them a pressure which urges them not to touch this most vulnerable, tenderest point of their union—to put it out of sight, so to speak. And the result? At length the couple will take the step, at first to their great distress, but with a final gain of outward peace, of in principle *renouncing* agreement in what *must* remain the matter of their highest concern. 'Let sleeping dogs lie', they will tell themselves. And after that? Step by step they will *lower* the fields of activity, the spheres of value, in which they still look for agreement, lower and lower, level by level; in other words, they will be less and less prepared to unite over general norms, aims, purposes, and will restrict their joint ventures more and more to whatever is technical or mechanical, *i.e.* not ends but rather means, such as transactions and similar business. Renunciation of a joint stand on the question of the *supreme* good sets in motion a process which of its nature *cannot* be checked. On and on it goes, passing first to the good which is next most high, then to a somewhat lower good, and so it proceeds. To what final state, then, will it reduce man and wife? It may be— if they are strong, efficient, well-endowed persons—that in the end they will represent an intelligent social organism of remarkable quality, dazzlingly organized in everything technical, superbly disciplined in managing the '*how* shall I do a thing, when I want to do it?'—in all such things a firmly integrated unit. But—the *central* goal-setting, pattern-making, norm-dictating forces of the mind, the powers which have to decide the *what*, not the *how*,—*What* shall I do? *What* is my mission in the world?'—these, like any other non-functioning organ, will have ebbed for want of use into a final decay.

This simile is truly applicable to the Europe which has lost its harmonious common reference to God in one Church. Like the thrown rider clinging to the reins of a runaway it is being dragged and whirled breathlessly along by the logic of its affairs, its machines, manufactures, methods and techniques, and at this very moment its economic warfare, its murder-machines. This internal logic of a predominantly technical, practical civilization is unrestrained by the unifying supervision of any commonly recognized moral authority.

No less significant is the disregard of the first principle in the commandment of love: Love God above all. It implies the withering of the central, guiding, goal-setting forces in the European mind. That is the meaning of humanitarianism. But if the Christian commandment of love is driven out of visible public life, if the moral energies of Christianity are frustrated of outlet into public life, in the frame of the Church, and forbidden to engage in the realm of objective judgment, the only result must be to confine the influence of those energies to the inner realm of the individual.

The *Enlightenment* therefore needed only to complete a piecemeal demolition of early Protestantism's topheavy structure of supernaturalism with its dangerous abandonment of the task of *inbuilding* God's kingdom into this intractable world; what then remained was pure humanitarianism, the picture of a mankind without a leader or pattern in its basic objectives. Left to the random impulses of its natural instincts, this mankind had lost with its common reference to God the highest warrant of its unity. As Augustine so long ago had seen, this was a theomorphous idea of man.[1] That a parallel anarchy of Europe, such as we are undergoing in

[1] See '*Zur Idee des Menschen*' in *Vom Umsturz der Werte*.

the present upheaval, did not immediately appear, that God-forsaking humanitarianism did not at once put forth its full destructive powers, can be ascribed to the fact that during the Enlightenment, in realms of mind beyond critical awareness, the common traditions inculcated by centuries of Christian edification upon the subsoil of ancient values continued to function long *after* their conscious relegation, like the afterglow of a sun which has set. Or we may say that, like musicians who go on playing for a time when the conductor has suspended operations, the nations of Europe still appeared to be rehearsing their Concert. But the final anarchy was inevitable. In what the great thinkers of the Enlightenment—Voltaire, Kant or Wolff—called autonomous 'reason', that assemblage of allegedly timeless and historically changeless principles in ethics, logic, economics, jurisprudence, etc., the light of eternity still shone in fitful glimmers: even where men had long since closed their eyes to Christianity, its light still shone through.

In the nineteenth century the increasing bias to realism and historicism steadily extinguished those glimmers too. In logical pursuit of the humanitarian ethos it gradually whittled down that idea of the uniformity of rational human nature into which the Enlightenment had gathered all concepts of truth and falsity, good and evil, right and wrong. More and more exiguous, abstract and formal grew all that was to be understood as common and normative for all men as men. At length it was invisible and impalpable to the masses. What else remained? The idea of conflicting groups following their interests or instincts, be they races, nations, states or classes—a picture of fluctuating conflict of every kind, in which only one thing is of deciding importance: the brutal issue. Everything in the nature of an idea or norm, whether it be of morality or justice, which formerly was intended to govern the relationships of men, is now pressed into the service of these interests and instincts as a bludgeon, knife or other weapon: it becomes epiphenomenal, an old mask behind which group-egoisms pharisaically hide.

What furnished the clearest and most accurate expression of this inner condition of Europe was none of the 'idealistic' general theories which—in some quarters—drift like frail and helpless bubbles on the surface of 'cultivated minds', but the ideological worlds of Darwin and Marx.

Before I go on to show how the Christian ethos of love was displaced by the other spiritual forces I have named, it will be necessary to elaborate the basic definition of the Christian *idea of community* in its broadest sense, to determine its characteristics as they evolve from the commandment of love.

2. THE CHRISTIAN IDEA OF COMMUNITY

It is impossible to form any judgment about concrete questions of community without touching on the fundamental questions, What is the *nature* of community? To what ends do its essential forms exist?

The first underlying proposition from which we must proceed is this: man, the finite personal spirit (and only *as* such), does not live a communal life with other finite personal spirits from pure accident and only *de facto* (for, say, historical reasons or prompted by his positive knowledge of nature). No; it is inherent in the *eternal, ideal nature* of an intelligent person that all its existence and activity as a spirit is *ab origine* just as much an outward-conscious, co-responsible, communal reality as a self-conscious, self-responsible, individual reality. The being of a man is just as originally a matter of being, living and acting 'together' as a matter of existing for himself.* Notice that this statement is divided not by a hair-splitting nuance but by an immeasurable chasm from this other one: 'All men of which we have knowledge through personal experience or historical documents lived or live in a community.' The first expresses an eternal and essential truth which is definitive *per se* and implies an essential necessity. The second expresses a contingent experience which like all such may be severely limited or more comprehensive but can never be complete and definitive. All that is established from contingent experience can also be undone by fresh contingent experience. Even the logical subjects of the two propositions are quite different in substance and scope. The first is true of *all possible finite spiritual beings*, even those outside our earthly ken (*e.g.* the angelic host) or hidden from us now (*e.g.* the souls of the dead). In so far as they exist—and we believe they exist—they live in community. But one may go further: the first proposition is true and the second, in its strict sense, is wholly untrue. It is simply not true at all that every man known in history lived in community with other men. There have been Robinson Crusoes—recluses, hermits, solitaries, anchorites of all kinds. But it is the Robinson Crusoe who can help us to clarify the implications of *our* proposition. It implies that the conscious experience of '*belonging*' to a community, of being a 'member' of it, was present even in him, present just as originally as his individual 'I'-feeling or self-aware-ness. It implies that awareness of membership is a characteristic even of persons living in such isolation, and that the *mental intention* in the direction of community exists quite independently of whether it finds or does not find fulfilment in the subject's contingent sensory experience of other men (via sight and other forms of apprehension)—and, further, irrespective of the number or kind of 'other' men. Even a hypothetical spiritual-corporeal being who had never been conscious of his fellows via the senses would ascertain his membership of a community, his 'belonging', precisely on account of a positive awareness that a whole class of intentions in his *essential* nature was craving and *not finding fulfilment*—all types of loving (love of God, of one's neighbour, etc.), promising, thanking, entreaty, obedience, serving, ruling and so on. Hence this imaginary being would not say, 'I am alone—alone in infinite space and infinite time; I am alone in the world, I belong to no community', but he would tell himself: 'I do not know the *actual* community to which I know that I belong—I must look for it—but I *know* that I do belong to one.' This, not the (nevertheless) half-true platitude that men normally live in nations, States, etc., is what the great proposition of the Stagirite means: ἄνθρωπος ζῷον πολιτικόν. Man, *i.e.* the vehicle of the rational psychic power, is a *communal* creature. *Where there is an 'I' there is a 'we'*, or 'I' *belong* to a 'we'.

But we may also say: Just as man *knows* himself to be from the beginning a member of a universal community, a community with a measureless realm of rational spirits like himself, so, as a rational spiritual being, he is *objectively* and originally oriented toward that community and realm. He is spiritually thus determined no less originally than in his physical aspect. Community, of course, is implicit in the creature of flesh and blood by reason of his very origin in the mother's womb, if not by virtue of dependence on her love and care, with its corresponding instincts of complementary mother-child love; this is not to mention his endowment with organs which direct him to the other sex and with gregarious instincts corresponding to this arrangement. Nevertheless, the spiritual rational community is no mere development from the natural biological community. One should not think that man loses his essential sociability as he lives more in the spirit. Thinkers like Darwin and Spencer make a great mistake when they suppose that *all* human community 'evolved' or can be derived from the natural biological community to be found, as 'animal societies', even in subhumanity, and when in consequence they explain all non-sensual love, sacrifice, sense of obligation, conscience and repentance as mere refinements and developments of the psychic powers holding the animal herd together.*

The spiritual and personal community of man exists in its own right and has its own origin. In both right and origin it is superior to the biological community. Its origin is as divinely spiritual as its right is divinely sanctioned.

The great importance of this becomes apparent as soon as we add a *second* proposition to our first. Because we have an awareness, as original as the self-awareness with which it is inextricably associated, of our organic membership in a universal community of spiritual beings, one which we cannot disregard, we have at the centre of our souls an urgent need and limitless pressure of spirit to *transcend* in thought, and aspire beyond in loving desire, not only our solitary, naked self but every one of the historically actual and sensually visible communities to which we belong; this implies in effect, when rationally determined, an urge to regard *every* actual community in its turn as the 'organ' of a still broader, more comprehensive and higher community of spirits. There is nothing clearer or surer to our hearts and minds than this: *not one* of these earthly communities (family, municipality, State, nation, circle of friends, etc.), would ever quite suffice to satisfy the demands of our reason and hearts, no matter what degree of perfection it might attain in history. But since all communities of this kind are communities not only of spirits but also of *persons*, this (in principle) boundless urge and the demand of reason for ever richer, more universal and higher community find only in *one* idea their possible conclusion and perfect satisfaction—the idea of communion of love and spirit with an infinite spiritual person who at the same time is the origin, founder and sovereign Lord of all possible spiritual communities as of all actual communities on earth. Just as certain kinds of love are implanted in the *nature* of our spiritual existence—kinds differentiated from the outset, before casual experience of their correlative objects, as emotional acts which demand fulfilment (love, for example, of children, parents, home, country)—so there is also a *supreme* kind of love, love of *God*, which we already feel and possess before we have a clear intellectual conception of the supreme being. That is why Pascal can say to God, 'I would not seek thee, if thou hadst not already found me'. We are equally clear in heart and mind that their intentions can be entirely fulfilled and satisfied only by this supreme and final union of love and reason in God, and that we are unable to envisage correctly the communities in which we know ourselves involved, unable to see them in a *true* light, until we are conscious of them against the *divine background* of this supreme and final community of all spiritual beings—until we see their shape against the illumination which only community with the personal God projects. In that community alone do peace and rest attend the endless questing of heart and mind beyond all finite visible communities: *Inquietum cor nostrum* (said Augustine) *donec requiescat in te*. It is in and through *God* that for the first time we are truly *bound in spirit* to one another. This is exactly the meaning of the 'first' and 'greatest' commandment (Mark 12.30-31), which merges self-sanctification and love of one's neighbour in their common root, the love of God. There are various kinds of natural evidence of God's existence. Every theme and thread of Creation, when we follow it, leads us back to God; we have only to imagine it protracted into infinity according to the law of being which governs the finite section known to us. All threads meet simultaneously in him. But here I should like to draw your attention to the existence of another independent and original evidence of the supreme being, which arises *solely* from the idea of a community of personal, spiritual beings. This 'sociological proof' of God, though it coincides with the goal of all the others, does not depend on them for logical support. Today it is perhaps unduly neglected.

Thus, if the natural light of the mind tells us that *all* community (on earth as in heaven) is directly or indirectly founded in God, that in him all true community has directly or (through intermediary creative causes) indirectly its origin, highest lawgiver, judge, lord and governor, the same light also tells us this: each individual is not responsible solely for his own character and conduct, responsible through his conscience before his Lord and creator, but each individual (likewise every comparatively restricted community) is also responsible to God—as originally as for self— for everything of moral bearing in the character and proceedings of the larger corporate selves of which he is an integral part. That is the *third* principle in the doctrine of community. For if community is more than a historically fortuitous, earthly co-operation of intelligent bodies, resting on artificial and arbitrary man-made contracts, if it necessarily proceeds from the *project* and divine, constructive intention of *one intelligent heart and mind*, if in the range of its ideal conception it embraces the suprasensual *ab origine*, including its very Lord and creator, the centre of all things—and if this central divinity is all that vouches for the sanctity of contracts, the possibility of truly binding reciprocal promises—then *from the outset* each one of us must be responsible for all, not only for himself (though he is that too!). Each and every one of us, then, is co-responsible for the collective guilt and collective merit which accrue to his community as a unit and integer, not as an 'aggregate' of the individuals called its 'members'.

From that you may see how perverted is the doctrine (introduced by Epicurus, later a basis for all 'liberal' theories of society up to Kant) which attempts to base the nature and existence of human community on human *contracts*, whether by imputing an origin in actual treaties or by contending that the legitimacy of every society must be decided by regarding it 'as if' it rested on contracts. For every contract presupposes a common standard incumbent upon both contracting parties, and this standard can only derive from a third party '*in whose eyes*' the contract is binding or not binding; again, the legitimate assumption of a promise on the part of a promise-receiver presupposes the co-responsibility of this receiver for the legitimacy of the promise which he is to assume.

This third great principle of ethics and religion is the principle of religious moral reciprocity or *moral solidarity*.* It does not mean something which is universally obvious—that wherever, or only where, we have consciously assumed a definite obligation, or know for sure, positively, that we were conscious participants and 'co-efficients' in an action, we have a share of the ensuing responsibility. Neither does it mean simply that when we are confronted by the guilt of others we would do better to think of our own guilt than to pass judgment on theirs. No; what it means is that we should feel ourselves truly co-responsible in *all* guilt. It means therefore that from the very beginning—even where the magnitude or extent of our actual participation are not clearly in view before our mind's eye—we must answer to the living God for *all* rise and fall in the moral and religious condition of the *collective whole* of the moral world, which is an intrinsically solidary unit.[1] Whatever precise or imprecise knowledge we may possess concerning our share of moral causation, its nature, extent, etc., merely shows to our inner self, which already knows itself originally co-responsible, the direction and degree in which we may also *judge* ourselves co-responsible. But it is not this knowledge alone which *creates* this co-responsibility as a *quality* of our persons. Even if we were able to place it in the endlessly intricate context of all the moral and religious action, reaction and interaction of men and souls, this knowledge could never set before our mental eye the full extent of what our conduct has indirectly added to us or subtracted from us in the way of collective merit and collective guilt. There is no moral gesture so trivial that does not radiate, like the splashing stone, an infinity of ripples—circles soon lost to the naked eye. But if a physicist can pursue the tremor beyond this natural barrier— how much farther can God the omniscient pursue the moral repercussion! *If* no impediments intervene, A's love of B not only awakens B's reciprocal love of A but stirs a natural growth of *general*, life-warming love in B's responding heart; hence B's love of C and D; and so the flood rolls on within the moral universe, from C and D to E and F *ad infinitum*. But the same is true of hatred, injustice, unchastity and all kinds of sin. Each one of us has been a partner in an immensity of actions good and bad, things of which he has—and *can* have—no inkling, but for which he nevertheless stands co-responsible before God. In the words of St Paul: 'But with me it is a very small thing that I should be judged of you, or of man's judgment:

---

[1] Whether we are in a leading or serving position in the community in question is a matter which determines only the degree (not the fact) of our responsibility.

yea, I judge not mine own self. For I know nothing by myself; yet am I not hereby justified: but he that judgeth me is the Lord' (I Cor. 4.3-4).

Though this is a principle of natural reason, it is also implied in the fundamental, central ideas of Christian faith: the idea of an all-embracing, catholic, unifying, Christian *ecclesia;* the idea that all men together fell 'in' Adam and rose 'in' Christ; that there is true hereditary *guilt*—not merely evil, pernicious hereditary traits; the doctrine of the Body of Christ—a pillar of the Holy Mass as much as of the dogma of the Church; vicarious suffering and sacrifice, intercession, the remission of sins, and much else.

To me it is a basic defect in the modern non-Christian ethos, with its corresponding philosophical ethics, that as modern individualism has unfolded, bringing with it the absolute State, nationalism and unrestricted economic competition, the sublime *principle of solidarity* has been lost to sight: the sense of it, aspiration toward it are gone, and its theoretic justification, its basis in reason are forgotten. One either, like Marx and Hegel, knows only an ideal leviathan of State, nation or 'society', which swallows into the maw of its worldly machinations the God-made personality, the family and their God-given rights (*e.g.* to educate children), abolishing the dignity of estates of the realm—denying the substantial existence of the personal soul; or one knows only the opposite extreme—that much-approved 'solitary soul and its God'—which thinks to win its own salvation and the world's by faith alone (*sola fides*), or by solitary mystical vision or in some other way which *need* not comprise love of one's brother's salvation: this is an attempt to circumvent God's appointed way to salvation, that of thinking, believing, hoping and loving *together* within the spiritual edifice of true community—the service of one another and the responsibility of each for all. In Protestant movements, moreover, it was their early abandonment of this great principle of original moral reciprocity which cast adrift their conception of a Church.

And so I see that one of our most essential missions in time to come will be to instil, justify and spread this sublime doctrine in the minds of men as much as we can; we must study its special implications for *all* kinds of communal relationship—in particular those of the contemporary world— and in practice build it anew into an almost entirely alienated world.

3. THE PRESENT RELEVANCE OF THE CHRISTIAN IDEA OF COMMUNITY

What now gives us ground for hope that this might happen is above all a fact in whose recognition Christians today know themselves at one with leading representatives of quite other points of view. We are one in feeling that we stand at the beginning of an age in world-history that may be described as a *positive* age of *belief*, in contrast to the modern era's devotion to unleashing the maximum earthly forces of man and nature, but at the same time as an age engrossed with *community*, with the spiritual mastery of forces where before they were irresponsibly unleashed, thus as an age of genuine organization. A period seems to be approaching in which the mind will once again, boldly and confidently, set about those forces which have broken free from the focal powers of will and intellect and have been exercising a quasi-fateful and mechanical, deterministic effect on the life of men. Such forces are found in the material economic processes, in the isolated intelligence of the business-mentality, in mechanical techniques, in the amassing of countless atomic particles of erudition, which no head could master any more: we feel that an age is coming in which the attempt will be made to channel them into the construction of a new and lasting dwelling-house for human society. This universal belief has been and is still shared by spirits as far apart as Auguste Comte, Joseph de Maistre, Saint-Simon, Fourier in France, in Germany by the unforgettable Adam Müller,· Rodbertus, the whole school of historical and 'doctrinaire' socialist national-economics (*e.g.* A. Wagner), and above all by socialists, Christian and non-Christian, of every kind and shade. In its general acceptance this idea represents the programme of intelligent men all over the present world. We must further expect that the Europe-wide anarchy of this war, or rather the gradually ripening vision of its ultimate springs of action, will raise this conviction to an even higher power and, when the war is over, that it will seep into all Europe as a still more potent tonic, re-creative and vivifying factor. But it is not only by the negative effect of destroying false doctrines that the war will help restore the Christian principle of solidarity. It will also work in this positive way: there has arisen among peoples a feeling closely linked with the wartime organizations that have had to be set up, a sense of being in the next man's shoes, of *deputyship* in work, responsibilities, suffering, death and sacrifices of every kind; this feeling we may shortly hope to see spreading across frontiers from its point of origin—the war—to establish a new European concord at least in colonial politics, but—what is far more important—we may also hope for its transference from the narrow emphasis of wartime exigencies, which engross but one aspect of the soul, to the *basic moral attitude* of the whole, fully active man.

For we have fortunately not come to the point where solidarity survives *only* in Christian tradition. The principle is active in workers' feelings of mutual responsibility for teamwork in factories. In the modern economic framework, if only for technical reasons, co-operation has become as necessary among employers as among the workers. Long before the war co-operation at the bench or machine, in the endless diversity of science and in every complex undertaking, had seized the imagination of working-groups as vital to their common *interests*. But gradually, too, it had produced and, up to a point, perfected the feeling of *moral* responsibility which lies *behind* mere 'interests'. Thus *technically* unified work-groups gave birth to leagues of interest. But out of these there have gradually arisen the *beginnings of an estate-consciousness*.[1] A strike-breaker for example (a strike, by the way, may be justified if there is no breach of contract)—a strike-breaker or the employer who refuses to join a syndicate of mere business-interests is, in the eyes of union or syndicate, more than a fool who fails to grasp his own interest and that of his class. In the eyes of the trade-union and professional guild he is above all a *traitor* with a moral taint. Thus even if the strike-breaker *correctly* saw it in his interest to break the strike, morally he *ought* to have refrained from that action for the sake of his brother-workers. And so in such cases we see a faint upsurge of the principle of solidarity, rising independently of Christian tradition, under the inner pressures of modern developments themselves. We see *interest* transformed into *ethos*, mere common economic cause or class-ties into ties of *estate*, estate-consciousness and conscience.

There are two streams, therefore, a higher and a lower, wherein the principle of solidarity may flow back into the hearts and consciences of Europe. Above there is the traditional Christian and Catholic idea of solidarity—Catholic because it is this very aspect of the Christian ethos that Protestantism has most neglected. Below is the modern stream gradually finding its way through the communities of interest; it has in its favour the *vitality* of the present age, yet it has still to extricate itself from entanglements of business and material welfare. It is now our task that we should lead these streams to fruitful confluence, that they may unite in a *single moral force*, the lower discovering its moral dignity in the light shed by the higher, the stream which flows from a source in God and the history of the Church. They must form one power of willing love and obligation, embracing all men in their work together, independently of mere

---

[1] This unnatural expression is an attempt to render *Standesbewusstsein*, where *Stand* (normally 'rank', 'standing') has the sense of 'estate of the realm' (as in the 'three estates'). Analytically one may take it to mean 'collective dignity of functional status', but in a later passage, p. 399. Scheler specifically relates it to the above meaning of 'estate', which word is used here to preserve the link with that passage. As will be seen, it expresses an ideal of co-operative function, opposed to all elements of antagonism and domination implied in the words 'class' and 'rank' (*Translator*).

communities of interest. Within the Christian Church itself the idea of moral reciprocity stands only to *gain* from the contact of old and new, losing nothing of its clear, firm, substance; that is to say, there should be a diminution of the danger which has threatened for so long—that it should decline into an idea only for Sunday and survive too exclusively in *formulae* of belief, not in the heartfelt faith which is a perpetual spring of action. The idea which is one of the cornerstones of the Church should make common cause with the daily round and common task, in order to bring about a more intimate contact between the Church and the life of the people.

But this is not all. It is equally important that the mighty period of organization at whose gates we stand, and in whose conduct one not unjustly allocates a special and outstanding rôle, rooted in their history, to the Central European powers, should be steered in a direction where it will not merely find a place within the Christian ethos and idea of society but number these among its chief guiding and *determining* factors.

Alike in the fields of political constitution, theory of State, international relations and economic theory and practice, the development of modern forms of State and society, in the predominantly critical and power-bent age, has produced *two opposing* sets of principles and ideals, each in permanent conflict with the other and *both* in like degree intimately repugnant to the spirit of Christian community.

In the theory of the State, the two sets read as follows: On one side there is the absolute, rigorously centralistic monarchy, sole arbiter of legality and 'sovereign', in the sense of dependence on no earthly power above its own will. Step by step (as first in France), on the fallacious premise that it alone was the source of all corporate rights, it had stripped the older, distinctive communities within its jurisdiction (nobility, priesthood, monastic orders, municipalities, down even to the family) of their traditional rights and privileges; this process had continued for so long that it had resulted in an almost total legal equality of individual subjects of the State. To this the counter-ideal is the no less sovereign lordship of the so-called popular will or *volonté générale*, and this means in effect— since this will is never homogeneous—the rule of the majority of citizens (the majority-principle, cf. Rousseau).

In international relations an analogous dichotomy prevails: The absolutely sovereign power-State, proclaiming a national 'way of life' and seeking the maximum of national unity, a State possessing no moral bounds to its expansion but only the limitations imposed by the power-will of other States of the same kind; *or* an international social world-republic, built on class-supremacy and seeking the maximum of uniformity.

In the cultural field we are asked to choose between an inbred, inward-looking national culture and a homogeneous world-culture.*

The corresponding economic systems are on the one hand an absolutely unrestricted competition of all individuals and corporate subjects, obedient only to their own economic interest, and as counter-ideal on the other a compulsory State-socialism, which progressively appropriates to State ownership and control the existing free and unfettered enterprise, together with the land it needs and its means of production, in order to distribute the collective yield of the State economy in accordance with an artificial yardstick.

Why, for what profoundest of reasons, do these four *pairs* of ideals—as much one side as the other—conflict with the inmost core of the Christian idea of community? And what *radically different* principle has this idea to offer in opposition to both factions? They conflict with it because to the same degree, though in opposite directions, they deny both the principle of solidarity as defined above and the closely associated principle that every individual and subdivision of society (family, municipality, State, etc.), shall, within a given circle, be as much an *independent* and legitimate authority in its own original right, as it is a free servant of the wider community and bearer of clearly definable duties corresponding to its rights: everyone a master, everyone a servant, and all together free, solidary servants of the supreme Lord over all community—God.

How and to what extent do they conflict with the principle of solidarity?

Let us first answer this question in reference to the *idea of the State*. This and this alone is the absolutely *new* thing in the idea of community which Christianity possessed from the beginning and brought into the world as a leaven—it unites in itself, and fuses into *one* indissoluble vision, *both* the following insights: on one side, the independent, substantial reality and independent, moral-religious responsibility for itself of each individual soul, its direct divine origin (creationism) and its supernaturally mysterious goal of beholding God in eternity; on the other side, the solidary membership and co-responsibility of all souls to God in *one* body which truly embraces them, is invisible in its source and as an entirety, but intrudes into the visible world, where it is powerfully active. Divine revelation teaches us to know this all-embracing collective body, of which all children of Adam are 'members', as the Body of Christ, as the *Church* which embraces all men, alive or dead, and all angels, with Christ as its mystic invisible Head and the successor of Peter as its visible Head.

In the right enjoyment of the Holy Eucharist we should become, certainly shall become, inwardly conscious in ever renewed bliss of our holy, supreme membership of the Body of Christ in love, suffering and service. But every secular corporation, every form of association without the Church, must *reproduce*, however faintly, the pattern of this *highest corporation* to which we belong. Each one of them must reproduce the strong, yet so fruitful *tension* which must always of necessity exist between the God-created, God-destined, independent, free, individual, personal soul and the original organic association of all such persons in one all-inclusive corporation.

The *Christian idea of corporation*, to be found in the earliest Fathers of the Church (Ignatius of Antioch, Cyprian, Cyril and Augustine, to name a few), is the highest *ideal and model of every human corporation*. Having spoken of a powerful tension, I would hasten to add that it may not be removed in favour of *one* of the elements of Christian community, whether the individual or the collectivity. Thus the Ancients, in their idea of community, were well acquainted with the principle of the State as a living organic community, with its constituent human beings bearing a mutual responsibility for the welfare and cultivation of the whole. But they were ignorant of the independent, Stateless, God-created, spiritual and immortal soul, superior in its inmost being to any possible State, possessing an inner world of religion and morality, a *private* realm of feeling and conscience. Likewise they were ignorant of the goal lying beyond the ends of welfare and cultivation for both the whole and the individual: the spiritual, supernatural *salvation* of men and mankind was a value beyond their ken. Man they confined, to the very roots of his being, in the State, which meant in effect a restriction to things of this earth. For that reason neither religion nor the higher culture of the mind were able to break free from the clutches of the State and make themselves independent within it. The ancient idea of community came once again strongly to the fore in theory and practice as Prussia developed; from the beginning it was more State than nation and its princes have always been unduly preoccupied with ancient models of State and public morality. Only recently scholars have put the idea forward in a particularly childish form. But make no mistake: it finds a hard and fast limitation in the freedom and conscience of the inmost personality. There it comes up against the one true *individualism*, which is to say the Christian individualism implicit in the Christian ideal of community, and there it must stop short.

For the word 'individualism', so Protean in meaning, has a sense in which it is not only an article of Christian faith but nothing less than what I would call the *magna carta* of *Europe*, as against Asia and even now

Russia, namely that *spiritual*—hence not primarily economic—individualism which categorically denies that the individual person is a mere 'modus' of some generality—the State, say, or society, or 'world-reason' or an impersonal self-generating historical process, whether it is called panlogical by Prussian State-philosopher Hegel, or a self-developing moral 'order' by Fichte or—by Marx—an economic process of history. Christian individualism denies that the smaller communities in the State or imperium (families, wards, parishes, municipalities, guilds, hereditary principalities, etc.), exercise only an *outward*-looking sphere of action and authority, on behalf of the enclosing whole; it insists they have equally, in their own original right, an *inward*-looking sphere of action and authority, which they do not derive from the overshadowing body politic. Even the nethermost term of all communities, the separate individual, has an original sphere of action and natural right which is all his own, is independent of the State and its legislation; therein he enjoys the exercise of those 'natural rights' which are innate in the essence of personality, rights such as those of existence and self-defence. Doubtless all communities founded on love and common life, such as family, township, State, people, nation, European civilization—as opposed to 'societies' formed in an arbitrary manner—outlive the *earthly* life of the individual, as the tree the leaves that fall. The State and nation have therefore an intrinsic right, in war for example, to require the physical life of the individual as a willing sacrifice to their weal or existence— but it must be the life of the visible organism, *not* the being and essence of personality, for that is immortal and therefore, even *during* earthly life, is not called upon to lose its identity by utter submission to nation or State.* It is not the being of the individual but the life of all these communities which in spite of their power to outlast the organic life of the individual is *finite* by nature, as shown by the histories of States and nations that have declined and vanished. And it is the spiritual, personal individuality which, in spite of its so much shorter and finite earthly life, is *infinite* in duration and effect. And only *because* it is essentially infinite may it and should it—chivalrously, as it were—give up the high good of its short physical life for the higher good of the life of the earthly communities, which 'live' so much longer but, as merely finite, are so much poorer in comparison. In this very war it is doubly important to cling to the right understanding of spiritual individualism. Why?

We see one of the surest signs of the rightness of our cause in this war in this, that we are helping to save not only ourselves but—indirectly and in the long run—also the States of our western and southern enemies, *all Europe* indeed, from inundation by the Russian hordes. At the same time we are helping to save them from the Russian mentality and Orthodoxy, to which the infinite worth of the *individual* soul—that *magna carta* of Christian Europe—is still unfamiliar. There race, tribe, mass and herd still engulf the personality. How absurd, then, it would be for us to jettison the very object of our struggle with the East—the value of the individual soul.

I have said that all ideas of community which have sprung from soil outside the Christian Church repudiate this necessary tension. The *absolute monarchy*, linked with the bourgeois nationalism that first served, later ruled it, robbed all corporations, the estates, nobility and priesthood, of their original rights and privileges. Its extreme concept of boundless power and sovereignty dared to exalt itself above the supreme authority of Christian law. It is scarcely surprising that one day absolute monarchy found a mass-revolt on its hands. France in 1789 offers the obvious instance, but it has happened to some extent everywhere, and at present it is taking place in Russia, for which country this war is but a prolongation of a revolution reaching hands across to that of the French. The mass-rising contested even the monarchy's 'absolute' right of existence and, falsely equating the mere will of the majority with the *volonté générale*, installed that will as the *absolute, sovereign people* in place of the absolute prince.

But both ideas of the State make State and nation into an *idol* denying Christian individualism as much as the Christian principle of solidarity, an idol to which is deliberately or unwittingly given the place due to the overlord of all community—God. They make the State into something which in theory is *only* the master of individuals or *only* their slave (slave, that is, of the majority's whim), whereas the Christian doctrine of society declares that none but God—no institution on earth—is 'master of all' and that *nobody* is a slave, but that every person and institution is *at once* a master and a free servant of a master. At length it was inevitable that both monarchic and popular extremes should foster that unbridled *nationalism* which, leaping out like a consuming flame, kindled the separate fires of ever smaller nationalities (lately Hungary, Bohemia, etc.—down to Esthonians and Latvians) and, finally overtopping itself in imperialism, has so fearfully collapsed in this war on the question of the idea of State in the Central European bloc. But who, if not the custodians of the Christian idea of community, hold the key to the ideas—as to strength and ability, them we must leave in God's hand—wherewith one may at least try to rebuild a true Christian Europe, snatched from the catastrophic dissolution of a Europe long quivering inwardly in moral and spiritual anarchy? What other idea may hope to *contain* the explosion of Europe?

And so this idea must oblige us to seek even in foreign affairs a system

N

of concord and reconciliation, at least in all matters concerned with the common European weal. It is simply untrue that the expansion of a State is limited *only* by the power-will of another similar State. In our *federal* form of political articulation, which for a long time has withdrawn from the individual State the property of 'sovereignty', we Germans and the Swiss have, constitutionally speaking, at least the beginnings of a great example showing how the genuine freedom of smaller historical regional and political units *can* in all things *co-exist* with the centralizing, technical necessities of modern industry, and even of an overall imperial economy. Let us hope that this kind of community-affiliation will become a *model* for Christian Europe in the coming age! For—still relatively speaking—*it is in the constitution of the federal State that the Christian idea of community is most present today*. Let us suppose it possible to extend the federal idea, modified no doubt as occasions demand, over the whole of Central Europe comprising our own and the Austro-Hungarian empire. Suppose this were done, gradually and prudently, in such a way that matters of common subsistence (first defence, later the economy) were strengthened by centralization throughout the federal realm, but that at the same time the individual races and federated States of our present imperium *gained* a considerable measure of autonomy in matters of religion, customs, culture and way of life—with a drastic diminution of the one-sided Prussian hegemony. If that were to come about an important advance in the Christian idea of community would have been achieved in the political field. The new federal body politic, presenting a materially greater, stronger and more centralized front to the outside world, but internally, spiritually, more *de*centralized, might also be legitimately imagined as a historical re-connection to the forces and ideas which sustained the mediaeval German empire; it would sound a recall to Germany's vocation as the heart of Europe (in the providence of geography and history), which is to mediate, in the formation of federal, *supranational* political organizations, between the idea and reality of Christian Europe (and ultimately a Christian world), and the self-seeking reality of peripheral European States and nations. It is my view that the post-1870 German Empire has, culturally speaking, been far too strongly and one-sidedly centred in the Prussian spirit and still clings far too fondly to the old outlook of the absolute monarchy, provoking the inevitable reaction of hyperdemocratic opposition. One could scarcely expect such an empire to exercise much power of attraction on surrounding peoples, even those of Germanic race; everywhere, even in Holland and Switzerland, it has been more *feared* than loved. But even this could alter under the impression of the newly rising federal pattern. If the surrounding peoples of Germanic stock saw that the last vestiges of the old Prussian absolutism had been expelled from the post-war *Reich*, if they saw that freedom, distinctiveness and regional loyalties were more encouraged among the constituent classes and races than ever before, with a much greater regional 'say' in the political conduct and government of the whole, they would automatically, after a time, lose their fear and suspicion. And it must have harmed Prussia itself that the *Reich* should have seemed a mere extension of its confines. In the process it lost its clear, proud and subtle spirituality; it lost—as Moeller van den Bruck has lately shown so well[1]—its style in art (its architecture!), in sociability and daily living.

No less compelling is the impact of the Christian idea of community on the restoration of normal psychological and cultural relations *between nation and nation*. Though condemning the political nationalism against whose aspirations the Central Powers, taking their stand on an ideal of Statehood, are above all waging their war, our ideal of community not only seeks to preserve the unity of mankind in Church and religion, but seeks also to uphold the right to *internal autonomy* of peoples and nationalities in all questions of language, culture, indigenous custom and distinctive forms of religion and piety. In my *Krieg und Aufbau*[2] I have shown how modern political nationalism is manifestly not of genuinely national origin, but represents, in aims as in origin, as uniform an *international class-phenomenon* (of nationally *engagé* bourgeois capitalism) as its antithesis, the internationalism of the working class, while on the other hand spiritual *cosmopolitanism* may justly be considered largely (though not of course wholly) a product of the German national spirit. (By spiritual cosmopolitanism I mean the view that all national spirits are called upon to complement one another in *solidarity* of culture. One is not interchangeable with another, but all are complementary in philosophy, science, art—and even in the diversified representation of the Kingdom of Christ.) The aim of political nationalism is to harness the forces of spiritual culture, which is necessarily rooted in visions of a single truth and beauty—but is prismatically divided into unique national capacities for recognizing the true, enjoying and producing the beautiful—to harness them in the service of its mere power-objectives and economic aims. If any kind of nationalism were to triumph, this political kind would be the very factor to extinguish the rich diversity of distinctive national

---

[1] *Der Preussische Stil*, Munich 1916.
[2] See the chapter entitled '*Soziologische Neuorientierung und die Aufgabe der deutschen Katholiken nach dem Krieg*'.

characters, products, ways of life—and to turn the world into a grey and desolate waste of uniformity.

And so the Christian idea of community enjoins us in *this* direction to do all we can to restore the cultural friendliness of European nations, to work against purely destructive hatred and to ensure that within the bounds of our country and of Austria a much greater respect than heretofore is accorded to the cultural characteristics of national minorities— for example, this spirit must be made effective in the government of Poland and Alsace. Logically, the 'one culture' State and the idea of a State embracing various nations, as our ideal requires, are mutually *exclusive*. 'One culture, one State' implies the closed nation-State.

For a nation's eternal right of existence lies *not* in the political or the economic sphere, but in its *culture*—its language, customs, literature, art. Just as sternly as it condemns the monolithic world-State idea, the Christian idea of community condemns the 'cultural State' which directly exercises an artificial control of culture (as in the imposition of uniform education), and does not rest content with ensuring the external *conditions* of culture with regard to welfare, the distribution of wealth, the free interplay of those likely to create culture. For the State can embrace several nations and truly rise above national passions as their rational master only if it also gives *cultural freedom* to the nations and refrains from spreading a uniform 'State culture' over the inhabitants of its territory. And in reference to our highest goods, those of holiness and religion, we men can form a true unity, one 'catholic' Church, only if—as much in political as in cultural respects—the earth contains a diversified *multiplicity* of independent groups, commensurate with the organic and spiritual evolution of peoples in history. For that reason true (*i.e.* Christian) cosmopolitanism eschews not only political nationalism but also the Jewish 'chosen people' belief made obsolete by Christ (an idea which England, by adoption from the Calvinist doctrine of election has incorporated in its ethos of State and 'Empire'); it rejects the dreary tedium of a monolithic 'world-culture' as much as the masonic farce of a 'world-republic'. It likewise condemns what has become the wretchedly broken idol of an international proletarian class-republic. Even the Church, for all its unique claim to unify all men in one embrace, for all its unique authority to pronounce on the supreme values, which are indivisible— even the Church should not wish, and does not wish, to exercise a *direct* control over culture: to put it more strongly, it does so only at the grave risk of particularizing itself. Its sole claim should be to protect the rich diversity of indigenous cultures from all political nationalism and imperialism, even what may be called spiritual imperialism, and to raise a clear voice of admonition where it sees a cultural trend causing harm to the Body of Christ or in some way challenging it.

Perhaps it was this very claim of the Church, or of its Head and supreme authority, to have oversight even over the plane of culture—where it touches on matters of salvation—which most repelled all nations of modern Europe from the Church before the War. Just as the Christian moral law was no longer seriously considered as the highest principle of foreign policy, so the Christian Church was no longer looked to for the inspiration of higher culture, art, philosophy and science; precisely because ties with this vital, cohesive inspiration of cultural fields and national cultures had been loosened in recent history, because it was more and more divorced, even in language, methods and styles, from an increasingly narrow and vehement cultural nationalism which denied the complementary nature of peoples, it was inevitable that any *démarches* of ecclesiastical authority should have affected the exponents of the non-Christian idea of culture as alien, arbitrary and inhuman encroachments from without. As a matter of principle the representative arbiters in nearly every State denied the right of the Church to infringe the alleged autonomy of reason and culture even in matters of salvation. But we have to bear the following in mind: since all human activities, even the highest activities of the spirit, are always at the same time *communal activities*, the particular nature and content of the idea of community holding sway over life at a given time is of the utmost importance for the continuance, spirit and fruition of these activities. Everywhere and in all ages the human condition forms a strict inner unity of style and pattern. Where for example the prevailing political form is the absolute State, and the economic form of free competition and business-expansion has prevailed over the rational subsistence-economy, where unrestrained individualism or un-compromising socialism has destroyed the Christian ideal of community, there you will find that the spiritual form of corporate faith within an *ecclesia*—and also the knowing together of co-operating aspirants to knowledge—have been done away. As in the Middle Ages generation on generation added stone to stone of the one church—yet leaving the building its identity of style—so generation after generation of mediaeval philosophers in many different nations, despite their differing windows on the world, all thought of themselves as adding their stone to the one *philosophia perennis*.

But as the modern spirit developed, two closely associated principles came to replace this organic and unselfconscious thinking, seeing and feeling together of times and peoples. One was the principle of *subjective criticism*, pervading a thousand minor manifestations, and the other was the principle of *rivalry*—rivalry among nations, rivalry in nations among 'schools of thought', rivalry among individuals within such factions. In another dimension a competition of historical periods and generations was encouraged: each should strive to outdo and overtop the preceding age, only to see itself cast into the wilderness—barely established—by the efforts of the succeeding. The tempo of this swing between birth and death was continually accelerated. The honest simplicity of loving *devotion* to the objective world in thought and understanding, with its constant awareness that the human mind originating in the divine fount of truth is able to grasp intelligently the very *being* of things, was replaced by an a-priori *mistrust* in one's mental powers and what I call the deep 'world-hostility' of modern thought, *i.e.* the refusal of all qualities, forms, values and patterns inhering in the world *itself*: a view of the world as an inchoate conglomeration of material, devoid of any destiny to salvation, from which man himself must construct something meaningful with his own intellectual operations. Kant's philosophy, for example, is a special case of this formula.* In strict consonance, the love-spurred co-operative alignment was replaced as the guiding genius of cultural activity by the vain urge to intellectual and aesthetic *competition*—the urge to produce something quite special and 'original' and, instead of working toward the truth by direct occupation with the matter in hand, the method of primary criticism, exposure of other thinkers' errors and delusions. That, as Goethe said and Augustine had seen, we can know things for what they are only in so far as we *love* them, that we can know things together only in so far as we first love one another and join in loving the same things —for God himself gave us knowledge of his inmost nature only through his loving will to redeem us in his son who offered himself for our sins; and only love in us can fully receive this communication—this was denied in principle. The individual's 'thought', isolated from the community and torn from the whole psychic context (cf. Descartes), if not some kind of sense-data equally isolated, was declared the sole legitimate source of knowledge.

It would certainly be foolish and unfair not to admit that both principles, subjective idealist criticism and self-outstripping competition, have produced magnificent results in philosophy, the sciences, the control of nature, of souls and of society; they have worked wonders in their way. *But*—and this *But* is the forceful lesson of a World War, God's summons to all Europe to a change of heart—even these results were only possible because the Christian era of mediaeval Europe had stored up in all nations and societies so great an *inner capital* of community-building spiritual powers that, secretly *in profundis*, and even in the ignorance of the parties involved, the centrifugal trends of society were still being contained. Owing to the greater powers of endurance of the older ways of thinking, Christian confidence in the ability of the mind to comprehend the world itself (not only its image within us) was not *wholly* destroyed by the new criticism. But the new fact that is with us now in Europe—news of such importance it should be cried from the rooftops—is indubitably this: apart from the faithful remnants of Christendom still to be found (and even they have been drawn into evil, as the polemical writings of French Catholics show), this capital, our unconscious legacy, is on the point of *exhaustion*.

Just as the experimental scientist isolates factor from factor so that he can see what each one is alone the cause of, so the World War can be said to have isolated the power of both the above-named principles in such a way that we may see whither they alone lead—to a veritable World War of minds, the building of a worldwide Tower of Babel. In so doing the World War has uncovered, for all willing to see, Europe's deepest mystery —that even among those of most secular outlook Europe has been secretly living on Christianity, on the spiritual legacy of the Church. This is a truth the war has written across the skies in letters of blood for all to read. It is not the lofty neutrality of Christianity, not the Holy Father's separate actions to alleviate the miseries of war, not the moving prayers of his Church for peace, which alone have led to the remarkable phenomenon that the Catholic Church and its Overseer are winning new respect and moral dignity even in the eyes of the most modern of modernists. Behind these pure and heartening effects there stands something more profound: the new insight that only a conscious return to the holy sources of life and spirit, which fed the history of Europe even to the hour when men would hear no more of them—only, in consequence, a return to the holy Church and the idea of community of which it is the guardian and sole agent— can yet preserve Europe as the foremost homeland of civilization. It was no mere error or succession of errors that led us so monstrously to over-estimate the ties holding Europe together (techniques of communication, workers' internationals, international finance, science, art, the 'European conscience', solidarity of the white races, international jurisprudence, the *jus gentium*, etc.). No, it was the fundamentally perverted *habit* of thinking and feeling as if the unconditionally necessary unity of the moral world-edifice could be *permanently* borne up 'from underneath' by earthly forces, as if it did not permanently and essentially need *at the outset*—not only for its progress but its continuance, no less—mighty focal forces 'from above' of a religious, spiritual and moral nature, *i.e.* not forces based only on common interest, on mere legal contracts, on the highly overrated 'uniformity' of human nature and mental equipment, but forces found only in revelation, grace, illuminated minds and hearts, and in a visible organization corresponding to these invisible powers, one on which the lower community-forming powers depend in turn for their efficacy.

If, as I have said, all those qualified to judge agree that we stand, economically and politically, on the threshold of an age devoted to the organization of forces that once were irresponsibly unleashed, then, given the vital interrelation of all aspects of social life, the life of the *mind*, thus art, philosophy and science, must also participate in that radical transformation. This too must gradually turn in the direction of Christian community. The whole of European cultural activity must win back the spirit of true and loving *co-operation* between man and man, school and school, nation and nation, generation and generation. Accordingly the principle of loving devotion to the objective world, together with the belief that its being may be directly known and perceived, will have to be accepted once again in place of that 'idealism' and 'criticism' which are so exclusively based on the attitude of 'world-hostility'. Moreover, all philosophy, art and science will have to learn once more to see, heed and love the essential constants of the world and their interrelations—the divine *essential ideas*, perceptible in individual contingent entities, in accordance with which God ordered the world—in place of what we merely find amenable to alteration and control. Thus the implications of the Christian idea of community are to be worked out anew in theory and practice over the whole of cultural life, and the Christian idea of *cultural* community should be brought forward to fill the vacancies left in the souls of men by the collapse of those overrated forces which, in the non-Christian view, used to unite man spiritually to man.

That must be one of our most urgent tasks in the reconstruction of community. Think for example of that unhappy sinner Friedrich Adler, who recently fired at Count Stürgkh. As a person he is as worthy of love as his fearful deed is worthy of hatred. Psychologically this frightful action is very understandable: it arose from his despair over the Internationale, which was the only thing the poor fellow knew that was above State, supranational, a force to bind men together. He was its secretary-designate for the abortive Vienna congress of 1914; with its existence he identified himself and his whole moral dignity; he believed in it as in an idol—as a man may believe in God but in *no* earthly institution; with its collapse his moral existence duly collapsed. Look at this figure of veritable Grand Guignol: beginning with a misconceived, immoderate condemnation of war as 'mass-murder' (a judgment leaving human sinfulness out of account) he ends as a *real* murderer—not for egoistic ends, no, but with the intrinsically pure and *high*-minded intention of sacrificing himself for an idea. Think of this figure as symbolizing the same or a similar disillusion in thousands of others, who were simply less fanatical—but also less true to themselves—and most of whom perhaps were only less *subjective* in their moral thinking. Then you will know what you have to do.

Just as important as the indications given by the Christian idea of community for the development of political and cultural community are its pointers to the position we should take in reference to the remaining dichotomy I have mentioned. I called it—simplifying—the system of *free economic competition* against *State-socialism*. In this case a specific economic system does *not* follow logically from the Christian idea of community or the basic principles of Christian ethics and the corresponding objective ladder of secular and spiritual goods. It could not so follow, for the very reason that the Christian idea of community and the objective scale of values are *eternal* and everlasting, whereas economic systems are subject to the most varied historical exigencies. They are even more subject to change than forms of political constitution. The existence and character of every economic system are dependent on absolutely innumerable causes that have nothing or little to do with the religious outlook of producers and consumers—or are concerned with it only in a very indirect way. They depend for example on the disposition of peoples, whether active or contemplative, on their temperament, national inventiveness, on the soil, climate, natural resources, state of technology, internal and foreign legal relationships and a host of other factors. But just as everywhere in nature and history it is spirit that moulds the body, so every economic system is also dependent at the beginning on a factor we may call the '*economic spirit*' or ruling 'economic ethos' of the governing circles, those who set the tone in a country. It is this factor which forms the binding inner vitality of the external organization and impresses its seal on every economic transaction and phenomenon, however trivial. But, acting through the medium of the economic spirit, the typical religious outlook, in particular the idea of community which it implies, incalculably affects the pattern of economic life. Only recently research on the part of that outstanding economist Max Weber, not to mention E. Troeltsch, W. Sombart and others, investigating in detail such subjects as the part played by Calvinism and other Protestant sects in the rise of capitalism, or the economic manifestations of the great religions of China and India,[1] has put this fact beyond the reach of doubt.

[1] See Max Weber's contributions to recent numbers of the *Archiv für Sozialwissenschaft und Sozialpolitik*.

I do not need to remind you that for a long time now the 'liberal' economic system of *laisser-faire*, whose spirit evolved into an acquisitive struggle of single economic units, unrestrained by any notion of reasonable consumption and a universal level of subsistence, has no longer had the wind of history in its sails. It denied the existence of any special problem of distribution (*i.e.* one of 'just' or equitable distribution) and was wholly engrossed with the problem of producing the *maximum* of material goods, expecting, against a religious background of deism, which produced an undoubtedly mistaken belief in the natural harmony of instincts, that an absolutely unrestrained *free competition* of economic subjects, with unrestricted free trade, would eventually result in the best distribution of goods. But for a long time now—as you know—we have been living in an age of far-reaching State activity, with a strong social programme in politics, including the German industrial legislation which Lloyd George has copied in England; we are in the age of the great workers' and employers' associations and, economically as well as in foreign affairs, in the age of what has been called neo-mercantilism, wherein the State blazes the trail for work, trade and exchange of goods—even, as we may now see, by force of arms. In addition the War has brought us the astonishing spectacle that our workers' organizations, especially the trades-unions (even the social-democratic—which scarcely sprang from a spirit friendly to the State), have joined with the State, and in many ways with the once hated employers' federations, to help close the ranks of one great national working-community. We have seen democratic socialism in our country cease to feel a State within the State, have seen it bury the greater part of its hopes for an international class-revolution; we have seen it actively and practically set about finding its place in the living organism of the State, seen it defer its faultfinding, shelve its utopian dreams in the face of work to be done here and now. We have also seen a major part of our leading industrial, commercial and financial interests step down, as it were, from their business rôles, not only contributing unprecedented monetary sacrifices toward the cost of the war but behaving as willing servants of the State; no longer have their thoughts been all for their business advantages and the expansion of industrial profits but they have been for the welfare of the whole. The spirit of *sacrifice*, the spirit of that most central idea of the Christian faith, which we see ever and again in its sublimest form when we participate in the mystic profundities of the Holy Mass, has seemed to fill the air we breathe and to seep through even to the most earthy layers of economic life.

Certainly these are great and profound transformations, experiences to move the soul! But in what *direction* should our Christian philosophy lead them? How should it try to protract the life of these newborn forces beyond the moment that occasioned their birth?

Now many, very many, of the most clearsighted Germans already see in all these processes something like the beginning of the realization of *socialism*,[1] not to be sure in exactly the form in which Marx dreamed of it —no, more in the form envisaged by Ferdinand Lassalle, *i.e.* a national commonwealth which though constitutionally monarchical is essentially State-socialistic in political effect. It is thought of in the following manner: the wartime organizations, with their far-reaching encroachments on the freedom of economic activity, will not only be preserved in large measure when the war is over (how far that is right is only a question of what *means* are appropriate to desired ends), but they will be used as the starting-point of a thorough-going *transformation* of our whole economic constitution. The War, that is to say, with what its hardship has won for us in terms of socialist measures and legislation, will be made the occasion of a permanent and essential revolution in our economy—a swing in a direction which, so they say, would be more in keeping with the historic German outlook, that for centuries maintained an organic economic pattern of estates, guilds and fellowships of all kinds. Demands such as that for a year of National Service for women—likewise originating in ideas strongly flavoured with socialism—or the demand for a uniformity of national schooling, doing away with schools providing for special sections of the community as well as class-differences from school to school, are readily aligned with this idea. Do we conform to the Christian idea of community if we welcome this way of thinking?

That question I answer with a decided No!

It would be utterly wrong first to distinguish (with many sociologists and economists, *e.g.* H. Dietzel) a so-called social and a so-called individual principle and then simply to place the Christian idea of community on the side of other ideas which can be ranged under the heading of the so-called social principle. For the Christian idea of community is a *third party*—neither one principle nor the other, nor a sorry conflation of the two.* Certainly the Christian idea of community has the internal motive capacity to *organize* the body politic economically into, say, a system of 'estates' and professional communities of various kinds. But if the spirit of the idea is to prevail this must, in the first place, be done in such a way that the individual, atomic psycho-physical unit whose core is the God-created soul retains, in its very existence as an economic being,

---

[1] Cf. my remarks, '*1789 und 1914*', on Joh. Plenge's book of that title, in the *Archiv für Sozialwissenschaft und Sozialpolitik*, Vol. 42, No. 2, and my article on Walter Rathenau's *Von kommenden Dingen* in *Hochland*, 1917.

its own free and *independent scope* for the exercise of its rights and legitimate activities. Secondly, it must be done in such a way that without initial compulsion from omnipotent centralized legislation that individual joins with his fellows, in an essentially co-operative spirit, into one moral whole made up of free components. In so doing he must be fired not by any State-imposed ideal but by a moral-religious insight—his consciousness, that is, of his natural and moral *membership* of a whole range of constitutionally different communities (differing according to the values and activities with which they are concerned, and ranking in accordance with the objective scale of those values). I have already made the following statement: 'In a human community organized under inspiration of religious thought the smallest piece of work of any person has a *meaning* far beyond its immediate object and his individual intention. He knows that in carrying out his task he is obeying a secret injunction which resounds in differing intensities through the various kinds of collectivity to which he belongs (estate, professional community, race, nation, etc.), but whose *original* point of departure is the total meaning which God has bestowed on the world-order of which he is the overlord. In modern man this *meaning* and the higher *dedication* of work have gone astray, and with them any kind of world-significance in a man's daily toil.'[1]

But this does not mean that every one of us should become in effect a kind of State-official or State-employee in one great beehive. No, it means that even without being an official or employee of the State a man should carry out his task, no matter how toilsome, willingly and joyfully, with a religious sense and consciousness that his work has the character of an *office* and dutiful service; in this frame of mind he should perform his industrial function in whatever higher or lower position God has called him to through his natural endowments, his estate and the course of history, which is in God's hands. To the extent that this occurs the *opposition* between bureaucracy and citizen, State and people, which was far too pronounced in our country before the War, is moderated and relaxed, thereby rendering the bitter pill of disruptive socialism—which presupposes the non-existence of a spirit of Christian community, hence the moral sickness of the body politic—a remedy no longer needed. For we must sharply distinguish the sense of personal *office*, which as it spreads makes officials redundant, from the socialist regimentation which would direct each person to his official function. We can at least say that the sense of office is as traditionally German as Catholic, and that there are

---

[1] Chapter on '*Soziologische Neuorientierung und die Aufgabe der deutschen Katholiken nach dem Krieg*' in *Krieg und Aufbau*.

very few basic elements of our moral consciousness where 'German' and 'Catholic' so happily and deeply coincide as here.

But at the same time we have to make a sharp division between an essentially *free* economy, which after the War would discard socialistic measures of merely passing necessity, and the old misconceived liberal system of unregulated *competition*. What is wrong in that system is *not* the freedom of the economy as an objective expression of equity but the *spirit* informing competition, the boundless craze to have more and be more, the struggle of all against all. There is, however, no reason in principle why this spirit of limitless *pleonexia*, this emphatically disagreeable spirit, this meanest destroyer of self-respect, should not pervade a State and imbue its economic officers with *exactly* the same facility as is habitually (but *not* necessarily) to be found in subjects of an essentially free economy. That is why it is so harmful and misleading to think, as many do, that the alternative of socialism 'or' free economy, as objective *moulds* of law and organization, is a statement with reference to the economic *spirit* of a nation. If for example the spirit of acquisitive competition is the *spiritus rector* of the leading minority, and the corporate body forsakes the forms of individualist economy to adopt the socialist mould, that spirit is simply transferred to the new subject, 'State', which now proceeds to satisfy this spirit of perdition in a new *form* and at the cost of other States and the non-ruling sections of the population. Thus there is no necessary reason why that spirit should disappear with the adoption of a socialist economy. Even with regard to the juster distribution of goods State-socialism is only of assistance *if* it really is the spirit of *justice* which animates the leaders and officials of the socialistic State. Otherwise socialism is as capable as a freer system of leading to the most unfair enrichment of the governing economic class. If it is the War which, having brought the financially powerful and its own *nouveaux riches* to the top, has necessitated the first steps toward a socialist economy, there is all the *less* reason for supposing that, when such measures no longer represent a sop thrown in emergency to the suffering masses, they will ensure a permanently more *equitable* distribution of wealth than a free economy.

One thing more we must add: We Christians believe that in general terms the authority of the State is held from God—not that this sanctions any given constitution or régime—and we believe that if the need arises the State has the right to interfere with and rearrange economic life, within limits to subordinate men as economic subjects. Yet we also believe that man is superior to the State, to all its interference and legislation, as a subject of *spiritual cultivation*, free speech and cultural self-expression, not to mention the *religious* subject and member of the Body of Christ. But if ever we were to fall under the dominance of a pervasive State-socialism and be wholly dependent on the State economically—thus for our hold on life—the State would be in a position to try to compel us even in *spiritual* matters, in the very sanctum of religious conscience, to adopt whatever dispositions accorded with the government of the day. And in our special case, here and now, we must be prepared to find that, simply on account of the *technical* problems which will follow the War in economics, finance and taxation, the type of German whose expert knowledge and experience promises the cleverest solutions will have obtained the controlling office of State—if not the supreme seat of power. Now, however respectful his representatives will be to us, they will bring to their offices more than their expert knowledge: they will bring their whole attitude to life, their outlook on the world. I hope I do not need to tell you how improbable it is that these will bear much resemblance to our Christian philosophy or be sympathetically disposed to it.

And so it is not a question of introducing a systematic State-socialism, but one of spreading an economic *spirit* in accord with the Christian idea of community. But at least there are two points at which we can make contact. Firstly, the fact, which is undoubtedly momentous, that the War has shattered the utopian idols of the masses; secondly, the present tendency of the best elements among the workers to emerge from an unstable anti-State and often anticlerical *class* into a stable *estate* equipped with firm rights and prepared as such to take its place in the organic life of the nation.

Knowing human nature and the ways of history one may certainly pour scorn on the 'State of the future' in which so many of our people placed their hope before the War. Of course it is a fetish which contravenes all the basic laws of human nature. But one should always pause to reflect that it is unloving merely to scoff at what the *soul* of a man privately lives by, builds on, hopes for, for whose sake it endures a hard life—even if it is mistaken. And here we have not one soul but very many. I do not know if you are aware that this modern idea of an ideal future State has a *religious* psychological root. You know that it stems from the ideological world of Karl Marx; you know that Karl Marx was a Jew and you know that even today believing Jewry has *Messianism* as one of the deepest roots of its faith. Judah bore all its vicissitudes with the strength of this Messianic hope which led it onward. Even those Jews who have lost their faith have retained this *form* of thinking and hoping toward the future, even if they have substituted quite another content, such as modern aspirations, for the coming of the Messiah. The material they have poured into the old mould they think to have derived from 'scientific' deliberation. We know that the psychological origin of the modern Utopia was this religious cast of thinking: religious Messianism, as exhibited by Marx.[1] And there is no doubt that over large sections of our population this ideal of the 'future State', itself of religious origin, has been functioning as the *surrogate* of a positive religion. It has been standing in the minds of men exactly where God should be, and the blessed hope of seeing him in the life of eternity. That is no strange thing. I believe one may contend and prove, in the philosophy and psychology of religion, that the finite mind *does not have* the choice of believing in something or not believing in anything. Any man who examines himself or his fellows will find that he identifies himself, or they identify themselves, with a particular good or kind of good in such a way that his (or their) personal relationship to that good may be summarized in these words: 'Without thee, in which I believe, I cannot be, I will not be, I ought not to be. We two, I and thou good, stand and fall together.' Of course the content of this good varies infinitely according to individuals, peoples, classes, etc. To the servants of Mammon it is money, to State-worshippers the State, to the nationalist the nation—or to anyone who makes the nation the 'supreme good'. To the child it may be a doll. *Thus man believes either in a God or in an idol. There is no third course open!* But it follows that if a man's faith in his idol is shaken, if he is *disillusioned* about the place it ought to occupy in his system of ideals, if the false god for which he felt such inordinate love, hope and faith is sent toppling, then all about him should look on that man with love and awe, arrested with emotion. Now is the time when something great may take place within him: he may grow ripe for belief in the one *true* God. To *that* God our hearts and minds have a natural bias, a natural link of significance. Once the idols are shattered and there is a *void* where every man can only be full, the soul inclines *of itself* to return to God, and to him it will return unless it is distracted and turns aside after new idols. So now this idol of great masses has been shattered we have boundless opportunities of action. Let us ensure that *faith* fills the countless voids and we will have done much to bridge the abyss between our people and the true beliefs to which they must return.

Secondly—and this is much more intimately linked with the first point than many think—let us work to this end: to transform the working *class* into an *estate*.[2] An estate is something stable, a standing or status, something wherein a man is self-sufficient, but which he nevertheless does not freely choose like a profession, since he merely finds himself 'placed' there. But to know one's estate is to be truly *at home* in the State, at home

[1] Cf. the striking arguments of J. Plenge in his *Marx und Hegel*, Tübingen 1911.
[2] This is the passage to which reference is made in my note to p. 380 (*Translator*).

in the consciousness of firmly defined and assured lawful rights on which no one may trespass. The idea of the estate and a certain order of estates, according to the values and functions with which each one is concerned, is totally inseparable from the Christian idea of community. On the other hand there is no reason why the number and character of estates, and their relationship to the State, should not change with historical circumstances. As you know, to the so-called three estates, priesthood, nobility and bourgeoisie, a 'fourth estate' was added after the French Revolution. But today it would be quite inaccurate to speak of only four estates. One should at least see the beginnings of new estates in the free-lance professions, intellectual or otherwise, which for a long time have sided rather with the fourth estate than with the capitalists with whom they have educationally more in common. However, I do not wish to probe that question here; it is better that I should attempt to define the characteristics of the 'spirit of *estate*' as opposed to the *class*-spirit.

The spirit of estate is characterized by love of the *work*, the created product and its quality, as the first motive of activity and labour, by care for the gross yield as second motive and by love of the net return (*i.e.* profit) only as the third motive. In contrast the naked class-spirit begins with the purely quantitative cash-value and every other consideration is reluctantly taken into account if and when it offers a means to the lucrative end. Class is Mammon. In the estate there is a *limit* to acquisitive toil, which finds a boundary in the family's needs for the preservation of living-standards fitting to the estate. In the class there is *no limit* to a man's acquisitive exertions, except that of bare *force majeure* in the competitive struggle of all against all. This is not to say that in the estate one neither compares oneself with other members of it nor strives to get ahead of them. But there is *not* this incessant comparison of oneself and one's position with members of *other* estates, a comparison which automatically produces monstrous envy and hatred. On the other hand, where there are only classes and all estates have disintegrated everybody must continually compare himself with everyone else, since here it is not the *substance* of the work which is felt as the positive motive of activity but always the being or having '*more* than my neighbour'. For that reason the phenomena of class-envy and class-hatred are inseparable. They are all the more inseparable as class-differences (which are always primarily differences of wealth) are seen to increase within one and the same formal status or legal standing of citizens. But, let us give thanks for it, that process has been halted for a long time now in Germany. Quite apart, then, from its particular qualities, a class-ridden society is laden with hatred and envy by virtue of its very structure.

Furthermore the estate has an 'honour' and a 'conscience', the class only a collective interest. The class has only the rights it has won for itself in battle, whereas the rights of the estate accrue by virtue of the *free, solidary union* in which it intrinsically joins with other estates and the State as a whole.

Now the social order in which we live at present is a remarkable mixture of estates and classes; on the one hand it is encumbered with a structure which is preponderantly—by a long way—a class-structure, but undeniably, on the other hand, it *tends* to reorganize into new estate-patterns. This tendency is one which our Christian idea of community commands us to further and assist on every occasion. It is a process for which no State-planning from above can substitute. It must above all be a process of *voluntary* self-organization, which, when the new-formed or re-formed estates have attained a certain maturity and viability, will be able to set the seal on them by obtaining a clear definition of their legal standing in the State.

I have intentionally refrained from touching too directly on practical problems. I have done so because nothing seems more important to me today than to place the *eternal values* of the Christian idea of community in relation with the great co-ordinates of world-history and evolution, so that those values may speak for themselves and live.

We have arrived, I feel, at a moment when the morning breath of spring, though faint, is discernible for our hopes of winning a great part of Europe back to the Christian idea of community. A host of signs announce the morning glow. Perhaps I shall have some other opportunity to speak of these signs and to try to interpret them. But this very task, this new situation brought about by God's great summons to conversion which the War has carried to all quarters of Europe, imposes a doubly sacred trust on all Christians.

Hitherto the Christian elements of Europe have had to spend the greater part of their energies on a mere *self-preservation* against the onslaught of modern civilization in all fields, on protecting the holy flame of their faith against the raging storms. Prudence, not to say alarm, dictated a contraction into the tightly-knit Christian community and a shutting-out of the world. But see what an attitude and atmosphere arose from this —a kind of ghetto-spirit, one which does not altogether correspond to the open, expansive, reverent catholicity, the breath of infinite compassion which constantly informs the inner spirit of the Church of Christ. It was a situation born of need. But now the very foundations of the modern secular civilization that has become estranged from the Church are rocking with no negligible violence—they are splitting and cracking more irreparably than history itself can tell!

As yet there is, to be sure, no more than a murmur of undermining doubt, the self-questioning of this civilization, the shaking of its beliefs. But its cry for help will grow louder and louder, and more and more bitter its plea for rescue. Already a new will to expiate and repent is germinating in its heart, and a grave disillusion over all that was the object of its prayers, all which it originally followed in a mood of triumph. After the War, when the nations become slowly *aware* of what they have done, this germ of sorrow will grow into a powerful tide, a river of tears sweeping through Europe. Nevertheless, repentance is the only path to renewal, the way to rebirth not only for individuals but also for society.

At this present time an immeasurable prize is staked on the hope that the Christian Church will heed that cry for help. All its adherents, in the strength of a vivified faith and morality to which they first must open their hearts, must open them wide and generously to pour forth the living stream of faith and love, now flowing secretly pent within the Church, into a world in sore need of faith and love—a world beginning to ask for them, a world desiring them as never before.

THE RECONSTRUCTION OF
EUROPEAN CULTURE

THE RECONSTRUCTION OF
EUROPEAN CULTURE

An Address

1. THE POLITICAL FRAMEWORK AND MORAL CONDITIONS OF CULTURAL RECONSTRUCTION IN EUROPE[1]

IN a recent work[2] I traced back to their various sources the waves of hatred by which the German people is besieged. At the conclusion of that work I described the moral attitude which it seemed fitting to adopt when faced by almost the entire world's hatred. Moving on from those findings my present question is this: how can we build anew the moral and spiritual culture of Europe, which has been shaken in its deepest foundations and now—to change the image—flutters in the wind like a flag in tatters over fields of dead? What spirit, what inner purpose must animate men to that end? What personal values, what incipient cultural trends are suited to that high purpose; which are to be encouraged and which to be condemned and combated? What kind of education, instruction, formation must the rising generation receive to assist the possibility of such a renewal? What substantially should be the *content* of our personal cultural ideal; and, if we are to succeed in the seemingly hopeless, Herculean enterprise, what exemplars of human personality should we hope to see at the head—whether as statesmen, teachers, educationalists, officials, priests or citizens—of States, nations and all kinds of cultural institution?

[1] The following thoughts were first expressed in the form of an address in the Urania at Vienna in the autumn of 1917. Though the opening passage, meant to suggest an approach to political problems of the day, no longer has topical significance, the author has thought fit to retain it. For one should not withhold from posterity the slightest proof that as early as 1917 it *was* possible to see where the German government's ruinous policies and the mentality of the Germanic peoples must inevitably steer the *Reich*.*

[2] *Die Ursachen des Deutschenhasses*, Leipzig 1917.

My theme is confined to the reconstruction of *culture*,[1] as distinct from political, judicial and economic forms.* But we may not forget that cultural reconstruction can only form a part of general reconstruction, nor that its scope will be determined by the provisions of political and even economic reorganization.

A truly objective mind, even if it owes allegiance to the outlawed Central Powers, cannot ignore that the parts of the world now hostile to us have been *united* in the three-year course of this war to an extent which a whole century of peace would scarcely have rendered possible, and this is true even in the cultural direction. Doubtless it is a terrible thought for us that the incentive to unification was in the first place a mere common hatred, a common struggling against the Germans, but there is no removing this great fact: this union, in any of its many forms, can and indeed will outlive its occasion, which is transitory though so bitter for us to contemplate. In that the quarters of the globe are not battling chaotically one against another but are united in directing their lances at our heart alone—at the heart of countries microscopic enough on earth—the problem of the evolving unity of world-culture, and in particular of the *European* mind, has been vastly simplified. Only one great step (the 'only' sets the scale of my observation) is necessary—the *one* great reconciliation with us Germans—and the world would be more united than it has ever been before. Whether this step is taken, and whether it succeeds, depends on our enemies as well as on ourselves. But for the present we can only take counsel of ourselves and urge courses on ourselves; of ourselves therefore let us speak.

Those uniform manners and institutions, those spiritual currents which we call *culture* certainly do not follow unerringly the path of political forms and institutions. From these they frequently part company and go their separate way—often they take the opposite path, as happened when Rome, having conquered Greece politically, was Hellenized in the process. Be that as it may, in our present situation we are faced with the problem of the political framework, on which the cultural structure of Europe is also

[1] Germans often refer to *Kultur* as Americans to their 'way of life' and Englishmen seldom willingly to anything. Therefore 'culture' in these pages often carries implications far beyond the aesthetic bias of common usage, and it need scarcely be said that when this is apparent the author has not inflated a concept equivalent to that commonly embodied in the English word. Unfortunately *Kultur* is not used in reference to self-cultivation or the implementation of cultural ideals in educational policy and less formal upbringing—the business of *faire un homme ou faire un citoyen*. Here the word is *Bildung* ('formation'), for which 'culture' is often the best word we have, so that the English word does double duty in the following pages (*Translator*).

directly dependent. Though the bare framework in no way *ensures* any cultural rebirth, it is nevertheless a prerequisite and indispensable.

The political provisions of the peace-treaty which concludes this war will also decide the fate of Europe's cultural reconstruction—decide, that is, whether Europe will henceforth be the geographical label for a lacerated body of jealous nationalities *or* a mighty spiritual unity which, having so long led the world, still has something important to *give* to it. As yet we can be sure of nothing with respect to the nature or content of the peace-settlement. Much is still shrouded in boundless fog. That we have made an armistice with Russia, that it is with her that we have first negotiated, wholly gratifies the wish and hope I expressed at the beginning of hostilities, and satisfies still more the group of requirements for cultural reconstruction which I mean to put before you today. First of all, however, I should like to express my feeling that the spirit of the Austrian Emperor's note to the Pope, and of Count Czernin's important *exposé* in his Budapest speech, expresses with fair accuracy that basic attitude to political and constitutional problems which avoids precluding cultural unity and reconstruction from the outset but offers, given other favourable conditions, a framework in which they may be attempted. Allow me just a few more remarks in connection with this problem in the *foreground* of our inquiry; in my opinion a certain form of political subdivision of Europe represents the minimum of requirements for cultural reconstruction.

I frankly confess that I am both more and less of a 'pacifist' than accords with the latest 'official pacifism' of the Central governments, even if you take into account the (quite rightly) very different shades of the word adopted in reference to Germany on the one hand or Austria on the other. I am *less* of one, because—even as a foreseeable historical goal—I think we hear too much of 'world-disarmament', and I think too many people are setting their hearts on it. I think it would be better to formulate our aims as 'systematic bilateral disarmament *within* the spiritual zone of European civilization'—and disarmament of nations only in proportion to their proximity to that zone or their partaking of that spirit. I am, or believe myself to be, *more* of a 'pacifist' because I should like to see true pacifism, the only Christian variety, the pacifism of serious peaceful *intent and conviction** still more sharply distinguished and set apart from the *ad hoc* pacifism of mere *necessity*, which combines with an understandable dread of intolerable costs for armaments after the War. That serious pacifism of peaceful intent is the only kind which I can regard as a contribution, within the scope of European life and spirit, to the atmosphere necessary for any cultural reconstruction.

But let us abandon that slogan of Utopian pacifism, that this is a 'war to end wars', a phrase quite heedless of world-history and the range of its future possibilities. Do we know for certain what lies ahead in Japan's expansionist drive against European cultural enclaves and the United States? We do not. For Japan, among others, there does not exist that power-political impasse which Count Czernin has turned into a vivid plea for world-disarmament. Moreover, the internal stresses which form the unity of the European family of peoples and for that very reason demand *here* and now the true spirit of peaceful intent—forces within whose ambit alone any cultural collaboration may thrive—these do not exist for this east-Asiatic people so utterly unlike us in ethos, spirit, manners and customs.

But the more we practise discretion, refraining from talk of the 'war to end wars', the more boldly we should press within the European cultural zone for something quite different from a disarmament imposed by necessity, *i.e.* the positive Christian spirit of true and serious conciliation and the erection of legal structures in accordance with it. Never and nowhere do legal treaties establish a true community of their own accord; at best they express it. If they are to be more than formulations *rebus sic stantibus* of reciprocal power-relationships, of economic advantages and disadvantages, treaties must be imbued with the warmth of peaceable spirit, good faith, understanding, the sense of justice and a feeling of spiritual kinship. And on yet a third point I should like to add a rider to Count Czernin's speech. It is not enough to pose the demand for European disarmament in a *hypothetic* form, conditional on the changing war-situation; it must be presented in an *absolute* form. Already the war-situation has changed so completely with regard to Russia and Italy[1] that to suppose the Count's sentiments valid only in the circumstances prevailing at the time of their utterance would be tantamount to destroy-ing the very sense of his speech. The very sense of the plea for a truly last-ing European peace-settlement—which I can claim to have seen from the beginning as the one thing which could make sense of the War[2]—will not tolerate dilution with hypotheses and reservations. I can call to mind no age in history which was more inclined to make an illusory virtue of necessity than these present war-years. Today there is for instance a pronounced socialism imposed on individuals and governments by *necessity*, and many are expecting it to work miracles when the War is over, expecting the emergence of a new era in mankind. The pacifism of

[1] These words were uttered directly after the successful offensive of the Central Powers against Italy.
[2] See the chapter entitled *'Die geistige Einheit Europas'* in *Der Genius des Krieges*.

necessity to which I have referred is a parallel phenomenon, and is no less distinct from the true spirit of peace than the socialism born of poverty or the socialism of equality by taxation is distinct from the true spirit of solidarity. Necessity can only occasion, it cannot create, though it may select ideas which are not only true for the moment but are *also* true and right *in themselves*. But here as always, in this question of disarmament, it is the spirit which forms the body and the legal organism. Just as a Galician Jew earning ten kronen a day may possess as strong a capitalist spirit as a Berlin banker in daily receipt of a thousand marks, so States with armies proportionally as small can be as unpacific as States with armies no matter how large, especially if all that limits the size of armies is the economic and financial restraint imposed by the *necessity* of the nation's affairs. As I see it, there are three signs in reference to the peace-settlement whereby we may distinguish the European and Christian spirit of peace from the pacifism of necessity and expediency: 1. recognition that for every belligerent party the *first* peace-question is—or should be—the total re-ordering of Europe into a new political organism; recognition that the sectional political interests of the belligerents should only come under discussion once the *framework* of the new order has been decided and established; 2. abandonment of reliance on so-called 'assurances' and 'solid guarantees'—a point on which unfortunately a gulf that cannot be concealed has opened between the Austrian and German governments—; 3. the belief that the new political order of European nations must itself be allowed to produce the positive peace, the character of the final settlement, *i.e.* the reverse of the notion that a new system of inter-European legal relations might proceed as afterthought and embellishment from a treaty concluded with an eye to redressing the so-called balance of power. Not international relations which legalize the upper hand of the sword, but only world-co-ordinations born of the strength and supremacy of the very ideas of *law and justice* hold out a promise of *permanence*—the stability alone conducive to that atmosphere in which a cultural reconstruction is possible.

If these basic principles were heeded and satisfied, there would be a further minimal condition for cultural reconstruction: the fulfilment of three requirements which I can here only indicate in brief. 1. The avoidance of a situation fomenting lasting passions of revenge in whole peoples (not merely in isolated interests within nations); this has particular reference to France and Russia, where we have the strongest temptations to make large-scale annexations. 2. Once for all we must reject a political method which of its *nature* was such that conflicts of interest in extra-European zones of colonization, selling-markets and colonial affairs not only exerted a back-pressure on internal European foreign policies and alliances (this can hardly be avoided) but even—quite probably— underlay and moulded them. Or, positively speaking, in extra-European affairs the States of Europe must learn to act in *solidarity*, *i.e.* in conformity with the principle of mutual responsibility and acting as one for the over-riding common interest. So far as possible England should be a party to this—but at *all* events the continental States must join together in this way. 3. Finally there must follow—in general terms—a devolution of many tasks and responsibilities, which have hitherto fallen to the lot of the huge political power-giants confronting each other in this war, upon a *multi-plicity* of bodies unattached to any State (some of them below the dignity of States, some above them in authority and others inter-State in function). At the same time there should take place everywhere a certain *loosening* of those abnormally centralized centres of power, culture and economic strength, a certain dismantling and *decentralization* in favour of their numerous subdivisions (nations, peoples, races, federated States, colonies), which must be such as to leave in essentials only *technical or co-ordinative*, hence innocuous, organizational tasks to the central authority. Thereby the power-romanticism of these centralisms would be dissipated and their claim to shape cultures permanently dismissed. What I have in mind may be summarized as the tendency to increasing *federalism* and the cultural *self*-government of each separate nationhood.

Unless these minimal requirements are satisfied I *cannot* seriously imagine any cultural reconstruction of Europe. In reference to the first condition the central question at present, the great, the decisive question, is that of Alsace-Lorraine; with it is linked the somewhat less urgent question of whether we should succumb to the temptation, fostered by English foreign policy, of making annexations in the East (thus mainly at Russia's expense) as compensation for what we cannot obtain, or do not wish to seek, in the West. It is not my business, nor is it the right time, to make positive suggestions with regard to Alsace. I would only say one thing: in handling this problem *all* kinds of political mysticism must be avoided like the plague. By political mysticism I mean a conception which refuses to look at this corner of land (whether from the French or the German point of view) in the only permissible manner for the purpose of lasting peace. That is, firstly with an eye to the real values (economic, military, etc.), bestowed by its possession and secondly as a component in the complex of all questions of a territorial or 'sphere of interest' nature. Political mysticism prefers to cast a veil of mystery over this plot of land, to make it a fetish, an object of infatuation, a kind of banner for whose possession one must fight to the last breath of the last European—

not for its real value as a piece of cloth but regarding it as a 'symbol and escutcheon' (to borrow Herr von Kühlmann's picturesque expression), or as something *torn* from the context of all other possible objects of negotiation and isolated as if it were an absolute and no merely relative thing. Even before the War the whole of Europe was suffering from this political mysticism with reference to Alsace, and it is time it were banned as a method of approach. However little we may seriously entertain the total or even partial reversion of Alsace-Lorraine to France, this whole question is one which must form the object of *negotiation*—direct negotiation with France, not in the first place with England; this for the simple reason that any negotiation with England would, just as England wishes, bind France more closely and irrevocably to her than is already the case. Negotiation and eventual agreement neither presuppose any cession of territory, nor do they imply in any way that our German sense of having won back Alsace-Lorraine legitimately in 1870 has weakened or faded. Negotiation could also lead to some kind of *quid pro quo* and other forms of settlement. If a nation noted for its morbid ambition has for forty years been obsessed with a plot of land it feels to have been snatched from it, it is difficult to imagine a psychological situation more favourable for the opposite party to strike a particularly good bargain, one wherein the wounded honour of one side is healed while the other side gains a very real improvement.

Both this dangerous mysticism over Alsace and the thirst for eastward annexations with which it is often associated form part of a policy, it seems to me, which fails to grasp that England—not from ill will but by virtue of its total historico-geographical position—must be the enemy of all continental solidarity in cultural and political fields—and will remain its enemy so long as some external force of circumstances does not compel her to conduct herself as a *member*, not (as heretofore) the master and judge, of Europe. The only kind of settlement which anyone may contemplate who does not want the perpetual starvation-peace of rearmament and the permanent exclusion of the Central Powers from sources of raw material— is a negotiated peace. If this is to come about we must reach *some* understanding with France even over Alsace, however difficult this may still appear. For the sake of the second requirement, that of European solidarity in extra-European affairs, this understanding must first be reached among the *continental* nations, bringing England into agreements only at a second stage and wherever possible. Again, to make forcible annexations in the East would foment a thirst for revenge which would nullify attempts at cultural reconstruction and bind Russia permanently to England.

Finally the third precondition of cultural reconstruction, the decentralization of the political power-giants, has now for the most part been satisfied in Russia, and is pressing to be satisfied with more and more success in the reborn Austria. It is also most likely that a similar devolution will ensue in the British Empire when the War is over—in the sense of an increase in self-government for Ireland and the colonies. If the result of this should be a slackening of the pressure from without upon Central Europe, in particular the German *Reich*, then it would be possible and desirable for the *counterpressure* to ease—that fearful (but hitherto necessary) reaction against encirclement which has produced the politico-military over-centralization of the German Empire under the hegemony of Prussia. Of course, given its overall economic and financial preponderance in Germany, Prussia can never become a simple *member* of the *Reich* while that *Reich* is thought, in the time-honoured way, to stand in the same relationship to a centralistic Austria as existed before the War. Prussia, however, could well become a genuine member of a Central-European whole which, as a whole, would be more united than before but which had decentralized its constitution in culture and internal politics. It could take its place therein without relinquishing its specific, valuable Prussian spirit to the extent that would be unquestionably necessary if it wished to remain the mere *master* of Germany. For in such a case it would have to become, in spirit and institutions, a pocket-edition of the *Reich*—the reverse, that is, of what Treitschke meant and advocated when he called the *Reich* an extended Prussia. But *both* are equally bad. A so-called 'democratization' of Prussia which mimicked the general conditions prevailing over the *Reich* would be no less deplorable than the generalization of Prussianism in accordance with Treitschke's formula.

Today[1] we have yet another factor come to justify the idea of an at least continental solidarity of Europe as a fundamental article of policy for every European State, with the decisive rejection of the formula hitherto guiding all internal European politics: *salus publica suprema lex*. This factor is the radical shift in *America's* position within the Entente since the onset of the German offensive in July 1918. We may express this change in the simplest way by saying that everywhere, obviously or discernibly, the chief seat of the united will to wage war against the Central Powers, the principal source of belligerent energy, has passed from France, and even from England, to the United States. This has happened so markedly and with such rapidity that even England, let alone France,

[1] The following passage, to the end of the introduction (p. 416 l. 4), was written in August 1918.

is reported to feel compelled by the American war-drive to carry on the conflict when special interests bid her end it and pave the way to peace-negotiations. The sense of this pressure is already very lively in France and England, and the latter's fear of falling into a lasting dependence on the U.S.A. in the event of being 'rescued' by Americans is already strongly conflicting with the hope of seeing the Central Powers vanquished by impact of huge forces which are fresh and unused.

Until very recently the importance of American intervention in the quarrels of Europe was underrated in a manner one might almost term scandalous—by the leaders of the Entente as much as by those of the Central Powers. Within the German alliance American psychology continued to be profoundly misread—even after abandonment of the childish argument that America's military preparations were principally aimed at Japan. The vested interests of American big business were still thought to motivate American war-spirit when it had long been known that the American masses were gripped with an *ideological, political* fervour that made it almost the badge of every upstanding citizen to further the 'crusade' against the German 'enemy of mankind'. Beliefs and expectations, which the facts did not warrant, such as that America could not seriously mean to deploy its full power in the War, that sub-marine warfare would sink all or most of her expeditionary forces, that American armies in Europe could never be adequately victualled—not to mention such irresponsible talk as that the American declaration of war was 'advantageous' to us, since it absolved us in the peace-treaty from respecting America and implementing Wilson's proposals for a league of nations—all these follies belittled the American danger in a manner which borders on wilful *self-delusion*. To put it no worse, there was mishandling, from the beginning of their arms-deliveries, of the moral offensive aimed at the psychology of Americans; it might have proved very effective. For it was not in those deliveries as such that the immorality of the American action lay—to them they had a *right* in international law —but in the fact that large areas of American industry had been turned over to the production of munitions to an extent far *beyond* the principles of rational economy and the greatest profit—conduct which even within the United States themselves had been bitterly stigmatized as an infringement of neutrality and 'immoral'.

But the Anglo-French Entente has been as incapable as the Central Powers of appraising the historical novelty of American armies appearing on European soil for the resolution of internal European conflicts; they have been equally slow to grasp the consequences of this epoch-making phenomenon as an example and precedent. They failed to see that the principle of 'America for the Americans', which seeks to restrict European participation in the affairs of the American continent and used to reflect America's basically defensive attitude to the dominance of Europe, now cries out to be *answered* by a much more firmly based slogan, one founded in the course of all history—that of 'Europe for the Europeans'. They failed to foresee the degree of dependence on America which they would incur in all directions if it were really the United States which decided the outcome of this war—and could then with good reason claim the right of supreme arbiter in European affairs, not only in drafting the peace-treaty but for all time to come.

At this time of day it seems to me that Europe can only be saved if both belligerent European parties recognize, openly confess and repudiate these deep-seated errors and delusions, so that on this basis of common insight a re-appraisal of so-called war-objectives might take place on both sides of the battlefront. No previous factor in this war could have afforded a chance of reshaping the war-policy of either side remotely similar to that presented by the manner of this American intervention. Even the collapse of Tsarism and the Russian revolution were unable to effect any bilateral transformation of war-aims, for the very simple reason that they came unilaterally to the help of the Central Powers.

Only now are we confronted with a fact which raises the *idea* of solidary European action in extra-European affairs from the plane and value of a *theoretical* political principle to the plane and value of a *practical* political necessity.

Now for the first time, with the transference of the *principal* seat of conduct of the war against the Central Powers, it is open for both they and the Anglo-French to revise their war-aims without fear of imputations of inconsistency or vacillation. There can be no doubt that in France, and still more in England, there are considerable circles of opinion to whom the thought of being 'rescued' by America is extremely unpalatable. But, if they go roundly to work, the Central Powers can greatly extend the area of these circles and strengthen their influence on their respective governments. To that end it would suffice if, simultaneously with an energetic moral offensive in this direction, we were to remove the main *barriers* which have so far stood in the way of a serious will to negotiate on the part of England and France. The first of these barriers is an invincible mistrust in our political leaders, the second concerns the fate of Belgium, the third that of Alsace-Lorraine.

With regard to the first we must put an end to a situation in which our government so obviously gives the impression of a transient, intermediary phenomenon, as has been the case of late. This impression, intensified by the personality of the present Chancellor, Count Hertling, who is essentially preoccupied with internal policy and stability, and by the lack—to all outward appearances—of a considered foreign policy at the head of affairs—this impression removes from the government's declarations the weight they must claim if we are to bring about a serious will to negotiate. Those of the Entente believe that all declarations vanish with the cabinet that voiced them, and each cabinet they see as a transitory affair. Setting aside the person of the present head of the government, one may even question whether the right man for the task can be a 'parliamentary' chancellor, *i.e.* one who, given the way in which he must have risen to his eminence, has to devote three-quarters of his energies to the appeasement of the parties by whose grace he largely holds office. Even if one firmly desires a *post*-War increase in the influence of Parliament on the conduct of affairs (which alone can educate the parties to increased political responsibility) one can still hold the opinion, without self-contradiction, that at present, in the prevailing mood of the parties, a parliamentary chancellor can scarcely be fitted to the tasks incumbent on him. Far more suitable, as it seems to me, would be a man accredited with a higher public dignity—if possible—who, possessing already in large measure the confidence of the Entente by virtue of his honourable wartime conduct, would be *directly* appointed by the monarch to a form of office which would proclaim him to all and sundry as *the* Chancellor of the Realm; to him, it would be made clear, would be entrusted the *final* conduct of the peace-negotiations. Such a man, I believe, even if he were equipped for the purpose with dictatorial powers, would be more to the point than a parliamentary chancellor.[1] If in internal politics the Crown—as shown by the Rescript issued in February on the subject of the Prussian franchise—has proved more ready to learn from the signs of the times than the parties, who have learned but little and forgotten next to nothing (witness wartime elections!), why should the Crown not make a similarly enlightened intervention in foreign affairs?

The second step which might lead to a serious readiness to negotiate on the part of our opponents is a short, clear, unambiguous declaration on Belgium. This must be unencumbered with talk of 'security-guarantees' or 'holding the country in pledge'—the metaphor is unfelicitous, neither is the attitude it expresses free from objections on grounds of legality and morality. It must therefore be a declaration implying a conscious retreat from our earlier handling of the question, a retreat justified in the

---

[1] This was written a month before the same considerations determined the appointment of Prince Max of Baden as an (ostensibly parliamentarian) *Reichskanzler* (*Translator*).

event of a new will to improve the position of Europe *vis-à-vis* America.

The third step would be the announcement of our readiness to negotiate over Alsace, with the proviso that any cession of all or part of the territory would be outside the scope of the discussion.

So much for the political framework which is the minimal external condition of a European cultural reconstruction. For of course all the above is a question of *external* framework. Even if we were to add as condition the maximal reduction of economic and tariff-warfare—and States are very unwilling to go far in this direction—we would still be discussing the nutshell, not the kernel!

But it is not in these things that the true, positive spiritual forces of reconstruction lie. They lie in freely willing *human beings*, in the private conscience of European man, in his change of heart, in the character and trend of the mental powers productive of culture, the powers that must be strengthened. And here for the first time we are on ground proper to our theme.[1]

All great matters of collaboration—such as this reconstruction—have a primary *moral* condition. Here this first condition takes the shape of the right inner picture which the individual, as a human being, must have or form of this most fearful of historical events. It is a question of how, if at all, he sees its evolution from the whole course of European history and civilization, and of how he reacts psychologically to this total picture.

Therefore I would say: A cultural reconstruction is only possible if an increasingly large proportion of the European population learns to look upon this cataclysm as resulting from a *collective guilt* of the European peoples, resting on their moral solidarity—as, therefore, a guilty evil which can only (if ever) be removed and inwardly conquered by common expiation, common repentance and common sacrifice, and which can only be replaced with the positive blessings of cultural community by dint of co-operative construction, mutual assistance, joint action consequent on solidary responsibility. These three things belong closely together and may not be dissociated: common guilt, common repentance and a common will to rebuild. This last must be a will to rebuild on the basis of a commonly accepted principle that every State, every people, every nation has its appointed place in God's scheme, being called to make a unique and indispensable contribution to a world-culture, and that in this wonderful co-operation of mankind throughout the ages Europe

[1] From this point what I have to say is irrespective of the political situation.

represents a special, comparatively unified circle of civilization with special qualities and a special mission.

First, therefore, must come the recognition that in the final analysis there is only *one* answer to the question, Who or what nation is responsible for this war? The answer is You, the asker of the question—by what you have done, or left undone. I do not say that once and for all the politician or historian must refrain from asking where the *political,* historical guilt for the definite occurrence lies, guilt for the outbreak of August 1914. Of such an interdict there can be no question; no doubt that is a problem which historians will argue to doomsday. What forms the object of collective guilt is not that the War did take place, still less the how and the when of its beginning, but that it *could* take place, that *such* an event was *possible* in this European quarter of the human globe, that it was an event of such a nature as we know it to be. The object of collective guilt is its possibility, then, and its quality, not its actual occurrence and real beginning. As you must be aware, within the individual the object of any deeper guilt-feeling is likewise not 'that I did it' but that I *could* so behave, was *such* a person as could do it.[1] Only this collective act of insight into the *reciprocity* of the shared responsibilities of every belligerent nation and all its subdivisions down to the family and individual can produce the psychological atmosphere from which European culture can arise renewed.

But the second requirement is common repentance, with the will to expiation and sacrifice. There is no psychic power more clairvoyant than repentance, none which more deeply sounds the well of past being, no greater power of healing than this liberating light of our history, which illumines our quintessential self. It is repentance indeed which enables man to acquire that kind of historical knowledge which not only describes the past but does the most important thing that historical knowledge can do—unburden from the past, free and strengthen the soul for a new future, a new power of action. I would like to think that the history of that bourgeois civilization which culminated in the War will be recounted for long years to come in such a way that it should appear to represent—in illustration and judgment—one great painful act of repentance. For before one can be prepared to build anew one must feel free of the past, and one must genuinely believe it possible to order the world otherwise than it was before the War, *i.e.* than the world which led to that war. On principle we must break with the old German vice of traditionalism, that false sense of historical determination in its thousand-and-one habitual forms, not to mention the ten-thousand-and-one academic theories it has fostered. And

[1] Cf. the section on 'Repentance and Rebirth'.

o

a new feeling of *freedom* is something we can only receive from our collective repentance for collective guilt. The 'modern era' is an unbroken *chain* of revolutions and semi-revolutions; its works have been *essentially* artificial works of arbitrary intellectual interference. Has it the right to talk of 'organic growths' we have a duty to preserve?

It thus goes without saying that there can be no question of reconstruction in the sense of merely *restoring* the cultural relations of the decades before the War. When I employ the word reconstruction in the title of this essay I do not mean restoration but only the regaining of the true *forces* which go to form the essential unity of Europe as a civilization— and an essential building *anew* by means of these forces.

We may not, then, follow the line of thought not uncommonly taken by foul-weather pacifists, that some genuine European spiritual community has been shattered and riven by a war conjured up by wicked rulers against the will of the people, and that we must now set about restoring the former concord. This is no truer than the proposition that the War created the hatred; of course it only brought it to light.[1] It is no truer than talk of the 'peacefulness of the democracies'. All this is the most repulsive national or popular pharisaism, and the very antithesis of the state of conscience in which one may begin to construct. It is a lie that the people were peaceable and only goaded into war by governments.[2] This, on the contrary, must be our point of departure, that genuine spiritual community, both among individuals and among those minorities which pre-eminently shape and represent culture, is absolutely *invulnerable* and cannot be rent asunder. Had such a community existed we could have been sure that it would have been revealed in the trial of war (had it failed to avert it altogether) and have asserted itself as a *spiritual* bond resisting the stress of division. Therefore, no truly *spiritual* bond held Europe together before the War. Why, it is a veritable definition of 'friendship' that it must be manifested in the fighting together against interests opposed to the friends. What passed for friendly relations before the War was no true spiritual bond of friendship but quite other things, things such as the exchange of diplomatic courtesies, international luxury and pleasure-seeking, international specialist interests in technology and science, declarations of good will, the boundless inanity of mutual back-scratching, the barrage of flattery designed to distract one another's attention from the widening abysses which long had yawned between one national spirit and another. That the War has uncovered and exposed this inner mendacity, this lying sham of European cultural community, long

---

[1] See the introduction to my book, *Die Ursachen des Deutschenhasses*.
[2] Cf. my *Krieg und Aufbau.**

corroded with the poisons of nationalism, subjectivism, relativism, capitalism—that the hidden wounds of Europe's soul have broken out in nauseating, eye-offending, evil-smelling but *healing* suppuration—for that thanks be even to this war! Here the War is not the cause of the disease but the diagnostic physician and analyst of the European soul. After all I have written before the War about the moral condition of Europe I hope I may appropriate the words of Stefan George in his poem '*Der Krieg*': 'Long have I known your devastating news'.[1] And so, when we bear in mind this moral causation, we must know there is no question of simply restoring the pre-war Europe by the external reconnection of scholar to scholar, artist to artist, etc., by the arrangement of international congresses, periodicals, institutes—in short, by purely external, *organizational* measures. Instead we must clearly recognize the movement of recent European history down the slope to the abyss, its spiritual self-destruction and moral dissolution. Now at least, at this eleventh hour, it behoves us truly to heed—to hear, as it were, with the ear of the soul—the divine ultimatum which this war delivers, for the sake of preserving the world-mission of our part of the earth and its total spiritual survival. Now in particular we must be mindful of the very real forces of destruction latent in the beginnings of that historical trend whose once-obscured goal and only possible *end* the stupidest eye can now see in this war.

No mere restoration, then, but *conversion* of culture; a radical change of heart and the serious will to build anew.

Undoubtedly there are European values for whose restoration we may rely on human egoism, on all kinds of vested interest, combined with geographical relationships, the unequal distribution of national riches, the varying nature of exportable assets and other values and forces. Forces of this kind will restore certain values in a quasi-automatic manner, whether or no there is any *crise de conscience*, change of heart and renewal of will. To such values belongs to a large extent (though one that can be overestimated) the free exchange of goods, for example our trade with the Russian granary—one will continue to buy what is best, cheapest and closest at hand. Trade, then, is in this category as well as the cross-fertilizing exchange of all those mental functions, services, values and products in which different nations, peoples, civilizations and their subjects can '*stand in*' for one another because what is *peculiar* to the individual spirits of these group-units is not represented. To a considerable degree what enters this category is not the already differentiated national *methods* of approach but the mere exportable *results* of mathematics and the exact

---

[1] '*Was euch erschüttert, ist mir lang vertraut*'—more literally, 'What you find so shattering is to me an object of long familiarity' (*Translator*).

sciences—technical advances, systems of weights and measures, terminologies, renowned international foundations for the furtherance of agri-
culture, geophysics, meteorology and countless other studies. And we may
add to the list, though already with more reservation, higher education
and the acceptance of international civil rights. Moreover, the human
pleasure-quest, encouraged by hotelier interests, will see to it that at no
far-off date the rich of Europe will once again be shaking hands, with
every external sign of affection, on the Riviera, in Cairo, in Monte Carlo
—with the kind of fraternization they now exhibit in Switzerland. The
senses and sensual enjoyment are as international as big-business—the
more so the lower the pleasure.

At bottom, however, none of these things have *anything* to do with
European *cultural* community. Far from moving within the range of the
European mind, they spread *wherever* there are self-indulgent men and
women capable of sensual or intellectual enjoyment—to Japan, say, or
China. No; for me the idea of *European* cultural community begins only
where the most universalized interests of international 'society' stop
working, in principle, in favour of unification; the need for the *will* to
bestir itself morally, the requirement of a change of heart begin only
where peoples are *inimitable*, unique, individual in their works and gifts,
in their spiritual inclinations and objects of love, where—so to speak—
they look down from a metaphysical viewpoint all their *own* into the one
cosmos of truth, beauty and goodness, at the same time beholding the one
God from their own special point of view. Certainly the damnable idea of
world-mastery by *one* nation or *one* State is not excluded by the mere
acknowledgment and existence—however widespread—of those imitable,
international products and phenomena. For the very reason that if
need be one nation can do duty for another in the production of such values,
there is no reason why even a *single* nation, having extended its sway to the
maximum, should not in theory represent every other nation, the whole of
mankind. Therefore, what makes the idea of world-supremacy damnable is
certainly not the international principle of society with its concomitant
utilitarian values and formal criteria of legality; it is the very *uniqueness*
and *irreplaceability* of national and ethnic individuality in the construction
of a coherent total culture of humanity.* Only from this principle does it
follow that *every* people, inasmuch as it shares in the construction of the
world-culture of the human spirit, is *ipso facto co*-responsible for the realization of the share which its neighbour or *any* other people is called by God
to perform and provide.

Thus, in respect of the higher spiritual culture, cosmopolitanism and the
insistence that culture is national are *not opposites*—they are not even two

different truths but only the *sides of a single truth*. And this one truth stands opposed to both internationalism *and* cultural 'nationalism'.

The *inimitable* values of distinctive religious and ecclesiastical forms, of art, history, the humanities, philosophy, the higher forms of manners and customs, are therefore beyond the competence of the above egoistic forces, which function automatically at lower levels, but cease here to be effective. Here for the first time a deliberate, consecrated will to preserve the best of one's own culture while respecting the best in others', to recognize the complementary nature of all cultures and assist their cross-fertilization, becomes a *necessity* for the construction of European cultural unity, something which transcends the mere gearing of interests. And so what are called common international interests, on one side, and, on the other side, the mutual co-responsibility of every people for what is *peculiarly* valuable in every other people (with a world-wide interplay of free cultures to the glory of God and for the sake of the world's value) are not equivalent in meaning but express the most different mental attitudes conceivable. Cultural values are invariably and *essentially* coloured by national character; when they come into question certain attitudes are therefore requisite which are inessential with reference to the merely international values of pre-war European civilization; these attitudes are a will to join one's culture with other cultures, not by coalescence but in a complementary harmony, then readiness to permit one's culture to be cross-fertilized by alien talents and values which it does not intrinsically possess, finally a heart open in love toward specially foreign cultural values *as such*. But these attitudes are only appropriate where cultures proceed from the peculiar spiritual *strength* of a nation, not when they are fabricated as a result of reflection on the national destiny.*

What I shall call the *moral requisite* for cultural reconstruction may therefore be summarized in these terms: a progression from the sense of common guilt through common repentance and expiation to the mutual respect of every European nation and cultural minority, thence finally to the solidary will to build anew.

When this change of heart is complete it will be fitting to inaugurate a new *intellectual* effort, on an unprecedented scale, an anthropological collaboration of all the humanities to establish where lie the true *unifying* forces of Europe and its culture, in what they consist, how they can be brought into the foreground from behind the nationalisms and purely negative internationalisms *both* of which have obscured them so long, how they may be strengthened by education and upbringing, by the formation of new and real friendships between the culture-shaping minorities—

strengthened in such a way that they once again become a truly leading spiritual force in the world. Unfortunately I cannot here investigate this enormous question of Europe's spiritual unity; I can scarcely embark upon the lengthy consideration it demands.[1] Moreover, one does not begin to see the true unity of the European spirit until one has some notion (more is impossible) of the spiritual individuality of other great civilizations and is capable of reducing correctly the multitude of phenomena (language, custom, arts, myths, political temper, religions, cognitive forms and objectives). However much scholarly experts have accumulated over the years in the *aggregate* of knowledge, their multifarious, departmental understanding is still very far from combining into one general European vision, one concerted reduction of cultural phenomena to characteristic spiritual forces with determinate structural qualities. To knowledge of this kind W. von Humboldt, W. Dilthey, Techet and Wölfflin have already made notable contributions.[2] But one may confidently assert that the average educated European has so vague and misty a sense of the essence and spirit of European culture that, just as in the days of Kant, Herder and Goethe, he is still inclined to take for *universally* human what is in fact only a vague and barely self-consciousness Europeanism. One of the primary *intellectual* requirements for a reconstruction, or better a building anew, of European culture is that this knowledge should be integrated in a systematic doctrine of civilizations typified according to the cultural spirit and the internal subdivision of the genius of humanity. This doctrine should be disseminated so that the European may grow truly conscious of himself, both of his positive strengths and his limitations, of his unifying features and his special tasks.

Let us here content ourselves with the more modest determination, in reference only to internal European history, of the unifying forces which it would be most advantageous to reinforce or reinstate.

2. THE FORMATIVE POWERS AVAILABLE FOR THE SPIRITUAL RENEWAL OF EUROPE

So far the spiritual life of Europe has known *three* radical ferments: 1. the cultural values of Antiquity, 2. Christianity, which in its externally

---

[1] I would refer the interested reader to my remarks on the subject in the chapter entitled '*Die geistige Einheit Europas*' in *Der Genius des Krieges*, as well as to my *Krieg und Aufbau*, chapters '*Über östliches und westliches Christentum*' and '*Zur soziologischen Neuorientierung, etc.*' (closing pages).

[2] See in addition the recent work of the Viennese cultural geographer E. Hanslick, also O. Spengler, *Der Untergang des Abendlandes*.

effective form has been overwhelmingly Augustinian, based on love, action and the in-building of God's kingdom into the world, rather than on speculation, contemplation, withdrawal and ascetic gnosis (as in the East), 3. something notably prominent since the Renaissance and only possible through the action of the two above legacies in the development of modern nations—a progressive interweaving and cross-fertilization, such as every departmental history discloses, of the arts, sciences, literature, techniques of every nation with those of every other.

Hitherto nothing has come to take its place beside the first two formative powers which is remotely comparable to them in value. And anyone anxious for the reconstruction of the European cultural zone can make no simpler inference than that every European nation must be prepared unconditionally to *preserve* both Antiquity and Christianity as the very cement and basis of *mores* and education, both higher and elementary. They must do more than preserve—revitalize. This simple formula will suffer neither dilution nor restriction; neither will the second, which is to call into being and everywhere assist a keen awareness of the *interweaving and interdependence* of all European national cultures, to make that awareness as universal as possible by the encouragement of linguistic studies and translations and in general by increased attention to cultural, as opposed to political and military history. Positively these formulae express but little. Negatively they are of great importance. Negatively they imply above all an *a limine* rejection of any attempt to place our formative culture and education on either an essentially *positivistic* basis, with a leaning to science and mathematics, or a largely *nationalistic* basis, disproportionately tied to the vernacular, to national history and legend.

This last trend is sub-European; the positivistic, though it takes one beyond the national frontier, also passes out of Europe itself—indeed it goes beyond the spiritual creature, man, who must after God be man's *first* object of inquiry. Neither can it be used as the normative basis of European reconstruction. The cultural ideals and educational objectives developed by a natural-positivistic philosophy like that of Comte, Mach or Ostwald can only promote the imitable, *interchangeable* values of international society; in other words, they offer moral support to what does not need it, because it creates its own support. It is not by their natural-scientific *results* that such cultural ideals foster an awareness of Europe as a psycho-biological community, but only by the meaningful *history* of mathematical, scientific and technological discovery, by epistemology and methodology. Yet this history and methodology lead back automatically to Antiquity as the native soil of European science.

But at present it is *inward-looking cultural nationalism* which looms as a far more dangerous enemy than positivism for the humanistic cultural ideal as the common European component in the cultural ideals of particular nations. Cultural nationalism, while less in evidence in England and Russia, has come strongly to the fore in Germany and the lands of the Romance languages. On one side we find a desire for a specifically 'Latin renaissance', *i.e.* an essentially rhetorical, formal culture, to which certain Franco-Italian circles have already pledged themselves.[1] In our country what a welter of aspirations! The pan-Germanic movement calls for a resolute exclusion from the 'German soul' of the ancient 'poison of the Renaissance' and the 'Jewish-Christian spirit' (as they make bold to term it). In the name of the Germanic myth, and usually demanding a one-sided concentration on the history of the fatherland's wars and heroes, the adherents of this movement seek the hermetic self-incapsulation of the Teutonic spirit. Altogether more reasonably, Ernst Troeltsch[2] desires no more than to modify the humanistic ideal in the light of the picture of mediaeval 'Gothic man' which we are gradually forming, the picture of a man endowed with an unresting, individually creative spirit, perpetually undoing and recreating forms in an endless movement of will and life— the man whose nature lies in unrestrained fantasy and fantastic unrestraint. Eduard Spranger,[3] again, sees in the humanistic ideal of our fathers (Goethe, W. von Humboldt) merely the correlate in personal culture of the individual, liberal idea of State normal before the nation-State; he therefore wishes to centre the new cultural and educational policy round the *idea of State* and focus it upon the individual's will to play his part within the State framework. But, however right Troeltsch and Spranger may be in various particulars, I can accept *neither* of their views.

Even so, Eduard Spranger's book is acutely sensitive and well worth reading. In it he affiliates his idea of humanistic culture largely to that of Wilhelm von Humboldt—of whose life and character he has also given us so charming an account. He was undoubtedly right to follow this course, since it is the Humboldtian ideal which has exerted the most powerful influence on the form taken in practice by higher education in Germany. But in our view this ideal of personal culture, with the conception of Antiquity which it embodies, contains *three* features which

---

[1] In his *Deutsche Renaissance*, Berlin 1918, C. Burdach has clearly shown, from the genesis of the Italian renaissance, which evolved throughout as a national Italic movement with an *anti*-French cultural bias, how unwarranted by the historical facts is the alleged unity of the Latin spirit.

[2] See *Humanismus und Nationalismus in unserem Bildungswesen*, Berlin 1917.

[3] See *Das humanistische und das politische Bildungsideal im heutigen Deutschland*, Berlin 1916.

cannot be simply retained but require correction. Firstly, it isolates Antiquity (already seen with disproportionate emphasis on the literary highlights of the 'classical' age) from its *Asiatic* origins and no less from its transition into Hellenism and Christianity. Though sprung entirely from Christian soil, and secretly far more moulded by Christianity than its originator would wish to concede—being therein like the ideas of Antiquity inspiring the heroes of our poetic art—Humboldt's ideal reads into the ancient a notion of pure 'humanity' which in fact is of *Christian* origin. In all respects this notion is remote from Antiquity, which was always circumscribed by the nation or imperium, but precisely because of its 'classical' label it has served at bottom to loosen 'man's' ties with God and all forms of grace, as accorded with the pantheistic spirit of Humboldt's age.

Secondly, Humboldt's ideal does not rise above the quasi-aesthetic individualism of striving to shape oneself into a 'perfect specimen of humanity'—like a work of art—and of referring all individual relationships with the community to this endeavour as the highest 'goal'. Thus in its internal assumptions it is as *utterly remote* as the ethics of Kant or Hegel from the *solidarity* which I have developed elsewhere[1] as the higher principle of social morality. If I am able to agree with Spranger that Humboldt's 'humanistic' cultural ideal can neither awaken a genuine sense of devotion to the *State* nor inculcate a proper concept of its meaning for the world, for history—or for higher culture itself—I cannot see this fact, like Spranger, as its *primary* fault but only as a consequence of its lack of reference to a far higher and more universal order.

Thirdly, as an ideal of education it places so disproportionate an emphasis on the *inner* formation of the personality, neglecting the individual's function and conduct in the frame of a highly developed community, that it is impossible to apply it or cling to it in our age.

Not even Spranger's proposals and suggested programme remedy, in my opinion, the first of these defects. As avowed Christians, clearly aware that in Christian values we possess something much higher and richer than Antiquity could ever provide, we must nevertheless learn to love Antiquity with understanding and to glean whatever is to be learned from it or in it. This attitude is firmly demanded not only by our re-awakened religious consciousness—which however diversified is at least not pantheistic—but also by our sharpened historical awareness of the limitations and national idiosyncrasy of the ancient values. Inevitably the secret seeping-in and overflow of Christian values into Antiquity (Goethe's *Iphigenia auf Tauris* offering only the most obvious example of the way of

[1] See Part 2 of *Formalismus in der Ethik und die materiale Wertethik.*

thinking which pervaded humanism) must cease once Christianity has regained its full dignity and rich diversity, while Antiquity regains its *real* historical character.

Undoubtedly Spranger has made a number of well-conceived proposals for overcoming the second defect I have named. And yet I would prefer, instead of the direct 'civic education' which he advocates in order to develop the sense of State, a continual indication, pervading *all* relevant instruction, of how this or that literature, art, science, philosophy *fitted* into the State of the time (*e.g.* how Greek literature into the organization of the *polis*), why certain groups of values—late-stoic philosophy for example—stood outside, which features were conditioned by the nature of the social groups exhibiting them, and which *could* have arisen—given cultural potentialities latent in existing forces—but were frustrated by political conditions. To my mind, this indirect cultivation of the sense of State and community, constantly drawing attention to the fact that even the highest fruits of the spirit are *inter*dependent with political and social conditions (thus the intellectualism of all Greek thought was dependent on the institution of slavery and slave-trading—and vice versa)—this method should renew the whole of thinking, in the direction of a deepened sense of State, much more intimately and permanently than any direct 'civic instruction' geared to the State of the day. But the most important consideration is that the sense of State (as I have already indicated) should be attained, if at all, only as a particular formulation of an intensified sense of community. If the pupil is to see and grasp *clearly* the actual ensemble and historical interplay of existing communities, the teacher must put before him a network of basic sociological concepts which is applicable irrespective of the particular variety of human group; the network must comprehend all *essential* forms of community, presenting the State as only *one* among many such forms—family, clan, race, people, nation, Church, sect, school, society, party, class, estate and so on. The goal of the new education must be more than the will to take one's place in the State: a differentiated will to play a part in a *multiplicity* of communities co-existing in their *own* right with their own aims and functions, together with a sense of the ever-present necessity to renounce and *sacrifice* any one of these communities in favour of the continuance and proper evolution of the higher. Spranger rightly draws attention to the fact that the new trend among young people to form leagues and communities—a tendency sharply divergent from conditions of only twenty years ago—spontaneously comes to meet this conversion of the older, individualistic cultural ideal. But when he complains that up to now these youth-societies have shown a great aversion to the State (and, we would add, take care with a certain exclusive jealousy that they are not regarded or used as 'citizen-training schools') I am unable to see any great harm in it. Surely this is only a sign that the State of the present is unable to exert a power of emotional attraction on the instincts of youth, and that new State-ideals are in process of growth from the native soil of youthful community-experiences *themselves*.

With reference to the third defect of the older humanistic ideal of personal culture, it seems to me that the older idea of self-cultivation (rather than preparation for one's communal function) deserves the rejection it incurs from Spranger less than two of its habitual corollaries. The first is the latent reflexion and excessive concentration on the taking-shape of the self—this as most obviously betrayed in the 'artefact' character of the personal life envisaged by Humboldt. The second is the erroneous and peculiarly German ideal of exclusive *inwardness*, wherein the intimate recesses of personality so disproportionately occupy the foreground that in reference to all participation in the conduct of public affairs there inevitably ensues a kind of resigned servility and quietism, together with a certain contempt for the whole social and political sphere.[1] Now, it is very possible to regard the self-shaping of the personality as the supreme *value* and *objective* end of education *without* admitting the *subjective intention* of self-cultivation or recommending it to the educator's special attention. But to avoid such a misplaced emphasis it is unnecessary to replace the ideal of *personality* in education by a preponderantly *functional* ideal related to the community. Far from setting personal models too constantly before youth, we have employed them too little. The separate function of the official in the mechanism of government has taken precedence over the evolution of the statesman; specialized technologists have been produced to the detriment of the personal, supervising scientific spirit that enables branches of knowledge to cross-fertilize each other; in economic matters the active middle class has been so taken up with business that it has lost its sense of political community as much as its taste for a higher life of the spirit. Against these impersonal trends the remedy is not to intensify the specialization of educational objectives but exactly the reverse. On the other hand something quite different from the functional ideal, with which Spranger appears too frequently to confuse it, must be fostered far beyond the framework of the older humanistic ideal of personal culture: this is the flair for the *public implementation* of what is accepted as right, and the constant feeling of *co-responsibility* for the character and ingredients of every public state of affairs.

[1] On this mistaken inwardness cf. my article '*Zwei deutsche Krankheiten*' in *Der Leuchter*, Darmstadt 1919.*

Again, the demand of Ernst Troeltsch that the German Middle Ages should be given a more important place in our higher education has much in its favour. Troeltsch is particularly justified in asking that our ideals of humanity should be more closely attached to that Franco-German Gothic which embodied a large measure of *general Europeanism*, which even maintained a deep subterranean relationship with Asiatic, especially Indian forms, but which, far from excluding the Christian, embraced it. Though the *national* element justifiably asks for a higher place within its limits as a formative factor, the mediaeval world as a whole demands no less attention as the greatest example of a sublime style of existence *organized* under the supervision of religious awareness embodied in a Church. In this connection, however, what is required is not the narrow extremes of emphasis advocated by R. Benz (and so brilliantly taken to task by C. Burdach) but that the whole of that *diversified* ramification which constitutes the cultivation of Germanic minds should win freedom of action and come into its own under the aegis of the Church and the exemplary lessons of Antiquity.

And so we see that these numerous modifications do not in the least contradict the requirement that cultivation of the classical values in the humanistic *Gymnasium* should remain the *starting*-point of higher education in all European peoples, if a cultural reconstruction is not to be built on sand. This alone is a matter for discussion: 1. which *aspects* or sectors of the ancient cultural values should be emphasized in this or that nation; 2. how these cultural values are to be fitted into the context of world-history, in particular their Asiatic antecedents, and how they are to be transplanted with this context into the narrower *national* ideals which, within their limits in the European framework, are perfectly legitimate. Given the histories of peoples it is understandable that the nations of the Romance languages should connect their culture and education more strongly to *Latin* antiquity, while in Germanic eyes *Greek classicism* is far more prominent, as is the *late Hellenic* for the Slavonic, especially the Russian world. But for the very reason that this is the obvious trend of history, the *will* governing the formation of *mores* must be focused on the task of 'filling in' from what is complementary to the historic national bias. For that very reason a deliberate, introspective *renaissance latine* would be thoroughly retrograde; for that very reason Germans and Slavs should keenly cultivate specifically Latin values—the sense of form and order, Latin practical logic and organization!

Advances in the study of Antiquity have had this result, that we can no longer see in ancient classical art, philosophy or ethos *eternal* models of heightened human existence. These very advances have shattered the esoteric, occupational *philologers' metaphysics* of 'eternal models' which could only see the Ancients in *opposition* to Christianity and fostered a kind of paganism. Everywhere a continuity, an only *relative* break of Greek culture with Asiatic forms was revealed, in archaeology, religion, philosophy, mythology, as was the impermanence of its national, social and political premises. Elements have been discovered, especially in Greek antiquity, which were wholly unknown to our humanistic forebears; among these I would name matriarchy and the mother-cult, orphism with its tragic pessimism, the beginnings of a code of civil law, social conflicts within the Greek cities, Greek natural science, mathematics and technology. The continual inpourings of things classical into the early Christian Church, via Hellenism, gnosis and late-classical religious forms, has been newly and forcefully brought to light. Nothing is now known with greater certainty than that the ancient 'classical' *cannot* be equated with the universally human and at most represents one of the earliest peaks in the values of the *European* mind.

What then? Well, above all, it does not follow from this historical relativization of the ancient values that we may no longer consider them a fit basis of European culture. It does not mean that we should regard them, say, as indifferent elements in a limitless historical flux and turn our culture to quite other objectives of, it may be, an excessively national or political character. Even if we may no longer call these values universally human, they are still normative for *Europe*. And even if they may no longer be called absolute models, they remain as necessary landmarks shared in common, as lighthouses at which the European nations should look not as goals on the course *before* them but as illuminated points lying *behind* them from which, turning their heads, they may constantly take bearings and know whether they are still in the path of the European spirit. I would wish that the common European relationship of nations to Antiquity, which is necessary to cultural reconstruction, might be understood in accordance with this metaphor of a 'lighthouse at one's back'.

But there is one other objective whose attainment is demanded by the common task of rebuilding European culture, in the particular world-situation which now prevails. It is a goal which our advances in historical knowledge assist us to achieve. It is a certain swing of our cultural life from its present preferential trend, which is for the East to look to the West, to the opposite, a *west-east* trend. In my estimation everything presses for this change. The excessively active, bustling European needs —I would say—a rest-cure in the profundities, the sense of eternity, in the repose and dignity of the Asiatic spirit. Moreover, since the Russo-Japanese war Asia has certainly ceased to be merely the passive object of capitalist investment or of Christian missions (which too often serve largely as trade-pioneers), and is everywhere *actively* stirring its wings, blinking the sleep of centuries from its eyes—in Asiatic Russia, Japan, China, India, the Muslim world. In this fact Europe has double incentive to *re-appraise* all its cultural property against what the East has to offer, as well as to re-assess what it holds in common with Asia.

Both in general terms and in detail the World War has prepared new adjustments, reductions of the differences in cultural level, which have been excessive. This is notably true in a qualitative sense. As Germany grows more democratic through the War, the English-speaking countries are becoming more centralized and socialistic; likewise, on a far larger scale, the War must inevitably result in a certain *parity of the specifically European and Asiatic.** And so from the outset we must put Antiquity before youth together with its Asiatic roots, also illuminating far more strongly than before the nodal points in the later history of ancient values where Eastern and Western mingled, as in Hellenism, Alexandrianism, etc., only to divide again into the separate streams of eastern and western history.

There is another reason for this reorientation of our central cultural interests: giving and taking will be a far more fruitful commerce in this direction than if we were to retain our too exclusive interest in western culture. For French culture (and to a lesser extent English also) has reached a self-contained maturity of form which—by human standards —could scarcely be surpassed. In France (as not in Germany or England) the middle class has so far failed to produce its own higher culture. In contrast to Germany's unpolitical bourgeoisie it has spent its energies in politics and social matters, living by grace of the *ancien régime* in all things of the spirit. It is improbable that now, long past its maturity, it will perform what it has always left undone in this direction. The real *novelties* of modern France, deviating from seventeenth- and eighteenth-century traditions—Bergsonian philosophy is an instance—have shown German and still more Russian influence in many ways. Whatever we are *capable* of absorbing from France—though admittedly it is rash to prophesy— we have already absorbed in essentials. The strict relation of culture to the social group is not so true of England but remains correct in a broad sense. At the core English culture is thoroughly aristocratic, though it hides under democratic labels to a far greater extent than French culture. On the other hand our German aristocrats (in so far as we have any) have remained almost wholly unproductive of culture. Their business has been government, war, politics. It is as improbable for them as for the French middle class that they should find any unusual spiritual fertility in their old age. In fact our culture, which socially has risen entirely from below, by its very sociology, its social conditioning, has more in common—in a profound sense—with the relations prevailing in the Slavonic and specifically the Russian world. Given also the incompleteness of cultural forms on both sides, *richer* fruits than are promised by a continuing western bias of attention are promised by the mutual *inter-completion* of Germanic individualism *and* Slavonic sense of community, the intellectual *and* the mystical, the marshalling attitude to life *and* respect for the strange claim to squander life, active Christianity *and* the contemplative devotion which releases from the clutch of earthly destinies.[1] Furthermore the social democrats of Russia and Germany, knowing themselves to be far more profoundly divided from the bourgeoisie than their western brothers, understand each other much better than could foreseeably be the case between German and western social democrats.

We should therefore give special encouragement to the spread of knowledge about Russia, and about the non-Russian Slavs as a bridge between that country and ourselves. In this, Austrian cultural life has a special rôle. But the German federal ministries of education must not neglect to endow new chairs of Russian history, civilization, language and literature.

National cultural ideals must move within the framework of the common European heritage and cultural foundation—they are not entitled to dislocate it, to shatter what is integrated. But within the frame they should enjoy the full measure of their rights.

However, every tendency toward 'pan-German' isolation must be strenuously resisted. It is senseless and even unGerman; it profoundly contradicts the very essence of the Germanic spirit. C. Burdach's Leibnizian definition of that spirit, in his *Deutsche Renaissance*, is quite correct. It is a 'creative mirror'—not so much a bundle of indigenous forms as the spirit of *synthetizing* all forms with an endless love of creative interconnection. Anyone who took *originality* as his only yardstick would have little to say for German culture, apart from its music and philosophy. For that very reason the German stands in far greater need of foreign stimuli than persons of another nationality; the entire history of his higher culture is taken up with the elaboration of foreign stimuli. Partly they originated in Antiquity and the Renaissance (humanism and classical poesy), partly in biblical antiquity (the Lutheran reformation), partly in France (our Enlightenment) and partly in England (Shakespeare, government, philosophy). 'Shakespeare, star of height sublime! Thee I thank for what I

[1] See the chapter entitled '*Über östliches und westliches Christentum*' in *Krieg und Aufbau.**

am'[1]—thus Goethe; 'Rousseau set me to rights . . . Hume roused me from dogmatic slumber'[2]—thus Kant. In all great Germans one finds sayings of this kind. What would Luther have been without Augustine or Paul? The German language has an *organic* need of supplementation by foreign words, *i.e.* a need rooted not in the historical fortunes of the German people but in *itself* and the laws of its formation and development. Yet, faced with these fundamental facts one dares to preach the cultural isolation of Germany! These trends are nothing but the ideology of an *economic* power-nationalism which has nothing, nothing at all to do with the German spirit except to misuse it wantonly in its own nefarious game.

But this general 'pan-German' trend is not all that deserves our resolute opposition. There are certain other ideological tendencies, hitherto vigorously supported by many of our most gifted men, which in my opinion are strong impediments to the reconstruction of European culture. Allow me to mention two.

First, that view of modern political history which came upon the scene with the proclamation of the German Empire and soon occupied the chairs of German universities, where it achieved most renown under the names of Treitschke and Sybel. Friedrich Naumann hit the nail on the head when he said that a conception of history which takes the straightest possible line from the Wartburg via Potsdam and Königsberg to Bismarck and his Little Germany no longer corresponds to the world we live in and is useless as a basis of cultural education. Once for all we must *give up* these politically tendentious constructions and reinstate the *fulness* of the German character. We must forswear not only the subjective tendency to think of history in this way but the hidebound political pathos it prompts in historians. We must return to the purer, more objective spirit of Leopold von Ranke, who was still filled with a true historian's joy over the wonderful *diversity* of the human in the historical world, a marvellous reverence for the *future* of humanity. Again, the German mediaeval world with its indigenous culture, the times of the great German emperors—in short, the periods of *organic universalism*— must take on quite another order of importance than hitherto for the average cultivated man. *Our* tasks are in the line of these times, not of Bismarck's Little Germany. It is the stations on the Wartburg-Potsdam line that have least to teach us at present.

Let us take as an example the age of the Reformation. Could there be

---

[1] *William, Stern der höchsten Höhe,*
   Dir verdank' ich, was ich bin.
[2] *Rousseau hat mich zurecht gebracht . . . Hume hat mich aus dem dogmatischen Schlummer geweckt.*

an age whose whole nature was more foreign to the claims made on us now? The individualism which first appeared then in religious guise and broke down the holy bulwarks present in the Christian idea of corporation and its reality, the Church—this individualism has today only too clearly outlived its *raison d'être*; even great Protestant theologians—Harnack, Troeltsch, Rade—are now confessing that today we must above all cultivate the Christian idea of community and solidarity in its *universal* essence, must restore its right to take part in the formation and organization of the public sphere. The age we are entering is not one of new schism but one of new *ecclesiastical syntheses*. In Russia, England, France and Italy the separation of Church and State, partly of long standing, partly (as especially in Russia and England) of recent development, opens new and important prospects in the great problem of the rapprochement of the Churches, which are thereby becoming free of national and political entanglements. This is true at once for the relations between the Anglican and the Roman, the Russian and the Greek Orthodox, the Roman and the Orthodox Churches (as defined, in respect of this last, by the Testament of Leo XIII). The middle-class citizenry, whose sociological creation was the nation-State and which used to set its face against feudalism and the Church, is dissolving into more and more new groupings and estates, or germs of estates. The absolute monarchy, which propagated the Reformation to an extent only recently appreciated, is opposed by the whole democratic upsurge of the times. Formerly the parts of Europe were bursting asunder in the development of new forces— nationally, politically, economically and in religion; today the watchword is the *levelling*, settling of differences: Europe has to pull itself together and not so much exploit any specific forces as *master* the overexploited with united spiritual and moral power.

But we have also least to learn from the spiritual leaders of that time. I say this with Ignatius of Loyola in mind as much as Luther, the Counterreformation as much as the Reformation. Certainly we must energetically throw off the correlation of an attenuated, exclusive mystical inwardness with near-Machiavellian power-doctrines of State and law: that it is which finally delivered the Church into the hands of the State, this which originated with Luther and lives on today in the shadow of Bismarck— this perilous German *dualism* of deed and conscience, faith and works, exclusively 'inner' freedom and political servility to temporal authority. But with no less energy we must throw off the dark fanaticism of the Counter-reformation and the narrow constraint it forced on the Catholic Church.

The second ideological trend to which I referred is the predominance of all kinds of *national* philosophy. This, to say the least, is a great hindrance to the cultural reconstruction of Europe. I mean both ideologies which are in fact too nationally restricted by nature and *consciously reflexive* national philosophies. In the first category I would place for example the ideal edifice of Kant, which is excessively permeated with the (narrowest) Prussian spirit in spite of the cosmopolitanism of its originator's *conscious, subjective* attitude. This is an assertion which I have no space to elaborate, but I would refer the interested reader to my philosophical writings.[1] When Schiller says in his study of aesthetic grace and dignity (*Über Anmut und Würde*) that Kant provided only for 'the servants of the house' and not for its 'children', he had already lighted on the gist of my meaning.

To become 'children of the house'—that is today the most pressing desire of the German people. Though Kant still felt himself wholly a member of the European 'republic of learning', in contrast to his speculative successors (Fichte, Hegel, etc.), nevertheless with him had already *begun* that phase of German thought which pressed the stamp of exclusive Prussian spirit on every officially recognized philosophical stirring and at the same time *narrowed* and *particularized* German philosophical development until it was entirely detached from the evolution of the *Christian European spirit*. Only compare Kant and Leibniz side by side, set Leibniz beside the Kantian trend, and the truth of this is clear. Leibniz still stands squarely in the great, broad tradition of European Christian philosophy, with its ancient bases in Plato, Aristotle, Augustine—this '*quaedam philosophia perennis*', as he calls it. In him we do not find the spirit of limitless construction and organization *in vacuo* with which Kant thought himself entitled to reduce nature to a scaled-up Prussian State, a synthetic construct of human intellect; nor do we find in him the excessive activity and vacuous, formalistic thirst for regimentation which typify Kant's attitude to the world; nor do we find the dissolution of all mental individuality to something in which, paving the way to pantheism, the only vital current is a tenuous ratiocination; nor yet in ethics do we find an idea of duty which is ruinously defective because at bottom void of *insight*; nor yet the insulation of moral incentives from the flow of all love and sympathy; nor again the emasculation of religion and the idea of God— their reduction to a mere 'as if' at the disposal of the dutiful citizen; nor the terrible old-Protestant doctrine, which Goethe found so deeply repugnant, of a radical wickedness in human nature; nor finally that cultivated scorn of happiness, that contempt which, unable to separate Greek *eudaimonia* or Christian bliss from the commonest sensual pleasure,

[1] Cf. my criticism of Kant's ethics in *Der Formalismus in der Ethik*, etc.

condemns both with like fanaticism—not only as conscious aims but also (alas!) as the soul's destined end.*

Kant is a forceful thinker, and we may not cease to come to terms with him, relate our thoughts to his. But his obscure, equivocal philosophy, not to mention the ingenious, self-willed subjectivisms of his speculative successors, is quite unsuited to be the general basis of higher education in *Gymnasium* and university. We need a philosophy which resembles, unlike the Kantian, not a closed fist but an *open hand*, which unites afresh the great heritage of Christian European thought and whose spirit must combine the *strictest objectivism* with recognition of the *essential* facts, eternal constants and interrelations inhering in the world and the mind of man. Only in the spirit of Leibniz, not in that of Kant, is it possible that philosophy in Europe should once again become a fruitful symphony— devoid of narrowly sectarian premises such as the Old Protestantism which pervades Kant's thinking in spite of an asserted autonomy of reason. It is even less acceptable that we should seek a basis in a *reflected* national philosophy like Fichte's or any 'I'-philosophies of a similar nature. It is our business not to puff up the German nonsensically into the 'originally free and rational' being but to know the character and merits, likewise the *limitations*, of our national individuality; similarly it behoves us not to think of the world as purely the indifferent 'material of endless duty'—such a conception is abominable—but to respond in *loving devotion* to its objective whole, with its rich diversity of distinctive, legitimate values and forms of being.

But I have also named another, higher European factor and value, which historically binds us together: *Christianity*, more especially in its western form.

Allow me to point out a few important elements in the Christian situation which embody points of moment for cultural reconstruction.

(*a*) First, it is highly significant that the Russian Orthodox system and Church, one of Christianity's greatest ecclesiastical forms, has not (as many of us expected) collapsed at the same time as the Russian autocracy, one of the most fearful power-States the world has known, but has survived the cataclysm and even been profoundly transformed by it.[1] The transformation comprises its divorce from the State, with a return to its pre-Petrine constitution and, in a certain sense, an independent spiritual head; further we may expect it to include a closer alliance with

[1] In this connection cf. Dimitri Merezhkovsky, *Vom Krieg zur Revolution*, Piper, Munich, 1918, in particular his account of A. V. Kartashov's address, 'The Fulfilment of the Church' ('*Die Erfüllung der Kirche*').

the Greek Churches of the Levant and the Balkans. The stimulus which this gives the mighty prospect of reunion between western and eastern Churches can hardly be overestimated. Several years before the War, referring to the pro-Roman party of Stundists, Harnack said (in *Das Testament Leo XIII*): 'Only by devious means is it able at present to influence political decisions, but once the petrified Erastianism of the Russian situation is no longer to be reckoned with—and who is to call it everlasting?—this party has a future, and one can understand why Rome is already making some account of it.' Already, indeed, efforts are being made in this direction, overtures exploring the possibility of an understanding between Rome and Orthodoxy. It is still too early, however, for one to be able to pass an opinion on them.

But there is a further lesson to be drawn from recent events in Russia. Western Europe has been shown the novel *example* of an alliance between the Christian ideology and its deepest impulses, on the one hand, and on the other social democracy and the justified sector of its demands, against the spirit of the capitalistic State. The Christian religion, while abhorring the external revolution of blood and violence, is from its beginnings, through and through, not *a* revolutionary but the *most* revolutionary force in history. Where it can work in the direction of its nature it makes all new. In all things rebirth is its underlying thought. In the West, particularly in Germany and Austria (where there has been a notably pronounced interweaving, not to say 'felting', of Church and ruling class), the Christian religion in all its outward forms and arrangements has become one-sidedly identified with the interests of the dominant bourgeoisie to a degree which has clipped the noble wings of its true, essential spirit. But in Russia the Christian religion, or very essential and important groups within it, has not only been dragged into a revolutionary movement but has even played no minor rôle in its production[1] (*e.g.* the Christian social revolutionaries); whatever dangers lurk in this movement for the ecclesiastical institutions of Christianity, at all events it has broken the one-sided bond of official religion with the ruling powers and, in particular, bourgeois capitalism and its spirit. This is a great, a sublime fact, and appears as such especially when one takes into account the new *readiness for reunion* which this divorce has created in the Churches of the West. We may remain in no doubt that this fact will have the strongest influence as an example to western Europe. Before the War, even, the great literature of Russia (Dostoyevsky, Tolstoy, Solovyev, etc.) was practically the *only* literary art-form of European stature which breathed a truly Christian inspiration.

[1] Even monks have played an active part in the conduct of this movement.

(*b*) At another great fact I have already hinted. Just as democratization, however modified from people to people, may be called (as by Franz Meinecke) a 'universal historical trend', which one can meet with foolish incomprehension or with wisdom and understanding as a sign of the times (but which at all events one is powerless to reverse), so we may rightly call a 'universal trend' the tendency for the Church to separate from the State and the State-spirit which produced the European anarchy of the War. To the extent that the Church has had to lean on the State for want of constructive religious vitality of its own, to the extent that men have been dragooned into Church, separation is a menace to its fabric. Thus it is more dangerous to Protestantism than to the self-contained Catholic Church, and to German Protestantism than to the Anglo-American system, with its greater measure of ecclesiastical self-government. But wherever political troubles may bring it to a head, separation represents a new and markedly invigorating ideal of gathering momentum—for such Churches as can sustain the operation of renewing their spirit and overhauling their organizations. See what idealism, strength of sacrifice, Christian reanimation of the profane arose in France before the War—exactly as foreseen by Pope Pius—when the Church was divorced from a bourgeois-capitalist régime! In the situation to which we have newly come we can eliminate many of the phenomena which, in my *Krieg und Aufbau*, I called the 'wrongful adaptation' of the German Catholics. In England, too, we find the same tendency to disestablishment, often strongly associated with the Romanizing elements of the High Church and occasionally identified with those who press for rapprochement with the Church of Russia.

In Prussia, certainly, denominational schooling would be endangered if, with the Constitution as it now stands, a majority of the Prussian House of Deputies based on the *Reichstag* franchise were to take the helm. But however gravely this shift of parliamentary power may for the time being affect Christian interests in Prussia, in the long view it will purify the forces of religion; its consequences will strengthen the Church's unifying spirit of solidarity across frontiers and divisions, leading finally to a deeper grasp of this idea: one cannot pledge one's services to the Mammon in a dechristianized society *and* to God. Readiness for union between Churches and sects—or at least for understanding, mutual understanding in learning, theology and worship—cannot but be strengthened by all these processes, which is to say they must strengthen the most important of the Christian forces which may contribute to Europe's cultural unity.

If, for the present, representatives of both Protestant and Catholic Churches have demanded specific assurances that the time-honoured relations of Church and State in Prussia will not be disturbed, this is probably only a question of the time-scale on which formal ecclesiastical adjustments take place; by a law of their being this scale must differ from that applicable to social or political change.[1] And in our view there is much to justify such demands. If, however, we do not go by the face-value of present events but exercise our political judgment to ascertain their probable course in the future, we will receive any assurances much more guardedly than usual. If the Church failed to retain the allegiance of the working masses in some *additional* way, failed to *win them over*, without relying on such legal safeguards as may be incorporated in a new constitution; if it failed to win them anew in an unfettered religious and spiritual mission, meeting the problems of the hour in the true spirit of Christian action—reliance on 'assurances' would come to resemble attempts to stem a torrent with a walking-stick.[2]

(*c*) The third factor I would phrase as a question: Stockholm *or* Rome —or—Stockholm *and* Rome?

Today these names represent two forces that have spoken out against continuing the War to the point of European suicide, two spiritual powers, also, demanding a permanent European order. Each name reminds us of the mighty endeavours of considerable groups towards whom the Central Powers have shown themselves notably more sympathetic than the Entente, particularly its western side. The Entente has failed to reply to the note of the Pope and, with the significant exception of Russia, has forbidden its subjects to attend the Stockholm talks. These very signs bear out what I contended in my book on the causes of hatred against Germany (*Die Ursachen des Deutschenhasses*): The[3] real starting-point of irreconcilable hatred against the heartlands of Europe does not lie in the fourth estate, so far as it has detached itself, nor in the powers of Christian cultural conservatism: it lies in the great capitalist forces and bourgeois groups of the western countries and in their corresponding individualist, atomistic, earthbound spirit. For that very reason, if we wished (as we do not) to divide the world into two armed camps according to ultimate moral motivations and spiritual allegiances—as the Entente has done with its ambiguous[4] slogan of 'political citizen-democracy versus autocracy and feudalism'—we could proclaim the following counter-formula: 'the united (or uniting) forces of Christian authority and moral standards *with* the genuine socialism of the fourth estate—*social* democracy—versus

---

[1] See Part 2 of *Der Formalismus in der Ethik, etc.**

[2] I need hardly remark that this judgment of two-and-a-half years ago has been all too thoroughly corroborated.*

[3] It is not clear where the self-quotation ends (*Translator*).

[4] In German the same word (*Bürger*) means 'citizen' and 'bourgeois' (*Translator*).

oligarchic plutocracy with its liberalism and rationalism in all the life of the spirit'. And here we would be entitled to place Russia on our side, particularly that great-hearted, vast-souled Russia still hidden from us in the smoke of political confusion.

Nevertheless, the endeavours which are summarized in the names of Stockholm and Rome have very different causes, are very different in spirit and goal. In the long run, will the first or the second throw a greater weight in the scales on the side of peace, or will both together? I venture to predict that on the answer to this question both the 'whether' and the 'how' of European cultural reconstruction will largely depend. Not only that. Whether or not these two forces of will and spirit succeed in concerting their efforts—no matter how in practice—toward a common goal *now*, surely after the War the inspiring memory of, objectively speaking, having worked toward similar ends will cause them to seek a new understanding, an alliance between the *social* (not bourgeois-liberal) democracy of the fourth estate *and* the forces of the Christian Churches striving for reunion? I mean specifically those forces which the trend toward separation from the State has rendered freer, more open, purer, more Christian: will they not work in the above direction? Could not the meaning of this unprecedented revolutionary upheaval of a continent lie partly in this, that the specifically bourgeois-capitalist spirit, this common enemy of the rising, struggling fourth estate and a Church clearly mindful of its *Christian* essence, is slowly but perceptibly being *brought to ruin* with all its works—false, merely sensual individualism, political nationalism, the centralistic capitalist State, imperialism?

Now at all events the question of the future interrelations of the Christian Church and social democracy is of the *utmost* importance for the cultural reconstruction of Europe.[1] For I will venture to say that neither one nor the other can accomplish the task alone; it is possible only for both together. If one or the other throws in its hand, there will be no true reconstruction at all.

My answers to these questions are none the less affirmative in direction, though I am well aware of the many obstacles in our path. But perhaps we have reasons to believe that these mighty obstacles are slowly diminishing. Let us turn our attention to some of these reasons.

No one may deny that there are strong antitheses on one side and the other. On one side the idea, inseparable from the Christian Church, of

---

[1] In a book of mine which will shortly appear, *Über Wesen und Werdensgesetze des Kapitalismus: Ein Weg zum christlichen Sozialismus,** I attempt a systematic solution of this problem, one exploring the ultimate spiritual, historical, philosophical bases of both capitalism and socialism.

authority in matters of belief and morality, together with the closely-knit government of the Church. On the other side the strong antipathy, taken over from bourgeois liberalism, against the idea of authority in any form. On that side also a strongly materialistic outlook on the world, in all things fixed on earthly considerations, expecting all of the class-war, nothing from a solidarity of estates, expressed in a host of ideologies of which Marxism is only the most important, and strongly associated with the kind of occupation which falls to the worker's lot in a civilization steeped in science and technology. But on this side again the sense of the supernatural, miracles and grace, the patient quest for one's place in a meaningfully, purposefully ordered world possessing fixed constants which govern a providential course—ideas which seem to hamstring all kinds of earthly activity, which drastically reduce—when once they are accepted —one's confidence in *human* power to order the world in a meaningful way. On the other side a still very active faith in the millennium, Utopia, Paradise on earth, coupled with an attitude to property and economic wealth which would like to abolish or restrict to a minimum the private ownership of land and the means of production, a desire to replace the natural and historical division of men into peoples and estates by a merely cross-sectional 'international' class-divison. On one side we have aware-ness that the end of man is a supernatural mystery proper to each in-dividual soul, that this world is full of sin and cannot permanently subsist without grace, redemption and an objective institution whereby they may be transmitted—cannot exist without hope and faith in a goal beyond this life. On this side also importance is attached to the principle of private property, to abandon which is to deny the individual, the spiritual person, the free exercise of his conscience in that direction, and the natural division of humanity into peoples and estates is accepted out of faith in providence. On the other side, be it remarked, considerable antagonism exists between the social democratic elements of different countries, but compared in importance and depth with the schisms of the Christian Church these divisions are perhaps only transitory phenomena inherent in the war-situation. Finally, up to the present we have had to reckon with the involvement of large sections of the Church in the remnants of feudalism and the rich bourgeoisie, and (on the other side) with the stubborn sense of class-unity.

All these profound antitheses I fully acknowledge; all will continue for years to come. But in every case, I maintain, their hard unyielding out-lines are undergoing a *softening* accelerated by the lessons of the War. In the process differences will increasingly diminish, they will above all seem small beside the *common* opposition of social democracy (especially in

Russia and Central Europe) and the world which still thinks and feels in Christian terms, to the spirit, ethos, institutions of bourgeois capitalism and its correlative ideologies.

The Christian idea of authority is opposed to democratic socialism only on the assumption that a form of solidarity exists between religious authority and some specific incorporation or constitution of *State* authority. It would be saying too little to say that the Church does not *teach* any such correlation: since the French Revolution, with the ensuing collapse of legitimism and the Holy Alliance, it has in *practice* disengaged itself little by little from any corresponding policy. A new Holy Alliance is the very last thing to expect in the future—unless we apply the term to a Christian *and* social democracy among the European peoples. All that the Church teaches in this connection is that the existence and validity of a superior authority, hence duty to obey its ordinances, are included —within the frame of natural right—in God's plan for the world. It leaves it to historical *causae secundae* (among which may be numbered wars and revolutions justified in providence) to determine the substance of the 'authority'. As I have said, the World War will considerably diminish whatever excessive feelings of solidarity remain here and there between outworn political forms of bourgeois dominance, on the one hand, and the Church on the other.

As to the antitheses of Weltanschauung, the following may be said: The first demand of belief in a supernatural destiny of the individual soul is for a social order wherein every man has *leisure* and inner *freedom* to be mindful of his soul, to *feel* that he has a soul—not only know verbally, theoretically, that he has a spiritual soul with its own personal ends and destiny. How few men—as Newman remarked—*feel*, experience their soul! Is it to be wondered at that the man of the fourth estate has so little noticed his soul, in this technical, industrial world so suddenly irrupting into the nineteenth century, that for *this* reason—not as part of the 'march of science' (which ideally is as abstract as truth itself)—he has been wont to think in materialistic, economic terms? And, at bottom, was it not the *bourgeois-liberal* spirit which, digging its own grave—today if ever!— provoked the ideologies which, spreading beyond the confines of learning, have been half-consciously pressed into the service of the fourth estate's material preoccupations and workaday ideals? But social democracy, with its great and just demands for an extensive social programme to be carried out with financial means released by unilateral disarmament— social democracy, with its eight-hour day and the abolition of irresponsible exploitation of labour, which sets free injurious nationalist-imperialistic world-competition—should provide the workers with the leisure they need to bethink them of their spiritual existence. Once they feel they have souls, they will at last be *able* to dwell on their spiritual destiny. Freedom of men *for* religion and the Church is the condition, not the consequence of the freedom of religion and Church in the world.

The spirit of the western Church, which, in the two-way intercourse, will also permeate and deepen that of the eastern, is not narrowly focused in all its forms (an exception being quietistic Lutheranism) on an *exclusively* transcendental kingdom of God. A *double*, upward and downward movement is characteristic of it: it *also* attends to the inbuilding of God's kingdom into the visible world of politics and public affairs.[1] As a potent, visible organization the Christian Church *should* work to affect history and the community not only on Sunday but on the weekday, for the workday. It is just this positive spirit of organization which, in an age eager to master hitherto anarchic forces, is *common* to the Christian Church and practical social democracy, as against the anarchic nature of bourgeois liberalism. Surely, when social democracy has a larger share of control, when it ceases to harp on negative criticism and acquires a sense of political responsibility, we may also expect a gradual, automatic change in its *picture* of the world. Shall not that change be a trend from the picture of blind economic forces hustling man hither and thither to one of a regulated order of things and values, over which there presides, as supreme governor, a free, intelligent power, a personal spirit—only one immeasurably more free and intelligent than the responsible, freely creative and ordering human mind (itself only definable by its likeness to God) can know to be mirrored in its own very depths? No human being (make no mistake, this is an unbreakable law of life!) can share in the responsible, intelligent ruling, ordering, control of the world *if* he at the same time believes that a blind atom, or a blind energy occupies the centre and basis of things. That is an intrinsic *impossibility* of the spirit. The belief in blind determinism can *only* be the attitude of subservience— such an outlook on the world as is found in disgruntled messenger-boys. It is an attitude in which one may utter any amount of irresponsible criticism, but in which one *cannot* exercise authority, take part in the control of affairs.

But the process which brings about the participation in government of social democracy, with its freedom from bourgeois prejudices, will also remove the greatest obstacle by far which has diverted the religious cravings of the fourth estate from their natural course to God and Christ. Like every hindrance to religious belief in the true God, this obstacle has been a *positive surrogate* of the highest good, an idol—an object of

---

[1] Cf. *passim* the article '*Über östliches und westliches Christentum*'.*

infatuation, as the old mystics would say—a wall of illusion blocking out the divine. A book could be written on all the God-surrogates whose ruin has been encompassed by this War in such a way as to release men's souls for God; its title might be 'The Decline of the European Idol'. For European social democracy the surrogate has been the *ideal State* of the future, the faith in automatic, smooth-running progress and 'evolution', which was to make Paradise of its own accord. In a word, it was faith in the very *possibility* of an earthly Paradise. When, in pursuance of his studies in the philosophy of history, Marx had formed the idea of the future State, he was under the demonstrable influence of Jewish *messianism*. With fearful derision the War's furious dance is trampling on these idols and already they are half in dust. An immeasurable void has been left in the great soul of the fourth estate, which in its honest inner hopes—in spite of much so-called revisionism before the War—has silently continued to *live* by these idols, class-reactive idols formed by conversion of middle-class and bourgeois liberal idols—those of imperializing Mammon and disorderly freedom. (Historically it was out of that same liberal middle class that the fourth estate arose—*without* initially possessing, *caught up as it was in an endless range of particularized work,* the time, leisure, freedom and intellectual independence requisite to conquer and replace the characteristic motives and theoretic attitude of that class.) There is then a void which requires, demands to be filled with truly religious types of good. It is the business of the Christian Church, its onerous, holy responsibility before God, to open at the right hour its arms of love and compassion in order worthily to receive the kind of European who will in future share the conduct of affairs, the (as we hope) wrongly thought lost son of the fourth estate—which the Church has too often deserted in favour of sons more correct in deportment, but far less worthy in the bottom of their hearts. Already the purely negative aspects of Marxism have been discarded to all intents, and no Christian thinker should allow himself to neglect the opportunity of collaborating in the formation of the fourth estate's *new ideology*. Up to now the fourth estate has seen all fields as controlled by only mindless or irrational forces. This will cease to be the case to the extent that it participates in the control of society.

However, like the view of history adopted by many recent and older German professors of philosophy, historical pantheisms, according to which world-history itself, *i.e.* the outcome of events, is the tribunal of the world (and God's final judgment at the end of time therefore superfluous), are equally alien to the spirit of any *Christian* way of thought. Such a way not only can, but *must* as Christian largely put to the account of sin the blind driving factors of hunger-instincts and baser passions in the history of mankind. It has, moreover, no reason to regard the 'spirit' as solely active in this fallen world—no reason to wear the rose-tinted glasses of pantheism.

Another field where rapprochement is discernible is that of the economic order, where extreme State-socialism has stood opposed to Christian teachings on social and property rights. In principle, of course, Christian philosophy teaches the unconditional respect of private property as a talisman of the freedom of the *unitary* psycho-physical human being. But it lays down no firm boundary for its positive ordering, the right of its free use and disposal, its obligations, onus, its total significance in State and society. Above all the Christian Church knows that what is most essential for the right shaping of the community's life is not the choice between a so-called free competitive economy and a State economy or any kind of planned, legislated collectivism—not any choice of right *system*—but a totally different kind of choice, one between the *spirit* of solidarity, co-operation and love-guided equity *and* the *spirit* of unmitigated competition, work against rivals and naked class-conflict, whether instigated from above or from below, whether between man and man, nation and nation, or State and State. And it knows that in the last resort it is a matter of total *indifference* whether the subject and vehicle of the economic ethos is called an individual or a State. For in *spirit* a State-socialism can be as imbued with capitalism as an essentially free economy by a sense of solidarity. To a very great extent these systems are questions of appropriate means to ends, and if present exigencies should prescribe a stronger measure of socialism in future for European States, only two things remain to be said:

1. If the State is to be more heavily laden with tasks and functions, and considerably fortified in its rôle of economic arbiter, we must ensure a sufficient admixture of democratic oil in the machinery to safeguard personal liberty, freedom of opinion and worship.

2. To a much greater extent than before, all cultural and religious matters (language, schooling, manners and customs, forms of worship, art, research, etc.), must be *removed* from the State, and every effort to 'organize' which goes too far in the direction of State-authority must be curbed more firmly than heretofore. Instead these matters must be yielded in trust more to the autonomous care of nations, races, federal units, municipalities, local government, so that the economically mighty State will not be tempted to overstep the regular *bounds* of its new jurisdiction. It is in *this*, not the political sense that we too demand a new self-determination of nations, races, peoples.

The involvement of the Church with the feudality has also lost a great deal of its reactionary character as the course of events has forced feudal elements into the *opposition* parties. That is very much the case in Prussia today. For in this way the outlook and ethos of both feudal remnants and the believing population will be *purged* of the stagnant prejudice into which both fell as a consequence of their over-close connection with the stratum of leading capitalists and the bourgeois spirit. It is plain for all to see in the history of the Prussian conservative party how all truly Christian conservative principles were sapped, subverted and abandoned. But already in Prussia there are—admittedly small—conservative circles which are beginning to remember the duties of a Christian conservative party as distinct from a class-coalition between the great landowners and heavy industry; evidence of this is provided by Herr von Kardoff's representations as well as the exchange of letters, which has attracted much attention, between Herr Thimme and Herr von Heydebrand. Indeed, I note that more and more young scions of the Prussian and Austrian aristocracies, men who have known and suffered in the War, are beginning to tread a path not unlike that strongwilled element of the Russian nobility which for decades has even led the Russian revolutionary movement. It is precisely the psychologically inhibited, politically all-too-subservient social democrats of Germany proper who need, more than any others, the collaboration and *leadership* of these untimorous, purposeful sections of the community, which are so greatly blessed—sadly over-blessed, one should say—with the hereditary instinct for mastery and leadership they have hitherto placed much too exclusively in the service of big business. But what concerns the politically uncommitted Christian citizenry (or shall we say its historical remnants?) is that the very marked decline of the middle class, which has taken place despite its implementation of many counsels of prudence, is certainly not inauspicious for the rapprochement of the Church and social democracy.

Taking all these things into consideration, we may conclude that 'Stockholm' and 'Rome' will come much closer together: in this way the *oldest and the newest* will be enabled to reinforce each other in the cultural reconstruction of Europe.

But now a few more words regarding the *younger generation* which will carry on its shoulders the Europe of the future and must revivify it for the reconstruction of its cultural unity.

1. The cultural ideal as applied to the upbringing of youth should as first consideration restore *man* to the centre of earthly life, and in man the spiritual, individual person with his co-responsible integration into the community; that is to say, man should oust from this central position

mere things, techniques, specializations, commodities, businesses or any kind of monstrous absolute—such as a State alleged to contain its own salvation. Doubtless in worth and purpose the State is superior to the mere welfare of the *physical* individual; but in relation to the *spiritual* individual it *ceases* to be an end in itself.

Similarly, it will be no bloodless, vaguely floating idea of law and order, no blind energy, no inanimate matter or impersonal cosmic spirit which will preside over such an outlook and appear to have the governance of the world, but the infinite *person* of God, to whom alone belongs absolute, unconditional obedience when he speaks to us through conscience and the Church. All other obedience is relative and conditional.

Within the frame of the European type of man, and not in opposition to this type, our youth will be led *not* by any shabby functional ideal but by a concrete *ideal of the personality* of the specifically German human being. It must be the ideal of a person who, down to the lowliest worker, has dignity, responsibility and freedom—a person whose service all mere 'organizations' must enter.

We wish to see our universities staffed by *persons*, by teachers who are *exemplars* of heart and mind, not by the one-eyed, Cyclopean heads of administrative drudges and pundits; our ministries we would fill with statesmen who have ripened in the open air of public life, not with placeholding machines. We do not fear the 'dilettantism' against which there is such an automatic outcry in Germany, as soon as man is found stronger than one department, office or business. On the contrary, we wish to have men at the top who are passionate *amateurs* of their concerns, with mere 'experts' and 'duty-doers' as their servants.[1] Let independent insight, not an unthinking *duty*-impulse, govern State and individual alike. The person will freely, as he should, fit into the dispositions of community and State—that lesson he has learned in the school of the War—but only in so far as material values are concerned, I mean those values which, while of great importance, are lower by nature than *spiritual* values; where *these* come into question, the person and the smaller community of spirits will carry their heads high towards all things of this earth, and bow them humbly only before God.

Moreover, this personal ideal will have to comprise certain internal distinctions and a gradation. At its centre stands man the *religious* person —a member of the all-embracing kingdom of God, the kingdom of all souls, of all men dead and living. There stands religious man, with every breath humbly thanking the creator that he *is* rather than is not, mindful

[1] Cf. the fine, searching words of the physicist A. Einstein in his address on the motives of research: '*Motive des Forschens*', Karlsruhe 1918.

of his share of responsibility for the rise or decline of this sublime realm, which never rises or falls but as *one* indivisible. Next in order stands man the *creative spirit*, in the context of his concrete national existence: he has a right to freedom of expression and cultural ideals, a right which the State must respect. The one-sided idol of the nation-State should be done away, that the ideal of free, spontaneously active national culture in the context of a State may gain in strength and vitality.

Only now comes the *citizen*, freely sharing the determination of his State's fate and conduct, awoken from his torpid immersion in business, from his 'subject'-mentality and blinkered functionalism. But just as the citizen in every man ranks *below* the cultural creative spirit, so he takes precedence over the *economic* subject, the producer-consumer. Thus economic man comes last after the inconceivably mysterious destiny of the individual religious essence, then the creative spirit and the citizen. To this we Germans will easily cling, who have always felt economic individualism as an element alien to our blood. Thus at one and the same time the State is *master* and *servant*: master of the economic individual, of all institutions and organizations making for the just distribution of wealth, but servant of the spirit, and in particular the servant of the soul and its individual goal in eternity.

2. But again this person will have as underlying strength that which has underlain all creative epochs of the human race—not world-*hostility*, not an attitude of antagonistic 'criticism', but friendliness, devotion and love for the objective world. Europe's whole way of thinking, the very *philosophy* of the bourgeois age from Descartes to Kant, has been, with all its forms of 'idealism' and subjectivism, the exact opposite of the type of mind and spirit which is needed to lighten the future path. At God and at the world, which it conceived as only a thing to be shaped, worked, controlled by man, this philosophy blinked skeptical eyes. And *since* one can control and move the world only in so far as it is a mechanism, the 'useful working-hypothesis' of man the technician, whereby he regards the world for convenience as if it *were* a mere piece of machinery, was unhesitatingly converted into a metaphysics: that is, into a (pre-given) 'true' picture of the world. On all fronts this grievous error is in retreat. Our latest literature is already inspired by this new force of great devotion, of fearless, imperturbable devotion to what *is*, reality itself, the heartfelt readiness to shake hands with facts. And already the new European philosophy, to elaborate which is beyond my present concern, is beginning to turn from the world-alienation of an outworn, subjective rationalism, which has ossified into formulae, to a living perceptual and empirical contact with things as they are.

Once again the meaning of human culture will be—to assist all things toward their particular meaning and goal by knowledge, love and creative activity, toward the meaning and goal to which they are appointed in the *ideas* which God has of them; and all this as may be achieved in the solidary co-operation of human cognitive effort, in loving endeavours—the collaboration of all individuals, communities, ages. Only in the shared work of redeeming all things, guiding them to God and their appointed ends, can the human person, with the help of grace, progress toward its own destination, which is to be as God has willed it to be.

If the German national spirit is willing to inscribe in this frame, so abstract as it stands, its own peculiar ends and aims—which may only be sensed intuitively—and if the German will seek to realize in work and deed the special ideal of German personality, which ages of authentic historical greatness inspire, then perhaps he will be able to do more than make a contribution to the cultural reconstruction of Europe. As is proper to his geographical position in the heart of Europe, and to the Germanic character that I have described, he may be able to lead and guide that reconstruction in community with the best in all other European nations.

EDITORIAL NOTICE[1]

by Frau Maria Scheler

This fourth edition of *Vom Ewigen in Menschen*, which forms Volume 5 in the collected edition now being undertaken (*Gesammelte Schriften Max Schelers*), comprises the same writings as the first and second editions (1921 and 1923), as well as the third of 1933, which the publishers styled a 'popular' edition. As the writer of this notice has already observed, in a postscript to Volume 2 of the collected edition (*Der Formalismus in der Ethik, etc.*, Berne 1954), it is the publisher's intention to arrange the nine volumes containing works that appeared in the author's lifetime in such a way that at least some of these volumes can bear titles under which the works of Max Scheler have come to be known.

The present volume appears under the title of *Vom Ewigen im Menschen*, by which name the author always referred to it and literature has always cited it. As indicated in the preface to the first edition, the subtitle 'Religious Renewal' (taken from the introductory section of 'Problems of Religion') originally served to distinguish this work from the two further volumes which the author planned but never published. The placing of 'Problems of Religion' before the two final essays corresponds not only to his original intention but also to the significance of this work within the volume as a whole. Only the fact that when printing had begun the manuscript was still incomplete (cf. below) caused the publisher, with Scheler's consent, to place 'Problems of Religion' last in the book, in order not to delay any further a publication which was taking place at a time of post-war difficulties and inflation.

The fresh type-setting of the work has afforded an opportunity of eliminating a number of textual defects existing in the first edition (and in the corresponding second and third, which suffered from a somewhat inadequate technical revision). Only in the case of certain works (see below) has it been possible to check against the manuscript. Much of 'Problems of Religion', especially, was set up in the first instance directly from the author's first draft, which in part had been hurriedly concluded; in the process, as fresh comparison with the manuscript has shown, a

[1] Appended to the fourth German edition (*Translator*).

P

rather large number of faults affecting the sense crept into the first impression. Such was Max Scheler's temperament, his carefree vitality, that when he had occasion to correct proofs he would not so much pay heed to removing the faults of the compositor as seize the opportunity to make alterations and additions to the text—a habit which by adding to the compositor's difficulties only increased the sources of textual error.

The appended list of corrections[1] gives information about corrections made in the text of this fourth edition.[2]

(. . .)

The *Annotations*, marked in the text and footnotes with asterisks, follow the policy adopted in our first published volume (*Formalismus* . . .) by supplementing in detail the mostly very general references of the author to his planned or published works. (In some cases the expansion has been made by the editress in the footnote itself.) Thus these Annotations provide information about the title, place, time of the author's later works, where they are mentioned, or on whether and where projected works appeared, whether any writings on the problem in question have been found among the author's papers, etc. Elsewhere the Annotations, in the absence of any reference by Scheler himself, draw attention to connections existing between the passage marked and other works of the author, especially those post 1921.

The *Bibliography* which has also been added to this volume, and to which there are many references in the Annotations, should furnish the reader with a cursory, overall picture of Max Scheler's work. At the same time it shows the projected arrangement of those works which are to enter Volumes 1 to 9 of the collected edition. In one of the later volumes a comprehensive bibliography will appear; through the loss of all author's copies, notably in the case of periodicals, and the disappearance of a comprehensive list which had been compiled over the years, it has not yet been possible to produce a bibliography without lacunae.

(. . .)

The following remarks concern the genesis of the separate works assembled here.

[1] Naturally absent from this English edition (*Translator*).
[2] Hereafter certain details of pagination, etc., relating only to the German editions, as well as a number of minutiae referring to manuscripts and other documents, have been omitted in translation. Where this is so, the omission is indicated by bracketed suspension-points, thus (. . .) (*Translator*).

'Repentance and Rebirth' (*'Reue und Wiedergeburt'*) first appeared as
'*Zur Apologetik der Reue*' in the quarterly *Summa* (Hellerauer Verlag, 1917,
No. 1, pp. 53 *et seq.*). In spite of various attempts the editress has been
unable to see a copy of this periodical (which ran for only a few numbers)
—as hinted above, the author's copy was lost in the post-war confusion of
1945—and it has not therefore been possible to establish whether, or to
what extent, Max Scheler revised the essay for inclusion in *Vom Ewigen
im Menschen*. Nor has the manuscript been found among his papers.

As '*Vom Wesen der Philosophie*', 'The Nature of Philosophy and the
moral preconditions of philosophical knowledge'[1] (*'Vom Wesen der
Philosophie und der moralischen Bedingung des philosophischen Erkennens'*) was
also first published in *Summa* (1917, No. 2, pp. 40 *et seq.*). This again is a
first publication of which the editress has been unable to trace a copy. But
fortunately the manuscript of the work, which was conceived as the
introduction to a projected book called *Die Welt und ihre Erkenntnis* ('The
world and knowledge of it'), has been preserved almost *in toto*. All that is
missing is the passage[2] (. . .). For these pages there has been found in the
author's files the carbon-copy of a dictated typescript, to which Max
Scheler refers in the marginalia of his manuscript. Comparison of this
document (uncorrected by the author) with the printed text reveals that
the dictation was searchingly revised. Elsewhere departures from the
manuscript are negligible. The manuscript must date from the end of
1916 or the beginning of 1917, and it is probable that the above pages
were inserted for the republication as part of this work.

While these two opening sections of the present volume were each set
down in one continuous spell of activity (this much is quite certain from
the manuscript in the case of 'The Nature of Philosophy'), the labours
which brought into being the most important and wide-ranging section
of the book, 'Problems of Religion' (*'Probleme der Religion'*), stretched over
a number of years: the drafts are visibly discontinuous. The manuscripts
(. . .) have been preserved with the exception of a few pages (. . .) for
which we have a corrected typescript. The drafts of course provide internal
evidence of the genesis and chronology of the various subdivisions. As
described in our postscript to the fourth edition of *Formalismus* . . . , the
gradual alteration of Max Scheler's handwriting over two decades has
become an important touchstone for the chronology of the author's
drafts—given the almost total absence of explicit time-references and the
relative lack of indirect indices

---

[1] Literally 'cognition' (*Translator*).
[2] A passage where Scheler defines his position *vis-à-vis* Edmund Husserl, in this
edition, pp. 80-83 (*Translator*).

The following details have been established:

The introductory section of the work (to p. 127 l. 10)[1] was originally published in the monthly *Hochland*, in the October number of 1918, under the title 'Religious Renewal' ('*Zur religiösen Erneuerung*'). All the rest of 'Problems of Religion' was first published in the frame of *Vom Ewigen im Menschen*. (. . .) For *Vom Ewigen im Menschen* the text of this section was set up from a typewritten transcript of the original manuscript, which had been worked over by the author and expanded by minor intercalations in the margin and longer insertions on handwritten sheets. (. . .) In the first edition (hence also in the second and third) Scheler's final insertion, here p. 127 l. 11–p. 128 l. 6, was blunderingly printed three pages too early— an error we have corrected. It is this passage which serves as a transition to the central sections of the whole work.

The two closing pages of the above original manuscript of the introductory section (two pages out of twenty-nine) have never been printed, either in *Hochland* or in 'Problems of Religion'. However, if we consider them in conjunction with the superscription on page 1 of the manuscript: ' "Religious Renewal"/I. The new world-situation / A. Internal Factors', these pages shed light for us on the manuscript's origin and genesis, as well as its relation to another section of the whole work. In them we find the following words (linking directly in the manuscript to what is represented by p. 127 l. 10 of the present edition):

'But to these more inward, psychical atmospheres in which religious renewal is taking place there are being added profound changes in public life, changes which are preparing a thoroughly new soil and climate for religion and the Church—to such an extent that many circles understandably cherish the hope of a *new religion*. Three of these are undoubtedly of universal significance.' (In the margin: 'Re-arrange!') 'The first change is the new universal tendency for Church and State to separate; the second is the awakening of the Asiatic peoples and the consequent entry of Asiatic forms of religion and *Weltanschauung* into the arena of European religious and ecclesiastical conflict. The third change concerns the basic coming to terms of religion and Church with the likewise universal tendency to political and social democracy.' (. . .)

On the last page of the manuscript, under the heading 'B. External Factors', we find:

'Before discussing these more external forms of the new religious and ecclesiastical spirit, the forms of its implementation and realization, I would like to address a few words to those who envisage the demand for

[1] This and all further references apply to the present translated edition (*Translator*).

religious renewal in quite a different manner from ours, and believe in the need for a new religion or new ecclesiastical structures.'

From these closing pages of the manuscript (as regards some of the 'external factors', cf. Section 2 of the last work in the present volume) it can be seen that the introductory section of 'Problems of Religion' arose independently of the central sections of the work. The original manuscript was in fact intended to be spoken, and was written in connection with the lectures given by Max Scheler in 1917-1918 in Switzerland and Holland, under the cultural auspices of the German Foreign Office. This explains the partly rhetorical diction of this section. Another thing that transpires is the intimate connection between the introduction and the concluding Section 3 of 'Problems of Religion' (religious renewal = new religion?)— whose first part is certainly not inconsistent in style with *its* origin as the spoken word. In the two relevant manuscripts the general character of the handwriting confirms that these sections took shape in close chronological proximity; both had perhaps already been drafted by the end of 1917, or by the summer of 1918 at the latest. (. . .) The last few pages of the final Section were added as a conclusion to the whole in 1920. (. . .)

As is clearly shown by the author's handwriting, within the central Sections 1 and 2 of 'Problems of Religion'—respectively 'Religion and Philosophy' and 'The Essential Phenomenology (*Wesensphänomenologie*) of Religion'—we must regard the last main chapter of Section 2, entitled 'Some recent attempts to provide a natural foundation for religion' ('. . . *einer natürlichen Religionsbegründung*'), as the earliest piece of work; it dates from 1917-1918. Only the closing paragraphs (. . .), written in 1920 as a transition to Section 3, are of a later origin. A private memorandum by the author, written on the back of a page in the manuscript, shows that this chapter existed as early as his stay in Holland in 1918. The fact that this chapter, devoted largely to critical reasonings, had an origin independent of and before the author's positive phenomenological investigations (which are recorded in Section 1 and the earlier part of Section 2) explains certain overlappings and repetitions. Section 1 and the remaining chapters of Section 2 were written between the end of 1918 and the end of 1920—but not continuously, as the manuscripts show. In any case, the chapters entitled 'Growth and decline of the natural knowledge of God' and 'Attributes of the divine mind' are of later origin than the sections on 'The Religious Act' which are printed after them. The very latest parts of the whole work are to be found within these two chapters; they are the passages on the 'functionalization of essential insight' and 'theism and the Fall', in the first and second respectively. They were not penned until the end of 1920.

The search for a solution of the problem of theodicy, based on the personalistic, spiritualistic Christian religion, in consequence of which Max Scheler saw himself impelled to sketch, in the last-named passage,[1] a tragic universal picture of the world—a world unredeemed—was a constant theme and point of reference in the steady transformation of his religious or metaphysical views over the years after 1920. In contrast to those who 'have been moved to unthinking dismissal by deep-seated ideological preconceptions' and have not wished or been able to recognize 'the simple philosophical logic' of the change in Scheler's metaphysical positions, Nicolai Hartmann, in his incomparable obituary of Max Scheler (in *Kantstudien*, 1929), has laid his finger on the central ontological problems which were decisive in this connection: 'The gravity of the problem of reality which gripped him more year by year compelled him to re-orient his outlook.' Hartmann calls the very 'wrestling and forward-thrusting of this life and thought' 'one great unswerving attestation of truth, truly philosophical at every step'. In the 'inner self-consistency of his gradual change' and the 'high art of progressive inquiry', the man who was Max Scheler's colleague for years at Cologne University places him 'in the same line as thinkers such as Fichte, Schelling, Nietzsche and even Plato'.

The paths of Christian theism in its Catholic form (with which Scheler, first increasingly, then decreasingly, identified himself in his writings from roughly 1912 to 1922) were regarded by Max Scheler himself as part of a genuine development in his thought, and as a necessary transition to the metaphysical views of his later years—views which he continued to profess even in the face of death, with the calm assurance of one who has found his road. On the other hand he insisted that in the context of a personalistic, spiritualistic conception of God the phenomenology of religion set forth in 'Problems of Religion' retained its validity and internal logic.

(. . .)

The address entitled 'Christian Love and the Twentieth Century' ('*Die christliche Liebesidee und die gegenwärtige Welt*') dates from 1917, as the author establishes with the text of the first page. Only one page of the manuscript has been found among the author's papers. So far as has been ascertained, this address was first published in *Vom Ewigen im Menschen*. For the rest, the reader is referred to the Annotations.

'The Reconstruction of European Culture' ('*Vom kulturellen Wieder-aufbau Europas*') also dates in essentials from 1917 (see author's footnotes to p. 405 and p. 412), but was first published in the monthly periodical

[1] On evil and the Fall, pp. 233 *et seq.* (*Translator*).

Hochland, 1918 (February, pp. 497 *et seq.*; March, pp. 666 *et seq.*). Max Scheler revised and expanded it for *Vom Ewigen im Menschen*. The manuscript has not been preserved, but we have the copy of the *Hochland* publication which, with the author's marginal interpolations and handwritten insertions on separate sheets, served as basis for the new impression in the frame of the larger work. (. . .) In order to preserve uniformity of appearance in the fourth edition the writer of this notice has provided headings, prompted by the text (. . .), for the two subdivisions (. . .) into which this section falls.

BIBLIOGRAPHY OF SCHELER'S
PUBLISHED WORKS[1]

1. *Beiträge zur Feststellung der Beziehung zwischen den logischen und ethischen Prinzipien* (Contributions to the ascertainment of the relation between the logical and ethical principles); Doctoral thesis, Jena 1897. Vopelius, Jena 1899. CE 1.

2. *Arbeit und Ethik* (Work and ethics); in the *Zeitschrift für Philosophie und philosophische Kritik*, Vol. 114, No. 2, 1899. (Cf. No. 19, below.) CE 1.

3. *Die transzendentale und die psychologische Methode*. (The transcendental and the psychological methods); 'A fundamental discussion of philosophical method'; 'habilitation'-treatise, Jena 1899. Dürr, Jena 1900. 2nd unrevised edition: Meiner, Leipzig 1922. CE 1.

4. *Über Selbsttäuschungen* (On Self-delusions); in the *Zeitschrift für Pathopsychologie*, I / 1, Engelmann, Leipzig 1911. (Cf. No. 10 below.) CE 3.

5. *Über Ressentiment und moralisches Werturteil* (On resentment and moral value-judgment); A Contribution to the pathology of culture (= civilization); in the *Zeitschrift für Pathopsychologie*, I / 2, 3, Leipzig 1912. (Cf. No. 10 below.) CE 3.

6. *Zur Phänomenologie und Theorie der Sympathiegefühle und von Liebe und Hass* (Contribution to the phenomenology and theory of sympathy-emotions and of love and hatred); with an Appendix on the reason for assuming the existence of other selves (. . . *des fremden Ich*). Niemeyer, Halle 1913. (Cf. No. 18, below.) CE 1.

7. *Der Formalismus in der Ethik und die materiale Wertethik* (Formalism in ethics, and the ethics of supraformal[2] values); with special reference to the ethics of Kant.
Part I, in the *Jahrbuch für Philosophie und phänomenologische Forschung*, 1st Year, Niemeyer, Halle 1913.
Part II, *ibidem*, 2nd Year, 1916.

---

[1] As appended to the fourth German edition: see Frau Scheler's remarks in her Editorial Notice, p. 450. Titles and headings have been translated literally, to furnish the English-reader with a synopsis of Scheler's work. CE = Collected Edition, Francke, Berne 1954 and after; the volume number is given in each case (*Translator*).
[2] Scheler's special use of (the German adjective) *material* is crucial in his thought. Cf. my note to p. 279 (*Translator*).

First edition, Parts I and II together, offprinted, with a foreword; Halle 1916.

2nd unrevised edition, with subtitle—'New endeavour to found an ethical personalism'—and a second foreword; Halle 1921.

3rd edition, with a third foreword and a subject-index; Halle 1927.

4th revised edition, edited by Maria Scheler, with a new subject-index; Francke, Berne 1954.   CE 2.

8. *Ethik: Ein Forschungsbericht* (Ethics, a report of research); in the *Jahrbücher der Philosophie* edited by Max Frischeisen-Köhler, 2nd Year, Berlin 1914.   CE 1.

9. *Der Genius des Krieges und der deutsche Krieg* (The presiding spirit of the War, and the German war.) Weisse Bücher, Leipzig, 3 editions, 1915-16-17.   CE 4.

10. *Abhandlungen und Aufsätze* (Essays and articles), 2 volumes.

First edition, Weisse Bücher, Leipzig 1915.

2nd and 3rd editions, retitled—

Vom Umsturz der Werte (On the overthrow of values), Nuer Geist, Leipzig 1919 and 1923.

Vol. I: The rehabilitation of youth

Resentment in the formation of overall moral attitudes (an expansion of No. 5, above)

The phenomenon of the tragic

The idea of man

Vol. II: The eidolons of self-knowledge (an expansion of No. 4, above)

In search of a philosophy of life

The psychology of the 'hysterical craving for security', and the true fight with evil

The meaning of feminism

The bourgeois

The bourgeois and the forces of religion

The future of capitalism   CE 3.

11. *Krieg und Aufbau* (War and (re-)building). Weisse Bücher, Leipzig 1916. (For republication of various sections, see No. 19, below.)

The War as a collective experience

On eastern and western Christianity

The national in French thinking

On the national ideas of the great nations

On the spirit and ideological bases of the democratic movements in the great nations

On the militarism of private outlook and ambition: a study in the psychology of militarism

Sociological reorientation and the task of the German Catholics after the War

On the meaning of suffering

Love and knowledge   CE 6.

12. *Die Ursachen des Deutschenhasses* (The causes of Germanophobia); 'A discussion to instruct the nation'. Wolff, Leipzig 1917. 2nd edition; Neuer Geist, Leipzig 1919.   CE 4.

13. *Von Zwei deutschen Krankheiten* (On two German maladies); in No. 6 of *Der Leuchter*, Reichl, Darmstadt 1919. (Cf No. 19, below.)

14. *Vom Ewigen im Menschen* (On the eternal in man), Volume 1: *Zur Religiösen Erneuerung* (Religious renewal).

First edition (in one volume); Neuer Geist, Leipzig 1921.

2nd edition (in two half-volumes), with a larger preface; Neuer Geist, Leipzig 1923.

3rd (unabridged 'popular') edition (in one volume); Neuer Geist, Berlin 1933.

Half-vol. I: Repentance and rebirth

The nature of philosophy and the moral conditions of philosophical knowledge.

The Christian idea of love and the twentieth century

The cultural reconstruction of Europe

Half-vol. II: Problems of religion   CE 5.

15. *Universtät und Volkshochschule* (University and *Volkshochschule*—National or People's College); contribution to symposium *Zur Soziologie des Volksbildungswesens*, ed. L. von Wiese (Cf. Nos. 20 & 22, below). Duncker and Humblot, Munich 1921.   CE 6.

16. *Die Deutsche Philosophie der Gegenwart* (German philosophy today); in *Deutsches Leben der Gegenwart*, ed. P. Witkop. Bücherfreunde, Berlin 1922.   CE 7.

17. *Walther Rathenau*; 'A tribute'. Marcan-Block, Cologne 1922.   CE 6.

18. *Wesen und Formen der Sympathie* (The nature and forms of sympathy); 2nd enlarged edition of No. 6, above. Cohen, Bonn 1923.

3rd and 4th editions; *ibidem* 1926 and 1929.

5th edition; Schulte-Bulmke, Frankfurt am Main 1948.   CE 7.

(English translation, *The Nature of Sympathy*, with general introduction to Max Scheler's work, Routledge and Kegan Paul, and Yale University Press, 1954—*Translator*.)

19. *Schriften zur Soziologie und Weltanschauungslehre* (Contributions to sociology and the study of *Weltanschauungen*); 4 small volumes. Neuer Geist, Leipzig 1923-24. (Cf. No. 11, above.)

I. *Moralia*

On sociology and *Weltanschauungen*
On the positivist historical philosophy of knowledge
On the meaning of suffering (ex No. 11, considerably expanded)
On the betrayal of joy
Love and knowledge (ex No. 11)
On eastern and western Christianity (ex No. 11)

II. *Nation*

On the national ideas of the great nations (ex No. 11).
The national in French thinking (ex No. 11)
The spirit and ideological bases of democratic movements (ex No. 11)
On militarism of private outlook and ambition (ex No. 11)
On two German maladies (cf. No. 13, above)

IIIa. *Christentum und Gesellschaft* (Christianity and Society): *Konfessionen* (Denominations)

Peace among the denominations
Sociological reorientation, etc. (ex No. 11)

IIIb. *Christentum und Gesellschaft: Arbeits- und Bevölkerungsprobleme* (Labour and population problems)

Prophetic or Marxist socialism?
Labour and ethics (cf. No. 2)
Labour and *Weltanschauung*
Population problems as questions of *Weltanschauung*   CE 6.

20. *Probleme einer Soziologie des Wissens* (Problems of a sociology of knowledge); contribution to symposium *Versuche zu einer Soziologie des Wissens*, ed. Max Scheler (Cf. No. 22, below). Duncker and Humblot, Munich 1924. Symposia mentioned in Nos. 15 & 20 represented Vols. I and II of the Annals of the *Forschungsinstitut für Sozialwissenschaften*, Cologne.

21. *Die Formen des Wissens und die Bildung* (The forms of knowledge, and the cultivation of persons). Cohen, Bonn 1925. (Cf. No. 27.)

22. *Die Wissensformen und die Gesellschaft* (Forms of knowledge, and society). Neuer Geist, Leipzig 1926.

  1. Problems of a sociology of knowledge (No. 20, expanded).
  2. Knowledge and work. A study of the value and limitations of the pragmatic motive in knowledge of the world.
  3. University and *Volkshochschule* (National or People's College) (Cf. No. 15.)   1 & 2: CE 8.   3: CE 6.

23. *Die Stellung des Menschen im Kosmos* (The place of man in the cosmos); in No. 8 of *Der Leuchter*, Reichl, Darmstadt 1927.

Offprinted 1st, 2nd, 3rd editions; 1928-29-31.

4th and 5th editions; Nymphenburger Verlagsanstalt, Munich 1948 & 1949. CE 9.

24. *Mensch und Geschichte* (Man and history). In *Neue Rundschau*, 37th Year, November 1926. (Cf. No. 27.)
Separate publication: 'Neue Schweizer Rundschau' Press, Zürich 1929.

25. *Idealismus—Realismus*; in the *Philosophischer Anzeiger* II. Cohen, Bonn 1927. CE 9.

26. *Der Mensch im Weltalter des Ausgleichs* (Man in the age of levelling); in *Politische Wissenschaft* ('Equality as destiny and task'). Publication of the *Deutsche Hochschule für Politik*, Berlin 1929. (Cf. No. 27.)

The following was posthumously published:

27. *Philosophische Weltanschauung*. Cohen, Bonn 1929. Pocket edition: Dalp-Taschenbücher No. 301, Francke, Berne, 1954.
Philosophische Weltanschauung
Mensch und Geschichte (cf. No. 24)
Der Mensch im Weltalter des Ausgleichs (cf. No. 26)
Die Formen des Wissens und die Bildung (cf. No. 21)
Spinoza: an address CE 9.
(E.T. *Philosophical Perspectives*, Beacon Press, Boston, Mass. 1954— *Translator*.)

The following have been published from the author's literary remains:

28. *Die Idee des Ewigen Friedens und der Pazifismus* (Pacifism and the idea of everlasting peace).
Neuer Geist, Berlin 1931.

29. *Schriften aus dem Nachlass* (From the literary remains of . . .), Volume I: *Zur Ethik und Erkenntnislehre* (On ethics and epistemology); edited with an appendix by Maria Scheler. Neuer Geist, Berlin 1933.
Death and life thereafter
On modesty and feelings of shame
Exemplars and leaders
Ordo amoris
Phenomenology and epistemology
Doctrine of the three facts

ANNOTATIONS[1]
by Frau Scheler

Prefaces

p. 11, l. 11.   The circumstances of time and place in which these works first appeared are further detailed in our Editorial Note.

p. 11, l. 13.   Cf. Editorial Note.

p. 12, l. 30.   A first draft touching the fundamentals of the philosophy of religion was found in the author's literary remains. It originated *c.* 1915–1916 in connection with work on Part II of *Der Formalismus in der Ethik und die materiale Wertethik*[2]. See the author's indications at the end of that section, and our own annotation in the appendix of the 4th edition, Berne, 1954.

p. 13, l. 35.   The two further volumes of *Vom Ewigen im Menschen*, announced here by the author, never appeared. Work intended for vol. 2 and discovered among his papers was published by the present editress, under the title 'Exemplars and Leaders', in the posthumous volume (1933) on ethics and epistemology, which collected together all the work arising from or projected in *Form.*: see No. 29 of bibliography. In respect of projects for vol. 3, cf. Nos. 11 and 19 (1); on the 'sociology of cognition' cf. *Probleme einer Soziologie des Wissens*, 1924, bibl. Nos. 20 and 22: Coll. Ed. vol. 8.

p. 17, n. 1.   Cf. bibl. No. 16 (Coll. Ed. vol. 7). The projected work mentioned p. 17 did not appear.

p. 23, n. 1.   See *Form.* §VI B, Ch. 2, 'Person and individual', and Ch. 4 *ad* 3. The present ensuing discussion of truth, universal validity, personal *versus* subjective, is related to *Form.* §VI A, 3c, 'Person and world'.

---

[1] As appended to the fourth German edition and indicated by asterisks in the text and footnotes (*Translator*).

[2] Hereafter referred to as *Form.* The references all relate to the fourth German edition, Berne 1954: Coll. Ed. vol. 2 (*Translator*).

p. 24, l. 2. Cf. section on 'phenomenological conflict' in *Phäno-menologie and Erkenntnistheorie* (1914), first published in the above-mentioned posthumous volume.

p. 25, l. 23. See especially *Form.* §II B, §VI B and subject-index.

Repentance and Rebirth

p. 39, l. 32. On the relation between the person and its psychic history, and in respect of what follows concerning the phenomenology of memory, see *Form.* §VI A3, Ch. g.

p. 44, l. 9. On the law underlying the relative order as data of value-content and symbolic or meaning-content, consult *Gegebenheit* and (*Bild-, Bedeutungs-, Wert-) Gehalt* in index of *Form.*

p. 50, l. 26. On the possible co-existence of such different levels or planes of feeling in the person, see *Form.* §V, Ch. 8.

p. 52, n. 1. Cf. also the later, expanded editions, *Wesen und Formen der Sympathie*, §A, Ch. 2, bibl. Nos. 6 and 18: Coll. Ed. vols. 1 and 7.

p. 58, l. 13. On collective, hereditary and tragic guilt, see *Form.* §VI B, Ch. 3, 'Autonomy of the person'.

p. 63, l. 10. Cf. 'Attributes of the divine mind' in 'Problems of Religion', Part 2.

The Nature of Philosophy

p. 80, l. 4. On the hierarchy of values, the ethos, and the principle of solidarity *versus* individualism, consult *Wertrangord-nung, Ethos, Solidarität* and *Individualismus* in index of *Form.*

p. 80, l. 37. 'Later': the present work was originally planned as an introduction to a larger work, *Die Welt und ihre Erkenntnis* (cf. p. 99), which never appeared.

p. 83, l. 22. Cf. also the essay *Weltanschauungslehre, Soziologie und Weltanschauungssetzung*, 1922, bibl. No. 19: Coll. Ed. vol. 6; likewise the above-mentioned *Probleme einer Soziologie des Wissens*.

p. 85, n. 1. On the 'restitution' of the Socratic proposition, cf. *Form.* §II (p. 89) and §III (p. 207).

p. 86, l. 17. On acts of emotional experience and the abstraction undertaken by explanatory psychology, see *Form.* §IV, Ch. 1 (pp. 209ff.).

p. 86, n. 1. See the above annotation of p. 13. On the text here cf. §III of *Form.*, pp. 153ff.

p. 88, l. 3. In this connection see 'Problems of Religion'.

p. 89, n. 1.   See the above annotation of p. 13.

p. 92, l. 13.   See the above annotation of p. 80, l. 37, and further cf. 'Problems of Religion'.

p. 92, n. 1.   'Later': see the above annotation of p. 80, l. 37. On phenomenological reduction see *Phänomenologie und Erkenntnistheorie*, *loc. cit.*, also, among later works, *Die Stellung des Menschen im Kosmos*, bibl. No. 23, and *Idealismus—Realismus*, No. 25: Coll. Ed. vol. 9.

p. 93, l. 21.   Cf. bibl. Nos. 21 and 27, *Philosophische Weltanschauung* (1927) and *Die Formen des Wissens und die Bildung* (1925), both republished 1954 in the pocket-volume *Philosophische Weltanschauung* (Francke, Berne).

p. 93, l. 24.   On the person-world and (corporeal) organism-environment correlates, see especially *Form.* §§III and VI B, A, 3g, also index.

p. 98, l. 18.   In the MS this section is headed 'Being in itself'. The work was to have been pursued (see annotation of p. 80, l. 37).

p. 99, n. 1.   See the above annotation of p. 80, l. 37.

pp. 102-3, n. 1.   On the function in a possible metaphysics of the supra-formal a-priori of realms of being, cf. pp. 295ff. in 'Problems of Religion', also the later writings *Die Stellung des Menschen im Kosmos* and 'Knowledge and work' in *Die Wissensformen und die Gesellschaft*, bibl. No. 22: Coll. Ed. vol. 8.

Problems of Religion

p. 111, l. 30.   See *Form.* §VI A: 'Micro- and macrocosm and the idea of God'.

p. 112, l. 40.   See discussion of Spinoza in *Philosophische Weltanschauung* (*v.s.* annotation of p. 93, l. 21).

p. 115, l. 17.   On 'functionalization' and the growth of the mind, see Part 2, 'Growth and decline of the natural knowledge of God'.

p. 118, l. 14.   For the criticism of all such 'need'-theories, see *Form.* §V, pp. 362ff.

p. 125, l. 27.   On the principle of solidarity, see *Form.* §VI B4, *ad* 4, and index.

p. 127, l. 37.   See the above annotation of p. 12.

p. 134, l. 35.   See 'Exemplars and leaders' (*op. cit.* in annotation of p. 13).

p. 137, l. 3.   For the criticism of Comte's law of three stages, see the 1921 essay on the positivist historical philosophy of knowledge, bibl. No. 19(1): Coll. Ed. vol. 6.

p. 143, l. 3.	On this point cf. the last heading of Part 2: 'Some recent basic theories of natural religion'.
p. 146, l. 12.	Cf. the foregoing arguments on pp. 134f. and pp. 138-42.
p. 155, l. 30.	See the above annotation of p. 143.
p. 155, l. 40.	Cf. Part 2, 'The religious act in its internal and external, individual and social aspects'.
p. 160, n. 1.	This footnote was evidently overlooked in the setting up of the first edition. The book referred to is E. Utitz, *Grundlegung der allgemeinen Kunstwissenschaft*, 1914 (see its introduction).
p. 162, n. 1.	See the above annotation of p. 13.
p. 163, l. 1.	*I.e.* on p. 154.
p. 167, l. 22.	On reality and resistance see *Form.* §III, pp. 154ff., 'Knowledge and work' (*op. cit. supra*) §VI, and *Idealismus—Realismus*, bibl. No. 25.
p. 170, n. 1.	Wundt's criticism of Husserl's *Logische Untersuchungen* is to be found in §VI, 'Psychologism and Logicism', of W. Wundt's *Kleine Schriften*, vol. 1 (Leipzig 1910). It also comes into play in the section on phenomenological conflict which, as mentioned in the annotation of p. 92, n. 1, forms part of the posthumous *Phänomenologie und Erkenntnistheorie*.
p. 172, l. 37.	'Infinitude'=essential consequence of God's aseity (cf. pp. 191 and 193). The word—a late addition to the MS—has been bracketed in this new impression.
p. 175, l. 9.	Cf. *Form.* §VI A, Ch. 3d, 'Micro- and macrocosm and the idea of God.'
p. 176, l. 39.	On awe and reverence see 'The rehabilitation of virtue' in *Vom Umsturz der Werte*, bibl. No. 10: Coll. Ed. vol. 3.
p. 180, l. 11.	On the ethos and absolute hierarchy of values, see *Form.* §V, Ch. 6.
p. 191, n. 1.	See the above annotation of p. 80, l. 37.
p. 192, n. 1.	Cf. the theory of memory in *Form.* §VI A3, Ch. g.
p. 196, n. 1.	Cf. *op. cit.* Part A IV; or A IV, Ch. 3, in *Wesen und Formen der Sympathie*.
p. 200, l. 2.	See criticism of the sensualist concept of sensation in *Form.* §§II and III (pp. 75ff. and 167ff.), and cf. §V of 'Knowledge and work'.
p. 200, l. 18.	See the theory expounded in *Form.* §II A, 'General nature of the a-priori and the formal', of a substantive, supraformal a-priori, together with a criticism of Kant's theory of the a-priori.
p. 202, l. 4.	On conscience and moral insight in general, see *Form.* §V, Ch. 7.

p. 202, l. 37.   See *Form.* §VI B4, *ad* 4, on the objectivity and hierarchy of values and on the co-operation of individuals or corporate persons to moral cognitive ends.

p. 204, l. 9.   See *Form.* §V, Ch. 7, and also *Die Stellung des Menschen im Kosmos,* bibl. No. 23.

p. 208, n. 2.   The projected publication did not ensue.

p. 215, l. 18.   On the overriding a-priority of love or hate, see *Liebe, Hasse* and *Apriorität* in index of *Form.*

p. 220, l. 29.   See the above annotation of p. 167.

p. 221, l. 41.   On the rôle of experience in the individual or general evolution of will, see *Form.* §III, pp. 143ff.

p. 222, l. 10.   On working and creating, cf. the early work, *Arbeit und Ethik,* 1899, bibl. Nos. 2 and 19(3b): Coll. Ed. vol. 1.

p. 222, l. 37.   On these types of persons correlative with certain a-priori values, see *Form.* §VI B4, *ad* 6b, and the above-cited 'Exemplars and leaders' (*v.s.* annotation of p. 13).

p. 225, n. 1.   See the above annotation of p. 13.

p. 230, l. 11.   On obedience and autonomy see *Form.* §VI B3, 'Autonomy of the person'.

p. 230, n. 1.   In the article adduced by the author there is no treatment of the matters mentioned. *Form.* would seem rather to be indicated.

p. 232, l. 2.   For criticism of Schopenhauer's and E. von Hartmann's teachings, see *Wesen und Formen der Sympathie* §VI, Part A, or 2nd Appendix of the 1913 original version, bibl. Nos. 6 and 18; Coll. Ed. vols. 1 and 7.

p. 236, l. 30.   The personal value-type of the artist is further discussed in the appendix, pp. 428ff. of the above oft-cited posthumous volume, 1933. Cf. also 'Metaphysics and art', article posthumously published in the bimensual *Deutsche Beiträge,* Munich 1947, No. 2.

p. 242, l. 31.   *I.e.* in *Form.,* *q.v.* in index under *Wert* II.

p. 243, l. 33.   See *Form.* §VI B4, *ad* 1, 'The being of the person as a self-value in history and community', also *Probleme einer Soziologie des Wissens,* Part I, and 'Man in the age of levelling', bibl. Nos. 26 and 27.

p. 246, l. 22.   See 'Attempts to form a philosophy of life' in *Vom Umsturz der Werte,* bibl. No. 10: Coll. Ed. vol. 3.

p. 248, n. 1.   See the above annotation of p. 118.

p. 250, l. 12.   On this distinction see *Akt* and *sozial* in index of *Form.*

p. 256, l. 28.   See the above annotation of p. 93, l. 24 and also the index of *Form.*

p. 258, l. 16.   On the assumption that one's fellow-men exist, see the criticism of these theories and Scheler's own positive theory in Part C of *Wesen und Formen der Sympathie*, or the appendix of the original version, 1913.

p. 263, n. 1.	See the above annotation of p. 118.
p. 265, l. 16.	On the moral intent (*Gesinnung*) and its attestation see Scheler's criticism of the ethics of success and the erroneous forms of an ethics of moral intent, together with his own positive theory, in *Form*. §III (see also *Form*. index under *Gesinnung*).
p. 265, l. 34.	See the above annotation of p. 236.
p. 265, n. 1.	See the above annotation of p. 85.
p. 268, l. 25.	The early MS on the philosophy of religion, mentioned in our annotation of p. 12, includes a phenomenological investigation of 'faith' and 'belief' as types of act.[1]
p. 269, n. 1.	On the Buddhist idea of Nirvana see article 'On the meaning of suffering', expanded and republished in *Moralia*, bibl. Nos. 11 and 19(1): Coll. Ed. vol. 6.
p. 270, n. 1.	These studies never appeared.
p. 271, n. 1.	See Part C of *Wesen und Formen der Sympathie*.
p. 273, l. 32.	See the above annotation of p. 258. With respect to the refuted theory inferring the reality of the past, see *Form*. §VI A3, g.
p. 288, l. 23.	On the value-cognitive character of emotional acts and the distinction between intentional 'feeling of . . .' and 'feeling', see *Form*. §V, Ch. 2, 'Feeling and feelings' (*Fühlen und Gefühle*)), and §II, pp. 83ff.
p. 289, l. 37.	Cf. criticism of Kant's attempt in *Form*. §V, Ch. 10.
p. 293, l. 3.	On ethics see especially §II A of *Form*.
p. 300, l. 28.	See *Probleme einer Soziologie des Wissens*, *loc. cit.*, as well as the closing section of 'The Reconstruction of European Culture', in this volume.
p. 300, n. 1.	See *Form*. §VI B, Ch. 3, *ad* 4.
p. 300, n. 2.	Essay first published in the monthly *Hochland*, 1920; bibl. No. 19: Coll. Ed. vol. 6.
p. 307, n. 2.	See entries *Gut—Böse* (*Irrige Lehren*) in index of *Form*.
p. 307, n. 3.	See *Form*. p. 227.
p. 308, n. 2.	And cf. §II B, Ch. 4.
p. 311, l. 28.	*I.e.* in *Form*. (see index under *Liebesakte*) and in the book on sympathy, all versions, Part B, §I.
p. 311, n. 1.	See *Wert* II in index of *Form*
p. 312, l. 37.	On this and the ensuing discussion see especially *Form*. §VI A and index under *Ich* and *Bewusstsein*.
p. 313, l. 31.	On the body and its perceptual status see *Form*. §VI A3, especially Chs. e and f (see also *Leib-* in index).

[1] The English words 'faith' and 'belief' are used in the German text (*Translator*).

p. 322, l. 26.   Cf. *Probleme einer Soziologie des Wissens, loc. cit.,* and *Form.* §VI B4, *ad* 4.

p. 323, l. 28.   On the unique character-designate, see *Form.* §VI B, Ch. 2 and Ch. 4 *ad* 3 (see also *individuelle Bestimmung* and *individuelles Gutes* in index).

p. 324, l. 31.   See criticism of ethics of goods and success in *Form.* §§I and III.

p. 335, n. 1.   Cf. *Wesen und Formen der Sympathie,* Part C III.

p. 339, l. 34.   On this contention see 1926 index of *Probleme einer Soziologie des Wissens,* entry *Fortschritt,* and what is said in *Form.* about the relation between a value's degree of perfection and its realizability (see *Wert* IId and *Solidarität* in index).

p. 341, l. 26.   Cf. passages on the holy in the above-cited 'Exemplars and leaders' from the posthumous volume of 1933.

p. 350, l. 29.   Cf. the criticism of these positivist doctrines in the essay 'On the positivist historical philosophy of knowledge', in bibl. No. 19(1): Coll. Ed. vol. 6.

p. 351, l. 32.   See the above annotation of p. 288.

Christian Love and the Twentieth Century

p. 361, n. 1.   On collective and hereditary guilt see *Form.* §VI B3.

p. 362, l. 26.   'Formal' must here be taken in the sense of a-priori, not, as in *Form.,* in opposition to 'substantive' and 'supraformal',

p. 363, l. 4.   Drafts for 'Politics and Morality', a course of lectures delivered in 1926-27, are to be found among the author's literary remains. See the conclusion of his foreword to the 3rd edition of *Form.*

p. 363, l. 9.   See the opuscule *Von zwei deutschen Krankheiten,* bibl. Nos. 13 and 19(2): Coll. Ed. vol. 6.

p. 364, l. 40.   On 'ethos' and 'morality' as dimensions of ethical evaluation, see *Form.* §V, ch. 6.

p. 366, l. 37.   In this fourth revised edition, the problems numbered 3 to 7 have been rearranged in the text according to the sequence in which they are treated in the final section, No. 3. The problems numbered 1 and 2 are treated in sections 1 and 2.

p. 367, l. 36.   See the above annotation of p. 339.

p. 368, l. 28.   Cf., in all versions of the book on sympathy, §B VI, Ch. 2, 'The facts concerning the "perspective of interests" '.

p. 373, l. 14.   See *Form.* §VI B 4, *ad* 4, 'The individual and the collective persons'.

p. 374, l. 35.	On the doctrine of the origin of sympathy, see the criticism of the naturalistic positivist theory in §A of the book on sympathy, chapter entitled 'The phylogenetic origin and extension of fellow-feeling'.
p. 377, l. 5.	See the justification of the solidarity principle and the criticism of the theory of social contract in *Form.* §VI B4, *ad* 4.
p. 382, l. 4.	On this erroneous alternative cf. §2 of 'The Reconstruction of European Culture', below. (Here too—see annotation of p. 366—the problems are in this edition introduced in the order of their subsequent treatment.)
p. 384, l. 26.	On the relation of State and person see *Form.* §VI B4, *ad* 4 and 5, and consult *Staat* and *Person* in the index.
p. 390, l. 17.	Cf. *Form.* §II A, pp. 86ff.
p. 395, l. 33.	In his lectures on 'solidarism' at Cologne, Max Scheler repeatedly exposed his doctrine concerning this 'third thing'. MSS relative to social philosophy are among the papers he left.

The Reconstruction of European Culture

p. 405, n. 1.	The reader is referred to our Editorial Note for closer details of additions to or insertions in the original MS of 1917.
p. 406, l. 2.	Cf. the immediately preceding work in this volume.
p. 407, l. 36.	On pacifism of inner conviction *versus* pacifism of expediency, see the posthumous opuscule, *Die Idee des Ewigen Friedens und der Pazifismus*, written in 1927 and published 1931 in Berlin (bibl. No. 28). Cf. also the end of the author's preface to the third edition of *Form.*
p. 418, n. 2.	Cf. bibl. Nos. 11 and 19: Coll. Ed. vol. 6.
p. 420, l. 35.	On the solidarity, complementariness and mutual unsubstitutability of individual peoples, see *Form.* §VI B4, *ad* 4, also what is said about emotional value-perspectivism and the due co-operation of times and peoples in §V, Ch. 6, *ad* 1, 'Variations of the ethos'.
p. 421, l. 27.	On the realization of values and 'intention towards own-value' in general, see *Form.*, index, under *Wertrealisierung*, *Eigenwert* and *Intention*. Cf. also p. 427, below.
p. 427, n. 1.	See the above annotation of p. 363, l. 9.
p. 430, l. 13.	Cf. the essay 'Man in the age of levelling' (1927),

	wherein the author delineates certain forms of levelling predestined. This work was published in *Philosophische Weltanschauung*, 1929; 2nd edition, Francke, Berne 1954.
p. 431, n. 1.	See bibl. Nos. 11 and 19(1): Coll. Ed. vol. 6.
p. 435, l. 2.	On the problem of eudaemonism, see *Form.* §V. especially Chs. 1 and 8-10, also the short essay 'On the betrayal of joy', bibl. No. 19(1): Coll. Ed. vol. 6.
p. 438, n. 1.	See *Form.* §VI B4, *ad* 4, on the a-priori reference of essential social forms to spatial and temporal diversity.
p. 438, n. 2.	From this footnote we may gather that the additions to the original MS (see Editorial Note) had already been penned in 1918.
p. 439, n. 1.	The book announced here never appeared. Preserved among Max Scheler's papers are drafts on the problem of capitalism and on Christian socialism (solidarism), drafts which date from these years.
p. 442, n. 1.	See the above annotation of p. 431, n. 1.

In twenty-nine footnotes the author's own bibliographical references have been made more explicit in this fourth edition, while thirteen more such references have been removed from the text and expressed as footnotes.

A NOTE ON THE AUTHOR[1]

by I. M. Bochenski

A. PERSONALITY, INFLUENCE, DEVELOPMENT

Endowed with an unusual personality, Max Scheler[2] was also beyond doubt the most brilliant German thinker of his day. His main strength lay in the field of ethics but his interest in religious philosophy, sociology, and other problems was no less intense. At all times his thinking is purposeful and close to life and his writings abound with problems. He is certainly the most original figure in ethical studies during the first half of the twentieth century.

The most varied currents afforded him inspiration. His first two books bear witness to the influence exercised on him during his earlier years by his teacher Rudolf Eucken, whose thought centres upon spiritual life, who accords supreme place to the spirit, despite being a sort of life-philosopher, and who has a profound admiration for St Augustine. Both these features reveal themselves in Scheler, for whom St Augustine is the great doctor of love, a love which the great saint conceives in an original manner such as the Greeks had never known; that is the line which Scheler chose to develop in his second period. After St Augustine, Scheler received the most lasting impressions from life-philosophy, Nietzsche, Dilthey, and Bergson, which accounts for his title 'the Catholic Nietzsche' (Troeltsch). Meanwhile he moved into the orbit of Edmund Husserl so that today he is considered to be the chief phenomenologist after the founder of the school, although his application of phenomenological methods to fresh problems leads him to modify the views of Husserl.

Scheler's life may be divided into three periods. As pointed out, the first period is dominated by Eucken. The next phase is that of his maturity

[1] This Note is reprinted by permission from *Contemporary European Philosophy* by I. M. Bochenski, translated by Donald Nicholl and Karl Aschenbrunner, University of California Press, Berkeley and Los Angeles, 1958.

[2] Max Scheler was born 1874 in Munich, became a pupil of Rudolf Eucken, and then taught in the Universities of Jena, Munich, and after 1919, Cologne. From Cologne he was called to Frankfurt a. M. but died there in 1928 before he could resume his teaching.

(1913-1922) in which he produces *Der Formalismus in der Ethik und die materiale Wertethik* (first published in Husserl's Year Book, 1913-1916), the most fundamental of his books; and then two collections of essays entitled *Vom Umsturz der Werte* (1919) and *Vom Ewigen im Menschen* (1921)[1]. During this time Scheler is a personalist, a theist and a convinced Christian. Then a profound change takes place within him, partly, it would seem, through his own restless nature and the violent crisis in his life; not only does he lose his previous faith, he even repudiates his theistic tenets. This conversion is already announced in *Die Wissenformen und die Gesellschaft* (1926) but receives its most pointed expression in *Die Stellung des Menschen im Kosmos* (1928). If his philosophy up to this point had turned upon the notion of God's personal love, now he maintains that man is 'the unique locus of the realization of the divine'. An early death robbed Scheler of the opportunity to amplify this latest phase of his thought.

B. EPISTEMOLOGY

Three types of knowledge are granted to man. The first is the *inductive knowledge* of the positive sciences, which is rooted in the urge for power and never attains to cogent laws; its object is reality. Scheler assumes the existence of reality but agrees with Dilthey that a creature which merely knew would have no reality because reality is whatever presents obstacles to our effort, and its existence is proved by our colliding with these obstacles.

The second type of knowledge enables us *to know the essential structure* of everything there is, the 'whatness' of things. As a condition of this knowledge we have to eradicate instinctive attitudes and to ignore the real existence of things, since such knowledge takes the *a priori* as its object. Along with Kant, Scheler asserts that there is *a priori* knowledge, interpreting as '*a priori*' all those ideal statements and units of meaning which are given to the thinking subject without his making any assumptions whatever. Nevertheless Scheler is led to contradict Kant upon several points at issue here. One is that what is comprised in the primary *a priori* is essences and not propositions. The sphere of *a priori* evidence has nothing to do with the formal sphere; there is an essential *a priori* which has content independently of experience and induction. Scheler rejects idealistic conceptualism and positivistic nominalism with unusual acrimony. Again, he will not concede to Kant that epistemology provides the fundamental theory of the *a priori*; he says that the basic error of the Kantians consists in asking 'how can anything be given?' instead of the fundamental question 'what is given?' Thus he treats epistemology as but one chapter in

[1] Here translated as *On the Eternal in Man*.

the theory of objective interconnections of essence. Finally, he considers the Kantian doctrine upon the spontaneity of thought to be radically false since it attributes all unification to the work of the understanding (or in certain cases, of the practical reason), whereas there is no such understanding which acts as law giver to nature. Convention is all that we can draw up, never laws. But the greatest error committed by Kant and all modern rationalist philosophers is to have equated the *a priori* with the rational; in fact, the whole of our spiritual life has *a priori* features—even the emotional faculties of the spirit such as feeling, loving, hating, and so on; there is an '*ordre du cœur*,' a '*logique du cœur*' (Pascal) in the deepest sense. By treating Husserl's phenomenology from this angle Scheler has extended it along original lines and opened up new vistas for it. He calls this doctrine 'emotional apriorism'.

The third type of knowledge is *metaphysical* and salvational and is arrived at by combining the results of the positive sciences with a philosophy centred upon essence. Problems on the borders of science (*e.g.*, 'what is life?') form its initial object, whence it proceeds to a metaphysic of the absolute. But the way to such a metaphysic cannot begin with objective being. It originates in philosophical anthropology, which sets itself the question, 'What is man?' Modern metaphysics has to be meta-anthropology.

c. VALUES

Values are the *a priori* grounds of emotion, the intentional objects of feeling. Though reason is blind to them they are as directly given to intentional feeling as colours are to vision. They are *a priori*.

Scheler carries out a devastating critique on the one hand of axiological nominalism, for which values are simply empirical facts, and on the other hand of ethical formalism. In this way he manages to achieve liberation from the dominant nineteenth-century prejudices very much as Bergson was able to do in the realm of theory. A presentation of this critique cannot here include the details, but has to limit itself to sketching the ground plan.

In human conduct Scheler distinguishes between the aspiration, the aim, the end, and the value. *Aim* is a content offered for realization; it is contained within the sphere of imagination and so it is always represented in consciousness. Not every aspiration necessarily has an aim. On the other hand, every aspiration does have an *end*, which is found in the very process of aspiration and is not conditioned by an act of imagination. In every end there is a *value*, which is its most intimate content. The assertion that man always aspires to pleasure is completely incorrect; ultimately, in fact, he never aspires to pleasure, nor to any emotional state whatever, but to values. And even when he takes pleasure as his end he does so under the impression that it is a value. However, to present a value does not imply producing an aspiration, because one can be aware of values (even ethical ones) without aspiring to them. It therefore follows that values are not dependent upon aim but are already present in the ends aspired to. Indeed values form the basis of our ends and only thereby can they form the basis of our aims. Furthermore one should not interchange value and obligation (*Sollen*). Ideal obligation is to be differentiated from normative (imperative) obligation; in the latter there is an ideal obligatory content related to aspiration as its condition. Value generates ideal obligation which in its turn generates normative obligation. To use the latter as a basis for ethics betrays a profound misunderstanding.

Values are anything but relative, they are absolute in the double sense of the word; their content is not relational; they belong to the category of quality, and they are unchanging. It is not the values themselves but our knowledge of them which is relative. There is an unmistakable vigour in Scheler's attack upon the various forms of relativism and particularly of relativist ethics. He subjects to examination first subjectivism, which traces values to human sources, and then relativism, which reduces them to mere life or regards them as conditioned historically. In this inquiry one discovers variations in the feeling for, and therefore knowledge of, values (ethos); variations in judgment upon value (ethics) in the models for institutions, ownership, and commerce; variations in practical morality concerned with the value of human behaviour; and, lastly, variations in custom and traditionally accepted habits. These are all subject to constant change, which nevertheless fails to disturb the ethical values; the latter may be clearly or less clearly conceived, defined, and formulated, but in themselves they remain absolute and unchanging.

Values form a closely knit realm held together by formal *a priori* laws and the interconnections of essence. Accordingly all values are classed either as positive or negative; the existence of a positive value is itself a positive value, its non-existence a negative one; the existence of a negative value is a negative value, its non-existence a positive one. The same value cannot be both positive and negative, every value that is not negative being positive and vice versa. The values are also classified into higher and lower. The most permanent ones, the least 'divisible' ones, those which generate others, those which produce a deeper satisfaction, and, finally, those which are least relative, are all higher values. The values are placed in their *a priori* hierarchy as follows: (1) values of sensible feeling, pleasant and unpleasant; (2) values of vital feeling, noble and vulgar; (3) spiritual values, beautiful and ugly, just and unjust, the pure knowledge of truth; (4) values of the holy and the unholy. Truth is not a value. This outline does not include the ethical (moral) values because these consist in the realization of other values which are relatively higher, or relatively lower, ones.

Finally, values are classified according to their subjects, the main division allotting some values to persons and others to things; the latter are all valuations of valuable things (goods), including among others cultural goods. Personal values are attached to the person himself and to his virtues and by their very essence are higher than those attached to things; ultimately the person alone is either good or evil. The secondary division of these values corresponds to tendencies in ethical capacity, the third one to the acts of a person. The ethical values are therefore personal values par excellence.

D. PERSON AND COMMUNITY

At the heart of Scheler's system lies the problem of the human person. To be a person is not the same as to have a soul or even to have selfhood; all men are not necessarily persons in the deepest meaning of the term, because the concept of person involves maturity and complete powers of judging and choosing. The person is not identical with the substantial soul, is not mental, and has nothing to do with psychophysical problems, character, or the health (as opposed to the sickness) of the soul. Neither substance nor object, it is much rather *the concrete unity of acts*, which is not in itself objective; the person is only revealed in its actions. But this does not mean to say that it is a vacant spring board (*Ausgangspunkt*) for acts, and still less that it consists in the sum of such acts, as Kant thought. The fact of the matter is that the whole person is committed in each act and varies in each act without exhausting its being in any one of them; and since the entire realm of action is spiritual, the person is essentially spiritual. *Spirit*, according to Scheler, does not consist of intelligence and the faculty of choice, for in this respect Edison and a clever chimpanzee differ in degree only, not in essence; it is a new principle, and is totally different from nature. The acts which the spirit generates are not functions of a self—they are non-mental (but not thereby physical) because acts are committed whereas mental functions occur. It is the act of ideation, that is, the ability to separate essence and existence, which constitutes the fundamental sign of the human spirit. Spirit is therefore objectivity (*Sachlichkeit*), the capacity of being determined by the objective nature of things.

The person is eminently *individual*; every man, in the degree to which he is a person, is a unique being and a unique value. (The contrast which

Scheler is stressing is between individual and general, not between individual and common.) To talk of a general person, or 'consciousness in general' (Kant) is nonsense. The person is doubly autonomous, firstly through autonomous personal insight into good and evil and, secondly, through autonomous personal volition for the good and the evil concretely given. Although the person is bound to his body he does not stand in a dependent relationship toward it because control over the body is one of the conditions for personal existence. Finally the person is never part of a 'world' but always its correlate, so that each person corresponds to a world (microcosm) and each world to a person.

But the person is differentiated into an individual person and a common person (*Gesamtperson*). The essence of the person is found in the fact that his whole spiritual being and activity is rooted both in individual reality (individual person) and in membership in a community. Therefore every finite person 'owns' both an individual and a common person, the latter springing from the manifold sources of experience which form the totality of shared experience. According to Scheler there are four types of social unity: (1) unity through slavish and infectious imitation (the masses); (2) unity through experiencing the same things together (*Miterleben*) or in retrospect; this produces an understanding between the members which, however, does not transcend the common experience (*Lebensgemeinschaft*); (3) artificial unity, in which all links connecting individuals have previously been shaped by particular and deliberate acts (society, *Gesellschaft*) there is no society, moreover, without a community (*Gemeinschaft*); (4) the unity of independent individual persons in an independent spiritual and individual common person. This latter unity is founded upon unity of essence in regard to a determinate value. Actually there are only two pure types of such common persons, (a) the church (salvational value) and (b) the nation or the cultural circle (the cultural common person, spiritual values of culture).

E. MAN AND GOD

The word 'man' has two meanings. According to the first, man as *homo naturalis* is a small pocket, a *cul-de-sac*, of life, an isolated relic of incessant evolution; man, in this sense, has not raised himself out of the animal world; he was an animal, he is an animal, and an animal he will remain to eternity. The humanity of the *homo naturalis* has neither unity nor greatness, and there is no misconception worse than that which led Comte to worship this humanity as the '*grand être*'. But 'man' has still another meaning; man is the creature who prays, the searcher for God (*Gottsucher*), the ultimate image of the living God—the lightning flashing through the cloud of mere natural existence and radiant with transcendent forms of meaning, value, and achievement: the 'person'.

Man enjoys an elemental and irreducible religious experience; the divine element belongs to the primitive givenness of the human consciousness. The formal designations of the divine essence are *ens a se*, infinity, omnipotence, holiness. The God of religion is a living God, he is a person, the person of persons; the God of pantheism is merely a poor reflection of theistic belief. The reproach of anthropomorphism against the latter is absurd and comical because it is not true that God is conceived according to man's image but rather that the only notion of 'man' which makes sense is 'theomorphism'. In the last resort every soul believes either in God or in idols, and even the agnostic believes in nothingness; God responds to this faith by making a revelation from his own side, and so religion and belief are only granted as a result of the workings of a personal God.

Metaphysics, which is always hypothetical, can never provide a basis for religion. Furthermore the God of philosophy is nothing but an inflexible first cause, and the real reason why the medieval proofs of God's existence carried conviction was simply because the Middle Ages had a wealth of religious experience. Yet metaphysics is an essential preliminary even for religious knowledge, and a culture without metaphysics is a religious impossibility; but then religion gives a fresh interpretation to this systematization of the world's nature (*system of conformity*). Nevertheless Scheler himself suggests a fresh proof of God's existence; all knowledge of God is knowledge through God; now there is such knowledge, for example any religious act, therefore God exists. He is given as the correlate of the world for just as there is an individual person corresponding to each microcosm so the person of God corresponds to the whole of the world (macrocosm).

F. LOVE

The thoughts so far presented are revolutionary enough both in form and content but it was Scheler's extremely radical theory of love which he first used to shake the complacency of nineteenth-century thought. In the first place love is not sympathy because it is not a feeling at all; it neither presupposes a judgment nor is it an act of aspiration; it contains within itself no social element and can just as well be directed toward oneself as toward someone else. There was a serious misunderstanding in regard to this at the root of all relativist nineteenth-century theories; they identified love with altruism, an absurd notion by which the other had to be loved as other; they made it into a love of humanity alone, love for something abstract, a fresh monstrosity; they identified it with the inclination to help or improve others, a feature which may certainly result from love, but cannot account for its essence. Scheler's far-reaching analysis proves that altruism and similar forms of modern sentimentality are based upon resentment, upon hatred of the higher values and, in the last resort, of God. An attitude of envy toward those who are the bearers of higher values leads to egalitarian and humanitarian ideals and these are the fundamental denial of love.

Genuine love (like genuine hatred) is always love for a person and never love for a value as such; Scheler even maintains that one cannot love even the good. Love goes through and beyond the value of the person; it is directed toward the person as reality. When we analyse our love for a person it becomes apparent that the sum of values attached to the beloved person can never come near to accounting for that love; over and above it there always remains an 'unaccountable'. What is 'over and above' is the concrete person of the beloved, the true object of love. The supreme ethical value of a person is only displayed to us when we share in the consummation of his loving act.

Love is a movement in which each concrete individual object that carries value achieves the highest possible value ideally destined for it. In striving to exalt the beloved it exalts the lover also. Understanding love is the plastic sculptor who in seeing a person's casual act or expressive gesture can bring out the highlights of his essential worth—unhampered by all that inductive and empirical knowledge which more often conceals the person's essence. For these reasons moral progress and the progress of values in general is bound up with the social exemplar, the genius, the hero and the saint.

The love of God, love at its highest pitch, is not to be thought of as love for God the all-bountiful, for it is participation in his love for the world (*amare mundum in Deo*). God is revealed as the supreme source of love; he endows the person with his ground of being, that is, his love. Such thoughts as these must in the end determine the theory of the community.

Toward the end of his life Scheler sketched out a philosophy which is largely a repudiation of his earlier notions; but this phase of his thought remained incomplete, and history will continue to regard him as a personalistic and theistic thinker. It will remain to his lasting credit that he broke away from nineteenth-century monistic prejudices and once more gave enhancement to the person; his wider significance is due to the fact that he made the transition to existentialism by emphasizing that the person could never be objectivized.

INDEX OF NAMES

Adam, K., 16, 27
Aquinas, Thomas, 12, 130, 238, 284, 307
Aristotle, 18, 71, 77f., 88, 135f., 149, 230, 288, 434
Auerbach, F., 239
Augustine, 13, 62, 135, 168, 197, 251, 260, 302f., 368, 371, 383, 390, 434
Avenarius, 217
Averroes, 114, 195

Balfour, J., 137
Barmgarten, O., 363
Bär, E. von, 241
Barrès, M., 137, 317
Bayle, P., 111
Bentham, J., 368
Benz, R., 428
Bergson, H., 75, 78, 116f., 137, 149, 220, 239
Berkeley, G., 186
Bernard of Clairvaux, 59
Biedermann, A. E., 340
Boltzmann, L., 239
Bonald, L. de, 137
Bruck, M. van den, 387
Brunetière, F., 137
Bruno, G., 87, 113
Buddha, 75
Bühler, K., 353
Burckhardt, J., 116, 236
Burdach, G., 424, 428, 431

Calvin, J., 49, 363
Cathrein, V., 324
Clement of Alexandria, 354
Cohen, H., 206
Cohn, J., 309, 316
Comte, A., 108f., 135ff., 298, 349, 352, 355, 379, 423, 464
Copernicus, 87
Cues, N. von, 227
Curtius, E. R., 116
Cyprian, 383
Cyril of Alexandria, 383

Darwin, C., 372, 374
Democritus, 111, 221
Descartes, R., 81, 87, 98, 104, 188, 247, 261f., 390, 447
Diederich, E., 332
Dietzel, H., 395
Dilthey, W., 81, 91, 422
Dostoyevsky, F. M., 436
Drews, A., 132, 340

Ehrenfels, C. von, 197
Einstein, A., 446
Eschweiler, K., 20
Eucken, R., 7, 144, 309, 312, 316

Fechner, T., 113, 149
Feuerbach, C., 108, 113

Fichte, J. G., 75, 78, 84, 91, 112f., 132, 179, 186, 189, 195, 202, 230, 233, 306, 308, 315, 384, 434f., 454
Fiedler, C., 265
Förster, Frau W., 129
Fourier, C., 379
Frederick the Great, 112, 331
Fries, J. F., 145

George, S., 419
Girgensohn, I. K., 16
Goethe, A., 56
Goethe, J. W. von, 114, 316, 356, 390, 422, 424f., 432, 434
Gomperz, H., 205
Grabmann, M., 303
Gratry, A., 283
Grünbaum, A., 353
Gründler, A., 16
Grützmacher, R. H., 21

Haeckel, E., 82, 113
Hanslick, E., 422
Harnack, A. von, 433, 436
Hartmann, E. von, 116, 132, 149, 179, 188ff., 195, 197, 224, 229f., 232f., 235f., 308, 340, 355, 466
Hartmann, N., 16, 454
Hegel, G. W. F., 20, 112ff., 132, 144, 149, 179, 195, 202, 204ff., 211, 215, 219f., 226f., 229f., 233, 306, 340, 355, 378, 384, 424, 434
Heiler, J., 16
Helmholtz, H. von, 271
Herbert of Cherbury, 146
Herder, J. G., 422
Herrmann, W., 144
Hock, C., 30
Hornbostel, E. M. von, 353
Horneffer, A., 21f.
Humboldt, W. von, 82, 422, 424f., 427
Hume, D., 156, 432
Husserl, E., 7, 9, 8off., 92, 151, 170, 310, 353, 451, 465

Ignatius of Antioch, 383

Jacobi, F. H., 112
Jaensch, E. R., 353
James, W., 291, 309, 328
Jellinek, K., 299

Kafka, F., 299
Kaftan, J., 144, 298
Kant, I., 7, 12f., 20, 29, 39, 78, 84, 104, 109, 113, 128, 130, 135f., 142ff., 153, 190, 199f., 202ff., 208ff., 235, 244, 257, 278, 283, 286, 289f., 292, 296ff., 306ff., 310, 349f., 362, 367, 372, 376, 390, 422, 424, 432, 434f., 447, 467
Kartashov, A. V., 435
Kerler, D. H., 261

Koffka, C., 353
Köhler, W., 256, 353
Külpe, 353

Lamarck, J., 118
Lammenais, R. de, 134, 137
Lang, A., 352
Lange, A., 203
Lask, E., 310
Lassalle, F., 395
Leibniz, G. W., 87, 149, 230, 234, 434f.
Leo the Great, 64
Leo XIII, Pope, 131, 433
Lessing, G. E., 112, 128
Lindworsky, J., 30
Locke, J., 104
Luther, M., 48f., 135, 247, 265, 289, 309, 369

Mach, E., 82, 143, 217, 423
Mager, A., 30
Maistre, J. de, 134, 137, 379
Malebranche, M., 16, 88, 135, 302
Malthus, T. R., 243
Mansbach, J., 347
Marx, K., 372, 378, 384, 395, 398f., 443
Maxwell, J. C., 239
Meinecke, F., 437
Meinong, A., 293
Merezhkovsky, D., 435
Messer, A., 347, 353
Mill, J. S., 349
Minot, C. S., 241
Möhler, J. A., 272
Müller, A., 379
Müller, J., 129, 332

Natorp, P., 174, 309
Naumann, F., 432
Neander, A., 59
Newman, J. H., 62, 235, 284, 441
Newton, J., 208
Nietzsche, F., 39, 52, 115ff., 129, 180f., 189, 261, 454
Novalis, F., 112

Origen, 354
Österreich, K. T., 15
Ostwald, W., 82, 113, 129, 423
Otto, R., 15, 145, 154, 169ff., 285ff., 306, 315

Pascal, B., 188, 266, 375
Paulsen, F., 113
Pflüger, A., 118
Plato, 18, 71, 73f., 77f., 81, 84, 90f., 135f., 434, 454
Plenge, J., 395, 399
Plotinus, 171, 215, 220, 226
Pythagoras, 276

Rade, M., 433
Rathenau, W., 395, 459

Renan, E., 113
Rickert, H., 84, 310, 314
Ritschl, A., 135, 144, 155, 298
Rodbertus, J. K., 379
Rohde, E., 116, 135
Rousseau, J.-J., 244, 368, 432

Saint-Simon, C. H. de, 379
Scheeben, M., 48
Schiller, F., 108, 434
Schlegel, F. von, 320
Schleiermacher, F. E. D., 12, 130, 143, 155, 264, 284ff.
Schmidt, W., 352
Scholz, H., 16, 27, 29f.
Schopenhauer, A., 18, 46, 112, 116, 132, 149, 229ff., 236, 271, 466
Shakespeare, W., 431
Sigwart, C. von, 111
Simmel, G., 246f.
Smith, Adam, 52
Solovyev, V., 436
Sombart, W., 393
Spencer, H., 203f., 234, 349, 374
Spengler, O., 422
Spinoza, B. de, 39, 49, 111f., 132, 179, 195, 215, 219f., 226f., 229f., 308, 337, 461, 464
Spranger, E., 424ff.
Starbuck, E. D., 291
Stern, W., 239
Strauss, D. F., 113
Strindberg, A., 124

Tagore, R., 360
Talleyrand, C. M. de, 244
Techet, C., 422
Tertullian, 61
Thomassin, 88, 284
Tönnies, F., 243, 355
Tolstoy, L., 126, 436
Troeltsch, E., 16, 22, 144, 354, 393, 424, 428, 433

Usener, H., 266
Utitz, E., 160, 465

Verworn, M., 82
Volkelt, J., 267
Voltaire, F.-M., 372

Wagner, A., 379
Walzel, O., 117
Weber, M., 393
Wertheimer, M., 353
Windelband, W., 84, 190, 212, 309ff.
Wobbermin, G., 144
Wölfflin, H., 422
Wolff, C., 372
Wundt, W., 113, 170f., 465

Zola, E., 108
Zwingli, U., 363

DATE DUE

4\v8			
JAN 3 0 1990			
GAYLORD			PRINTED IN U.S.A